CHATTER~~LEY COURT~~ESANS AND
OTHER SARDONIC SKETCHES

LUCIAN was born probably around AD 125 in Samosata, on the Euphrates, in the Roman province of Syria. Although the facts of his life are not known independently, Lucian was the author of a vast number of prose works, ranging from essays and speeches to dialogues and stories, and it is from these writings that the biographical details we generally accept have been inferred. He tells us that he was apprenticed to his uncle, a sculptor, but soon turned his attention to the study of philosophy and rhetoric, for which purpose he mastered Greek, which was not his native language.

Lucian also says that he entered the public sphere as an orator, travelling widely in Greece, Ionia, Italy and Gaul. He later gained a reputation as a sceptic and satirist, and made attacks upon several contemporaries – including philosophers, rhetoricians and one famous religious-cult leader. Lucian describes his own writing career as falling into two parts: the first being his 'condemning tyrants and praising princes', and the second – after his fortieth birthday – being his experimentation with comic dialogue.

Lucian moved to Egypt in his old age and became an official in the imperial administration, in charge of bringing cases to the prefect's court. He hoped to become an imperial procurator, and it is possible he had at some point become a Roman citizen. A reference to the death of Marcus Aurelius shows that Lucian was still alive in the early 180s. His best-known works include *The Philosopher Nigrinus*, *Timon the Misanthrope* and *True Histories*.

KEITH SIDWELL is Professor of Latin and Greek and Head of the Department of Classics at University College Cork. As well as Lucian and his influence, his scholarly interests include Greek tragedy and comedy and Renaissance Latin, especially in Ireland.

LUCIAN

Chattering Courtesans and Other Sardonic Sketches

Translated with an Introduction and Notes by
KEITH SIDWELL

PENGUIN BOOKS

PENGUIN BOOKS

Published by the Penguin Group
Penguin Books Ltd, 80 Strand, London WC2R ORL, England
Penguin Group (USA) Inc., 375 Hudson Street, New York, New York 10014, USA
Penguin Books Australia Ltd, 250 Camberwell Road, Camberwell, Victoria 3124, Australia
Penguin Books Canada Ltd, 10 Alcorn Avenue, Toronto, Ontario, Canada M4V 3B2
Penguin Books India (P) Ltd, 11 Community Centre, Panchsheel Park, New Delhi – 110 017, India
Penguin Group (NZ), Cnr Airborne and Rosedale Roads, Albany, Auckland 1310, New Zealand
Penguin Books (South Africa) (Pty) Ltd, 24 Sturdee Avenue, Rosebank 2196, South Africa

Penguin Books Ltd, Registered Offices: 80 Strand, London WC2R ORL, England

www.penguin.com

This translation first published 2004
1

Set in 10.25/12.25pt PostScript Adobe Sabon
Typeset by Rowland Phototypesetting Ltd, Bury St Edmunds, Suffolk
Printed in England by Clays Ltd, St Ives plc

Contents

Acknowledgements

It has been a privilege to spend the last few years in the company of such an attractive and interesting writer as Lucian, knowing that I have a chance to bring to a new generation some idea of the pleasure his works hold. In the end, however, no translation can do justice to words written in another tongue and I hope that my readers will be inspired by my renditions to go back to the original Greek and enjoy the full bouquet of this Syrian vintage.

I have tried here alongside my versions to mediate recent research work on the satirist and his influence, occasionally adding a few cent (as we in the Euro zone are barbarously instructed to write the plural of our new pence) of my own. I am ever mindful, however, of the difficulty of writing as a scholar about a writer who made his living satirizing pedants, and can offer nothing better as an antidote than the handwritten epigraph left on the flyleaf of my copy of Lt.-Col. H. W. L. Hime's *Lucian the Syrian Satirist* (for which, see further Introduction, section 6, n. 43):

> Alas! Lt.-Col. Hime,
> In writing this you lost your time:
> For Lucian is always Lucian
> In spite of critics Lilliputian.

I have a number of debts to acknowledge. First, to John Dillon, who first suggested to Penguin (an embarrassingly long time ago now) that they interview me for the job. Secondly, to David Braund, who read my version of *The Scythian* carefully and made some useful suggestions for the notes. Thirdly, to Adam Bartley, who communicated to me some interesting ideas about Thucydides in the *True Histories* prior to their publication. Fourthly, to my colleague Noreen Humble, to whose collaboration in work on Lucian's *Dream* I owe valuable new insights into Lucian's literary sophistication and who suggested the new title for *Dialogues of the Courtesans* which (dis)graces the cover of this selection. Fifthly, to Malcolm Garrard, whose knowledge of Tucholsky helped me add a solid final punch to the section of the Introduction on Lucian's reception. Sixthly, to Stephen Ryan, my copy-editor, whose vigilance was Argos-like, and whose intelligent and sympathetic probings have helped to improve the final product enormously. Finally, to my mother, Joan Gladys Sidwell (née Little), who always encouraged me to pursue whatever it was that interested me, even if that did turn out to be Ancient Greek and even if that was not among the burgeoning professions. She was summoned aboard Charon's wherry on 4 May 2001, during the writing of this book, and it is only fitting that it be dedicated to her memory. But how much more would I have preferred to see her smile and protest mildly at her son's suspect taste as she leafed through *Chattering Courtesans*!

Introduction

1. 'A man seriously committed to raising a laugh'[1]

Eunapius, writing at the end of the fourth century AD, around two hundred years after the death of Lucian, captures in his throwaway assessment an essential truth about Lucian's writings. Lucian is a comic writer, whose ironic tone is pervasive and whose unexpected angle of vision exposes absurdity or pretentiousness in a unique way which has always delighted his readers. His combination of three quite separate ancient genres – the satirical comedy of Athens (Old Comedy), as written by Aristophanes, Eupolis and Cratinus,[2] the philosophical dialogue, the chief models for which were Plato, Xenophon and Aristotle, and Menippean satire, a serio-comic form mixing prose and verse developed by the third-century BC Cynic writer Menippus of Gadara – produced a body of work which has no equal in antiquity and has exerted an enormous influence upon literature since the Renaissance. However, to focus attention purely on the comic aspects, as Eunapius does, is to miss an underlying seriousness, detected and mobilized by many of his imitators. For Lucian's comedy is not merely comic; it is *serio-comic*. Following a tradition of Cynic philosophical writing of this kind, it uses laughter to promote sensible and honest living, whether the lesson is purely ethical, as in the case of the tyrant in the Underworld who cannot stop weeping at the loss of his worldly goods and power, or literary, as in the following example from *How to Write History* (paragraph 26), where he is criticizing the lies and narrative excesses of an unnamed historian of the Parthian War (AD 162–6):

Then, because Thucydides had inserted a funeral speech over the first dead in that famous war, this fellow too thought he ought to have a valediction spoken over Severianus. You see, all of them are vying with Thucydides, despite the fact that he is in no way responsible for the troubles in Armenia. So after giving Severianus a magnificent burial he brought up onto the tomb one Afranius Silo, a centurion, to challenge Pericles. His rhetorical flourishes were so mighty that I swear I wept copious tears . . . of laughter, and especially at the end of the oration when Afranius, crying and groaning piteously, mentioned all those extravagant dinners and toasts of Severianus'. Then he capped the speech with an action borrowed from Ajax. He drew his sword, very nobly and as befitted an Afranius, and in full view of everyone committed hara-kiri on the grave. Mind you, he deserved to have perished long before if his speech really was as reported. Our historian comments that the crowd who had watched this were all struck with admiration and praised Afranius to the skies. For my part, I did have a very low opinion of him for his near mention of sauces and frying-pans and his tears at the memory of pastries, but my main complaint was that he had died without first butchering the historian who had produced this drama.

2. An Elusive Life

It would be good to be able to continue this introduction with a set of agreed facts about Lucian and his life. However, as is the case with many ancient writers, external sources are (with one exception) late and (for various reasons) untrustworthy, while a growing suspicion among literary historians in general about the reliability of biographical data provided by authors themselves is compounded in Lucian's case by his irony and his sophisticated use of allusion. For example, *The Dream, or Lucian's Career*,[3] an introductory piece (*prolalia*: see section 3 below), addressed to an audience in his home town, Samosata (*The Dream* 18), describes the author's choice of culture against the family business of sculpture. Apprenticed to his uncle, on the basis that he had been good at modelling wax as a child, he spoiled a piece of marble on his first day and was beaten for it.

He ran home and complained to his mother about her brother's
treatment of him, then fell asleep to dream that two women,
Culture and Sculpture, were presenting him with their credentials so that he could make his career choice. He ran into the
arms of Culture, who then mounted him on a chariot drawn by
winged horses and took him on a journey from East to West,
during which he sowed something (he can't remember exactly
what) and was cheered by the peoples over whom he passed.
When he returned, he was dressed in a garment with purple
decoration. The question is whether there is anything at all here
that we can trust. Despite the panoply of literary allusion which
supports the piece, some scholars are prepared to believe that
Lucian had this dream, or at the very least that he cannot have
lied about his family background to an audience in his home
town.[4] However, even this is not certain. Socrates was believed
in antiquity to have been a sculptor before turning to philosophy, and the picture of the little Lucian making wax figures at
school recalls the ambivalent figure of Pheidippides in Aristophanes' *Clouds*. Both Lucian and Pheidippides have to make a
choice between good and evil which mirrors that of Heracles in
Prodicus' *Seasons* (probably known to Lucian through Xenophon's *Memorabilia* 2.1.21f.). Can we be sure that this sophisticated web of literary allusion has been chosen because it suits
the facts of Lucian's background rather than because it provides
an appropriately ambiguous and ironic picture of a would-be
Socrates whose ambitions are far removed from what it will be
realistic for him to achieve? This is by way of a 'health warning',
then. In what follows, I gather together the apparently autobiographical references plus one contemporary allusion to Lucian,
attempting to allow for irony and literary games.

Lucian's birthplace he himself claims to be Samosata, a city
in the formerly independent kingdom of Commagene, in the
Roman province of Syria (*How to Write History* 24). His date
of birth is uncertain, but various indications suggest *c.* AD 125.[5]
We cannot know for certain whether he really was of the artisan
class (see above), but it has been plausibly argued recently that
his self-description as '(As)syrian' and 'barbarian' (*Two Charges
of Literary Assault* 27, 34; *The Scythian* 9; *The Dead Come to*

Life 19; *The Ignorant Book-Collector* 19; *The Goddesse of Surrye* 1) chimes in with his close acquaintance with the temple and rituals of the goddess Atargatis-Juno at Hierapolis-Bambyce in Syria (*The Goddesse of Surrye*) and an allusion to an Aramaic term (*The Goddesse of Surrye* 33) to suggest that he was from the Semitic and not the imported Greek population.[6] His education in Greek, then, was a process of cultural as well as linguistic assimilation. His career took him into the public sphere as a speaker. In one work, he has Plato allude to him as 'an orator and advocate and a rhetorical rogue' (*The Dead Come to Life* 9). Later in the piece, Diogenes also describes him as an orator, but one who has left judicial oratory behind to concentrate on abusing philosophers (paragraph 25). His self-representative 'Syrian' in *Two Charges of Literary Assault* has Rhetoric (his wife) mention not only his education in Greek (and his irregular enrolment as a (Greek) citizen) but also their travels together in Greece, Ionia, Italy and Gaul (27). In a late work, where he defends his earlier attack on those who took paid employment in Roman aristocratic houses, he alludes to his time in Gaul, when his dedicatee Sabinus knew him as a man 'who brought in the highest fees for public oratory . . . and was numbered among the high-earning sophists' (*Apology for the 'Salaried Posts in Great Houses'* 15).[7] If *The Dream* really was delivered in Samosata (see above), then it belongs to the period after his return to Greece and Asia, to which a number of other works seem to allude, and which would fit in the 160s. *How to Write History*, which deals with historians of the Roman (co-)emperor Lucius Verus' Parthian campaign, probably belongs to the years 166–8.[8] *Images* and *In Defence of 'Images'*, which have as their subject Verus' mistress, Panthea, seem to mention the emperor as still alive, and so probably belong before 169. Lucian purports to have been an eyewitness of the self-immolation of the Cynic philosopher Peregrinus (*The Passing of Peregrinus* 35f.), an event which occurred most probably after the Olympic Games of 165.[9] Other travels took him, he tells us, to Abonuteichos on the Black Sea, where he claims to have tried to unmask the new cult of Glycon-Asclepius founded by one Alexander (*Alexander the False Prophet* 55f.),[10] and to Macedonia (*Zeuxis* 7–8, *The Scythian* 9). His claims to have attempted to face down imposters like Peregrinus and Alexander gain some credence from the only external contemporary mention of him. Galen of Pergamum (129–?199), the famous doctor, speaks of a Lucian who exposed the ignorance of a well-known philosopher by faking a work of Heraclitus and having it passed on to him, and also did the same sort of thing with some grammarians.[11] In his old age, possibly in the reign of the emperor Commodus (after 180), Lucian moved to Egypt, where he took a position in the imperial administration, probably that of *eisagogeus*, an official in charge of bringing cases to the prefect's court (*Apology for the 'Salaried Posts in Great Houses'* 1, 12).[12] He had ambitions, he reports (12), of becoming an imperial procurator, and this, together with his move and his position, may suggest that he had become at some stage a Roman citizen and aspired to higher status (that of an *eques*, 'knight').[13]

Lucian's self-representative 'Syrian' in *Two Charges of Literary Assault* 32, divides his writing career in two, placing rhetorical exercises such as 'condemning tyrants and praising princes' in the period up to near his fortieth birthday and after that his experiments with the 'comic dialogue', his mixture of Platonic dialogue with Old Comedy, with something of the Cynic writer Menippus of Gadara thrown in (see section 1 above and section 5 below). In *Hermotimus* 13, an interlocutor of the sceptical Lycinus, often taken to represent Lucian himself, suggests Lycinus/Lucian is about forty at the time of this conversation in which the advice he gives to the ardent student of philosophical dogmas is 'to live the common life' (84), exactly the view whispered by Tiresias to Menippus in the comic dialogue *Menippus* (21). These statements have sometimes been used in attempts to find a chronology for the works.[14] However, it has to be said that the relatively few pieces which can be described as purely rhetorical (*The Tyrannicide, Disowned, An Encomium of Fatherland, Phalaris I, II,* possibly *Hippias, or The Bath, The Consonants at Law* and *Praising a Fly*) do not constitute much of a corpus for a writing career of some fifteen to twenty years, while the vast amount of material which seems to represent generic experimentation, exposure of phonies and other literary innovation (and thus is to be placed on this schema after Lucian's fortieth year or so) is as great as that of the corpora of most of his contemporaries spread over a lifetime. The explanation may be that he suppressed much of his earlier output and that he was later a highly prolific producer. At any rate, Lucian's own apparent autobiographical indications are not especially helpful in dating those works for which there is no clear external evidence.

3. The Lucianic Corpus

However, as it happens we have another problem: establishing precisely what Lucian wrote. Eighty-six items have come down to us under the name of Lucian (listed in the Appendix in the order of Macleod's Oxford Classical Text, the numbering used in my notes). Seven are certainly – or almost certainly – spurious.[15] Doubts are usually expressed over another eight.[16] Another four, stigmatized at times in the past, are now generally regarded as genuine.[17] There was at least one more lost work (the *Sostratus*, mentioned at *Demonax the Philosopher* 1).

Outside of the small number of works which fall into established rhetorical genres (see previous section), it is extremely difficult to categorize Lucian's writings effectively according to form or theme. This is certainly a measure of his originality. But this originality was achieved, as Lucian himself is at pains to point out (see section 5 below), within the boundaries of contemporary literary theory, which operated on the principle of *imitation*. None the less, a few remarks can be made which will give an idea of the spread of genres and material he covers.

A large number of works are in dialogue form. These might be divided between the realistic and the fantastic. The works in the first category cover an enormous range of themes, from eulogy to literary vituperation,[18] from attacks on philosophers and philosophical schools to philosophical attacks on Rome,[19] from discussions of athletics, friendship, pantomime and love to conversations between courtesans and a demonstration of the futility of not facing facts.[20] The second category, the fantastic, can be subdivided into pieces with an Underworld setting, those with an Olympian setting, those in which gods and humans interact or gods come to the human world, those in which the conversations are with long-dead figures from the past or an animal and one where a fantastic cure is effected.[21] There is no thematic consistency here either, though a playful focus on moralistic notions such as the futility of power and possessions in the face of death, and the satirical treatment of dogmatic philosophy, are strong tendencies.

The remaining works exhibit just as great a diversity. One group contains short pieces thought to have served as introductions to longer works, often, probably, dialogues. These are known as *prolaliai* and I have included two in the selection ('*So You Think I'm the Prometheus of the Literary World?*' and *The Scythian*).[22] Another category comprises personal attacks on contemporaries, either named or anonymous.[23] A third group centres on literary theory and literary satire.[24] A fourth category includes generic attacks on various types of human behaviour.[25] A fifth group consists of pieces written in Ionic Greek,[26] and a sixth contains two self-defences.[27] A seventh group consists of a mock-tragic poem that shows Lucian adept at poetic parody,[28] and the verse *Epigrams* (usually thought spurious). Finally comes a eulogistic biography of a philosopher, *Demonax the Philosopher*, a work which might be taken as a guidebook to a set of concerns which pervades the entire corpus: philosophical eclecticism, the centrality of practical ethics, the importance of wit in the puncturing of pretension, fearlessness in criticizing those who have power (even Romans), the importance of friendship, physical fitness and self-sufficiency, the necessity of being involved in the affairs of the community (though at enough distance to be a fair critic) and above all the attempt to live the life of the ordinary man.

4. A Syrian Greek in the World of Rome

The world into which Lucian was born and in which he operated was controlled by the Romans. Though he himself appears to have been from the non-Greek, Semitic population of Samosata (see section 2 above), the culture by which he defined himself was Greek. Yet he knew Latin (*A Slip of the Tongue in Greeting* 13) and when we last hear of him he was in the imperial administration of Egypt, probably a Roman citizen. These paradoxes have led to a long discussion of Lucian's cultural identity and his attitude to the Roman empire.[29]

The issues are not yet (and perhaps cannot be) definitively settled. Evidence of various kinds suggests that a variety of self-definitions were available to the Greek-speaking educated elite of the East. During the second century AD, it became increasingly normal for Greeks to hold high office at Rome (for example, the Athenian Herodes Atticus was consul in 143). And dedicatory inscriptions could allude to both the *polis*-based Greek identity of the dedicatee and his Roman affiliations.[30] At this level, then, being Roman was entirely compatible with being Greek. The fact is, though, that the literary products and sophistic displays of Lucian's age tended to marginalize Rome and to concentrate on the Greece of the distant past, in the period of independence, the fifth and fourth centuries BC.[31] And this focus was also promoted by the preferred linguistic register of such works, the Attic Greek of that period.[32]

That said, Lucian does not completely ignore Rome and the Romans, though they always appear in contexts where the primary focus is culturally Greek. For example, Alexander of Abonuteichos has a strong network of support among the Roman elite (*Alexander the False Prophet* 30) and Lucian too has his Roman protectors (55), but the cult of Glycon-Asclepius is Greek and belongs to a Greek city (*polis*). Similarly, the criticisms of Rome in *The Philosopher Nigrinus* and those of individual Romans in *Demonax the Philosopher* are made by Greek philosophers, while the attack in *On Salaried Posts in Great Houses* is aimed at educated Greeks, to persuade them not to demean themselves, rather than primarily at the Romans who abuse them.

One group of works, however, associated with the emperor Lucius Verus, has tended to suggest a more positive attitude to the Roman empire.[33] *How to Write History* (prompted by the Parthian War of AD 162–6), *The Dance* (apparently a staunch defence of a popular genre beloved of Verus), *Images* and *In Defence of 'Images'* (seemingly encomia of Verus' mistress Panthea) are usually read as attempts to curry favour and break into the charmed imperial circle.[34] However, the strong stance against the use of history for eulogistic purposes in *How to Write History* 38–41 and the demand that the historian be 'subject to no king' (41) rather suggest the assertion that even the emperor must subject himself to the unvarnished truth, and the other works cannot, in consequence, remain unsuspected of a level of irony only revealed by a close examination of the network of literary allusion which is woven through them (see below, Preface to *Images* and *In Defence of 'Images'*). It may be better to conclude that, like Demonax, Lucian was not prepared to suffer fools gladly, whether they were Greeks or Romans, and that, when they were Romans, he was prepared to find safe ways to make fun of them when they crossed the limits of his tolerance.

5. The *Pepaideumenos*, Writer and Reader

Lucian's prospective audience was the *pepaideumenos* ('trained individual'), a word constantly used in this period to denote a person (almost always male) who had been educated in the prevailing Atticist literary culture. What was involved can partly be seen in the handbooks of the rhetoricians Hermogenes, Aphthonius and Theon of the second and third centuries AD, whose *progymnasmata* ('preliminary exercises') teach the neophyte how to dress up and vary a theme. It might be treated by extended comparison (*synkrisis*) or by working proof and disproof (*kataskeue* and *anaskeue*) of the same proposition, or enlivened by simile or description (*ekphrasis*). Those who continued beyond these preliminaries studied with a sophist.[35] The focus here was on *meletai*, 'practice exercises' or 'declamations' on 'display' (epideictic) themes such as 'a Spartan advises the Lacedaemonians not to receive the men who had returned from Sphacteria without their weapons' or 'an endeavour to recall the Scythians to their earlier nomadic life, since they are losing their health dwelling in cities'.[36]

The location of these themes in the classical age of Greece is indicative of another feature of the education of the *pepaideumenos* in this period, the emphasis on the study of classical Greek literature, especially Homer, Herodotus, the Attic historians, dramatists and orators, and the philosophers Plato and Aristotle. With the insistence on the use of classical Attic Greek as the predominant dialect came also the whole paraphernalia of purism, including glossaries of Attic usage, which was created by and also fuelled the social inclusion and exclusion zones of the elite. This training, which involved minutely detailed analysis of texts, conspired towards the production of practitioners and recipients of literature whose antiquarian antennae were ever deployed for the appreciation of stylistic borrowing and the detection of allusive meaning.[37]

In *The Dead Come to Life*, Lucian defends himself to the angry philosophers (Plato, Diogenes, etc.) who have begged a day off from Pluto and come back to earth to attack the blackguard who has blackened their names in his facetious *Philosophies for Sale* as follows: 'Where else but from you did I get the material I've gathered like a bee, which I use in my public displays? The audience applaud and recognize each of them the allusion, its source and how I have collected it, in their view envying me for my flower-picking, but in fact envying you and your meadow.' The writer's art lies in 'understanding how to select and intertwine and fit together [the various coloured flowers], so that they aren't out of harmony with one another' (6). It is possible to take this too literally and to brand Lucian as a plagiarist, who has done nothing except steal material from older (and better) writers.[38] But elsewhere (e.g. *'So You Think I'm the Prometheus of the Literary World?'* and *Two Charges of Literary Assault*), he asserts his originality in combining Old Comedy, the philosophical dialogue and Menippean satire[39] to create a strange new hybrid – the comic dialogue. So the procedure of simply digging down to discover the roots of his art is not exactly what Lucian expects of his audience. In effect this literary material forms a substructure which can carry meanings for the *pepaideumenos* which it will not for the person who cannot spot the reference, recall its traditional interpretation (or interpretations) and set them against the context in which it has now been placed.

The question of how Lucian's works reached his learned audience is difficult to resolve. In some cases, for example *The Scythian*, a piece is addressed to a plurality[40] and so looks to have been designed for live performance to a specific audience (in this case, to the citizens of a Macedonian city (paragraph 9)). In others, notably *True Histories*, the work is explicitly spoken of as designed for reading (1.1–2): 'When they have finished a long spell of reading more serious material, they ought to allow their intellect some recreation . . . Their recreation will be of the right kind if they spend their leisure on the sort of reading [etc.] . . .'[41] Given that reading was itself a performative act, done aloud rather than silently, the gap between 'reader' and 'auditor' may have been less obvious in antiquity than it is for us. However, the problem still remains of whether Lucian's dialogues were designed for public performance rather than private reading and, if so, whether they would have been presented by Lucian himself in a virtuoso act in which he played all the parts, or whether he would have handed over to actors (or other orators) once he had performed the *prolalia*.

6. Blasphemer, Philosopher and Disgusting Semite: The Afterlife of a Satirist

In modern times, Lucian's place in the classical canon has been marginal. A large part of the responsibility for this must lie with the attitude of German classical scholars of the early twentieth century, many of whom disputed his originality, branding him a mere imitator, of Menippus in particular. To quote one, he was a 'light-fingered, sensation-mongering, irresponsible columnist'.[42] For some, in a display of proto-Nazism which makes the contemporary reader shudder, he was even 'a Syrian half-breed', his understanding limited to 'the spirit whom he resembled, namely the whole cross-bred, debased, degenerate world around him'.[43] But it was not always like that.

Despite the lack of attention in the period after his death from Philostratus, the early third-century historian of the sophists,[44]

Lucian's works were preserved, read and imitated in later
antiquity: authors such as Alciphron, Aristaenetus and the
emperor Julian imitated him,[45] and the Christian writers Lactantius and Isidore of Pelusium alluded to his satire of the pagan
gods.[46] His *Slander* was even paraphrased in Syriac in the sixth
century.[47]

His success in Byzantium was more spectacular. His works
were much copied and annotated, early examples being the
scholia (commentator's notes) of Basilios, archbishop of Adada
in Pisidium (*fl.* 870) and Arethas, archbishop of Caesarea
(*fl.* 907). The patriarch Photius (d. *c.* 893) wrote a lengthy
book-report on his works in his *Library* (item 128). And imitations appeared regularly from the tenth to the fifteenth century.[48]
He was used in Byzantine schools as an author whose style and
literary techniques were both admired and found useful.

It was this established position in the Byzantine curriculum
that ensured Lucian's centrality when Greek studies began again
in the West. To be precise, for his Greek classes in Florence from
1397 to 1400, Manuel Chrysoloras (*c.* 1353–1415), the first
officially appointed teacher of ancient Greek of the Renaissance,
used a manuscript of Lucian he had brought with him from
Greece. Part of this was copied and survives with interlinear
glosses in Latin by a pupil in his seminar.[49] From these small
beginnings, Lucian's vast influence in the early Renaissance can
be traced.

One of my subsidiary purposes in making the selection I have
(see further Translator's Note) has been to present some of the
pieces that found favour, and hence Latin translators, in the
earliest period after Lucian's works had reached the West.
Timon the Misanthrope was among the first two works to be
translated. The earliest manuscript of this version (by a certain
Bertholdus) is dated to 26 May 1403 and is likely to have
emerged from the seminar of Chrysoloras, since it was among
the works glossed in his pupil's manuscript. *Slander* was also
among the classroom works of Chrysoloras and found no less
than four Latin translations during the fifteenth century in Italy
alone, the earliest by Guarino da Verona, who also translated
Praising a Fly (later also done by an anonymous scholar) and

About the Parasite. Slander's central pictorial motif (the *Calumny of Apelles*) was brought specifically to the attention of artists by Leon Battista Alberti in his *De Pictura* of 1435. The version realized by Sandro Botticelli is only the most famous of the Renaissance reuses of the motif.[50] *Toxaris* was translated by the Sicilian humanist and manuscript collector Giovanni Aurispa before 1430. *Demonax the Philosopher, A Few Words about Mourning* and *An Encomium of Fatherland* were translated by Lapo da Castiglionchio il Juniore before 1438, and *An Encomium of Fatherland* found another translator in Antonio Pacino da Todi at around the same time. The earliest version of *True Histories* was made by Lilio Tifernate in the 1440s and *The Journey down to Hades* was Latinized by Cristoforo Persona before 1470.[51] Many of these versions found wider distribution with the introduction of printing in the second half of the century, and when the great Dutch humanist Desiderius Erasmus teamed up with Thomas More in 1506 to produce a new set of Latin translations, the printed version of that became an enormous success and ran into many editions.[52]

Lucian's place in the library of the humanists and then the school curriculum rested upon a positive image projected by those who translated his works. He was characterized as 'a most learned man', 'a philosopher very well known among the Greeks of his own day', 'weighty in speech' with 'propriety in diction', 'wise', 'vehement and biting in criticizing vice', a writer who combined 'jollity with severity'.[53] But another set of evaluations, which had existed since Byzantine bishops had annotated his works, was lying in wait for his reputation. The tenth-century dictionary *Suda* had asserted that Lucian had died torn apart by wild dogs, and had commented dryly, 'he was adequately punished in this world, and in the next he will inherit eternal fire with Satan'. All this venom centred on Lucian's patronizing description of the early Christians whose credulity is used by his arch-villain, the Cynic Peregrinus, to further his own cause (*The Passing of Peregrinus* 11–13). On that passage a Byzantine (or earlier Christian) commentator had written, 'what is this drivel, you accursed man, against Christ the saviour?'.[54] In the white heat of the Reformation, Lucian and his friends and imitators (people like Erasmus and More) suffered a backlash from both sides, which emerged from this earlier, hostile evaluation of the satirist.[55]

Yet Lucian continued to be a school text, and in the seventeenth and eighteenth centuries vernacular translations – the French of Nicolas Perrot d'Ablancourt (1654), the English 'by various hands' known as 'Dryden's Lucian' (1711), the German by Christoph Wieland (1788–9) – brought him to a much wider public.[56] One Lucianic genre which had enormous success between 1680 and 1780 was the Dialogue of the Dead. Fontenelle's collection (1683) was followed by that of Fénelon (1700–18), while Lord Lyttleton's was published in 1760.[57] Another English devotee was the essayist and novelist Henry Fielding (1707–54), who at one time planned a complete new translation.[58]

In the nineteenth century, imitations continued to be produced. Walter Savage Landor's *Imaginary Conversations of Greeks and Romans* (1853) contains a dialogue, first published in 1846, between Lucian and the fanatical Christian Timotheus. But as the century wore on, the professionalization of scholarship by the universities, first in Germany, then in the other European nations, meant that the focus now was rather study than creative reuse of classical sources.[59] In Germany in the nineteenth century six Greek editions (not all complete) were published (there had only been some ten separate ones between 1496 and 1743).[60] All the stranger, then, the sudden about-turn of scholarly literary opinion there at the beginning of the twentieth mentioned in the opening paragraph of this section.

The most familiar twentieth-century image from Lucian also has its origin in an earlier German enthusiasm. The translation of Christoph Wieland appears to have galvanized Johann Wolfgang von Goethe (1749–1832) into producing a version of a story from *The Lover of Lies* – that of the magician's feckless sidekick who learns only half the spell, getting a broom to grow hands and carry water, but unable to stop it flooding the house. This was his ballad *Der Zauberlehrling* ('The Sorcerer's Apprentice') of 1797. A century later, the French composer Paul Dukas based his symphonic poem *L'Apprenti sorcier* on Goethe's text.

In 1938, when Walt Disney had the idea for a cartoon animation of Dukas's piece, his research team tracked it back to its origins and re-created very largely the Lucianic version – with the sorcerer's apprentice played by Mickey Mouse.[61]

But the greatest tribute to Lucian's spirit – and one which ran against the grain of early twentieth-century Teutonic evaluations of his works – came from the German satirist Kurt Tucholsky (1890–1935). His poem 'To Lucian' makes his admiration clear, and his no-nonsense exposure of the Führer's new clothes in his other writings demonstrated a real-life commitment to the Lucianic exposure of phonies that led to banishment, depression and finally suicide.[62]

NOTES

1. Eunapius, *Lives of the Philosophers and Sophists* 454.
2. Further information on named individuals, places, etc. mentioned in this edition may be found in the Glossary.
3. See Appendix: List of Lucian's Works. In the Introduction, prefaces and notes, I have used my own titles for works in this selection and those of Harmon–Kilburn–Macleod (see References) for the rest.
4. Believers include Jones 1986, 9–10, Swain 1996, 308–9 (see References for full bibliographical details).
5. Firm dates show Lucian grown up, well connected and able to afford travel in the 160s (see p. xii). His allusion to 'conversion' from rhetoric at the age of nearly forty (*Two Charges of Literary Assault* 32), after his various jobs elsewhere, allows this conjecture – so long as we accept that his self-description is not itself ironic.
6. Swain 1996, 299–308. *The Goddesse of Surrye = The Syrian Goddess*. The archaic English of the Loeb translation, whose title I use (see n. 3 above), was intended to reproduce something of the effect of Lucian's use in this piece of the Ionic dialect to counterfeit the manner of Herodotus.
7. A 'sophist' could be defined as an orator involved in teaching (a position of considerable emolument), and as such is distinguished from a mere public speaker (a 'rhetor'). However, for Philostratus, writer of *Lives of the Sophists* in the early third century

AD, the title also implied brilliance of reputation (and distinguished birth). Lucian does not appear in Philostratus' account and it is possible that Lucian is actually here distinguishing his position as 'rhetor' from that of 'sophist' at the same time as claiming that in Gaul he was paid quite as much as if he had been a sophist. See Swain 1996, 96–100.

8. See Jones 1986, 60.
9. Jones 1986, 117 and 125 with n. 34.
10. Jones 1986, 17–18 dates the trip around 165.
11. The passage is in a part of his commentary on Hippocrates' *Epidemics* which has survived only in Arabic. See Strohmaier 1976, Macleod 1979 and Jones 1986, 19.
12. See Jones 1986, 20–1.
13. This is roughly the argument of Jones 1986, 21.
14. Schwartz 1965. For criticism, see Hall 1981, 56f.
15. In Macleod's list, nos. 75, 81–86.
16. Macleod nos. 12, 18, 39, 49, 58, 72, 74, 76 (but see Branham 1989, 237–8, n. 4). For details, see Anderson 1976, Hall 1981.
17. Macleod nos. 16, 33 (*About the Parasite*; see Nesselrath 1985, 1–8), 44 (see Swain 1996, 304f., Elsner 2001, 124–5), 48.
18. Eulogy: *Images, In Defence of 'Images', In Praise of Demosthenes, About the Parasite*. Literary vituperation: *The Sham Sophist*.
19. Attacks on philosophers and philosophical schools: *The Carousal, The Lover of Lies, The Eunuch, Hermotimus*. Philosophical attack on Rome: *The Philosopher Nigrinus*.
20. Athletics: *Anacharsis*. Friendship: *Toxaris*. Pantomime: *The Dance*. Love: *Affairs of the Heart*. Conversations between courtesans: *Chattering Courtesans*. The futility of not facing facts: *The Ship*.
21. Underworld setting: *The Journey down to Hades, Menippus, Dialogues of the Dead*. Olympian setting: *Prometheus, The Judgement of the Goddesses, The Parliament of the Gods, Dialogues of the Sea-Gods, Dialogues of the Gods*. Gods and humans interact or gods come to the human world: *Zeus Catechized, Zeus Rants, Icaromenippus, Timon the Misanthrope, Charon, Philosophies for Sale, Two Charges of Literary Assault, The Runaways, Saturnalia*. Conversations with long-dead figures from the past: *The Dead Come to Life, A Conversation with Hesiod*. Conversation with an animal: *The Dream, or The Cock*. Fantastic cure: *Lexiphanes*.
22. Other *prolaliai*: *Dionysus, Heracles, Amber, The Dream, or*

Lucian's Career, The Dipsads, Herodotus, Zeuxis, Harmonides.
For surveys of these, see Branham 1985 and Nesselrath 1990.

23. Personal attacks on contemporaries, named: *The Passing of Per-egrinus, Alexander the False Prophet*; anonymous: *The Ignorant Book-Collector, A Professor of Public Speaking, The Mistaken Critic.*

24. Literary theory: *How to Write History.* Literary satire: *True Histories.*

25. *Slander, A Few Words about Mourning, On Sacrifices, On Salaried Posts in Great Houses.*

26. *The Goddesse of Surrye, Astrology.*

27. *A Slip of the Tongue in Greeting, Apology for the 'Salaried Posts in Great Houses'.*

28. *Gout.*

29. From Peretti 1946 to Bowersock 1969, Jones 1986, Swain 1996 and Whitmarsh 2001a.

30. The first-century AD Greek writer Plutarch, for example, was a Roman citizen (L. Mestrius Plutarchus), information which is gleaned from an inscription (*SIG* 829a; see Whitmarsh 2001a, 22 with n. 95).

31. See Bowie 1970, Swain 1996, Whitmarsh 2001a.

32. See Swain 1996, 17–64.

33. See Swain 1996, 312–15.

34. Jones 1986, 66–7.

35. See n. 7.

36. These are reported by Philostratus (b. *c.* AD 170) as the topics of speeches by, respectively, Marcus of Byzantium and Alexander Peloplaton ('Clay-Plato'), *Lives of the Sophists* 1.24 and 2.5. The other types of rhetoric, the forensic (for lawcourt speeches) and political (for public assemblies) were in general less important at this period.

37. See Swain 1996, 17–64.

38. See further my remarks in section 6.

39. All that survives of the works of the originator of Menippean satire (a genre imitated at Rome by Marcus Terentius Varro in the first century BC and Seneca the Younger in the first century AD in his *Apocolocyntosis*) are a few titles reported in the first half of the third century AD by Diogenes Laertius (*Lives of the Philosophers* 6.101), such as 'Descent to Hades' (cf. Lucian's *Menippus, or The Descent into Hades*) and 'Sale of Diogenes' (cf. Lucian's *Philosophies for Sale*).

40. Cf. paragraph 10, where the verbs addressing the audience are all second person plural.

41. Cf. *Images* 23, where the conversation between Lycinus and Polystratus becomes a book, which is then sent off to Panthea for her to read.

42. R. Helm's *Lukian und Menipp* (*Lucian and Menippus*) (Leipzig and Berlin 1906) argued the case for plagiarism (and branded Lucian a 'mayfly'). The source of the quotation is W. Schmid and O. Staehlin's *Handbuch der Altertumswissenschaft* (Munich 1924). See Holzberg 1988, 206.

43. The quotation is from the *Grundlagen des 19. Jahrhunderts* (1899) of Richard Wagner's son-in-law, Houston Stewart Chamberlain, which appears to be the source of much of the racially based prejudice against Lucian which emerges around the turn of the century in German classical scholarship. For references and discussion, see Holzberg 1988, 207 and Baumbach 2002, 217f. Such racist attitudes were not entirely confined to Germany, however. Note Lt.-Col. Henry W. L. Hime's 1900 monograph *Lucian the Syrian Satirist* and the comment on page 2 about Lucian's reaction to his uncle's blows (*The Dream, or Lucian's Career* 3–4): 'The course he took ... was the natural one: a beating always puts an Asiatic to flight.'

44. For Philostratus, see n. 7 above. Lucian is only mentioned by Eunapius as a source, for the life of Demonax (*Lives of the Philosophers and Sophists* 454, quoted in the heading of section 1 of this Introduction).

45. Alciphron (second/third century AD) and Aristaenetus (fifth century AD) both wrote *Letters of Courtesans* and Aristaenetus acknowledges Lucian's paternity (in his *Dialogues of the Courtesans*) and Alciphron's debt by composing a letter to Lucian from Alciphron and a reply by Lucian to the same man. Julian the Apostate (d. 363) seems to follow Lucian's literary approach to satire in his *Misopogon* and *Caesares*.

46. Lactantius (d. *c.* 320), *Divine Institutes* 1.9; Isidore of Pelusium (360–*c.* 435), *Letters* 4.55, p. 1105C (J.-P. Migne, *Patrologia Graeca* 78).

47. The manuscript dates from the eighth or ninth century, but scholars place the translation much earlier.

48. Examples are *Philopatris* (*The Patriot*; mid eleventh century?), *Timarion* (twelfth century), *Mazaris* (late fourteenth to early fifteenth century). See Robinson 1979, 68–81 and Seminar Classics 609 1975.

49. Berti 1985, 1987a and 1987b.

50. See Cast 1981 and Massing 1990 for a detailed history of the motif in art.

51. Details of translations in this paragraph are from Sidwell 1975, but can now be more easily accessed in Marsh 1998.

52. Thompson 1940.

53. Sidwell 1975, 75–84.

54. Jacobitz, IV, 247.

55. Martin Luther said to Erasmus 'your breath smells of Lucian' (*On Non-Free Will* (1524), 127) and condemned his *Colloquia Familiaria* (1519) as worse than Lucian. Alberto Pio da Carpi from the Catholic side condemned his use of Lucian in both the *Colloquia* and the *Praise of Folly* (1509). Robinson 1979, 168 and Caccia 1907, 37–8.

56. On 'Dryden's Lucian' see Craig 1921.

57. See Robinson 1979, 145f.

58. Robinson 1979, 198. Lucian's influence on Fielding in his style and other ways (first suggested by Miller 1961) has been brought into question by Mace 1996.

59. This is not to suggest that such creative reuse died out. A good twentieth-century example is *1920 or Dips into the Near Future* (London 1917), written under the pseudonym 'Lucian'.

60. Lehmann (Leipzig 1822–31); Jacobitz (Leipzig 1836–41 and 1851); Bekker (Leipzig 1853); Dindorf (Leipzig 1858); Fritzsche (Rostock 1860–82) (30 works); Sommerbrodt (Berlin 1886–99) (incomplete).

61. Their knowledge of the Lucianic version is suggested by two things, (1) the fact that the film's narrator introduces the story by alluding to its antiquity and (2) divergences from Goethe and convergences with Lucian. See Sidwell 1990.

62. See Baumbach 2002, pp. 230–2.

Further Reading

Branham, R. B., *Unruly Eloquence: Lucian and the Comedy of Traditions* (Cambridge, Mass. 1989). An excellent general introduction, especially good on Lucian's humour and its sources.

Hall, J., *Lucian's Satire* (New York 1981). A detailed study of Lucian's life and works, closely argued and sensible.

Holzberg, N., 'Lucian and the Germans', in *The Uses of Greek and Latin: Historical Essays*, ed. A. C. Dionisotti et al. (London 1988, 199–209). A fascinating essay which traces Lucian's reception in Germany from its zenith to its anti-Semitic nadir.

Jones, C. P., *Culture and Society in Lucian* (Cambridge, Mass. 1986). A closely argued study of Lucian the thesis of which is that there is much more close observation of the contemporary world in his oeuvre than was thought by critics such as Bompaire, who believed Lucian to be operating merely in the 'world of books'.

Marsh, D., *Lucian and the Latins: Humor and Humanism in the Early Renaissance* (Ann Arbor 1998). A study of the first contact between Italian humanists and Lucian, detailing translations and examining imitations by genre (Dialogue of the Dead, paradoxical encomium, etc.).

Robinson, C., *Lucian and His Influence in Europe* (London 1979). A wide-ranging account of Lucian's works and their influence in Byzantium and from the Italian Renaissance to the Enlightenment, with special emphasis on Erasmus and Fielding.

Swain, S., *Hellenism and Empire: Language, Classicism and*

Power in the Greek World, AD 50–250 (Oxford 1996). A detailed but wide-ranging study of Greek identity, politics and culture in the Roman empire, with studies of several writers of the period, including Lucian.

Translator's Note

The works selected have been chosen to cover diverse aspects of Lucian's output, while avoiding unnecessary overlap with other available collections.[1] As I have mentioned (Introduction, section 6), many of the works chosen (the majority in fact) were among those favoured by the earliest humanist translators and were consequently very influential in the creation of new literary genres. These are *Demonax the Philosopher*, *Slander*, *A Few Words about Mourning*, *The Journey down to Hades*, *Timon the Misanthrope*, *The Scythian*, *Toxaris*, *An Encomium of Fatherland*, *Praising a Fly*, *About the Parasite* and *True Histories*. *'So You Think I'm the Prometheus of the Literary World?'* and *Two Charges of Literary Assault* were selected because of their importance for Lucian's self-presentation, both as narrator and as character. *The Philosopher Nigrinus*, while not Lucian's most attractive dialogue, commands attention because of the closeness of many of its themes to Roman satire. *The Ship, or Prayers* once more shows Lucian dealing with an ethical theme with what many consider is his *alter ego*, Lycinus, centre stage. *Images* and *In Defence of 'Images'* appear both because of their originality and intrinsic interest as 'eulogies' cast in dialogue form, and because they face us with one of the most serious problems of interpretation in Lucian, the question of his attitude to Rome. *Chattering Courtesans*, the title piece, was partly translated into Italian (not Latin) around 1471 by Niccolò da Lonigo, but my main reason for its inclusion is that it deserves to be better known. As to arrangement, I have tried to gather works into groups which will be mutually revealing (e.g. eulogies, comic dialogues, diatribes) and to order them in such a way as to move from Lucian as self-conscious literary innovator through those innovations to the most complex and famous of them, *True Histories*. Each work selected has its own distinctive contribution to make in the creation of an overall view of the nature and tone of the Syrian satirist's oeuvre. Hence, the collection is designed to serve as a useful overview, if read in sequence, with the Notes and the Glossary.

Lucian's Style and the Translation

Lucian is unique not only in his manipulation and merging of ancient literary genres, but also in his style. Like most ancient rhetoricians, he favours the extended sentence, though he can write in shorter, punchier sentences where necessary. However, his treatment of the period tends to be rather informal, with plentiful interruptions of the main flow and a tendency towards parataxis ('and ... and ... and') rather than subordination, reflecting parallel tendencies in two of his three bases for imitation, Old Comedy and Platonic dialogue. Despite this structural informality, his vocabulary is both wide-ranging (drawn from comedy, history, tragedy, philosophical dialogue and oratory) and non-idiomatically deployed. In addition, he drips with classical allusion and his choice of words is often designed to recall quite specific ancient writers.

Any ancient text presents a challenge to the translator, but this set of demands is especially difficult to meet in full. The sophisticated verbal intertextuality can only be communicated by notes and glossary. In regard to the humour of Lucian's language, I have tried to keep some idea of the high style he employs, while occasionally dipping – as he himself does – into lower registers, but I have used the modern colloquial abbreviated forms (e.g. 'isn't', 'can't') to suggest the witty informality that none the less attends Lucian's writing. However, Lucian was writing not in the everyday language of the Samosatan street, but in an idiom specifically revived for cultural prestige (see Introduction, section 5). So whatever the English translator does, short of borrowing the language of Chaucer or Shakespeare, this aspect of Lucian's style must be held out as a carrot to induce readers to learn classical Greek and taste the source for themselves.

NOTE

1.   Reardon 1965 and Macleod 1991.

Note on the Texts

Lucian's works, like those of all Greek authors of antiquity, were transmitted in manuscript form. Over a hundred manuscripts of Lucian survive, some complete and some incomplete, the earliest from the beginning of the tenth century. Since the appearance of the first printed edition (Florence 1496) many scholars have undertaken the task of establishing a sound text, by sorting out the relationships between manuscripts (there appear to be two distinct families), by critically assessing the variant readings and by making conjectures where no manuscript makes adequate sense. For a brief account of the principal manuscripts and printed editions, see volume 1 of the Harmon–Kilburn–Macleod Loeb Classical Library edition, pp. xiii–xiv. I have based my translation upon the text of the most recent complete edition, the Oxford Classical Text edited by M. D. Macleod, which is both reliable and accessible. I have drawn attention to and where necessary explained my very occasional divergences from this in the notes to the relevant works.

For ease of reference to the Greek text, I have used the Macleod OCT paragraph numbering throughout.

Maps

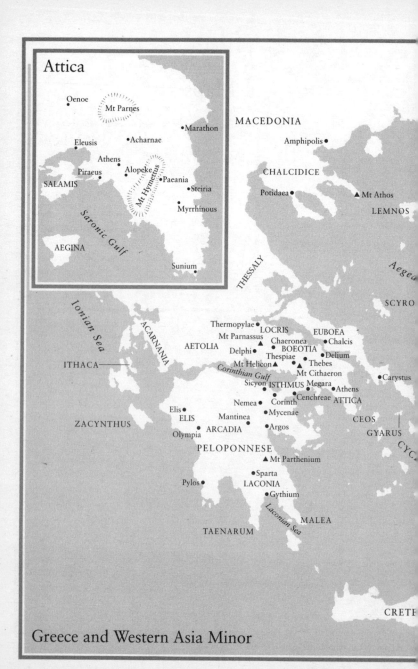

Attica

Oenoe

Mt Parnes

Marathon

Eleusis

Acharnae

Athens

Piraeus

Alopeke

Paeania

Steiria

SALAMIS

Mt Hymettus

Myrrhinous

Saronic Gulf

AEGINA

Sunium

MACEDONIA

Amphipolis

CHALCIDICE

Potidaea

▲ Mt Athos

LEMNOS

Aegea

SCYRO

THESSALY

Ionian Sea

ACARNANIA

Thermopylae

LOCRIS

Mt Parnassus

Chaeronea

EUBOEA

Chalcis

AETOLIA

Delphi

BOEOTIA

Delium

Thespiae

ITHACA

Mt Helicon ▲

Thebes

Corinthian Gulf

Mt Cithaeron ▲

Carystus

Sicyon

ISTHMUS

Megara

Nemea

Corinth

Cenchreae

Athens

ATTICA

Elis

Mycenae

CEOS

ELIS

Mantinea

Argos

ZACYNTHUS

ARCADIA

GYARUS

Olympia

CYC

PELOPONNESE

▲ Mt Parthenium

Sparta

Pylos

LACONIA

Gythium

MALEA

Laconian Sea

TAENARUM

CRETE

Greece and Western Asia Minor

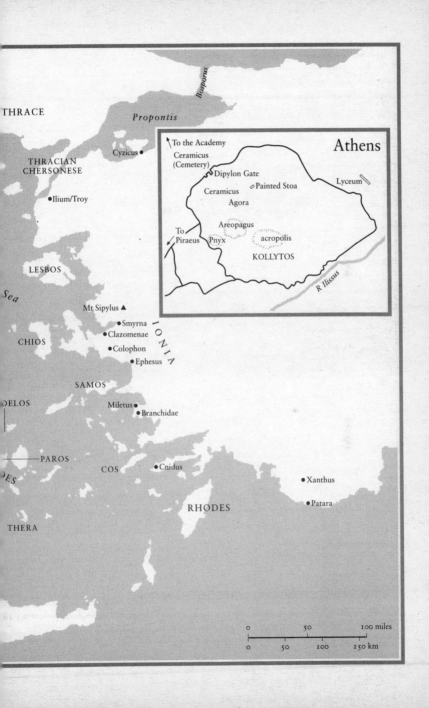

THRACE

Propontis

Bosporus

THRACIAN
CHERSONESE

Cyzicus ●

●Ilium/Troy

LESBOS

Sea

CHIOS

Mt Sipylus ▲

●Smyrna
●Clazomenae

●Colophon

●Ephesus

IONIA

SAMOS

DELOS

Miletus ●
●Branchidae

PAROS

COS

●Cnidus

ES

RHODES

THERA

●Xanthus

●Patara

Athens

↖ To the Academy
Ceramicus
(Cemetery)

Dipylon Gate

⌀Painted Stoa

Lyceum

Ceramicus

Agora

Areopagus

To
Piraeus

Pnyx

acropolis

KOLLYTOS

R Ilissus

0		50		100 miles

0	50	100	150 km

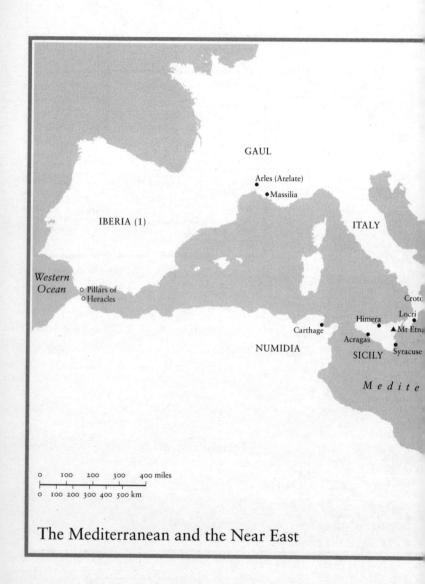

GAUL

Arles (Arelate)
•Massilia

IBERIA (1)

ITALY

Western
Ocean   o Pillars of
         o Heracles

Crot

Himera   Locri

Carthage   ▲ Mt Etna

NUMIDIA   Acragas

         SICILY   Syracuse

Medite

o   100   200   300   400 miles

o   100 200 300 400 500 km

The Mediterranean and the Near East

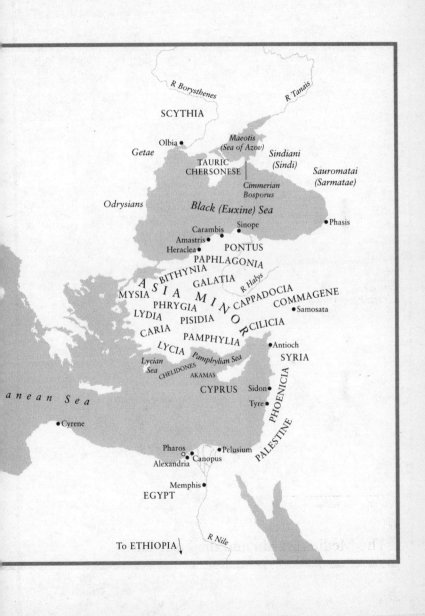

R Borysthenes

R Tanais

SCYTHIA

Olbia •

Maeotis (Sea of Azov)

Sindiani (Sindi)

Getae

TAURIC CHERSONESE

Sauromatai (Sarmatae)

Cimmerian Bosporus

Odrysians

Black (Euxine) Sea

• Phasis

Carambis • • Sinope

Amastris •

Heraclea •

PONTUS

PAPHLAGONIA

BITHYNIA

GALATIA

R Halys

A S I A

CAPPADOCIA

COMMAGENE

MYSIA

M I N O R

PHRYGIA

• Samosata

LYDIA

PISIDIA

CARIA

PAMPHYLIA

CILICIA

LYCIA

Pamphylian Sea

• Antioch

Lycian Sea

CHELIDONES

AKAMAS

SYRIA

anean Sea

CYPRUS

Sidon •

Tyre •

PHOENICIA

• Cyrene

Pharos

• Pelusium

Alexandria • Canopus

PALESTINE

Memphis •

EGYPT

To ETHIOPIA ↓

R Nile

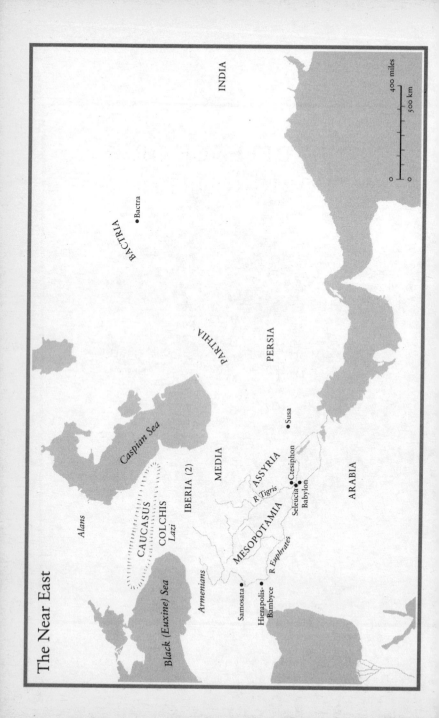

The Near East

INDIA

400 miles
500 km

BACTRIA
•Bactra

PARTHIA

PERSIA

Caspian Sea

•Susa

MEDIA

ASSYRIA

Ctesiphon
Seleucia•
Babylon

ARABIA

R Tigris

Alans

CAUCASUS
COLCHIS
Lazi
IBERIA (2)

MESOPOTAMIA

R Euphrates

Armenians

Black (Euxine) Sea

Samosata•
Hierapolis-
Bambyce•

IN DEFENCE OF
ORIGINALITY

Preface

This section comprises two works of different types, a *prolalia* (see Introduction, section 3), 'So You Think I'm the Prometheus of the Literary World?', and a comic dialogue, *Two Charges of Literary Assault*.[1] Dating can only be relative: at *Two Charges* 32, 'The Syrian' (Lucian) is past the age of forty, and the claimed change of life and literary goals after this age would also place 'So You Think I'm the Prometheus' at a similar period. Both works purport to be literary defences of Lucian's originality in combining the philosophical dialogue of Plato with the comic fantasy of Athenian Old Comedy, as written by Aristophanes and Eupolis in particular (*Two Charges* 33 – but note that this is the way the *prosecution* puts the case). Such self-conscious parading of the author is absolutely typical of Lucian, whether it is done in first person narrative (as in 'So You Think I'm the Prometheus') or in dramatic form (as in *Two Charges*). At the same time, the persona presented is hedged about with literary reminiscences, often presented in enigmatic form, as a sort of challenge to the audience to use their education to spot citation or allusion, recall its context and the scholarship which surrounds the text, and then read between the lines. In *Two Charges*, for example, the framework of the accusations against his *alter ego* 'the Syrian speech-writer' by his wife Rhetoric is formed upon the plot of a famous Old Comedy by Cratinus, *The Wine-Flask*, unfortunately lost to us, except for a brief and incomplete plot outline.[2] In the play, the central character (a comic poet) was accused by his wife Comedy of abuse. Now, Lucian certainly did not intend, in a work which focuses on his use of Old Comedy, that his audience should miss this reuse of

Cratinus. But what can it mean? Part of our problem is that we are unclear about the details of Cratinus' plot, though we do know how it was generally read in later antiquity – as a self-defence of Cratinus.[3] By appropriating Cratinus' motifs and redeploying them with himself as the central outspoken Old Comic poet figure, Lucian reinforces his right to use frank and abusive speech (he represents himself in another dialogue, *The Dead Come to Life*, as Parrhesiades, 'Freespeechson'), and at the same time displays his own literary virtuosity. The allusion, that is, must be spotted and set in its intellectual context for the full value of Lucian's literary game – and his defence – to become clear. The modern reader must also be prepared to be challenged by these procedures.

NOTES

1. The Greek titles translated literally are 'To one who said "You're a Prometheus in words"' and 'Twice accused'.
2. The plot outline is preserved in the scholia to Aristophanes' *Knights* 400a in the *Suda*. See *PCG* IV, 219, Cratinus Testimonia on *Pytine* [*The Wine-Flask*] ii.
3. This is made clear by the item mentioned in the previous note.

'SO YOU THINK I'M THE PROMETHEUS OF THE LITERARY WORLD?'

So you're saying I'm a Prometheus,[1] are you? Perhaps, my dear man, you mean that, like him, I also fashion my works from clay. If so, I recognize the point of comparison. I am like him. I don't deny that I'm a potter, even if the clay I use is inferior, from the crossroads, you might say, and next of kin to mud. On the other hand, if you're applying the name of the cleverest of the Titans to my works as a way of praising them – way above their merit – as masterpieces of invention, there's a danger that people will think your good opinion has a subtext rife with irony and the old Attic nose-in-the-air attitude. Go on, tell me where my inventiveness lies. What exactly is the remarkable cleverness and Promethean quality my writings possess? As far as I'm concerned, it's enough if they don't seem too earthen or entirely deserving of being pegged out on the Caucasus. Anyhow, it would be much more reasonable to make the Prometheus comparison with you people who have great reputations for pursuing your cases as lawyers in accordance with the dictates of truth. What you create is really living and breathing, and, by Zeus, its heat is intense. Now that is Promethean, except for one thing, of course, that it isn't from clay that most of your creations are made, but from pure gold.

Those of us who are popular entertainers and compose this type of lecture are only putting on show empty images. On the one side, as I said a minute ago, the work is done completely in clay, like that of the doll-manufacturer. But, on the other, there's no movement that could be compared to that produced by Prometheus, and nothing to indicate there's a soul present. The thing is just idle enjoyment and entertainment. So I suppose I'm wondering whether you might mean by 'Prometheus of the literary world' what the comic poet said about Cleon. I think the quotation about him goes:

Cleon's a Prometheus *after* the event.[2]

The Athenians themselves actually used to call potters and oven-makers and all workers in clay 'Prometheuses', punning on the material they used and also, I suppose, on the fact that they had to bake their products. If that's what you mean by calling me a Prometheus, you not only hit the target spot on, but with a strong dose of sharp Attic wit as well. I mean, what I make can also be easily broken, just like their pots: all it takes is to throw a small stone, and, smash, the whole lot's in pieces.

3   And yet someone who wanted to console me might say, 'No, this wasn't the basis of the comparison with Prometheus at all. What he's praising is your originality, the fact that you had no model to work to. Just like Prometheus, in fact. Men didn't yet exist. He thought them up and then made them. Think of all those living creatures he shaped and kitted out so that they moved properly and were lovely to look at. To put it in a nutshell, he was the master-craftsman, even if Athena did help a bit by breathing on the clay and making his creations live.' That's what my comforter might say, thinking that the *bon mot* was designed to be laudatory. And maybe this was what the expression meant. For me, though, it's not really enough for someone to think that I'm original, and to be unable to point to something more ancient than my creation, of which it was, as it were, the offspring. I can tell you, if it didn't seem pleasing, I'd be ashamed of it. In fact, I'd stamp on it and rub it out. As far as I'm concerned, the originality would be absolutely no impediment to its destruction as an eyesore. Moreover, if I didn't think that way, I would certainly deserve to have my liver pecked at by sixteen vultures, for not understanding that ugliness is exponentially increased by strangeness.

4   Let me give you an example. Ptolemy, the son of Lagus, brought two novelties to Egypt. One was a jet-black Bactrian camel. The other was a man with skin of two colours. One half

of him was completely black. The other was gleaming white. And he had exactly the same amount of black skin and white skin. Ptolemy gathered the Egyptians together into the theatre and put a great many things on show. His pièces de résistance, however, with the sight of which he expected to astonish the crowd, were the camel and the black-and-white man. When they saw the camel, they almost got up out of their seats and ran off, they were so terrified, despite the fact that the beast had been completely decked out in gold, had purple robes[3] thrown across it, and a gem-encrusted bit, a treasure once belonging no doubt to Darius, Cambyses or Cyrus. The man mostly provoked laughter, though there were a few who were merely disgusted, thinking that he was a monster. So Ptolemy, realizing that he had gained no increase in his status by showing them and that the Egyptians had not been smitten with wonder by their novelty, but regarded harmony and beauty as prior qualities, took them away and no longer valued them as he had before. The camel died of neglect. The two-tone man he gave as a gift to the piper Thespis when she had given a good performance at a drinking-bout.

I'm afraid my work may be a camel among the Egyptians, so to speak. What people admire is its bit and purple saddle. Even the fact that it's made up of two absolutely splendid things, dialogue and comedy, I mean, will be insufficient to create beauty, unless the mixture is also harmonious and measured. Because, you know, it's perfectly possible to produce something grotesque out of mixing two lovely things together. Take the obvious example, Centaurs. You wouldn't be inclined to describe them as loveable beasts. They're actually pretty objectionable, if you give credence to the painters who show them getting drunk and committing murder. But then, you'll say, it's surely possible to combine two really excellent ingredients and make something beautiful, isn't it? For instance, the combination of wine and honey is top class. I agree. Not that I can go so far as to claim this quality for my own writings. On the contrary, I'm afraid that the mixture may have spoiled the beauty of each of the two ingredients.

It has to be said that dialogue and comedy were not firmly

compatible friends when they started out. One (Dialogue) stayed at home and kept himself to himself, or spent time with a few associates in the shaded walks. The other (Comedy) gave herself up to Dionysus and spent time in the theatre, having a ball, raising laughs and making snide remarks about people. She walked in rhythm, sometimes accompanied by the pipe, riding high on anapaestic metres,[4] spending most of her time rubbishing the companions of Dialogue by calling them 'thinksters' and 'air-heads' and the like. The only reason she had for living was to deride them and pour down the licence of the Dionysia festival over them, sometimes showing them walking on air and consorting with clouds, sometimes measuring the distance a flea can jump, actually discussing in great detail airy nonsense.[5] Dialogue, on the other hand, kept his social affairs strictly above board, philosophizing about nature and virtue. The result is, as the musicians say, there's two octaves between them, from highest to lowest. None the less, I was bold enough to bring together two things which had this contrary relation to each other, and to fit them together, even though they weren't too keen and put up with the cohabitation with some discomfort.

7   Now that I come to think of it, I'm afraid I may appear to have done another thing like your Prometheus, in causing intercourse between female and male. Perhaps that's what I'm charged with. I rather suspect that there's another thing, though. Maybe it's that I've deceived my audiences by giving them a feast of bones covered in fat, I mean, comic laughter hidden under philosophy's solemnity.[6] As to the charge of theft – also made against the same god – come off it! This at least is something you couldn't say my works are guilty of. Who would I have stolen from? Of course, I may be mistaken. Someone else has also possibly put together a set of sea-horses and goat-stags like these. But what's a man to do? I've made my bed, and I'm going to have to lie on it. After all, it's Epimetheus' job to have second thoughts, not Prometheus'.

TWO CHARGES OF
LITERARY ASSAULT

ZEUS: Oh to hell with the philosophers who say that happiness
exists only among the gods! If they knew what we go through
for the sake of human beings, they wouldn't be so eager to
envy us the blessings of nectar and ambrosia. In any case,
their evidence is taken from Homer, who was blind and a
fraud. Fancy calling us 'blessed' and telling tales about what
goes on in heaven, when he couldn't even see what was
happening on earth![1] I mean, look at the Sun here, for
example. He yokes up his chariot and spends the whole
day trekking through the sky, clothed in fire and radiating
sunbeams. He'd be lucky if he got a second to scratch his ear,
as they say. A moment's carelessness, and his horses have
slipped their reins, veered off course and burnt everything to
a crisp.[2] The Moon too. She gets no sleep, going round and
shining for revellers and people who leave their dinner-dates
late. And it's a pretty troublesome art that Apollo's taken on
himself to practise too. He's been virtually deafened by people
bothering him for prophecies. One minute he's got to be
in Delphi, in a bit he runs off to Colophon, from there he
skips over to Xanthus and then at a run heads for Delos
and Branchidae. You might say that whenever his priestess
sips from the holy spring, chews some laurel leaves, shakes
the tripod and bids him be present, without even catching
his breath he must be there right away to help her deliver
the oracles. If he doesn't, bang goes his professional reputation. I won't even mention all the tricks they try on him
to test his mantic skill, cooking up lamb-and-tortoise stew.[3]
If he hadn't had a sharp sense of smell, the Lydian[4] might

well have had the last laugh on him. As for Asclepius, the Healer,

> he looks on dreadful things, lays hands on worse,
> and reaps a harvest full of private grief
> from others' sorrows.[5]

I could mention the Winds, who make the crops grow, send ships on their way and breathe on the work of winnowers. I could cite Sleep, who flies into everybody's bed, or Dream, who stays the night with him and helps him expound the gods' will to men. The gods toil away at all this because they love human beings and each of them in his or her separate way contributes to life on earth.

2   But what the others have to put up with is mild compared with the unpleasantness and trouble I, the father and king of all, have to endure, with my mind divided between so many concerns. In the first place, I have to supervise the work of the other gods who have responsibilities under my regime, to make sure they don't slack in their duties. Then I have a million tasks to perform myself, scarcely manageable because of their complexity. It's not as though I simply have the major administrative task to perform, I mean managing and organizing the weather – rain, hail, wind and lightning – before I can sit down and take a break from my assigned worries. I've got to do all this and at the same time keep a watch in all directions and supervise everything as though I were that herdsman at Nemea:[6] people stealing, people perjuring themselves, people sacrificing. Has someone made a libation? Where's the sacrificial smell and smoke coming from? Who has called for me in sickness or at sea? But the most onerous task of all is being in so many places at the same time: Olympia for a hecatomb, Babylon for a battle, with the Getae to hail, with the Ethiopians to feast.

Even so, it's very hard to stop people bemoaning their lot. Time and again 'the other gods and men in helms sleep out the night' but for Zeus, that's me, there's no Homeric 'sweet sleep' to hold me in its bosom.[7] And just say we do nod off for a few minutes? Then Epicurus is immediately justified with his claims that we take no thought for earthly affairs. And it's not a negligible danger we face if people believe what he says. As a consequence we'll have no garlands on our temples, no smell of roasting in our streets, no libations poured to us from the mixing-bowls, the fires will go out on our altars and there'll be a total lack of sacrifice and offering. We'll certainly starve.[8] That's the reason I'm standing up here alone at the stern like a steersman, with the steering-oar in my hands. The crew can sleep if they happen to have had one over the eight. But I take thought for everyone 'in my heart' and 'in my mind',[9] sleepless and supperless. The only reward I get for this is that people consider me the boss. I 3 wish I could ask the philosophers who think only the gods are happy when the hell they think folk with so many problems to deal with have any down time to drink nectar and eat ambrosia!

Take an example. We're so damned busy, we've got an enormous backlog of old lawsuits not dealt with. They've been stacked there so long, they've fallen apart with mildew and they're covered in spiders' webs. I'm thinking in particular about the ones taken out against certain individuals associated with the intellectual arts and the crafts. Some of them are absolutely ancient. The litigants themselves are bawling on every side, grinding their teeth, calling for justice and accusing me of tardiness. What they don't realize is that it's not through contempt that these decisions have passed their sell-by-date. It's because of that state of bliss they think we live in. That's the name they give to our complete lack of spare time.

HERMES: Actually, Zeus, I've also heard lots of people making 4 complaints like this while doing my duties on earth, but I've never dared to tell you. But now you've broken the silence, I do feel free to mention them. What they're really upset about, father, and censure – they aren't able to say it openly, but can only mutter as they put their heads together – what they really accuse you of is the time-lag. They each ought long ago to have known the result and been able to come to terms with it.

ZEUS: What do you think we should do, then, Hermes? Should we set up a lawsuit market[10] now, or do you want us to announce it for the new year?

HERMES: We mustn't put it off. Let's do it now.

ZEUS: OK. You fly down and announce that there'll be a lawsuit market on the following terms. All those who have suits pending should come to the Areopagus today. There Justice will allot them juries from the Athenian citizen body according to the amount of damages claimed. Anyone who thinks that the decision is unfair has the right to appeal to me, and have the case heard again from the beginning as though it had never been tried. My daughter, you go and sit beside the Dread Goddesses. It's your job to allot juries to the cases and scrutinize the proceedings.

5 JUSTICE: What? You want me to go back to earth again? All that will happen is that I'll have to run away from human life once more when I can't stand the mocking laughter of Injustice.

ZEUS: You should have better expectations. At all events the philosophers have by now persuaded people to pay you more respect than Injustice. The key player in all this was the son of Sophroniscus.[11] He really gave justice a good press and demonstrated that it was the greatest good of all.

JUSTICE: Well, the fellow you mentioned got a fantastic reward for his lectures about me. He was handed over to the Eleven,[12] put in prison and drank the cup of hemlock. The poor man, he hadn't even offered the cockerel he owed to Asclepius.[13] That's the advantage his accusers had. They produced the opposite philosophy, with Injustice as its focus.

6 ZEUS: But in those days philosophical discourse was still a foreign country to most people. So it's no wonder the lawcourts swung the way of Anytus and Meletus. Things are different nowadays. Don't you see how many old cloaks, sticks and begging-bowls there are? Everywhere you look there are long beards and books in the left hand. And everyone has you on his philosophical lips. The shaded walks are packed with people meeting each other in squadrons and phalanxes, every man jack of them claiming to be a foster-child of virtue. Why, lots of them have abandoned the skills

they had before, made a dash for the begging-bowl and the little cloak, got themselves an Ethiopian tan and hey presto are now philosophers instead of cobblers or carpenters, and go around singing the praises of you and your virtue.[14] It's the old proverb, really. You'd sooner miss hitting a plank if you fell down on board ship than not see a philosopher wherever you cast your eye.

JUSTICE: But they scare me to death, Zeus, with the quarrels they're always having with each other, and with their unfeeling attitude in the discourses they hold about me.[15] I've heard that most of them only pretend to honour me, but actually won't let me anywhere near their houses. In fact, people say they would obviously shut me out if I arrived at their doors, because Injustice is a long-honoured guest of theirs.

ZEUS: They're not all of them bad, daughter. It's enough if you run into just a few good men. But off the two of you go now, so that you can get a few cases settled today.

HERMES: OK, Justice, let's go. It's this way. We go straight past Sunium, just under Hymettus keeping Mount Parnes on the left, where those twin peaks are. I imagine you've forgotten the way, it's been so long. Why are you crying and making such a fuss? Don't be afraid. Things have changed for the better in the lives of men. All those Scirons, Pityocampteses,[16] Bousirises and Phalarises that you used to fear are dead. Wisdom, the Academy and the Stoa hold the field now. Everywhere they're in search of you and talking about you, craning their necks to see if you might fly back down among them from somewhere.

JUSTICE: Well, at least you'll tell me the truth, Hermes, even if you're the only one who will. You've spent much of your time among them, hanging around in the gymnasia and the market-place. At any rate they call you 'Hermes of the market-place' and you're the one who makes announcements at assemblies. What kind of people have the Athenians become? Will I be able to stay among them?

HERMES: Well, it certainly would be wrong of me not to tell my sister the truth. Most of them have received clear benefits from the study of philosophy. At the very least, they're more moderate in their sins out of respect for the costume they wear. I have to admit, though, that you'll still run into some bad eggs among them, and some who are in between – either half-philosophers or half-bad. To take a metaphor from dyeing, when wisdom took them over, those who absorbed the colour completely turned out to be really good men. There were no traces of any other hue at all. These are the ones who will welcome you with open arms. There are others who were too coated in old dirt for the colour to stay fast. These are better than the rest of humanity, true. But the job isn't finished. They have spots and marks and are dappled like leopards. There is another group, though. They have touched the outside of the dyeing vat with the tips of their fingers, wiped off a bit of soot and think they've been sufficiently imbued as well. Obviously, you'll only be staying with the best sort, though.

9   But while we've been talking, Attica's come into sight. Let's keep Cape Sunium on the right and head off towards the acropolis. When we land, you sit down on the Areopagus and look down at the Pnyx until I've finished my announcement of Zeus' decree. I'm going up onto the acropolis. That's the easiest place to make sure everyone hears me.

JUSTICE: Don't go away, Hermes, without telling me who this is coming along. He's got horns, a pipe and hairy legs.

HERMES: You mean you don't recognize Pan, the most bacchic of Bacchus' servants? His old home was on Mount Parthenium. But when Datis sailed up and the barbarians landed at Marathon, he came to help the Athenians without being called.[17] Since then he's taken up residence in this cave under the acropolis, just above the Pelasgicum. He now pays tax as a resident foreigner.[18] He's obviously spotted us nearby and is coming to greet us.

10 PAN: Hello, Hermes. Hello, Justice.

HERMES: Hello to you too, Pan, champion musician and dancer among the satyrs,[19] champion warrior at Athens!

PAN: What can have brought you here, Hermes?

HERMES: Justice will give you the full story. I must head for the acropolis to make my announcement.

JUSTICE: Zeus has sent me down to allot juries to the cases, Pan. How are things for you in Athens?

PAN: Well, on the whole I'm not doing as well among them as I had hoped – in fact rather worse. After all, I did get rid of all that hurly-burly created by the barbarians. However, two or three times a year they do come up and make sacrifice to me. They always choose a billy-goat with a full set of equipment and a particularly rancid smell, and then feast on the meat, making me only a viewer of their enjoyment and honouring me with nothing but their hullabaloo. Still, I do get a kick out of their fun and laughter.

JUSTICE: And have they really improved in other areas because of the philosophers, Pan? 11

PAN: Who are these philosophers you're talking about? Do you mean those depressives who huddle together in groups, the ones with beards like mine, the natterers?

JUSTICE: That's them.

PAN: Well, I'm not completely sure what it is they're actually saying and I don't understand their philosophy. I'm from the hills and I've never learned that smart city-slicker type of language. Where would you get a sophist or a philosopher from in Arcadia? I'm good at the transverse chanter and the pan-pipe. I can herd goats, dance, and fight, if I have to. All I do is listen to them shouting and talking about 'virtue' and 'forms' and 'nature' and 'the incorporeal', strange words[20] absolutely beyond my ken. When they begin their conversations with each other, they're peaceable enough. But as the meeting goes on, they gradually raise the pitch of their voices until they reach screaming point. The result is that they strain their larynxes with wanting to talk at the same time as everyone else, their faces become red, their necks swell up and their veins stand out. They look just like pipers trying to force the air through the pipe when all the holes are closed. So they throw the discussion into confusion, and go their separate ways after nullifying the premise of their original inquiry. Most of them have words of abuse for each other as they go, wiping the sweat from their brow with bent fingers. The winner is the one who shouts louder and behaves more recklessly than the others and leaves the crumbling discussion last. I have to say, though, that the majority of people admire them greatly, especially those who have no pressing claims on their time. They stand around absolutely spellbound by their brazen bawling. To me their behaviour made them seem like complete frauds. And besides, I was irritated by the way their beards looked like mine. I couldn't tell you if there was any public benefit accruing from their shouting or whether any good was likely to spring up from their words. But if you don't mind my telling you the truth without trimming my sails, I can tell you this – because, as you can see, I virtually live in a watchtower – late in the afternoon I've often seen lots of them . . .[21]

12   JUSTICE: Hold on, Pan. Hermes is about to make his proclamation, don't you think?

PAN: Yes, it looks like it.

HERMES: Hearken, O ye people. We are going to establish today, the seventh of Elaphebolion, with the favour of fortune, a lawsuit market. Those who have suits pending should make their way to the Areopagus, where Justice will allot the juries and preside over the judging herself. The jurors will be chosen from the Athenian citizen body as whole. The pay will be three obols[22] for each case. The number of jurors will vary in accordance with the charge. Those who registered their suit but died before it came to court are to be sent up from the Underworld by Aeacus. Anyone who considers that he has received an unjust judgment will be able to appeal. The appeal will be heard by Zeus.

PAN: Good Lord, what a row! Did you hear how loudly they shouted, Justice, and do you see how eagerly they're gathering together, dragging each other up towards the Areopagus? Ah, look, here's Hermes back again. Why don't you two busy yourselves with the lawsuits, allotting and judging the way you usually do, and I'll slink back to my cavern and play a love-song on my pan-pipes. It'll be one of the 'needling Echo' genre. I've enough rhetorical disquisitions and legal arguments every day of my life, listening to all the cases in the Areopagus.

HERMES: Come on, then, Justice, let's call the cases.   13

JUSTICE: Good idea. As you can see, they're arriving in crowds, making a din, buzzing like wasps around the top of the hill.

AN ATHENIAN: I've got you, you scoundrel.

ANOTHER: It's a false charge.

ANOTHER: Now, finally, I'm going to get satisfaction from you.

ANOTHER: I'll prove you did a dreadful deed.

ANOTHER: Give my case the first slot in the timetable.

ANOTHER: Come with me to the court, you scum.

ANOTHER: Don't throttle me.

JUSTICE: You know what we should do, Hermes? Let's postpone the rest of the cases until tomorrow and just allot today the ones brought by the Crafts, Lifestyle and Intellectual Arts lobbies. Hand me the suits that fall into these categories.

HERMES: Intoxication versus Academy. Charge: kidnapping Polemon.

JUSTICE: Seven jurors to be allotted.

HERMES: Stoa versus Pleasure. The charge is malicious damage by seduction of her lover Dionysius.[23]

JUSTICE: This only needs five jurors.

HERMES: Luxury versus Virtue. Aristippus is the bone of contention.

JUSTICE: Five jurors should also be allotted to this case.

HERMES: Merchant Banking versus Diogenes. Charge: escaped from slavery.

JUSTICE: Just allot three.

HERMES: Painting versus Pyrrhon on a charge of desertion.

JUSTICE: We should have nine jurors for this case.

HERMES: Do you want us to allot jurors for these two cases,   14 Justice, the ones recently brought against the orator?

JUSTICE: We'll deal with the old ones first. We'll judge these tomorrow.

HERMES: But they're of a similar kind. The charges may only just have been brought, but they're like those you've just allotted jurors for. It seems reasonable to take them with the others.

JUSTICE: It looks as though you have a vested interest in granting this request, Hermes. Still, if you think it's right, let's allot jurors for these – but only the two of them, mind. We've got enough cases to deal with. Hand me the indictments.

HERMES: Rhetoric versus the Syrian. The charge is neglect. Dialogue versus the same. The charge is wanton abuse.[24]

JUSTICE: But who is he? His name hasn't been written on the charge-sheet.

HERMES: Allot the jury to him as the Syrian orator. There's nothing to stop his being arraigned without a name.[25]

JUSTICE: So! We're going to try cases involving absolute foreigners, now, are we, in the Athenian Areopagus, when they ought to be tried on the other side of the Euphrates? All right. Give him eleven jurors. But they have to judge both cases.

HERMES: Good housekeeping, Justice! That will save a lot on juror pay.

15 JUSTICE: Academy and Intoxication's will be the first case. Pour the water into the clock.[26] Intoxication, you have the first speech. Why is she saying nothing and nodding at me? Go and find out, Hermes.

HERMES: She says she can't conduct the prosecution, because she's tongue-tied from drinking unmixed wine.[27] She's afraid of making herself a laughing-stock in the courtroom. As you can see, she's barely able to stand.

JUSTICE: Well then, let her have one of these clever advocates stand up and speak for her. There are any number ready and willing to burst their lungs for three obols.

HERMES: The trouble is, there's no one who will want to be openly associated with Intoxication as a lawyer. However, she has a plan which she considers reasonable.

JUSTICE: What is it?

HERMES: She says that Academy is always equipped for both sides of a case and takes special pride in her skill at being able to present the opposing argument well.[28] So she says Academy should speak first for her, and then for herself.

JUSTICE: That's unusual. None the less, present both sides of the case, Academy, since you're well able for it.

16 ACADEMY: Pay attention, jurors. My first speech will be on Intoxication's behalf. It's her water that's running through the clock first.

The poor thing has been caused the most grievous injury by me, Academy. There was only one slave she had who was well disposed and faithful to her, and who did not consider shameful anything she might tell him to do. That was Polemon. Her complaint is that I have stolen him away. In the past he used to go revelling during the day through the middle of the market-place, accompanied by lyre-players and a singer from dawn till dusk. He was always drunk, had a perpetual hangover and wore flowery wreaths on his head. All the Athenians can bear witness to this. They never saw Polemon sober. Then one day he revelled right up to the doors of the Academy, the way he usually did to everyone's. I kidnapped him and snatched him from the grasp of Intoxication by force. I then seduced him, forcing him to drink water and training him to stay sober. I tore his wreaths into pieces and then, when he ought to have been lying down drinking,[29] I taught him all sorts of appalling enigmatic expressions, loaded with deep thoughts. As a consequence, his complexion has lost its rosy bloom. He's become pale and shrivelled, the poor creature. He's forgotten all his songs and sometimes doesn't eat or drink until midday. He just sits and babbles all the sorts of rubbish that I, Academy, teach him. The worst crime, though, is that I've given him such airs that he actually mocks Intoxication now and is prepared to list her crimes by the ten thousand.

The case for Intoxication rests. Now I shall speak on my own behalf. Pour in my portion of water now, please.

JUSTICE: What on earth will she say to that? But pour her an equal measure, anyhow.

ACADEMY: Well, jurors, what the advocate has said on Intoxi- 17 cation's behalf is all very reasonable. But if you're prepared to give me a fair hearing, you'll realize that I've done her no wrong at all.

She claims that Polemon here is her slave. However, he's not naturally bad nor an acolyte of Intoxication. He's instinctively similar to me. But when he was still young and tender, Intoxication got in and grabbed him first, with help from Pleasure, who often acts as her partner in crime. She corrupted the poor fellow, giving him over lock, stock and barrel to carousals and courtesans. In the end, he hadn't an ounce of self-respect left. So the arguments she thought just now were in her favour, are actually more in mine. The wretched man used to go around from early morning garlanded, sozzled, accompanied by pipers in the middle of the market-place, never sober, revelling at everyone's door. He was a complete disgrace to his ancestors and the whole city, and a figure of fun for foreigners.

So he came to my house. As usual, I had thrown my doors open to those of my friends who were around, to conduct a discussion about virtue and sensible behaviour. He arrived with his pipe and his garlands and first of all started bawling and trying to break up our meeting by heckling. None of us took the slightest notice of him. But he obviously wasn't terminally bedrenched by Intoxication, because gradually the arguments started to sober him up. He took off his garlands and made the piper stop playing. He began to feel ashamed of his purple cloak.[30] He was like someone awaking from a deep sleep. He suddenly saw his true condition and gave a guilty verdict on his past life. And indeed the rosy bloom of Intoxication did leave him. Instead, he grew red at the thought of his misconduct. In the end, he ran away just as he was and deserted to my camp. I had said no word of encouragement. I had brought no force to bear, as Intoxication claims. He came willingly, because he thought this was the better option.

Now call Polemon to the stand. I want you to find out how I'm treating him. Jurors, I took this man over when he was a laughing-stock. He couldn't even speak or stand up for the unmixed wine in his system. I set him on the straight and narrow, sobered him up and showed him to be a fine man, sensible and valued highly by the Greeks. What's more, he's grateful to me for this, and so are his family.

I rest my case. Please consider now which of us is the better companion for him.

18   JUSTICE: Right. Don't hang about. Cast your votes and get out. There are other cases to try.

HERMES: Academy wins by six votes to one.

JUSTICE: Well, it's no surprise that someone actually voted for   19
Intoxication. Take your seats, jurymen in the case of Stoa
versus Pleasure on the subject of the seduction of her lover.
The water's in the clock. It's you to speak first, the one with
the paint and elaborate highlights.[31]

STOA: I'm well aware, jurors, that I'm going to have to speak   20
against a very attractive opponent. I can see most of you
looking in her direction and smiling at her. You have only
contempt for me, because I wear my hair cropped close, have
a masculine look and appear hard-faced. However, if you're
prepared to listen to what I have to say, I'm sure that I'll
present a juster case than her.

You see, my present complaint is this. By dressing herself
up like a courtesan, and giving him seductive glances, she has
gulled my lover Dionysius, once a sensible man, and drawn
him over to her camp. In fact, the previous case judged in this
court is a blood-relation of this one. What we are examining
here also involves a choice between two opposing lifestyles.
Should we live like pigs, with our heads bent low over the
trough of pleasure, and have no serious or lofty thoughts?
Or, alternatively, should we live the free life of free-thinking
philosophers, putting pleasure in second place to virtue, not
fearing pain as something ineluctable, nor slavishly preferring
pleasure and seeking happiness in honey and figs? The latter
are the bait with which she traps the foolish. She also uses
painful labour as a bogeyman. Between the two techniques,
she manages to bring over the vast majority of people to her
way of thinking. Among them is this poor fellow. She watched
for a moment when he was sick and then got him to take off
our harness and cut loose. If he had been in full health, he
would never have entertained her arguments.

But what use is there in my getting upset at her, when she
doesn't even spare the gods? In fact, she flatly questions their
providential role. So if you're wise, you'll lay a charge of
impiety against her as well. Now I've heard that she's not
even going to be bothered to plead her own case, but is going
to use Epicurus as an advocate. That's the kind of contempt

she has for the court. But what about this? Ask her what sort of characters would Heracles and your very own Theseus have turned out, if they'd avoided their painful labours because pleasure had sweet-talked them? There would have been nothing to stop the earth being full of injustice, if they hadn't laboured painfully.

I'm going to rest my case now. I don't very much like long speeches. However, if she acceded to a small cross-examination from me, it would soon become obvious what a nothing she is. At any rate, you must remember your oath when you cast your votes. If you're to keep it, you mustn't believe Epicurus when he claims that the gods have no role in overseeing human affairs.

JUSTICE: Step down. Epicurus, speak for Pleasure.

21   EPICURUS: I shan't be speaking for long, jurors. I shan't need many words.

Now, if Pleasure had used spells or drugs to force this man Stoa says was her lover to stay away from her and to look only at herself, Pleasure would with reason have appeared to be a sorceress and could have been condemned of misconduct for entrancing other people's lovers. But this is a case of a free man, in a city which claims to be free, with no legal impediment finding distasteful the unpleasantness preached by her and judging nonsense the happiness she tells him is the reward for his painful labours. He escaped from those arguments which resemble labyrinths in their complexity, and with gladness in his heart deserted to Pleasure. He cut away the coils of argument as though they were chains. His conclusion, that painful labour is indeed laboriously painful, and pleasure pleasurable, is entirely human and sensible. Now in these circumstances, should she have locked him out? He was like a man swimming to harbour after a shipwreck, longing for calm. Should she have pitched him back headlong into painful labour and handed the poor fellow over completely to perplexity? But he was like a suppliant at the Altar of Pity when he fled to Pleasure's protection. And handed back for what? So that he could climb the steep slope, sweating profusely, and finally glimpse his goal, the much-vaunted

Virtue, and then, after labouring painfully his whole life, claim happiness only after death?

But here's the clinching argument. What better judge of the matter could you possibly have than Dionysius himself? He knows Stoa's arguments if anyone does. At one time, he thought that the only good is virtue. Then he realized that painful labour is a bad thing, and chose what he considered to be the better option. I suppose he must have seen that the people who talked so much about endurance and putting up with hardships were privately devotees of Pleasure. They make promises in public but at home live according to the laws of Pleasure. They feel compunction at the appearance of slackening their strings and betraying the doctrine, and so experience something of the fate of Tantalus, the poor things. So wherever they expect to be able to break the laws with impunity, without anyone seeing, they stuff themselves with pleasure by the mouthful. At any rate, if someone had given them Gyges' ring and its gift of not being seen when you had it on, or the cap of Hades, I can tell you for a fact they'd have bid painful labour adieu and shoved their way into Pleasure's palace. Yes, they'd all have followed Dionysius' lead. In fact, up till his illness, he'd hoped to gain some benefit from those arguments about endurance. But when he started having aches and pains and the full reality of painful labour had come home to him, he saw that his body held philosophical doctrines absolutely opposed to those of Stoa. He put his faith in his body's philosophy, not hers, and realized he was a man with a man's body. From then on he stopped treating his body like a statue. He knew now that the man who speaks in useless condemnation of Pleasure, as Euripides has it,

is taking joy in words; his mind's elsewhere.[32]

I rest my case. Jurors, bring in your verdict.

STOA: No. Let me cross-question him a bit.
EPICURUS: Ask away. I'll give you answers.
STOA: Do you consider painful labour to be a bad thing?
EPICURUS: Yes.

STOA: And you think pleasure is a good thing?

EPICURUS: Of course.

STOA: Very well. Do you know what 'material' and 'immaterial' mean? And 'approved' and 'disapproved'?[33]

EPICURUS: Of course.

HERMES: Stoa, the jurors are saying they don't understand these polysyllabic questions. So pipe down. They're casting their votes anyway.

STOA: But I'd have won, if I could have examined him on the third figure of indemonstrables.[34]

JUSTICE: Who has won?

HERMES: Pleasure, five votes to nil.

STOA: I'm lodging an appeal before Zeus.

JUSTICE: Good luck to you. Hermes, call another case.

23 HERMES: Virtue and Luxury. They're at loggerheads over Aristippus. Call Aristippus as well.

VIRTUE: I should speak first. I'm Virtue. Aristippus is mine, as his words and deeds quite clearly demonstrate.

LUXURY: No, I should speak first. I'm Luxury. The man's mine, as you can see from his garlands, his purple cloak and his perfumes.

JUSTICE: Don't be so eager for the fray. This case is also going to be held over until Zeus makes a judgment in the Dionysius case. It seems to be quite similar, anyway. So, if Pleasure wins, Luxury will also win Aristippus. However, if Stoa wins, Aristippus will by the same token be adjudged the property of Virtue. Bring on another case. Oh, by the way, the last jurors must not be paid. Their case didn't come into court.

HERMES: So it's for nothing that old men have made such a long uphill journey?

JUSTICE: Well, it'll be all right if they're given a third. Off you go. Don't be annoyed. You'll get a chance to judge another time.

24 HERMES: It's time for Diogenes from Sinope to be in court. Merchant Banking, you are to speak.

DIOGENES: If she doesn't stop harassing me, Justice, it won't be a charge of escape from slavery she'll be making, but of grievous bodily harm. I'm going to bash her right away with my stick and . . .

JUSTICE: What's this? Merchant Banking has run off, and he's chasing her with his stick raised. She looks to be going to get beaten pretty badly. Call Pyrrhon.

HERMES: Painting is here, Justice. But Pyrrhon hasn't come up at all. I reckoned he would do this.

JUSTICE: Why, Hermes?

HERMES: Because he doesn't think there's any such thing as a true judgment.[35]

JUSTICE: Well, they must condemn him by default. Now call the Syrian speech-writer. Though I must say that it was only yesterday the charges were laid against him and there was no urgency to make a decision. Still, since that's what we've decided to do, bring on Rhetoric's case first. My word, what a crowd has gathered to listen!

HERMES: That's natural, Justice. After all, it's not a stale case, but novel and strange. As you said, it was only lodged yesterday. The expectation of hearing Rhetoric and Dialogue making prosecution speeches in turn, and the Syrian defending against both, is what's brought many flocking to the court. Begin your speech, Rhetoric.

RHETORIC: Athenians, first of all I pray to all the gods and goddesses to grant me for this trial as much goodwill from you as I have always shown towards your city and all of you. Next, I ask the gods to allow you to hear me make my prosecution speech as I have planned and designed it. Let them command my opponent to hold his peace meanwhile. This is only just. As far as I can see, there is an irreconcilable difference between the treatment he has meted out to me and the language he uses. His words, I mean, will be very similar to those I am using. But his actions have gone so far, you will see, that I am bound to look for ways to make sure that I get no worse treatment in future.[36] However, I don't wish to make a long preamble. The water in the clock is already running away with no purpose served. I shall begin my prosecution.

It was I, men of the jury, who came upon this man, still wandering around Ionia not knowing what to do with himself, took him up and trained him. He was pretty young, still spoke a barbarian language and was a hair's breadth from

going native and wearing an Assyrian-style kaftan. He seemed
to me to be a good student and his gaze was firmly fixed on
me. In those days he did me obeisance, flattered me and was
in complete awe of me and me alone. So I left all my other
wealthy, handsome and nobly born suitors and betrothed
myself to this ungrateful individual, a poor man with no
connections. I brought with me an enormous dowry – a
copious supply of wondrous words. What's more, I introduced him into my tribe and sneaked him onto their lists, thus
making him a citizen.[37] The suitors who had missed out were
mortified. He decided to travel. He wanted to show off the
good-fortune he'd derived from his marriage. I didn't stay
behind. I was dragged around, up and down, following him
everywhere. I made him world famous by giving him my
resources and protection. I'll not make too much of the jour-
neys in Greece or Ionia. But when he wanted to travel to Italy,
I sailed with him across the Ionian Sea. In the end, I even took
ship with him as far as Gaul, and there brought him material
success.

28   Well, for a long time he followed my instructions in everything. He was with me all the time. He didn't sleep a single
night away from my side. But when he'd procured enough
verbal supplies and thought he was well enough endowed
with the trappings of fame, he changed his tune: up went his
eyebrow, his nose was in the air. In short, he took no notice
of me any more. In the end, he actually left me. He fell
passionately in love with that bearded fellow, Dialogue – the
one you can spot just by his costume – who claims to be the
son of Philosophy.

He's with him now – love for the 'older man', I suppose.
Without a blush, he's curtailed the free flow of my language
and confined himself in a prison of short and snappy questions
and answers. Instead of saying whatever he likes in a penetrat-
ing voice, he weaves a few brief arguments together and
speaks them in a conversational tone. He won't receive a
standing ovation or tumultuous applause that way. All he'll
get from his audience is a smile, a restrained movement of the
hand, a slight nod of the head, a little sigh of approval at his

words. This is what he's conceived a passion for, the fine fellow. This is his reward for scorning my attentions. But I hear that he can't even keep the peace with his new lover. He's treating him appallingly as well, I suppose.

I submit that he's an ungrateful person. He's liable under the laws about mistreatment on several counts. He left his lawfully wedded wife in this disgraceful manner after he'd received the great benefits already described and the fame he now enjoys. He's chosen to grasp novelty instead, despite the fact that I'm the sole object of everyone's admiration and that everyone wants to enrol me as his patroness. So many suitors! They bang on my door and call out my name in loud voices. But I hold out against them. I won't open up, nor will I pay them any heed. I can see that they bring nothing more than an ability to shout. Even so, this fellow does not turn his face towards me. He looks at his lover. What on earth does he think he has to gain from him, ye gods? He knows his only possession is a worn-out cloak. 29

I rest my case, jurors. Don't allow him to use my form of discourse for his defence speech. It would be hard-hearted of him to sharpen my own dagger to use against me. Let him defend himself in the manner of his beloved Dialogue, if he can!

HERMES: I'm not convinced by this last point, Rhetoric. He can't possibly do a Dialogue when there's only one of him.[38] He must have a proper speech as well.

THE SYRIAN: I'm not going to make a long speech, jurors, especially since my opponent has expressed her annoyance at the prospect given that it was from her that I actually gained the ability to speak. I shall leave you to examine the whole matter after I've dealt with the key points in the prosecution case. It's true that she trained me, that she travelled abroad with me and that she made me into a Greek. On these counts, I'm grateful for the marriage. You must now hear my reasons for leaving her and turning to Dialogue here, jurors. Do not suppose for a minute that I will lie to serve my own current needs.[39] 30

There came a time when I saw that she was not behaving 31

sensibly any longer, nor retaining the seemly dress which she wore when the famous demesman of Paeania[40] took her as his bride. Instead, she was wearing jewellery, had coiffeured hair, had rubbed rouge all over her cheeks and had a black line drawn under each of her eyes. I was immediately suspicious and I watched to see where she turned her gaze. I can pass over everything else. I'll just tell you this. Every single night our side-street was packed with drunken lovers revelling up to her door and knocking on it. Some of them even tried to force their way in in a most disorderly manner. She would laugh and enjoy the proceedings. Often enough she would peep out from the roof, listening to them singing love-songs with their rough voices. Or she would actually open the door when she thought I wasn't looking and debauch herself with adulterous acts in their embrace. I could not put up with this. But rather than indict her for adultery, I thought it better to go to my neighbour Dialogue and ask him to take me in.

32   This is the great wrong I've committed against Rhetoric. In any case, even if she'd done nothing of the sort, it would've been time for me to quit all that noisy hubbub in the lawcourts and leave the jurors to have some peace. After all, I was almost forty years old. High time to stop condemning tyrants and praising princes, and to betake myself to the Academy or the Lyceum. Time to wander round with my very good friend Dialogue, engaging in gentle conversations which have no need of ovations and applause.

I shall stop here, though I've by no means exhausted my subject. It's up to you to vote in accordance with your oath.

JUSTICE: Who's the winner?

HERMES: The Syrian wins by ten votes to one.

JUSTICE: I suppose it'll be an orator who cast the only opposing vote.

33   HERMES: Dialogue, please address the same jurors. Jurors, please remain seated. You'll receive a double fee for hearing both cases.

DIALOGUE: I would have preferred, jurors, to speak in small doses, as is my wont, rather than deliver an extended oration. But I shall follow the legal conventions in my prosecution, even though I am a complete and utter novice in these matters, without a grain of technical expertise. That's my preamble done with.

Now, I'm going to tell you how this man has wronged and mistreated me. I used to be majestic. I inquired into subjects such as, 'the gods', 'nature', 'the universal periodic cycle'.[41] I 'trod on air', high above the clouds, where 'great Zeus driving his winged chariot' is borne along. I was actually flying through the vault of heaven and climbing 'the sky's back',[42] when this fellow dragged me down, broke my wings and made me live the same life as ordinary people. He took off my sensible tragic mask and put on another, comic, satyr-like and almost ridiculous. Then he shut me up in the same room with joking, iambus,[43] cynicism, Eupolis and Aristophanes – men terribly clever at criticizing serious things and pouring scorn on what is right and proper. Finally, he even dug up one of the ancient dogs,[44] Menippus. And he had a reputation for much barking and biting. The Syrian put him in with me. A truly terrifying dog he is too, only you don't notice his bite, because he laughs while he's biting you.

Is this not contemptuous treatment? I've lost my natural character. I'm a comic, I'm a clown who has to act bizarre roles for him. The most absurd thing of all is that I've been stirred into a paradoxical mixture. I'm not prose and I'm not poetry.[45] The audience looks on me as some sort of Centaur, a strange and compound monster.

HERMES: What will your reply to these charges be, Syrian?   34

THE SYRIAN: I'm stunned, jurors, to be facing this charge before you. I would never have expected Dialogue to make an accusation like this. When I took him over most people thought he was sullen-looking and withered with continuous question and answer sessions. Because of this, of course, they thought he deserved respect. However, he wasn't at all pleasant and the general public didn't like him. The first thing I did was to get him used to walking on the ground like normal people. Then I washed off a lot of the accumulated dirt, forced him to smile and so made him more pleasant to look at. But the most important thing I did was to yoke him up with Comedy.[46]

I managed by this device to bring him an enormous amount of goodwill from his audience, even though before they'd been wary of handling him. They were afraid of his prickles, I suppose, as though they were picking up a sea-urchin.

Actually, I know what it is that's really upsetting him. It's the fact that I don't sit down and engage in all that nit-picking logic-chopping with him. 'Is the soul immortal?' 'How many ladles of the unmixed essence of real being did the god pour into the mixing-bowl in which everything was combined when he constructed the universe?' 'Is Rhetoric only a phantom of a portion of politics, or is it a quarter of the art of flattery?'[47] He's incredibly attached to this type of logical minutiae. He's like a man scratching an itch. When it's put to him that not everyone can see the truth about the Platonic Ideas[48] as sharply as he can, he finds the thought most pleasant and gives himself airs on that account.

I suppose that it's this that he's looking for from me. He wants those wings of his back. He's always looking up. He can't see what's at his feet. I can't think that he would have any other grounds for blaming me. He can't say, for example, that I've torn off his Greek cloak and put him into barbarian costume, even though people think I am a barbarian. That would certainly have been a crime, to steal his native dress.

That's my defence, as far as it goes. Please vote the same way as you did in the last case.

35   HERMES: Good grief! You win, ten votes to one. The same dissenter as before. I suppose he makes this a habit and always casts the voting-pebble with the hole.[49] I hope he never stops this campaign of hatred against the great and good. Jurors, go home now and good luck to you. We'll decide the rest of the cases tomorrow.

FAVOURITE PHILOSOPHERS

Preface

Demonax the Philosopher purports to be the biography of the philosopher of that name, and *The Philosopher Nigrinus* is the report of a diatribe against the city of Rome by another philosopher.[1] *Demonax* must date from some time after AD 174, the probable date of the death of Herodes Atticus' favourite, Polydeuces (see *Demonax* 24 and 33), but there is no sound way of dating *The Philosopher Nigrinus*. Both pieces present serious problems of interpretation. First of all, nothing certain is known about either of these men outside Lucian's works.[2] Secondly, despite his usual classification as a 'Cynic',[3] Demonax appears to be extremely eclectic, so that there must be some doubt as to whether the remarkable fit between his preoccupations and those of Lucian is based on the reality of Lucian's claim to have spent time with him and been influenced by him (*Demonax* 1–2) or whether it is not, rather, an indication that he is a figment of Lucian's own biographical fiction – a designer philosopher, constructed deliberately to give validation to Lucian's own brand of eclectic Cynicism.[4] As for Nigrinus, the question has been raised whether he in fact represents a parodic reference to the Platonic philosopher Albinus (Latin *nigr-* ('black') being substituted for *alb-* ('white')).[5] The third problem, this one specific to *The Philosopher Nigrinus*, relates to its form. The comic frame for the denunciation of Rome seems to some scholars to undercut the seriousness of the central panel.[6] It seems likely that resolutions to these difficulties will only come by acceptance as a starting point of the deliberately enigmatic nature of Lucian's approach. In the meantime, we can note that in the ascription to others (Demonax and Nigrinus) of remarks critical of aspects of the imperial power which ruled the Greek-speaking world, Lucian could effectively distance himself from charges of subversion, and by the use in *The Philosopher Nigrinus* of motifs which were at home in the native Latin tradition of Roman satire (see Notes, pp. 363ff.) he could claim to be doing nothing not sanctioned by Roman literary precedent.[7]

NOTES

1. The Greek titles literally translated are 'The life of Demonax' and 'The philosophy of Nigrinus'.
2. About thirty 'sayings of Demonax' have survived in a separate tradition. But were they made up *after* Lucian and on the basis of his work? No Platonic philosopher by the name Nigrinus is recorded anywhere.
3. Jones 1986, 90f.; *OCD*³, s.v. 'Demonax'.
4. This radical suggestion was made to me in conversation independently by Noreen Humble and by E. L. Bowie. See also Branham 1989, 57–63.
5. Tarrant 1985.
6. See Anderson 1978. The most recent discussion is that of Whitmarsh 2001a, 265–79.
7. For Lucian's attitude to Rome, see Introduction, section 4 and further Swain 1996 and Whitmarsh 2001a.

DEMONAX THE
PHILOSOPHER

Apparently it was the will of the gods that life even in our day   1
should not be utterly bereft of memorable and noteworthy men.
It was destined to bring forth an amazingly strong physical
specimen and a supremely intelligent philosopher. My first reference is to the Boeotian Sostratus, whom the Greeks called –
and actually believed to be – Heracles. My second is to the
philosopher Demonax. I saw them both with my own eyes and
the sight amazed me. In the company of one of them, however,
Demonax, I actually spent a long time. I have written another
monograph dealing with Sostratus,[1] where I have recorded his
great size, his colossal strength, his outdoor life on Mount
Parnassus, his uncomfortable sleeping arrangements, his mountain diet and his deeds, which were not dissonant with his
nickname: I mean all that removing of robbers, walking of the
unwalkable and crossing of crevasses.

Now, it is only right and proper for me to talk about   2
Demonax. There are two goals I am trying to achieve. First of
all, as far as I am able, I want to make the great and good
remember him. Secondly, I am eager that the noblest young
men, whose bent is towards philosophy, should not only have
the ancient role-models to emulate, they should also have an
exemplar from our own lifetime before their eyes. Demonax is
the best philosopher I am acquainted with and a fine example
for them to follow.

He was born in Cyprus, from a family not undistinguished   3
for nobility and wealth. He overcame this obstacle, however.
Thinking himself worthy of the finest things available, he turned
to philosophy. It was certainly not the encouragement of his

predecessors, Agathoboulus or Demetrius, or even of Epictetus,
which drove him. None the less, he did spend time with all of
these men and also with Timocrates of Heraclea, an intellectual
whose mind and ability to express himself were on a par with
each other. Demonax was not 'called' by any of these men, as I
said. He had his own inbuilt impetus towards philosophy, which
amounted to a passion. Right from his boyhood this drove him
on to scorn all worldly goods. He devoted himself completely
to freedom and unfettered expression of his views and continued
living a life which was upright, healthy and unimpeachable. His
intellect and his philosophical sincerity were a model for those
who saw and heard him.

4   But you shouldn't think that he rushed off into this field with
unwashed feet, as the proverb has it.[2] He was weaned on the
poets and knew most of them by heart. He had been trained in
rhetoric. He had a knowledge of the philosophical doctrines
that was not, as the saying goes, skin deep.[3] He had exercised
his body into shape and was inured to physical hardship. He
had made it his overall objective to need no one else. Consequently, when he realized that he was no longer self-sufficient,
he departed from life of his own free will, leaving behind a fine
reputation among the most noble Greeks.

5   He did not apportion to himself only one sort of philosophy.
On the contrary, he mixed many philosophical systems together.
He did not in fact make it very clear which one he found most
congenial. He seems to have modelled himself most closely on
Socrates, even though in his dress and his free and easy lifestyle
he appears to have emulated the man from Sinope.[4] But he never
debased the currency of daily routine to gain the awed attention
of those who encountered him. He lived the same way as everyone else. He went on foot. Not for a moment did he display
affectation in his dealings with people. He joined in the work of
the city with everyone else.

6   There was no Socratic irony about him.[5] On the contrary,
conversations with him were full of Attic charm.[6] As a result,
those who had dealings with him went on their way with no
trace of contempt for him as a worthless individual, or desirous
of escaping the hard edge of his criticisms, but were uplifted by

joy, better behaved, brighter and more hopeful for the future.

No one ever saw him shouting or losing control of himself or becoming angry, even if he needed to reprimand someone. He corrected the sin, but forgave the sinner. His example was taken from the way doctors administer their treatments. They never get upset with patients. His reasoning was this. To err is human,[7] to put right such slips divine – or the work of a godlike human being.

Because he lived this sort of life, he had no wants of his own. But he always helped his friends, as you might expect. Those among them who thought they were fortune's favourites he would remind gently that they were giving themselves airs on the basis of illusory and short-lived goods. Those who complained of their poverty or bore their exile badly or blamed old age or illness for their discomfort he would console with a joke. They could not see that their troubles would very soon cease, that the difference between good and bad would be forgotten, and a long freedom would shortly overtake them.[8]

He also took the trouble to effect reconciliations between brothers at odds with one another and to be a peacemaker between disaffected wives and their husbands. There were occasions on which he spoke reason to popular assemblies in a state of turmoil and persuaded most of their members to give due service to their native land.

This was his style of philosophy, humane, mild and cheerful. The only thing that upset him was when a friend was ill or died. You see, he considered friendship the greatest of human blessings. For this reason he befriended everyone and considered any human being as his close relation. Of course, he did enjoy some people's company more than that of others. But the only ones he avoided were those who had in his view strayed beyond all hope of a cure. All this he did and said with the aid of the Graces and Aphrodite herself. You could use the famous phrase of the comic poet, and say that always 'Persuasion sat upon his lips'.[9]

For these reasons there was enormous respect for him among the whole Athenian people and their leaders. They always regarded him as one of the greats. Nevertheless, when in public office he had annoyed some of them. His independent spirit together with his habit of saying exactly what he thought had won him among the people the sort of hatred they had once accorded Socrates. There was no lack of Anytuses and Meletuses to make the same accusations against him as their ancestors had against Socrates. He had never been seen making a sacrifice and was the only person among all of them never initiated into the Eleusinian Mysteries. He bravely put on a garland[10] and a clean cloak, went to the assembly and made a defence speech which mixed his normal moderation with the rough side of his tongue. He answered the charge of never having sacrificed to Athena as follows: 'I don't think you should be surprised, Athenians, that I have not in the past made sacrifice to Athena. I did not suppose she needed any offerings from me.'[11] As to the other charge, the one related to the Mysteries, he gave the following account of his reasons for not joining them in the ritual. If the Mysteries were worthless, he would not hold his peace, but would try his best to dissuade non-initiates from the rites. On the other hand, if they were good, his love of humanity would force him to reveal them to everyone. The Athenians had been holding stones in their hands, ready to use against him. But at once they became mild and well-disposed towards him. From that moment began the process leading from honour and respect to veneration. And yet right at the beginning of his speech before them he had used tough language as a preface. 'Athenians,' he said, 'you can see that I am wearing a garland. So you should proceed at once with the sacrifice. The omens you got from your previous victim, Socrates, were not good enough.'

12   Now I want to give you some examples of his witty and well-aimed remarks. A good place to start is with what he said to Favorinus.[12] Favorinus had heard that Demonax was making fun of his lectures. He was getting a special rise out of the effeminate verses they contained. He had condemned them as slavish, womanish and quite unsuitable to philosophy. Favorinus went up and asked Demonax who he thought he was to make fun of him. Demonax replied, 'I'm an Athenian, with ears well-trained to detect phonies.' The sophist pressed him with a further question, however: 'What credentials did you carry to

cross the border from the training camp to the heartland of philosophy?' Demonax replied, 'Balls.'

On another occasion Favorinus approached Demonax and 13 asked him which philosophical doctrine he subscribed to. Demonax asked in reply, 'Who told you I was a philosopher?' As he was leaving Favorinus, however, he gave a little chuckle. When Favorinus asked why he was laughing, Demonax replied, 'I just thought it was amusing that your criterion for regarding someone as a philosopher is a beard, when you don't have one yourself.'

When the sophist from Sidon[13] was in high favour at Athens, 14 he made great claims for himself. He had tested out every philosophical school, he said. But it would be better to give you his actual words. 'If Aristotle summons me to the Lyceum, I shall go with him. If Plato invites me to the Academy, I will be there. If Zeno asks me, I shall spend my time in the Painted Stoa. If Pythagoras calls, I shall seal my lips in silence.' Demonax stood up in the middle of the audience, shouted his name out loud and said, 'Hey, Pythagoras is calling.'

A pretty young man called Python, one of the Macedonian 15 gentry, once quizzed Demonax on a sophistic question. When he demanded the answer to the syllogism, Demonax replied, 'The only thing I know, my child, is that we are dealing here with a trespass on your premises.'[14] When the boy took umbrage at the double entendre and threatened that he would show him a man if he wanted one, Demonax laughed and asked, 'Do you have a man, then?'

Another time he had ridiculed for being seen in public wearing 16 a flowered robe an athlete who had won an Olympic crown. The athlete hit him on the head with a rock. There was blood everywhere. All the onlookers were as angry as if they had been wounded themselves and insisted that he should go to the proconsul. Demonax merely said, 'Gentlemen, there is no way that I shall visit the proconsul. I am on my way to the doctor.'

Once when he was walking down the street he came across a 17 little gold ring. He put up a notice in the market-place, asking the person who owned the ring and had lost it to come to him. He would get the item back if he could give details of its weight, stone

and setting. A pretty young man arrived, saying that he was the
one who had lost it. However, nothing he said was correct. So
Demonax dismissed him with these words: 'Go away, my boy,
and take care of your own ring,[15] since you've not lost this one.'

18   A Roman senator once introduced his son to Demonax at
Athens. He was very pretty, but exceptionally effeminate. The
senator said, 'My son greets you, sir.' To which Demonax
replied, 'He's a fine lad, worthy of you and the spitting image
of his mother.'

19   He would never call the Cynic philosopher who went round
in a bearskin by his real name, Honoratus. To Demonax he was
'Arcesilaus'.[16]

20   Someone once asked him what his definition of happiness
was. He said that only the free man is happy. When his interlocutor made the point that there were a lot of free men, he replied,
'Well, the man I consider free is the one without hopes or fears.'
'How can anyone achieve this, though?' asked the other. 'We
are all pretty much enslaved by these.' 'Well,' replied Demonax,
'if you really understand human life, you'll discover that it
doesn't merit hope or fear. After all, both our irritations and
our pleasures are destined to have an end.'

21   Peregrinus Proteus berated Demonax for not taking things
seriously and for satirizing human beings, saying to him, 'You're
not a Cynic.' Demonax replied, 'You're not a human being.'[17]

22   A physical scientist was once giving a disquisition about the
antipodeans.[18] Demonax made him get up, took him to a well,
showed him his own reflection and asked, 'Is that what these
antipodeans look like?'

23   There was also a fellow who claimed to be a magician. He
said he had spells strong enough to persuade anyone to give
him whatever he wanted. Demonax said to him, 'That's not
especially startling. I myself possess the same skill as you. If you
care to follow me to the bread-seller's, you'll see me persuade
her to give me some bread using just one spell and a tiny charm.'
His real meaning, of course, was that money had the same power
as his magic spell.

24   Demonax went up to the exalted Herodes Atticus when he
was mourning for Polydeuces, who had died young. He had had

the boy's chariot yoked, with the horses standing by, as though
at any minute the lad would climb aboard. His place was also
laid at dinner. Demonax said to him, 'I have brought you a
letter from Polydeuces.' Herodes was overjoyed to think that
Demonax too was falling in with the general indulgence of
his grief and said, 'What is it that Polydeuces wants, then,
Demonax?' 'He's annoyed with you for not joining him sooner.'

Another time, there was a man who had shut himself up in   25
the dark to mourn his dead son. Demonax came to him and
claimed to be a magician. He told the man he had the power to
bring up from the Underworld the shade of his son, if he could
name three human beings who had never mourned for anyone.
He thought and thought, but eventually gave up (I suppose he
couldn't name any such individual). Demonax then said, 'You
fool, when you can see that no one lacks his share of grief, why
do you think you are the only one who is having to bear the
unbearable?'

He was also a great mocker of people who used strange   26
and archaic vocabulary in their discourses.[19] On one notable
occasion, he asked one fellow a question and received a reply
the language of which was more Attic than that of the ancient
Athenians themselves. Demonax said, 'My friend, I asked a
question in the present era. But you have given me a reply as
though we were living in Agamemnon's time.'

One of his friends once asked him to go to the temple of   27
Asclepius to pray for the healing of his son. Demonax replied,
'You must think Asclepius awfully deaf, if he can't hear us
praying from where we are now.'

He once noticed two philosophers holding a really ignorant 28
dispute on some problem. One of them was asking strange
questions, and the other was making irrelevant replies.
Demonax said, 'My friends, don't you think it's rather as though
one of them was milking a billy-goat and the other was trying
to catch the milk in a sieve?'

The Peripatetic Agathocles[20] was boasting that he was not 29
only the best logician but the only one. Demonax demurred:
'My dear Agathocles, if you are the best, then you are not the
only, if the only, then not the best.'

30   Cethegus the consul[21] said and did many ridiculous things on his way through Greece to Asia to serve as legate[22] to his father. One of Demonax' friends saw him and said he was a major piece of refuse. Demonax demurred: 'Not major.'

31   Demonax once saw the philosopher Apollonius leaving town with many of his students. He had been called to tutor the emperor and was just setting out. Demonax remarked, 'There goes Apollonius with his Argonauts.'[23]

32   Someone else once asked him whether he thought the soul was immortal. He replied, 'It's immortal – like everything else.'[24]

33   Nevertheless, he had a remark apropos of Herodes Atticus: 'Plato was right to claim that we don't have merely one soul each.[25] The man who writes those amazing speeches can't be the same as the one who still invites Regilla and Polydeuces to dinner even though they're dead.'

34   He once even took the risk of asking the Athenians publicly, after hearing the proclamation which opens the Mysteries, why they exclude barbarians from participation, when it was a barbarian, Eumolpus from Thrace, who had set the ritual up for them in the first place.

35   On one occasion, he was planning a voyage in winter. One of his friends asked him whether he wasn't afraid that the boat might capsize and he be eaten by the fishes. He replied that he would be an ungrateful sort of fellow to fear being shared out as a meal among fishes, when he had eaten so many fish himself.

36   An orator had given a horrendously bad performance and Demonax advised him to practise and rehearse. The orator replied, 'But I'm always speaking my material over to myself.' Demonax said, 'Well it's no wonder you speak as you do, then, since you have such a stupid audience.'

37   He once saw a fortune-teller predicting the future for a fee. He commented, 'I don't see the justification for your fee. If it's possible to change any of the things already fated, then whatever you charge will be too little. But if everything is going to turn out the way the god has decided, what's the point of your prophesying?'

38   A Roman veteran who was in good shape gave a display of armed combat, using a post as his target. He then asked

Demonax, 'What do you think of my battle-skills?' Demonax replied, 'They're fine, so long as you have a wooden opponent.'

Even when he was asked apparently insoluble questions, he 39 was always prepared with an answer that hit the target. Someone once set him the following problem, in an attempt at mockery: 'If I were to burn a thousand minas[26] of wood, Demonax, how many minas of smoke would there be?' Demonax replied, 'You have to weigh the ashes: the rest will be smoke.'

A completely uneducated man called Polybius,[27] who was 40 prone to solecism, told Demonax, 'The emperor has me with Roman citizenship honoured.' Demonax replied, 'I wish he'd made you a Greek rather than a Roman.'[28]

He once saw a rich man giving himself airs because of the 41 breadth of his purple stripe. He leant over and whispered in his ear, taking hold of the garment and pointing to it, 'For all that, a sheep wore this before you and was no more than a sheep.'[29]

On one occasion, the water at the baths was boiling and he 42 decided not to go in. Someone said he was a coward. Demonax asked in reply, 'Tell me, was I being asked to risk life and limb for my country?'

When someone asked him, 'What do you think it's like in 43 Hades?', he said, 'Wait around and I'll send you news when I get there.'[30]

A bad poet called Admetus[31] told Demonax that he had 44 composed a one-line epitaph, which he had instructed in his will should be engraved on his tombstone. There's no harm in actually quoting it, I suppose:

Admetus' husk the earth hath ta'en, but he is gone to heaven.

Demonax laughed and said, 'It's such a fine epitaph, Admetus, that I wish it was already in place.'

Someone noticed on his legs the sort of marks that you find 45 on old men, and asked, 'What's this, Demonax?' He smiled, and replied, 'Charon bit me.'

Another time, Demonax saw a Spartan whipping his own 46 servant. He exclaimed, 'Stop treating your slave as though he were your equal!'[32]

47   When a woman called Danae was in dispute with her brother, Demonax told her to go to court. 'After all,' he said, 'you may share her name, but you're not actually the daughter of Acrisius.'[33]

48   His greatest campaigns were fought against those who practised philosophy for display rather than in a search for truth. For instance, he saw a Cynic one day wearing a worn cloak and a beggar's pouch, but with a long, thin pestle instead of a stick, shouting and claiming that he was a follower of Antisthenes, Crates and Diogenes. 'Don't be such a liar,' said Demonax. 'You're a student of Pestleson.'[34]

49   When he saw that many athletes were fighting dirty and breaking the rules of the *pankration*[35] by biting, he remarked, 'I can see now why their fans call present-day athletes "lions".'

50   An equally witty and biting comment was the one he made to the proconsul. He was the type who used pitch-plaster to remove hair from his legs and the rest of his body. A Cynic philosopher got up on a rock one day and condemned him for this practice, saying that it showed the proconsul was a passive homosexual. The proconsul saw red and had the Cynic dragged down. He was on the point of punishing him with a beating or even exile, when Demonax happened upon the scene. He pleaded for mercy for the man on the grounds that his brazen behaviour was only an expression of traditional Cynic outspokenness. The proconsul let him off for Demonax' sake. But he asked, 'What do you think would be a suitable punishment if he has the audacity to do something like this again?' Demonax replied, 'Well, *then* you should order him to undergo depilation by pitch-plaster.'

51   There was another individual entrusted by the emperor with command of legions and a vast province who asked Demonax' advice on the best way to govern. Demonax replied, 'Don't get angry; talk little; listen a lot.'

52   He was asked whether he too ate honey-cakes. He replied, 'Do you think it's only for fools that the bees make their honey?'

53   One day he spotted a statue near the Painted Stoa with one hand missing. His comment was that it had taken a long time, but at least now the Athenians had finally honoured Cynegeirus with a bronze image.[36]

In the same vein, he noticed that Rufinus the Cypriot – the 54
lame Aristotelian, I mean – spent a lot of time in the covered
walks around the Lyceum. His comment was: 'There's nothing
more brazen than a lame Peripatetic.'[37]

Epictetus once criticized him for not marrying and having 55
children, and advised him to do so, on the grounds that this too
befits a philosopher – to leave nature another to take his place.
Demonax' response was just as sharp: 'All right, Epictetus. Give
me one of your daughters, then.'[38]

It's also worth mentioning what he said to Herminus the 56
Aristotelian. Demonax knew that Herminus was a complete
villain and had done Aristotle's reputation immeasurable harm.
He had also noted that Herminus always had Aristotle's ten
Categories on his lips. He commented, 'Herminus, you are truly
worthy of ten categories in their other sense – prosecutions.'[39]

The Athenians were considering the setting up of gladiatorial 57
contests in competition with the Corinthians. Demonax came
forward and said, 'Don't vote this measure through until you've
removed the Altar of Pity.'[40]

On one occasion, he went to Olympia and the people of Elis 58
voted to erect a bronze statue of him. He said to them, 'Men of
Elis, you should not do this, in case people think you are
criticizing your ancestors. After all, they didn't put up statues
of Socrates or Diogenes.'

I once heard him making the following remark to a legal 59
expert. 'I'm afraid that laws may be useless, whether they're
made for the bad or the good. The good don't need them and
the bad won't be made any better by them.'

The line of Homeric poetry he quoted most frequently was: 60

The wretch and hero find their prize the same.[41]

He also singled out for praise the figure of Thersites, whom 61
he saw as a sort of Cynic popular orator.

He was once asked which of the philosophers was his favour- 62
ite. He replied that they were all worthy of admiration. 'But I
revere Socrates, admire Diogenes and love Aristippus.'[42]

He lived to be almost a hundred. He was never ill or in pain. 63

He troubled no one and asked for no man's help. He was helpful to his friends and never made an enemy. The Athenians and all the rest of the Greeks loved him so passionately that, when he went by, magistrates would step aside and everyone would fall silent. In the end, when he was very old, he would enter any house he happened to be passing and be given dinner and a bed. The residents would consider it a sort of divine epiphany, as though a good spirit had entered their house. When he passed, the women who sold bread would compete with each other to give him free loaves and the winner would consider it a piece of good fortune to have been the supplier. Even the children would call him 'father' and bring him fruit.

64   Once there was a political crisis at Athens which produced an acrimonious division of opinion in the assembly. Demonax simply came into the meeting and by his appearance alone silenced them. When he saw that they regretted their previous actions, he left again without having uttered a word.

65   When he came to the point where he was no longer able to be self-sufficient, he quoted to his companions the verses used by the heralds to end the games:

> The contest which has custody of all the noblest prizes
> Is closing and time calls on you to stay no longer here.

Then he refused to eat or drink and left life cheerfully, with the same way of treating people as always.

66   Just before he died, someone asked him about his preferred funeral arrangements. He replied, 'You don't have to worry. The smell will get me buried.'[43] When his friend objected that it was a terrible thing for the body of such a great man to be given as food for the birds and dogs, his comment was this: 'There's nothing especially unusual, is there, in trying to be useful to the living even in death?'

67   Despite all this, the Athenians gave him a magnificent public funeral and mourned him for a long time. In honour of the man, they even paid homage to and garlanded the stone seat on which he used to take a rest when he was tired. Their feeling was that even the stone on which he used to sit was sacred. Everyone

attended the funeral, including the full complement of philosophers. In fact it was they who lifted up his body and carried it to the tomb.

These are just a few notes from a vast amount of material. But they will allow my readers a way of judging the sort of man the great Demonax was.

THE PHILOSOPHER
NIGRINUS

A LETTER TO NIGRINUS[1]

Greetings to Nigrinus from Lucian.

As the saying goes, 'Owls to Athens',[2] the point being that it would be ridiculous for anyone to bring owls there, since they have lots of them. If I wanted to show off my verbal dexterity and wrote a book and sent it to Nigrinus, I would truly be the butt of that owl-bringing joke. However, since all I want to do is to reveal my current opinion to you, how I feel at this moment and that it is no cursory attachment I have formed to your discourses, I suppose I might reasonably also escape the terms of the Thucydidean dictum 'ignorance leads to brazenness', but proper consideration renders people timid.[3] For it is obvious that ignorance on its own is not to blame for an act of such effrontery. It is also my passion for your words. Fare well.

THE PHILOSOPHY OF NIGRINUS

1   FRIEND: What a snooty and high and mighty return you've made to our shores! Do you think we're no longer worth a glance? Aren't you going to give us the benefit of your company or share in our conversations? You've undergone a sudden change, it seems, and become arrogant. I'd really like you to tell me how you come to be acting so strangely and what the reason for it is.

     TRAVELLER: What else can it be, my friend, except good fortune?

FRIEND: What do you mean?

TRAVELLER: It's as a by-product of my journey that I return to you favoured by the gods, fortunate and – to use the theatrical word – 'thrice-blessed'.[4]

FRIEND: Heracles! So quickly?

TRAVELLER: Yes.

FRIEND: What on earth can this great blessing be that makes you give yourself such airs? Let's have a full and accurate account, so we don't merely get the pleasure of the nub of it.

TRAVELLER: Don't you think it's amazing, in the name of all that's holy, that I've become a free man instead of a slave, a truly rich man instead of poor and instead of a demented fool a more moderate man?

FRIEND: Of course I do. But I don't yet quite understand what it is you're actually saying.   2

TRAVELLER: Well, I left for Rome,[5] wanting to see an eye-specialist, because my eye problem was getting worse.

FRIEND: I knew all that, and I prayed for you to hit upon someone good.

TRAVELLER: I had meant for ages to pay a visit to the Platonic philosopher Nigrinus. So I got up early, went to his house, knocked on the door and was called in after the slave had announced me. I went in and found him with a book in his hands, surrounded by portrait-busts of the ancient philosophers. In the middle was a board covered with geometrical figures and a sphere apparently constructed as a model of the universe.

He greeted me very warmly and asked how I was doing. I   3 told him everything, and then in turn I thought I should ask how things were with him and whether he had decided to make the journey to Greece again.

He began right away to talk about these things, my friend, and to tell me his views. In doing so he sprinkled over me such an amount of ambrosial language that he rendered obsolete the famous Sirens (if they really existed), the nightingales and the Homeric lotus.[6] That was how divine his voice sounded.

He went on to give a eulogy of philosophy itself and the   4 freedom it brings in its wake. The things generally thought to be beneficial, and much admired not only by the public at large but hitherto even by me, he derided – I mean wealth, fame, power, honour, oh and gold and purple too. I took this in with an earnest and open mind. All at once I had no idea what had happened to me. I was all over the place. One moment I was aggrieved that the things I held most dear, wealth, hard cash and fame, had been proved false friends, and was almost in tears at their condemnation. The next, I thought them worthless and contemptible, and I rejoiced as though I was able to see again after emerging from the gloomy fog of my former life into a clear sky and brilliant sunshine. Consequently, something very strange occurred. I began to forget about the sickness of my eye, and in a short time began to see more clearly with my soul. I hadn't realized that I'd been going round mentally blind.

5   I eventually progressed to the point you accused me a few minutes ago of being at. I'm arrogant and have my head in the clouds as a result of what Nigrinus said, and I scarcely notice little things any more. I think the same thing has happened to me in respect of philosophy as they say did to the Indians[7] in relation to their first experience of drinking wine. They are a naturally excitable race themselves and when they drank such a strong concoction they immediately went crazy, and in double measure too because of the unmixed wine. It's just the same with me: what you see is a man enthused, going about drunk on Nigrinus' philosophy.

6 FRIEND: That's not drunkenness. It's being sober and sensible. But I'd like to hear the things he actually said, if that's possible. I don't think it would be right at all for you to begrudge this, especially when the person who wants to hear is a friend who has the same interests as yourself.

TRAVELLER: Don't worry, my dear fellow. It's a case of 'spurring a willing horse' (to adapt Homer).[8] In fact, if you hadn't got in first, I would have begged you to listen to me telling the story. You see, I want to make you my witness to the general public that my madness is not irrational. In any case, I take such pleasure in the constant recollection of his words that

I've made them a memory-exercise.[9] Even if there's no one there to listen, two or three times a day I run over to myself what he said.

I'm a lot like lovers when the object of their affection[10] is   7
away. They beguile their lovesickness by remembering certain things the beloved would do or say and dwelling on them, as though he were actually there with them. Some even go so far as to hold imaginary conversations with the absent one. They take pleasure in what they heard in the past as though it had only just been uttered, and avoid the irritation of present troubles by fixing their minds upon the world of memory. This is what I do with respect to philosophy. Though she isn't here, I gather up the words I heard at the time and gain great comfort from as it were unrolling for myself the book which contains them. I'm like a sailor riding the sea at night: Nigrinus is like a beacon that I look to for guidance. I imagine that the great man is there in everything I do and that I'm continually hearing him repeating to me the same message. Sometimes, when I concentrate very hard, I can even see his face and hear the echo of his voice in my ears. As the comic poet once said, he has really left his sting in his audience.[11]

FRIEND: Stop backing water, my dear fellow. Pick up what was   8
said from the beginning and tell it to me. This merry dance you're leading me is wearing me out completely.

TRAVELLER: Well said! That's certainly what I must do. But I've one thing more to add, my friend. Have you ever seen a bad tragic actor, well it might even be a comic one, I suppose? I mean the sort who are booed because they ruin the poetry, even though the dramas themselves are good and have won prizes.

FRIEND: I've seen lots of actors like that. What's your point?

TRAVELLER: I'm afraid that while I'm talking I might do a passable imitation of people like these, and make a fool of myself. I might put some things in the wrong order, and sometimes spoil the ideas themselves through my own feebleness. If I do, you might gradually become inclined to despise the play itself. It's not for myself that I mind. But I'd be really unhappy if the play was a failure because of the disgraceful way I'd played my role.

9   So remember this all the time I'm speaking: the author is
not to be held accountable for this type of error; in fact, he's
sitting somewhere a long way away from the stage, and has
absolutely no interest in what happens in the theatre. It's I
who am putting myself to the test, to see how well I can act out
what I remember. I'm exactly like a messenger in a tragedy.
Consequently, if anything I say seems a little lacking, just
keep it in mind that it was better in the original and that the
author may have put it differently. But as for me I won't take
it much amiss even if you boo me off the stage.

10   FRIEND: By Hermes, what a fine prologue![12] You've followed
the rhetorical handbooks to the letter.[13] I thought for a minute
you were going to add that other stuff – you know, 'I didn't
spend very long with him' and 'I haven't come prepared to
speak' and 'it would have been better to hear this from his
own lips' because 'I've only gathered in my memory the few
words I could manage'. Weren't you going to say this? Well
then, you don't need any more of that as far as I'm concerned.
Consider the prologue spoken in full. I'm ready to shout and
applaud. But if you delay any further, I shall hold it against
you during the competition[14] and boo you very loudly.

11   TRAVELLER: As a matter of fact, I would have wanted to say
the things you just mentioned, as well as this: I'm not going
to speak in an ordered way, as he did. That would be impossible for me. I'm just going to give you a speech dealing with
the main ideas. And I'm not going to put words into his mouth
either. I don't want to resemble those actors I mentioned in
another respect as well. I mean, the way they often put on the
mask of Agamemnon or Creon or Heracles, get dressed up in
golden robes, and look fearsome, with their gaping mouths,[15]
but then speak in a small, feeble, womanish voice, weaker
even than that of Hecabe or Polyxena. So in order not to be
found out for having put on a mask much too big for my own
head and bringing disgrace on the costume, I want to talk to
you from my own unadorned face. I don't want to fall down
and drag the hero I'm playing into the dirt with me.

12   FRIEND: The man is going to spend the whole day treating me
to metaphors from the tragic stage!

TRAVELLER: No, I'm not. I'm just about to turn to the subject in hand. He started his remarks with a eulogy of Greece and of the men of Athens, for being companions of philosophy and poverty. According to him, they never like seeing anyone, citizen or foreigner, trying to force the introduction of luxurious living onto them. Anyone so inclined who arrives there is gently corrected and given remedial education to put him back onto the true way of living.

He gave as a example one of those millionaires. He came   13
to Athens, highly visible and annoying because of the crowd of hangers-on. He reckoned all the Athenians would envy him and look to him as the embodiment of happiness because of his expensively woven clothes and his gold. But they actually thought the poor fellow was a victim of misfortune. They tried to educate him, but not in a harsh way: it wasn't in their minds simply to forbid him from choosing his own lifestyle in a city where freedom reigned. But when he got on people's nerves in the gymnasia and the bathhouses, crowding and squeezing everyone he met out of the way with his slaves, someone would remark in an undertone, pretending secrecy and as though not referring to the man in question at all, 'He's afraid he'll be killed while bathing. Yet the baths have been pacified for ages. So there's no need for an army.' As he heard such remarks, he gradually learned better. As for his fancy clothes and his purple cloaks, they managed to get those off him pretty wittily, by joking at the flowery colours he wore: 'It's spring already, then,' they would say, or 'Where did that peacock come from?' or 'Perhaps it belongs to his mother' and similar things. They gave the same jovial treatment to his other excesses, whether it was the number of his rings, his elaborate hair-style or the licentious way he lived. Gradually, he came to his senses and went away much the better for his public education.

The Athenians are not ashamed of admitting their poverty.   14
This he exemplified for me by recalling an utterance he said he had heard everyone give common voice to during the Panathenaic contests. One of the citizens had been arrested and brought before the festival controller because he was

attending in a dyed cloak. But the onlookers took pity on him and, when the herald announced that it was against the law for him to be watching the proceedings in such clothes, with one voice they all shouted out as though they had planned it beforehand that he should be forgiven for his garment, because, they said, he didn't possess any other.

Nigrinus praised this and also the freedom they enjoy, the way they live their lives without envy, their peacefulness and apolitical attitude: none of these qualities is in short supply among them. He made it clear that spending time with such people is in harmony with philosophy and has the power to keep one's character pure. Moreover, life in Athens is far the best suited to the serious individual who has trained himself to despise wealth and has made the conscious choice of living in accord with what is naturally good.

15   As for the other types of man – the sort who has a passion for wealth, is beguiled by gold and measures his happiness by his purple or his power (and thus balances his virginity in freedom with his absolute inexperience of candid speech and his inability to see the truth, child of flattery and slavery that he is in every respect), or the sort who has handed his whole soul over to pleasure and has determined to serve only this (and is as addicted to extravagant banquets as he is to drinking and sex, a man full to the brim with trickery, deceitfulness and falsehood), or the sort who loves listening to twanging and trilling and to effeminate songs – these are the ones whom life at Rome (where he lives) fits like a glove.

16   The reason is this: at Rome 'every street and every forum is full'[16] of the things they hold most dear. They can let in pleasure through every gate, through the eyes, through the ears and nose, through the gullet, or through the loins. Pleasure's foul stream runs ceaselessly and widens all the access routes. That's because with her enter adultery, acquisitiveness, perjury and that whole gang of pleasures, while a sense of shame, virtue and justice is swept aside as the soul is completely flooded by them. The soul's land, bereft of their presence, becomes a thirsty desert and the only flowers that bloom there in plenty are wild desires.

This was the picture he drew of the city,[17] as a teacher of   17
all that was worthwhile. He continued as follows: 'When I
first returned from Greece, I stopped when I got near Rome
and asked myself why I was coming here. I had the famous
Homeric line on my lips:

> Why then, you wretch, leaving the sun's bright light,[18]

that is, Greece with its prosperity and freedom, have you
come here? I suppose to see the chaos, the *sykophantai*,[19] the
haughty greetings, the dinners, the flatterers, the murders, the
legacy-hunting and the false friendships? What else do you
think you're going to do, when you can't get away from things
the way they are and you can't get involved with them either?

'This was how I thought it out. Then I pulled myself out   18
from the volley of weapons, as Zeus did to Hector,

> out of the killing field, the blood and din.[20]

I chose to live out the rest of my days at home, and I took on
this womanish sort of existence that most people think is
cowardly. I pass the time in conversation with philosophy,
Plato and the truth, and by seating myself really high up, as
it were, in a packed theatre I watch what goes on.[21] This can
give me a great deal of entertainment and amusement, but it
also has the capacity to test a man's real resolve.

'I don't suppose one should eulogize evil. But one might   19
well say one couldn't imagine a better training-ground for
virtue or a truer test for the soul than this city and its way of
life. It's no small feat to resist such great temptations, such
sights and sounds which drag you in from every direction and
grab hold of you. You really do have to follow Odysseus'
example and sail past them.[22] However, it would be cowardly
to have your hands tied and your ears stuffed with wax. You
must hear the Siren-song free and truly raised above its level.

'This way it's possible to admire philosophy as one sits on   20
the sidelines watching such mindless behaviour. One can have
contempt for the good bestowed by fortune as one sees, as

though on a stage, in a drama with a cast of thousands, this fellow become a master instead of a slave, that one poor instead of rich, another a satrap or a king instead of a pauper, this man his friend, that one his enemy and a third an exile. The most astonishing thing is this, that although Fortune bears witness to the games she plays with human life and confesses that nothing is stable, nevertheless every day men, with open eyes, grasp after wealth and power, and all go around full of unrealized expectations.

21   'Now I'll explain what I meant a minute ago when I said that it's possible to get entertainment and amusement from these goings-on. It's obvious that the wealthy provide a good laugh: those purple cloaks they display and those rings they hold out and those accusations of bad taste they're always making! The oddest thing, though, is the way they greet those they meet through an underling.[23] Presumably they reckon people should be content with just a glance. The haughtier actually wait to receive homage. It doesn't happen at a distance or in the Persian manner. You must approach and bow down, abasing your soul and making it plain that its condition matches that of your body. Then you kiss the man's chest or right hand. You'll be an object of envy and admiration to those who miss out on this. And the fellow stands there ready to allow himself to be deceived for hours. I must say, though, that what I find praiseworthy in their misanthropy is that they refuse to let us near their lips.

22   'However, their clients and hangers-on are even more ridiculous.[24] They get up in the middle of the night, they run round and round the city, they get locked out by slaves, and have to endure hearing themselves called dogs and toadies. And the reward for this bitter round of theirs? That vulgar thing the dinner party, the cause of so many troubles, where they eat too much, drink more than they want, blurt out secrets and end up going off complaining or feeling ill, saying the dinner was no good, or accusing the host of insulting behaviour or meanness. The alleys will be full of them vomiting and fighting in front of the brothels. During the day, most

of them take to their beds and give the doctors reason for *their* rounds. What's very peculiar, though, is that some of them don't even have time to be ill.

'In fact I consider the flatterers to be much more abominable   23
than the flattered and virtually responsible for their arrogance. What else do you think they will get into their heads, when people admire their vast wealth and praise their gold, fill their atria in the mornings and go up and address them as though they were their masters? If they made a common decision to stop doing this for even a short while, don't you think the opposite would happen? Wouldn't the rich be coming to the doors of the poor pleading with them not to leave their happiness unseen and unwitnessed, and the beauty of their tables and the size of their houses without profit or use? You see, it's not so much the wealth they love as being regarded as fortunate because of it. This is the way it is: a fine house is useless to the owner, and so are gold and ivory, unless there's someone to admire them. They should have reduced and nullified their power this way, by building a fortress of contempt for wealth. As it is, however, they push them towards lunacy by their servility.

'Now, one might perhaps take a less stern view of such   24
actions in the case of ordinary people who openly admit their lack of education. But when many of the men who claim to be philosophers do even more ridiculous things than these, it is absolutely the worst thing that could happen.[25] How do you think I feel when I see one of them, especially an older man, mixing with a crowd of toadies, acting as bodyguard to one of the great and chatting with the people who issue dinner-invitations, particularly given that he's easier to spot and more obvious than the rest because of the way he's dressed? The thing that annoys me most is that they don't change their costume as well, seeing that they're playing their part in the drama in every other respect.

'As for their behaviour at drinking-parties, can we see any   25
of the virtues in that? They're the most tastelessly gluttonous, the most openly intoxicated, the last of all to leave the table

and claimants of the right to carry away a bigger share of the leftovers than the rest. The more charming among them have even been induced to sing.'

These things he considered risible. But he mentioned in particular the philosophers who take payment for their skills and put virtue on sale as though they were in a market. He called their schools brothels and taverns. He reckoned that anyone who is going to teach contempt for wealth will first have to show that he is above the profit motive.

26   Of course, he always practised what he preached. Not only did he give free instruction to those who wanted it, he also helped those in need and held all surplus in contempt. So far was he from grasping at things which didn't belong to him, that he didn't even take care to avoid the deterioration of his own assets. He possessed an estate not far from the city, but didn't bother to set foot on it for many years. Indeed, he wouldn't even say that it was his. I suppose his idea was that we are none of us owners of such things by nature. It is convention which allows us to inherit the use of them. We take them over for an indeterminate period, and for a brief time are regarded as masters. When the time comes, someone else takes over and has the benefit of that title.

He also provides no minor example to those who wish to imitate him in the simplicity of his diet, the moderate nature of his exercise regime, the respectful look on his face and his restrained manner of dress. On top of all these, there are his well-trained intellect and his gentleness of character.

27   He advised his pupils not to procrastinate with the good. That's what most people do, setting as deadlines festivals or holy days, from which they intend not to tell any more lies and to do what is right. He thought that the beginning of the voyage towards the good should not be a matter for delay. It was obvious that he had contempt for those philosophers who regard it as an exercise in virtue if they train young men to withstand many toils and tortures. Many of them tell their charges to take cold baths, others whip them, while the more refined actually scrape their skins with knives.

28   His view was that one should aim to make sure that it's the

soul that is toughened up and freed from emotion first. The man who is trying to choose the best way of educating people will take account of the soul, the body, the age and the previous education, so as to avoid being accused of giving someone tasks beyond his powers. He claimed at any rate that many deaths had occurred through subjection to unreasonable strain. And I even saw one person myself who had had a taste of the bad treatment meted out by the others, but as soon as he heard the truth had run away and come to Nigrinus without a backward glance. He was obviously now in a much easier frame of mind.

Then he left the philosophers and turned to the rest of 29 mankind again. He told of the hullabaloo and jostling in the city, of the theatres, the circus, the statues of the charioteers, the names of the horses and the conversations about these things in the alleyways. Horse-fever is really rife, and has even taken a grip now upon many seemingly serious individuals.[26]

After this he touched on another drama, the one enacted 30 among those who spend their lives on funerals and wills. He added the comment that the sons of the Romans only say one true thing their whole lives: and that they put in their wills, presumably so that they won't profit from their own veracity.[27] While he was talking, he made me laugh out loud at people reckoning it fine to bury their own idiocies with them and admitting their want of feeling in writing. Some of them command that from among their prized lifetime possessions their clothing be burned with them on the pyre, others have slaves stand by at their tombs and yet others enjoin the garlanding of their gravestones with flowers. What they have in common is that they remain senseless even after their deaths.

So he felt sure he could guess what they'd done during their 31 lives, if these were the sort of instructions they gave about their posthumous existence. These will have been the buyers of expensive fish, the people who serve wine flavoured with saffron and spices at their drinking-parties, those who are surfeited with roses during the winter, loving the rarity and unseasonableness of them, but turning their noses up at things that are in season and natural, because they're cheap. These will be the sort who actually drink perfumed oils. But his most astringent criticism was aimed at their not knowing how to make use of their desires. They break the laws and overstep the limits even in these, allowing luxury to trample their souls in every way. Their behaviour mirrors that commonplace of tragedy and comedy – breaking in when you could easily use the door.[28] His phrase for this phenomenon was 'hedonistic solecism'.

32   In the same spirit he made the following observation also, in close imitation of the words of Momus.[29] Just as Momus criticized the god who designed the bull[30] for not putting the horns in front of the eyes, so Nigrinus accused those who wear garlands of not knowing the right place for them.[31] He expressed his reason as follows: 'If it's the scent of the violets and roses they enjoy, then they ought to wear the garlands under their noses, as close as possible to where they breathe, so that they can derive the most olfactory pleasure.'

33   He also ridiculed people who display a remarkable enthusiasm for food, with their fancy flavourings and curious cakes. His claim was that they were giving themselves endless trouble in their passion for what would only be a short-lived and small pleasure. At any rate he demonstrated that they were undertaking their toil for the sake of the breadth of four fingers – the length of the longest human gullet. For none of what they had purchased could give them any pleasure before they had eaten it, and after consumption satiety is no more pleasant for having been produced by expensive food. It follows that it is the pleasure obtained during the food's journey down the throat that they buy so dear. He remarked that they deserved all they got for failing to recognize, through stupidity, the truer pleasures. For people who choose to take pains the sponsor[32] who provides all these is philosophy.

34   He had many other tales to tell about things that go on in the baths, including the size of people's entourages, insulting behaviour and people who lean on their slaves and are almost ready for their own funerals. But there was one thing he

seemed especially to despise, a thing which is very fashionable in Rome and its baths: as their masters proceed, the slaves have to shout out and tell them to watch their step, if they're about to pass a high or a low spot, and – strangest of the strange – to remind them that they're actually walking. He thought it a dreadful thing, since they don't need another's mouth or hands while they're dining, nor another's ears while they're listening to something, that in the fullness of health they should need someone else's eyes to help them see what's in front of them and that they should put up with hearing words suitable for the unfortunate and incapacitated. Even governors of cities allow this sort of thing to happen to them in the market-places in broad daylight.

When he'd related a lot of other such stories he concluded his discourse. For some while I'd been listening to him in amazement, fearful that he might fall silent. And when he did stop, I had an acute attack of the Phaeacian syndrome.[33] For ages and ages I just looked at him in absolute enchantment. Then I was seized by confusion and dizziness, I was bathed in sweat, and when I tried to speak I fell short and stopped in mid sentence, my voice left me and my tongue failed.[34] In the end I was so distressed, I began to weep. It was no superficial or chance effect that his words had had on me. The wound was deep and mortal, the speech had taken deadly aim and, if one can say so, had pierced my soul to the core. For if I may now use philosophical discourse for a moment, this is the way I have come to think about these things.

The soul of the naturally good man resembles a very soft target. Life has many archers with quivers full of complex words of many kinds, but they are not all so good with their aim. Some draw the bowstring too tight and fire their arrows too vigorously. They strike their target, it is true, but their arrows do not stay in their mark. The excess force drives them through and they fly onwards, merely leaving the soul with a gaping wound. Others do the exact opposite. The tension of their bowstring is so weak that their arrows don't even reach the target, but often lose momentum halfway and fall to the

35

36

ground. When they do very occasionally reach the mark, they only 'graze the surface',[35] and do not make a deep wound, because they were not shot forcefully.

37   The good archer, like Nigrinus, first of all takes a detailed look at the target, to see whether it is too soft or too hard to take the shot (there are targets which are impenetrable). When he has taken note of this, he then smears the tip of his arrow, not with poison (in the Scythian fashion), nor with acid (like the Curetes), but with a slightly pungent, slightly sweet drug. When he has made these preparations, he takes a skilful shot. The missile, fired with exactly the right string tension, breaks right through into the target, doesn't pass through but stays there and releases a great deal of the drug, which spreads out and circulates throughout the soul. It's this that makes people joyful and tearful as they listen (this was my experience too), because the drug is quietly running round the soul. That's why it came into my mind to cite to him that line of Homer:

Fire thus. Thou mightest bring salvation's light.[36]

For, just as not everyone who hears the Phrygian pipes goes mad,[37] but only those who are seized by Rhea, recalling their emotional propensity at the sound of the melody, so not everyone who hears philosophers becomes enthused and goes away wounded, but only those who have some natural inclination towards philosophy.

38 FRIEND: What a wondrous, majestic and divine tale you've told, my friend! I hadn't realized just how truly full up you were with ambrosia and lotus. Consequently, as you were speaking, my soul was actually affected in some way. Now that you've stopped, I'm upset and – to borrow your metaphor – wounded. You shouldn't be surprised. You're well aware that people who are bitten by rabid dogs aren't the only ones who go crazy: in their madness they even dispose others to the same symptoms, and these people also lose their wits. Somehow the condition is transmitted through the bite, the virus spreads and the madness claims many successors.

TRAVELLER: So you also admit to feeling the same passion as I feel?

FRIEND: Absolutely. What's more, I want you to think up some treatment we can share.

TRAVELLER: Well then, we must do what Telephus did.

FRIEND: What do you mean?

TRAVELLER: We must go to the man who caused the wound and beg him to heal us.[38]

DAMNING DIATRIBES

Preface

This section puts together under the heading 'diatribes' – a moralistic form of prose writing developed by Cynic writers – two works which deal with ethical topics, *Slander* and *A Few Words about Mourning*. There are no good criteria for dating either work, though just possibly *Slander* might be reckoned a 'rhetorical' work, and hence belong before Lucian's fortieth year (see Introduction, section 2). *Slander* is mainly remarkable for its description of a painting by Apelles which found its way into the bloodstream of Western art during the early Renaissance through the agency of Alberti (*De Pictura*, 1435). Botticelli's exquisite version, which hangs in the Uffizi gallery in Florence, is only the most famous re-creation. The subject was also treated by Mantegna, Rembrandt, Raphael, Dürer, Bruegel, Rubens and dozens of others.[1] *Ekphrasis* such as this (see Introduction, section 5) is a rhetorical mode used elsewhere by Lucian to striking effect (cf. *Zeuxis* and *Herodotus*). However, the tone of this work is serious and the turn of phrase (though it employs metaphor from drama and dramatic criticism to good effect) lacks the wit and verve of the second piece, which is more characteristic of the author. *A Few Words about Mourning*, like its companion work *On Sacrifices*, takes a Cynic view of these human activities, with the presenter deliberately distancing himself from his subjects, rather like an anthropologist observing the curious customs of some primitive tribe, but with the addition of a sharp irony which suggests the folly of those unwittingly monitored. This posture is found in many other places (e.g. *Menippus* and *Icaromenippus*) and has links to the serio-comic writing of the third-century BC Cynic writer Menippus.[2]

NOTES

1. See Massing 1990 for an exhaustive catalogue.
2. For Menippus, see Introduction, notes 39 and 42.

SLANDER

And the Right Degree of Scepticism to Treat It With

Ignorance is a dreadful thing and has caused no end of damage   1
to the human race. It pours a sort of mist over everything,
darkens the light of truth and casts a shadow over everyone's
life. At all events, we are all like people wandering about in the
dark, or rather, we have the same experience as the blind: we
stumble against one object with no reason, and we jump over
another when there's no need; we don't see what is nearby and
under our feet, but we fear the deleterious influence of things a
very great distance away. In sum, in everything we do we slip
up more often than not. And so such experiences have already
provided innumerable subjects for the plays of the tragic poets
– the Labdacids, Pelopids and other similar families.[1] In fact,
the intelligent observer will discover that the majority of the
disasters that find their way up onto the stage have been chore-
ographed by Ignorance, as though it were some god from a
tragedy.[2]

Besides making a general point here, I'm alluding in particular
to untrue and slanderous accusations made against relatives and
friends. These have often caused the ruin of families and the
complete destruction of cities, the mad fury of fathers against
their children, brothers against their siblings, children against
their parents and lovers against their beloved. Many a friendship
has been broken off and many an oath broken by a readiness to
believe slanderous accusations.

So then, in order that we may fall foul of such accusations as   2
seldom as possible, I want to demonstrate graphically in speech
the nature and origins of slander and to catalogue its effects.

Actually, the painter Apelles of Ephesus long ago pre-empted this picture of mine. He too had been slandered.[3] A report had reached Ptolemy Philopator claiming that he was a co-conspirator with Theodotas in Tyre, though in fact Apelles had never seen Tyre, and didn't even know who Theodotas was – apart from having heard that he was one of Ptolemy's governors, in charge of Phoenicia. None the less, a rival painter, Antiphilus by name, envied the regard in which the king held him and was jealous of his artistic skill, and so accused him before Ptolemy of having been involved in the whole plot.[4] He said someone had seen Apelles at dinner with Theodotas whispering privately in his ear throughout the meal. His final thrust was ascribing the revolt of Tyre and the capture of Pelusium to the advice of Apelles.

3   Now, Ptolemy had not shown himself especially sensible in other matters. After all, he had been brought up in an atmosphere in which a master was told exactly what he wanted to hear. This incredible piece of slander brought his anger to an instant conflagration and so upset him that he gave no consideration to what had probably happened. He didn't stop to think that the slanderer was a rival artist nor that a painter was too small a player to orchestrate such a large conspiracy. He didn't take account of the fact that Apelles had been well treated by himself and that any other painters you asked spoke highly of him. He didn't even enquire whether Apelles had ever journeyed to Tyre. He had simply blown his top at once and filled the palace with cries of 'the ungrateful so-and-so', 'the traitor' and 'the conspirator'. Indeed, if it hadn't been for one of his fellow-prisoners who was angry at Antiphilus' effrontery, took pity on poor Apelles and declared that the fellow had had nothing to do with their conspiracy, the painter would have lost his head and shared the reward for the troubles in Tyre when he had done nothing to deserve such a fate.

4   They say that Ptolemy was so remorseful and ashamed at what had happened that he gave Apelles a hundred talents[5] as a bonus and made Antiphilus his slave. Apelles' response to his narrow escape was the following painting – a warning against slander.

5   On the right sits a man with huge ears – almost like those

of Midas – stretching out his hand towards Slander, who is approaching, but still some distance away. By him stand two women: I think they are Ignorance and Prejudice. From the other side Slander is approaching, an extraordinarily beautiful woman, but with a tendency to passion and excitability, her demeanour displaying fury and anger. In her left hand she holds a blazing torch, and with the other she is dragging by the hair a young man stretching out his hands and calling the gods to bear witness to his innocence. Leading this procession is a pale and ugly man, with sharp eyes, who looks like people do who have lost a lot of weight through a long illness. It would be reasonable to guess that this was Envy. There are two other women at hand who are encouraging Slander, attending meticulously to her toilette. The guide who explained the painting told me that one of them was Treachery and the other Deceit. Following behind was a woman dressed in funeral attire, in a torn and tattered black garment. I think she was called Remorse.[6] At any rate, she was turning to look behind her, weeping and casting a very shamefaced glance at the approaching figure of Truth.

This was the way Apelles imaged in the painting the danger 6 he had faced. If you like, let us follow the example of the Ephesian artist's craft and describe the attributes of slander. First, however, we must define it. This will make our picture clearer. Slander, then, is an accusation which is made with no grounds, which is not known about by the accused, but is believed incontestably after only one side has been heard. This is the subject of my discourse. As in the comedies, there are three actors:[7] the slanderer, the slandered and the person to whom the slander is communicated.[8] Let us examine each of them to see how things are likely to happen.

First, then, if you like, let us bring on stage the drama's 7 leading actor, I mean the person responsible for the slanderous accusation. I suppose everyone recognizes that this is not a good person, since no one who is good would do harm to his neighbour. Good men gain their reputation and an additional renown for benevolence from the good they do for their friends, not from the accusations they wrongly bring against others and the hatred they thus inspire.

8   Secondly, it is easy to realize that such a man is unjust, a law-breaker, irreverent and harmful to his friends. For who would not admit that equality in all things and not taking more than one's fair share are marks of justice, while inequality and greed are indices of injustice. The man who employs slander secretly against an absent individual is obviously greedy. He appropriates his hearer entirely, he pre-empts his ears, blocks them and makes them completely impassable to a second argument, because they have been filled up with slander. Such a proceeding is the height of injustice. The best of our lawgivers, such as Solon and Dracon, would admit this, since they made the jurors swear an oath to listen to both sides impartially and accord the litigants the same degree of goodwill, until the arguments of the second speaker had been laid out and could be seen to be either better or worse than those of the other.[9] They considered it completely impious and sacrilegious to give a judgment before one had compared the defence to the prosecution case. In fact we would say that the gods themselves would be angry if we allowed the prosecutor to say what he wanted with impunity, but blocked our ears to the accused or stopped his mouth and cast our votes convinced by the first speech. Hence one may claim that slanders contravene justice, law and the juror's oath. However, in case there is anyone who is not convinced by the lawgivers' instructions to give judgments so just and impartial, I think I shall bring on the supreme poet to help the case. He gave a very good opinion about this, or rather, he laid down the law, saying:

Do not judge a case until you have heard both speeches.[10]

He was also, I think, of the view that, though there are many injustices in life, you could not find anything worse or more unjust than the condemnation of a person without trial and without the right to speak. But it is this above all that the slanderer tries to achieve, by bringing the slandered person without a trial to meet the anger of the hearer and by pre-empting his defence by his secret accusations.

9   Such a man, who evades the privilege of free speech, is a

complete coward. He does nothing openly, but fires his arrows
from a hideout, like people who set up an ambush. The result
of that is that it is impossible to institute countermeasures of any
kind. One must simply submit to being wiped out in frustrated
ignorance of one's adversary. And this is surely the greatest
proof that slanderers are not telling the truth. For when a man
knows he has true accusations to make, he makes them openly,
I think, plays straight and uses arguments as the basis for his
legal challenge. The military analogy is instructive. No one who
can win a pitched battle ever uses the tactic of ambush and
subterfuge against his enemies.

The easiest place to see such people is in the courts of kings. 10
They are held in high esteem in the coteries of those who wield
power and influence, where envy is rife, suspicion has a thousand
voices and the opportunities for flattery and slander are legion.
It is a maxim that where you find greater expectations, you will
always also find deeper jealousies, more dangerous hatreds and
more subtly managed rivalries. Everyone keeps a close eye on
everyone else. They are like gladiators[11] watching for an exposed
area of their opponent's body to attack. In the frantic desire to
be top dog, everyone shoves and elbows the man next to him
out of the way and tries to pull back or trip up the one in front.
In these circumstances, the good man is simply upended at once,
dragged to one side and in the end dishonourably discharged,
while the man more adept at flattery and more persuasive at
such malignant actions is held in high regard. The rule is that
he who strikes first wins the contest outright. These people
prove the absolute truth of the Homeric dictum:

> The War God is impartial – he kills the killer too.[12]

The contest is not for small stakes. That is why they think up
cunning stratagems against each other, the swiftest and most
dangerous being that of slander. It takes its beginning from envy
or hatred based on great expectations. But the end it leads to is
more pitiful, tragic and disaster-laden.

One should not, however, suppose that this is a small and 11
uncomplicated matter. On the contrary, it calls for a great deal

of skill, no little shrewdness, and diligent attention. Slander could never cause such problems if it did not rest on some plausible ground. It would never overpower the truth, a mightier force than any other, if it had not equipped itself with attractive and plausible arguments and a thousand other weapons against those who are going to listen to it.

12   The most frequent victim of slander is the person who is held in high regard. It is this which renders him an object of envy to those whom he has left in his wake. The reason such people fire their arrows at him is that they see him as a sort of stumbling-block. Everyone thinks that he himself will occupy the top position if he has laid successful siege to the chorus-leader and removed him from the charmed circle. This sort of tactic is employed at the games by runners. There, too, the good runner takes off as soon as the starting-gate is lowered[13] and concentrates only on what is ahead, his mind focused on the finishing-post. His hope of victory is in his feet. He does no harm to his closest rival and has no concern at all with anything to do with the other competitors. It is the bad and untrained contestant who turns to cheating, because he realizes that his speed gives him no hope. His absolutely only goal is to watch for a chance to hold back the leader, hinder him and curb his progress, knowing that if he fails to do so he can never win. The same thing happens with the friendships of these rich men we are talking about. The man who stands out is at once the target of plots. Caught without a bodyguard in the midst of his enemies he is done away with. The slanderers are made the object of affection and are thought to be friends because of the harm they decided to do to others.

13   Nothing is left to chance in the verisimilitude of their slanders. They are entirely governed by the fear that they might employ a charge which does not chime in with the victim's circumstances or character. So they mostly alter some known fact about their victim for the worse and thus make their accusations credible. For example, they slander the doctor by saying he is a poisoner, the rich man by claiming he wants to be a dictator, and the dictator by calling him a traitor.

14   Sometimes, though, it is the hearer himself who supplies the

bridge-head for the slander and these vile individuals take good aim by suiting the accusation to his personality. For instance, if they know he is the jealous type, they will say, 'He nodded to your wife during dinner and sighed when he looked at her. Stratonice[14] did not seem ill-disposed towards him.' Slanders addressed to such a man are all to do with love and adultery. But if he is a poet and thinks highly of his own work, the line will be: 'I swear to you, Philoxenus[15] poured scorn on your epic. He pulled it to bits. He said its metre and structure were flawed.' To the pious man who loves the gods, the friend is slandered as a godless and sacrilegious person, who rejects the divine and denies the existence of providence. The hearer, stung through the ear by the poisonous gadfly, at once becomes inflamed, as you might expect. He turns his back on his friend without waiting for exact proof.

In a nutshell, the slanderer thinks out and says precisely those things which have the power to incite the hearer to anger. He knows where each of his subjects can be most easily wounded, and that's where he fires his arrows and aims his javelin. As a result, the hearer is shaken by his instantaneous rage and no longer has any patience for investigation of the truth. Even if the slandered man wishes to make a defence, he won't allow it, because he is now predisposed to treat the unexpected news as the truth.

As a matter of fact, the most effective form of slander is that which claims opposition to the hearer's deepest desires. For example, someone once gave the Ptolemy nicknamed Dionysus the false information that the Platonic philosopher Demetrius drank only water and was the only person who didn't put on women's clothing at the Dionysia. He was summoned at daybreak, and in full sight of everyone drank wine, dressed up in a diaphanous gown, played the cymbals and danced to their beat. If he hadn't, he would have been killed for not taking pleasure in the king's lifestyle, but instead setting himself up as a critic and rival of Ptolemy's luxury.

In Alexander's court, claiming that someone did not reverence and worship Hephaestion gave opportunities for the greatest slander of them all. The reason was that on Hephaestion's death

Alexander's passion determined him to add to the rest of his mighty achievements that of making the dead man into a god. In a flash the cities were setting up temples, sanctuaries were being founded, and altars, sacrifices and festivals were being instituted in honour of this new deity. The most powerful oath anyone could swear was 'by Hephaestion'. But for anyone who smiled at what was going on or did not appear to be giving full devotion to the cult, the statutory penalty was death. The flattering classes seized on this childish desire of Alexander's and began fanning it to rekindle its ardour. They related dreams of Hephaestion, attributed epiphanies and cures to him, and even ascribed prophecies to him. In the end, they began sacrificing to him as a god who could help ward off evil. Alexander was delighted to hear this and in the end became a believer. He thought highly of himself on the grounds not just that he was the son of a god,[16] but that he could also create gods. It is worth a thought just how many of Alexander's friends at that period gained from the divinity of Hephaestion the reward of being falsely reported as dishonouring the god whom everyone worshipped, driven out because of it and deprived of the king's goodwill.

18   It was at that time that Agathocles from Samos, an infantry commander of Alexander's and highly regarded by him, barely escaped being shut up with a lion when he was reported for having shed a tear while passing the tomb of Hephaestion. They say that Perdiccas came to his assistance by swearing a great oath by all the gods, including Hephaestion, that while he was out hunting the god had appeared to him in broad daylight and told him to instruct Alexander to spare Agathocles. Allegedly, the god had explained that Agathocles had wept not because he was an unbeliever or thought that Hephaestion was dead, but in memory of their former friendship.

19   It was precisely at this spot that a combination of flattery and slander worked effectively on Alexander's emotions. After all, when besieging a city, the enemy don't approach the high, precipitous, well-defended parts of the wall. They advance with full force against the place they see is unguarded, weak or low, because they reckon that it is here they will be able to break in and

capture the city. Slanderers operate the same way. They look for the soul's weak spot, where it is close to collapse and easily accessible, and attack there. They bring up their siege-engines and eventually capture the beleaguered soul because there is no one to stand against them or even to notice that they have entered the gates. Once they are inside the walls, they set everything on fire, burning, slaughtering and expelling, doing all the things you might expect when a soul is captured and enslaved.

The siege-engines they use against their hearers include deceit, 20 lies, oaths, persistence and brazenness, among thousands of other villainies. But the greatest of these is flattery, a close relative, well, rather, a sister, of slander. At any rate, no one is noble enough and so well fortified with an adamantine wall before his soul that he would not give way before the attacks of flattery, especially if slander were undermining and removing the foundations.

This is what is happening on the outside. Meanwhile, within, 21 many treacheries stretch forth their hands to give assistance, throw open the gates and use every method to aid in capturing the hearer. In pride of place there is the love of novelty, which all men naturally possess. Then comes fickleness, and next the propensity towards the unusual.[17] We are all hopelessly addicted to hearing secrets and gossip and suspicions whispered in our ears. For my part, there are lots of people I know whose ears are as thoroughly titillated by slanders as though they were being tickled with feathers.

With all these allies, then, when they attack, they are over- 22 whelming, in my view. The victory could not possibly be difficult when there are no troops lined up to defend against the assault. The hearer surrenders voluntarily, while the victim of the slander knows nothing of the plot. The slandered are like people slaughtered in their sleep when a city has been captured in the night.

But here is the most pitiable thing of all. The victim, knowing 23 nothing of what has occurred, meets his friend with a bright face, since he is unconscious of any misdeed, and speaks and acts the usual way, although the poor fellow has been set up for ambush by every possible means. If the hearer has any trace of a noble, open-minded and free-speaking disposition, he immediately gives vent to his anger and pours out his rage, eventually allows a defence to be made and learns that he has been provoked against his friend for no reason.

24   But if he is of a less noble and lower sort of character, he will receive his friend with a smile which plays only on the edges of his lips, while really he despises him, grinds his teeth secretly and, as the poet has it, 'broods in his soul's depth'[18] over his anger. Personally, I cannot think of anything more unjust or slavish than to bite one's lip and hide one's bile while allowing the hatred locked up inside to increase, concealing one thing in one's heart, but saying something else.[19] This is just to act with a bright comic mask a heart-rending tragedy brim-full of woes.

This is experienced most often when the slanderer, despite appearing to be a long-standing friend of the slandered, attacks him none the less. In such circumstances, people refuse even to listen to what the men slandered or their defenders have to say. They are completely predisposed to give credence to the accusation because of the supposedly long-standing friendship. They don't take into account that even among the best of friends there often arise many reasons for enmity which are not perceived by others. Sometimes, too, it happens that when a man is guilty of a crime himself he tries to escape the charge by anticipation and accuses his neighbour. And it is a rule that no one would dare to slander an enemy. The accusation immediately lacks credibility because its motive is so obvious. Slanderers attack those who appear to be friends because their purpose is to display goodwill towards their hearer. And they do this by showing that they do not even hold back from implicating their nearest and dearest to serve his needs.

25   Some people, even if they find out later that their friends have been unjustly slandered to them, none the less do not deign to receive them any more or even to glance in their direction. They are too ashamed by what they were brought to believe. They react as though they themselves have been wronged because they have found out that the friend was innocent.

26   As a result of such easily believed and unexamined slanders, life has been filled with a multitude of disasters. For example, Anteia said:

Die, Proetus, or cut down Bellerophon,
Who wished to lie in lustful bed with me, who wished it not,[20]

but she was the one who had made the move and been rejected.
The young fellow was almost killed in the struggle with the
Chimaera. That was the penalty he paid for self-control and
respect for his host, all through the plots of a lustful lady.
Another instance in point is Phaedra. She too made a similar
accusation against her stepson, Hippolytus. She caused him to
be cursed by his father Theseus, when he had done nothing, ye
gods, absolutely nothing wrong.

At this point, someone may say, 'That's all very well. But 27
sometimes the slanderer merits belief precisely because he
appears in other respects to be just and sensible. People have to
pay attention to what he says because he would never commit
such a crime.' All right. But can you think of anyone juster than
Aristides? Despite his nickname,[21] he plotted against Themistocles and stirred up the people's anger, so the story goes,
under the impulse of some political rivalry. Aristides may well
have been just in comparison to others, but he was still a
human being himself, possessed of the usual capacity for anger,
partisanship and hatred.

There's another example to hand, too, if the story about 28
Palamedes is true. The most intelligent of the Achaeans and in
other respects a mighty hero, Odysseus, is said to have been the
author of that secret conspiracy, aimed at a man who was a
comrade-at-arms, a friend, and had sailed to face the very same
danger as himself. This shows just how deeply rooted in human
nature is the propensity to go astray in matters like this.

There is a whole string of examples one could mention if one 29
wished. For instance, Socrates was unjustly slandered to the
Athenians as an impious plotter, while Themistocles and
Miltiades fell under suspicion of treason against Greece after so
many glorious victories. But there are thousands of examples,
and almost all of them are already well known.

So how should the sensible person act, if he lays claim to 30
virtue or respect for the truth? I reckon he should follow the
advice given by Homer in the allegorical story of the Sirens.[22]

He tells us to sail past those destructive aural pleasures, to block up our ears and not to open them to people whose passion has induced them to prejudge the issues. Instead, we must put reason in strict charge of the door to check everything that is said. He will admit and take on board what is worthwhile. What is worthless he will lock out and push away from the door. After all, it would be silly to have doorkeepers for one's house, but to leave one's ears and mind unguarded.

31   So when someone arrives with this sort of tale to tell, look at the story on its own merits. Take no notice of the age of the speaker, or the rest of his way of living, or his shrewdness of speech. The more plausible a person is, the more careful the investigation needs to be. You must not trust someone else's judgement, or rather inimical mis-judgement, of the accused. You must yourself be the guardian of the process of discovering the truth. The slanderer's envy must be allowed for, the testing of the mind of the slandered person done openly and the person who has undergone the process of scrutiny accorded disapproval or approval in consequence. To make a judgement before doing this because you have been stirred up by the first slanderous accusation is absolutely childish, base and the very image of injustice.

32   As we said at the start, though, the cause of all these things is ignorance and the fact that a person's character lies shrouded in deep shadow. If a god were to take the lid off our lives, slander would flee into the abyss and vanish. It would have no place when our affairs were illuminated by the searchlight of the truth.

A FEW WORDS
ABOUT MOURNING

It is actually worth the trouble to conduct a close examination 1
of the behaviour and words of the general public when they are
in mourning, as well as of the platitudes offered them by their
would-be comforters. One may observe how unbearable people
who are grieving consider what is happening not only to them
but to those they mourn, although I swear by Pluto and Persephone that they have absolutely no clear knowledge whether
the latter is bad and worth their pain or on the contrary is
pleasant and better for those who undergo the experience. They
just put their sorrow in the hands of convention and habit. This,
then, is what they do when someone dies . . . Well, no, I would
rather give you first an account of the various beliefs they hold
about death itself. That way it will be clear why it is they perform
these strange rituals.

Hoi polloi, known to the philosophical classes as 'laymen',[1] 2
put their trust on these matters in Homer, Hesiod and the other
storytellers, regarding their poetry as law. They suppose that
deep beneath the earth there is a place called Hades. Apparently,
it is large and spacious, but dark and sunless (so I've no idea
how on earth they think there can be enough light to see each
of the things inside). The king of the great void is a brother of
Zeus, called Pluto, 'the Rich Man'.[2] An expert on the subject
told me that he is honoured with this appellation because he is
rich in corpses. This Pluto has organized his state and the life
below in the following way. The jurisdiction allotted to him
gives him absolute authority over the dead. Once he has received
them and taken them into his charge he binds them fast in unbreakable bonds. He allows no one at all to reascend (though

there have been in the vast course of history a very few exceptions[3] granted for extraordinary reasons).

3   The country is encircled by vast rivers, whose very names strike fear into the heart – 'Wailings', 'Fireblazings'[4] are the sorts of thing they're called. The most important thing, though, is that the Lake of Acheron lies in front and is the first thing to face the dead. You can't cross it or go round it without the ferryman. It's too deep for fording, and too broad to swim. Even the feathered dead wouldn't be able to fly across.[5]

4   At the downward path, where there is an adamantine gate, stands Aeacus, a cousin of the king, who is in charge of the watch. Accompanying him is a very jagged-toothed, three-headed dog,[6] who gives a friendly and peaceable glance at the new arrivals, but barks at those who attempt to escape and terrifies them with its gaping jaws.

5   After the journey across the lake, a great meadow planted with asphodel[7] receives the voyagers. There is also a drinking-fountain which is inimical to memory. I suppose that's why it's called 'Forgetfulness'.[8] Of course, this information was vouchsafed to our forebears by those who had come back – the Thessalians Alcestis and Protesilaus, Theseus the son of Aegeus, and Homer's Odysseus,[9] all very eminent and credible witnesses. I imagine they didn't drink from the fountain, otherwise they wouldn't have remembered these things.

6   According to these sources, Pluto and Persephone are the rulers and are in complete control of everything. But they have a huge crowd of servants to help them administer their kingdom. There are Furies, and Punishments and Terrors, and Hermes – though he isn't there all the time.

7   There are two lieutenants – satraps[10] you might say – who judge in the court, the Cretan pair, Minos and Rhadamanthys,[11] both sons of Zeus. When they have gathered a lot of people together, they send the good, just men who have lived a virtuous life to the Elysian Fields – as if to a sort of colony[12] – to live the good life.

8   Any wicked individuals they get hold of they hand over to the Furies and send to the place reserved for the impious to be punished in line with their crimes. There isn't any type of suffer-

ing they don't undergo there – being racked, burned, nibbled by vultures, whirled round on a wheel, and having to roll rocks.[13] Tantalus[14] is even standing right near the lake's edge dry as a bone, in danger of dying of thirst, the poor fellow.

People who have lived a middling sort of life – and these are   9 in the majority by a long way – wander about in the meadow as shadows with no bodies and vanish like smoke if you try to touch them. They live off the libations we pour and sacrifices we make on their tombs. Consequently, any dead person who hasn't a friend or relative left above ground doesn't get fed and lives there under starvation conditions.

This account of the Underworld has so thoroughly penetrated   10 the consciousness of the general public that when a relative dies the first thing people do is place an obol[15] in his mouth, intended as payment for the ferryman for the passage across to Hades. They don't bother to enquire beforehand what coinage is acceptable currency in the world below. Which obol is the standard, the Athenian, the Macedonian or the Aeginetan? And not for a moment does it occur to them that it would be much better not to have the fare for the ferry ready to hand. That way the ferryman would refuse to take them on board and they would be sent back to the world of the living once more.[16]

The next step is to wash the corpse – as though the infernal   11 lake wouldn't give them a good enough dousing when they reached it. What's more, they rub the body with the finest scented oils when it's already well on the way towards the odour of decomposition. Then they garland it with flowers of the season and lay it out after clothing it magnificently.[17] I suppose this is so that the corpses won't get cold along the way or be seen naked by Cerberus.

There follow groans and wails from the women, tears from   12 the whole assembly, the beating of breasts, the tearing of hair and the scratching of cheeks until they're raw. A bit of garment-rending and pouring of dust over the head might be thrown in too, rendering the living more pitiable than the corpse. On the one side, then, you'll have the mourners rolling about in the dirt, beating their heads against the ground, and on the other the deceased, elegant and beautiful, garlanded to complete excess, lying in state raised on a high platform as though dressed for a festival.

13   And then the mother or even, by Zeus, the father steps forward from the midst of the mob of relatives and throws his arms around him (I'm supposing the deceased is a good-looking young man, just to wring the most out of the drama they'll perform over him). His father will emit strange and useless utterances – and the corpse would have a ready reply, if he could only speak. The old man will say something like this, using a sorrowful tone and lingering over every expression: 'My dearest child, you have gone away and left me, you have died, you were snatched away before your time and left poor me bereft. You didn't marry, or have children, or join the army, or till the land or become an old man. You will never go revelling again, my child, you will not fall in love nor will you get drunk with your friends at drinking-parties.'[18]

14   This is the sort of thing he'll say, then. He thinks his son still needs these things and desires them even after death but can't get hold of them. However, I don't know why I'm concentrating on such a minor folly. How many people have sacrificed horses, concubines and even cupbearers over the tomb,[19] and burned the clothes and other paraphernalia of the deceased along with them or even buried it in the grave for them to use there and to take advantage of in the Underworld?

15   None the less, the old man who expresses his grief in all the ways I've mentioned, and even more, does not appear to be performing this tragic scene for his son's sake (he knows very well that he won't hear him even if he shouts louder than Stentor) nor even for his own (after all, it would be enough just to know and think these things even, without shouting aloud; no one needs to shout at himself). The only possible motive left for this nonsense is the impression it will make on the other mourners. After all, the fellow doesn't know what has really happened to his son, or where he has gone to. What's more, he hasn't really bothered to inquire into the nature of life itself. If he had, he wouldn't be so inclined to fuss over the transition from it as though it were something terrible.

16   If his son could get permission from Aeacus and Aidoneus to

put his head out of the Underworld's narrow entrance for a moment to stop his father's foolish words, he would say: 'You poor man, why are you shouting? Why are you bothering me? Stop plucking at your hair and scratching the skin on your face. Why are you reproaching me and calling me wretched and ill-fated, when I have attained a far better and happier state than you? Can it be that you think something bad has happened to me? Is it because I haven't become an old man like you, with a bald head, a wrinkled face, hunched of back and slow of limb, completely worn out by time with all the months and Olympiads you've endured, and to cap it all losing your mind in front of so many witnesses? You fool! What do you think there is in life that's of any use which we can't share? No doubt you'll mention drink, food, clothes and sex. You're probably afraid that I may be dying of their absence. Don't you realize that not being thirsty is much better than drinking, not being hungry than eating and not being cold than having a well-stocked wardrobe?

'Come now, since you seem to be in the dark, let me instruct   17
you in the true art of mourning. Go back to the beginning and cry, "Poor child, you will no longer be hungry, thirsty or cold. Ill-fated one, you have left me and escaped disease, to fear no more the heat of a fever, the wrath of an enemy, the cruelty of a tyrant. Erotic passion will no longer trouble you, sex will not torture you, and waste your energy two or three times a day. What a disaster! You won't suffer the contempt an old man does and you will never blight the eyes of the young."

'If you say this, father, don't you think it will be far truer and   18
more noble than the other? For goodness' sake, don't let it upset you thinking about the shadowland and deep gloom we exist in, and fear that I might suffocate shut up in my tomb. You must reason it out. In a while my eyes will have rotted (or been burned, if you've decided to cremate me), so I won't need to see darkness or light any more.

'Still, all this might perhaps be regarded as reasonable. But   19
what benefit do you think I'm going to get out of your wailing and this breast-beating to the sound of pipes and the women's immoderate lamentations? What's the point of the garlands on my tombstone? What good will it do for you to pour unmixed

wine on it? Do you think it'll drip down to us and reach Hades? I suppose even you can see that in sacrifices the smoke takes the most nutritious part of what is offered up with it as it disappears into the sky. That's of no use at all to us below ground. What's left, the ashes, is useless, unless you believe that we eat ash. The kingdom of Pluto is not so unsown and unfruitful and so lacking in asphodel that we have to send to you for supplies. As Tisiphone is my witness, I've been longing to have a good belly-laugh at what you've been doing and saying. The only things stopping me were the linen shroud and the wool you used to tie up my jaws.'

Thus, then, he spoke and death's finality covered him o'er.[20]

20   In Zeus' name, if the corpse turned his head, leaned on his elbow and said this, wouldn't we consider his words absolutely right? Instead, the fools start shrieking and call in a mourning expert,[21] who has gathered a formidable repertoire of well-worn wails. They use him as a fellow-player and chorus-leader for their idiocy and sing their laments in tune to his prompting.

21   As far as lamentation goes, everyone shares the same inane custom. Burial rites, however, tend to be differentiated according to race. The Greeks use cremation, the Persians inhumation. The Indians cover their dead in glass,[22] the Scythians eat them and the Egyptians embalm them. Your Egyptian – and here I speak from personal observation[23] – desiccates the corpse and then keeps him to share his dinners and his drinking-parties. It often happens that a financially embarrassed Egyptian solves his problem by having kept his dead brother or father on hand and using him for surety.[24]

22   As for funeral mounds and pyramids and gravestones and inscriptions, they last only a short while. They are completely superfluous and childish.

23   Some people even set up games,[25] and deliver funeral orations over the tomb.[26] It's as though they're acting as advocates or witnesses for the dead before the infernal jury.

24   Then on top of all this, there's the funeral feast. The relations are all there, comforting the parents for the loss of the departed

and persuading them to taste food (though the pressure they come under isn't by any means unwelcome, by Zeus, since they're by now fainting with hunger after three days of abstinence). What they'll say is: 'How long are we going to mourn, man? Let the soul of the blessed departed have a break. And even if you have made a firm decision to keep the weeping up, that is itself a very strong reason for not starving yourself; you'll need your strength to match the extent of your mourning.'

This is the point at which everyone trots out two lines of Homer,[27] as though they were rhapsodes:[28]

> Even Niobe of the fair tresses bethought herself of food

and:

> The Achaeans should not mourn the dead with their bellies.

So they reach out for the food, but at first they are ashamed and afraid to appear still bound by human necessity after the death of their nearest and dearest.

Anyone who observes what goes on at funerals will see these and much more ridiculous things. And all because most people regard death as the greatest misfortune of them all.

OLD COMIC DIALOGUES

Preface

This section contains three comic dialogues, the innovative form of which the author seems to have been most proud, to judge from his remarks in various *prolaliai* and in *Two Charges of Literary Assault*. Dating of these pieces is difficult, though on the grounds of form they should belong after Lucian's fortieth year or so (see *Two Charges* 32 and Introduction, section 2), if we agree to see them as fitting Lucian's description of the new genre.[1] Operating with the Platonic dialogue form, but with the language and fantasy of Old Comedy and the Cynic alienation of Menippus, Lucian contrives to freshen up some well-worn ethical topoi – the ultimate vanity of human wealth and power (*The Journey down to Hades*), the way wealth attracts hypocrites and false friends (*Timon the Misanthrope*) and the folly of fantasizing, as opposed to facing reality (*The Ship, or Prayers*). The dialogues are, however, of different types. *The Journey down to Hades* is an Underworld piece, having its parallel in the series of miniatures entitled *Dialogues of the Dead* (cf. also *Menippus*). *Timon the Misanthrope* takes much of its inspiration from Aristophanes' *Wealth*, where the god of Wealth, Plutus, is given back his sight and begins to give his bounty to the just rather than the unjust. *The Ship* is much more Platonic in its basic conception, beginning rather like the *Republic* with a walk to and from Piraeus and involving as the main interlocutor Lycinus, usually read as a cover-name for Lucian himself.[2] It is possible that Lucian was here following the Platonic tradition also in populating his dialogue with recognizable individuals, who are however presented (like himself?) under pseudonyms in the manner ascribed in Lucian's time to

Old Comedy (see *Two Charges* 14 with n. 25). Their addiction to unrealistic dreams despite their philosophical interests is thus enigmatically satirized (see further *The Ship*, n. 54 and compare the method used in *True Histories*).

NOTES

1. Jones 1986, 168 places *The Journey down to Hades* after AD 165 on the grounds of an identification with a contemporary (but see my note 15 on paragraph 6 of the work). He tentatively suggests that *The Ship* belongs in the mid-160s, because paragraph 34 alludes to fighting in Mesopotamia and Lucius Verus' Parthian campaign belongs at this time.
2. See Whitmarsh 2001a, 247–94 for a sceptical view of the 'express-ive-realist' theory which he takes to underlie attempts to track down the 'real Lucian'.

THE JOURNEY DOWN TO HADES, OR THE TYRANT[1]

CHARON: Right, Clotho, this ferryboat of ours has been ready 1
for ages and thoroughly prepared for departure. The bilges
have been bailed, the mast raised, the sail hoisted and every
oar oarlooped.[2] As far as I'm concerned, there's nothing to
stop us weighing anchor and sailing off. It's Hermes that's
holding us up. He ought to have been here ages ago. But, as
you can see, the boat is empty of passengers, even though we
could have made three trips already today. Why, it's almost
supper-time and we haven't earned a single obol[3] yet. I know
Pluto's going to assume that I'm lazing about among the
customers here, even though the fault lies with someone else.
As it is, that noble corpse-guide of ours[4] just like anyone else
has drunk the water of Lethe up above and forgotten to come
back to us. He's either wrestling with the ephebes[5] or playing
the lyre or rehearsing a speech to show off his capacity for
nonsense. Maybe the dear man is even engaged in a bit of
thievery on the side – after all, that's one of his skills too.
Well, whatever it is, he's treating us a bit too freely, even
though he's actually half ours.

CLOTHO: How do you know it's not some business he has to 2
attend to. Zeus has probably had need of his services for a bit
longer to deal with things on earth. After all, he's his master
as well.

CHARON: But he shouldn't try to control a mutual possession
unfairly, Clotho. After all, we've never stopped him when he
had to leave. No, I know what the reason is. All we've got
here is asphodel, and various offerings to the dead, in liquid
and solid form. Everything else is gloom, mist and darkness.[6]

Now, by contrast, in heaven everything's bright and the ambrosia is plentiful and the supply of nectar is unstinted.[7] So he thinks it's more pleasant to linger among the gods. Well, he does fly off from here like a jailbird escaping from prison. But when it's time to come down, he finally arrives after a very leisurely walk.

3 CLOTHO: Stop complaining, Charon. You can see he's nearby now and he's bringing quite a crowd with him. Actually, they look more like a herd of goats as he drives them all in a bunch with his magic wand.[8] Hello, what's this? I can see a fellow among them tied up and another laughing, and one equipped with a beggar's pouch and carrying a stick in his right hand,[9] looking stern and hurrying the others along. Can't you see Hermes himself dripping with sweat, his feet covered with dust? He's panting too. I can see how he's trying to get his breath back. What's up, Hermes? What's the rush? You look a bit hot and bothered to me.

HERMES: This vagabond here ran away, Clotho. I chased after him and nearly left you all in the lurch today, that's all.

CLOTHO: Who is he? Why did he try to run away?

HERMES: That's obvious. He preferred to stay alive. He must be a king or a tyrant, to judge from his laments and the things he's wailing about. He claims he's been deprived of great happiness.

CLOTHO: So the fool tried to run away, as though he could continue living, when the thread spun for him had already run out?[10]

4 HERMES: Tried to run off, you say? He would have got clean away if this fine fellow here, the one with the stick, hadn't helped me to catch him and tie him up. Ever since Atropos had handed him over to me he'd spent the whole journey resisting and pulling in the opposite direction, digging his heels into the ground and generally being difficult to control. At times he begged and supplicated me, asking for a short remission and promising me an enormous bribe. Obviously, I could see he was after the impossible and I didn't release him. Well, when we had got right up to the entrance to Hades, and, as usual, I was counting the corpses for Aeacus and he

was checking them off against the tally sent him by your sister,[11] somehow this complete scoundrel slipped away and vanished. So we were one corpse short in the books. Aeacus raised an eyebrow and said, 'You mustn't employ your thievery for everything, Hermes. You ought to save these games for when you're in heaven. The accounts we keep of the corpses are accurate and transparent. As you can see, the log has one thousand and four names written in it, but you've come to me with one short. I don't suppose you're going to tell me that Atropos got her figures wrong, are you?'

I blushed at what he said and then I soon remembered what'd happened on the way. I looked round and couldn't see him anywhere. So I realized he'd run off and I went in pursuit as quickly as I could on the road leading back to the sunlight. This fine individual followed me of his own accord. Off we ran like runners out of their traps.[12] We caught up with him when he was already in Taenarum. That's how close he came to getting away.

CLOTHO: And there we were already accusing you of negligence,   5
Hermes!

CHARON: Well, what are we still waiting for? Haven't we already had enough of a delay?

CLOTHO: Well said. Get them on board. I'll get the book and sit by the gangplank, as usual, and check each passenger to find out name, place of birth and manner of death. Charon, you take them on board and pack them together in their places. Hermes, put these infants on board first, will you? They can't answer my questions.

HERMES: Here you are, ferryman. There are three hundred of them, counting the exposed infants[13] along with the others.

CHARON: My, what a good catch! But these are unripe corpses you've come with.

HERMES: Clotho, would you like me to put the unlamented on board next?

CLOTHO: Do you mean the old? Yes, make it so. Why should I   6
give myself trouble inquiring into the period before Eucleides' archonship?[14] Come forward now those over sixty. What's this? They can't hear me. Their ears are bunged up through

age. You'll probably have to pick them up to bring them on board as well.

HERMES: Here you are. Three hundred and ninety-eight of them, every one melt-in-the-mouth ripe, picked absolutely at the right moment.

CHARON: Too true! They're all raisins already.

CLOTHO: Bring on the wounded next, Hermes. First of all tell me how you died to get here. No, it's better if I examine your cases in relation to what I have written here. There's supposed to be eighty-four who died yesterday in Media, including Gobares the son of Oxyartas.

HERMES: Present and correct.

CLOTHO: There are seven suicides from love, including the philosopher Theagenes,[15] whose motive was the courtesan from Megara.

HERMES: Here they are, right next to you.

CLOTHO: Where are the ones who died fighting each other for the monarchy?

HERMES: They're standing next to you.

CLOTHO: And the fellow killed by his wife and her lover?

HERMES: Right beside you.

CLOTHO: Well then, bring on the ones from the lawcourts, I mean those put to death on the frame and the cross.[16] And where are the sixteen who were killed by brigands, Hermes?

HERMES: They're here, the wounded ones you can see. Do you want me to bring on the women at the same time?

CLOTHO: Yes, and those who died in shipwrecks as well, please. After all, they died the same way and at the same time. Next those who died of fever (they also went together) and Agathocles the doctor along with them.[17]

7   Now where's the philosopher Cyniscus,[18] who's supposed to have died after eating Hecate's dinner[19] and the eggs from the purificatory offerings and on top of that a raw squid?[20]

CYNISCUS: My dearest Clotho, I've been standing at your side for ages. What did I do wrong for you to leave me in the land of the living for so long? The thread you spun me seems to have taken up the whole spindle. I can't say I didn't try to cut the thread and come here many times. Somehow I just couldn't break it.

CLOTHO: I left you there to observe and cure human sins. Well, come on board and good luck to you.

CYNISCUS: No, no. Not before we get this prisoner on board. I'm afraid he might plead with you and persuade you to let him go.

CLOTHO: Let me see who he is.

CYNISCUS: Megapenthes,[21] son of Lacydes, a tyrant.

CLOTHO: Get on board, you.

MEGAPENTHES: No, no, my lady Clotho. Let me go back up for a little while. Then I'll come back of my own accord, with no summons from anyone.[22]

CLOTHO: And why is it that you want to go back?

MEGAPENTHES: Just let me finish my house first. I left my residence half-completed.

CLOTHO: You're talking nonsense. Just get on board.

MEGAPENTHES: I'm not asking for long, O Fate. Just let me stay this one day, until I've given my wife instructions about my money and told her where I've buried my huge treasure.

CLOTHO: The decision's fixed. You won't get what you want.

MEGAPENTHES: So all that gold's going to be lost?

CLOTHO: Not at all. You can rest easy about that, anyway. Your nephew Megacles[23] is going to get hold of it.

MEGAPENTHES: But that's completely unjust. He was my enemy and only laziness stopped me from killing him before I died.

CLOTHO: The very man! What's more, he'll outlive you by a little over forty years. Oh, and he'll take over your concubines, your clothes and all your gold.

MEGAPENTHES: It's wrong of you to distribute my goods among my deadliest enemies, Clotho.

CLOTHO: My noble friend, but didn't you take these very things over from Cydimachus,[24] after murdering him and killing his children over his still-breathing body?

MEGAPENTHES: But they're mine now.

CLOTHO: Well, your lease on the property has now expired.

MEGAPENTHES: Listen, Clotho. I've something to say to you

privately, with no one else listening. You lot, just move off a few steps. If you let me run away, I guarantee I'll give you a thousand talents[25] of stamped gold today.

CLOTHO: You ridiculous man, have you still got gold and talents on your mind?

MEGAPENTHES: All right, if you want, I'll throw in the two wine-mixers[26] I took when I killed Cleocritos.[27] Each of them weighs a hundred talents of refined gold.

CLOTHO: Drag him on board. It doesn't look as though he's going to embark willingly.

MEGAPENTHES: I'm telling you, my city wall and the dockyards aren't finished yet. I could have completed them if I'd lived another five days.

CLOTHO: Forget them. Someone else will do it.

MEGAPENTHES: No, look, here's an absolutely reasonable request.

CLOTHO: What is it?

MEGAPENTHES: Just let me live long enough to conquer the Pisidians, to impose tribute on the Lydians and to set up an enormous monument to myself with an inscription recording all the great deeds and military successes of my life.

CLOTHO: Hey you, it's not this one day you're asking for any more, but something like a stay of twenty years.

10 MEGAPENTHES: Look, I'm ready to give you the names of guarantors of my speedy return. If you want, I'll even give you my lover as a hostage instead of me.

CLOTHO: You scoundrel! When you prayed so often that he would live after you?

MEGAPENTHES: That prayer was ages ago. Now I see what's better.

CLOTHO: Well, he's going to be joining you soon. He'll be killed by the new king.

11 MEGAPENTHES: Well, O Fate, don't refuse me this request, at least.

CLOTHO: What is it?

MEGAPENTHES: I want to know how things will turn out after me.

CLOTHO: I'll tell you, because you'll be more upset if you know.

Midas your slave will have your wife. In any case, he's been her lover for ages.

MEGAPENTHES: The scoundrel! And after I'd set him free at her request?

CLOTHO: Your daughter is going to join the list of the present tyrant's concubines. The portraits and statues of you which the city set up to honour you long ago will provide a good laugh to the people who see them pulled down.

MEGAPENTHES: Tell me, isn't any of my friends angry at what's being done?

CLOTHO: Did you have any friends, I mean, anyone who had a good reason to be one? Don't you realize that all the people who bowed down and praised everything you said and did were acting through fear or hope? They were friends of your power and they had an eye to opportunity.

MEGAPENTHES: But they poured libations at drinking-parties, praying loudly for great happiness for me. They even claimed to be ready to die in my place, if they could. They went so far as to swear by me.

CLOTHO: That was why you died after a dinner yesterday with one of them. That last drink he had you brought was what sent you here.

MEGAPENTHES: So that was why it tasted slightly bitter. But why did he do this?

CLOTHO: You've got a lot of questions. You ought to be getting on board.

MEGAPENTHES: There's one thing that's really bothering me, Clotho. It's the reason why I was wanting to pop back up into the daylight, even for a short while.

CLOTHO: What's that? It's obviously something really important.

MEGAPENTHES: As soon as my slave Carion[28] saw that I was dead, he came back to the room where I was laid out late in the afternoon. He didn't have to hurry – there was no one guarding me – he brought in my concubine Glycerion[29] – I think they'd been having an affair for some time – he pulled the door shut and started going at it with her as though there was no one else in the place. When he'd satisfied his desires, he looked over at me and said, 'As for you, you revolting little specimen, you often struck me when I'd done nothing wrong' and as he said it started plucking my hair out and hitting me over the head. Finally, he hawked deeply and spat on me and left with the parting shot: 'Off with you to the abode of the impious!' I was absolutely burning with rage, but I had no way of doing anything to him, because I was already dry and cold. My revolting slave-girl heard the noise of people approaching and smeared her eyes with spittle as though she'd been crying over me. She left me, wailing and calling my name. Now, if only I could get hold of them . . .

13 CLOTHO: Stop making threats and get on board. It's time for you to keep your appointment at the courtroom.

MEGAPENTHES: And who's going to dare to cast his vote against a tyrant?

CLOTHO: Well, against a tyrant, no one would. But against a corpse, it'll be Rhadamanthys. You'll see straight away that he's absolutely just and gives each individual the penalty he deserves. So don't delay now.

MEGAPENTHES: Well, just make me a private citizen, O Fate, one of the poor, or even a slave instead of the king I was just now. Only let me live again.

CLOTHO: Where's the man with the stick? Hermes, help him to drag the fellow on board by the foot. He won't get on of his own accord.

HERMES: Follow me now, runaway. You take him, ferryman, and, you know, make sure he's safely –

CHARON: Don't fret. I'll tie him to the mast.

MEGAPENTHES: But I should be sitting in the best seat.

CLOTHO: Why?

MEGAPENTHES: Well obviously because I was a tyrant and had ten thousand bodyguards.

CYNISCUS: Well then it was right that Carion plucked at your hair, stupid man that you are. I'll make you regret your tyranny when you taste my stick.

MEGAPENTHES: What, Cyniscus is going to dare to strike me

with a stick? Didn't I nearly have you pinned to the board[30]
the other day for being too free and rough and critical?

CYNISCUS: That's the reason you're now staying pinned to the
mast yourself.

MICYLLUS: Tell me, Clotho, have you no account of me? Or is   14
it because I'm poor that I have to get on board last?

CLOTHO: Who are you?

MICYLLUS: Micyllus the cobbler.[31]

CLOTHO: And you're fed up with the delay? Didn't you see the
amount the tyrant was prepared to offer for just a brief
postponement? I'm amazed that the delay doesn't please you
as well.

MICYLLUS: Listen here, kindest of the Fates. Frankly, I'm not
especially delighted with the Cyclops' gift, viz. his promise
that 'I'll eat Nobody last'.[32] Whether it's first or last, the same
teeth are waiting. In any case, my position is different from
that of the rich. In fact, as the saying goes, our lives are diametrically opposite.[33] Your tyrant here appeared to be blessed
during his life. Everyone feared him and looked up to him. It
was reasonable for him to be upset at leaving such a pile of
gold and silver, clothes, horses, dinners, lovely boys and pretty
women. When he was separated from them, he was sad. The
soul somehow sticks to this type of thing as if it's glued and
doesn't usually let go easily, since it's been clinging fast to
them for so long. Really it's more like an unbreakable chain
that they happen to have been bound with. Of course, even if
you use force to pull them away, they wail aloud and suppli-
cate. They may have been bold as brass in the face of everything else, but the road which leads to Hades finds them
lily-livered. They keep turning round to look back. They're
like people disappointed in love, who want to see the world
of light even if they can only glimpse it from afar. That's the
way this fool acted in running away as we were travelling
here and begging you to let him go when he got here.

  I on the other hand had no security in my life. With no   15
farm, no tenement, no gold, no furniture, no reputation and
no pictures, I was as you might expect ready to travel. Atropos

had only to give me the nod, and I gladly threw away my knife and piece of leather (I had a boot in my hands at the time), jumped up right away with no shoes on and followed without even bothering to wipe the polish off me. Actually, I led the way, looking straight ahead. There wasn't anything behind me to make me turn round or to call me back. Indeed, I can already see that all your arrangements are lovely. I note that there are no debt-collectors demanding payment here, and no taxes to pay. The most important thing, though, is that there's no shivering in the winter, no getting sick and no being beaten by people who have more power. Everywhere there's peace and everything's upside down. What I mean by that is, we poor folk are smiling, while the rich folks are distressed and moaning.

16   CLOTHO: So that was why I saw you laughing a while ago, Micyllus. But tell me, what was it that made you laugh most?

MICYLLUS: I'll tell you, goddess whom I honour the most. I used to live next door to a tyrant up on earth and got a pretty close look at all that went on at his place. I must say that then I regarded him as a sort of demi-god. I thought he was truly happy when I saw the lustre of his purple robes, the number of his servants, his gold, his cups studded with precious stones and his couches with their silver feet. What's more, the smell of what was being made for dinner used to drive me crazy. Consequently, I saw him as superhuman with all the gods' blessings upon him and all but the most handsome of men, taller by a whole royal cubit than others, raised aloft by fortune, with a proud step and a haughty demeanour which struck fear into everyone he encountered. But when he died, it wasn't just him I realized was completely absurd when he had put aside the trappings of luxury. I also laughed derisively at myself for having admired such a piece of scum and for judging his happiness from the smell of cooking and counting him among the blessed on account of the blood of little molluscs from the Laconian Sea.[34]

17   It wasn't just him, though. I saw the moneylender Gniphon[35] groaning and regretting that he hadn't had any enjoyment out of his money, but had died without tasting it. *And*

he had left it to the spendthrift Rhodochares,[36] since he was the nearest relative and was legally entitled to the first claim on the property. Well, that made me laugh uncontrollably, especially when I remembered how pale and dirty he always was. His brow was full of anxiety and he was really only wealthy at the tips of the fingers he used to count up his millions. He was painstakingly collecting what the delighted Rhodochares would take a few moments to dispose of.

But why aren't we off yet? We can laugh at the rest as we sail, watching them weep and wail.

CLOTHO: Get on board so the ferryman can weigh anchor.

CHARON: Hey you, where do you think you're going? The boat's already full. Stay here till tomorrow. We'll take you over in the morning. 18

MICYLLUS: That's a crime you're committing, Charon, leaving behind a corpse that's already starting to stink. Watch out or I'll bring a suit against you before Rhadamanthys for proposing an unconstitutional measure.[37] Oh, what a disaster! They're already sailing off.

And I'll be left all on my ownsome here.[38]

Wait a minute, why don't I swim after them? There's no fear of me giving up the effort and drowning when I'm already dead. In any case, I don't even have the obol for the fare across.

CLOTHO: What's this? Hold on there, Micyllus. It's not proper for you to cross that way.

MICYLLUS: Actually, I may even get there before you.

CLOTHO: No, no. Let's steer towards him and pick him up. Come on, Hermes, help to pull him on board as well.

CHARON: Where's he going to sit now? As you can see, everywhere's full up. 19

HERMES: If you like, he can sit on the tyrant's shoulders.

CLOTHO: That's a nice idea Hermes has had.

CHARON: Get up then and tread on the scoundrel's neck. Now let's enjoy the voyage.

CYNISCUS: Charon, it's a good idea to tell you the truth here. I won't be able to give you the obol when we come to port. I've nothing more with me than the beggar's pouch you can see and this stick here. However, if you want I can man the bilges, or I'm perfectly happy to take a turn at rowing. You won't find me wanting, if you'll just give me a strong and well-made oar.

CHARON: All right, you do the rowing. That'll be enough to pay your fare.

CYNISCUS: Do you think I'll need to give the time?[39]

CHARON: Certainly, by Zeus, if you know any of the shanties.

CYNISCUS: Oh, I know lots of them, Charon. But you can see how these people who are weeping are moaning a different rhythm. If I sing, they'll only interrupt.

20 THE RICH: Alas, my possessions! – Alas, my farms! – Woe is me, what a fine house I have left behind! – What a pile of money my heir will waste when he inherits! – Ah, my young children! – Who's going to harvest the grapes I planted last year?

HERMES: Micyllus, haven't you any laments to make? It's not proper form for anyone to cross without a tear.[40]

MICYLLUS: Get away with you! I've nothing I want to complain about on a nice trip like this.

HERMES: None the less, just give us a little groan to satisfy custom.

MICYLLUS: All right, then, Hermes, I'll lament, if you think I should. Alas, my bits of leather! Alas for my old boots! Woe is me for those rotten sandals. Poor me, I'll never again stay hungry from dawn till dusk, and I won't go round in the winter with no shoes and hardly a stitch on with my teeth chattering from the cold. Who is going to inherit my knife and awl?

HERMES: That's enough threnodies. We're almost in port.

21 CHARON: Right. First you must all pay me your fares. You give me yours as well. Now I've got everyone's. Where's your obol, Micyllus?

MICYLLUS: You must be joking, Charon. As the saying goes, you're trying to write on water if you're expecting an obol from Micyllus. To start with, I've no idea whether an obol is square or round.

CHARON: Huh! What a fine, profitable trip I've had today! Well, get off anyway. I'll go back for the horses, cattle, dogs and other animals. They have to sail over here now as well.

CLOTHO: Get them together and take them off, Hermes. As for me, I'm sailing back over to the other side to bring the Chinese Indopates and Heramithras[41] here. They died fighting one another over the boundaries to their property.

HERMES: Let's get moving, you lot. No, it's better if you form a line and follow me in a group.

MICYLLUS: Heracles, what a gloomy place! Where's the hand- 22 some Megillus now? And how could anyone tell in this place whether Simiche was more beautiful than Phryne?[42] Everything's the same even monochrome and there's neither positive nor comparative of the word 'beautiful'. Why now even my old cloak that seemed so ugly is on a par with a king's purple robe. The reason is that both of them are invisible and submerged in the same darkness. Cyniscus, where ever are you?

CYNISCUS: I'm right here, Micyllus. Let's walk together, if you like.

MICYLLUS: Well said. Give me your right hand. Tell me, Cyniscus – I'm presuming you were initiated into the Eleusinian Mysteries – don't you think things here bear a remarkable resemblance to what we saw there?

CYNISCUS: You're right. At any rate, here's a woman approaching with a torch, with a dreadful threatening look.[43] She can't be a Fury, can she?

MICYLLUS: Well, she is if her appearance is anything to go by.

HERMES: Take charge of these people, Tisiphone. There are one 23 thousand and four of them.

FURY: Here's Rhadamanthys. He's been waiting for you for ages.

RHADAMANTHYS: Bring them forward, Fury. Hermes, please be our herald and call their names out.

CYNISCUS: Rhadamanthys, bring me forward and examine me first, in the name of your father.[44]

RHADAMANTHYS: Why?

CYNISCUS: I'm really eager to prosecute a tyrant and give

evidence of wicked deeds I know he committed during his life. But what I say won't have any credibility if my own character and the way I lived my life aren't known first.

RHADAMANTHYS: Who are you?

CYNISCUS: Cyniscus, sir. And I'm philosophically inclined.

RHADAMANTHYS: Come here and be the first to face judgment. Hermes, call his accusers.

24 HERMES: Anyone who has anything to say against Cyniscus here should step forward.

CYNISCUS: No one's coming forward.

RHADAMANTHYS: That's not enough, though, Cyniscus. Take your clothes off so that I can examine you from your markings.

CYNISCUS: How did I get to be a marked man?[45]

RHADAMANTHYS: Every bad deed any of you has done in his life leaves an invisible mark on the soul that you carry about with you.

CYNISCUS: Here I am, then, standing naked before you. So now look for those things you called 'markings'.

RHADAMANTHYS: He's completely clean, apart from three or four very faint and unclear marks. Wait a minute, what's this? There are lots of traces and signs of branding, but somehow they've been rubbed out, or rather cut out. How did this happen, Cyniscus? How did you get clean again?

CYNISCUS: I'll tell you. Long ago I was wicked, because I didn't know any better. So I earned myself lots of marks for that reason. But as soon as I began to practise philosophy, bit by bit I washed the stains from my soul.

RHADAMANTHYS: Well, that was a good and effective medicine you used. Go to the Isles of the Blest to spend your time with the heroes.[46] But first prosecute the tyrant you mentioned. Hermes, call the others.

25 MICYLLUS: My case is small and only needs a brief examination, Rhadamanthys. That's why I've been naked for some time. So please examine me.

RHADAMANTHYS: Who are you?

MICYLLUS: The cobbler Micyllus.

RHADAMANTHYS: Well done, Micyllus. You're completely

clean and without a single mark. You too can go and join Cyniscus here. Now call in the tyrant.

HERMES: Megapenthes the son of Lacydes is to come forward. Where are you going? Come here. It's you I'm calling, the tyrant. Get him into the centre, Tisiphone. Shove him in head first.

RHADAMANTHYS: Now Cyniscus, give the prosecution speech and expose the man. He's right here.

CYNISCUS: Well actually, there really didn't need to be any speeches. You can tell the sort of person he is right away from the marks. None the less, I'll expose the man's character for you myself as well and bring him more out into the open through my arguments. I think I'm going to pass over the things this vile character did when he was a private citizen. I'll concentrate on what he did after he'd got together a group of the most reckless companions, brought in some bodyguards, attacked the city and became tyrant. He killed more than ten thousand without trial and appropriated the property of every one of them. When he reached the pinnacle of wealth, he left no form of excess unexplored, and employed every type of cruelty and injustice against the hapless citizens. He deflowered virgins and made ephebes perform disgusting acts. In every way he abused his power against his subjects. There's no way you could exact any penalty from him that would match what he deserves for his disdain, his pride and his insolence to those he met. It was easier for someone to stare straight at the sun than to look at him without blinking. And how could anyone give an adequate account of the cruel novelty of his punishments? He didn't even exempt his own family. If you call as witnesses the people he killed, you'll discover that this is not a lot of empty slander that's being slung at him. Actually, as you can see, they've come without a summons and are standing round him in a circle throttling him. All of these, Rhadamanthys, died at the villain's hands. He plotted against some because they had beautiful wives. Some lost their lives because they got angry that he had taken their sons away to abuse them. Others died because they were

26

rich. Others perished through being upright and sober men who didn't like what he was doing.

27 RHADAMANTHYS: What's your reply, you vile man?

MEGAPENTHES: I'm guilty as charged of the murders and the rest. But about the adulteries, the abuses of ephebes and the deflowerings of virgins, Cyniscus is lying.

CYNISCUS: Well then, Rhadamanthys, I'll bring you witnesses for these things as well.

RHADAMANTHYS: Who do you mean?

CYNISCUS: Call up his oil-lamp and bed,[47] please, Hermes. They were there and will give eyewitness accounts of what they know he did.

HERMES: Call Megapenthes' Bed and Oil-lamp. I'm glad to say they've answered the call.

RHADAMANTHYS: Tell me what you know about Megapenthes here. Bed, you speak first.

BED: All the accusations Cyniscus made are true. But I'm ashamed to relate these things, my lord Rhadamanthys. He did such awful things on me.

RHADAMANTHYS: Your evidence is very clear, even though you can't bear to mention the deeds themselves. Now it's your turn to give evidence, Oil-lamp.

OIL-LAMP: I didn't see what happened during the day. I wasn't there. And I hesitate to tell you what he did and had done to him at night. But I saw many unspeakable things which exceeded every imaginable type of unwarranted abuse. There were many times when I voluntarily stopped drawing up oil because I wanted to go out. But he always brought me up close to the action and totally defiled the light I gave.

28 RHADAMANTHYS: That's enough witnesses. Take off your purple robe so that we can see how many marks you have. My goodness! He's livid and completely covered. Actually, I'd say he was black with markings. How can we punish him? Should we throw him into Pyriphlegethon or hand him over to Cerberus?

CYNISCUS: Not at all. If you like, I'll suggest a novel punishment which will fit the crimes.

RHADAMANTHYS: Tell me. I'd be very grateful for your advice.

CYNISCUS: It's usual for all the dead to drink the water of Lethe, isn't it?

RHADAMANTHYS: It is, of course.

CYNISCUS: Well, let him be the only one not to drink it.

RHADAMANTHYS: What effect will that have?   29

CYNISCUS: He'll find it a hard punishment remembering the man he was and what power he had on earth and reviewing his life of luxury.

RHADAMANTHYS: Good idea. I rule that he be condemned to be taken off and chained next to Tantalus, to remember what he did during his life.

TIMON THE MISANTHROPE

1   TIMON: O Zeus, god of friends and companions and hearth, lord of the lightning and of oaths, cloud-gatherer and loud-thunderer and any other name the insane poets call you by (especially when they have a metrical problem, because that's when they start giving you all those different epithets to prop up their verse schemes and fill up a gap in the scansion), where on earth is that thunderous lightning and raucous thunder and that blazing, shiny, fearful thunderbolt of yours?[1] All that now appears to be nonsense and simply a poetic smokescreen – apart from the impact of the words. Somehow, that renowned far-shooting[2] weapon you always had to hand has been completely snuffed out. It's cold, and retains not a spark of outrage to use on the unjust.

2   At any rate, if a man wants to commit perjury, he'd sooner be afraid of a guttering wick than of the flame from the all-subduing thunderbolt. As far as they're concerned, the burnt-out torch you threaten them with brings no fear of fire or smoke. The deepest wound they reckon to suffer is a faceful of soot.[3]

    This is the reason Salmoneus had the audacity to thunder in rivalry against you. And he wasn't entirely without credibility, a reckless fellow boasting against a Zeus whose temper had cooled so completely. Of course he wasn't. You're sleeping the sleep of the drugged. You don't hear the perjurers, you don't spot the wrongdoers, you have short-sight and cataracts as far as what goes on is concerned and your ears are as deaf as those of the aged.

3   It was different when you were still young. You had a keen

temper then and your anger was sharp. Against the unjust and violent you were always taking action. There was never any idea of a truce with them then. Your thunderbolt was always in complete working order, your aegis[4] was shaken, your thunder was crashed out and your lightning was forever being waved like a javelin ready for a skirmish. You produced earthquakes as though you were shaking a sieve, snow in heaps and hailstones like half-bricks, to speak in low style. Your storms were furious and violent,[5] and every raindrop was a river, so that in Deucalion's time in the twinkling of an eye there was such a great shipwreck that everything was submerged, and just one little chest managed to escape and berth near the shrine of Apollo Lycoreus, preserving a spark of human seed for the sowing of greater evil.

It's for this reason you're reaping the current reward for your laziness, when no one sacrifices to you any more and no one garlands your statues except as a by-product of the Olympic Games (and they don't do that because they think they have to, but merely as a contribution to established custom). They're almost at the point of showing you up, most noble of the gods, as another Cronus, and removing you from your position of authority. I will forbear to mention the number of times they've ransacked your temple. Why, they even laid their hands on your statue at Olympia. You, the 'high-thunderer',[6] hesitated to rouse the guard dogs or call the neighbours, so that they could rush to your aid and catch the thieves when they were packed and ready to escape. No, instead you sat there, the noble slayer of the Giants and conqueror of the Titans, allowing them to give you a haircut, and you with that fifteen-foot thunderbolt in your right hand![7]

When are you going to stop letting these crimes so carelessly alone, O wondrous one? When are you going to punish criminality of this magnitude? How many Phaethons or Deucalions would it take to pay for such overwhelmingly unjust lives?

Now let me leave these general complaints and turn to my own problems. I raised lots of Athenians to a great height and made them rich instead of poor, seeing to their every need, or, rather, emptying out my great pot of wealth to help my friends. But now that I've become poor because of my beneficence, the people who used to bow and scrape before me and hang on every nod of my head don't even acknowledge me any more. In fact, whenever I meet any of them in the street, they pass me by as though I were the gravestone of a long-dead individual, toppled onto the ground through age, which they don't even notice. If they spot me from a distance, they'll even turn off onto another path, regarding their recent saviour and patron as an ill-omened sight they'd rather not see.

6   In consequence of these troubles, I've moved to this hinterland, where I work the soil, hired for four obols a day,[8] wearing a leather tunic and philosophizing to the wilderness and my mattock. Well, at least I can count among my blessings the fact that I won't have to see so many people prospering undeservedly. That would be even more painful.

So, now, at long last, son of Cronus and Rhea, shake off this deep, sweet sleep of yours (you've already been dozing longer than Epimenides), take a fan to your thunderbolt or make it flame brightly by getting a light from Mount Etna, and please show some anger worthy of the young and manly Zeus – unless of course the Cretans are right when they say that you're dead and buried on their island.

7   ZEUS: Hermes, who's that fellow, the one shouting from Attica, by the foot of Mount Hymettus, the filthy dirty, unwashed chap in the leather tunic? I think he's digging, bent over. He's a mouthy, brazen individual. Maybe he's a philosopher. Otherwise he'd never have used such impious language to attack us.

HERMES: What do you mean, father? You really don't recognize Timon from Kollytos, the son of Echecratides? This is the one who often gave us a feast involving perfect victims – the nouveau riche, the whole-hecatomb[9] man. We used to have splendid feasts with him at the Diasia.

ZEUS: My, what a change! Is it really that handsome fellow, the rich man who used to be surrounded by so many friends? How is it he's in this state, dirty, run-down, a hired ditch-digger by the look of it, with that heavy mattock he's wielding?

HERMES: Well, one way of putting it is that his own kind- 8
heartedness and philanthropy and compassion for everyone
brought him down. To tell you the truth, though, it was
stupidity, simple-mindedness and a lack of critical judgement
in regard to his friends. He didn't realize that he was doing
favours for crows and wolves. He was having his liver pecked
away by a great crowd of vultures,[10] but he thought they were
his friends and comrades and were enjoying their feast because
they really liked him. In fact, they laid his bones completely
bare and gnawed on them, taking great care to suck out any
marrow that was left in them, before they went off and left
him a dried-out husk with even his roots chewed away. Now
they don't acknowledge him any more or even cast a glance
in his direction – why would they, indeed? – still less give him
help or support in their turn. This is the reason he's become
the mattock-and-leather-tunic man you can see. Shame made
him leave the city. Now he tills the soil for a wage, embittered
and depressed by his dreadful situation – especially the fact
that the men who became rich through his agency pass him
by with their noses in the air, not even knowing if his name is
Timon.

ZEUS: Well, we mustn't ignore the man. We have to take care 9
of him. It's perfectly understandable that he was upset at his
misfortunes. If we forget a man who's burnt so many fat-laden
thighs of bulls and goats on our altars[11] (my, I can still smell
their savour), we won't be acting any differently from those
wretched toadies of his. It's just that with so much work and
the deafening din of the perjurers, thugs and thieves – not to
mention my fear of the temple-robbers (there are crowds of
them, they're hard to anticipate and they hardly allow us to
take forty winks) – it's a long time now since I even took a
glance towards Attica, and especially since philosophy and
its verbal disputations surfaced among them. While they're
fighting one another and shouting I can't even hear the
prayers. The only choice I have is either to sit there with my
ears stuffed up or to have to put up with them going on in
loud voices about 'virtue' and 'incorporeality'[12] and other
nonsense. That's the reason it's happened that this fellow

too has suffered from my neglect, though he's not a bad type.

10   Still, Hermes, take Wealth and go off to him at once. Wealth can bring Treasure with him and both are to stay with Timon and not to be separated from him so easily, even if his kind-heartedness tries to chase them out of the house again. As for those toadies and the ingratitude they displayed towards him, I'll be looking into that another time, and they'll be paying the penalty – when I get my thunderbolt mended. The two biggest rays were smashed and blunted when I threw it a bit too ambitiously the other day at Anaxagoras the sophist, who was trying to persuade his pupils that we gods don't exist at all. As it happens, I missed him – he was under Pericles' protection – the thunderbolt glanced off the temple of the Dioscuri,[13] set it on fire and was almost completely shattered on the rock. Anyway, in the meantime it'll be sufficient punishment for them to see Timon as a billionaire.

11   HERMES: Well, it obviously pays to shout loudly and to be a brazen troublemaker. It's a useful skill, and not just for law-court speech-makers, but for people who are praying too. Look at this! Timon's going to become rich instead of an absolute pauper, just because he shouted and said what he thought in his prayer and caused Zeus to change his mind. If he'd carried on digging, bent over, he'd still be digging away unnoticed.

WEALTH: No, Zeus, I'm not going to him.

ZEUS: My dear Wealth, why on earth not, when I've given you a direct order?

12   WEALTH: Because, by Zeus, he gratuitously mistreated me, carried me out like a corpse and divided me into lots of pieces, even though I was an ancestral friend of his. Why, he almost pitchforked me out of the house like a man tossing a hot coal from his grasp. So am I really going back to be given to parasites and toadies and prostitutes? Send me to people who'll enjoy the gift, Zeus, who'll treat me well, people who honour and desire me. Let those idiots stay with poverty, since they prefer her company to mine. They can get a leather tunic and a mattock from her and enjoy bringing in their

four obol wages, the wretches, when they've thrown away
ten-talent[14] gifts without a care.

ZEUS: Timon's not going to do anything like that with you any   13
more. If he's not got a completely insensitive backbone, that
mattock's really taught him that you're a better choice than
poverty. Anyway, I think you're just a grumbler, impossible
to please. Now you're attacking Timon for opening his doors
and letting you wander about freely, not shutting you in and
playing the jealous guardian. But at other times I've heard
you complaining about the fact that the rich have you locked
in with bars and keys and special seals, so that you can't even
get a peek at the daylight. Well, that was what you were
moaning about to me, claiming you were suffocating in complete darkness. That was why you looked pale and full of
worries, with your fingers contracted through the habit of
doing accounts, and threatened to run away from them if you
got the chance. You regarded the whole situation as absolutely
appalling, having your virginity guarded in a bronze or iron
chamber (very Danae-like), under the tutorship of a pair of
careful and dreadful guardians, Interest and Accounting.

You used to say that what they were doing was absurd;   14
they were head over heels in love with you, but didn't dare to
take the pleasure that was clearly available to them, and
although they were empowered to do so they were afraid to
indulge their passion. Instead, they stayed awake and guarded
their possessions, unblinkingly staring at the seals and the
door-bolts. Apparently, they considered it a sufficient reward
not to benefit themselves but to stop anyone else from
enjoying them. They were like the dog in the manger, who
didn't eat the barley himself but wouldn't allow the starving
horse to eat it either. What's more, you used to mock their
thrift, their security measures and their paradoxical jealousy
of themselves, as well as their ignorance of the fact that a
wretched slave or a steward made for fetters will get in on the
quiet and have a drunken ball, leaving his wretched and
unloveable master to stay awake over his interest receipts to
the light of a dim and narrow-necked oil-lamp with a thirsty

wick. Now tell me, isn't it wrong of you to have made these accusations in the past and now to be making the opposite complaints against Timon?

15   WEALTH: But if you investigate properly, you'll realize that both of these sets of accusations are reasonable. You'd find that Timon's completely lax attitude is uncaring and doesn't display goodwill towards me. As for those who shut me up under guard behind locked doors and in darkness, to make me heavier and fat and swollen through their solicitousness, not touching me themselves and not allowing me into the light of day, in case someone else might see me, I considered them criminal fools, making me rot in those huge chains when I'd done nothing wrong, and not realizing that very soon they'd be going off and leaving me to some other wealthy individual.

16   Consequently, I'm not in favour of either the stingy or the overgenerous. My vote goes to those who'll put some sort of limit on the thing, neither refusing to touch their wealth at all nor giving it all away.[15]

Think of it this way, Zeus, by Zeus. If a man contracted a legitimate union with a beautiful young woman and then didn't keep a close eye on her and watch out for rivals at all, but allowed her to go where she wanted night and day and to consort with anyone who wanted to consort with her, or, to make it more graphic, took her to her lovers himself, opening his doors, acting as her pimp and inviting all and sundry to come to her, would you think that a man like this was in love? No, Zeus, you wouldn't say so, at any rate, with all your vast experience of the passion.[16]

17   Now take the opposite case. A man takes to his house a free woman, in accordance with the law, for the procreation of legitimate offspring. But he never lays a finger himself upon this beautiful young maiden and he allows no one else to get a glimpse of her. Instead, he shuts her up and keeps her a virgin, barren and childless, even though he claims that he's in love with her (and obviously is, to judge from his complexion, his wasting flesh and his sunken eyes). There's no way you wouldn't think he was absolutely bonkers, is there? He should be getting her pregnant and enjoying his marital

rights, but instead he puts a lovely, desirable girl on a life-long diet, as though she were a priestess of the Lawbringer.[17] Well, this is my complaint too, that some people kick me around, gobble me up or pour me away like bilge-water, while others chain me up, like a runaway slave with a brand on his forehead.

ZEUS: I don't know why you're so annoyed about them. Both [18] lots pay a fair price for their behaviour. One group are like Tantalus, thirsty, hungry, with dry mouths, just gaping at gold. The others resemble Phineus, with the food snatched from their gullets by the Harpies. Now get moving. I'm sure you'll find Timon a lot more sensible now than he was before.

WEALTH: Well, will he ever stop emptying me out hurriedly as if he was using a leaky bailer, trying to stop the deluge before I've completely rushed in, in case I overflow the bilges and swamp him as I arrive? I feel as though I'm pouring water into the jar of the Danaids. I'll be pouring to no purpose – the vessel won't hold the liquid. What's poured in runs out almost before it's run in. So much wider is the hole that lets it out, the outflow is unstoppable.

ZEUS: So, if he doesn't stop up the gaping hole and it's been [19] opened once and for all, you'll run out in a very short time and he'll easily rediscover his leather jerkin and mattock in the dregs from the jar. Now get off with you and make him rich. And Hermes, please remember when you come back to bring me the Cyclopes from Mount Etna. I need them to sharpen and repair my thunderbolt. We're soon going to need it to have a fine edge.

HERMES: Right, Wealth, let's get moving. What's up? Are you [20] limping? My dear fellow, I hadn't noticed that you were lame as well as blind.

WEALTH: I'm not always like this, Hermes. But whenever Zeus sends me to someone, somehow I'm slow and lame in both legs. I have real difficulty in reaching my goal and sometimes the recipient has grown old before I arrive. On the other hand, when I have to leave a man, you'll see me growing wings. Then I'm faster than a fleeting vision. The starting-gate is no sooner lowered[18] than I'm declared the winner. I jump clean out of the stadium, and sometimes the spectators don't even see me go.

HERMES: That's not true. I could name loads of people who one day didn't even have a penny to buy a rope to hang themselves with, but on the next were suddenly conspicuously wealthy, driving out in a carriage drawn by two white horses when they'd never even owned a donkey before. Still, they go around dressed in purple, with gold rings on their fingers, hardly able to believe themselves that their riches aren't a dream.

21   WEALTH: That's another type of thing, Hermes. In those cases I don't make my own way and I'm not sent to them by Zeus, but by Pluto, god of the dead, in his capacity as bestower of wealth and giver of largesse.[19] So when I have to move houses, they put me in a wax tablet, carefully sealed, pick me up like a bundle and take me to the new owner. The dead man is laid out in a dark corner of the house, covered from the knees up with an old linen shroud, a battleground for the wild cats. Meanwhile the hopefuls hang around in the market-place waiting for me with their mouths open, for all the world like a nest of little swallows chirping as their mother flies towards them with food.

22   The seal is removed, the thread which ties the tablet is cut, the will is opened and the name of my new owner is announced. He may be a relative, or a hanger-on, or a homosexual slave esteemed for his services as a lover who still keeps his chin shaved and with the reward the fine fellow receives being large enough to make up for those varied and specialized pleasures he served up for his master even when he was already himself well past his prime. Well, whoever the heir is, he grabs me along with the will and runs off with the spoils, now bearing the name[20] 'Megacles' or 'Megabyzus' or 'Protarchus' instead of his former 'Pyrrhias' or 'Dromon' or 'Tibius'. He leaves behind the group who have had their mouths open to no avail to suffer a distress which is very real. It's a very large fish indeed that has just slipped out of the bottom of their net and the bait he's gulped down is substantial enough.[21]

As for the vulgar, thick-skinned individual who has sud-   23
denly chanced on me, still afraid of chains, pricking up his
ear in case some passer-by should casually offer him a whipping, and bowing down before the mill[22] as if it were a temple,
he becomes absolutely unbearable to those he encounters. He
wantonly abuses the free-born and whips his fellow-slaves,
testing to see if he too can do such deeds. Eventually, he'll run
into some little whore or he'll get the itch to raise horses, or
he'll surrender himself to toadies who'll swear he really is
more handsome than Nireus, from a better family than Cecrops or Codrus, more intelligent than Odysseus and richer
than sixteen Croesuses put end to end. In the wink of an eye
the poor fellow will run through the wealth accumulated bit
by bit from a multitude of perjuries, acts of theft and bits of
crooked dealing.

HERMES: Well that's almost exactly what happens. But tell me,   24
when you go on your own feet, how is it you can find your
way when you're blind? How can you tell which are the
people Zeus has judged worthy of wealth and is sending
you to?[23]

WEALTH: Do you really think I find the people who are like
that? Well, I don't at all, by Zeus. If I did, I'd never have left
Aristides and gone to Hipponicus and Callias and lots of
other worthless Athenians.

HERMES: So, what is it you do when you're sent down?

WEALTH: I wander up and down, going around until I bump
into someone. Whoever it is who chances to be the first to run
into me takes me off home and keeps me there. But it's you,
Hermes, that he gives humble thanks to for the windfall.

HERMES: So you're saying that Zeus has been deceived when   25
he thinks that you enrich the people he considers deserve it
according to his own criteria?

WEALTH: Yes, and rightly too, my friend, given that he know-
ingly sends a blind man in search of a thing which is both
difficult to find and has for a long time been all but extinct
among humans. Why even Lynceus would be hard pushed to
spot such a dark and minute object. Hence, given the paucity
of good men and the general control of affairs in cities

exercised by the immoral majority, it's easier for me to meet the latter as I go around and to be netted by them.

HERMES: Well then, how is it that you get away so easily when you abandon them, since you don't know the way?

WEALTH: It's the opportunity to escape and nothing else that makes me become sharp of eye and sound of foot.

26   HERMES: So answer me another question, then, which I really have to ask. How is it that a blind man like yourself, with the additional disadvantages of a pallid complexion and heavy legs, has so many lovers?[24] Everyone has his eyes fixed on you. The ones who get you think they're lucky. The ones who miss out can't bear to carry on living. At any rate I know that quite a few have been so desperate of your affections that they've even thrown themselves 'off beetling cliffs into the deep and yawning main',[25] thinking that you've passed them over when you didn't even see them in the first place. But I know perfectly well that even you will agree with me – if you have a scrap of self-knowledge – when I say that people who fall for a lover like that are suffering from Corybantism.[26]

27   WEALTH: Do you really think they see me the way I am, lame or blind or with all the other problems I have?

HERMES: But how do they not, Wealth, unless they're all blind as well?

WEALTH: They do have eyes, my friend. It's just that Ignorance and Deceit[27] (current lords of all they survey) darken their vision. And I do something on my own account, to avoid the appearance of absolute ugliness. To meet them, I put on a really attractive mask, full of gold and studded with precious stones, and dress in an elaborate robe. They think that they're seeing my beauty face to face. So they fall in love and can't live with not having me. If someone stripped me completely and showed me to them, obviously they would condemn themselves for being so extraordinarily short-sighted and for falling in love with such unloveable and unlovely things.[28]

28   HERMES: So how is it they're still not disabused of their error when they actually become rich and put on the mask them-selves? Indeed, if someone claims it from them, they'd rather lose their head than that mask. It's unlikely that when they

can see it all from the inside they don't know that your beauty is all face-paint.

WEALTH: There are quite a few things which help me here too, Hermes.

HERMES: Such as?

WEALTH: When a person first encounters me and opens up his doors to receive me, there enter unseen beside me Pride, Folly, Boastfulness, Weakness, Wanton Injustice, Deceit and a whole host of other, similar vices.[29] His soul is taken over by all of these, and so he admires what he should not admire and tries to get what he should shun. The father of all those incoming vices, myself, protected by that bodyguard, he holds in awe. He would be prepared to have anything done to him rather than lose me.

HERMES: How smooth and slippery you are, Wealth! You're hard to get a grip on and easily lost. You give no secure handhold. You're like eels or snakes. Somehow you slip through people's fingers. By contrast, Poverty[30] is sticky and easy to grasp. She has thousands of little hooks which grow from all over her body. Consequently, when anyone gets close, they're held fast at once and can't easily get free. But while we've been idly chattering we've let something really important slip our notice.

WEALTH: What's that?

HERMES: We haven't brought Treasure with us. But he's the one we needed most.

WEALTH: Well, there's no need to worry about that, anyway. I always leave him on earth (well, actually, in the ground)[31] when I come back up to see you. I tell him to stay inside and lock the door and not to open for anyone, but only if he hears me calling.

HERMES: Well then, let's get onto Attic soil now. You catch hold of my travelling cloak and follow me until I reach the border.

WEALTH: It's a good idea to lead me by the hand, Hermes. If you let me go, I'll probably wander round and bump into Hyperbolus or Cleon. But what's that noise? It sounds like iron against stone.

31   HERMES: It's Timon here, digging nearby on a little stony patch of ground on the mountainside. My goodness! Poverty's with him as well,[32] not to mention Toil there. There's Endurance, Wisdom, Courage and the whole crowd of the sort of virtues that are drawn up under the influence of Hunger. They're a much better bunch than your bodyguard.

WEALTH: Why don't we just go away, Hermes, as quickly as we can? We can't achieve anything worthwhile with a man surrounded by an army that size.

HERMES: Zeus' view was different. So let's not be cowards.

32   POVERTY: Where are you taking that man whose hand you're holding, Slayer of Argos?[33]

HERMES: We've been sent by Zeus to Timon here.

POVERTY: What! Wealth is coming to Timon? But when I found him, he was in a dreadful state because of Luxury. I handed him over to Wisdom and Toil here and made a noble and valuable man of him. I suppose you consider Poverty to be so contemptible and easy to wrong that you can claim from me the only possession I have who has been thoroughly trained in virtue. The intention is, I suppose, for Wealth to take him and put him in the hands of Wanton Injustice[34] and Pride again, turn him back into the weak, ignoble fool he was and hand him back to me when he's reduced to a ragged remnant.

HERMES: This is Zeus' idea, Poverty.

33   POVERTY: Well, I'm off then. Follow me, Toil, Wisdom and the rest. He'll soon find out the sort of woman he's going to desert. I'm a good workmate. I teach what is best. Being with me has made him physically healthy, and mentally strong. He's come to live the life of a real man, looking to his own resources and regarding all that excess as what it truly is, alien to him.

HERMES: They're going. Let's approach him.

34   TIMON: Who are you, you wretches? Why have you come here to annoy a man who's trying to earn his living? Well, you won't get away scot-free, dirty swine that you are. I'm going to break your bones right away with a shower of clods and rocks.

HERMES: No, Timon, don't throw anything. You won't be attacking humans. I'm Hermes and this is Wealth. Zeus heard your prayers and has sent us down. So leave off your labours and accept affluence and good fortune.

TIMON: You'll soon be sorry too, even though you claim to be gods. I hate all gods and men equally. And I think I'm going to bash this blind fellow with my mattock, whoever he is.

WEALTH: Let's go, Hermes, in the name of Zeus, in case I get something nasty to take with me. I think the man's completely crazy.

HERMES: Don't do anything stupid, Timon. Lay down that wild   35
and rough attitude, put your hands out and receive good fortune. Be rich again, take your place among the leading Athenians, take no notice of those ungrateful individuals. It's you alone who is happy.

TIMON: I need nothing from you. Don't bother me. My mattock is wealth enough for me. As for the rest, I'm most happy when no one comes near me.

HERMES: That's a very misanthropic attitude, my good friend.

Am I to bring to Zeus this rough reply, strong words like this?[35]

Well I suppose it's reasonable that you would hate human beings, since they've done you so much harm. But there's no reason for you to hate the gods, when they've taken such care of you.

TIMON: And I'm very much obliged to you and Zeus for the   36
concern, Hermes. But I won't take Wealth here.

HERMES: Why not?

TIMON: Well it's because in the past he was the cause of countless problems for me. He put me in the hands of toadies. He pointed plotters in my direction. He aroused hatred against me. He ruined me with luxurious living. He made people envy me. And then, to cap it all, unbelievably and treacherously he all of a sudden left me. By contrast, my dear Poverty has trained me by labours of the manliest sort. Her company, with its concomitant dose of truth and frankness, gave me all the necessities through my own work and taught me to have contempt for great wealth. She made me hang my expectation of life on myself alone and showed me what riches I did possess – the sort that couldn't be removed by the flatteries of a toady, the threats of a *sykophantes*,[36] the passions of the people, the votes of the assemblymen or the machinations of a tyrant. So now I'm hale and hearty because of the hard work I do industriously tilling this piece of ground. I see none of the city's problems and I have a lasting source of sufficient food in my mattock. So go back where you came from, Hermes, and take Wealth back to Zeus. It would suit me perfectly well if the whole of mankind, young and old alike, came to a sticky end.

HERMES: No, no, my friend. Not everyone deserves to come to a bad end. Leave off this childish tantrum and accept Wealth. There's no way you can reject the gifts Zeus gives you.

WEALTH: Do you want me to put my case,[37] Timon? Or will you get annoyed if I speak?

TIMON: Go on, then. But make it quick and don't give me a whole load of introductory waffle like the wretched politicians. I'll put up with a few words from you for the sake of Hermes here.

WEALTH: Well, I think I should've been allowed to give a long speech, given the large number of charges you've made against me. However, just consider whether I've done you any harm, as you claim. I was the one who was responsible for all those delights you enjoyed – honour, front-row seats, garlands and the rest of the trappings of the good life. It was because of me that you were looked at, talked about and longed for. It's not my fault if your toadies did you harm. On the contrary, it's I who was more wronged by you, since you put me so dishonourably in the way of scoundrels who praised you and bewitched you and used every device in conspiring to get hold of me. Your final accusation was that I'd betrayed you. Actually, it's I who should throw this charge at you, the way you drove me off and pushed me head first out of your house. That's why Poverty (whom you hold in such great regard) has clothed you in this leather tunic in place of the soft cloak of yore. Hermes here will bear witness to the way I begged

Zeus not to make me come back to you, since you'd attacked
me so virulently.

HERMES: But you can see the sort of man he's turned into now,   39
can't you, Wealth? So have confidence and live with him.
You, Timon, keep on digging the way you are. Wealth, I want
you to bring up Treasure under his mattock. He'll listen once
you call him.

TIMON: Well, Hermes, I'm constrained to obey and to be
wealthy again. What can a man do when the gods force the
issue? I just want you to notice what trouble you're putting
me in the way of, unlucky man that I am. Up to a moment
ago, I lived a really happy life. Now suddenly, though I've
done no wrong, I'm going to receive all this gold and all those
worries to go with it.

HERMES: Do it, Timon, for my sake, even if it's difficult and   40
unbearable. This way you can make those toadies burst with
envy. I'm going to fly back to heaven using the route over
Mount Etna.

WEALTH: Well, he's gone, I reckon (I'm guessing from the
flapping of his wings). Timon, you stay here. I'm going to go
off and bring Treasure up for you. No, better, you knock on
the ground. Hey you, Golden Treasure, listen to Timon here
and let yourself fall into his hands. Keep digging, Timon,
and make your mattock strokes deep. I'm going to get out of
your way.

TIMON: Right, now, mattock, be strong and don't tire as you   41
summon Treasure into the open out of his deep hiding-place.
O Zeus the wonder-worker, friendly Corybants and Hermes
god of gain, where did such a huge amount of gold come
from? Maybe I'm dreaming. I'm afraid I'll find it's just charcoal when I wake up. No, it's gold all right, stamped, with a
reddish tinge, heavy and lovely to look at.

O Gold, a mortal's greatest pride and joy![38]

Night and day like blazing fire you shine.[39] Come, dearest and
most desirable creature. Now I can really believe Zeus became
gold once. What virgin would not have opened her lap to

receive so handsome a lover as he streamed down through the ceiling?[40]

42   Now Midas and Croesus and you offerings at Delphi, you turn out to be nothing compared with Timon and his wealth. Why, even the king of Persia can't match it!

Now, mattock and trusty leather tunic, the best thing is to set you up here as offerings to Pan. I'm going to buy all this border land. I'm going to build a tower over my treasure just big enough for me to live in. And I think I'll be buried there when I die as well.

'I hereby decree[41] that for the rest of my life the following law shall be in force: refusal to mix with anyone, refusal to recognize anyone and contempt for everyone. Friends, guests, comrades and the Altar of Pity[42] I shall regard as absolute nonsense. To take pity on someone who weeps or to help someone in need is illegal and will be a breach of my ethical code. My way of life will be as lonely as that of a wolf. I shall 43 have one friend only – Timon. All other people are to be seen as enemies and conspirators. It will pollute me even to be in their company. If I even see someone, it will be declared a black day. In a word, as far as I'm concerned human beings are to be no different from statues of stone or bronze. We are to receive no heralds from them nor make a treaty. The wasteland is to be our boundary with them. As for member-ship of clan, phratry, deme and even the fatherland[43] itself, these are merely cold and useless names and things in which only fools take pride. Timon is to be rich alone. He is to ignore everyone else. He is to wallow in luxury alone, free from flattery and cheap eulogies. He is to sacrifice and feast the gods alone, acting as his own neighbour and shaking off everyone else. When he dies, I decree that he shall pay him-44 self the final respects and put a garland on himself. The name he favours is to be "the Misanthrope", and the signs of his character bad-temperedness, roughness, awkward-ness, anger and moroseness. If I ever see a person dying in a fire and begging me to put it out, I am to try to extinguish it with pitch and oil. If a river in spate carries off someone, and he stretches forth his hands asking me to grab hold, I am to push him right under so his head goes below and he can't stick it out again. This is the way they will receive what's coming to them. Law drafter, Timon son of Echecratides of the deme Kollytos. Proposer, the same Timon.' Right, let that be my decree and let me ensure I stick by its provisions manfully.

On the other hand, I would've really liked people to know 45 about my superabundant wealth somehow. It would be torture for them if they did. But what's this? My goodness, what speed! They're running up from all directions, covered with dust and struggling to catch their breath. Somehow they've caught a whiff of my gold.[44] So shall I climb onto this outcrop and drive them away, showering them with stones from the higher ground? Or shall I break the law just a little bit and just once meet them all together, to make them feel the sting of my contempt more fully? I think the latter course might be better. So let me stand my ground now and receive them. Let me see who the first one is. Ah, Gnathonides[45] the toady, the one who offered me a noose the day before yesterday when I asked him for a loan, even though he'd thrown up whole vats of wine at my place. I'm glad he came, anyway. That means he'll be the first to get what's coming to him.

GNATHONIDES: Didn't I always say the gods wouldn't neglect 46 a good man like Timon? Greetings, Timon, handsomest, sweetest and most clubbable fellow.

TIMON: The same to you, Gnathonides, greediest of vultures and most cursable of men.

GNATHONIDES: Oh, you always like a joke. But where's the drinking-party? I've brought a new song with me from one of the recent dithyramb productions.[46]

TIMON: Well, it's going to be elegies[47] that you'll be singing in a genuinely heart-rending way when my mattock gets to work on you.

GNATHONIDES: What's this? Are you hitting me, Timon? Witnesses! By Heracles, ow ow! I'm going to bring a case of grievous bodily harm against you in the Areopagus.

TIMON: Well, if you'll hang on a bit, it's possible it'll be a charge of murder.

GNATHONIDES: No, no. You can cure the wound completely if you just smear on a little gold. It's amazingly effective as a staunching agent.

TIMON: Are you still here?

GNATHONIDES: I'm going. But you'll regret turning from a good man into such an awkward customer.

47 TIMON: Who's this balding fellow coming up? It's Philiades,[48] the most disgusting of all the toadies. He got a complete farm from me and a two-talent dowry for his daughter. I was paying him back for praising me. When I'd sung and everyone else stayed silent, he was the only one to laud me to the skies. He swore that I was more melodious than the swans.[49] He saw me a few days ago when I was ill and I went up and asked him for some help. The good fellow gave me a sound beating.

48 PHILIADES: Have you no shame? So you acknowledge Timon now? It's now Gnathonides is a friend and drinking companion? Well his ingratitude has earned him his just deserts. Those of us who are his long-standing acquaintances, people who were ephebes[50] with him and are fellow-demesmen,[51] have a sense of moderation, so as not to appear to be jumping in too soon. Greetings, master. Make sure you guard against these revolting toadies. They're only interested in your table, and in other respects are no different from carrion crows. You can't trust anyone now. They're all ungrateful scoundrels. I was bringing you a talent to use for your pressing needs when I heard on the way, when I was almost here, that you'd become astonishingly wealthy. So I've just come to give you this warning. Mind you, you're so wise that you probably don't need my words. Actually, you could even give the right advice to Nestor.

TIMON: All in good time, Philiades. But come here so that I can greet you – with my mattock.

PHILIADES: Help! The ungrateful rascal has broken my head, just because I was giving him some sound advice.

49 TIMON: Look, here's a third one coming. It's the orator Demeas.[52] He's got a decree in his right hand and he's claiming to be my kinsman. He's the one who paid the city within one day a fine of sixteen talents, which he'd got from me. He'd

lost a case and then been put in prison for not paying up what
was due. I took pity on him and paid the fine to get him out.
Then the other day, when he was allotted the Erechtheus
tribe's post for the distribution of the theoric fund[53] and I
went to ask for the usual dole, he declared that he didn't
acknowledge me to be a citizen.

DEMEAS: Greetings, Timon, the great benefactor of our tribe,   50
the support of Athens, the bulwark of Greece. The people has
long been gathered, as have both councils,[54] and they await
your presence. But listen first to the decree which I have
proposed on your behalf:

'Inasmuch as Timon, son of Echecratides, of the deme
Kollytos, a man not only noble, but also wiser than any
other in Greece, will continue for ever performing the most
extraordinary acts for the city, and has won the Olympic title
for boxing, wrestling and running on the same day, as well as
for the horse-drawn chariot and the pair –'

TIMON: Hey, I've never even been as an official delegate to
watch the Olympic Games.

DEMEAS: So what? You'll go later. It's better to have lots of
things like this to hand. 'And he gained distinction recently
near Acharnae and cut to pieces two Spartan divisions –'[55]

TIMON: What? I wasn't even put down on the call-up roster,   51
because I had no weapons.

DEMEAS: You're being modest about yourself, but we'd be
ungrateful if we didn't remember. 'Moreover, also in his
proposals of decrees, his counsels and his generalships he has
given no small contribution to the city's welfare. In the light
of all these facts, let it be the settled will of the council and
people and the Eliaea court in its tribal divisions and of all
the demes both individually and collectively to dedicate a
golden statue of Timon next to Athena on the acropolis with
a thunderbolt in his right hand and sunrays on his head[56] and
to award him seven golden crowns and to have these crowns
publicly proclaimed today at the Dionysia when the new
tragedies are performed – because for his sake we have to
celebrate the Dionysia today. The proposal was put by the
orator Demeas, Timon's closest relative and his student (for

Timon also happens to be the finest orator and everything else he'd like).'

52   There's your decree. I was also wanting to bring my son to present to you. I've named him Timon after you.

TIMON: How is that, Demeas, when you've never even got married, as far as I know?

DEMEAS: Well, god willing I'll get married in the new year, I'll have a child and that child (it's going to be a boy) I'll be calling Timon.

TIMON: I don't know if you'll ever get married, you scoundrel, when you feel the size of blow I'm going to give you.

DEMEAS: Ow! What's this? Are you trying for a tyranny, Timon, and beating free men when you're not completely free or a citizen yourself? Well, you'll soon pay the penalty for all your crimes, including the burning of the acropolis.

53   TIMON: You rogue, the acropolis hasn't been set on fire. You're obviously a *sykophantes*.

DEMEAS: What's more, your wealth comes from a robbery you staged on the temple treasury.

TIMON: Well that hasn't been broken into, either. So this charge is also incredible.

DEMEAS: It'll be broken into later. But as things stand you got everything which was in it.

TIMON: Well then, you can have another smack.

DEMEAS: Ow, my back!

TIMON: Don't screech or I'll give you a third thump. After all, I'd look completely ridiculous if I'd cut to pieces two Spartan divisions with no weapons, and I couldn't put paid to one miserable little guttersnipe. That would make my Olympic boxing and wrestling crowns worthless.

54   But what's this? Isn't it Thrasycles[57] the philosopher? The very man. I can see him approaching with his beard spread out and his eyebrows raised, muttering something to himself, with the glance of a Titan and his hair piled up over his forehead, the very image of Boreas or Triton as painted by Zeuxis. This is the fellow with the fine posture, the calm walk and the sober dress sense, who spends his mornings telling countless anecdotes about virtue, attacking pleasure-seekers

and praising self-sufficiency. But when he's had his bath and arrives at dinner, and the slave hands him a cup that's large (and he prefers his wine with less water too), it's as though he's drunk the water of Lethe – he displays exactly the opposite qualities to those he's lauded in his morning lectures.[58] He grabs at the savouries first like a kite and elbows his neighbour out of the way. He gets his beard full of gravy, stuffs himself like a dog, leans over the dishes as though he expects to find virtue in them, wipes the bowls clean with his finger so as not to leave behind even a trace of the salad-dressing, is always 55 dissatisfied with what he receives, even if he's the only one of the company who gets the whole cake or the boar. The crowning achievement of his greed and gluttony is that his drunken excesses don't stop at singing and dancing: no, he quarrels and gets angry. What's more, over his cups, he pours out many speeches, especially at that point about sobriety and proper demeanour. And he says these things when he's already feeling bad from the unmixed wine and lisping ridiculously. Then on top of this he throws up. In the end, a couple of people pick him up and carry him away from the party, both his hands firmly clasped around the pipe-girl.[59] Now, this is a man also who when sober is the equal of anyone in lying, sheer audacity and greed for gold. He's also the leading toady and a ready perjurer. His herald is trickery and his travelling-companion brazenness. What a piece of work he is! Perfect from every angle, a complete paragon! Good fellow that he is, it's not going to be long before he too gets what's coming to him. What's this? My goodness, it's Thrasycles. You're late.

THRASYCLES: I've not come in the same spirit as this mob here, 56 Timon. They're astounded by your wealth and have gathered in haste in the hope of silver and gold and expensive dinners. They'll display boundless flattery, when you're a straightforward sort of man who shares his belongings with others. You know that a barley-cake is enough of a meal for me, and that I prefer thyme or cardamom as my relish, or, if I let myself have a fling once in a while, a bit of salt. My drink is provided by the public fountain. My old cloak here is better than any purple robe you could mention. My view is that gold is of no more value than the pebbles on the seashore. Actually, it's for your sake I've come here, to make sure you're not corrupted by this dreadful possession, wealth, which brings plots in its wake and has been for many on many occasions the cause of appalling disasters. If you take my advice, your best course will be to throw the whole lot into the sea. It's of no real use to a good man who can see the real wealth in philosophy. But don't drop it in the open sea, my dear fellow. Just go in up to your waist and put it where the waves break. Let me be the only witness. If you don't want to do this, here's a better plan still. Take it out of your house right away and don't leave an obol for yourself. Share it out among those in need, five drachmas to one, a mina to another, half a talent[60] to a third. But it would be right to give a double or triple share to any philosopher among them. As for me – well, I'm not asking for myself, but to be able to give my friends who need it a share – it's quite enough for you to fill up this pouch here. It doesn't hold even two complete Aeginetan bushels.[61] The philosopher should be moderate, make do with little and not think beyond his pouch. ·

TIMON: You have my approval for what you've said, Thrasycles. But before I fill your pouch, bring your head here and let me measure out with my mattock some knuckle-sauce to fill that with.

THRASYCLES: O Democracy! O Laws! I'm being drubbed by this scoundrel, in a free city!

TIMON: What's your problem, my dear fellow? Have I given you short measure? Look, I'm willing to throw in four pounds extra. But what's this? Crowds of them are gathering. There's Blepsias and Laches and Gniphon[62] and the whole cohort of the people who are shortly going to walk in darkness. Why don't I get up on this rock, give my mattock a well-earned rest from its long labour, pile a load of stones together and send down a hail of missiles on them from a distance?

BLEPSIAS: Don't start throwing, Timon. We're off.

TIMON: Not without a few drops of blood and unwounded, you're not.

THE SHIP, OR PRAYERS

LYCINUS:[1] Didn't I say that it'd be easier for a decomposing
corpse lying out in the open to evade the attention of the
vultures than it would for any unusual sight to pass Timolaus
by, even if he had to go as far as Corinth at a run and without
stopping for a breather. You really are a born tourist and
completely resolute in your vocation.

TIMOLAUS: But what else could I have done, Lycinus? I was
entirely at leisure when I heard that this absolutely massive
ship had put into Piraeus. It's one of the grain-ships that make
the run from Egypt to Italy.[2] Anyway, it's my guess that you
and Samippus here have also come from the city with nothing
else in mind but to take a look at the ship.

LYCINUS: Absolutely. And Adeimantus from Myrrhinous also
came with us, but somehow he's wandered off and got lost in
the crowd of sightseers. We got as far as the ship together,
and as we were approaching it I think you were leading,
Samippus, and Adeimantus was just behind you. I was behind
Adeimantus, holding on to him with both hands. He held my
hand and saw me safely up the gangway, as he was barefoot
and I had shoes on. I didn't see him any more, either on board
or after we disembarked.

SAMIPPUS: Do you know when he must have left us, then,
Lycinus? I reckon it was when that nice-looking young man
came out of his lair, the one wearing the white linen tunic,
with his hair tied back, drawn off his forehead on both sides.
If I know Adeimantus at all, my guess is that when he spotted
a sight as elegant as that he decided he'd had enough of the
Egyptian shipwright who was doing the guided tour, and

stood there weeping, as usual. The man is a tear-fountain when it comes to affairs of the heart.

LYCINUS: But I didn't think the young fellow was particularly pretty, Samippus. Well, not enough to stagger Adeimantus. After all, he's got a whole gaggle of beautiful boys following him in Athens, all worth standing and weeping at, all free-born, good talkers and smelling of the wrestling ground.[3] This one on the other hand, in addition to being dark-skinned, with protruding lips and skinny legs, spoke too quickly, slurring his words and running them together – in Greek, it's true, but with the accent and timbre of his native language.[4] What's more, the fact that his hair is pulled into a plait behind argues that he's not free-born.

3 TIMOLAUS: No, Lycinus, this is a sign of noble birth among the Egyptians, the hair. All Egypt's free-born boys braid their hair until they reach the age of ephebes.[5] It's the opposite of what our ancestors did. They reckoned it good for the old men to have long hair and to tie it in a top-knot, held in place with a golden cicada.

SAMIPPUS: That's a nice citation of Thucydides' histories, Timolaus. You're referring of course to the prologue, where he spoke about our former love of luxury among the Ionians, when that generation first became colonists.[6]

4 LYCINUS: Hey, Samippus, I've just remembered the point at which Adeimantus went missing. It was while we were standing by the mast, looking up for ages, counting the layers of hide in the sails and staring in wonder at the sailor climbing up the rigging and then running safely along the yard-arm, hanging on to the yard-ropes.

SAMIPPUS: You're right. But what should we do? Will we wait for him here or do you want me to go back to the ship again?

TIMOLAUS: No, let's go on. He's probably already gone ahead of us in his hurry to get to the city, realizing he couldn't find us any more. If that's not the case, well, Adeimantus knows the way, and there's no fear he'll get lost just because we've left him behind.

LYCINUS: Nevertheless, it might seem a bit rude to leave a friend behind and go off ourselves. However, if Samippus thinks it's all right, let's go.

SAMIPPUS: I do think so, especially if we might find the wrestling ground still open.

By the way, though, what a massive ship! The shipwright said it was a hundred and twenty cubits long, more than a quarter of that in breadth and twenty-nine cubits from the deck to the bottom at the deepest part of the hold. As for the rest, the mast was massive. It was held in place by an enormous forestay and supported a huge yard-arm. The stern stood up above the rest, gently curving and with a golden goose[7] on it. At the other end, the prow likewise swept forward and went higher, with the ship's name – 'The Goddess Isis' – written on both sides. As for the rest of the equipment, it all seemed wonderful to me – the paintings,[8] the fiery-red topsail, but more particularly the anchors, the capstans, the windlasses and the cabins at the stern. As for the crew, you might have compared them to an army. They said it could carry enough grain to feed everyone in Attica for a whole year. And the safety of this huge vessel was in the hands of a tiny little old man, who controls the massive steering-oars with a minute tiller. He was pointed out to me, a curly headed chap with a bald patch, called Heron, I think.

TIMOLAUS: The passengers said his skill was marvellous. He knows the sea better than Proteus, according to them.

But did you hear how it was they put in here, what happened to them during their voyage and how the star saved them?

LYCINUS: No, Timolaus. But we'd very gladly listen to an account now.

TIMOLAUS: The captain himself told me the story. He was a nice man and very approachable. He said they'd set sail from Pharos with a light wind and after seven days were in sight of Akamas. Then a westerly started blowing and drove them sideways as far as Sidon. From there, through a gale, they made it through the straits to the Chelidones on the tenth day. That was where they almost went down lock, stock and barrel.

8   I've sailed past the Chelidones myself and I know how high the waves can be there, especially with a south-westerly wind which has a little help from the south as well. This is the spot where the Pamphylian Sea is divided from the Lycian. The surge from the many currents around the headland is broken up – there are sheer and jagged rocks there, sharpened by the pounding of the waves – and makes the place where the breakers crash fearsome with the huge echo and the waves often reaching the height of the cliff itself.

9   Those were the sort of conditions the captain said greeted them too. But it was also still night and the darkness was intense. But the gods were moved to pity by their cries and showed them a fire from Lycia so that they could recognize that place. What's more, one of the Dioscuri set a bright star at the masthead,[9] which guided the ship, which was heading straight for the cliffs, into the open sea to port. After losing their course, they sailed on through the Aegean against the Etesian trade winds and put in at Piraeus yesterday, on the seventieth day out from Egypt. What a long way they've been set back! They ought to have had Crete on their right, sailed past Malea and be in Italy already.

LYCINUS: Well, this helmsman Heron you've mentioned is a wonder-man, to get his navigational calculations so wrong. He's at least as old as Nereus.

10   What's this though? Isn't that Adeimantus?

TIMOLAUS: It is indeed. The very man. Let's give him a shout. Hey, Adeimantus! It's you I'm calling, the son of Strombichus from Myrrhinous.

LYCINUS: It can only be one of two things. He's annoyed with us or he's gone deaf. At any rate, it's not a case of mistaken identity. That is Adeimantus. I can see quite clearly now. That's his cloak and his walk and his close-cropped hair. Still, let's walk a bit more quickly to catch up with him.

11   Adeimantus! Apparently, if we don't grab your cloak and make you do an about-turn you won't respond to our shouts. My, you really look like someone deep in meditation. It looks to me as though you're trying to tease out something neither small nor contemptible.

ADEIMANTUS: It's nothing deep, Lycinus. It's just that a novel
notion struck me as I was walking along which caused me to
ignore your shouts because I was concentrating all my attention on it.

LYCINUS: What is it? Don't be afraid to tell us, unless it's one
of those things you really shouldn't tell anyone. But in any
case, as you know, we've been initiated into the Mysteries[10]
and we've learned how to keep our mouths shut.

ADEIMANTUS: Actually, I'm ashamed to tell you. You'll just
think my notion is adolescent.

LYCINUS: Oh, it's not an affair of the loins, is it? If you tell us,
you certainly won't be talking to the uninitiated, but to fellows
who've gone through the initiatory rituals to the light of a
bright torch.[11]

ADEIMANTUS: It's nothing like that, my friend. Actually, I was   12
daydreaming myself a pile of money, the sort of thing *hoi
polloi*[12] call 'empty happiness'. You came across me just as
I'd reached the height of my fortune and luxury.

LYCINUS: Well then, Adeimantus, it's a case of the well-worn
proverb, 'finders sharers'.[13] Bring your money-pots and set
them out in the open. It's quite reasonable that his friends
should benefit from a share of Adeimantus' luxury.

ADEIMANTUS: I got separated from you right at the ship's
entrance, just after I'd got you safely on board, Lycinus.
Somehow you left while I was measuring the thickness of the
anchor.

Still, when I'd seen everything, I asked one of the sailors   13
how much revenue the ship brought in for its owner on a
yearly average. He replied, 'Twelve Attic talents,[14] to reckon
it at its lowest.' So from that point on as I was coming back I
was mulling over what a life I would live and how I would
help my friends if some god suddenly made that ship mine.
Sometimes I'd sail on board myself, and sometimes I'd send
my slaves. And then I'd already built myself a house from the
twelve talents in a fine spot just above the Painted Stoa,
abandoning my ancestral home on the banks of the Ilissus.
I'd bought slaves and clothes and chariots and horses. Just
now I'd actually been on the point of starting a voyage, being

reckoned a happy man by the passengers, but feared by the sailors and virtually called 'monarch' by them. I was still arranging the things on the ship and glancing back at the harbour in the distance, when you came up to me, Lycinus, and sank my money-bags and capsized my vessel when it was speeding nicely along with the following wind of wish-fulfilment.

14   LYCINUS: Well, then, my dear friend, why don't you grab hold of me and bring me to the general to accuse me of piracy on the high seas, since I've caused such a mighty shipwreck – even though we're on dry land, on the road from Piraeus to the city? But come on. Here's how I'll console you for your loss. If you like, here's five ships right away, bigger and better than the Egyptian one. The most important thing is, though, that they can't be sunk and each will bring five cargoes of corn per annum from Egypt. Now, you star among captains, you'll obviously become impossible for us to deal with. After all, if you couldn't hear us calling you when you were as yet the master of only one ship, get hold of another five, all three-masters and unsinkable, and you quite clearly won't even see your friends. So, my dear fellow, have a good voyage and we'll sit here in Piraeus and ask people who sail in from Egypt or Italy whether by any chance anyone's spotted Adeimantus' great ship the *Isis*.

15   ADEIMANTUS: See? This is why I was afraid to tell you what I was thinking about. I knew you'd ridicule and satirize my wish. So I'll just go over here for a while until you've gone on, and I'll sail off again on my ship. It's much better to chat with the sailors than to be the butt of your ridicule.

LYCINUS: We'll support your enterprise too and go on board with you.

ADEIMANTUS: I'll go on first and pull away the gangway.

LYCINUS: Well, we'll swim after you then. Do you think that you can get hold of vessels as big as these easily without buying or building them and we can't pray to the gods for the ability to swim for many miles without tiring? Why, only a few days ago, as you know, the whole lot of us friends went over to Aegina for the rites of Enodia.[15] We were packed into a tiny boat and made the crossing for four obols apiece. Why didn't you get upset then that we were sharing the voyage, but you're so annoyed now that we're going to climb aboard with you that you're going on first and removing the gangway? Adeimantus, you're too full of yourself. You're not even spitting in your lap.[16] Now you're a shipowner you've forgotten who you really are. You've become so high and mighty because of that house you've had built in a nice part of the city and the vast numbers of servants you have. Still, my good friend, in the name of Isis, I'd be grateful if you'd remember to bring us back some of those dried small fry from the Nile or some myrrh from Canopus or an ibis[17] from Memphis. If the ship has space, maybe you'd also bring us one of the pyramids.

TIMOLAUS: That's enough satire, Lycinus. Look how you've made Adeimantus blush. You've swamped his vessel with waves of laughter. The bilges are overflowing and the ship can't hold on any more against the inflow. 16

Anyway, we've still a long way to go before we reach the city. So let's divide the journey in four and each ask during the stades[18] allotted to him for whatever he'd like from the gods. That way we won't notice our tiredness and simultaneously we'll get pleasure from falling as it were into a pleasant daydream which will pamper us as much as we want. By this I mean that each of us will determine the limits of his wish and we're to assume that the gods will grant it, even if it's against the laws of nature. Most importantly, though, the scheme will be a way of showing who would use his wealth and his wishes to the best ends, because it will reveal clearly what sort of person each would have been if he'd become wealthy.

SAMIPPUS: Good idea, Timolaus. I'm right behind you. When the moment comes, I'll pray for what I'd like. I don't reckon we even have to ask Adeimantus if he wants to play the game. He's got one foot on his ship as it is. But Lycinus must agree too. 17

LYCINUS: All right, let's be rich, if that's the best thing. I don't want you thinking I begrudge the good fortune we'll all share.

ADEIMANTUS: Who's first, then?

LYCINUS: You go, Adeimantus. Then after you Samippus here, then Timolaus. I'll join the prayerfest only about half a stade before the Dipylon Gate – and I'll try to cover the distance at a run.

18 ADEIMANTUS: Well, I'm still going to stick with my ship. However, since the rules allow it, I'm going to add a few things to my prayer. I pray that Hermes the god of gain will grant everything. Let me possess the ship and everything in it – cargo, merchants, women, sailors.

SAMIPPUS: There's something you've forgotten you have on board, the possession that will give you the most pleasure of all.

ADEIMANTUS: Ah, you mean the boy with the long hair, Samippus. Yes, let him be mine as well. And I'd like the grains of wheat on board converted into an equal number of darics.[19]

19 LYCINUS: What do you mean, Adeimantus? Your ship will sink. The wheat grains don't weigh the same as the equivalent number of gold coins would.

ADEIMANTUS: Don't be a begrudger, Lycinus. When your turn comes, you can pray for the whole of Mount Parnes there to be turned to gold and I won't say a word.

LYCINUS: I was only pointing it out for your safety. I didn't want everyone going down with the gold. I'm not so bothered about your plight. But the pretty young man will drown. The poor thing doesn't know how to swim.

TIMOLAUS: Don't worry, Lycinus. The dolphins will pick him up and bring him safely to land. After all, they saved a musician[20] and paid him in kind for his singing. And the dead body of another lad was brought to the Isthmus on a dolphin's back.[21] Do you think that Adeimantus' newly acquired slave will be without a dolphin to serve the cause of passion?

ADEIMANTUS: Are you doing a Lycinus on me as well, Timolaus, with this pile of sardonic comments? This game was your suggestion, you know.

20 TIMOLAUS: Well, it would be better if you made the wish more credible. Discover a treasure buried under your bed, then you won't have any bother about transferring the gold from the ship to the city.

ADEIMANTUS: Good idea. I decree that a treasure trove has been dug up under the stone Herm in my courtyard. It contains a thousand bushels of gold coin.[22] So my immediate priority, as Hesiod would have it, is a house,[23] so that I can live as conspicuously as possible. I've already purchased all the land around the city that isn't just thyme and rocks. I've bought the seashore at Eleusis and a few acres around the Isthmus for the sake of the games, in case I want to go there for the Isthmia, and the plain of Sicyon. In a word, every bit of Greece that has thick shade, a good water supply and decent crops will belong to Adeimantus in a trice. I'll have gold plate to eat off. My cups won't be those flimsy things Echecrates[24] uses, but will each weigh two talents.[25]

LYCINUS: How's the cup-bearer going to be able to handle such a heavy cup when it's full? And are you going to be able to take it from him without struggling, when it's not a cup he's giving you but more like a Sisyphean weight.[26]

ADEIMANTUS: Don't spoil my wish, man. If you don't shut up, I'll have my tables and couches made of solid gold, and my servants as well.

LYCINUS: Well just watch out that you don't follow Midas' example and have your bread and wine turn into gold. Then you'd be a poor little rich man dying of very expensive starvation.

ADEIMANTUS: You can make a more convincing job of your own wishes in a minute, Lycinus, when it's your turn.

On top of all this, I want purple robes and the most luxurious lifestyle. I'll sleep sweetly for as long as I like. My friends will come to me with cap in hand. Everyone will be afraid of me and bow and scrape. People will walk up and down outside my doors every morning early,[27] and among them will be the high and mighty Cleaenetus and Democrates.[28] When they come up and expect to be admitted ahead of the others, seven doormen, huge barbarians, who are standing in attendance will slam the door shut in their faces, the way these fellows do now. At a time of my own choosing, I'll peek out like the sun. I won't cast even a glance in their direction, though. But if there's a pauper around, as I was before I found the treasure, I'll be kind to him and tell him to come to dinner at the usual time, after his bath. The rich will choke with rage as they see my chariots, horses and good-looking slaves, about two thousand of them, the choicest from every age group.

23   Then I'll dine off gold plate – silverware is cheap stuff and not my style at all. And on the menu there'll be dried fish from Iberia, wine from Italy and Iberian olive oil as well. The honey will be ours,[29] and fresh. There'll be dainties from everywhere. I'll serve boar, hare and every kind of winged creature, including the bird from Phasis,[30] the Indian peacock and the Numidian cockerel. The cooks in every case will be experts, with specialisms in pastries and sauces. Anyone I propose a toast to, asking for a cup or a bowl, can take the vessel away with him as well after he's drunk what's in it.

24   The people who are now rich will all look like imitations of Homer's beggar Irus[31] in comparison with me. Dionicus will stop displaying his silver dishes and cups in the procession,[32] especially when he sees my slaves using so much silverware. What's more, I'd make the following special provisions for the city. Every month I'd distribute a hundred drachmas to each citizen, and fifty to each metic.[33] Funding for public projects would include fine theatres and bath-houses, a great canal to bring the sea as far as the Dipylon Gate and a harbour there, so that I can moor my ship nearby in sight of the Ceramicus.

25   As for you, my friends, I'd tell my steward to measure out twenty bushels of gold coin for Samippus, five litres for Timolaus and only one for Lycinus, level measure at that, because he's a prattler and satirizes my prayer.[34] This is the life I'd like to live, being massively wealthy, living in the lap of luxury and making unstinted use of every possible pleasure. That's all I have to say. I pray that Hermes, god of luck, will make it happen for me.

26 LYCINUS: You do realize, don't you, Adeimantus, that all this wealth of yours is hanging by a terribly thin thread, and that if it breaks everything will vanish and leave you with a sack of charcoal instead of a treasure trove?

ADEIMANTUS: What do you mean, Lycinus?

LYCINUS: My dear man, just that it's not clear how long you're going to live as a rich man. Who knows, you may be sitting at your gold table, and before you can stretch out your hand and taste the peacock or the Numidian cockerel, you'll breathe your last little breath and leave all this stuff for the vultures and the crows. I don't suppose you want me to give you a list of the people who have died before being able to enjoy their wealth. And I won't mention the group deprived of what they owned while they were still alive by some divinity jealous of such things. No doubt you've heard the stories of Croesus and Polycrates. They were much wealthier than you and lost all their riches in the twinkling of an eye.

But leaving them aside, can you be absolutely sure that 27 you'll stay in good health? Can't you see that lots of rich men live a miserable life because they're constantly in pain? Some of them can't walk, others are blind or suffer from some intestinal complaint. I'm absolutely certain that for twice the wealth you wouldn't choose to take on the sufferings of the rich Phanomachus[35] and to be as weak as him, even if you won't admit it. I won't mention all the plots against your money, the thieves, the envy, and the hatred of the general public. Do you see the sort of problems your wealth is responsible for?

ADEIMANTUS: You're always against me, Lycinus. I'm not even going to give you your litre, now that you've treated the last part of my prayer with contempt.

LYCINUS: You're already starting to behave like most rich men, trying to duck out of your promises and reneging on them. However, it's your turn to have your wish, Samippus.

SAMIPPUS: I'm a landlubber, as you know, an Arcadian from 28 Mantinea. So I won't be asking for a ship. I wouldn't be able to show it off to my fellow-citizens. And I'm not going to be finicky with the gods and ask for treasure and gold measured out in bucketfuls. The fact is, the gods can do everything, even what seems most extraordinary. And Timolaus' rule for our wishes was that we shouldn't be afraid to ask for anything, because they aren't going to refuse any of our requests. So, my wish is to become a king. But not like Alexander son of

Philip or Ptolemy or Mithridates or anyone else who inherited his kingdom from his father. I'll start as an outlaw with about thirty absolutely trustworthy and devoted comrades and confederates. Then gradually the number will grow to three hundred as various people join up. Then it'll be a thousand and pretty soon ten thousand. Eventually, I'll have fifty thousand hoplites[36] and around five thousand cavalry.

29   I'll be chosen as leader by unanimous popular vote, because the men think I'm the best general and policy-maker. This is already a better start than the other monarchs have, to rule because you've been selected by the army for your courage, and not simply to take on the mantle of kingship someone else has worked for. That would be analogous to Adeimantus' treasure. There's no comparison with the pleasure gained from knowing you've got hold of power through your own merits.

LYCINUS: My word, Samippus, nothing small scale for you! You've asked for the crème de la crème of good fortune, to be chosen as the best by fifty thousand and to lead such a mighty force. We had no idea Mantinea had brought up such an amazing king and general for us. However, carry on with your regime. Lead your soldiers, arrange your cavalrymen and your men at arms. What I want to know is where this vast army of yours is going to proceed from Arcadia. Who are going to be the first poor creatures to have you arrive on their doorstep?

30 SAMIPPUS: Listen, Lycinus. Or better, if you like the idea, come along with us. I'm going to make you cavalry commander of my fifty thousand.

LYCINUS: For the honour you do me, my liege, I'm grateful to you. In Persian mode I bow down and do obeisance to you, bringing both my hands behind my back as I honour your upright tiara and your diadem.[37] But make one of these strong fellows your cavalry commander. As you know, I'm dreadfully unhorsey and have never in my whole life so far mounted a charger at all. I'm afraid that when the trumpeter gives the signal I'll fall off and be trampled in the chaos under so many hoofs or that the horse in its high spirits will take the bit between its teeth and carry me into the middle of the enemy or that I'll have to be tied onto the saddle if I'm to remain on board and hold onto the reins.

ADEIMANTUS: I'll lead your cavalry, Samippus. Give Lycinus 31 the right wing. It's only fair that I should get something really big from you when I gave you so many bushels of gold coin.

SAMIPPUS: Let's ask the cavalrymen themselves if they'll accept you as their leader, Adeimantus. Raise your hands, you cavalrymen who think Adeimantus should be your commander.

ADEIMANTUS: As you can see, Samippus, they've voted for me unanimously.

SAMIPPUS: Right then. You command the cavalry and Lycinus can have the right wing. Timolaus here will be stationed on the left. I'll be in charge of the centre, as is the rule for the kings of Persia when they join the fray themselves.[38]

Let's pray to King Zeus and set out on the road to Corinth 32 by the mountain route. And once we've conquered every part of Greece – there'll be no opposition to such overwhelming forces as we possess, so we'll win with no effort – we'll embark on our triremes,[39] put our horses aboard the horse-transport vessels and cross over to Ionia (all the preparations, including sufficient food supplies and the right number of ships, will have been made in advance at Cenchreae). Next we'll sacrifice to Artemis on the Ionian shore,[40] take the cities easily, as they're unfortified, leave governors in them and proceed towards Syria by way of Caria, Lycia, Pamphylia, Pisidia and the seashore and mountain regions of Cilicia until we arrive at the Euphrates.

LYCINUS: My liege, if you wouldn't mind, please leave me 33 behind as satrap of Greece.[41] For one thing, I'm a coward, and for another, I wouldn't like to be a long way away from things at home. It looks as though you're off to fight Armenians and Parthians, warlike tribes with a reputation for accurate archery. So hand over the right wing to someone else and leave me in Greece as a sort of Antipater,[42] in case someone hits poor me with an arrow where my armour doesn't cover me when I'm leading your phalanx[43] near Susa or Bactra.

SAMIPPUS: You're deserting the line, Lycinus, because you're a coward. But the legal penalty for desertion is decapitation. Now, we're already beside the Euphrates and the river has been bridged. What's more, behind us every region we've passed through is safely in our hands – lieutenants have been assigned to each race and are in complete control – and we've sent parties to secure Phoenicia, Palestine and Egypt for us. So you cross over first with the right wing, Lycinus. I'll follow you and Timolaus here will follow me. Finally, you bring the cavalry, Adeimantus.

34   All the way through Mesopotamia we've met with no resistance. People have willingly surrendered themselves and their citadels. Our arrival in Babylon was unforeseen by the inhabitants. We got inside the walls and now have the city in our control. The king heard of our approach while at Ctesiphon. He then went to Seleucia and got together an enormous cavalry force, also sending for archers and slingers. Our scouts tell us that the army already gathered numbers around one million, including two hundred thousand mounted archers. Even so, the Armenians, the inhabitants of the Caspian Sea area and the people from Bactra are not here yet, and the force consists only of those from the vicinity of the capital itself. That was how easy it was for him to collect so many thousands. So it's time for us to consider what we ought to do.

35   ADEIMANTUS: My view is that we ought to send the foot-soldiers on the road to Ctesiphon and leave my cavalry here to guard Babylon.

SAMIPPUS: Are you ducking out of it through cowardice as well, Adeimantus, now you're in sight of danger? What do *you* think, Timolaus?

TIMOLAUS: We should march towards the enemy in full force and not wait until they're better prepared and their allies have arrived from all sides to swell their numbers. Let's attack them while the enemy are still on the road.

SAMIPPUS: Well said. What's your opinion, Lycinus?

LYCINUS: I'll tell you. We're tired out from our quick walk down to Piraeus this morning and from the thirty stades or so we've now come on the way home. The sun is blazing hot, because it's already around midday. I propose we sit down under this olive-tree on that upturned gravestone and take a rest. Then afterwards we can get up and finish the rest of our journey to the city.[44]

SAMIPPUS: Goodness me, Lycinus, do you think you're still in Athens? Right now you're on the plains before Babylon in the midst of a great army discussing battle strategy.

LYCINUS: I'm glad you reminded me. I thought I was still sober and telling you my opinion as if we were wide awake.

SAMIPPUS: We'll advance, then, if you think that's the right strategy. Make sure you are brave men in the midst of dangers and that you don't betray the spirit your Greek forefathers gave as your inheritance. The enemy are already engaging us. The battle signal is to be 'Ares, God of War'. When the trumpeter sounds the advance, raise a great shout, bang your spears against your shields and try to engage the enemy as soon as possible. Get inside the range of the archers so that we don't give them the chance of striking at us from a distance. Now we're in hand-to-hand combat, the left wing under Timolaus routs their right, which consists entirely of Medes. But round me, the battle is equal, because I'm facing Persians led by the king himself. The whole body of the barbarians' cavalry is charging at our right. So, Lycinus, be a brave man and encourage your troops to hold firm under their attack. 36

LYCINUS: Just my luck! It's me the whole enemy cavalry is charging at. Somehow they seem to think I'm the only foe worth bearing down on. If they're going to treat me roughly, I reckon I'll desert by running into the wrestling ground and leaving you to fight it out.[45] 37

SAMIPPUS: No, don't do that. You're well on the way to defeating them already. As for me, as you can see, I'm actually going to go into single combat against the king. He's issued a challenge and it would be an absolute disgrace for me to back away.

LYCINUS: Oh, my word, and you've immediately been wounded by him too. I say this because it's a mark of royalty to be wounded while fighting for power.

SAMIPPUS: You're right. But the wound is superficial and not on the visible parts of my body. I wouldn't want the scar to be unsightly later on. But did you see how I charged, threw my spear and pierced him and his horse right through with one blow? Then I cut off his head, took off his diadem and am now king. Everyone is falling down to do obeisance to me. Only the barbarians, mind you.[46]

38   You I shall rule with the title of supreme commander, following Greek custom. After this victory, can you imagine how many cities I'll found bearing my name or how many I'll capture and raze to the ground, when their citizens show any tendency to treat my regime with contempt? That rich man Cydias[47] will be the special object of my revenge. We were neighbours. He started encroaching on my land, gradually pushing inside the established boundaries.

39 LYCINUS: Stop there, Samippus. It's time for you to celebrate your victory in Babylon after winning such a huge battle. I think your command has gone over the space limit we set and now it's Timolaus' turn to make whatever prayer he wants.

SAMIPPUS: So, Lycinus, what do you think of what I asked for?

LYCINUS: Well, most wondrous of kings, it was far more laborious and violent than Adeimantus' wish. All he wanted was a life of luxury, toasting his drinking companions from heavy gold cups. But you were actually wounded in single combat, you felt fear and you worried night and day. And it wasn't only your enemies who gave you reason to be afraid. There were any number of plots against you instigated by your companions, not to mention their jealousy, hatred and toadying. No one was a real friend. Everyone appeared to like you, but did so merely through fear or expectation. And you never actually enjoyed the delights of success. All you had was glory, purple robes embroidered with gold thread, a white victory ribbon wrapped round your forehead and a band of spear-bearers marching in front. All the rest was unbearable toil and a plethora of unpleasantness, receiving a delegation from your enemies, judging court cases or sending instructions to your subordinates. There's always a rebellion to deal with or an attack from one of the peoples bordering on your empire. Your lot is fear and suspicion of everything. Other people may count you happy. You'll be the only one who denies it.

Here's something equally bad. You get ill exactly the same   40
as private individuals. Fever has no way of telling that you're
a king. Death isn't afraid of your bodyguards. When he thinks
it's the right moment, he just comes along and leads you away
wailing. He has no respect at all for your diadem.[48] You, high
and mighty as you are, will be dragged down off that kingly
throne of yours and go on the same journey as the common
crowd, driven off among the herd of corpses on an equal
footing. You may leave behind you above the ground a huge
mound, a large gravestone or a beautifully designed pyramid,
but these will be honours that come too late and that you
won't be able to appreciate. As for those statues and temples
the cities dedicated to please you, they'll all gradually slide
away and vanish, neglected along with your great reputation.
And even if they do remain for a long time, what use will they
be to you? You'll have no way to appreciate them then. So
you can see the trouble you're going to have while you're
still alive, the fears, the anxieties and the hard work, not to
mention how things will stand when you're dead.

However, it's your turn to make your wish, Timolaus. Be   41
sure to outdo these fellows. I'm sure you will. You're intelligent and well versed in the ways of the world.

TIMOLAUS: Well then, Lycinus, see if my prayer deserves your
reproaches and what there is in it to give adverse judgement
on. It was reasonable for you to denounce the wish for gold,
treasure troves, bushels of coin, kingdoms, war and all the
fears that come with power. These are all unstable acquisi-
tions which bring with them a host of plots and which contain
much more trouble than pleasure.

What I want is a meeting with Hermes where he give me   42
some rings with the following powers. The first will make my
body strong, healthy and altogether invulnerable. The second
will allow its wearer to be invisible, like the one Gyges had.[49]
A third will give me the strength of more than ten thousand
men and allow me to pick up effortlessly on my own a weight
that ten thousand together would scarcely be able to budge.
Ring number four will let me fly high above the earth,[50] and

numbers five and six will give me the power to put to sleep anyone I choose and to loosen the bars and bolts on any door I approach and open it.

43   The seventh and last is to grant the best and sweetest power of them all. When I put it on, it'll make me desirable to every pretty boy, to every woman and even to whole peoples. In fact, there'll be no one who doesn't fall in love with me, conceive an enormous craving for me and talk about me all the time. Many women will be unable to bear their passion and will hang themselves. Young men will go out of their minds and will think they're in heaven if I even cast a glance in their direction. If I ignore them, they'll also die of grief. In a word, I'll put Hyacinthus, Hylas or Phaon from Chios in the shade.

44   Now, I'm to have all these without the short term of life which is usual for human beings. I must live on for a thousand years, continually having my youth renewed. I'll stay about seventeen years old, sloughing off my old age like a snake. With these rings in my possession, I'll have everything I need. After all, whatever anyone else possesses could be mine, since I'll be able to open his doors, put his guards to sleep and enter without being seen. Are there unusual sights in India or among the Hyperboreans or things worth having or nice things to eat or drink? I won't have to send for them. I can fly off myself and enjoy them to my heart's content. Even the griffin, a winged beast, or the Indian phoenix which no one else has ever seen, I'll be able to look at. I'll be the only one who knows where the source of the Nile is, how much of the globe is uninhabited and whether the southern hemisphere is inhabited by antipodeans.[51] I'll also be able to find out readily about the nature of the stars, the moon and even the sun itself – I'll be immune to the heat, of course. The thing that'll give me most pleasure, though, will be the capacity to announce the news of Olympic victories in Babylon the same day they've been won. I could even, maybe, have breakfast in Syria and dinner in Italy. I could repay an enemy by using my invisibility to pick up a rock and smash his skull with it. My friends, on the other hand, I could help by pouring them out a heap of

gold while they're asleep. Any arrogant individual, say a wealthy tyrant with no respect for anyone else, I could lift up into the air and then let drop to crash over the cliffs twenty stades away. As for my favourite boys, I'd be able to get together with them without hindrance. I'd enter invisibly and put everyone to sleep except only them. Imagine what it would be like too to watch a battle floating in the air above, beyond the range of missiles. If I liked, I could help the losing side by putting the victors to sleep and handing victory to the side that had fled, reversing their flight. To sum up, I'd regard human life as a game, everything would be mine and other people would regard me as a god. Now, that's the peak of happiness: no death, no plots against me and perfect health during a long life.

Anything to fault in my prayer, Lycinus?   45

LYCINUS: Nothing, Timolaus. Actually, it wouldn't be safe to oppose a man with wings and the strength of ten thousand men. I'll ask you this, though. Among all those peoples you flew over, did you see any other old man who'd so utterly lost his senses, borne by a little ring, able to move whole mountains with the tip of his finger and an object of desire to everyone, despite his total baldness and his snub nose? Tell me this as well. Why on earth can't you have one ring to do all this? Instead, you're going around wearing all these, with every finger on your left hand weighed down. No, I'm wrong, there are more rings than fingers. You'll have to get the right hand to help as well. However, you still lack the most important ring of all, the one that'll stop you playing the fool and wipe away all this drivel. I dare say, though, that it's nothing a good strong dose of hellebore couldn't cure.[52]

TIMOLAUS: Well, now it's your turn to tell us your wish, Lycinus. Then we'll be able to find out what the chief be-grudger of everyone else can ask for that's unexceptionable and unimpeachable.   46

LYCINUS: But I don't need a prayer. We're already near the Dipylon Gate and my fine friend Samippus here with his single combat around Babylon and you, Timolaus, with your breakfast in Syria and dinner in Italy, have used up my portion of the journey. I'm glad you did. I'd really hate to have to put up shortly with the annoyance of eating my barley-cake without any condiments after this brief experience of empty wealth. That's what you're going to be doing in a little while, when your happiness and huge riches fly off and vanish. You'll climb down from your treasure troves and diadems as though you'd woken from a lovely dream to find that things at home are not like that at all. You'll be the image of those tragic actors who play kings on the stage, but leave the theatre for the most part with their bellies empty, even though a minute before they were Agamemnon or Creon.[53] So you'll be upset, I reckon, and dissatisfied with what you've got at home. That applies most especially to you, Timolaus, when the same thing happens to you as happened to Icarus. Your wings will fall apart, you'll fall from the sky, all those rings will moult from your fingers and vanish, and you'll be left walking on the ground. It's quite sufficient for me to swap your treasures and Babylon itself for the chance to have a good laugh at the inordinate wishes you've made, even though you're dedicated followers of philosophy.[54]

NEW COMIC DIALOGUES

Preface

This section contains the whole of *Chattering Courtesans* (the original title, in a straight translation, is *Dialogues of the Courtesans*), one of Lucian's four collections of miniature dialogues.[1] There is no evidence on which to date the pieces. Lucian nowhere says anything about the innovation of a short conversation in prose based on themes from poetry, which is a way of describing what is common to all these series. However, he clearly scores another first here and it is not enough to ascribe his inventiveness merely to the resources of a rhetorical tradition which exercised schoolboys in 'transposition'.[2] In *Chattering Courtesans*, Lucian combines two pre-existing poetic genres and their themes, the New Comedy (of Menander, Philemon, Diphilus and others) and the 'mime' (*mimos*) (now represented for us only by Hero(n)das, a writer of the Hellenistic period, probably mid third century BC).

New Comedy, which began its development in the mid fourth century BC at Athens, is 'situation comedy' and its central theme the romantic attachments formed by young Athenian males, with their complications (often the apparent status of the beloved) and happy resolutions. Courtesans were often important characters, as is, for example, the Samian woman in Menander's play *The Woman from Samos*. The mime, a literary genre (and not to be confused with 'mime' in the modern sense), probably originated in Sicily, where Sophron (fifth century BC) wrote pieces in rhythmic prose in the Doric dialect. The central role played by scenes in dialogue of ordinary life can be judged from Hero(n)das' first mime, written in choliambic metre and Ionic dialect. Here an old woman attempts to persuade a younger one to take a new lover while her man is away in Egypt. Lucian's innovation is to combine the earthy realism of the mime with the more sophisticated language (and social context) of New Comedy, and to return to the mime's prose origins.

Though the surface appears to belie it, once more the pieces in *Chattering Courtesans* might be argued to explore ethical themes (the power of lust, the unsatisfactory nature of deviant sexual practices, etc.) in a fresh and attractive way, by utilizing the realistic mode and argumentative variety associated in antiquity with New Comedy, and following the tendency of ancient writers to interpret New Comedy as essentially moralistic.[3]

NOTES

1. The others are *Dialogues of the Gods*, *Dialogues of the Sea-Gods* and *Dialogues of the Dead*.
2. See Bompaire 1958 *passim*.
3. Cf. the famous dictum 'Menander and Life, which of you imitated the other?' of the Alexandrian scholar Aristophanes of Byzantium (*c.* 257–180 BC), and the praise by the Latin rhetorician Quintilian (b. *c.* AD 35) of Menander's ability as an orator (*Training an Orator* 10.1.69–72). The existence of collections of 'Menandrian' *monostichoi* ('single lines') at any rate seems to point to a widespread ethical interpretation of New Comedy in later antiquity.

CHATTERING COURTESANS[1]

I

Glycerion[2] and Thais

GLYCERION: Thais, do you know the soldier, the Acarnanian, the one who used to have Abrotonon,[3] and after that fell in love with me? The well-dressed fellow I mean, the one in the cloak. Or have you forgotten the man?

THAIS: No, I know him, Glycerion, and he was drinking with us yesterday at the Haloa. What of it? It looks as though you're going to tell some story about him.

GLYCERION: That absolute witch Gorgona has seduced him and taken him away from me. And she's supposed to be my friend.

THAIS: And now he won't go near you and has made Gorgona his lover?

GLYCERION: Yes, Thais, and the whole thing's got to me badly.

THAIS: Well, it's bad, but not unexpected, Glycerion, in fact the sort of thing that usually happens when we good-time girls are involved. So you shouldn't be too upset or hold it against Gorgona. Abrotonon didn't blame you on his account, even though you were friends. What I'm surprised about is this. What on earth did this soldier find to praise in her, unless he's completely blind? Didn't he see she has thinning hair and a receding hairline? Her lips are livid, her neck is thin and you can see the veins in it. She has a big nose. There's only one good point. She's tall and straight and has an alluring smile.

GLYCERION: So you think it's by her beauty that the Acarnanian has been captivated? Don't you realize that her mother Chrysarion is a witch, a Thessalian who knows spells and brings the moon down to earth? They even say that she flies at night. It's she has driven him mad with love, by pouring him potions to drink. And now they're plucking his grapes.

THAIS: And you'll soon be plucking someone else's, Glycerion. Let this one go hang.

2

Myrtion and Pamphilus and Doris

1 MYRTION: So, Pamphilus, you're marrying the daughter of Philon the shipping magnate. In fact, they say you're already married, don't they? So all those enormous oaths you swore and the tears you shed have vanished in the twinkling of an eye, and you've forgotten Myrtion now, and at that when I'm already eight months pregnant, Pamphilus? This is the only profit I've had of your passion, that you've made my stomach this size and I'll have to look after a child soon – a very difficult thing for a courtesan. I say 'look after' because I'm not going to expose it,[4] especially if it's male. I'm going to call him Pamphilus and have him as a consolation for our love. And he will one day throw it in your face that you were unfaithful to his poor mother. Anyway, the girl you're marrying is no beauty. I saw her recently at the Thesmophoria with her mother. Of course, I didn't know at the time that it would be her fault that I would never see Pamphilus again. Well, take a good look at her first, and see her face and her eyes. Don't be distressed that she has absolutely grey ones and that they are squinty and look into each other. No, you've seen the father of the bride, Philon, and you know his face. So there won't be any more need to see his daughter.

2 PAMPHILUS: Am I going to have to listen to you babbling about marriageable girls, Myrtion, and telling me about mercantile marriages? And do I know any marriageable girl, whether snub-nosed or pretty? Or even at all that Philon from Alopeke

– I suppose he's the one you mean – had a daughter ready for marriage? He's not even a friend of my father's. In fact, I remember that my father recently took him to court over a contract. It was a talent,[5] I think, that he owed my father and didn't want to pay. My father brought him before the naval court.[6] He paid the sum over under protest, and not in full, my father said. Anyway, if I really had decided to get married, would I be marrying the daughter of Philon, when I would have to let go Demeas' daughter, with her father a general last year and also a cousin on my mother's side? Where did you hear this from? You've been fighting shadows, Myrtion, and discovering for yourself some empty grounds for jealousy, haven't you?

MYRTION: So you're not getting married, Pamphilus?   3

PAMPHILUS: Are you mad, Myrtion? Or is it just a hangover? It can't be that, I suppose. We didn't get particularly drunk yesterday.

MYRTION: It was Doris here who gave me the bad news. She'd been sent to buy wool for the child in my womb and to pray to the goddess of childbirth[7] for me. She said that Lesbia met her ... But why don't you tell him what you heard, Doris, that is if you didn't make the whole story up?

DORIS: May I be struck down if I told any lie at all, mistress. I was near the prytaneum,[8] when Lesbia met me with a smile and said that your lover Pamphilus is marrying Philon's daughter. She said if I didn't believe her I should put my head into Pamphilus' alleyway and see how everything was garlanded, and the pipe-girls and the din and singers chanting the song to Hymen.[9]

PAMPHILUS: So did you put your head round the corner, Doris?

DORIS: Of course I did, and I saw everything she'd mentioned.

PAMPHILUS: Now I understand the basis of the misconception.   4
It wasn't all lies Lesbia told you, and you have told Myrtion the truth. Only, you've both been upset for nothing. The wedding wasn't at our house. Now I remember my mother telling me, when I came back from your place yesterday. She said, 'Pamphilus, Charmides, our neighbour Aristaenetus' son, is already getting married and showing sense. How long

are you going to be with a courtesan?' I took no notice of this sort of stuff and went to sleep. Then next morning I left the house early and so saw none of what Doris saw later. If you don't believe me, Doris, go back yourself and don't just look at the alleyway, but see which door it is precisely that has been garlanded. You'll find it's our neighbours'.

MYRTION: You've saved my life, Pamphilus. I would have killed myself if anything like that had happened.

PAMPHILUS: But it wouldn't have happened, and I wouldn't be mad enough to abandon Myrtion, especially when she's pregnant with my child.

3

Mother and Philinna

1 MOTHER: Did you just go mad, Philinna, or what happened to you at yesterday's drinking-party? Diphilus came to me early this morning in tears and told me what you'd done to him. He said you'd got drunk, stood up in the middle and danced, even though he tried to stop you, and after that kissed his friend Lamprias. And when he got angry with you, you left him and went over to Lamprias and gave him a hug, and left Diphilus choking with rage while this went on. I don't think you even slept with him last night. You left him crying and lay down on your own on the next bed, singing and upsetting him.

2 PHILINNA: That's because he didn't tell you what he'd done, mother. If he had, you wouldn't even have talked to him, the brute,[10] leaving me and having a private conversation with Thais, Lamprias' courtesan, when Lamprias wasn't yet there. And when he saw that I was upset and I tried to signal to him what he was doing, he grasped the lobe of Thais' ear, bent her neck back and kissed her so passionately that she could hardly pull her lips away. And I started crying, but he laughed and said a lot of things into Thais' ear, obviously getting at me. And Thais smiled as she looked at me. When they saw

Lamprias coming and had had their fill of kissing each other, I none the less lay down on the couch beside him,[11] so he shouldn't have that excuse later on. But Thais was the first to get up and dance, showing a lot of ankle, as though she was the only girl who had pretty ones. Lamprias kept quiet and said nothing. But Diphilus praised her sense of rhythm and her costume to the skies, saying how well her foot followed the lyre and how pretty her ankle was and ten thousand other things, as though he were praising the 'Sosandra' of Calamis[12] and not Thais. You've seen her when we've bathed together and you know what she's like. But Thais immediately started actually making smart remarks against me, saying, 'If a girl's not ashamed of having spindly legs, she'll get up herself as well and dance.' What could I say, mother? I got up and danced. What should I have done? Put up with it, have the joke seem to be true and let Thais be queen of the party?

MOTHER: You acted too competitively, my girl. You should have paid no attention. But tell me what happened next.

PHILINNA: Well, the others praised my dancing, but Diphilus just threw himself back on the couch and started looking at the ceiling until I was exhausted and stopped.

MOTHER: And is it true that you kissed Lamprias? And that you changed places and hugged him? Why aren't you saying anything? These aren't things you can be forgiven for, you know.

PHILINNA: I wanted to hurt him back.

MOTHER: And then you wouldn't sleep with him, but sang while he cried? Don't you realize, daughter, that we're paupers? Don't you remember how much we've received from him, or how we would've had to survive last winter, if Aphrodite hadn't sent him to us?

PHILINNA: What do you want, then? Should I put up with being mistreated by him?

MOTHER: You can get angry, but don't mistreat him back. Don't you know that lovers stop being in love if they're mistreated? Then they give themselves a good talking-to. But you've always been too hard on the man. Just watch out we don't stretch the proverbial cord too far and break it.

3

4

Melitta and Bacchis[13]

1   MELITTA: Bacchis, if you know any old women of the sort they say abound in Thessaly, the ones who utter spells and make men fall in love, even if the woman is really hateful, please do me a favour and bring her along to see me. I'd gladly throw away my cloaks and these gold trinkets if only I could see Charinus come back to me hating Simiche[14] as he now hates me.

BACCHIS: What do you mean? Has Charinus left you and gone off to Simiche, Melitta, after enduring so much anger from his parents when he refused to marry that rich girl who was reputed to be bringing along with her a five-talent dowry? I heard this from you. That's how I know about it.

MELITTA: All that's a thing of the past, Bacchis. It's five days since I've even seen him at all. He and Simiche are drinking together at the house of his fellow-ephebe[15] Pammenes.

2   BACCHIS: What a dreadful situation, Melitta! But what drove a wedge between you? It can't have been anything trivial.

MELITTA: I really can't tell you the whole story. Only that a few days ago when he came back from Piraeus, where he'd gone to collect a debt at his father's request, he didn't even look at me when he entered and he didn't let me near him when I ran up to him, as I usually do, and he shook me off as I tried to hug him, saying, 'Go to Hermotimus the shipowner, or read what's written on the walls in the Ceramicus, where your two names have been written up.' I replied, 'Who's this Hermotimus and what inscription are you talking about?' But he didn't answer, had no dinner and slept turned away from me. You can imagine how many tricks I tried after this, hugging him, turning towards him, kissing his back as he was turned away. He didn't soften the tiniest bit, but only said, 'If you bother me any more, I'll go away now, even if it is the middle of the night.'

3   BACCHIS: All the same, did you know Hermotimus?

MELITTA: Bacchis, if I know any shipowner called Hermotimus, I hope you'll see me in an even worse state than I am now. The only thing is, Charinus had gone off early, after waking as soon as the cock had crowed, and I recalled that he'd said that the name was written up in the Ceramicus on some wall. So I sent Acis to have a look. The only thing she found was this, written as you enter on the right by the Dipylon, 'Melitta loves Hermotimus' and, a bit lower down still, 'Hermotimus the shipowner loves Melitta.'

BACCHIS: Those meddling young fellows! I understand it now. Someone wanted to upset Charinus and wrote the inscription knowing he's the jealous type. He believed it straight away. If I see him, I'll tell him. He's naive and still only a child.

MELITTA: But where are you going to see him, when he's locked himself in and is spending his time with Simiche? His parents are still looking for him at my place. But, as I said, Bacchis, if only we could find an old woman. If she turned up, she might save the day.

BACCHIS: Well, my dearest, there is a really useful witch, a 4 Syrian, still fresh and solid, who once reconciled Phanias to me when he was also angry for no reason, like Charinus. It had been four whole months, and I'd already given up hope, when he came back again to me, because of the spells.

MELITTA: What did the old woman do, if you still remember?

BACCHIS: Well, she doesn't take a very large fee, Melitta, just a drachma and a loaf of bread. You have to add seven obols,[16] brimstone and a torch, along with salt. The old woman takes these. You must fill a wine bowl to the brim, but only she can drink it. You'll have to have something belonging to the man, such as a cloak or boots or some of his hair or suchlike.

MELITTA: I've got his boots.

BACCHIS: She hangs them from a peg and fumigates them 5 with the brimstone, sprinkling some salt onto the fire. She pronounces both names, his and yours. Then she brings out from her pocket a magic wheel and turns it, uttering a spell with a quick tongue, foreign words to make your hair stand on end. This is what she did on that occasion. And it wasn't very long before Phanias came back to me, mostly under the influence of the spell, even though at the same time his fellow-ephebes criticized him, and Phoebis, his paramour, pleaded with him a great deal. The Syrian woman also taught me the following charm to induce in him hatred of Phoebis. I was to watch for her footprints, whenever she left, rub them out and step with my right foot onto the impression of her left. I had to do the same with my left foot to her right footprint and say, 'I have climbed on top of you and am above.' And I did as I was told.[17]

MELITTA: Bacchis, don't delay, don't delay. Call the Syrian woman now. Acis, go and get the bread, brimstone and all the rest ready for the casting of the spell.

5

Clonarion and Leaena[18]

1 CLONARION: Well, Leaena, it's a strange thing we're hearing about you. Apparently the wealthy Megilla from Lesbos loves you as though she were a man, and you're having intercourse together, though I've no idea what it is you do with each other. What's the matter? Is that a blush? Come on, tell me if this is the truth.

LEAENA: Yes, Clonarion, it's true. But I'm ashamed. It is a bit odd.

CLONARION: What's going on, by Aphrodite? What's the woman up to? More important, what do you actually do when you're having intercourse? Do you see? You don't love me. Otherwise you'd never have hidden things like this.

LEAENA: I love you more than anyone. But the woman is awfully manly.

2 CLONARION: I don't understand what you really mean, except that she's a woman's courtesan. They say that there're women like this on Lesbos.[19] They're masculine-looking. They don't want to have men do it to them, but have intercourse with women as though they themselves were actually men.

LEAENA: It's something like that.

CLONARION: All right, then, Leaena, tell me this. How did she make the first move? And how did you manage to fall in with what happened next?

LEAENA: She and the Corinthian Demonassa threw a drinking-party. Demonassa is also well-off and plies the same trade as Megilla. She'd brought me along to play the lyre for them. After I'd played, and it had got a bit late and was time to sleep, and they were a bit the worse for drink, Megilla said, 'Come on, Leaena, it's time for bed. Sleep here with us. You can be in the middle.'

CLONARION: So you agreed? What happened next?

LEAENA: First off, they started kissing me like men. It wasn't just lip-to-lip stuff. They were opening their mouths, cuddling me and feeling my breasts. Demonassa even bit me while she was kissing. I had absolutely no idea what was going on. Eventually Megilla got all hot and bothered and took off her wig – it was very realistic and close-fitting. She was close-cropped like one of those really masculine athletes. I was taken aback when I saw this. But she said, 'Leaena, have you ever seen such a beautiful young man?' I replied, 'Well, Megilla, I don't see any young man here.' 'Don't feminize me, with your "Megilla". I'm called Megillus and I've been married for ages to Demonassa here. She's my wife.' I laughed at this, Clonarion, and said, 'So, Megillus, you've fooled the lot of us. All the time you've been a man, hiding like Achilles among the maidens.[20] And I suppose you've got that thing men have and do Demonassa with it like the fellows?' 'No, I haven't got one of those, Leaena. But I've absolutely no need of one. You'll see me using a special technique, much more pleasurable by far.' I replied, 'Good grief, are you a hermaphrodite, then, with both sets of organs? They say there're lots.' At this point, Clonarion, I was still in the dark. 'No,' she said, 'but I'm a man, none the less.' And then I said, 'I heard the Boeotian pipe-girl Ismenodora telling a local story. Apparently, there was someone in Thebes who changed from a woman to a man. The same fellow was also a fabulous seer. His name was Tiresias. Is this the sort of thing that happened to you too?' 'No, Leaena,' she said. 'I was born the same as the rest of you. But my way of thinking and my desire and everything else about me are the same as a man's.' 'So desire is enough, then?' I asked. 'Try for yourself, if you don't believe me,' she said, 'and you'll soon find I don't fall short of men in any respect. I've something in place of the male thing.[21] Come here. You'll see.' So I yielded, Clonarion, after she'd pleaded a lot and given me an expensive necklace and some fine linen dresses. Then I hugged her, as if she were a man, and she started the action, kissing me and breathing heavily and to all appearance enjoying herself enormously.

CLONARION: What did she do, Leaena? How? Please tell me this.

LEAENA: Don't ask for the details. It's too shocking. By Aphrodite, I won't tell.

6

Crobyle and Corinna[22]

1   CROBYLE: So, Corinna, you've now discovered that it wasn't at all as bad as you'd imagined, losing your virginity. You were with a nice-looking young man, and what's more you've earned your first mina.[23] And from that, I'm going to buy you a necklace right away.

CORINNA: Yes, mummy dear. Can I have one with bright red stones, like Philaenis'?

CROBYLE: Yes, I'll get you one like that. Now, let me tell you the other things you must do and how to behave yourself with men. We've no other way of earning a living, you know, daughter. Do you realize how badly we've lived these last two years since your blessed father died? While he was alive, we had everything, with no problem. He worked metal and had a great name in Piraeus. Everyone swears that there'll never be another smith like Philinus. When he died, first of all I sold his fire-tongs and his anvil and his hammer for two minas. And we managed to live off that for seven months.[24] Then I earned our daily bread with difficulty, sometimes by weaving, sometimes by spinning the two kinds of thread, for woof and warp.[25] I was feeding you, daughter, waiting for you to fulfil my expectations.

CORINNA: Do you mean the mina?   2

CROBYLE: No. But I reckoned that when you were the age you are now, you'd be able to look after me, and easily get yourself clothed well, grow rich and have purple robes and maids.

CORINNA: What do you mean, mother? How?

CROBYLE: By spending your time with young men, drinking with them, and sleeping with them for money.

CORINNA: Like Daphnis' daughter Lyra?[26]

CROBYLE: Yes.

CORINNA: But she's a courtesan.

CROBYLE: There's nothing wrong with that. You'll get rich just like her and have lots of lovers. Why the tears, Corinna? Don't you realize how sought after courtesans are and how much money they make? Look, I can tell you for a fact, O beloved Adrasteia,[27] that Daphnis used to wear rags before her girl became old enough. Well, you can see how she goes about now, can't you, gold and flowery clothes and four maids.

CORINNA: How did Lyra get this?   3

CROBYLE: First of all by dressing nicely, keeping trim and being pleasant to everyone, not to the point of laughing out loud at the drop of a hat, as you usually do, but by giving a sweet and enticing smile, then by being clever company, by not cheating anyone who makes an approach or sends a gift and by not grabbing hold of men herself. And whenever she gets paid to go to a dinner, she doesn't get drunk – that's ridiculous and men hate girls who do – and she doesn't fill herself up with food in a vulgar way. She holds it with the tips of her fingers, puts it into her mouth quietly and doesn't stuff it into both cheeks. She drinks slowly, not in great gulps, but with regular pauses.

CORINNA: What, even if she's really thirsty, mother?

CROBYLE: *Especially* when she's dying of thirst, Corinna. And she doesn't speak more than she has to, or make fun of anyone there. And she looks only at the man who has hired her.

That's why they like her. And when she has to go to bed, she won't do anything coarse or uncaring. Her one goal throughout is to attract the man and make him her lover. That's what everyone praises in her. So, if you can learn to do this as well, we too will be rich. At any rate in everything else she's less ... But I'm talking nonsense, O beloved Adrasteia.[28] My only wish is for Corinna to live long.

4　CORINNA: Tell me, mother, are all the men who hire girls like Eucritus,[29] the one I slept with last night?

CROBYLE: No, not all of them. Some are better, others are already men and some are not particularly good-looking.

CORINNA: And will I have to sleep with men like that?

CROBYLE: Oh yes, daughter. These are the ones who'll pay more. The good-looking ones wish only to be good-looking. But you need to think about getting more, if you want everyone to be pointing you out with their fingers very shortly and saying, 'Do you see how very rich Crobyle's daughter Corinna is and how completely blissful she's made her mother?' What do you say? Will you do it? I know you will. And you'll outrun the rest easily. Now go off and bathe, in case that young man Eucritus comes by today as well. He did promise he would.

7

Mother and Musarion[30]

1　MOTHER: Well, Musarion, if we can find another lover like Chaereas,[31] we're going to have to sacrifice a white goat to the goddess of earthly love, a kid to the goddess of heavenly love, the one in the gardens,[32] and also garland the statue of the giver of wealth,[33] and we'll be utterly wealthy and completely blissful. You can see now what great gifts we get from the boy. He hasn't ever given you an obol, not a piece of clothing, no shoes, no perfume. All you've ever got are excuses, promises, high hopes and lots of 'if my father ...,[34] and I get hold of my inheritance' and all that stuff. You tell me he's even sworn to make you his lawfully wedded wife.

MUSARION: Well, mother, he did swear by the two goddesses[35] and Athena Polias.

MOTHER: And you presumably believe him. And because of that, yesterday, when he had no contribution to make to his meal,[36] without telling me you gave him your ring, and he sold it and drank the proceeds away. That's what he did to the two Ionian necklaces, each worth two darics,[37] that the Chian shipowner Praxias brought back for you from Ephesus. I suppose Chaereas needed to give a contribution to a meal for his fellow-ephebes. I don't have to mention the linen and tunics, do I? He's come to us as a complete godsend and a great help.

MUSARION: But he's good-looking and he hasn't grown a beard yet and he says he's in love with me and he cries and he's the son of Deinomache and Laches the Areopagite.[38] And he says that we'll get married and we have great expectations from Laches, if only the old man would take his last sleep.

MOTHER: So, if we need shoes, Musarion, and the shoemaker asks for the two drachmas,[39] we're going to say to him, 'We don't have the cash, but you can have a few of our hopes.' And we'll say the same to the bread-man too. And if someone comes for the rent, we'll say, 'Can you wait until Laches dies? I'll pay you straight after the wedding.' Aren't you ashamed of being the only courtesan not to have earrings, necklaces and diaphanous gowns?

MUSARION: So what, mother? Are they more fortunate or better looking than me?

MOTHER: No. They're just more intelligent and they know how the courtesan business works. They don't trust words and young men with oaths on their lips. But you, the 'faithful wife', don't even go near anyone but Chaereas. Why, only the other day that farmer from Acharnae came with two minas. He didn't have a beard either, and he had with him the money for the wine his father had sent him to sell. But you cursed him off and slept with your Adonis, Chaereas.

MUSARION: Well? Should I have left Chaereas and taken in that farmhand, stinking of goat? Chaereas is smooth, as the saying goes, but the Acharnian's a little pig.[40]

MOTHER: All right, then. So that countryman doesn't smell too good. Why didn't you take in Antiphon the son of Menecrates[41] either, even though he promised you a mina? Isn't he good-looking, sophisticated and the same age as Chaereas?

4 MUSARION: Chaereas said he'd kill both of us if he caught me with him.

MOTHER: How many others make the same threat? And because of that, I suppose you'll remain without lovers and live chastely, as though you were some priestess of the Lawbringer[42] rather than a courtesan? I'll leave it at that. Today's the Haloa. What's he given you for the feast?

MUSARION: He's doesn't have any money, mummy.

MOTHER: Is he the only one in the world not to have found a way to get round his father, who can't send a slave to do the deception for him, or who hasn't asked his mother, under threats of sailing off to be a soldier[43] if she doesn't provide? He just sits there, destroying us, not giving us anything himself and not allowing us to take anything from those who will. Do you think you're always going to be eighteen? Or that Chaereas will feel the same way when he's rich himself and his mother finds him a marriage worth multiple talents? Will he still remember the tears or kisses or oaths, do you think, when he's looking at maybe a five-talent dowry?

MUSARION: He'll remember. And I can prove it. He still isn't married. He said no, even though he was under enormous pressure.

MOTHER: Well, I hope I'm wrong.[44] But I'll remind you of this when he does marry, Musarion.

8

Ampelis and Chrysis[45]

1 AMPELIS: If a man isn't jealous, Chrysis, doesn't get angry, doesn't ever hit you or cut off your hair or tear your dress, he can't be in love any more, can he?

CHRYSIS: So, are these the only proofs of passion, Ampelis?

AMPELIS: Yes. These show a man in the heat of love. The rest, kisses and tears and oaths and often coming to see you, are the marks of incipient passion, when the plant is still growing. The fire of passion, though, depends totally upon jealousy. So if Gorgias[46] is actually hitting you and acting jealously, as you say, expect good results and pray that he always acts the same way.

CHRYSIS: The same way? What do you mean? That he'll always hit me?

AMPELIS: No, but that he'll be upset if you don't look only at him. After all, if he's not in love, why would he be angry at your having a lover?

CHRYSIS: But it isn't as though I actually do have one. He just presumed, without reason, that the rich fellow was in love with me, because I happened to mention him casually in conversation.

AMPELIS: Now that's a good thing, that he should think that rich men are after you. That'll make him more upset and more eager to make sure his rivals don't outdo him.

CHRYSIS: But all he does is get angry and hit me. He doesn't give me a bean.

AMPELIS: He will, though – he's jealous – and especially if you hurt him.

CHRYSIS: Somehow you want me to get beaten up, Ampelis.

AMPELIS: It's not that. In my opinion, though, the way great passions come about is if lovers think they're being neglected. But if he thinks he's the only one who has you, somehow the desire withers away. I'm telling you this with twenty full years' experience of the courtesan business, and you're only eighteen, or less, aren't you? If you want, I'll tell you about an experience I had just a few years ago. Demophantus the moneylender, the one who lives behind the Painted Stoa, was in love with me. He'd never given me more than five drachmas[47] and thought he owned me. His love, Chrysis, was one of those surface things. He didn't groan, or weep, or arrive at my door in the middle of the night. All he did was sleep with me sometimes, usually with long intervals in between. Then one night he arrived and I locked him out.

Callides the painter had sent me ten drachmas and was in the house. At first he just went away saying a few choice words. Then, after several days had gone by and I hadn't sent for him, because Callides was still with me, Demophantus finally started getting warm and burst into flames of passion himself for the affair. He stood and waited for the door to open and wept, hit me, threatened to kill me, ripped my dress and tried everything. In the end, he gave me a talent and had me exclusively to himself for eight whole months. His wife told everyone I'd used magic charms to drive him mad. The only charm I used was jealousy. So, Chrysis, you should use the same charm on Gorgias. That young man's going to be rich one day, if something happens to his father.

9

Dorcas and Pannychis and Philostratus and Polemon[48]

1 DORCAS: We're done for, mistress, we're done for. Polemon's back from the wars, and with piles of money, they say. I've actually seen him myself. He was wearing a full purple cloak fastened with a brooch and had lots of attendants. When his friends saw him, they ran up to him to greet him. While that was happening, I spotted his servant following behind, the one who'd gone away with him. So I asked him a question. I greeted him first and then continued, 'Tell me, Parmenon,[49] how did you get on? Have you come back from the wars with anything worth having?'

PANNYCHIS: You shouldn't have asked that straight out. You should've said, 'We're deeply grateful to the gods, especially Zeus the protector of strangers and Athena, goddess of the army, for your safe return. My mistress was always trying to find out what you were doing and where you were.' It would've been even better if you'd also added the information that she kept weeping and remembering Polemon.

2 DORCAS: All of that was what I used straight away as a preamble at the beginning. I didn't tell you, because I wanted to tell you

what I'd heard. This was the way I actually started with Parmenon: 'I imagine, Parmenon, that your ears were buzzing. At any rate, my mistress was always bringing you up with tears, especially if anyone had come back from battle and reported grave loss of life. Then she would tear her hair and beat her breast and go into mourning at every message.'

PANNYCHIS: Good, Dorcas! Exactly right.

DORCAS: So then, after a little pause, I asked him the important question I told you about, and he replied, 'We've come back in splendour.'

PANNYCHIS: Did he put it just like that, too, without saying first that Polemon had kept me in mind or missed me or prayed to find me alive on his return?

DORCAS: Of course he said lots of things like that. But the main news was of 'great riches, gold, clothes, servants, ivory'. He said they couldn't even count the money they brought back, but had had to measure it out in bushels – and it came to loads of bushels.[50] Even Parmenon had a ring on his little finger, huge, polygonal, set with one of those three-coloured stones, deep red on the surface. He wanted to tell me how they'd crossed the river Halys and killed someone called Tiridates and of Polemon's starring role in the battle against the Pisidians.[51] But I left him and ran off to tell you all this, so that you could see what to do about our current circumstances. If Polemon arrives on our doorstep – and he's bound to do that when he's shaken off his friends, what do you think he's going to do when he finds that Philostratus is at our house?

PANNYCHIS: Let's see if we can devise a plan to get us out of this mess, Dorcas. On the one hand, it wouldn't be a good idea to send Philostratus away when he's recently given us a talent and anyway is a merchant and has promised much more. On the other, it's no use not receiving Polemon when he's returned in such style. Besides, he's the jealous type and even when he was poor he was pretty unbearable. What wouldn't he do now?

DORCAS: Well, he's actually just coming up the street.

PANNYCHIS: I've absolutely no idea what to do, Dorcas. I'm all a-quiver.

DORCAS: And here comes Philostratus as well.

PANNYCHIS: What am I going to do? Why doesn't the earth open up and swallow me?

4 PHILOSTRATUS: Why don't we have a drink, Pannychis?

PANNYCHIS: You – you've ruined me. Oh, hello Polemon. It's been a long time.

POLEMON: Who's this fellow coming up to speak to you? Nothing to say? Fine. Get lost, Pannychis. To think I flew back from Thermopylae in five days, rushing for a woman like this! It serves me right. I ought to be grateful, though. At least I won't be robbed by you any more.

PHILOSTRATUS: And who are you, my fine fellow?

POLEMON: You must have heard of Polemon of Steiria, from the Pandionis tribe. First I was a chiliarch[52] and now I command five thousand men. I was Pannychis' lover, when I thought she still had her feet on the ground.

PHILOSTRATUS: Well, right now, mercenary captain, Pannychis is mine. I've given her one talent, and she'll soon have another, when I've disposed of my goods. So come with me now, Pannychis, and leave this fellow to be a chiliarch among the Odrysians.

POLEMON: She's free and she'll go with you if she wants.

PANNYCHIS: What shall I do, Dorcas?

DORCAS: We'd better go inside. It's no use being there when Polemon gets angry. He'll only be worse now that he's jealous.

PANNYCHIS: All right, let's go in.

5 POLEMON: I'm telling you, this drink you take today will be the last, unless it's for nothing I've arrived here schooled in slaughter. Parmenon, get the Thracians together. Tell them to come here armed and block the alleyway in formation. Let's have the hoplites[53] at the front, the slingers and archers on either side and the rest behind.

PHILOSTRATUS: You're talking to us as though we were babies, you mercenary, and threatening us with the bogeyman. Have you ever killed a cockerel or even seen a war? Well, maybe I'll do you the favour of believing that you've guarded a fence as a platoon leader.

POLEMON: Well, you'll soon find out, when you see us coming with our serried spears glinting in the sun.

PHILOSTRATUS: Oh, get yourselves ready and come. Tibius here – my only ally – and I will throw a few stones and potsherds and set you running so you won't even know where you've gone off to.

10

Chelidonion and Drosis[54]

CHELIDONION: Doesn't the young man Cleinias[55] come to visit 1
you any more, Drosis? I haven't seen him at your place for ages.

DROSIS: No, he doesn't, Chelidonion. His teacher has stopped him coming near me any more.

CHELIDONION: Who is he? You don't mean the trainer Diotimus,[56] do you? He's a friend of mine.

DROSIS: No. It's that philosopher Aristaenetus,[57] curse him.

CHELIDONION: You mean the frowning, hairy, long-bearded fellow who usually walks around with the young men in the Painted Stoa?

DROSIS: That's the fraud I mean. I'd love to see him come to grief, with the public executioner dragging him along by the beard.

CHELIDONION: How on earth did he manage to persuade 2
Cleinias to do such a thing?

DROSIS: I've no idea, Chelidonion. All I know is that a fellow who's never been away from my bed since he started going with women – and I was the first – hasn't even approached my alleyway for three whole days now. And when I started to get upset – somehow I feel this way on his account – I sent Nebris[58] to take a look at him, whether he was spending his time in the market-place or in the Painted Stoa. She said she saw him walking around with Aristaenetus and gave him a nod from a distance. But he apparently went bright red and looked down and wouldn't meet her eye any more. Then they walked off together to the Academy. She followed them as far as the Dipylon Gate. But he didn't even turn round. So she came back without anything clear to report. How do you think I'm doing after that, not knowing what's happened to my boy? Have I accidentally caused him pain, I was saying, or has he taken against me because he's fallen in love with someone else? Has his father stopped him coming? In my distress I turned over lots of thoughts like this. And then just now, this afternoon, Dromon[59] came to me with a letter from him. Here, read it, Chelidonion. I think you know how to read, don't you?[60]

3 CHELIDONION: Let's see. The writing's not very clear. In fact, it's very sloppy. Probably written in a hurry. It says, 'The gods are my witness to how much I loved you, Drosis.'

DROSIS: Oh, dear me. He didn't even write 'Dear Drosis' at the beginning.[61]

CHELIDONION: 'Even now, it's not because I hate you that I'm leaving you, but because I'm being forced to. My father has handed me over to Aristaenetus to study philosophy with him. He knew everything about the relationship between us, and gave me a tremendous dressing down about the disgrace involved in the son of Architeles and Erasicleia[62] being involved with a courtesan. He said it was much better to prefer virtue to pleasure.'

DROSIS: Curse that babbler, teaching the boy such rubbish!

CHELIDONION: 'So I have no choice but to obey him. He's always with me, keeping close watch. It's absolutely impossible for me even to glance at anyone but him. If I'm good and take his advice in everything, though, he promises I'll be completely happy and, because I'm virtuous, I'll be predisposed by my training to withstand troubles.[63] I'm writing this with difficulty, in secret. Have a good life and remember Cleinias.'

4 DROSIS: What do you think of the letter, Chelidonion?

CHELIDONION: Well, most of it's like the proverbial 'Scythian answer',[64] but the 'remember Cleinias' has a little bit of hope left in it.

DROSIS: I thought that as well. But as you know, I'm dying of love. And none the less, Dromon did say that Aristaenetus is a lover of boys and it's only in pretence at study that he spends his time with the most beautiful of the young men and in his private conversations with Cleinias is making great promises that he'll make him into a demi-god. He's also reading with him speeches about love composed by the ancient philosophers for their students,[65] and he's absolutely taken by the boy. Dromon even threatened to tell all this to Cleinias' father.

CHELIDONION: Drosis, you should've given Dromon a free meal.

DROSIS: I did. Anyway, he'd have been in my pocket even without that. He's smitten with Nebris as well.

CHELIDONION: You can be confident that everything will be fine, then. I think I'm actually going to write on the wall in the Ceramicus,[66] where Architeles usually takes his stroll, 'Aristaenetus is corrupting Cleinias'. That way there'll be other evidence to support Dromon's useful accusation.[67]

DROSIS: How are you going to do the inscription without being seen?

CHELIDONION: I'll get a lump of charcoal from somewhere and do it during the night.

DROSIS: Wonderful! Just be my ally in the campaign against the fraud Aristaenetus.

11

Tryphaena and Charmides[68]

TRYPHAENA: What! Someone hires a courtesan for five   1 drachmas, pays her, and then turns away, and tries to go to sleep, weeping and moaning? I don't think you even enjoyed the drink and you were the only one who didn't want to eat. I know. I saw you crying even during dinner. Even now you haven't stopped sobbing like a baby. Why are you doing this, Charmides? Don't hide it from me. I'd like to get this satisfaction also out of a night awake with you.

CHARMIDES: It's love, Tryphaena. It's killing me. I can't hold out against it any longer.

TRYPHAENA: Well, it's obvious it's not me you're in love with. Otherwise when you had me with you, you wouldn't be ignoring me and pushing me away when I want to cuddle you. And you certainly wouldn't have made a wall down the middle of the bed with your cloak between us, because you were afraid I might touch you. But anyway, tell me who she is. You never know, I might be able to give you a bit of help to fulfil your passion. I know how to manage these things.

CHARMIDES: Actually, you know her pretty well and vice versa. She's quite a well-known courtesan.

2 TRYPHAENA: Tell me her name, Charmides.

CHARMIDES: It's Philemation,[69] Tryphaena.

TRYPHAENA: Which one do you mean? There are two. The one from Piraeus, who's just lost her virginity. Damylus, the present commander's son,[70] is her lover. Or is it the other, the one they nickname Mantrap?

CHARMIDES: It's Mantrap, and I've been trapped by her, unlucky that I am. She's really got a hold on me.

TRYPHAENA: So it's because of her you were crying?

CHARMIDES: Of course.

TRYPHAENA: Have you been in love with her long or are you, as it were, a neophyte?[71]

CHARMIDES: No, I'm not a 'neophyte'. It's almost seven months since I first saw her at the Dionysia.

TRYPHAENA: Have you seen *all* of her close to? Or have you just seen her face and the better bits of her body she leaves on show, as a woman already past forty-five is obliged to do?

CHARMIDES: But she swore she'd be twenty-two next Ela-phebolion.

3 TRYPHAENA: Which would you rather believe, her oaths or your own eyes? Examine her close up. Take a glance at her temples. That's the only place she has her own hair. The rest is a full wig. Right by the temples, when the dye she uses wears off, you can see the hair is completely white. And that's not all. Force her to undress so that you can see her naked.

CHARMIDES: She's never let me go that far.

TRYPHAENA: I'm not surprised. She knew you'd be disgusted at her white hairs. And she's as spotty as a leopard from head to toe. And you were crying over not having intercourse with her? I suppose she tried to hurt you and wouldn't take any notice of you?

CHARMIDES: Yes, Tryphaena, even though she'd had a lot of presents from me. And the last thing is, now she's asked for a thousand drachmas. I can't find a sum like that easily, given the stingy father I'm being brought up by. So she took Moschion[72] in and shut me out. In revenge, I picked you up, because I wanted to hurt her back.

TRYPHAENA: By Aphrodite, I wouldn't have come, if I'd known that this was the reason, to get back at someone else, and at that, Philemation the coffin.[73] I'm off. The cockerel's already crowed three times anyway.

CHARMIDES: Not so fast, Tryphaena. If what you say about Philemation is true – the wig, the dyeing and the pock-marks – I couldn't even look her in the face any more.

TRYPHAENA: Ask your mother if she's ever been to the public baths when she was there. Actually, your grandfather will tell you her age, that's if he's still alive.

CHARMIDES: Well look, if that's what she's like, let's take the barrier down and hug and kiss each other and make love properly. And Philemation can go to blazes!

12

Ioessa and Pythias and Lysias[74]

IOESSA: Are you giving me the cold shoulder, Lysias? I suppose that's fair enough, seeing that I never asked you for money, or locked you out when you came to the door and said there was someone else inside. And I didn't force you to cheat your father or steal from your mother in order to bring me something, as the other girls do. Right from the start I took you in without charge, without asking for a contribution to expenses. And you know how many lovers I sent on their way. There was Theocles, who is currently a *prytaneus*,[75] Pasias the shipowner, and your fellow-ephebe Melissus, even though his father had only just died and he'd come into his property. But I only had my Phaon.[76] I didn't look at anyone else and I didn't let anyone near me but you. I was stupid enough to believe your oaths, and so I devoted myself to you, and kept my chastity like Penelope, despite my mother's protests and accusations to her friends. But when you knew that you had me under your thumb and that I was head over heels in love with you, you first of all flirted with Lycaena right under my nose, to upset me, and then, when you were lying at dinner with me, you praised the lyre-girl Magadion.[77] This makes me cry. I know I'm being treated badly. Then, the other day when you were drinking with Thrason and Diphilus,[78] the pipe-girl Cymbalion and Pyrallis[79] were also there. Pyrallis is my sworn enemy. You knew that. It didn't bother me much that you kissed Cymbalion five times. You were showing contempt for yourself by kissing a woman like her. But Pyrallis – well, you kept nodding to her, and when you drank you'd raise your cup to her, and when you gave it to the slave you'd whisper in his ear that he shouldn't fill it if Pyrallis didn't ask. Finally you took a bite out of your apple, when you saw Diphilus was busy talking to Thrason, leant forward and with good aim threw it into her lap.[80] You didn't even try to make sure I wasn't looking. She kissed it and stuffed it under her girdle, between her breasts. Why are you doing this? What wrong, big or small, have I done you? How have I hurt you? What other man have I looked at? Don't I live just for you? It's a great thing you're doing, Lysias, making a poor woman upset who's mad about you. The goddess Nemesis sees such things anyhow. Perhaps you'll be upset when you hear I'm dead, whether I've hanged myself or jumped into the well head first or found some other means of ending it all so that the sight of me won't annoy you any more. I suppose you'll be really swaggering then, as though you've achieved some great and glorious success. Why are you looking at me like that and grinding your teeth? If you've any charges to bring, please tell me, and let Pythias here be our judge and jury. What? You're going off and leaving me without even answering? Pythias, do you see what Lysias is doing to me?

PYTHIAS: Such savagery! Not even taking pity when you're crying your eyes out. He's a stone, not a human being. I must say, Ioessa, though, that the truth is you've ruined him by loving him too much and letting it show. You shouldn't have lionized him so much. If lovers spot this, they get uppity. Come on, stop crying, you poor thing. If you'll take my advice, you'll lock him out once or twice when he comes. You'll soon see him getting warm and falling madly in love for real.

IOESSA: Don't! Lock Lysias out? Don't even say it. I only hope he won't leave me first.

PYTHIAS: Hey, he's coming back again.

IOESSA: You've done for me now, Pythias. He's probably heard you say 'lock him out'.

LYSIAS: I haven't come back for her, Pythias. I wouldn't even   3
look at her any more, the way she's behaved. I've come back because of you, so you won't condemn me and say that Lysias is hard-hearted.

PYTHIAS: Well, actually, that's what I was saying.

LYSIAS: So, Pythias, do you expect me to put up with Ioessa's tears now when I myself stood over the bed where she was sleeping with a young man and being unfaithful to me?

PYTHIAS: To put it in a nutshell, Lysias, she's a courtesan. But how did you find them sleeping together?

LYSIAS: It's about five days ago now. That's right, by Zeus. It was the second of the month and today's the seventh. My father locked me in and told the doorkeeper not to open up. He knew that I'd been in love with this fine specimen for ages. I couldn't bear not sleeping with her. So I told Dromon to crouch down by the cornice of the courtyard, where it's lowest, and let me get on his back. I could more easily climb up that way. To cut a long story short, I climbed over, got to Ioessa's house and found the courtyard door firmly closed. It was, after all, the middle of the night. So I didn't knock. I just gently lifted up the door, as I'd done on other occasions, twisting the pivot from its socket,[81] and slipped in without making a noise. Everyone was asleep. I got to the bedside by following the wall with my fingers.

4   IOESSA: O Demeter, I'm in agony. What are you going to say next?

LYSIAS: When I realized there was more than one person breathing, I thought at first it was Lyde[82] who was sleeping with her. But that wasn't the case, Pythias. I felt around and discovered a beardless man, very soft, shaven-headed, also smelling of perfume. I wouldn't have hesitated, I can tell you, when I saw this, if only I'd brought a sword with me. Why are you both laughing, Pythias? Do you think my story deserves guffaws?

IOESSA: Is this what's upset you, Lysias? It was Pythias here who was sleeping with me.

PYTHIAS: Don't tell him, Ioessa.

IOESSA: Why can't I tell him? It was Pythias, my darling. I'd called her to sleep with me. I was upset that I didn't have you.

5   LYSIAS: Pythias, with a shaved head? Then how has she managed to grow such a fine head of hair in five days?

IOESSA: She had to shave her head because of a disease, Lysias. Her hair was falling out. Now she wears a wig. Show him, Pythias, show him that it's true. Make him believe me. There! Here's the young man, the lover you were so jealous of.

LYSIAS: And why not, Ioessa? I was in love and I did actually touch him.

IOESSA: So now you're convinced. Do you want me to hurt you to get my own back? It's reasonable for me to be angry in my turn.

LYSIAS: No, let's have a drink instead, and Pythias too. It's only right and proper for her to be present at the peace.[83]

IOESSA: Fine by me. But what I've had to go through because of you, Pythias, you noble youth!

PYTHIAS: Well it's me that's brought you back together. So don't be angry with me. Only one thing, Lysias – don't tell anyone about my hair, will you?

13

Leontichus and Chenidas and Hymnis[84]

LEONTICHUS: Tell her how I rode out in front of the rest of the   1
cavalry on the white horse in the battle against the Galatians,[85]
Chenidas, and how they, though mighty warriors, trembled
as soon as they saw me and left their positions to a man. Then
using my lance as a javelin, I drove it right through the cavalry
commander and his horse. Some of them had held their
ground, but they had re-formed from a phalanx[86] into a
hollow square. I drew my sword on them and driving forward
with all my strength I knocked over as many as seven of their
front line just by my horse's impetus. I brought down my
sword on one of their two platoon leaders and split his head
in two, helmet and all. It wasn't long after that that the
rest of you arrived, Chenidas, when the enemy were already
running away.

CHENIDAS: Wasn't that also a feat of derring-do, Leontichus,   2
when you engaged in single combat with the satrap in
Paphlagonia?[87]

LEONTICHUS: I'm glad you reminded me of that. Not a trivial
incident, I'd say. The satrap was a huge fellow and had the
reputation of being the best hoplite in the business. He had
nothing but contempt for us Greeks. He jumped out into the
middle and challenged all and sundry to a duel. The rest of
the platoon commanders and the taxiarchs[88] were scared to
death. So was the general himself, and he was no mean man.
I'm talking about Aristaechmus the Aetolian, our best javelin
thrower.[89] I was still a chiliarch at the time. I took my courage
in both hands and shook off the comrades who were holding
me back – they were terrified for me when they saw the gold
armour of the barbarian glinting and the size of his fearsome
crest, and the way he was brandishing his lance –

CHENIDAS: I was afraid for you then too, Leontichus. You
know how I held on to you and begged you not to put yourself
in danger. Life would've been unliveable for me if you'd died.

3   LEONTICHUS: But I took heart and strode out into the middle.
I wasn't wearing armour inferior to the Paphlagonian's. In
fact, I was also clad completely in gold. A great shout arose
right away, both from our side and from the barbarians. Even
the enemy had recognized me, I suppose, from my small round
shield and the bosses and crest on my helmet. Tell her who
everyone said I looked like at that moment, Chenidas.

CHENIDAS: None other than Achilles, by Zeus, the son of Thetis
and Peleus, your helm shone so conspicuously, your cloak
gave such a purple glow and your shield sparkled so daz-
zlingly.

LEONTICHUS: We engaged. The barbarian wounded me first. It
was a flesh wound made with his spear just above my knee. I
drove my pike through his shield and speared him right
through the chest. Then I ran up and with no bother cut off
his head with my sword. I returned carrying his armour and
bringing his head stuck on the tip of my pike, completely
bathed in his blood.

4   HYMNIS: Don't, Leontichus! That's a disgusting and terrifying
tale you're telling about yourself. No one could even look at
you the way you gloat over gore, let alone drink with you or
sleep with you. I'm off, anyhow.

LEONTICHUS: What if I pay you double?

HYMNIS: I couldn't bear to sleep with a murderer.

LEONTICHUS: Don't be afraid, Hymnis. All that happened in
Paphlagonia. Now I'm at peace.

HYMNIS: But you're polluted.[90] The blood from the barbarian's
head you were carrying on your pike was dripping down over
you. And I'm supposed to hug and kiss a man like that? Never,
by the Graces! You're no better than the public executioner.

LEONTICHUS: And yet, if you'd seen me in my armour, you'd
have been smitten, I can tell you.

HYMNIS: I'm feeling nauseous and goose-bumpy just listening
to you, Leontichus. I imagine I'm seeing the shades and phan-
toms of those you killed, and especially the ghost of the poor
platoon commander whose head you split in two. What do
you think I'd have felt like if I'd actually witnessed the action
and the blood and the corpses lying there? I think I'd have

died on the spot. I've never even seen a cockerel being killed.

LEONTICHUS: You can't be such a coward and so lacking in spirit as that, Hymnis. I thought you'd enjoy hearing my stories.

HYMNIS: If you can find some Lemnian women or Danaids,[91] you'll find they like your tales. But I'm off back to my mother while it's still daylight. Come on, Grammis.[92] Farewell, great chiliarch and murderer of millions.

LEONTICHUS: Wait, Hymnis, wait . . . She's gone.   5

CHENIDAS: That's because she's a simple young girl, Leontichus, and you terrified her by shaking your crest and telling her tall tales of your prowess. I saw at once how green she went while you were still relating that story about the platoon commander, and how she wrinkled her face up and shuddered when you said you'd cut his head in two.

LEONTICHUS: I thought I'd appear more attractive to her. But you didn't help at all, Chenidas, in suggesting the single-combat stuff.

CHENIDAS: You're telling me I shouldn't have abetted your deceit, when I could see why it was you were bragging? You just made it too frightening. I mean, all right, you cut the poor Paphlagonian's head off, but why did you have to stick it on your pike, so his blood ran down all over you?

LEONTICHUS: Yes, I suppose that really was horrible, Chenidas,   6 when the rest of the tale hadn't been badly put together. Why don't you go off and try to persuade her to sleep with me?

CHENIDAS: So, shall I say that the whole thing was a pack of lies you told her because you wanted her to think you were a hero?

LEONTICHUS: That would be too shaming, Chenidas.

CHENIDAS: Well, she won't come otherwise. So you have a choice. You either have Hymnis hate you because she thinks you're a mighty warrior, or you get to sleep with her by admitting that you lied.

LEONTICHUS: Both are tough. But I'd rather have Hymnis. So go off and tell her that I made it up – but not completely.

14

Dorion and Myrtale[93]

1 DORION: So, it's now you start shutting the door on me, Myrtale, now, when you've drained every penny out of me? Yet I was everything to you, lover, husband, master, when I was bringing you all those presents. And now I'm a completely dry husk, and you've found the Bithynian merchant as a lover, I'm shut out and stand in front of your door weeping, while he gets his nightly dose of love, and he's the only one inside your house, and he's the one who stays all night long. You even claim you're pregnant by him.

MYRTALE: This is what makes me especially choke with rage, Dorion, when you keep telling me about all those presents you gave me and how I'm the cause of your poverty. Come on, then, reckon up everything you brought, starting at the beginning.

2 DORION: All right, Myrtale. Let's reckon it up. First of all there's the shoes from Sicyon, worth two drachmas. Put two drachmas onto the account.

MYRTALE: But you slept with me for two nights.

DORION: And when I came back from Syria, you got a jar of myrrh from Phoenicia. That was worth two drachmas as well, by Poseidon.

MYRTALE: But when you sailed off I gave you that little thigh-length cloak to wear when you were rowing, the one the bow-officer Epiuros[94] left here by mistake when he was sleeping with me.

DORION: Epiuros recognized it not long ago in Samos and took it back, after an enormous battle, as the gods are my witness. And I brought you onions from Cyprus, five sea-bass, and four perch[95] when I sailed back from the Bosporus. What's more, ungrateful woman, you got a basket of eight dried ship's loaves, and a jar of dried figs from Caria, and later from Patara a pair of gilded sandals. I also remember once bringing you a huge cheese from Gythium.

MYRTALE: That probably comes to about five drachmas for the lot, Dorion.

DORION: That's all a fellow could afford who was a plain sailor, making trips for pay, Myrtale. But now I've risen in rank to command the right-hand bank of oars and you choose to take no notice of me? What about the silver drachma I placed on your behalf as an offering at Aphrodite's feet at the last Aphrodisia? What's more, I gave your mother two drachmas for shoes and have often put two or three obols in the hand of Lyde here. When you add that up, it's all a sailor could possibly possess.

MYRTALE: You mean onions and sea-bass, Dorion?

DORION: Yes, because I never had more to bring you. I wouldn't have been a rower if I'd been wealthy. My own mother never got so much as a head of garlic from me. I'd love to know what the Bithynian's presents to you are.

MYRTALE: Well, first of all do you see this little tunic? He bought it for me, and the heavy necklace too.

DORION: He bought that? I know you've had it for ages.

MYRTALE: The one you knew was much lighter and had no emeralds. He gave me these earrings and that carpet. What's more, the other day he paid our rent, two whole minas. There's no sandals from Patara and cheese from Gythium and rubbish like that.

DORION: You've missed out one important point. What's he like to go to bed with? He's fifty if he's a day, he's going bald and he's got skin like a prawn. And haven't you seen his teeth? He's absolutely dripping with charm, by Castor and Pollux, especially when he sings and tries to be sophisticated. He's the proverbial ass accompanying himself on the lyre. Well, good luck to you.[96] You deserve him. I pray that you have a child who looks like his father. I'm going to look for Delphis or Cymbalion[97] among my friends, or your neighbour the piper, or at any event someone. We don't all have carpets and necklaces and rents of two minas to squander.

MYRTALE: What a lucky girl your new lover's going to be, Dorion! You'll be bringing her onions from Cyprus, no doubt, and cheese when you sail back from Gythium.

15

Cochlis and Parthenis[98]

1 COCHLIS: Why are you crying, Parthenis? Where're you coming
from with your pipes[99] all broken?

PARTHENIS: The Aetolian soldier who's in love with Crocale
slapped me when he found me playing the pipes at Crocale's
house. I'd been hired by his rival Gorgus.[100] He burst in while
they were in the middle of dinner, broke my pipes, overturned
the table and upset the wine bowl. Then the soldier – I think
his name's Deinomachus[101] – together with his friend dragged
the countryman Gorgus out of the party by the hair. Then
they stood over him and beat him up. He's so bad, I'm not
sure he'll live, Cochlis. There was blood pouring from his
nose and his face is completely swollen and black and blue.

2 COCHLIS: Did the man go mad or was it a fit of drunken
rowdiness?

PARTHENIS: It was a fit of jealousy, Cochlis, arising from an
extraordinary passion. I think Crocale had asked for two
talents for sole use of her services. When Deinomachus
couldn't pay, they say she slammed the doors in his face and
locked him out when he turned up. Instead, she received
Gorgus from Oenoe, a rich farmer and a nice man, who'd
been in love with her for ages, drank with him and brought
me along to play the pipes. The drinking had been going on
for a while, when I started to play a Lydian reel, the farmer
got up to dance, Crocale was playing the castanets and everything was fine. While this was going on, we heard a crash and
shouting. The courtyard door was being broken down. Soon
afterwards about eight really hefty young fellows burst in, the
Megarian[102] in their midst. At once everything was turned
upside down and, as I said, Gorgus was beaten up and
trampled as he lay on the ground. Crocale got out and somehow escaped to her neighbour Thespias'[103] house. Deinomachus slapped me, said, 'Get the hell out of here' and threw
my broken pipes after me. Now I'm in a rush to tell my master

all this. The farmer himself is also off to see some friends from the city who are going to hand over the Megarian to the *prytaneis*.[104]

COCHLIS: This is what you get from loving soldiers – nothing   3
but violence and lawsuits. What's more, they may claim to be generals and chiliarchs, but if you ask for anything, they say, 'You'll have to wait till payday, when I get my wages, and then I'll see you right.' They can go to hell, the frauds. In any case, I'm right not to receive them at all. What I wish for is someone on my level – a fisherman, or a sailor, or a farmer – who doesn't have a lot to offer on the flattery front, but who brings loads of presents.[105] As for the fellows who shake their crests and tell you war stories – empty noise, that's all they are,[106] Parthenis.

SCYTHIANS

Preface

This section groups together two pieces concerned with Scythians, *The Scythian, or The Honorary Consul* and *Toxaris, or Friendship*. *The Scythian* appears to have been delivered in a Macedonian city (paragraph 9), possibly in Beroea,[1] with the purpose of gaining the patronage of two of its prominent citizens, a father and son (10–11). It is possible that this *prolalia* was designed as an introduction to *Toxaris*.[2] There is no useful criterion by which to date *Toxaris*, but if *The Scythian* was designed to operate thus it must belong at the same time, and probably after Lucian's fortieth year or so (see Introduction, section 2).[3] Lucian's interest in barbarians who become fascinated with Greek culture (*Anacharsis* is another example) seems to mirror his own self-presentation as a Syrian Hellenophile (see Introduction, section 4). The way he uses these outsiders is similar to the way he employs Menippus of Gadara, other Cynic figures (e.g. Cyniscus in *Zeus Cathechized*) and also Lycinus (see *The Ship*, *Images* and *In Defence of 'Images'*) to promote a viewpoint which will startle his audience into awareness of their own cultural preconceptions. *Toxaris* uses this technique to deal with the theme of friendship. The eponymous interlocutor is challenged by Mnesippus, a Greek, to explain why the Scythians honour Orestes and Pylades, who, according to myth, did them great harm. The Scythians' focus on the close friendship of the pair reflects well on the outsiders, who, despite being barbarians, appear to have a better grip on the real ethical essentials than the Greeks (and are more charitable). The ensuing 'friendship competition', consisting of five stories from the Greek and five from the Scythian, has not yet received a fully satisfactory interpretation. A few points may be made. First, the literary references surrounding the opening of the competition would have suggested to the audience that the narratives will be fictitious. Secondly, the stories are set in the contemporary world, and touch on aspects of the Roman empire. Thirdly, the audience are invited to spot the holes in the narratives and to derive amusement from so doing. This invitation to a critical stance does not, however, affect the ethical point of the piece, which is underlined when the competition ends without a victor and the two become friends.

NOTES

1.   See Jones 1986, 11.
2.   Similar claims are sometimes made for *Dionysus* vis-à-vis *True Histories*. See Georgiadou and Larmour 1995. It must be noted, though, that the stories in *Toxaris* are set in the Roman world (see below), so that the Toxaris of the dialogue shares only a name with the more venerable peer of Solon in the *prolalia*. On the other hand, see note 6 to *The Scythian*.
3.   Jones 1986, 169 infers from *The Scythian* 9 that Lucian is young. But there can be no certainty about this.

THE SCYTHIAN, OR THE
HONORARY CONSUL[1]

Anacharsis[2] wasn't actually the first Scythian to arrive in Athens   1
out of eagerness for Greek culture. Toxaris was there before
him. He was a wise man, who loved what was good and was an
eager student of the best accomplishments. However, at home
he didn't belong to the royal family nor to the 'pilophoric' class,[3]
but was one of the Scythian *hoi polloi*,[4] from the common people
they call 'octapods', which means being the owner of two oxen
and one wagon.[5] This Toxaris[6] never actually returned to Scythia, but died at Athens. Not long after his death he came to be
regarded as a hero,[7] and the Athenians sacrifice to him as the
'Foreign Physician', the name he acquired after he achieved hero
status. But maybe it wouldn't be a bad idea to tell you why he
received this sobriquet, the reason for his enrolment into the
ranks of the heroes and what led to his reputation as one of
the sons of Asclepius. That way you'd discover that it's not just
Scythians who customarily immortalize human beings and 'send
them to Zamolxis'.[8] It's actually possible for Athenians to make
gods out of Scythians on Greek soil.

During the great plague[9] the wife of Architeles,[10] a member   2
of the Areopagus, had a vision. The Scythian[11] stood near her
and told her to tell the Athenians that they would be released
from the grip of the plague if they sprinkled their alleyways with
large quantities of wine. This was done on numerous occasions
(the Athenians heard the advice and did not disregard it) and it
actually stopped the plague in its tracks. It's unclear whether
the smell of the wine extinguished some noxious vapours, or
the hero Toxaris gave the advice because of some greater insight
he had in his capacity as a doctor. Whatever the truth is, he still

today receives payment for his successful treatment, in the form
of the sacrifice of a white horse at his tomb, on the spot Deimainete[12] pointed out as the place from which he approached her
and gave the instructions about the wine. They actually discovered that Toxaris was buried there, recognizing him by the
inscription (even though it was no longer completely legible),
but more particularly by the sculpture on the gravestone of a
Scythian, holding in his left hand a strung bow, and in his right,
apparently, a book. Even today you can see more than half of
the figure and all of the bow and the book. But the ravages of
time have now damaged the upper part of the stone including
the face. It's not far from the Dipylon Gate, to your left as you
go towards the Academy. The mound is rather small and the
gravestone is on the ground. None the less, it's always covered
in garlands and the story goes that individuals have been cured
of fever by him. And, by Zeus, that's not at all incredible,
considering that he once cured the whole city.

3   But let me get back to the reason for mentioning Toxaris in
the first place. He was still alive when Anacharsis sailed into
Piraeus and was making his way from there up to the city. As
you might expect in a barbarian stranger, his mind was still
pretty confused. Everything was new to him, the noise of most
things made him nervous and he didn't know what to do. He
realized that his clothes made him an object of derision to those
who saw him, he couldn't find anyone who spoke his language
and he was already full of regret at having made the journey. In
fact, he'd already made up his mind just to visit Athens and to
turn straight round, board a ship and sail back to the Bosporus,
from where it would be a relatively short journey home to
Scythia. Anacharsis was in this frame of mind when like an
angel of mercy[13] Toxaris ran into him when he'd reached the
Ceramicus. In the first place what attracted his attention was
the dress of his native land, but then it wasn't going to be hard
for him to recognize Anacharsis himself, given that he was from
the most prominent family and one of the leading men in Scythia.
But how could Anacharsis have recognized Toxaris as a fellow-
Scythian, when he was in Greek clothing, with his hair shaved
close, no beard, no belt and no sword, already a chatterbox[14]

and indistinguishable from the autochthonous inhabitants of Attica? That was how much time had changed his appearance.

Anyhow, Toxaris came up to him and said in Scythian, 'Aren't   4 you Anacharsis the son of Daucetas?'

Anacharsis wept for joy at finding someone who spoke the same language and knew his position in Scythia, and asked, 'But how do you know me, stranger?'

He replied, 'I'm from there too and of your race. My name is Toxaris. I'm not from the nobility, so that it wouldn't actually be familiar to you.'

Anacharsis said, 'You're not the Toxaris I heard about are you, the one who caught a passion for Greece and went off to Athens, abandoning his wife and young children, and now lives there, respected by the great and good?'

Toxaris replied, 'That's me, if people still talk about me at all among the Scythians.'

Anacharsis' response was this: 'I must tell you, then, that I've become your pupil and an emulator of the passion for seeing Greece which engulfed you. In fact, this is the trading venture which has brought me so far from home. I've had a thousand adventures among the peoples between home and here. If I hadn't bumped into you, I'd already decided to go back on board ship before sunset. That was the state I'd got into, seeing that everything was strange and unknown. However, in the name of Acinaces[15] and Zamolxis, our ancestral gods, take me under your wing, Toxaris. Be my guide and show me the finest things in Athens and the rest of Greece, including the best of their law codes, the greatest of their men, their customs, their festivals, their way of life and their civil organization, everything which made you, and me after you, make such a long journey. Don't let me go back home without seeing them.'

'What you've mentioned, turning round and leaving when   5 you've only reached the doors, is hardly the act of a person in the grip of a passion,' said Toxaris. 'Still, take heart. You won't leave, as you claim. The city won't let you go so easily. She's not so lacking in charms to employ on strangers. In fact, she'll really take a grip on you. If you still have a wife and children, you'll completely forget them.[16] Now I'm going to tell you how you may see the whole city of Athens as quickly as possible – no, the whole of Greece and the beauties of the Greeks. There's a wise man here, a native, mind you, but one who's spent a great deal of time abroad in Asia and Egypt, and who's mingled with the best of humankind. Despite that, he's not one of the wealthy, but is actually quite poor. What you'll see is an old man dressed in a very plain fashion. However, the Athenians have great respect for him because of his wisdom and his other virtues. Consequently, they have him as their lawgiver in matters of civil organization and think it right to live their lives in accordance with his precepts. If you made a friend of him and found out the sort of man he is, you could consider that you had the whole of Greece in him and that you'd know the most important of the good things to be found here. There's no greater favour I could possibly do you than to introduce you to him.'

6   'Let's not delay, then, Toxaris,' said Anacharsis. 'Take me to him. However, I'm afraid he might be difficult to approach and might not take seriously your intercession on my behalf.'

'No words of ill omen, please,'[17] replied Toxaris. 'I suspect I'll be doing him the biggest favour of all by giving him an opportunity to do a good turn for a stranger. You'll soon find out how great his respect for the god of strangers[18] is as well as all the rest of his admirable qualities of propriety and goodness. But no, by good fortune this is him coming towards us. He's the one deep in thought, talking to himself.'

He followed this immediately by addressing Solon in these words: 'I've brought with me this enormous gift, a stranger in need of friendship. He's a Scythian, one of our noblemen, but none the less he's left behind all he has there to spend time with you Greeks and to see the best Greece has to offer. And I've found this short-cut for him, the easiest way for him both to learn everything for himself and to become known among our best men. That short-cut was bringing him to you. Now, if I know Solon, you'll perform this task, serve as his honorary consul[19] and turn him into a genuine citizen of Greece.[20] As I just told you, Anacharsis, once you've seen Solon, you've seen everything. He is Athens, he is Greece. You're no longer a stranger, everyone knows you and everyone is your friend.

That's the influence that's associated with this old man. Being with him, you'll forget about everything in Scythia. Now you have the prize for your journey abroad, the object of your passion. Here is the yardstick of Greece, here is a sample of Attic philosophy. I say this so that you'll realize that the man who spends time with Solon and has him as a friend is the happiest on earth.'

It would be a long story, if I were to tell you the joy Solon felt 8 at the gift, the things he said and how they spent the time afterwards in each other's company. Solon was the educator, teaching what was best. He made Anacharsis friends with everyone, introduced him to the cream of the Greeks and took every care to make his sojourn in Greece as pleasant as possible. Meanwhile, Anacharsis was beguiled by Solon's wisdom and was never willingly more than a step away from him. Just as Toxaris had promised, through this one man, Solon, he learned everything in a trice and everyone knew who he was. He was also respected because of Solon. For Solon's praise was no small recommendation, and in this area too people were ready to trust him as a lawgiver: they showed affection for those he approved and believed that they were men of the best stamp. In the end, Anacharsis was the only barbarian to be initiated into the Eleusinian Mysteries, after being awarded Athenian citizenship (if we can believe Theoxenus, who also records this about him).[21] Indeed, if Solon hadn't died, I don't think he would ever have returned to Scythia.

Do you want me to tell you the end of the story? After all, it 9 wouldn't do for it to be wandering around without a head. It's time for you to be told why it is that these two fellows Anacharsis and Toxaris have just now made the trip from Scythia to Macedonia, bringing with them also from Athens the old man Solon. What I'm saying is that I've had a similar sort of experience to that of Anacharsis. Now, I beg you in the name of the Graces not to be annoyed at my presumption in comparing myself to a man of royal blood. For, after all, he was a barbarian too, and I don't think you'd say that we Syrians are any lower down the scale than the Scythians. But actually it isn't at all for the royal aspect that I'm introducing my own experiences into the comparison. It's for this. When I first came to your city from abroad, I was immediately overawed when I saw its size and beauty, the number of its citizens, the rest of its power and its total splendour. Consequently, for a long time I was entranced by these things and could not take in the wonder of it. My feelings were like those of the famous young islander when he sees the house of Menelaus.[22] I was bound to feel this way when I saw a city at the absolute peak of its development and as the famous poet says

aflower with all the good things that make a city bloom.[23]

10   In this frame of mind I started to consider what I should do. I had actually decided long before to display some of my rhetoric to your citizens. (For to what other audience could I have displayed it, if I'd passed by such a great city without speaking?) Because what I was trying to find out (and I won't hide the truth from you) was who the outstanding men were and who it was a person might approach, enlist as patrons and use as his allies for everything. In this city my informant wasn't (as in the case of Anacharsis) one individual and a barbarian at that (Toxaris), but many: in fact everyone I asked said the same thing in different words: 'Stranger, there are lots of other good and clever men all over the city (in fact, you wouldn't find so many fine individuals anywhere else). But we have one pair of noble men in particular who are outstanding above everyone in their birth and reputation, and who merit comparison with the Ten Attic Orators for their education and the power of their oratory. The common people's goodwill towards them is indeed a passion,[24] and whatever they wish is done. And this is because they want what is best for the city. Their goodness, their kindness towards strangers, the lack of reproaches despite their greatness, their benevolent respectfulness, their gentleness and their approachability you will be telling others of a little later, when you've experienced those qualities for yourself.

11   'What's even more amazing is this. The two of them belong to the very same household. They're father and son. For the former, you can imagine him as a Solon, a Pericles or an Aris-

tides. As for the son, even his appearance will attract you straight away, he's so tall and good-looking in a completely masculine way. Let just a word fall from his lips, though, and he'll be off with you tied to him by the ears, so much of Aphrodite does the young man have on his tongue.[25] The whole city listens to him open-mouthed whenever he comes forward to speak in the assembly, just as they say the Athenians of the time did with the son of Cleinias.[26] The difference is that they soon had cause to regret the passion they had conceived for Alcibiades,[27] whereas the city doesn't just love him, but has already thought fit to revere him, and, in sum, our one public good and a great boon to all is this man. So, if he and his father welcome you and make you their friend, you have the whole city. All they have to do is wave a hand, and your success is no longer in doubt.'

I swear by Zeus that this is what everyone told me (if I really need to bolster up what I'm saying with an oath). But now my own experience suggests that they told me only a very small part of their virtues.

> So now's no time for sitting still or for procrastination

as the poet from Ceos[28] says. I must pull on every rope, and do and say everything to make friends of such men. If this goal is achieved, everything else will be plain sailing, with a following wind, a calm sea and the harbour near at hand.

TOXARIS, OR FRIENDSHIP

1   MNESIPPUS: What's that, Toxaris? Do you Scythians actually
      sacrifice to Orestes and Pylades in the firm belief that they're
      gods?

  TOXARIS: We do sacrifice, Mnesippus, yes, indeed, but not
      because we think they're gods. We do it because we think
      they're good men.

  MNESIPPUS: So it's customary for you to make sacrifice to good
      men when they die as though they're gods?

  TOXARIS: Oh, that's not all we do. We also honour them with
      various kinds of festivals.

  MNESIPPUS: What is it you're looking for from them? I take it
      you can't be making sacrifice to them purely through
      goodwill, given that they're dead.

  TOXARIS: Well perhaps there'd be no harm if the dead too were
      well disposed towards us. However, we actually reckon that
      we're going to be benefiting the living by remembering the
      best men and that's why we do them this honour. This way
      we think we'll have lots of men who want to be like them.

2   MNESIPPUS: Well, in that way of thinking you're quite correct.
      But tell me, what is it in particular that you admire Orestes
      and Pylades for that you've put them on a par with the gods,
      even though they were foreigners and, what's more, enemies?
      After all, the Scythians of the time took them prisoner after
      they'd been shipwrecked, and took them off intending to
      sacrifice them to Artemis. They attacked their jailers, over-
      powered the guards, killed the king and not only grabbed the
      priestess, but actually stole Artemis herself and sailed away,
      making a laughing stock of the Scythian state.[1] If this is why

you honour the men, then it won't be long before you've created a whole swathe of people like them. After that, you can judge for yourselves with reference to what happened in ancient times whether it suits you to have a whole crowd of Oresteses and Pyladeses putting into Scythian ports. It seems to me that this would be the quickest way for you to become impious and godless, when the rest of your gods had been exported from your land in the same way as Artemis. At that point, I suppose, to replace all your gods you'll deify the men who came to carry them off and will sacrifice to the robbers of your temples as gods.

If this isn't what you honour Orestes and Pylades for, 3 Toxaris, tell me what other benefit they've conferred on you which has made you change your view of them? In olden days you didn't think they were gods, but now your sacrifices to them demonstrate that you do. Now you're bringing sacrificial victims to offer to men who were once almost sacrificial victims themselves. This might seem ridiculous, and contradictory to the views of your ancestors.

TOXARIS: Actually, Mnesippus, even the deeds that you've listed done by those men were noble. There were only two of them, yet they undertook this great venture. They sailed an enormously long way from their own country to the Black Sea, which was at that time still unexplored by any Greeks, with the single exception of those who'd served aboard the *Argo* on the expedition to Colchis.[2] They weren't terrified by the stories about the region, and the fact that it was known as 'Inhospitable',[3] because, I suppose, the tribes on its shores were savages, held no fears for them. When they were taken prisoner, they managed the situation with conspicuous bravery. And they weren't content merely to escape, but they punished the king for his outrageous treatment of them and sailed away with Artemis on board. How could anyone who admires courage not regard this as astonishing and on everyone's part well worth the kind of honour given to a god? However, it's not this that we've observed in Orestes and Pylades that makes us treat them as heroes.

MNESIPPUS: Well, please get on and tell me what other fine and 4

godlike deed it is they've done. For as far as their voyage and
foreign travels are concerned, I could show you lots of people
distinctly closer to the gods. I mean the merchants, and
particularly the Phoenicians among them, who haven't
merely sailed into the Black Sea as far as Maeotis and the
Bosporus,[4] but have plied the seas all over, Greek and barbarian. Every year they explore so to speak every headland
and every shore and only return to their native land late in
the autumn. Your logic dictates that you should regard them
as gods as well, even though most of them are traders and
sometimes fishmongers.[5]

5   TOXARIS: My admirable friend, listen to me and see how much
more reasonable our barbarian judgement of good men is
than yours. At Argos or Mycenae you won't see a fine tomb
for Orestes and Pylades, yet we can even show you a temple
to them. And it's dedicated to both of them, as you might
expect, given that they were friends. They receive sacrifices
there, and all the other honours, and the fact that they were
foreigners and not Scythians makes no difference to the judgement that they are good men and to the honour paid to them
by the Scythian nobility. We don't ask about the provenance
of the bravest and best or feel pangs of jealousy if they've
done brave deeds when they aren't our friends. We praise
what they've done and we make them our own because of
their deeds. The thing that has most struck us about these
men and has led us to praise them is this. We think they were
the best friends of all and can be set up as exemplars to others,
laying down the law that friends must share both good and
bad fortune.

6   An account of all the things they did together or for each
other was written up by our ancestors on a bronze plaque
which they set up in the temple of Orestes.[6] What's more,
learning by heart this inscription was established by law as
the very first lesson their children had to learn when they
began their education. Each of them would have sooner forgotten the name of his father than fail to have known the
deeds of Orestes and Pylades.

    On the walls of the temple, too, the same deeds mentioned

by the plaque are represented in pictures painted by the ancients: Orestes sailing with his friend; next their ship wrecked
on the cliffs; Orestes captured with Pylades and prepared for
sacrifice; Iphigenia already consecrating the victims. On the
opposite wall, Orestes is pictured already out of his chains
and in the process of killing Thoas[7] and many other Scythians.
The final scene has them sailing off in possession of Iphigenia
and the goddess.[8] The Scythians are vainly trying to grab hold
of the boat, which is already in motion, hanging from the
steering-oars and trying to climb on board. Then, when they
make no headway, they swim back towards land, some of
them wounded and others fearing they will be. And here's
where one can see in detail how much affection they displayed
towards each other, that is in the engagement with the Scythians, because the painter has shown each of them ignoring the
enemies ranged against himself, but warding off the ones
attacking the other, trying to meet their arrows before his
friend does and regarding it as nothing to be killed so long as
he saves his friend's life and forestalls the blow aimed at him
by taking it on his own body.

This enormous affection of theirs, their companionship in   7
troubles, their loyalty, their love of friendship, the truth and
firmness of the passion that they felt for each other we considered were not characteristic of human beings, but of some
nobler cast of mind than most men can aspire to. Generally
speaking, while the voyage is going smoothly, people get
annoyed with their friends if they don't give them equal shares
in their pleasures, but if the wind starts blowing even a bit in
the opposite direction, they're gone, leaving them alone to
face their perils. I want you to be aware that Scythians think
there is nothing more important than friendship and that
there is nothing that a Scythian would pride himself on more
than joining a friend in his travails and sharing the dangers
that face him. By the same token, among us there's no greater
source of shame than to be considered a betrayer of one's
friendship. It's for this reason that we honour Orestes and
Pylades. They were the best exponents of the things the Scythians consider good and excelled in friendship, which we regard

as the most important of all. The name we have given them, 'Korakoi', reflects this. Translated into Greek, this Scythian word would mean something like 'Spirits of friendship'.

8   MNESIPPUS: So, Toxaris, the Scythians turn out not only to be good at archery and better warriors than others, they're also the most persuasive speakers of all. At any rate, although a while ago I had a completely different view, I'm now convinced that this deification of yours of Orestes and Pylades is justified. But I had no idea, my good friend, that you were also a fine artist. That was an exceptionally clear picture you drew of the paintings in the temple of Orestes, of the battle the men fought and the wounds they sustained for each other. The thing is, though, I wouldn't have thought that friendship was a thing the Scythians prized so highly. My impression was that, because they are inhospitable and savage, their constant companions are enmity, anger and wrath, and that they never make friends even with those closest to them. I inferred this from other things we hear about them, but especially from the fact that they eat their fathers when they die.[9]

9   TOXARIS: Well, now would not be the time to contest with you whether we are juster and more pious than the Greeks in other things, including our behaviour towards our parents. But it's easy to demonstrate that Scythian friends are far more loyal than Greek friends and that friendship is regarded more highly among us than among you. And I beg you in the name of the Greek gods not to get annoyed with me when you hear me talking about what I've noticed during the considerable time I've now spent in Greece.

You Greeks seem to me to be better than others at talking about friendship, but when it comes to the reality, not only do you not practise properly what you've preached, but you think it's quite enough to praise it and show what a terribly good thing it is. When an emergency arises, you betray your arguments and run off somehow from the realities. When the tragic poets bring friendships like these up onto the stage and show them to you, you praise the participants, you applaud them, and most of you actually shed tears when the friends

are taking risks for each other. But you never dare yourselves
to offer any action done for your friends' sake that's worth
an encomium. If your friend happens to need something, all
those tragedies fly off out of sight like dreams, leaving you
looking like those empty, dumb masks with their exaggerated
mouths stretched into an enormous rictus, which don't emit
the slightest sound.[10] We're the exact opposite. We make up
for all that we lack in talking about friendship in our practice
of it.

So, if you agree, let's do as follows. Let's leave ancient   10
friendships in peace, any from time gone by that either we or
you could list. The reason is that you would have the lion's
share here, because you'd bring in the poets as witnesses –
and there'd be a whole lot of them with a high degree of
credibility – to sing in the most elegant words and verses of
the friendships of Achilles and Patroclus, and of the comrade-
ship of Theseus and Pirithous and the rest.[11] Instead, let's
select a few examples from our own time and tell their stories.
I'll do the Scythians, and you do the Greeks. Whoever prevails
in the provision of exemplars of friendship will be the victor
himself and will proclaim his country the winner. And he'll
have fought in a very fine and noble contest. Indeed, I think
I'd find more pleasure in losing in single combat and having
my right hand cut off (the standard penalty for defeat in
Scythia) than in being adjudged worse than another in the
realm of friendship, especially than a Greek, given that I'm a
Scythian myself.

MNESIPPUS: Well, Toxaris, it's no mean task to go into the lists   11
against a warrior like you, so well armed with sharpened
words, aimed securely at their target.[12] However, I'm not
going to yield to you and betray the whole Greek cause
so ignobly and so quickly. Actually, it would be absolutely
appalling if those two on their own could defeat as many
Scythians as shown by the stories and those ancient paintings
of yours you described a minute ago in such finely honed
tragic mode,[13] but all of the Greeks together, in the great
number of their tribes and cities, should be condemned by
you by default. If this happened, it would be right for my

tongue to be cut out – and not my right hand cut off, as you Scythians do. Now, do you think we should put a limit on the number of these deeds of friendship? Or should the victory go to the one who can cite more examples?

TOXARIS: No. The victory shouldn't lie in the number of examples. We should each have the same number. If yours seem better and sharper,[14] obviously they'll inflict more-serious wounds on me and I'll succumb more quickly to your blows.

MNESIPPUS: Well said. Let's decide what the right number would be.

TOXARIS: I think five each would be right.

MNESIPPUS: I agree.

TOXARIS: You speak first. But you must swear that you'll speak the truth, the whole truth and nothing but the truth.[15] Otherwise it wouldn't be very difficult to invent such things and it would be hard to refute them.[16] But if you swore an oath, disbelief would be tantamount to impiety.

MNESIPPUS: We'll swear oaths, then, if you think we need to. Which of our gods would be acceptable to you? Zeus in his guise as god of friends?[17]

TOXARIS: Certainly. And I'll swear the normal Scythian oath when it's my turn to speak.

12   MNESIPPUS: Be it known therefore to Zeus the god of friendship that I swear the examples I shall give to you either are personally known to me or have been learned from others with as great a degree of accuracy as was possible. I shall add no tragic frills of my own.[18]

My first story will be about the friendship of Agathocles[19] and Deinias, which became famous among the Ionians. This Agathocles was from Samos and lived not long ago. His deeds showed that he was an aristocrat in friendship, but in other respects he had no advantage over the generality of Samians either in birth or in the rest of his resources. He had been friends with Deinias the son of Lyson from Ephesus since childhood. Now, Deinias became exceedingly wealthy, and, as you might expect from a nouveau riche, he had a lot of other people around him. They had the capacity to be drinking companions and to be pleasant company. But their deficiency in true friendship was enormous.

For a while, Agathocles was also one of their number. He kept company and drank with them, although he didn't take much pleasure in such a lifestyle. Deinias valued him no more than he did his toadies. In the end, Agathocles offended Deinias by his constant criticisms. He came to appear irksome because he was always reminding Deinias of his ancestors and telling him to take care of what his father had acquired with enormous effort and then left to him. Consequently, Deinias stopped inviting Agathocles to his revels. He began revelling on his own with his toadies, and tried to do it without Agathocles knowing.

Came the day when the poor wretch was persuaded by his 13 entourage that Charicleia,[20] wife of Demonax, was in love with him. Demonax was a noble and a leading light in Ephesian politics. Letters from the woman started reaching Deinias along with half-withered garlands and apples with a bite taken out of them[21] and all the other devices procuresses employ against young men. Little by little they construct passions for them. The first step in the process of lighting their fire is to make them think they're the object of someone's desire. This is a sure method of attracting their attention, especially if they think they're good-looking. Eventually, they're in the net before they realize it.

Charicleia was a witty little lady. But she was awfully courtesan-like[22] and would always be anyone's, even if he only wanted her for a very short time. A man had only to glance at her and she would say yes. There was no need to be afraid that Charicleia would ever refuse an offer. Her skills covered many areas, but she was an expert comparable to any courtesan you could name at drawing in a lover, subjecting him to her will when he was still making up his mind, putting him on the rack when he was hooked, and then adding fuel to the flame of his passion by getting angry and being flattering in turn, then shortly afterwards ignoring him completely and pretending to be interested in someone else.[23] The woman was fully trained in all aspects of her craft and was armed with many weapons to use in the siege of her lovers.

14   So this was the woman that Deinias' toadies drew towards the young man at that time. They played a supporting role in the comedy,[24] pushing him into a love affair with Charicleia. She had already caused many young men to fall from their saddles, acted in countless dramas of passion[25] and ruined many a super-wealthy dynasty. When she got into her clutches a callow young man who was unschooled in such devices, she did not let the grip of her talons loosen. No, she held him tightly all round and stuck her claws in. When she was in complete control, though, she was the victim of her own successful hunting expedition, not to mention the pile of troubles she caused the wretched Deinias.

The first step she took immediately was to employ the old letter-routine against him and to send her maid constantly to tell him of her tears, her insomnia and the poor woman's intention to commit suicide from unrequited passion. Eventually, the lucky fellow was persuaded that he was good-looking and that the women of Ephesus were lusting after him. So, after many entreaties, he met Charicleia.

15   From then on it was always going to be easy for him to be ensnared, as you might expect, by a beautiful woman who knew how to be pleasurable company, to cry on cue, to moan pitiably while in the middle of a conversation, to grab him when he was already on his way out of the house, to dash up to him when he came in, to dress to please him as much as possible and what's more to sing and play the lyre as well.

She used all these tactics against Deinias. And when she could see that he was in a bad way, was already saturated with passion and had become nicely tender, she thought of another trick on top of these and began to destroy the poor fellow. She claimed that she was pregnant by him (enough on its own to fan the flames of a stupid lover) and stopped going to him, with the excuse that her husband had discovered their affair and was guarding her.

Deinias couldn't stand it any longer, nor could he bear not seeing her. He wept and sent in his toadies. He kept on

invoking Charicleia's name. He carried her statue with him
(he'd had one made of marble). He would wail continually.
In the end he started throwing himself on the floor and rolling
around. His condition had reached the point of plain madness.
For now his gifts weren't returned to her in terms of apples
and garlands. Now it was whole apartment blocks, farms,
maidservants, embroidered dresses and as much gold as she
could want. Need I say more? In the twinkling of an eye, the
house of Lyson, which had had the greatest reputation in
Ionia, was drained and left empty.

Next, when Deinias was now a dry husk, Charicleia left   16
him and started hunting down another young man of the
gilded elite, a Cretan. She changed over to him and was
already passionate about him. The Cretan believed her.

So Deinias was now neglected not only by Charicleia, but
by his toadies as well, who had also switched over to the
camp of the new Cretan beloved. He went to Agathocles, who
actually had long known that his affairs were in a bad way,
and although at first he was shamefaced, none the less told
him the whole story, of his love, his lack of money, the
woman's disregard and his rival the Cretan. He ended by
saying that he couldn't live without Charicleia. Agathocles
decided that it was not the time to remind Deinias that he was
the only one of his friends Deinias had not allowed near him
and that he had at that time preferred his toadies to him. He
sold the only house he'd inherited from his father, in Samos,
and came to Deinias bringing the proceeds, which amounted
to three talents.[26]

When Deinias got hold of the money, he was instantly
not invisible to Charicleia, having somehow regained his
attractiveness. In came the maid again with the letters and the
reproach that it was ages since his last visit. The toadies also
gathered with their fishing lines ready, when they saw that
Deinias still had some flesh to be picked off.

When he'd promised to come to her, had arrived late at   17
night and was inside, Demonax, Charicleia's husband,
whether he'd found out some other way, or had agreed the
plot with his wife (both versions are current), got out of

bed as though emerging from an ambush and ordered the courtyard door to be locked and Deinias to be seized. He threatened to brand and whip him and drew his sword as against an adulterer.[27]

Deinias, realizing the extent of his predicament, seized a wooden bar that was lying nearby, hit Demonax with it on the temple and killed him. Charicleia he dispatched not with a single stroke, but with multiple blows and later with Demonax' sword. The slaves had for a while stood there speechless, stunned by the unexpectedness of the events. Then they tried to grab him, but ran away when he started to attack them with the sword as well. So Deinias slipped away after perpetrating a deed of this magnitude.

Until dawn he stayed with Agathocles. The two of them went over what had happened and tried to discern what the results would be in the future. When dawn came, the generals arrived and arrested Deinias, for the crime had already become widely known and Deinias did not deny that he'd done the murders. They took him off to the then harmost of Asia and he sent him to the great king.[28] Not long afterwards, Deinias was sent off to the island of Gyarus in the Cyclades, ordered by the king to remain there in perpetual exile.

18   Agathocles stayed with him even when he sailed to Italy.[29] He was the only one of his friends who went into the court with him and he helped him in everything. When Deinias was exiled, even then Agathocles did not abandon his friend. He condemned himself to exile, lived on Gyarus and shared Deinias' banishment. When they were utterly bereft of means, he put himself in the hands of the purple-fishers,[30] dived with them and earned a wage with which he fed Deinias. When Deinias fell ill he nursed him for a long time. When he died, Agathocles had no wish to return to his own land again, but stayed there on the island, ashamed to abandon his friend even after his death.

This is what a Greek friend did and it all happened not long ago. It may not even be five years since Agathocles died on Gyarus.

TOXARIS: I wish you hadn't sworn an oath, Mnesippus. Then

I'd have been able to disbelieve your tale, so much does
Agathocles recall the Scythian style of friendship. However,
I'm afraid you may have another, similar one to tell me about.

MNESIPPUS: Well, Toxaris, listen to another one, then. This is 19
the story of Euthydicus[31] from Chalcis. It was Simylus the
merchant from Megara who told me about him, with a solemn
oath that he'd actually been an eyewitness to the deed. He
said that he was sailing from Italy to Athens at the time when
the Pleiades set,[32] carrying passengers picked up in various
places. Among them was Euthydicus and along with him
Damon, also from Chalcis, his friend. They were the same
age, but Euthydicus was healthy and strong, while Damon
was pallid and weak, as though he had just got up after a long
illness.

Well, as far as Sicily, said Simylus, the voyage went
smoothly. But when they'd passed the straits and were now
sailing on the Ionian Sea, they were struck by a tremendous
storm. Most aspects of it would be among the usual common-
places: huge waves, whirlwinds, hailstorms and all the other
horrors of a tempest. They'd sailed as far as Zacynthus, with
the yard-arms bare of sail, and also trailing cables in their
wake to help counter the force of the waves breaking over the
ship. About midnight, Damon, feeling seasick, as you might
expect he would in such a swell, was leaning over the rail
and vomiting into the sea. Then the ship must have pitched
violently in the direction he was leaning. The waves swept
him in the same direction and he fell head first into the sea.
The poor fellow wasn't even undressed, which would have
made it easier for him to swim. He gave a shout, but he was
choking and having difficulty even keeping himself afloat.

Euthydicus was lying in bed, naked, when he heard the 20
shout. He jumped into the sea, grabbed hold of Damon, who
was already at his last gasp, and swam along with him, helping
to buoy him up. Simylus could see most of this, he said,
because the moon was shining. He reported that those on
board had wanted to help and were full of pity for the men's
mishap, but they were in the grip of a strong following wind
and were powerless. All they could do was throw out to them

a lot of pieces of cork and some poles for them to use as floats, if they could catch hold of one. In the end they also threw them the gangway itself, which was not small.

Now tell me, in the gods' name, if you can think of any firmer proof of a person's affection for a friend who'd fallen overboard at night into such a raging ocean than being willing to share his fate. Picture in your mind's eye the towering waves, the roar of the water as they broke, the boiling foam all around, the darkness and Damon's despair. Now imagine him as he chokes and barely keeps his head above water, stretching his hands out to his friend, and then Euthydicus without hesitation leaping after him, swimming alongside him, afraid that Damon will die first. This way you'll discover that the Euthydicus whose story I've told was also no ignoble friend.

21 TOXARIS: Did the men die, Mnesippus, or were they unexpectedly saved? Tell me, because I'm terribly afraid for them.

MNESIPPUS: Don't worry, Toxaris, they reached safety. Actually, they're still in Athens, both practising philosophy. All Simylus could relate was what he'd seen that night, Damon falling overboard, Euthydicus jumping in after him and the two swimming. But he could only see for so long, given that it was night-time. The sequel was related by the people in Euthydicus' circle themselves. First of all, Damon and Euthydicus managed to find some pieces of cork and supported themselves on them, swimming away weakly. Later on, around dawn, they spotted the gangway, swam up to it, climbed on board and stayed there until they made an easy landfall at Zacynthus.

22 Now, in my view, these are no mean examples of friendship. But I'm now going to ask you to listen to a third tale which is in no way inferior.

Eudamidas the Corinthian was friends with Aretaeus from Corinth and Charixenus[33] from Sicyon. They were wealthy men, but Eudamidas was a complete pauper. When he was on his deathbed, he left a will which others may perhaps find ridiculous, though I don't know if you will, given that you're a good man who respects friendship and that you're compet-

ing for first place in this area. These were the terms of the
will: 'To Aretaeus I leave my mother to feed and care for in
her old age, and to Charixenus my daughter to marry off with
as large a dowry as he can manage from his own resources' –
at this point I'll mention that he had an aged mother and a
daughter already of marriageable age – 'and should either of
them die in the mean time, the other is to have that share as
well as his own.' When the will was read, people who knew
how poor Eudamidas had been, but not about his friendship
with these men, regarded it as a joke. They all left laughing
and saying, 'Lucky old Aretaeus and Charixenus! What a
splendid legacy they'll be receiving if they pay Eudamidas'
price! They're alive, but it's the dead man who's going to
inherit.'

However, when the legatees of this inheritance heard about   23
it, they came at once to sort out the provisions of the will.
Charixenus, though, died, outliving Eudamidas by only five
days. But Aretaeus, the acme of legatees,[34] took on his own
portion and that of Charixenus. He looks after Eudamidas'
mother and has only recently married off his daughter. From
the five talents he possessed, he gave as dowry two to his own
daughter and two to his friend's daughter. He even went so
far as to celebrate both their weddings on the same day.

What do you think of this fellow Aretaeus, Toxaris? Has
he given us a bad example of friendship, receiving a legacy
like this and still not betraying the last will and testament of
his friend? Or can we count him too as validly balloted among
our five?

TOXARIS: He's also a fine exemplar. As for me, though, it's
Eudamidas I'm more admiring of for the confidence he had
in his friends. What he was showing was that he'd have done
the same for them. Even if this hadn't been written in a will,
he'd have come before the others to claim such a legacy as a
nuncupative heir.[35]

MNESIPPUS: Well said. Now, my fourth example will be the   24
story of Zenothemis[36] the son of Charmoleos from Massilia.

When I was in Italy on an embassy for my native land,[37] I
had a tall, good-looking man pointed out to me. He looked

to be wealthy. Beside him on the carriage he was travelling in sat a woman who'd have been ugly in any case, but in addition had a withered right side and one eye missing. She was a hideous horror,[38] to be given a wide berth. I expressed my amazement that a good-looking man like this who was in his prime could bear having a woman like her riding beside him. But the person who'd pointed him out told me the circumstances that had obliged him to marry her. He knew all the details of the story, being from Massilia himself.

'Zenothemis,' he said, 'was a friend of Menecrates,[39] the father of the deformed woman. They were on a par with each other in wealth and position. Later on, however, Menecrates was deprived of his property through a court ruling, when he actually lost his citizen rights at the hands of the Six Hundred[40] for publishing an unconstitutional measure.[41] This is the way the Massiliotes punish anyone who has made an unconstitutional proposal. So Menecrates was naturally distressed at the judgment against him – after all, in a short space of time he'd become poor instead of rich and without status instead of a member of the elite. But what really upset him were the consequences for his daughter. She was now eighteen and of marriageable age. Yet no one, noble or poor, would have readily agreed to take her in marriage, even if her father had given as a dowry the entire fortune he'd had before the ruling, so unfortunate was she in her looks. She was even reputed to have the falling sickness at the waxing of the moon.

25   'When he was airing these troubles to Zenothemis, his friend replied, "Don't worry, Menecrates. You won't be without what you need to live on and your daughter will find a bridegroom worthy of her birth."

'As he said this, he took him by the right hand and led him into his house and gave him a portion of his property, which was substantial. Then he had a dinner prepared and gave a feast to his friends and Menecrates, pretending that he'd persuaded one of his comrades to promise to marry the girl. When the dinner was over and the libations to the gods were done, Zenothemis raised a cup brimming with wine to Menecrates and said, "Now, Menecrates, accept a cup of friendship from the bridegroom. For today I'm going to marry your daughter Cydimache.[42] I've received the dowry – twenty-five talents – long ago."[43]

'Menecrates responded by saying, "No, no, Zenothemis. Not you. I hope I'm not mad enough to allow a good-looking young man like you tie the knot with a girl who's an ugly cripple." But as he was making this point, Zenothemis picked his bride up bodily, went off to the bedroom and came out a short time later having taken her virginity.[44]

'Since then, he's been with her. He treats her with enormous affection and, as you can see, takes her round everywhere with him. So far is he from being ashamed of his marriage, he actually seems to take pride in it, demonstrating that he despises the criteria of physical beauty and ugliness, wealth and reputation, and looks only towards his friend.[45] As for Menecrates, Zenothemis doesn't consider that the value of his friendship has been lessened at all by the votes of the Six Hundred.

'However, fortune has now recompensed him for all this in the following way. This extremely ugly woman has borne him a really fine-looking child. The other day, the proud father picked it up and took it into the council chamber wearing an olive wreath and dressed in black to make its appearance induce greater compassion for its grandfather. The infant smiled at the council members and clapped its hands, and the council, moved to pity by the child, cancelled Menecrates' sentence. So now he's regained his citizen rights, by employing an advocate of such tender age to plead his case with the assembled councillors.'

This was what the man from Massilia said Zenothemis had done for his friend. As you can see, it was no small favour, and not many Scythians would've done it, given their reputation for making sure even the concubines they choose are absolutely the prettiest.

My fifth example remains to be given. I think I'm going to tell you about Demetrius of Sunium. It wouldn't be right to forget him and give you another story.

Well, Demetrius sailed off to Egypt along with his childhood

26

27

friend Antiphilus[46] from Alopeke. They'd been fellow-ephebes.[47] Now they were together getting an education. Demetrius was following the Cynic training under the famous sophist from Rhodes, while Antiphilus was studying medicine.[48] Now, one time Demetrius happened to be on a sightseeing trip into Egypt to visit the pyramids and the statue of Memnon. He'd heard that the pyramids, though tall, cast no shadow, and that the statue of Memnon cries aloud at sunrise. Demetrius had sailed off down the Nile, then, in his eagerness to see the pyramids and to hear Memnon's statue. He'd now been away five months. He'd left Antiphilus behind because he'd had qualms about the journey and the heat.

28   But while Demetrius was away, Antiphilus suffered a catastrophe that required a really noble friend. His slave, whose name and nationality were 'the Syrian',[49] fell in with some temple-robbers and with them went into the shrine of Anubis and stole two golden chalices, a herald's staff (also made of gold), some silver baboons and other, similar objects. They then deposited them with the Syrian. Then they were caught trying to sell some of the stolen goods, and put in prison. Under torture on the rack they immediately told the whole story and led the way to Antiphilus' house, where they produced the stolen goods, which were hidden in the darkness under a couch. The Syrian was immediately put in chains, and so was his master Antiphilus. In fact, he was dragged off in the middle of listening to a lecture by his teacher. No one came to his assistance. His one-time comrades all turned their backs on him as the robber of the shrine of Anubis, and considered it an act of grave impiety that they'd ever drunk and feasted with him at all. His other two slaves gathered together everything in the house, ran away and disappeared.

29   So Antiphilus had already been chained up for a long time. Of all the criminals in the prison he was considered the most appalling. The Egyptian warder, moreover, was a god-fearing man who thought that he'd gain favour with the god and avenge him at the same time by guarding Antiphilus harshly. Whenever he defended himself by saying that he hadn't done any such deed, he was considered devoid of shame and made

himself even more hated for doing so. He'd consequently begun to fall ill and was in a bad state, as you might expect, seeing that he was sleeping on the ground and couldn't even stretch his legs out fully at night because they were locked into the stocks. Apparently, during the day it was enough for him to wear a collar and have one hand chained, but he had to be completely restrained for the night. What's more, the stench and the stifling heat of the cell, the fact that many were chained and packed into the same area so that they could hardly breathe, the noise of the iron shackles and the lack of sleep, all these took their toll and were hard to bear for a man unused to these things and untrained for such a harsh way of living.

He was on the point of exhaustion and was refusing even 30 to take food when Demetrius returned. He knew nothing of what had happened. As soon as he found out, he went to the prison, running as fast as he could. It was evening, and he was refused admission. The prison warder had locked the door some time before and was asleep, and had given his subordinates instructions to keep guard. At dawn, however, he got in after much pleading. As he went forward, he searched for a long while for Antiphilus, who'd become unrecognizable because of his suffering. Demetrius went round examining each prisoner carefully, like a person looking for his relatives in the battle-lines among the dead bodies already beginning to decompose. Indeed, if he hadn't shouted out his name, calling 'Antiphilus son of Deinomenes',[50] he'd have taken even longer to recognize him, so greatly had his afflictions altered his appearance. When Antiphilus heard his voice, he shouted aloud, and when Demetrius approached he parted his hair and pulled the dirty, matted locks away from his face to reveal his identity. The unexpected sight made both of them fall down in a dead faint.

After a while, Demetrius picked himself and Antiphilus up and learned from him clearly the details of what had occurred. He told Antiphilus to take heart and, tearing his cloak in half, he put one piece on and gave the rest to Antiphilus, after stripping off the squalid and threadbare rags he was wearing.

31   From then on he did all he could to be with him, looking
out for his welfare and taking care of him. The way he
managed this was by providing his services to the merchants
at the harbour from daybreak until midday. This portering
work brought him quite a good income. He would then return
from his job and give half his wage to the prison warder to
keep him peaceably co-operative with him. The rest was quite
enough to allow him to look after his friend. During the rest
of the day, he stayed with Antiphilus and comforted him. At
nightfall, he went to sleep just in front of the prison gate, on
a palliasse he'd made and laid out on a pile of leaves.

32   They lived like this for a while. Demetrius went in without
hindrance and Antiphilus bore his misfortune more easily.
Later on, however, a brigand in the prison died of poison, or
so it was conjectured, and after that the watch was strict and
no one who asked was let into the jail. Demetrius was upset
at this turn of events and didn't know what to do. With no
other way of being beside his friend, he went to the harmost[51]
and incriminated himself in the conspiracy to rob Anubis.

When he'd made this declaration, he was marched straight
off to the prison and brought to where Antiphilus lay. And at
least he was able to prevail upon the warder, after many pleas,
to be chained up next to him in the same set of collars. This
was where he demonstrated most particularly the affection he
had for Antiphilus. He ignored his own personal discomfort,
though he also fell ill, concentrating instead upon ensuring
that his friend got enough sleep and suffered less hardship.
This way, by sharing their miserable lot, they bore it more
easily.

33   After a while, though, the following event put an end to
further misfortune on their part. One of the prisoners had
somehow got hold of a file. He conscripted many of the
prisoners into the plot, managed to saw through the chain
into which their collars were inserted to chain them in a row,
and released everyone. The prisoners easily killed the small
number of guards and made off in a pack. Most of them
were recaptured later, having scattered immediately after the
breakout wherever they could. But Demetrius and Antiphilus

stayed where they were, and also took hold of the Syrian as he was on his way out. When day dawned, the prefect of Egypt[52] learned what had happened. He sent a posse to track down the escapees, but sent for Demetrius' party and had them released from their chains, praising them for being the only ones who'd not run off.

But they didn't take kindly to being released in this way. Demetrius shouted and made a commotion, claiming that it was a great injustice if they were going to be seen as villains who had been let off out of pity or as a reward for not running away. Eventually they forced the judge to investigate the affair properly. When he discovered that they'd done nothing wrong, he praised them, expressing particular admiration for Demetrius, and set them free. As compensation for the unjust imprisonment they'd undergone as punishment, he awarded Antiphilus a thousand drachmas[53] and Demetrius double that sum.

Antiphilus is still in Egypt. Demetrius left his two thousand drachmas with him and went off to India to the Brahmins.[54] All he said to Antiphilus was that he might be reasonably forgiven for leaving him at this point. He himself didn't need the money, since he was able to manage on very little so long as things continued the way they were, and Antiphilus no longer needed a friend, now that his affairs had become settled.

This is what Greek friends are like, Toxaris. And if you hadn't already slandered us by claiming that we pride ourselves upon our oratory, I'd actually have recounted to you the many noble words Demetrius spoke in the court. His defence focused not on himself, but on Antiphilus. He wept, he pleaded and he was prepared to take the whole blame upon himself, until the Syrian was whipped and his evidence set them both free.[55]

These that I've related to you, the first ones that sprang to mind, are a few of many more good, firm friendships. Now I'm going to step off my platform and let you fulfil your side of the bargain. Now, if you have any thought for that right hand of yours and you don't want it cut off, you'll take good care to make your Scythians not worse, but far better than my Greeks. You must be a bold warrior. After all, you'd look foolish after praising Orestes and Pylades in so sophistic a manner[56] if you showed yourself a poor advocate of your native Scythia.[57]

TOXARIS: Good for you, Mnesippus, for encouraging me to speak as though it didn't bother you at all that you may have your tongue cut out if I defeat you in the story contest. Anyway, I'm going to start straight away, without literary embellishments of the sort you used. That's not the Scythian way,[58] especially when the actions speak louder than the words needed to describe them. Nor should you expect from me any of the sort of tales you've told and given high praise to. A fellow marrying an ugly woman with no dowry, someone giving a friend's daughter two talents of silver when she marries, and especially a man who allows himself to be imprisoned when he's obviously going to be released a short while later are all footling matters with nothing great or brave about them. What I'm going to relate are blood-baths, wars and deaths endured for a friend's sake, so you'll realize what child's play your examples are when judged by the Scythian criterion.

None the less, what's happened with you is perfectly rational, and your praise for these petty examples is quite understandable. You live in an atmosphere of profound peace,[59] and so you have no exceptional occasions for the proof of friendship. You wouldn't be able to find out a helmsman's capacities during calm weather either. It would take a storm for you to be able to judge that. On the other hand, among the Scythians, wars follow each other in endless succession. We're either attacking someone else, or retreating in the face of an attack, or fighting at close quarters over pasturage or booty. These are the circumstances in which the need for good friends is fundamental. And it's for this reason that we contract friendships as firmly as possible, because we consider it's the only weapon we have which is irresistible and impossible to defend against.

First I want to tell you how we make our friends. We don't

do it on the basis of drinking together, or being ephebes at
the same time or because a fellow lives next door, like you
Greeks. No, when we see a good man who can do great deeds,
we all make a rush towards him. In the realm of friendship,
we imitate the procedures you have for marriage. We go
through a long courtship and we do everything together with
our chosen person to avoid losing the friendship and getting
the reputation of cast-offs. And when a friend has finally been
picked out ahead of the rest, the next thing we do is make a
pact and take the solemnest of oaths, swearing to live with
each other and, if necessary, to die for each other. And this is
what we actually do. From the moment we make that single
cut in our fingers, let the blood drip into a cup, dip the tips of
our swords in it and both of us together put it to our lips and
drink,[60] there is nothing after that which could separate us.
The maximum number of such pacts we're allowed to enter
on is three. The man with many friends seems to us like those
adulterous women whose sexual favours are in the common
pool. We reckon that his friendship can't be equally strong
when its affections are divided in so many directions.

   I'll begin with the story of Dandamis, events which took   38
place recently. It was in the engagement with the Sauromatai,
when his friend Amizoces had been taken off as a prisoner,
that Dandamis . . . But, no, first I'd better swear the Scythian
oath to you, since I agreed to this also at the start. The tales I
shall tell to you about Scythian friends, Mnesippus, shall
contain no falsehoods. I swear this by the wind and by the
dagger.[61]

MNESIPPUS: Well, I didn't really need you to swear at all. None
   the less, you were right not to invoke any gods when you
   made the oath.

TOXARIS: What do you mean? Don't you consider the wind
   and the dagger to be gods? Have you been ignorant thus far,
   then, of the fact that there are no greater forces for human
   beings than life and death? When we swear by the wind and
   the dagger, we make the oath on the assumption that the
   wind is responsible for giving life, and the dagger for causing
   death.

MNESIPPUS: Well, if that's the reason, then you could have a lot more gods like Dagger – Arrow, for example, and Lance, and Hemlock and Noose, and others of the same kind.[62] This god death is a many-faceted character and the paths he engineers which lead to him are countless.

TOXARIS: Look how captious and litigious you're being. You're interrupting me and spoiling my story. I kept quiet while you were speaking.

MNESIPPUS: I won't do it again, Toxaris. Your criticism is well taken. Carry on with what you have to say from now on in the full confidence that I'll be as quiet as though I weren't even present at your discourse.

39   TOXARIS: It was the fourth day since Dandamis and Amizoces had confirmed their friendship by drinking each other's blood. The Sauromatai came into our land with ten thousand cavalry and their infantry forces were reputed to be three times as strong again. We hadn't expected their incursion, so they routed us completely, killed many of our warriors and led others off alive. There were some who managed to escape by swimming to the other side of the river, where half of our army and wagons were. We'd pitched our camp this way on that occasion, on both banks of the river Tanais. The decision had been made by our nomad chiefs, but I couldn't tell you why.

All at once, then, the cattle were being rounded up, the prisoners brought together, the tents plundered and the wagons seized, most of them being captured with the people still in them. They were abusing our concubines and wives right in front of our eyes, and we were bridling at what was
40   happening. Amizoces had been taken prisoner and as he was being led away he called his friend's name aloud, bound so dreadfully as he was, and reminded him of the cup of blood. When Dandamis heard this, he delayed no longer, but with everyone watching he swam across into the midst of the enemy. The Sauromatai raised their javelins and charged towards him with the intention of spearing him. But he shouted 'Zirin'.[63] When someone says this word, they no longer attempt to kill him. They accept that he's come for the

purpose of paying a ransom. He was brought before their
leader and he asked for his friend. The leader asked for
ransom. He said he wouldn't release him unless he got a high
price in return. But Dandamis said, 'You have plundered
everything I possessed. But, if there is anything I can pay
naked as I am, I'm prepared to promise it to you. Ask for
whatever you wish. If you like, do whatever you like to me in
exchange for this man.' The Sauromate replied, 'There's no
need for us to keep you entirely, especially as you've come as
"Zirin". You can take away your friend if you leave part of
what you possess.' Dandamis enquired what it was he wished
to receive. The Sauromate asked for his eyes. At once
Dandamis allowed them to put them out. And when they'd
been put out and the Sauromatai now had their ransom, he
took Amizoces and returned, leaning on him. They swam the
river together and returned safely to us.

This event comforted all the Scythians. They no longer 41
considered that they were beaten, seeing that the enemy hadn't
taken away the most important of our treasures. We still
possessed great resolve and trust in our friends. And the same
event terrified the Sauromatai not inconsiderably. It made
them wonder what sort of men they'd be fighting when they
were prepared, even though this time they'd prevailed through
surprise. Consequently, when night fell, they abandoned the
majority of the cattle, burned the wagons and made off in
flight. Amizoces, however, could no longer bear to have the
power of sight himself now that Dandamis was blind. So he
blinded himself with his own hands. Now both sit there,
looked after with every honour by the Scythian people from
public funds.

What similar example would you Greeks be able to relate, 42
Mnesippus, even if I were to give you another ten to add to
your existing five, and, if you like, without having to swear
an oath, so that you could add a whole lot of lies to your
stories? And yet I've given you the facts bare. If you'd been
telling a story like this, I know exactly how much ingenious
padding you'd have filled it up with – Dandamis' supplication,
an account of his blinding, his words on that occasion, his

return, the welcome he received from the Scythians, their loud applause and all the other kinds of devices that you Greeks usually employ when you give rhetorical displays.

43   So, now I want you to listen to the story of Belitta, Amizoces' nephew, a man on a par with my first example. Belitta was hunting together with his friend Basthes, when he witnessed Basthes being dragged off his horse by a lion. The lion quickly clasped Basthes, got him tightly by the throat and began tearing at him with his claws. Belitta leapt down from his horse as well, fell on the beast from behind and tried to divert his attention, provoking the lion into changing course to attack him, putting his fingers between its teeth and trying as hard as he could to rescue Basthes from the lion's jaws. Eventually, the lion left Basthes already more dead than alive, turned round, locked himself around Belitta and killed him too. But, as he died, he was at least able to get a blow in with his dagger on the lion's breast. Consequently, they all died together and we buried them in two large mounds near to one another, one for the friends and, opposite, one for the lion.[64]

44   The third story I'm going to tell you, Mnesippus, is about the friendship between Macentes, Lonchates and Arsacomas. The last of these, Arsacomas, fell in love with Mazaia, the daughter of Leucanor, king of Bosporus,[65] when he was on an embassy on the matter of standard tribute-payments on which the Bosporines were now three months in arrears. When he saw at the feast Mazaia, a tall and beautiful girl, he conceived a passion for her and was in a bad way. The tribute business had already been dealt with, the king was paying what was due, entertaining him to a feast and already giving him a send off. Now, in Bosporus it's the custom for suitors to ask at the feast for the girls they wish to marry and to declare the status they have to claim acceptability for the marriage. What's more, it happened that there were many suitors there at the feast, kings and kings' sons, including Tigrapates, the king of the Lazi, Adyrmachus, the ruler of Machlyene, and many more. Each suitor must first declare his intention to woo, then sit down quietly and dine with the others. At the end of the feast, he must ask for a wine bowl,

pour a libation over the table and ask for the girl's hand in marriage, giving in the process an encomium on the breeding, wealth or power he might possess.

Now, there were many individuals who poured the customary libations and made their bids, enumerating their positions of power and the extent of their wealth. Arsacomas was the last to ask for the wine bowl. He didn't make a libation, because it's not our custom to pour wine away: we think this is a wanton act of disrespect towards the god. Instead, he drank it in one go and said, 'Give me your daughter Mazaia to have as my wife, King Leucanor. I'm much more suitable than these men, at any rate when it comes to the extent of my wealth and possessions.' The king was taken aback. He knew that Arsacomas was poor and was from the ordinary class of Scythians. So he asked him, 'How many cattle or wagons do you have, Arsacomas, since this is what you Scythians count as wealth?' Arsacomas replied, 'I have no wagons or herds of cattle. My wealth lies in two fine, brave friends the like of whom no other Scythian has.'

What he said caused laughter at the time. He was ignored, in the belief that he was the worse for drink. Next morning, Adyrmachus was chosen ahead of the rest and made plans to take his bride off to the Machlyans along the shore of Maeotis. Arsacomas went home and told his friends how he'd been dishonoured by the king and laughed at during the banquet because they thought he was poor. 'And yet,' he said, 'I told them what great wealth I had in you, Lonchates and Macentes, and of your affection, which is much superior to and firmer than the power of the people of Bosporus. As I related this, he derided and despised us, and allowed Adyrmachus the Machlyan to take the bride away, just because he was rumoured to possess ten golden wine bowls, eighty four-berth wagons and hordes of sheep and cattle. This then was the way he set above brave men the possession of herds of cattle, elaborate drinking-vessels and heavy wagons. Now, my friends, I'm upset for two reasons. I'm in love with Mazaia, for one thing. And, for another, the gross insult[66] Leucanor perpetrated before so many men has touched me to the quick.

45

46

My feeling is that you've been wronged as well. A third of the dishonour done to me belongs to each of you, at any rate if we're still living the way we have since coming together, that is as one man with the same troubles and the same joys.' 'It's not just a third,' pronounced Lonchates. 'Each of us was wholly insulted when you had these things done to you.'

47   'Well,' said Macentes, 'what are we going to do now?' 'Let's divide the job between us,' said Lonchates. 'I guarantee Arsacomas that I'll bring him Leucanor's head, and you must return his bride to him.' 'Let's do it that way, then,' replied Macentes. 'In the mean time, Arsacomas, since it's reasonable to suppose we'll need to gather an army and fight a war afterwards, you wait for us here, get together weapons and enlist cavalry and as many other forces as you can muster. It should be very easy for you to get together a great number, since you're brave yourself and we've a lot of relatives. But you'll have most success if you sit on the oxhide.' This was agreed. Lonchates went towards Bosporus just as he was, and Macentes to the Machlyans, both on horseback. Arsacomas stayed at home, spoke to his comrades and got an armed force together from among his relatives. Finally, he also sat upon the hide.

48   Our custom in relation to the hide is as follows. When a man has been wronged by another and wants to hit back, but realizes that he can't win the battle by himself, he sacrifices a bull, then he cuts the flesh into pieces and boils it, then spreads out the hide on the ground and sits on it, putting his hands behind his back like a prisoner with his arms bound. Among us, this is the most powerful way of making a supplication. The bull's flesh is set down next to the hide. People – including relatives and anyone else who wants to – come up, each take a piece of meat, step onto the hide with their right foot and promise help according to their ability, one man saying that he'll give five horsemen without asking for food or pay, another that he'll send ten, another more, another as many hoplites[67] or light-armed infantrymen as he can and, the poorest, just himself. Sometimes a very large force is assembled 'on the hide' and this sort of army is certain to hold together

and prove irresistible to its enemies precisely because it's under oath. You see, stepping on the hide is actually an oath.

So this was what Arsacomas was doing. He raised a force of around five thousand cavalry and twenty thousand hoplites and light-armed infantry.

Lonchates got to Bosporus unrecognized. He approached 49 the king as he was conducting some state business and said he'd come from the Scythian people, but was bringing some important private news also. Leucanor told him to speak and Lonchates said, 'The Scythians have the usual request to make, namely that your herdsmen should not cross the plain but only pasture their flocks as far as the rocky ground. In respect of the brigands you accuse of overrunning your country, the Scythians deny that they're being sent because of a public policy. They're marauding individually for private gain and if you catch any of them you're at liberty to punish them.

'This is what they've instructed me to say. But my own 50 news is that a great expedition against you is on the point of being sent by Arsacomas, the son of Mariantes, who came here a little while ago on an embassy. I think it's because he asked for your daughter's hand and was refused that he became angry. He's been sitting on the hide for seven days now and has gathered a large force.'

'I'd heard myself,' said Leucanor, 'that an army was being gathered from the hide. But I didn't know that it was being put together to attack us and that Arsacomas was the driving force behind it.' Lonchates replied, 'Well, the preparations are intended against you. But Arsacomas is my enemy. He's irked by the fact that the elders hold me in higher honour than him and that I'm more highly regarded in all respects. If you promise your other daughter Barcetis to me in marriage, though, since I'm in any case not unworthy of you, I shall soon return bringing you his head.' 'You have my promise,' said the king, who'd become very frightened. He acknowledged that the matter of the marriage had given Arsacomas cause for his anger and in general he was always very timorous before the Scythians.

Lonchates said, 'Solemnly swear that you'll keep our pact, and that you'll not renege on it when this has been done.' But when the king raised his hands up to heaven with the intention of making the oath Lonchates said, 'Not here, in case one of the bystanders suspects what we're swearing an oath about. Let's go into the temple of Ares here, shut the doors and make the oath so that no one can hear us. If Arsacomas got to know any of this, I'm afraid he would have me sacrificed as a pre-war offering, given that he's already managed to gather a large force.' 'Let's go in, then,' said the king. 'You others, stay as far away as possible. No one should enter the temple unless I summon him.'

They entered the temple and the guards stood down. Lonchates drew his dagger, covered the king's mouth with the other hand to stop him shouting and struck him in the chest. Then he cut off his head and went out with it beneath his cloak, apparently still in the middle of a conversation with the king and telling him that he'd come back soon, as though he'd been sent on some errand by him. This way he arrived at the place where he'd left his horse tied up, mounted up and rode off back to Scythia. There was no pursuit, because the Bosporines knew nothing of what had happened for a long time. When they did find out, they became embroiled in a civil war over the kingship.

51 This was what Lonchates did. He kept his promise to Arsacomas by handing over Leucanor's head. Macentes had heard the news of events in Bosporus as he was on his way and when he came to the Machlyans his first act was to report the murder of the king. 'Adyrmachus,' he said, 'as you're the king's son-in-law, the city is summoning you to be king. So you should go on ahead and take over power, making your appearance while things are in a state of confusion, but the maiden should follow behind in the wagon train. This way, you'll find it easier to bring over to your side the majority of the Bosporines, if they have sight of Leucanor's daughter. As for me, I'm an Alan and a relation of this girl on her mother's side. It was from us that Masteira came, the woman Leucanor married. Now I've come here from Masteira's brothers in

Alania. Their advice is for you to proceed as quickly as possible to Bosporus and not allow the kingdom to fall into the hands of Eubiotus. He's the illegitimate brother of Leucanor and is a constant friend of the Scythians, but an enemy of the Alans.'

This was what Macentes said. He was dressed like an Alan, and spoke the Alan language. These things are in fact common to Alans and Scythians, except that the Alans don't wear their hair as long as the Scythians. However, Macentes had imitated the Alans in this aspect of his appearance as well and had had his hair cut as much shorter as you'd expect an Alan to wear it than a Scythian. Consequently, these things gave him credence and people thought he was a relative of Masteira and Mazaia.

'Now, Adyrmachus,' said Macentes, 'I'm ready to travel   52 with you to Bosporus, if you wish, or to stay, if it's necessary, and conduct the girl.' 'The latter is what I'd much prefer,' said Adyrmachus, 'that is for you to conduct Mazaia, since you're a blood relation. If you came with me to Bosporus, we'd only be one horseman the more. But if you were to conduct my wife, you'd be worth a whole troop.'

So this is what happened. Adyrmachus drove off, after handing Mazaia over to Macentes to bring. And she was still a virgin. During that day, he conveyed her on the wagon. But when night fell, he put her on horseback (he'd made arrangements beforehand for another horseman to follow him), leapt onto his own horse and no longer pursued his course along the Maeotis, but turned off into the inland areas keeping the Mitraean mountains on his right. He gave the girl a rest now and then, and reached Scythia from the territory of the Machlyans on the third day. When his horse stopped running, it stood for a few moments, then died. Macentes   53 handed Mazaia over to Arsacomas, saying, 'Now you have what I promised you as well.'

Arsacomas was astonished by the unexpectedness of the sight and had begun offering his thanks, when Macentes said, 'Stop making me into someone different from yourself. To thank me for what I've done is like someone's left hand thanking his right for looking after it when it was wounded and taking care of it in a kind way while it was injured. We'd also be doing something ridiculous if after being joined together for so long and having as far as possible become one person we still considered it a major event if part of us did something good on behalf of the whole body. He does it for himself, because he's part of the whole which is being benefited.'

54   This is what Macentes said to Arsacomas when he thanked him. Adyrmachus, however, when he heard of the plot, didn't continue towards Bosporus, because Eubiotus was already in power. He'd been summoned home from among the Sauromatai, where he'd been spending his time. Instead, Adyrmachus returned home, mustered a large army and invaded Scythia through the mountains. It wasn't long before Eubiotus also attacked, leading in full force his Greeks, and twenty thousand each of Alans and Sauromatai whom he'd called up. Eubiotus and Adyrmachus joined forces, making in all an army ninety thousand strong, a third of them mounted archers.

Our side (I say this because I was myself[68] a member of their expedition, having contributed at that time 'on the hide' a hundred self-supporting cavalry) awaited their attack gathered together in a body in numbers not many fewer than thirty thousand, cavalry included. Our general was Arsacomas. When we saw them approaching, we advanced against them, sending in the cavalry as a vanguard. There followed a fierce battle which lasted a long time. Eventually our side began to give ground. The phalanx[69] had been broken and in the end the whole Scythian contingent had been split in two. One part was gradually retiring. It hadn't suffered a clear defeat and was withdrawing rather than fleeing, and the Alans didn't dare to pursue it for long. The smaller part, however, was surrounded by Alans and Machlyans, who were cutting it to pieces by firing unending volleys of arrows and javelins from all directions. Consequently, those of our men who were surrounded were in great distress and many had already thrown down their weapons.

55   It happened that Lonchates and Macentes were in this

group. They'd already sustained wounds by putting themselves into the danger zone of the front line. Lonchates had been hit in the thigh by the bottom spike of a spear,[70] while Macentes had sustained a head wound from an axe and a shoulder wound from a pike. Arsacomas was in our group, but he'd seen all this. Considering it would be a dreadful thing if he went off and left his friends behind, he spurred his horse, gave a great shout and drove through the enemy ranks with raised scimitar. The Machlyans didn't even attempt to stand up to the surge of his spirit. Instead, they parted and allowed him to get through.

Once he'd regained his friends, he encouraged all the rest and made a rush at Adyrmachus. He struck him with his scimitar by the neck and split him in two as far as his belt. When he'd fallen, the whole Machlyan army broke up, and that of the Alans soon afterwards, followed by the Greeks. The upshot was that we were on top once more and we'd have carried on killing for a long time if night hadn't stolen our opportunity.

Next day ambassadors came as suppliants from our enemies begging us to make friends with them. The Bosporines promised to pay double their current tribute, the Machlyans said they'd give hostages, and the Alans undertook as restitution for their invasion the subjugation to our power of the Sindiani (who'd been in revolt for a long time). These conditions persuaded us, though Arsacomas and Lonchates were by far the first to be consulted and peace was concluded with them as negotiators of the detailed arrangements.

This is the sort of boldness of action Scythians undertake for their friends, Mnesippus.

MNESIPPUS: It's a highly tragic tale, Toxaris, which smacks of   56
fable.[71] I pray that Dagger and Wind, the gods you swore by,
mayn't take it amiss. At any rate, no one could really blame
a person for not believing the story.

TOXARIS: My noble friend, you should make sure that your
disbelief isn't jealousy. Anyway, your scepticism is not going
to deter me from relating other stories like this of deeds I
know done by Scythians.

MNESIPPUS: Well make them brief, my friend, and don't employ such a prolix narrative technique. As things stand, with all this running up and down through Scythia and Machlyene, and back and forth to Bosporus, you've completely used up my silence.

57 TOXARIS: I suppose I'm going to have to obey this new law of yours and speak briefly, in case I exhaust you with these aural peregrinations. Listen instead now to the service my friend Sisinnes did for me personally.

When I was on my way from home to Athens, out of enthusiasm for Greek culture,[72] I put into Amastris on the Black Sea. The city isn't far from Carambis, and is right on the route for people sailing from Scythia. I was accompanied by my childhood friend Sisinnes. We'd found lodgings at the harbour, transferred our belongings there from the ship and were out shopping at the market, not suspecting that anything bad might happen. While we were out, though, thieves forced the lock on our door and stole everything, not leaving us even enough to last out the day.

When we returned home and found out what had happened, we decided it wasn't a good idea to take out a case against the many neighbours or the landlord. We were afraid that most people would think we were *sykophantai*[73] when we claimed that someone had stolen four hundred darics,[74] a lot of clothing and rugs, and everything else we possessed.

58 Instead we considered what to do about our situation, now that we were completely without means in a foreign country. My view was that there and then I should stick my dagger between my ribs and leave this life before I was forced to an ignoble end by hunger or thirst. But Sisinnes comforted me and persuaded me not to do anything of the sort, since he had a good idea where we could get enough to live on.

For the time being, he worked at the harbour, carrying wood, and came home with food he'd bought for us from his wages. The next morning, as he was walking round the market-place, he told me, he saw a procession of fine, good-looking young men. They'd been enlisted to fight in single combat for pay and would be contesting in the arena[75] in

three days time. When he had found out how everything stood
with them, Sisinnes came to me and said, 'Don't call yourself
a pauper any more. In three days time I'll be making you a
rich man.'

This was what he said. We survived with difficulty in the   59
mean time, but on the day of the show we too went to watch.
Sisinnes actually took me along to the theatre on the pretext
that we were going to enjoy a strange Greek spectacle.[76] We
sat down and watched first of all wild beasts being attacked
with javelins, hunted by hounds and set on men who were
tied up (we reckoned they must be criminals). When the
gladiators came in, a herald led forward a huge young man
and announced that anyone who wanted to fight against him
should come into the middle of the arena.[77] The payment for
the contest would be ten thousand drachmas. At this moment,
Sisinnes stood up, leapt down into the arena, engaged to fight
and asked for his weapons. He received his payment of ten
thousand drachmas, brought it over to me and put it in my
hands, saying, 'If I win, Toxaris, we'll go off on our journey
with enough to live on. If I die, bury me and go back to
Scythia.'

My response to this was to begin lamenting. But he took   60
up his arms and put them all on, except the helmet. He stood
and fought with his head bare. He was the first to be wounded.
His opponent's curved sword cut his hamstring and caused a
stream of blood to flow. I was already dead from fright.
However, Sisinnes waited for his adversary to make a rather
audacious assault and struck him in the chest. The weapon
went right through and the man immediately fell down at his
feet. Sisinnes sat down on the corpse, weary from his own
wound and almost gave up the ghost. I ran over to him, lifted
him to his feet and offered words of encouragement. He was
declared the victor and allowed to leave. I picked him up and
carried him back to the house. After a long convalescence
he recovered and is still in Scythia. He married my sister.
However, he still limps because of the wound.

Now, this didn't happen among the Machlyans or in
Alania, Mnesippus, giving you the chance to be sceptical

because there are no witnesses. There are plenty of citizens from Amastris around who remember the Sisinnes fight.

61   I'm going to tell you one more story, my fifth, and then stop. It concerns what Abauchas did. This Abauchas arrived one day at the city of the Borysthenites. He brought with him his wife, whom he loved very much, and their two children. One was a boy, still at the breast, and the other was a seven-year-old girl. With him on this foreign journey was his friend Gandanes. Gandanes was unwell as a result of a wound he'd sustained along the road when brigands had attacked their party. He'd put up a brave resistance against them, but had been struck in the thigh, so that he couldn't even stand, because of the pain. Now, their lodging was in an attic room. While they were asleep one night, a huge fire started, all exits were cut off and flames surrounded the house on all sides. At this point, Abauchas awoke. He abandoned his weeping children, shook off his wife as she clung to him and begged him to save her, picked up his friend and managed to burst out through a place not yet completely consumed by the fire. His wife followed, carrying the infant, and told the little girl to come with her. But she was already badly burnt and barely managed to jump through the flames after letting the baby fall from her arms. The little girl managed to get through with her, though she also came very close to death. Later on, someone criticized Abauchas for having abandoned his children and his wife and carrying Gandanes out of the fire. His reply was, 'It'll be easy for me to have more children in the future. In any case, it's unclear whether they'll turn out well. But I couldn't find another friend like Gandanes if I searched for a very long time. He's given me many proofs of his affection.'[78]

62   I've finished, Mnesippus. These are the five I've chosen from many possibilities. Now it's time for us to have the decision made as to which of us has to have his tongue cut out or right hand cut off. Who's going to judge?

MNESIPPUS: No one. We didn't set anyone up to judge our discussion. But do you know what we'll do? Since we've fired our arrows just now without a target, let's choose an arbitrator another time and relate some stories of different friends in front of him. Then the loser can have his amputation performed, either my tongue or your right hand. No, that would be too crude. Since you've chosen to praise friendship and I myself consider human beings can have no better or finer possession than this, why don't we also make an agreement to be friends with each other from now on and for ever? Let's be content to share the victory, taking with us the greatest prize of all, that's to say, that each of us has acquired in place of one tongue and one right hand two of each, and also four eyes, and four feet, and in fact double everything. The sort of thing that happens when two or three friends combine their resources is analogous to the way painters portray Geryon as a six-handed, three-headed man. In my opinion, Geryon was three men acting in concert in everything, as friends ought to.

TOXARIS: Well said. Let's do as you say.   63

MNESIPPUS: However, Toxaris, let's not call in the blood or the dagger to confirm our friendship. The current discussion and the shared goals we have are a much more reliable basis for trust than that cup you Scythians drink. In my view, friendship is a matter of conviction, not compulsion.

TOXARIS: I approve of what you say. Let us be friends from this moment and hosts[79] too, you for me here in Greece and I for you if you ever come to Scythia.

MNESIPPUS: You can rest assured, Toxaris, that I'd go even further than that if it meant I'd encounter friends such as you have proved yourself to me to be from your stories.[80]

THE ART OF THE EULOGY

Preface

This section focuses on the genre of encomium, bringing together five diverse pieces of eulogy – or apparent eulogy. *An Encomium of Fatherland* is a highly conventional rhetorical piece which exemplifies the genre in its straightforward use. It is most unlike Lucian to toe the line so completely.[1] There is no hint of irony, the literary references lack any suggestion of a subtext which runs counter to the surface (see below on *Images* for a different approach), and the language and rhetorical decoration are quite plain (contrast the use of *ekphrasis* and imagery from drama and dramatic criticism in *Slander*). If it is genuine, then it belongs with rhetorical exercises like *The Tyrannicide* and *Disowned* (though the latter have the merit of presenting clever arguments rooted in bizarre circumstances and being written in a lively style).[2] In any event, it provides a neat introduction to the more normal Lucianic flavour of the other pieces. *Praising a Fly* and *About the Parasite* are both 'paradoxical encomia', that is, pieces which take as their subject things which are not generally thought worthy of praise.[3] *Praising a Fly* is a brief piece, which elegantly presents the fly's case with a panoply of literary reference. *About the Parasite*, on the other hand, is in the form of a full-blown Platonic dialogue, which uses Socratic dialectic (ironically) to prove that 'parasitic' is not merely an art, but the best of all of the arts. *Praising a Fly* is thus less ambitious than *About the Parasite*, and it may belong to that small body of writing which predates Lucian's fortieth year or so (see Introduction, section 2). In *About the Parasite*, there is more than a hint of a subtext not merely adverting to the possibility of perverting dialectic, but even critical of the notion that dialectic is in any sense the way to approach philosophical problems and truth. Demonax, at any rate (see *Demonax the Philosopher*), though he uses argument and wit to articulate his ethical values, never employs the Socratic method, and the later development of this into the conundrums of the Stoics is often satirized elsewhere in Lucian (e.g. *Philosophies for Sale* 21f.), while there is continual stress on the straightforwardness of the best life (that of the ordinary man: see the conclusion of *Menippus*) versus the impossibility of choice between the dogmas of the philosophical schools (see *Hermotimus*). The link with *Hermotimus* also suggests a date after Lucian's fortieth year or so (see again Introduction, section 2).

Images and *In Defence of 'Images'* relate to the sojourn in Antioch of Marcus Aurelius' co-emperor Lucius Verus (reigned AD 161–9) and so cannot predate his arrival there in 163, while the fact that he seems to be mentioned as living gives a probable terminus of 169. This pair of dialogues centres around the figure of a real person, Panthea, the mistress of Lucius Verus. In the first, Lycinus is induced by his friend to create a portrait (in words) of the beautiful woman he has seen. He does this by borrowing features from well-known ancient statues and paintings. His friend, who recognizes her from the description, completes the portrait by describing and praising the woman's non-physical attributes, again with copious use of classical exemplars. In the second, the friend returns from offering their book to Panthea with a list of criticisms, which Lycinus then rebuts. Like *The Ship*, these are dialogues with Lycinus (= Lucian?) as main interlocutor. However, here he is anything but the cynical spoiler we see elsewhere. Modern readers put this change of heart down to Lucian's attempts to get into Verus' circle.[4] However, what we know of the contemporary view of Panthea's relationship with Verus does not require us to believe that people accepted it uncritically or that Panthea was really that *rarissima avis* in the period, a well-educated woman.[5] In fact, the pattern of literary references creates a subtext which for Lucian's learned audience would have cut right across the generic stance (eulogy). For example, the method by which Panthea's image is created (and her name) recalls Hesiod's Pan-

dora, fount of all ills for men;[6] Polystratus insists that if Lycinus
heard Panthea sing he would think he heard the Sirens, everywhere in late antiquity interpreted as the temptation of lust; and
the Xenophontic parallel for Verus' mistress, Panthea the wife
of Abradatas, turns out to be a moral counter-example to this
Panthea, because the Persian king Cyrus did not have a liaison
with her, but instead kept her chaste for her husband and thus
gained an indomitable ally by his moral actions. There is a case,
then, for reading *Images* and *In Defence of 'Images'* as ironical
works, which interact with an atmosphere in Syria which was
highly critical of Verus' liaison. Only the truly educated, however, who could spot the literary allusions and understand them
correctly, would have been able to see past the generic surface
statement. These would, naturally, not have included Panthea,
while a simple defence in the face of Lucius Verus would have
been the claim that they really were eulogies.[7]

NOTES

1. Contrast the way Favorinus of Arles, in his treatise *On Exile* (a
   fragment of which survives), uses that theme to redefine the
   whole notion of 'fatherland'. See Whitmarsh 2001a, 302–24 for
   a translation.

2. In *The Tyrannicide*, a man has killed a tyrant's son, leaving the
   tyrant so distraught that he kills himself with the killer's sword:
   the killer now claims the prize for tyrant-slaying. In *Disowned*, a
   son disowned by his father studies medicine and then cures his
   father of madness. When asked to cure his stepmother of madness,
   he refuses and is disinherited again by his father. He argues
   against this second decision. This theme is found in the *Contro-
   versies* (4.5) of Seneca the Elder (c. 55 BC–between AD 37 and
   41). Also 'rhetorical' in this ironical manner are the two *Phalaris*
   pieces, where the tyrant of Acragas, who was said to have tortured
   people by putting them inside a bronze bull which was then heated
   over a fire, defends himself and has his defence upheld by a neutral
   listener.

3. Compare the *Praise of Hair*, *Praise of the Gnat* and *Praise of the
   Parrot* of the sophist Dio Chrysostom (c. AD 40–after 111). Only
   the first of these is extant, embedded in the *Praise of Baldness* of

the fourth- to fifth-century writer Synesius. See the Loeb Classical
Library edition of Dio, vol. 5, 332–43.

4.   See Jones 1986, 75–7.
5.   External sources are *Historia Augusta*, *Verus* 7.10 and Marcus
     Aurelius, *Meditations* 8.37. For educated women, see Swain
     1996, 64, n. 75.
6.   For Pandora, see Korus 1981.
7.   See further Sidwell 2002. Goldhill 2001b, 184–93 offers a rather
     different reading of these texts.

AN ENCOMIUM OF
FATHERLAND[1]

The news has been spread abroad long since that 'there is 1
nothing sweeter than one's fatherland'.[2] Can it be that nothing
is more pleasant, but that there is some other thing which is
more majestic and divine? Yet it is their fatherland that is
responsible for teaching men about everything they think majestic and divine, since it begets, nurtures and educates them. Many
admire cities[3] for their vast size, their fame and their priceless
possessions, but everyone loves his fatherland. And no one even
of those who have succumbed completely to the pleasures of
sightseeing has ever been taken in so much as to allow the
excessive wonders to be found elsewhere to make him forget his
fatherland.

The man who gives himself airs because he is a citizen of a 2
wealthy city seems to me to be unaware of the honour he ought
to give to his fatherland. I think such a person would be upset
if a less well-off place had been allotted to him. The more
welcome course seems to me to be to give honour to the very
word 'fatherland'. The reason is this. If you try to compare
cities, you have to find out their size, their beauty and the
abundance of the goods they have on sale. Yet wherever people
can choose, no one would pick a more famous city and let go of
his fatherland. He might pray for his fatherland to be put on
equal terms with the rich ones, but he would still choose it
whatever state it was in.

This is exactly what right-minded children and good fathers 3
do. An upstanding young man would not give anyone more
respect than his own father, and a father would not neglect his
son and give his affection to another youngster. In fact, so

overcome are fathers by their natural affections that they ascribe to their sons all the superlatives – best-looking, biggest, most accomplished in everything. The man who does not make such a judgement about his son does not seem to me to have a father's eyes.

4   In the first place, then, the word 'fatherland' is the closest to home of all. For there is nothing closer to home than a father. And if a man apportions the appropriate respect to his father (as custom and nature require), then it would be proper for him to give his fatherland preference. For his father is himself a belonging of the fatherland, as are his father's father and all those related to them in previous generations. Moreover, the name proceeds in its ascent right up to the gods of one's fathers.

5   For the gods also take pleasure in fatherlands and although seemingly they watch over all the deeds of mankind, considering the whole earth and sea their possession, none the less each of them gives preference before all other cities to the one where he was born. Cities are the more majestic for being the fatherland of a god and islands are more divine when they are celebrated in song for the birth of divinities.[4] At any rate, people consider that the gods are especially gratified by those rituals which are celebrated on their home territories. And if the word 'fatherland' is honoured by the gods, how can it not be honoured even more by men?

6   Every human being first saw the sun from his fatherland. Consequently, even though he is a god shared by all, none the less everyone reckons him a deity belonging to his forefathers because he had his first sight of him from that place. This was also the place where he began to speak, learning to chatter in the local tongue, and first learned about the gods. Even if a person has drawn as his lot the kind of fatherland which leaves him needing another to complete his higher education, he still ought to be grateful to his fatherland for this training. For he would not have even known the word 'city' if he had not learned it because he had a fatherland.

7   In my opinion, all information on any subject which is collected is brought together by men because they aim to make themselves more useful to their fatherland. What's more, their

acquisition of money is also a result of their competitive desire
to spend it upon projects which benefit the community of their
fatherland. I think that's what you might expect. People who
have gained the greatest benefits must show gratitude to their
benefactors. And if, as is only just, whenever anyone has done
us a good deed, we show gratitude for such benefits to the
individuals involved, we are much more obliged to repay our
fatherland in due measure. There are, after all, laws in the cities
against mistreatment of one's parents.[5] We should regard our
fatherland as the common mother of us all and repay her for
the gift of upbringing and our knowledge of the laws themselves.

The man has never been seen who is so unmindful of his   8
fatherland that he does not care about it when living in another
city. Those who are doing badly during their foreign sojourns
continually proclaim that their fatherland is the greatest good
of all. Those who are doing well, even if successful in other
respects, none the less consider that the biggest disadvantage is
not living in their fatherland, but in exile from it.[6] Being domi-
ciled abroad is a matter for reproach. People who have become
famous during their time abroad, either through their acquisition of wealth or a great reputation, through demonstrating
their education or by being praised for bravery, one can see all
hurrying back: they can't think of a better place to show off
their finery. And a man's enthusiasm for regaining his fatherland
is in direct proportion to the size of his reputation among others.

Young people too long for their fatherland. But the extent   9
to which wisdom increases when men have reached old age
compared to their youth matches the increase in longing for the
fatherland in the elderly. Every old person wishes and prays to
end his life in his fatherland: his aim is for his body to be set
down once more in the soil which nourished him and where he
began life, and to have its common share in the funeral rites of
his forefathers. Everyone thinks it a dreadful thing to be convicted of being an alien[7] even after death, lying in the grave in
some foreign land.

The amount of benevolence that the truly legitimate citizen   10
has towards his fatherland can be judged from the autochthonous races. Mere incomers are like illegitimate children – they

change homes easily, neither knowing nor having affection for the word 'fatherland'. They reckon they will find all the necessities of life anywhere, and set as their measure for contentedness the pleasures of the belly. But those who regard their fatherland as a mother, love the land on which they were born and reared, even if what they have is small, rough and thin soiled.[8] Even if they are unable to praise the goodness of the soil, they will find no shortage of encomia to utter over their fatherland. If they see others preening themselves on open plains and meadows distinguished by all sorts of plants, they too do not forget how to praise their fatherland: they pass over its horse-breeding potential and concentrate on praising its potential for child-rearing.[9]

11   A man hastens to his fatherland, even though he be an islander, well able to live the good life among others. Offered immortality, he will not accept it, preferring a tomb in his fatherland. Even the smoke from his fatherland seems brighter to him than fire elsewhere.[10]

12   The high value placed by everyone on his fatherland can be judged by the observation that lawgivers everywhere have imposed exile as the most severe penalty for the greatest crimes. And it is not that lawgivers are a special case, and the commanders of armies think differently. No, the greatest encouragement that can be given to the troops drawn up for battle is this – that the war is being fought for their fatherland. No one who heard this appeal would wish to be found wanting. What makes even the coward brave is the word 'fatherland'.

PRAISING A FLY

The fly isn't the smallest of the winged creatures, when you [1] compare her,[1] say, with gnats and mosquitoes and the even tinier bugs. In fact, the fly is about as much bigger than those creatures as she is smaller than the bee. She doesn't have the same sort of feathers as the other winged creatures, some of which have bodies covered all over with them, while others have quill-feathers. She's parchment-winged, like locusts, grass-hoppers and bees, but her wings are as much finer than theirs as Indian cloth[2] is thinner and softer than Greek. What's more, anyone who takes a close look at one when she spreads out her wings and flutters them in the sunlight will see that they are decorated like the peacock's.

Her flight isn't like that of bats, with a constant oar-like [2] movement of the wings, nor is it like that of locusts, with a leap, nor with a whirr like that of wasps, but with a graceful curve to whatever part of the air she has set her sights upon. She has another quality also, not flying in silence, but accompanied by a melodic sound, not a harsh noise like that of mosquitoes and gnats, nor the deep buzz of the bee or the terrifying threat of the wasp. There is the same qualitative difference in the sweet clarity of her song as there is between the reed pipes[3] on the one hand and trumpets or cymbals on the other.

Let me turn to the rest of her body. The head has a very [3] slender connection with the neck and easily turns round. It is not of one piece with the body, like that of locusts. The eyes are prominent and have a very horn-like surface. The upper body is compact and the feet are directly attached to the waist,[4] which is not narrow like that of the wasp. The belly is armoured, and looks like a cuirass, with broad bands and scales. But her defence system is not at the rear, like that of the wasp and the bee. She uses instead her mouth and proboscis. With the latter, which she has in common with the elephant, she forages, takes hold of her prey and keeps a grip by hanging on to it with a tip which resembles a sucker. From the proboscis there protrudes a tooth with which she pricks the skin to drink blood. I should add that she drinks milk as well, but likes the taste of blood too, and does not hurt her victims unduly when she bites. She has six feet; she walks with four only, while the front pair she actually uses like hands. If you wish, you can observe her walking on four legs and holding a piece of food up in her two hands, very much in the way we human beings do.

4   She is not born this way from the start, but in fact emerges first as a grub from the dead bodies of human beings or other animals. Then after a while she puts forth feet and grows wings and changes from a creeping thing to a winged creature, becomes pregnant and bears the larva which will soon afterwards become a fly. The fly is brought up with man, and as his companion and his table-mate will taste everything, except olive oil. If she drinks that, it means certain death. However, as she is fated to die early[5] (for her life has been measured out into a comparatively short span), she loves the daylight most of all and does her citizen duties during that time. At night, she stays at peace, doesn't fly or sing, but goes to ground and keeps still.

5   I can tell you that she displays no mean intelligence in escaping from the enemy which preys on her – the spider. She watches carefully for ambushes and keeps an eye focused on the spider as she takes evasive action so as not to be netted and caught after falling into the creature's web. As for her courage and prowess, it is not my part to mention them. We can leave it to the most grandiloquent of the poets, Homer. When he wishes to praise the greatest of the heroes he doesn't compare his prowess to that of a lion or a leopard or a wild boar, but to the courage of the fly and her fearlessly persistent style of attack.[6] The reason is that it isn't bravado but bravery[7] that he ascribes to her. And this is because, even when she is fended off, she doesn't let up, but goes for the bite.[8] Homer has such great

praise and affection for the fly that he mentions her not once, nor even just a few times, but often. So much does her mention enhance his verses. In one place, he will narrate her gregarious flight towards the milk.[9] In another, when Athena diverts the arrow aimed at Menelaus so that it doesn't reach his vital organs, he likens her to a mother taking care of her sleeping child and once more introduces the fly into his simile.[10] He even adorned them with a very beautiful epithet, calling them 'thronging', and using for a swarm of them the word 'tribes'.[11]

The fly is so strong that her bite can penetrate not only the skin of a human being, but also that of cattle or horses. She can even bother an elephant by getting down into its wrinkles and inflicting with her own proboscis a sting proportionate to her size. The fly enjoys a great deal of freedom in the realm of Aphrodite – marriage and copulation. The male moreover does not behave like the cockerel, mounting the female only to leap away at once, but rides the female for a long time. The female carries her mate and they soar aloft in that well-known display of aerial intercourse which is not spoilt by the fact that they are flying. When a fly has her head cut off, she will continue to live and breathe for a long time with the rest of her body.

Now I want to tell you about the greatest natural asset flies possess. And it's the only example of the phenomenon which Plato seems to have overlooked in his discussion of the immortality of the soul.[12] When a fly dies, if you pour ashes over her, she will get up again, experience rebirth and have another lifespan right from the beginning. This example should completely convince everyone that the fly's soul is also immortal, since it can go off and return again, recognize and resuscitate the body it left and make the fly airborne again. It also confirms the truth of the story about Hermotimus of Clazomenae. They say his soul often left him and went off on trips by itself, then came back and reoccupied his body and raised Hermotimus from the dead.

The fly is an idle beast who does not labour, but lives off the fruits of others' toil and always has a full table wherever she goes. Goats are milked for her benefit, and the bee does its work no less for flies than for humans. Cooks sweeten their dishes for her, and it is she who tastes food even ahead of kings, trampling round their tables, joining in their feasts and enjoying everything.

9 She does not set up a nest or a lair in one place. She has entered upon a pattern of flight which is nomadic, like that of the Scythians,[13] and she makes her hearth and bed wherever nightfall happens to overtake her. But, as I said, she does nothing during the darkness and does not think she can get away with doing something then, nor does she think of committing any bad deed which would bring disgrace in its wake were it performed in daylight.[14]

10 Legend tells us too that there was once upon a time a human called Muia,[15] a very pretty girl, but a chatterbox, forever babbling and singing. She was Selene's rival for the affections of Endymion. Then, when she kept on disturbing the boy's sleep with banter and songs and revelry, Endymion got upset, and Selene in anger changed Muia into this creature. It is for this reason that she even now begrudges sleepers their rest, especially those who are young and tender, because she still remembers Endymion. And the fly's actual bite and her blood-quaffing are a sign not of her savagery but of her passion and her love of humanity. As far as she can, she enjoys plucking some of the flowers of beauty.

11 The ancients also report the existence of two women of the same name, the one a poetess,[16] of great beauty and wisdom, the other a well-known courtesan[17] among the Athenians. The comic poet said of her:

> Muia stung him to the heart.[18]

So the charm of comedy did not spurn or shut out from the stage the name of the fly. And parents have found no shame in calling their daughters by this name. But tragedy also mentions the fly with great praise, for example in these verses:

> 'Tis strange indeed that flies with strenuous might
> Leap on men's bodies, to take their fill of gore,
> But hoplite soldiers fear the hostile lance.[19]

I might also have been able to say a great deal about Muia the Pythagorean,[20] if her story were not well known to everyone.

There exist also some enormous flies, called by most people 12 'soldier flies', but by others 'dog flies'. They make a very rough buzzing noise and are exceptionally fast in flight. They are also very long-lived and survive the whole winter long with no food, snuggling down especially under roofs. Another remarkable thing about them is that they perform the sexual duties of both male and female, riding and being ridden in the manner of the child of Hermes and Aphrodite,[21] who was of mixed sex and had both male and female beauty. I still have a great deal to say. But I will bring my discourse to an end at this point. After all, I don't want you to think I'm making the proverbial elephant out of a fly!

IMAGES[1]

1   LYCINUS: Those who looked on the Gorgon's head must have had the sort of experience I've just undergone after spotting a really beautiful woman, Polystratus. It's just like what the story says, anyway, your friend has almost become a stone instead of a human being, solidified by amazement.

POLYSTRATUS: By Heracles, it must have been a pretty extraordinary sight and awfully powerful for a woman to have struck Lycinus. I know it's very easy for you to have such experiences when you see young men (in fact it would be easier to shift the whole of Mt. Sipylus than to stop you standing round good-looking boys with your mouth open and shedding a frequent tear in an excellent imitation of the daughter of Tantalus).[2] But tell me, who is this stone-turning Medusa and where is she from? I'd like to see her as well. I'm sure you won't begrudge us the view and be jealous about it, if we ourselves also are fated to be solidified alongside you when we get up close.

LYCINUS: Well, you ought to be aware that even if you only get a bird's-eye view of her, it'll leave you with your mouth open and with less mobility than a statue. And yet looking at her yourself is probably the more peaceable option and the wound you'll receive will be less likely to be lethal. But if she looks back at you, there'll be no way you'll be able to keep away from her. She'll have tied a line to you and lead you wherever she wants, the same way Heracles' stone[3] attracts iron.

2   POLYSTRATUS: Stop weaving fantasies of remarkable beauty, Lycinus, and tell me who the woman is.

LYCINUS: Oh, you think I'm exaggerating, do you, when I'm

afraid that if you see her you'll judge me a rather weak encomiast, so much superior will she seem to my description. Anyhow, I couldn't say who she is. However, she was the focus of much attention, and all the other paraphernalia around her was magnificent – a whole host of eunuchs and lots and lots of beautiful girls. All in all, I thought the whole arrangement smacked of something bigger than a private fortune could manage.

POLYSTRATUS: Didn't you even find out the woman's name?

LYCINUS: No. Well, only that she's Ionian. I found that out because one of the onlookers turned to his neighbour as she passed and said, 'Well, that's typical of the beauty you find in Smyrna. Anyway, it's no wonder that the most beautiful city in Ionia should have produced the most beautiful woman.' Actually, I reckoned the man who said this was from Smyrna himself, to judge from his pride in her.

POLYSTRATUS: All right, then, since you acted just like a stone 3 in not following the man from Smyrna and asking him who she was, tell me as best you can in words what she looks like. Maybe that way I might recognize her.

LYCINUS: Don't you see what an enormously large undertaking you've asked me to embark on? Words – and especially my words – can't represent such a remarkable image. Why, Apelles, Zeuxis or Parrhasius – or even Phidias and Alcamenes – would scarcely have seemed up to it. The weakness of my technique will only make me do damage to the original.

POLYSTRATUS: Nevertheless, Lycinus, tell me what her face was like. It's not a dangerous enterprise to show her image to a friend, whatever your drawing is like.

LYCINUS: Even so, I think the safer course will be for me to summon some of those famous ancient craftsmen to help me in the task of drawing the woman's portrait.

POLYSTRATUS: What do you mean? How on earth could they come to you when they've been dead for so many years?

LYCINUS: Easily, if you aren't afraid to answer a little question.

POLYSTRATUS: Ask away.

LYCINUS: Did you ever visit the city of the Cnidians, Polystratus? 4

POLYSTRATUS: Of course.

LYCINUS: So obviously you'll have seen their Aphrodite?

POLYSTRATUS: Yes indeed. It's Praxiteles' finest sculpture.

LYCINUS: No doubt you've also heard the story the locals tell about it, then. How a young man fell in love with the statue, managed to stay behind unnoticed in the temple and had intercourse with it – well, as far as it's possible with a statue.[4] Anyway, I merely mention this by the way. You've seen the Aphrodite. So now answer me this. Did you ever see the statue by Alcamenes in the gardens at Athens?[5]

POLYSTRATUS: Come now, Lycinus, I'd be the laziest man alive to have passed over the most beautiful of Alcamenes' creations.

LYCINUS: All right, then, I'm not going to ask you if in your many trips up onto the acropolis you've seen Calamis' Sosandra.

POLYSTRATUS: I've seen that many times as well.

LYCINUS: That's as much as I need. Now, which do you think is Phidias' finest work?

POLYSTRATUS: Well, it must be the Lemnian Athena. Phidias was proud enough of it to carve his name on the base. And, by Zeus, there's also the Amazon leaning on her spear.

5 LYCINUS: You're right, these are the finest. So we won't need any other artists. So, now, let me piece together a single image using all these as best I can, taking the bit I want from each of them.

POLYSTRATUS: How are you going to do that?

LYCINUS: It's easy, Polystratus. From now on we'll put our images in the hands of Discourse to rearrange, put together and fit as elegantly as possible, taking care to balance the variety with the need for consistency.

POLYSTRATUS: That's a good idea. Let Discourse, then, take them over and display them. I want to know how he'll use them to put together from so many a single consistent image.

6 LYCINUS: Look now, though! Already Discourse is allowing you to see the image as it takes shape. He's fitting things together in the following way. He's taking just the head from the Aphrodite from Cnidus. He won't need the rest of the body, since it's naked. Now, the hair and the forehead and

the fine line of the eyebrows he's going to leave her just as Praxiteles fashioned them. He's also going to preserve the same languishing quality of the eyes and the same brightness and charm as Praxiteles imagined. But her cheeks and the front parts of the face he's going to take from Alcamenes' Aphrodite in the gardens. He's going to borrow from the same statue also the fingertips and the finely proportioned wrists and the finely tapering fingers. Phidias' Lemnian Athena will provide the outline of the face as a whole, the softness of the cheeks and the well-proportioned nose. The same artist will offer the arrangement of her mouth and her neck, though this time from his Amazon. Calamis' Sosandra will provide her with the adornment of modesty, and her stately smile, barely perceptible, will also be taken from this model. The correct and orderly style of dress is also from the Sosandra, except that the woman's head won't be veiled. As for her stature, this should most closely resemble the Cnidian Aphrodite. So we'll take the measurements for this from Praxiteles as well.

What do you think, Polystratus? Will the image be beautiful?

POLYSTRATUS: It'll be extremely lovely – when it's complete in all its details. For in bringing everything together into the same place you've still left out an aspect of beauty which lies outside sculpture.

LYCINUS: What's that?

POLYSTRATUS: My friend, it's not the least important thing, unless you consider that the right complexion in the right parts makes no contribution to good looks – that is, that the dark bits should be dark, the white white, that there should be a surface tinge of red and so on. There's a danger the most important thing is still missing.

LYCINUS: Well, where are we going to get this extra material from? Obviously we should summon the painters to our aid, especially the ones who were best at mixing and applying their colours effectively. So look, let's imagine we've called Polygnotus, the famous Euphranor, Apelles and Aëtion. They'll divide the work between them. Euphranor is to supply the hair colour he used for his Hera.[6] Polygnotus will give her eyebrows the same appearance and her cheeks the same blush as he gave to his Cassandra in the hall at Delphi.[7] The same painter will also make for our portrait clothes fashioned in the flimsiest material, drawn so that what must be covered is covered, but most flies free in the wind. Apelles is to be the artist for the rest of her body. He should copy his own Pacate[8] most closely, giving her a complexion which is not too pale, but shows fully her vigour by its red tinge. Aëtion is to paint her lips the way he did Roxana's.[9]

8   But no, actually here's a better idea. We may have Euphranor and Apelles to hand, but we're also in possession of the best painter of them all, Homer. Let's make her overall complexion the sort of colour he attributed to Menelaus' thighs when he used the image 'like ivory with a tinge of blood-red'.[10] The same word-artist can paint her eyes as well, making her 'ox-eyed'.[11] The Theban poet[12] can also help Homer with the work on the eyes. Doesn't he have the epithet 'violet-eyed'?[13] Homer will also make her 'laughter-loving', 'white-armed' and 'rosy-fingered'.[14] All in all, the image comparison he'll make between our model and 'golden Aphrodite' will be much more to the point than his own between the goddess and Briseus' daughter.[15]

9   This then will be the work of the sculptors, the painters and the poets. But who could mimic the feature which enlivens the whole picture, grace – or rather the whole band of Graces together and all the Cupids dancing around her?

POLYSTRATUS: What you're talking about is a wonder, Lycinus, and truly divine in origin, the sort of thing you'd find in heaven. But what was she doing when you spotted her?

LYCINUS: She had a book scroll in her hands, with the two ends rolled up. It looked as though she'd already read some of it and was continuing with the rest.[16] As she continued her journey, she was saying something or other to one of her companions. I couldn't hear what it was. But it made her smile, and, Polystratus, I've no way of telling you how white were the teeth she revealed, or how even and regular. If you've ever seen a fine necklace made of gleaming pearls of equal size, that's the way her rows of teeth grew. And they were enhanced by the redness of her lips. That brief appearance of her teeth reminded me of the Homeric phrase 'like sawn ivory'.[17] That's to say, most women have some teeth wider than others, and some protruding or with gaps. Not her. All hers were the same both in colour and in size and were equally close to each other. The whole thing was amazing. It was a sight which far outstripped all human beauty.

POLYSTRATUS: Hold on! I know now very clearly who the woman is you're talking about, both from the details you've given and from her city of origin. You did say that she'd some eunuchs in her train, didn't you? [10]

LYCINUS: I did indeed. She also had some soldiers.

POLYSTRATUS: Then, my dear man, this woman you're talking about is the famous consort[18] of the king.[19]

LYCINUS: What's her name?

POLYSTRATUS: Oh, that's also elegant and lovely, Lycinus. She has the same name as the beautiful and famous wife of Abradatas, king of Susa.[20] You know what it is. You've heard[21] Xenophon often enough praising her as a right-minded[22] and beautiful woman.[23]

LYCINUS: I have indeed. Whenever I get to that passage, it's as though I can see her and almost hear her speaking the words attributed to her and see the manner in which she armed her husband and her demeanour when she sent him into battle.[24]

POLYSTRATUS: My dear fellow, you've only seen her once, like a flash of lightning zipping by. Consequently, your eulogy seems to encompass merely the obvious thing, by which I mean her physical beauty. You haven't witnessed her mental capacities. So you're unaware of the beauty of her soul. I can tell you, it outstrips her physical beauty by a long way and is really more akin to divinity. I on the other hand am an acquaintance of hers and I've participated in discussions with her many times, being from the same city. In any case, as you well know, I'd always praise gentleness, the capacity to love one's neighbour, generosity, sound judgement[25] and culture before beauty. I think it's right to give priority to these things over the body. After all, it would be irrational and ridiculous [11] not to, just like being struck by the clothes rather than the physique. Actually, in my view, complete beauty consists in the simultaneous presence of both internal excellence and external comeliness. Actually, I could give you lots of examples of women who are physically well furnished, but disgrace their beauty in other respects. As soon as they speak, it loses its bloom and withers away, shown up as unseemly and cohabiting, unworthily, with a soul that's a bad mistress. I'd compare women like these to Egyptian temples. There too you'll find a very lovely, very tall building, adorned with expensive stone and decorated with gold and paintings. But if you seek out the god inside, you'll discover it's a monkey, an ibis, a goat or a cat.[26] You can find lots of women like that.

Beauty on its own simply isn't sufficient. It has to have the right accoutrements. By that I don't mean purple robes and necklaces. I'm talking about the things I mentioned before, virtue and sound judgement and fairness and the capacity to love one's neighbour, and all the other qualities which define virtue.

12 LYCINUS: All right, then, Polystratus, swap me word for word, in the same measure, as the saying goes, or even better, since you *are* able.[27] Why don't you draw an image of her soul and show it to me, so that my admiration for her can be complete and not half-formed, as it is now.

POLYSTRATUS: That's no small task you've set me, my friend. It's not the same thing to use words to praise what's seen as it is to use them to bring into the open what's invisible. I think I'm going to need some help for the image as well. And it won't be just sculptors and painters. I'm going to need philosophers too, to make sure I line my statue up to their rules and display a product which measures up to the standards of ancient sculpture.

13   So let's imagine the image is before us. First of all, she speaks 'with human voice' and 'clear'.[28] In fact, Homer's phrase about the famous old man from Pylos, that words fell from his tongue 'sweeter than honey',[29] is apter when applied to her. The whole tenor of her voice is as soft as can be. It's not as deep as a man's, but it isn't very thin either or weak,

the way a woman's can be. It's like that of a boy who hasn't yet reached adolescence. It's sweet and gentle and sinks softly into the hearing, so that when it stops the sound lingers and a fragment of it stays behind to resonate around the ears, like an echo which prolongs the auditory experience and leaves in the soul honey-flavoured traces of her words, filled to the brim with persuasiveness.[30] Ah, but when that lovely voice sings, and especially to the lyre, that's the signal for halcyons, cicadas and swans[31] to keep their peace. In comparison with her, they've no music in them at all. Even Pandion's daughter is a talentless amateur by contrast, 'much-echoing' though the voice be she sends forth.[32]

Orpheus and Amphion were very successful at drawing in   14
their audiences. They could even get inanimate objects to come and listen to their songs. But if they'd heard her, they'd have left their lyres to one side and come themselves to listen. She can hold the pitch accurately without compromising the rhythm at all. Her singing rises and falls in precisely the right measures, her lyre keeps pace and her plectrum strikes the same beat as her tongue. The gentle touch of her fingers and the fluidity of the harmonic line are qualities the famous Thracian could never have acquired, let alone the fellow who did his lyre practice in between cattle-watching duties on top of Cithaeron.[33]

Consequently, Lycinus, if you ever actually hear her singing, it won't be that Gorgon experience you'll be having any more, becoming stone instead of human, you'll also know what it was like to listen to the Sirens.[34] You'll stand next to her absolutely enthralled, forgetting home and family completely. Even if you stuff your ears up with wax, the tune will reach you through the barrier. That's how powerful her performance is. She must have learned it from the Muses themselves, Terpsichore, Melpomene or Calliope, considering the myriad charms of all sorts it contains. I can sum it up briefly. I'm asking you to imagine you're hearing the sort of song that you'd expect to come from between such lips and from between those teeth. You've seen the woman I'm talking about. So now imagine that you've heard her.

15   We shouldn't be surprised at the accurate pitch and the pure
Ionic of her voice, nor that she can speak readily when you
meet her and with plenty of Attic charm.[35] This is inherited and
ancestral. Indeed, she should be no other way, sharing as she
does in the Athenian heritage by virtue of Smyrna's original
status as an Athenian colony.[36] And least of all should I express
surprise at her joy in poetry and the time she spends with it. She
is after all a fellow-citizen of Homer.[37]

Here's one image for you, then, Lycinus. It portrays her
beautiful voice and her singing, though it images them inad-
equately. Now look at the rest of my images. I've decided,
you see, not to make one grand masterpiece by putting it
together from many, as you did. There's bound to be tension
between the elements of a complex model when you compile
it this way. I'm going to describe the totality of her qualities
of soul one by one and thus draw the exact image of my
original.

LYCINUS: What you're inviting me to, Polystratus, is a festival
and a feast. At any rate, I reckon you're really going to give
me back more than I doled out.[38] Dole away, then. There's
nothing you could do that would please me more.

16 POLYSTRATUS: All right, then. Since culture must be the foremost of all the best qualities, especially of those that can be
acquired by practice, let's now put this together too, though
as something varied and multiform, so that we don't fall short
of your sculptural paradigm even in this aspect. So here
she is, portrayed with the complete panoply of Helicon's
bounty.[39] She's not like Clio, Polymnia, Calliope and the other
Muses, who have only one skill each. She possesses the skills
of all of them, and in addition those of Hermes and Apollo
as well.[40] Let the image be adorned with all the material
tricked out in metre by the poets, all the speeches published
by clever and powerful orators, all the historians' narratives
and all the ethical teachings of the philosophers. And this is
to be no surface colouring only. Our subject is steeped deeply
in these matters, and the dye used has been full and perma-
nent. You must forgive me if I can't give you an archetype of
this painting. No such phenomenon in terms of culture is

mentioned in the ancient writers.[41] If you like, though, let's dedicate this offering as well. I don't think we can fault it.

LYCINUS: No, Polystratus, it's absolutely lovely and all its lines are accurately drawn.

POLYSTRATUS: After this we've got to paint the image of wis- 17 dom and intelligence. We're going to need plenty of paradigms for this, most of them ancient, and one actually Ionian as well (its painters and artisans are Aeschines the friend of Socrates and Socrates himself, the most successfully realistic of all the craftsmen, because they also had a passion for their subject).[42] As a notable example of intelligence, we have the famous Aspasia from Miletus, whose consort was none other than the remarkable Olympian himself.[43] She was experienced in the ways of the world, had a sharp eye for politics, was shrewd and had a witty tongue. Let's bring all this into our image using an accurate plumb line. The only difference is that Aspasia's portrait appeared on a small plaque, but our lady is the size of a colossus.[44]

LYCINUS: What do you mean by that?

POLYSTRATUS: I mean, Lycinus, that the images are similar, but they're not the same size. The city of Athens as it was then and the present Roman empire[45] are nowhere near equal to one another. Consequently, even if there's a close resemblance between Aspasia and our subject, the latter is far superior, given that she appears drawn on a very broad canvas.

For examples number two and three, we'll take the famous 18 Theano[46] and the poetess from Lesbos.[47] And let's add to them Diotima. What Theano brings to the picture is high-mindedness. Sappho adds the elegance of her calling.[48] Our subject will resemble Diotima not only in the aspects Socrates chose for his eulogy, but in the rest of her intelligence and capacity to give advice. There you are, Lycinus. This is the sort of image we can hang up as well.

LYCINUS: Yes, indeed, by Zeus, Polystratus, it really is a 19 remarkable one. Now paint the rest.

POLYSTRATUS: Do you mean, my friend, those images which will depict her goodness and her capacity to love her neigh-bour, and display her gentle character and her kindness towards those in need? Let's borrow for her the image of the famous Theano wife of Antenor,[49] and Arete, and her daughter Nausicaa,[50] and anyone else who retained sound judgement of fortune when at the pinnacle of affairs.

20   Next after this one we should paint the portrait of sound judgement itself and of goodwill towards one's companion. The closest model here is the daughter of Icarius, 'secure of mind' and 'thoughtful' as she's described by Homer (that was the sort of image of Penelope that he painted).[51] But there's also her namesake, the wife of Abradatas whom we mentioned a little while ago.[52]

LYCINUS: This is also a lovely one you've made, Polystratus. And now you're almost at the end of your images. You've reviewed her whole soul in your praise of the individual parts.

21   POLYSTRATUS: Not all of it. The most important part of my eulogy is still to come. What I mean is this. She finds herself in the midst of great pomp and circumstance. Yet she hasn't let her good fortune make her supercilious and she hasn't trusted her luck so far as to lose the human perspective even at the heights she's reached. She's kept her feet on the ground. She has no tasteless or vulgar thoughts. She greets those who come to her democratically and as equals. Her handshakes and her embraces of welcome are all the sweeter to those who join her company inasmuch as there's no pomposity attached to them, even though they come from a superior. People who've used their great power, not to show contempt, but actually to do good are the ones seen to be most worthy of the gifts given them by fortune. They're the only group who'd justly escape envy. No one would envy the prominent man if he saw him behaving moderately in his good fortune rather than behaving like Homer's famous Ate[53] and treading on the heads of men, trampling down his inferiors. Those with weak intellects are prone to act this way from vulgarity of spirit. When Chance quite against the level of their expectations suddenly mounts them on a winged chariot in mid air, they don't rest with their present situation and they don't look down, but always push onward. That way, just like Icarus, as soon as the wax has melted and their wings have started to

moult, they raise laughter at their own expense as they plunge head first into the raging seas. But those who've used their wings like Daedalus and haven't flown too high, knowing that they're made with wax fixtures, but instead have carefully steered their flight with an eye to their human condition, preferring to be carried along just above the waves, so that their wings are always a little damp but they never expose them just to the sun, these are the people who've completed their flights safely and with good judgement. That's what we should praise in our subject too. That's why she has a deserved reward from everyone. And everyone prays that these wings of hers remain and that she be showered with even greater fortune.

LYCINUS: Let it be so, Polystratus. Her merits are not confined 22 to her body, like the beauty of Helen. She has an even lovelier and more loveable soul hidden within. It's only right that the great king,[54] good and kind as he is, should have the good fortune (along with all the rest of the blessings he has) that in his time such a woman should have been born, should be his consort and should reciprocate his affection. It's no mean stroke of luck to have a woman of whom without exaggeration one could cite Homer's famous comparison, that she rivals 'golden Aphrodite' in beauty, and in her works is a match for 'Athenaia' herself.[55] As Homer says, all in all no woman could surpass her 'in body or in stature, in thinking or in action'.[56]

POLYSTRATUS: True, Lycinus. So, if you think it's a good idea, 23 let's now put together the images, the ones you fashioned of her body and those I painted of her soul. We'll make one single image out of all of them, and put it down in a book for everyone to admire, both our contemporaries and those of future generations. It will last longer than the paintings of Apelles, Parrhasius and Polygnotus. It will also be much more pleasing to the lady herself than such things, since it's not made of wood and wax and paint, but has been imaged with the devices of the Muses. This will be the most accurate image, since it reveals at one and the same time both physical beauty and excellence of disposition.

IN DEFENCE OF 'IMAGES'

1   POLYSTRATUS: This is what the lady says: 'Lycinus, I could see in your work a great deal of affection and respect for me, of course. No one would have heaped up such undeserved praises, if he hadn't been well disposed to his subject. But just let me tell you what my opinion is. In general I don't have much time for people of a flattering disposition. I think they're cheats who have a natural predisposition towards duplicity. And especially when it comes to encomia and I receive vulgar, overblown praises from someone which are completely out of proportion to their subject, I find myself blushing and almost trying to block my ears.[1] What's being said seems more like a joke to me than a eulogy.[2]

2   'The reason is that encomia are only bearable if their subject can acknowledge that each element is appropriate to him. Anything beyond this is alien and the intention to flatter is obvious.'[3]

She continues: 'Yet I know that lots of people really enjoy it when someone attributes to them in a eulogy qualities they don't possess. For instance, someone might praise an old man for his youth or might clothe an ugly fellow with the beauty of Nireus or Phaon. I suppose they imagine that the encomia will make their physique change as well and bring back their lost youth, the way Pelias thought would happen to him.

3   'But it just isn't like that. Eulogy would be a really valuable thing if such hyperbole could actually bring a practical benefit to its subject. As things stand, however, the players in this game resemble a man who brings a handsome mask and an ugly individual whom he puts it on. The ugly fellow starts

giving himself airs because of his beauty, even though it's detachable and subject to accidental breakage – in which event he would attract a greater degree of ridicule, appearing then with his own face so that people could see the sort of individual he was and what sort of mask he'd been hiding under. Another equally extreme example would be a short man who put on thick-soled boots[4] and then started arguing who was taller with people who have a cubit on him when they stand on the ground.'

She also mentioned another, similar instance. A noble   4 woman, beautiful and attractive in other respects, but much shorter than the average, was eulogized by a poet in a song for being, among other things, beautiful and tall. In fact, he used the poplar as an image for her tall, straight stature. She was delighted with the encomium, as though she was actually growing to the music. She kept shaking her hand and the poet kept repeating the same thing over and over, since he could see how much she enjoyed being praised. Finally, one of the company leaned over and said in his ear, 'Enough, you fool, before you make the woman stand up!'[5]

She said that Stratonice the wife of Seleucus had done   5 something much more ridiculous even than this. She set up a poetry contest with a prize of one talent.[6] The theme was 'an encomium of Stratonice's hair'. Actually, she was bald and hadn't a hair of her own. Even so, though this was the condition of her head and everyone knew that it had happened because of a long illness, she actually listened to the wretched poets calling her hair 'hyacinthine', braiding curly ringlets and using the wavy celery as an image for the non-existent locks.[7]

So she was contemptuous of all these types of people who   6 put themselves in the hands of flatterers. She added that the phenomenon was not confined to eulogies. Lots of people like to submit to similar flattery and deceit in their portraits as well. What she said was: 'At any rate they get most enjoyment out of the painters who image them as better looking than they really are.' She maintains that there are some who actually instruct the artist to make their nose a bit shorter, or their

eyes a bit darker, or to add whatever other feature they
would desire to have. Then they forget that the images they're
garlanding with praise are alien and bear no resemblance to
them at all.[8]

7   These were the sorts of things she said, praising most of
your work, actually, but singling out one thing she couldn't
bear, the fact that you compared her image to the goddesses
Hera and Aphrodite. Her actual words were: 'Such comparisons are not just above my level, they're above all human
beings. I wasn't even prepared to have you compare me to the
heroines Penelope, Arete and Theano, let alone to the greatest
of the goddesses. That's especially so when I have an
extremely superstitious and jumpy attitude towards the
divine.[9] I'm afraid I'll be thought to be following Cassiepeia's
example if I accept a eulogy like this. Yet she was comparing
herself with the Nereids, and was respectful towards Hera
and Aphrodite.'[10]

8   Consequently, Lycinus, she's asked you to change these
parts. Otherwise, she'll call the goddesses to witness that
you've written against her wishes, and she says that you're
aware that the book will distress her if it circulates in its
present form, with its disrespectful and impious attitude
towards the divine. Her attitude is that it would be her act of
impiety and her sin if she allowed herself to be compared with
the Aphrodite from Cnidus and the one in the gardens.[11] She
asked me to remind you of what you said about her at the
end of the book. You claimed she was moderate and without
arrogance; she didn't try to overreach her human condition,
but flew close to the ground. But despite your words you've
made the woman mount above the heavens themselves by
going so far as to compare her image to the goddesses.

9   And she didn't expect you either to consider her less intelligent than Alexander. An architect promised to alter Mt. Athos
completely and shape it so that the whole mountain became
an image of the king holding two cities in his hands. Alexander
refused to countenance this prodigious promise. He thought
the enterprise was above his status and he stopped the fellow
from fashioning unconvincing colossi. He told him to leave

Mt. Athos as it stood and not to diminish such a great mountain by making it bear the likeness of a tiny body. She praised Alexander for his strength of mind. She said that this would stand as a monument greater than the Athos statue in the minds of all who would know of him in the future. It took no small intelligence to reject such an extraordinary honour.[12]

So, while she praises your inventiveness and your idea of the images, she doesn't recognize the likeness. She says she's not worthy of such comparisons. She's not even close, just as no other human female is. Consequently, while she honours you and acknowledges with piety the originals which you used as examples, her instructions are to praise her in human terms and not to make the shoe too big for her foot. 'I don't want it to hamper me when I walk about in it', as she said.

She also told me to tell you this. Her words were: 'I've heard lots of people saying (you men will know whether it's true or not)[13] that even Olympic victors are not allowed to set up statues that are bigger than life-size. The *Hellanodikai*,[14] they say, are charged with the task of ensuring that they are true to life, and the examination of the statues is even more demanding than that of the athletes. So just make sure that we don't get accused of falsifying our measurements, and then have the *Hellanodikai* knock down our image.'

That was what she said. So it's up to you now, Lycinus, to ensure that you change the book so as to take away all of this type of thing and avoid impiety. It was this that really upset her. She bristled at it and shuddered as the words were read out and kept praying the gods to be propitious to her. You must forgive this feminine response.[15] Though, if truth be told, I actually felt a bit the same myself. When I first heard it, I couldn't see anything wrong with what was written. But as soon as she pointed things out I started to notice the same things in the work, and I had a similar experience to the one we have when we look at things. If we examine something close up and right under our eyes, we don't see anything clearly. If we back off a bit and look at it from the right distance, everything becomes clear, both the good things and the flaws.

13   As for imaging a human female as Aphrodite and Hera, what else can this be but open disparagement of the goddesses? I say this because in such cases the comparison doesn't so much enhance the status of the lesser party, as diminish that of the greater, by dragging it down to a lower level. Take the example of two people walking along together. One of them is a giant and the other's a dwarf. Imagine we have to make them equal, so that one doesn't tower over the other. This parity of height won't be achieved if the smaller one tries to stretch himself upwards, even if he raises himself right onto the tips of his toes. If they're going to appear the same size, then the taller will have to bend over and make himself look smaller. It's exactly the same with these sorts of images. If someone images a human being as a god, it doesn't so much enhance the man as diminish the divinity, as it's bound to, when it's made to bend into the form of the inferior being. What's more, if someone were to extend his discourse to heavenly comparison because there was nothing on earth to suit the purpose, such a speaker would be less likely to be accused of doing it from impiety. In your case, there were multitudinous examples of human beauty to choose from. There was no need brazenly to image your subject as Aphrodite and Hera.

14   So, remove what's extravagant and invites the gods' jealousy, Lycinus. It's not like you anyway to be like this. You've never been very quick and ready with your praise in other circumstances. For some reason you've now had a complete change of character. You're positively ladling it on, and where once there was a praise miser there's now a praise prodigal. And you shouldn't feel ashamed of altering the piece that's already been published. The story goes that even Phidias did this after he'd finished the statue of Zeus at Elis. He stood behind the doors just after he'd opened them to display the work publicly and listened to what people said about it in praise or blame. One person said that the nose was too broad, another that the face was too long and so on. When the visitors had gone, Phidias shut himself up again and revised the statue to fit the views of the majority. He reckoned that

the advice of such a large section of the populace was not insignificant: in fact, he believed in the axiom that the many see better than the one, even if the one is Phidias.[16]

This is the message I've brought you from her. My advice as a friend and well-wisher is to accept it.

LYCINUS: I'd no idea you were such an accomplished speaker, 15 Polystratus. Anyway, the prosecution speech you've made against my work was so long and thorough that I don't even have any hope that I can defend myself now. The only thing I'll say is that you of all people shouldn't have contravened legal process this way, giving a judgment on the book by default, in the absence of its advocate. As the proverb has it, it's the easiest thing in the world to win a race when you're the only competitor. There's nothing surprising, then, in the fact that I've actually been convicted, not having been given the chance to make a defence speech or the measure of water by the water-clock in which to speak.[17] Actually, the strangest thing of all is that the case had you, the prosecutors, also acting as the jurors.

What do you want me to do, then? Shall I acquiesce in the judgment and say nothing? Do you think I should act like the poet from Himera and write a palinode?[18] Or are you going to give me a chance to appeal against the conviction?

POLYSTRATUS: By Zeus, of course you can appeal, if you've anything reasonable to say. You're not going to be making your defence speech in the antagonistic atmosphere of a court-room, as you've put it, but among friends. In fact I'm quite prepared to join your side in the case.

LYCINUS: It upsets me, though, that I can't make my appeal in 16 her presence, Polystratus. That would've been far better. As things stand, I've got to defend myself by proxy. Nevertheless, if you carry my message to her as well as you carried hers to me, then I'll risk casting the die.

POLYSTRATUS: Don't worry on that score, Lycinus. You won't find me delivering your defence speech badly. But try to speak succinctly, so that I can remember it better.

LYCINUS: Well, I really needed a very long speech to answer such a vehement prosecution speech. But for your sake I'll cut my defence short. So tell her from me what I'm about to say.

POLYSTRATUS: No, no, Lycinus. Speak as though she were actually here. Then I'll imitate your voice when I repeat it to her.

LYCINUS: All right, Polystratus, if that's the way you think it should be. Let's imagine she's here and has just made from her own lips all the points you reported. Now I must begin the second speech. I don't mind telling you, though, somehow you've made the situation more nerve-racking for me now. You can see how I'm already sweating and fearful. I can almost see her in front of my eyes. It's put me into great confusion. None the less, I'll start. There's no way of getting out of it now she's here.

POLYSTRATUS: She is, indeed, and what's more her face has an expression of great kindness on it. She's cheerful and receptive. So say your piece with confidence.

17 LYCINUS: Most excellent of women, even though I, as you say, have praised you beyond measure, I don't see that I've offered you an encomium as great as the one you've produced on your own behalf in the great importance you attribute to respect for the gods. This feature almost outweighs the whole of what I've said about you and I hope you'll forgive me for not having added its image to my gallery: ignorance is my excuse. Consequently, in this respect I can claim that I've not only not been hyperbolic in my praises, but that I've eulogized you far less than you deserve. Consider for a minute what a huge lacuna this is and how greatly it would have contributed to revealing your good nature and good sense. People who make respect for the gods a central feature of their lives are likely to be the best at dealing with human affairs too. So, if it becomes necessary for me to alter my discourse and correct my image of you, I wouldn't presume to take anything away from it, but I shall add this feature as the crowning glory of the whole work.

But on top of this I must confess that I owe you a very great debt of gratitude. I praised your moderate ways and the fact that the current great fortune of your situation hasn't engendered in you any high-and-mighty behaviour or filled

you with arrogance. The kinds of criticisms you've made of
my eulogy have actually confirmed its truth. Not to seize upon
such points in my encomium as your due, but to be ashamed
of them and to say that they're above your merits, is in fact a
sign that you have a disposition both moderate and democratic. However, the more you incline to take this view of
praise, the worthier an object of encomium you show yourself
to be. Your predicament has virtually come to embody the
axiom of Diogenes. Someone asked him once how one could
become famous. His reply was, 'By having contempt for
fame.' If someone asked me, 'Who are the people most deserving of praise?', I would answer, 'The people who dislike being
praised.'[19]

However, that's all possibly beside the point and not what's   18
at issue. The thing I have to defend is my use of the Aphrodites
in Cnidus and the gardens[20] and of Hera and Athena as images
for my portrait of you. In your view this spoilt the rhythm of
my discourse by as it were putting in too many syllables.[21] It's
about this matter that I'll speak.

It's an ancient saying that poets and painters aren't accountable.[22] It applies even more fully in my view to encomiasts,
even if they walk prosaically along the ground, like me, and
aren't mounted on the chariot of verse.[23] Eulogy is a rather
free genre. There are no laws which govern how long or short
it should be. Its central goal is simply to use every means to
express admiration for its subject and to create the impression
that he is to be envied. But I'm not going to walk along that
road, in case you think it's because I don't know what else
to say.

What I will say is this. The material for our eulogistic genre   19
is such that it requires the encomiast to bring images and
comparisons to bear in addition. In fact, one could almost
say that creating good images is his most important task. And
the criterion for judging the success of the encomiast does not
lie in comparisons with equal or inferior objects, but in his
capacity to bring the object of his praise as close as possible
to what is superior.

For instance, would you think that an encomiast who

praised a dog by saying it was bigger than a fox or a cat was a master of his craft? You surely wouldn't. Indeed, even if he were to say that the dog was the same size as a wolf, this would be faint praise. How will the special objective of encomium be achieved, then? If he says the dog resembles a lion in both size and strength. This is what the poet did who eulogized Orion's hound. He called him 'lion-taming'.[24] Now that was the way to fulfil the criteria for the encomium of a dog.

To take another example. Just suppose someone wanted to praise Milon of Croton or Glaucus from Carystus or Poly-damas and what he said was, 'Each of these is stronger than a woman'. Don't you suppose he'd be ridiculed for the stupid-ity of his encomium? But even if he'd said that his subject was better than a specific male object of comparison, that wouldn't have been sufficient to achieve the objective of eulogy. Now ask how a renowned poet praised Glaucus. Here's how. He said that 'not even the mighty Polydeuces or the steely child of Alcmene'[25] could have put a glove on him. You see the sort of gods he used to image Glaucus, don't you? Actually, he made him appear better than either of them. Yet Glaucus himself didn't get annoyed for being praised above the gods who are the overseers of athletes, nor did they take action against either Glaucus or the poet for impiety in the encomium. On the contrary, both of them gained renown and were honoured by the Greeks, Glaucus for his strength, the poet most especially for this particular song.

There's no call, then, for you to be startled if I too, in my wish to use images as encomiasts are duty-bound to do, employed a lofty paradigm. Reason dictated this approach.

20   You also mentioned flattery. Now, I approve of your detes-tation of toadies. Your attitude is the only sensible one. But I'd like to tell you what the vital distinction is between the task of the encomiast and the hyperbole of the flatterer.

The toady is using praise to further his own personal inter-ests. Consequently, he takes little notice of the truth and thinks that he must praise everything to the skies. He invents and embellishes most of the material from his own stock. He wouldn't scruple to present Thersites as handsomer than

Achilles, and Nestor as the youngest of the expeditionary force against Troy. He'd swear too that Croesus' son had sharper hearing than Melampus,[26] and Phineus better eyesight than Lynceus,[27] so long as he hoped to gain something from the lie. The encomiast would never lie or add some quality which the subject did not possess at all.[28] What he would do is to take the subject's natural abilities, even if not particularly distinguished, enlarge them and make them seem greater. If he wanted to praise a horse, he'd be bold enough to say of the animal which is above all those we know light on its feet and a natural runner that:

it ran across the tops of stalks of corn and did not make them bend.[29]

And, again, he wouldn't shrink from mentioning 'the course of storm-swift horses'.[30] And if he praises a beautiful house which has been built really well, he'll say:

Olympian Zeus' court was surely thus within.[31]

The toady would use this expression even to describe the swineherd's hut,[32] if only he hoped to get something from the swineherd. Take Cynaethus, Demetrius Poliorcetes' flatterer. He'd used up all his stock of flatteries. So when Demetrius was afflicted with a troublesome cough, Cynaethus praised him for hawking melodiously.

This isn't the only mark of difference between the two, I mean that toadies don't shrink from actual falsification for the sake of pleasing the subject of their praise, while encomiasts try to enhance what the subject actually possesses. It's also no small distinction between them that toadies employ hyperbole as often as possible, while encomiasts are sensible even in their use of it and stay within the proper limits. 21

I could have said a lot more. But these are a few of the signs which distinguish flattery from true praise, to help you avoid suspicion of encomiasts *tout court*, and instead tell the two things apart and employ the correct yardstick for each.

So now, if you will, bring both standards to bear on what 22

I said, to find out which set it conforms to. If I'd said that some ugly individual was like the statue of Aphrodite at Cnidus, I could really be considered a cheat and even more of a toady than Cynaethus. If however I said it of a woman who's actually as beautiful as everyone knows she is, then what I tried boldly to do wasn't a long way from the reality.

23   Perhaps you might say – well, actually, you already have: 'Well, all right, then. You were allowed to praise my beauty. But you should have composed the encomium so that it couldn't invite divine jealousy by imaging a mere human female by reference to goddesses.' Actually – and now she's going to oblige me to tell the truth – it wasn't by reference to goddesses that I imaged you, my dear lady, but to works created by good craftsmen, fashioned from stone, bronze or ivory. It's not impious, I suppose, to use human creations as images for human beings. Unless perchance you were under the misapprehension that the statue Phidias made really was Athena or that what Praxiteles created not all that many years ago in Cnidus was the heavenly Aphrodite. Beware, though, of the potential impiety in thinking such thoughts about the gods. I for my part suppose their true images are unattainable by human mimesis.

24   In any case, if I'd really and truly imaged you with reference to the goddesses themselves, it wouldn't have been my own idea. I wouldn't have been the first traveller on that particular road. Before me there had been a crowd of fine poets, not the least among them your fellow-citizen Homer. In fact, I'm going to bring him to the stand as well, to help me plead my case (otherwise there's no way he's going to avoid being convicted with me on the same charge).

So I'll ask him ... No, better, I'll ask you on his behalf, since you remember distinctly (and a fine achievement it is too) the most graceful of the verses he stitched together. What do you think of the passage in which he says of the captive Briseis that as she grieved for Patroclus she 'resembled golden Aphrodite'?[33] Then a little later, as though it won't suffice for her to resemble Aphrodite alone, he says:

Then spoke the woman weeping, like the goddesses to behold.[34]

So when he makes remarks like these, do you despise him as well and throw the book away, or do you grant him the licence to be a little free in his encomia? Even if you don't grant it, the whole great stretch of the ages since has done so. There's no one who has censured him for this, not even the critic who dared to whip his image or the one who obelized the verses he considered inauthentic.[35]

So, is he to be allowed to image a barbarian woman, and one in tears at that, with reference to the golden Aphrodite, but I'm to be prohibited from comparing to images of the gods, I won't say your beauty, because you can't bear to hear of this, but a radiant woman, normally smiling (a feature humans have in common with the deities)?

Now look at the case of Agamemnon. How sparingly   25
Homer uses the gods and how restrained was his custodian-ship of their images! His eyes and head are like Zeus', his waist is like Ares', his chest is like Poseidon's. He divides the fellow up limb by limb to match the images of all these gods. Again, he claims Hector resembles 'manslaying Ares'. And he does this with different heroes in diverse ways. The son of Priam, the Phrygian, he calls 'godshaped', and Peleus' son he often dubs 'godlike'.[36]

But I'll go back to female examples again. No doubt you've heard Homer saying:

like Artemis or golden Aphrodite

and

as Artemis goes down the mountainside.[37]

In fact, it isn't just humans themselves that Homer images   26
with reference to gods. He even imaged Euphorbus' hair with reference to that of the Graces, even though it was drenched in blood.[38] All said, there are so many things like this that there isn't any part of his poetry that's not embellished with

divine images. Consequently, either there should be an edict that these should be deleted as well, or I should be permitted to make an equally bold gesture. But there is so little account-ability[39] in terms of images and comparisons that Homer didn't even scruple to praise the goddesses themselves using inferior objects as terms of comparison. At any rate, he imaged Hera's eyes with reference to those of cows.[40] And someone else called Aphrodite 'violet-eyed'.[41] And is there anyone who's spent even the smallest amount of time with Homer's poetry who doesn't know the epithet 'rosy-fingered'?[42]

27   Now, to say that someone resembles a god in appearance is quite a moderate thing by comparison with the widespread practice of imitating the names of the gods. How many people have there been called Dionysius or Hephaestion or Zeno or Poseidonios or Hermeias? The wife of Evagoras the king of Cyprus was called Leto, but the goddess didn't get cross with her, though she had the power to turn her into stone as she'd done with Niobe. I won't even mention the Egyptians – they're the most god-fearing of all peoples, yet they use the names of their divinities to excess. At any rate, almost all their names are taken from heaven.

28   So, it's not down to you to be so timid of praise. You're not to be held to account for any sins my writing has committed against the gods, unless you think there is an accounting process for listening.[43] It's me the gods will take it out on, when they've dealt with Homer and the other poets ahead of me. However, they've not yet even punished the best of the philosophers[44] for saying that man was made in god's image.

I still have lots to say to you, but I'll stop here for the sake of Polystratus here. I want him actually to be able to remember my words.

29 POLYSTRATUS: I don't know whether that's possible any more, Lycinus. Even what you've said has been long and has exceeded the amount of water poured out for you. None the less, I'll try to remember it. As you can see, I'm already in a hurry to be off to her. And I've stuffed up my ears[45] so that nothing else can get in to upset the arrangement of your ideas and make the audience hiss me off the stage.

LYCINUS: It's up to you, Polystratus, to act your part as well as you can. As for me, now I've handed the drama over to you, I'll stand to one side. When they announce the votes of the jury, I'll be there in person to see the result of the contest.[46]

ABOUT THE PARASITE: PROOF THAT PARASITIC IS AN ART[1]

1   TYCHIADES:[2] Why is it, do you think, Simon, that while other people, slaves and free, have all learned an art which makes them useful to themselves and others, you seem to have no occupation through which you may profit yourself in any way or have something to share with others?

SIMON:[3] I'm not yet certain what you mean by this question, Tychiades. Try to put it more clearly.

TYCHIADES: Is there any art you happen to have acquired, such as music?

SIMON: Not music, by Zeus.

TYCHIADES: What about medicine?

SIMON: Not that either.

TYCHIADES: How about geometry?

SIMON: No.

TYCHIADES: How about rhetoric? As for philosophy, you're as far from that as is wickedness itself.

SIMON: I'd be even further away if I could, too. So don't think you're casting this insult at someone who's unaware of what he's like. I admit I'm a bad man – and far worse than you think.

TYCHIADES: Yes. But maybe you didn't learn any of these arts because of their scope and difficulty, but you acquired one of the artisan accomplishments, such as carpentry or shoe-making? As far as I can tell, at any rate, you aren't in a position to do without an art even of this kind.

SIMON: You're right, Tychiades. But it isn't any of these things that I've knowledge of.

TYCHIADES: What else could it be?

SIMON: What else? In my view, a noble art. If you learned it, I expect you'd hold it in high esteem too. In fact, I'd say that I'm already successful at it practically, though I can't say whether I can manage the theory yet.

TYCHIADES: What is it?

SIMON: I don't yet feel confident that I've mastered the theoretical discourse about it. So it's enough for now that you know I do have an art. You ought to drop your irritation with me on this account. What it is, I'll tell you another time.

TYCHIADES: I'm not going to put up with that.

SIMON: The trouble is that you'll probably think the focus of the art rather strange when you hear it.

TYCHIADES: Well, that's a good reason for me to be eager to find out.

SIMON: Another time, Tychiades.

TYCHIADES: No. Tell me now, unless of course it's something you're ashamed of.

SIMON: It's parasitic.

TYCHIADES: Come on, Simon, no one would call *that* an art,   2 except a lunatic.

SIMON: Well, I do. And if you think I'm a lunatic, you'd better regard the fact that I know no other art as a product of my lunacy and free me immediately from these accusations. As a matter of fact, they say that this particular spirit, though she has the disadvantage of being hard for those whom she takes hold of to put up with, at least forgives them their sins, taking them upon herself[4] like a teacher or a tutor.

TYCHIADES: So 'parasitic' is an art, then, Simon?

SIMON: It is, and I'm a practitioner of it.

TYCHIADES: So you're a parasite?

SIMON: That's a terrible insult, Tychiades!

TYCHIADES: How can you call yourself a parasite without blushing?

SIMON: Why should I blush? Actually, I'd be ashamed not to say it.

TYCHIADES: So, when we want to explain who you are to someone who doesn't know you, when he requires the information, we're to call you 'Simon the parasite', are we?

SIMON: It would be much better to call me this than to call Phidias a sculptor. I can tell you, I'm just as proud of my profession as Phidias was of his Zeus.[5]

TYCHIADES: Well, I must say, now I look at the matter closely, this presents me with a wonderful occasion for a laugh.

SIMON: What's that?

TYCHIADES: I'm wondering whether we're going to have to put at the top of letters we send you, in the usual place, 'to Simon the parasite'.

SIMON: Actually, that would please me even more than it would have pleased Dion if you'd addressed a letter to him 'to the philosopher'.[6]

3 TYCHIADES: It matters little or nothing to me what you like being called. What we need to examine is the remaining absurdity.

SIMON: Which one is that?

TYCHIADES: The one that follows if we're planning to include this art in the register along with the rest. The consequence will be that if someone asks what sort of art this is we must answer that it's 'the parasitical', like 'the grammatical' or 'the medical'.

SIMON: For my part, Tychiades, I'd be much more inclined to call this an art than any of the others. If you'd like to hear it, I'd like to explain my thinking, even though, as I've already said, I'm not completely prepared for the task.

TYCHIADES: It won't make any difference, even if you say very little, so long as it's true.

SIMON: Come, then, if you like, let's look first to see what we mean by the generic term 'art'. This way, we might be able to understand whether the individual arts according to their nature actually partake correctly of its essence.[7]

TYCHIADES: Well, what is 'art'? You know, I'm sure.

SIMON: Absolutely.

TYCHIADES: Well, if you know, don't hold back from telling me.

4 SIMON: As far as I can remember the definition given by a philosopher I once heard, 'art is a system of perceptions trained together to fulfil some goal useful for life'.[8]

TYCHIADES: You've remembered his definition correctly, if that's what he said.

SIMON: So if 'parasitic' were to meet these conditions, what else could it be than an art itself too?

TYCHIADES: If things were like that, it would be an art.

SIMON: All right, then. Let's try fitting 'parasitic' to the defining characteristics of an art and see if its theoretical basis is in tune with them. It'll be like knocking a faulty pot to see if it rings true or not. Like every other art, then, parasitic too must be a system of perceptions. The first of these lies in the ability to scrutinize and distinguish the sort of person suitable to look after one's needs and for whom one wouldn't later regret having begun to play the parasite. Or are we going to accept that the assayer possesses an art, since he knows how to distinguish counterfeit coins from the real ones, but that the parasite judges between the counterfeit and the honourable man without any art? It's not as though men are like coins, immediately clear in their nature – and the wise Euripides has some critical remarks on this very subject:

> If someone needs to spot the wicked man,
> No natural hallmark's there to pick him out.[9]

In this respect, the art of the parasite is actually the greater, since it apprehends and takes note of things so indistinct and unclear better than the art of prophecy.

As for understanding how to use the right sort of language and do the right sort of things to become friends and show oneself really well disposed towards one's benefactor, don't you think this requires formidable intelligence and perception?

TYCHIADES: It certainly does.

SIMON: And what about making sure that one leaves the dinners themselves with more than anyone else and gets a better reputation than those who haven't acquired the same art as oneself, do you think this can be achieved without some sort of theory and wisdom?

TYCHIADES: Not at all.

SIMON: Now then, do the ability to distinguish good and bad food and a close and active interest concerning delicacies seem to you the marks of a man without art? Yet our noble Plato tells us that 'when a feast is being prepared, the judgement of the person who will be enjoying it will be less trustworthy if he is not skilled in cookery'.[10]

6   At any rate, it'll be easy for you to understand from the following consideration that parasitic arises not merely from perception but from trained perception.[11] In the case of the other arts, the perceptions may often remain out of training for days, nights, months or years, and yet the art of the practitioner is not damaged. But in the parasite's case, if his perception is not practised every day, it'll be the end not merely of the art but also of the practitioner himself.

7   As for whether parasitic has a goal useful for life, it would be madness to undertake an inquiry on this topic. For my part, I can't find anything more useful in life than eating and drinking. In fact, survival isn't possible without them.

TYCHIADES: Indeed it isn't.

8 SIMON: Yet parasitic isn't the same sort of thing at all as beauty and strength. So it can't be defined as a faculty rather than an art.

TYCHIADES: That's true.

SIMON: Nor on the other hand is it a lack of art.[12] A lack of art can never secure anything for the person who has it. Tell me, if you put yourself in charge of a ship at sea during a storm without knowing how to steer, would you save your skin?

<TYCHIADES: Absolutely not.>

<SIMON: And if someone took charge of horses when he wasn't a charioteer?>[13]

TYCHIADES: He wouldn't save his hide either.

SIMON: And this would happen through his not possessing an art with which to save himself, wouldn't it?

TYCHIADES: It would.

SIMON: It follows, then, that the parasite wouldn't save his skin by parasitic if it were a lack of art.

TYCHIADES: It does.

SIMON: So he's saved by art, not lack of art?

TYCHIADES: Indeed.

SIMON: So it follows that parasitic is an art, does it not?

TYCHIADES: Apparently, it does.

SIMON: Now, I can cite many examples of good steersmen being shipwrecked and of skilful charioteers falling from their vehicles, some sustaining serious lacerations and others not living to tell the tale. But no one can give you a comparable instance of a parasite's disaster.

So, if parasitic is neither a lack of art nor a faculty, but a system of trained perceptions, clearly we've agreed today that it's an art.

TYCHIADES: From what you've said so far, I'd infer that it is. 9
But now give us a proper definition of parasitic.

SIMON: You're right, I should. My feeling is that the best definition would be as follows: 'Parasitic is the art of drinking and eating and the language which their acquisition requires. Its objective is pleasure.'

TYCHIADES: Well said! That's a wonderful definition of your art. But you'd better be on your guard in case you get into a fight with some of the philosophers about your objective.[14]

SIMON: Well, it'll be enough to discover whether their 'happiness' has the same goal as parasitic does.

It'll be made clear from the following. The sagacious Homer 10 admires the parasite's life as being the only one that's blessed and enviable:

> I claim that there is no more pleasing goal
> Than when delight obtains throughout the land,
> And feasters in the palace hear a bard
> Seated in rows, beside them tables filled
> With bread and meat, and when the steward draws
> Wine from the bowl and pours it in their cups.[15]

And as though he hadn't expressed his admiration for this sufficiently, he makes his own opinion even clearer with the fine line:

> My heart considers this the finest thing.[16]

From what he says, it's being a parasite which he considers the happy life. It isn't as though he's given these words to any old character, but to the wisest of them all. Yet had Odysseus wanted to praise the goal of the Stoics,[17] he could have mentioned it when he brought back Philoctetes from Lemnos, when he sacked Ilium, when he stopped the Greeks from fleeing, when he whipped himself and entered the city of Troy in mean Stoic rags. But at those moments he didn't say that that goal was the 'more pleasing'.[18] Even when he lived the Epicurean life with Calypso, when he was able to pass his time in idleness and luxury and screw the daughter of Atlas and enjoy all the soft pleasures,[19] not even then did he dub that goal 'more pleasing', but rather the life of parasites ('feasters' was the vogue name for parasites at that time). So what does he mean? It's worthwhile reporting his verses once more. There's nothing like listening to them being constantly repeated: 'Feasters sitting down in a row'[20] and

> beside them tables filled
> With bread and meat . . .[21]

11 As for Epicurus, he was absolutely shameless in his misappropriation of the goal of parasitic for the objective of what he defines as happiness. You can be quite sure that it was misappropriation and that pleasure is the concern of the parasite and not Epicurus from the following considerations. In my opinion, pleasure subsists primarily in the absence of physical distress, and secondly in the absence of mental stress.[22] The parasite hits both of these targets, but Epicurus neither. For the person who inquires into the shape of the earth and the boundlessness of the universe and the size of the sun and distances in space and primary elements and the existence or otherwise of the gods and is always at war and in dispute with people about the actual objective of life is up to his neck not just in human but in cosmic distress.[23] By contrast, the parasite reckons that everything is fine and trusts that things couldn't be arranged any better than they are. So, since there's nothing of the sort to distress him, with complete impunity and

calm[24] he eats and sleeps on his back, stretching out his feet and hands, like Odysseus sailing home from Scheria.[25]

However, this isn't the only respect in which pleasure has 12 nothing to do with Epicurus. There's also the following consideration. Epicurus here, the self-styled sage, either has the means to eat or has not. If he has not, then there's no way he'll live pleasurably – he won't live at all. If he does have the means, then it's either from himself or from someone else. Now, if he were to get his food from someone else, he'd be a parasite and not the person he claims. But if he has it from himself, then he'll not live pleasurably.[26]

TYCHIADES: What do you mean, he won't live pleasurably?

SIMON: Supplying one's own sustenance brings with it a lifestyle involving many unwelcome consequences, Tychiades. Look how many there are. Tell me, should the person intent upon living pleasurably satisfy all the desires arising in him or not?

TYCHIADES: I think he should.

SIMON: Well, this is perhaps possible for the man who has a lot of money, but not for the fellow who has little or none. So a poor man couldn't become a sage or attain the objective, I mean, pleasure. Actually, though, even the rich man who gives his desires full funding from his own resources won't be able to attain this goal.

TYCHIADES: Why on earth not?

SIMON: Because the person who spends his own money can't avoid encountering many unpleasant situations. For example, if the chef makes a mess of preparing the food, he either has to argue with him or eat bad food and miss out on his pleasure. Or if his steward manages the house badly, he has to take issue with him. Isn't this how it is?

TYCHIADES: It certainly is, in my opinion too.

SIMON: So it's likely that anything could happen to Epicurus to stop him from achieving his objective. But the parasite has no chef to get upset with, he has no farm, no steward and no money whose loss could cause him pain. What's more, he's got everything at his disposal so that he can eat and drink without anyone causing him the sort of distress which the others have to encounter.

13   From this and the other arguments, I've now demonstrated
sufficiently the fact that parasitic is an art. It remains to show
that it's also the best, and not this simply, but first that it's
superior to the rest in general and then that it's specifically
better than each of them.

Its superiority to all the rest in general lies in the following.
Every art has as a necessary prelude the learning process with
its hard work, its terrors and its beatings. There's no one who
wouldn't wish them away. It seems that parasitic is the only
art which you can learn without hard work. Or did you ever
know anyone to leave a dinner in tears, the way we see some
pupils leaving their teachers' houses? Did you ever see anyone
going off to dinner with a frown on his face, the way those
setting off for school look? In fact, the parasite sets off willingly for dinner, really enthusiastic for his art, while those
who learn the others hate them to the point where some
actually run away because of them.

I think you also ought to take note of the fact that mothers
and fathers most often reward progress in the other arts the
way the parasite is rewarded every day. 'The boy's written
well,' they say. 'Give him something to eat.' Or, 'He's written
badly. Don't give him anything.' Study seems so full of the
promise of rewards and punishments.

14   What's more, the other arts have this reward later, after the
learning process is over and they receive the fruits of their
labours with pleasure. For there is a great 'and steep pathway
that leads to' them.[27] Parasitic is the only one which benefits
immediately from the art during the learning process, and
aims at and achieves its objective simultaneously.

There's also the fact that every single one of the other arts
exists merely to provide a means of sustenance. The parasite
has his sustenance straight away, as soon as he starts to
acquire his art. I suppose you realize that the farmer doesn't
farm for the sake of farming, any more than the carpenter
does woodwork for its own sake? The parasite, however,
has no other objective: his task and its motive are exactly
the same.

15   What's more, everyone knows that practitioners of the

other arts slave away the rest of the time and only have a couple of days' holiday each month, while cities have some yearly and some monthly festival days when they reckon to enjoy themselves. The parasite is on holiday thirty days each month,[28] because he regards every day as sacred to the gods.

Another thing is that those aiming at success in the other 16 arts put up with diets of limited solids and limited liquids, like invalids. Not for them the enjoyment of learning along with full bellies and bumpers of wine!

The other arts are useless to their practitioners without the 17 tools of the trade. I mean, you can't pipe without pipes or strum without a lyre or ride without a horse. Parasitic is so good and gentle on its practitioners that they can practise it without any implements at all.

It seems, moreover, that we have to pay money down to 18 learn other arts. We're paid to learn parasitic.

The other arts have teachers. Parasitic does not. It's like 19 poetry as defined by Socrates – it appears as a gift from the gods.[29]

One final point. You'll note that it's impossible to carry on 20 the other arts while we're travelling or sailing. Parasitic can be practised while one is on the road or at sea.

TYCHIADES: That's true.   21

SIMON: What's more, Tychiades, the other arts in my opinion are covetous of parasitic, while parasitic has eyes for no other art but itself.

TYCHIADES: But tell me, don't you think that people who take what belongs to someone else are doing wrong?

SIMON: Of course I do.

TYCHIADES: Well then, how is it that the parasite is the only person who doesn't do wrong when he takes what's someone else's?

SIMON: I've no idea. But to continue, in the case of the other 22 arts, the start is always a lowly and skimpy affair, while with parasitic it's magnificent. And the reason for this is that you'll discover the root cause of parasitic in that well-worn word 'friendship'.

TYCHIADES: What do you mean?

SIMON: Well, no one invites an enemy to dinner or a fellow he doesn't know at all, nor even someone he's only moderately well acquainted with. The man's first got to become his friend before he can share in his libations and his table and the mysteries of this art. At any rate, I've often heard people saying, 'How can he be a friend when he's never eaten or drunk with us?' Their view is obviously based on the idea that the only reliable friend is someone who's drunk and eaten with you.

23   Anyway, you can infer that parasitic is the most regal of the arts not least from the following consideration. It isn't just that the other arts are practised with hard labour and sweat, but they're also done sitting or standing: these practitioners are slaves to their arts. The parasite, however, takes in hand the tasks allotted to his art reclining,[30] like a king.

24   I needn't mention another thing that makes him a happy man, namely the fact that he's the only one (to borrow the wise Homer's words) who neither plants nor ploughs, but gathers 'everything without ploughing the fields or scattering'.[31]

25   And there's nothing to stop a rhetorician or a mathematician or a sculptor practising his art even if he's a wicked or stupid individual. The parasite simply can't get away with being a blackguard or a fool.

TYCHIADES: My goodness, what a marvel you're making parasitic out to be! I'm even on the point of wanting to take it up myself instead of the profession I currently practise.

26 SIMON: So I think that I've now demonstrated that parasitic is a cut above all the other arts generally. Let's move on to see how it also surpasses each one individually. Now, it would be complete folly to make a comparison between parasitic and the banausic arts – really more the act of a man trying to minimize the reputation of his art. What I have to do is show that it's superior to the greatest and most prestigious arts. Everyone accepts that rhetoric and philosophy <are the greatest>, and for some their nobility makes them branches of science.[32] So when I've managed to demonstrate that parasitic is far greater than these, it'll obviously be agreed that it's as far

above the other arts as Nausicaa excelled her handmaidens.[33]

In general, to start with, parasitic outdoes both rhetoric   27
and philosophy in its substantiveness. Parasitic subsists,[34]
while the others don't. The reason for saying this is that we
don't all have the same unitary view of what rhetoric is, on
the one side, with some regarding it as an art, others as the
complete opposite, another group as a defective art and others
as something different again. In the same way, our definition
of philosophy isn't pat and self-consistent either. Epicurus
has one view of how things stand, the Stoics another, the
Academics yet another and the Peripatetics another. In a
nutshell, everyone has a different idea of what philosophy is.
As things stand right now, there's no consensus about the
correct view and their art doesn't appear unified. The inference we must draw is obvious. My principle is that what has
no substance cannot be an art. I mean to say, how is it that
arithmetic is always one and the same thing – two twos
are four among both us and the Persians, and Greeks and
barbarians are at one over this – but we have on view many
different philosophies, which agree with each other neither in
their starting points nor in their definition of goals?

TYCHIADES: What you say is true. They say that philosophy is
unitary, but then fragment it themselves.

SIMON: Now, if there were something inconsistent in the other   28
arts, you'd think it forgivable and walk on by: after all, their
apprehensions are mediocre and not immutable.[35] But who
could stand the thought that philosophy wasn't unitary and
was more out of tune than a musical instrument can be? I
conclude that philosophy isn't unitary, since I see that it has
no boundaries. However, there can't be many 'philosophies',
since philosophy is unitary.

Likewise one could say the same things about the substan-   29
tiveness of rhetoric. The situation which occurs when there's
a battle involving conflicting doctrinal tendencies rather than
universal agreement about a single proposition, is the most
powerful demonstration of the non-existence of the phenomenon in the first place, since there's no single direct apprehension of it. In fact, the very search for a preferred definition

and the lack of agreement as to its essential singleness destroys the very existence of the object of inquiry.[36]

30   Parasitic isn't like this. It's the same among Greeks and barbarians, with the same premises and practices (one couldn't say that different people practise parasitic in different ways). There don't appear to be parasitic sects (in the mould of Stoics or Epicureans), with different doctrines. On the contrary, there's universal agreement about its nature and harmony in defining its tasks and its goal. Consequently, my view is that on these arguments parasitic might possibly be the same thing as wisdom.

31 TYCHIADES: I certainly think that you've explained this well enough. But how are you going to demonstrate that philosophy is inferior to your art in other respects as well?

SIMON: Well, the first thing I have to say is this. No parasite has ever fallen in love with philosophy, while there are droves of philosophers who are recorded as having been struck with desire for parasitic – and to this day there are philosophers who lust after her.

TYCHIADES: Which philosophers could you name as enthusiasts for parasitic?

SIMON: Are you really asking which ones, Tychiades? I think you know full well which ones, but you're pretending not to know because in your mind there's shame in this allegiance rather than honour.

TYCHIADES: By Zeus, no, Simon. I really am completely at a loss about whom you might find to mention.

SIMON: My dear fellow, I reckon you must be ignorant of their biographers, otherwise you'd be absolutely in a position to recognize whom I'm talking about.

TYCHIADES: I can tell you, though, by Heracles, I'm bursting to hear who they are.

32 SIMON: Well then, I'm going to give you a list. And, mind you, these aren't the insignificant ones, but the very best and the ones you'd least expect. Aeschines the Socratic, the author of all those long and witty dialogues, arrived one time with his works in Sicily, to see if they'd help him get an introduction

to the tyrant Dionysius. He read out his 'Miltiades', was judged a roaring success and spent the rest of his life in Sicily as Dionysius' parasite, waving goodbye to the Socratic way of life. Now, tell me this. Don't you regard Aristippus from 33 Cyrene as one of the leading philosophers?

TYCHIADES: Of course.

SIMON: Well, he too at around the same period spent time in Syracuse playing the parasite for Dionysius. And there's no doubt anyway that he was the most well-thought-of of all his parasites. For one thing, he'd a greater natural capacity than the others for the art. So much so, in fact, that Dionysius used to send his cooks to Aristippus every day to learn from him.

He's a person who's agreed to have actually brought credit 34 to the art. But turning to your fine Plato, he also came to Sicily for the same purpose. He spent just a few days as parasite to the tyrant before he was dismissed from the post for innate lack of talent. He returned to Athens, worked hard and prepared himself for a second trip. He arrived in Sicily, dined with Dionysius for another very few days and was sent away because of his ignorance of the art. Plato seems to have had very much the same experience of Sicily as Nicias.[37]

TYCHIADES: And who is our source for this information, Simon?

SIMON: Well, there are lots. But in particular I'm thinking of 35 the musician Aristoxenus. He's a very reputable individual and was himself a parasite of Neleus.

Anyhow, I'm sure you're aware that Euripides was Archelaus' parasite right up to his death and that Anaxarchus did the same for Alexander.

As for Aristotle, he made only a preliminary study of para- 36 sitic – as he did with all the other arts.[38]

Well now, I've shown that philosophers took to parasitic, 37 just as I said. But no one can give you the name of a parasite who wanted to be a philosopher.

What's more, though, if happiness consists in not being 38 hungry or thirsty or cold, this is a unique attribute of parasitic. You could find lots of philosophers who were cold and hungry, but not a single parasite. If he were cold and hungry, he wouldn't be a parasite, but a fellow down on his luck or a beggar or someone rather like a philosopher.

39 TYCHIADES: That's enough of that. How are you going to demonstrate that parasitic is superior to philosophy and rhetoric in other respects as well?

SIMON: In a man's life, my dear friend, there are seasons, one for peace, in my view, and another for war. It's during these that the arts and the quality of their practitioners must come out into the open. If you agree, let's first look at wartime, to see who would be the most useful individuals both to themselves and to the city as a whole.

TYCHIADES: That's no mean competition you're proclaiming. I'm already chuckling to myself at the thought of the comparison between the parasite and the philosopher.

40 SIMON: Well, to forestall your amazement and your tendency to sneer at this matter, let's pretend that news has been announced of a sudden enemy invasion of our territory. This brings with it the imperative of going to meet the challenge and not allowing the land outside the city to be laid waste. The general calls up onto the list all the men of military age. They all assemble, including some philosophers, rhetoricians and parasites. So let's first of all take their clothes off (obviously, those about to arm must first strip). Take a close look at the men, my good friend, and make an assessment of their bodies. One group you'll see is thin and pale from want of food, shivering as though they've already been left wounded. It would be ridiculous to claim that such men could put up with a real contest, a long battle, pushing and shoving, dust and wounds when what they need is a pick-me-up.

41   Now turn and take a look at the condition of the parasite. Is he not first of all big of body and sound of complexion (I mean, not dark or white – the latter denotes a woman and the former a slave), but also full of guts, with a great, fierce, bloody glare like mine (it's not a good thing to bring into battle an eye that has a fearful and effeminate glance)? Wouldn't someone like this be a fine hoplite[39] when he was alive, and a fine corpse if he happened to be killed?

But what's the point of drawing imaginary pictures when   42
we have real examples? To put it simply, when you consider
the recorded behaviour of rhetoricians or philosophers, you'll
find that some of them wouldn't even venture to step outside
the walls, while any one of them that ever did, I maintain,
was forced to join the line and then turned tail and left it.

TYCHIADES: All of this is quite astonishing and what you
promise to prove is no meagre matter. None the less, continue.

SIMON: I'll deal with the orators first. Not only did Isocrates
never go to war, he never even entered a lawcourt. It was cowardice, in my view. That was also the reason he didn't have the
voice for it. What next? Didn't Demades and Aeschines and
Philocrates give up the city and themselves to Philip through
fear straight away after his declaration of war and ever afterwards continue promoting his policies at Athens, although he
more than anyone was making war on the Athenians at this
time? Among them, Philip was a friend. On the other side,
Hyperides, Demosthenes and Lycurgus are regarded as braver
individuals, with their constant brouhaha in the assembly
meetings and their abuse of Philip. But what outstanding act
did they ever perform in the war against him? Hyperides and
Lycurgus not only never went out to battle, they didn't even
dare stick their heads outside the gates a fraction. They just sat
there inside the walls already under siege by the Macedonians,
putting together nugatory resolutions and proposals. And
what about their ringleader, the one who was continually
saying in assembly meetings, 'Philip the Macedonian is a
scoundrel. No one would ever even buy a used slave from
him'?[40] He did have the courage to go as far as Boeotia. But
before the armies clashed and came to blows, he'd thrown
away his shield and run off. Don't tell me you've never heard
any of this before from anyone? It's not just every Athenian
who knows it. It's also common knowledge in Thrace and
Scythia – the birthplace of the piece of scum.[41]

TYCHIADES: I know this. But these men were politicians, trained   43
in speaking, not in virtue. What are you going to say about
the philosophers, though? There's no way you can make the
same kind of accusations against them.

SIMON: On the contrary, Tychiades, these people who discuss
bravery every day and wear down the word 'virtue' by constant use will be seen to be much more cowardly and unmanly
than the rhetoricians. Look at it this way. First of all, no one
could name a philosopher who's died in battle. Either they
never served in the army at all, or if they did they all ran away.
On the one side, then, Antisthenes, Diogenes, Crates, Zeno,
Plato, Aeschines[42] and Aristotle and that whole crew never
even saw a battle-line. The only one who had the courage to
go to fight at the battle of Delium was their sage, Socrates.
He ran off out of the battle from Mount Parnes and took
refuge in the wrestling school[43] of Taureas. He thought it
much more pleasant to sit billing and cooing with the young
lads and to pose conundrums to people he met than to fight
a Spartan.[44]

TYCHIADES: My dear fellow, I already knew this from other
people too, who'd absolutely no intention of deriding and
blaming them.[45] So I've no sense that you're telling lies about
the men in order to support your own art.

44   Nevertheless, if now seems the best time, why don't you
tell me what kind of disposition the parasite displays in battle
and whether parasites existed among the ancients.

SIMON: Come now, my friend, no one, even the completely
uneducated, is so ignorant of Homer that he doesn't know
that his mightiest heroes were parasites. The famous Nestor,
from whose tongue words flowed like honey,[46] was the parasite of the king himself. And Agamemnon praises and admires
no one as he does Nestor, not Achilles, who was regarded as
– and indeed actually was – the finest physical specimen, nor
Diomedes nor Ajax. It's not ten Achilleses or ten Ajaxes he
prayed to have. He'd have taken Troy ages before, he
reckoned, if he'd had ten soldiers like this parasite of his,
however old he might be.[47] Homer likewise mentions that
Idomeneus the descendant of Zeus was Agamemnon's
parasite.[48]

45 TYCHIADES: I'm aware of all this myself too. But what I don't
think I've yet grasped is in what sense these two individuals
were Agamemnon's 'parasites'.

SIMON: Well, my dear man, try to recall those verses in which
    Agamemnon himself is speaking to Idomeneus.
TYCHIADES: Which ones?
SIMON:

> Thy cup stands ever brimming
> Like mine, to quaff whene'er thine heart commands.[49]

What he means here by 'Thy cup stands ever brimming' is not
that Idomeneus' beaker stands fully charged whether he's
fighting or sleeping, but that he's the only one who has the
privilege of dining with the king every day of his life, and not,
like the other soldiers, by invitation on specific days.

Homer tells us in relation to Ajax that after his finely
contested single combat with Hector 'they led him to godlike
Agamemnon'.[50] He'd rather late in the day been judged
worthy of the honour of dining with the king. Idomeneus and
Nestor, by contrast, were the king's daily table-companions,
according to the bard himself. I reckon Nestor to have been
a particularly fine professional royal parasite. I say this
because he didn't begin to practise the art with Agamemnon:
he had earlier experience with Caeneus and Exadius.[51] In fact,
I don't think he'd ever have stopped being a parasite, if
Agamemnon hadn't died.
TYCHIADES: Well, this is a good example of a parasite. But see
    if you can name any others.
SIMON: Come now, Tychiades, wasn't Patroclus Achilles' para-   46
    site, even though he was a young man physically and mentally
    inferior to none of the other Greeks? In fact, I think that he
    was on the same level as Achilles himself, to judge by his
    actions. It was Patroclus who thrust Hector out of the encamp-
    ment after he'd broken down the gates and was fighting inside
    by the ships. And it was Patroclus who put out the fire already
    blazing on Protesilaus' vessel,[52] even though the soldiers on
    board it at the time were not the dregs, but in fact the sons of
    Telamon, Ajax and Teucer, the one a fine hoplite and the
    other a great archer. And this parasite of Achilles killed many
    of the barbarians, including Sarpedon,[53] the son of Zeus.

What's more, his death was quite different from that of the others. Achilles killed Hector and was in turn killed by Paris. But to kill the parasite, it took a god and two human beings.[54] And his last words as he died weren't like those of the noble Hector, who fell at Achilles' feet and pleaded for the return of his corpse to his nearest and dearest, but the sort you'd expect from a parasite. What were they?

> If twenty men like him had tackled me,
> They'd all have perished, conquered by my spear.[55]

47 TYCHIADES: Well that's enough about that. But try to tell me why it is that Patroclus must be called Achilles' 'parasite' rather than his friend.

SIMON: I'll present you with Patroclus himself, Tychiades, saying that he was a parasite.

TYCHIADES: That's astonishing.

SIMON: Well then, listen to the actual verses:

> Lay not my bones, Achilles, far from thine,
> But with them, as in your house was I fed.[56]

A bit further on he again says, Peleus then

> Taking me in,
> He fed me kindly and named me as thy squire.[57]

This means he had him as a parasite. If he'd wanted to call Patroclus Achilles' friend, he wouldn't have used the word 'squire'. After all, Patroclus was a free man. What are these 'squires' he mentions, if they're not slaves or friends? Obviously, parasites. It's for the same reason he calls Idomeneus' Meriones a 'squire' also. I infer that this was what parasites were known as back then. Note, by the way, that although Idomeneus was the son of Zeus, it's not him that Homer calls 'the image of Ares', but his parasite, Meriones.[58]

48   Now tell me this. The poor common citizen Aristogiton was the parasite of Harmodius, wasn't he, according to Thu-

cydides?[59] Now go on. Wasn't he also his lover? (It's a general rule that parasites are also the lovers of their patrons.) Well now, this 'parasite' turned round and freed the city of the Athenians from tyranny and is now standing in a bronze version with his lover in the Agora.[60]

You must confess that men of this mettle were excellent parasites.

Now, what sort of fighter do you think the parasite will make? First of all, a man like this will have breakfast before he goes into the battle-line, just as Odysseus also recommends.[61] According to him, there's no other way of fighting a battle, even if you're obliged to fight it at dawn. What's more, the time when the rest of the soldiers are all doing other things through fear – one fitting his helmet properly onto his head, another putting on his cuirass, a third actually trembling because he guesses how dreadful battle will be – our man is eating, with an extremely cheerful face. And as soon as battle is joined, he's right away fighting it out in the front line. His benefactor, however, is lined up behind his parasite, and the parasite covers him with his shield (as Ajax did for Teucer)[62] and protects him, exposing his own body while the missiles fly. He's far keener to save his benefactor than himself. 49

And even when a parasite died in battle, you wouldn't find anyone, officer or common soldier, ashamed at his corpse, which would be large and like someone who's taken his place on the couch at a fine drinking-party. It'd be worthwhile to see a philosopher's corpse lying beside our parasite's – dry, dirty, with a long beard, a weak fellow who'd already died before battle was joined. Who wouldn't despise a city whose soldiers he could see were such a poor bunch? Wouldn't he be likely to conjecture, seeing the corpses of weedy individuals with pale skins and long hair, that the city had been stuck for allies, and had released the criminals from the prison to do the fighting? 50

That's how parasites are in war compared with orators and philosophers. In peacetime, though, I think parasitic is as superior to philosophy as peace is to war. 51

First of all, if you agree, let's examine the locations of peace.

TYCHIADES: I don't yet understand what on earth that means. But let's do it anyway.

SIMON: Well, what I'd say is that the market-place, the lawcourts, the wrestling schools, the gymnasia, hunts and drinking-parties[63] are civic locations.

TYCHIADES: Yes, they are.

SIMON: Well, the parasite won't enter the market-place and the lawcourts, I suppose because these places are much more suitable for *sykophantai*[64] and nothing tolerable is ever done there. It's the wrestling schools and the gymnasia and the drinking-parties he frequents and of which he's the crowning glory. Tell me, has there ever been a philosopher or an orator who's stripped in a wrestling ground who could be compared physically to a parasite? Isn't it rather the case that any one of them seen in a gymnasium has brought a blush of shame to the place? What's more, none of them would stand his ground if he met a wild beast in the wilderness. The parasite has learned to despise them at his feasts,[65] and so awaits their charge and easily manages it. No stag or wild boar can give him the jitters and panic him. If the boar bares his tusks at him, the parasite bares his own back. As for hares, he's better at chasing them than the hounds are. And when it comes to the drinking-party who can compete with a parasite, whether he's joking or eating? Who can put the drinkers in a better frame of mind, this man with his songs and jokes, or an unsmiling fellow, reclining in a tattered cloak and looking at the ground, as though he's come to a funeral and not a party? In my view, a philosopher at a party is a bit like a dog in a public baths.

52   So now let's move on from this to the actual life of the parasite. We'll investigate it and at the same time effect a comparison.

First of all, one can see that the parasite always has contempt for reputation and doesn't care a jot about what people think about him. On the other hand, in the case of rhetoricians and philosophers, the addiction to vanity and reputation – and not only to reputation, but, what's worse, to money – is not confined to a few here and there but is general among them. The parasite's attitude to money is as careless as one's attitude towards pebbles on the seashore, and for him gold is no better than fire. Now, the rhetoricians, and, what's more terrible, those who claim to be philosophers, have an awful attraction towards these things. There's no need to give examples of the rhetoricians. They regularly get convicted of taking a bribe when judging a lawsuit for bribery. But among the philosophers currently rated high in their profession one acts the sophist[66] and gets his pupils to pay for his services, while another demands a salary from a king in exchange for his company[67] and doesn't feel ashamed of being for this reason away from home as an old man and taking a wage as though he were an Indian or a Scythian prisoner of war. Not even the name he's called brings a blush to his cheek.

And this isn't all you'll find looking at these people. They're   53 also susceptible to other emotions – pain, anger, jealousy and desires of all kinds. The parasite stands apart from all this. He doesn't get angry – he has forbearance. And besides, there's nothing for him to get angry about. And if he ever does become vexed, his irritation has no untoward or gloomy effects: it's more likely to cause smiles and to delight his companions. He suffers less pain than anyone else: this is because his art has provided him with the gift of having nothing to pain him. He has neither money nor house nor slave nor wife nor children, the loss of which necessarily inflicts pain upon their possessor. And he has no desire for reputation or money, nor even for a pretty catamite.

TYCHIADES: But Simon, it's obvious he'd be troubled if he   54 didn't have enough to eat.

SIMON: Tychiades, you seem unaware that the person who doesn't have enough to eat is not, from the first, a parasite (any more than the brave man can be brave if he lacks bravery, or the intelligent man intelligent without intelligence).[68] Any other way, he wouldn't even be a parasite. Our inquiry had as its premise the actual parasite, not the non-existent one. If the brave man is brave only because of the presence of bravery and the intelligent man intelligent only because of the presence of intelligence, it follows that the parasite is a parasite because of the presence of free food and drink. If he doesn't have this, then our investigation will concern someone else, but not a parasite.

TYCHIADES: So the parasite will never want for a meal?

SIMON: That seems to be the case. Consequently, there's nothing else for him to be upset by.

55   What's more, the whole pack of rhetoricians and philosophers live in fear. You find most of them wandering about with a stick. They wouldn't be armed, of course, if they weren't afraid. They also lock up their doors very tightly, presumably frightened that someone will attack them during the night. The parasite shuts his house door any old way just so that the wind won't blow it open. If there's a noise during the night, it doesn't bother him any more than if there's none. When he goes into the wilds, he travels without a sword. He's not afraid of anything anywhere, you see. But I've often seen philosophers packing a bow,[69] when there's no trouble about at all. They even take a stick with them when they visit the baths or go out to a meal.

56   No one can accuse a parasite of adultery or grievous bodily harm or theft or any other crime at all. The reason is that a man like this wouldn't be a parasite, but just a man wronging himself. Consequently, if he's caught in adultery, along with the crime, he now adopts the name of the crime and is called 'an adulterer'. Just as the wicked man doesn't take on the name 'good' but that of 'bad', so I imagine if the parasite commits a crime he'll lose this title and take on the one appropriate to his misdeed. On the other hand, of such misdeeds by rhetoricians and philosophers we know countless examples, not only in our own day: we have written documentation of their crimes in literature. We have a 'Defence Speech' by Socrates, Aeschines, Hyperides, Demosthenes and practically the majority of rhetoricians and sages.[70] But no 'Parasite's Defence' exists and no one can tell you of a suit brought by anyone against a parasite.

57   In any case, though, if the parasite's life is superior to that of rhetoricians and philosophers, will his death be worse?

No, on the contrary, it'll be far happier. We're well aware that all, well, the majority of, philosophers have been bad men who died a miserable death, some as the result of a judgment against them in court, after being convicted of the greatest crimes, by means of hemlock, others completely consumed by fire, others wasting away from kidney failure, others in exile.[71] No one can give you an example of a death like this for a parasite. They die a very happy death, eating and drinking. If a parasite appears to have died violently, he'll have met his end through indigestion.

TYCHIADES: That seems sufficient to defend the parasite against   58 the philosophers. Now try to tell me finally whether this is a good and useful thing for the patron to have. My opinion would be that the rich feed them in a spirit of philanthropy and beneficence, and that this brings disgrace upon the man who is given free board and lodging.

SIMON: I'm surprised at your naivety, Tychiades, if you can't tell that a rich man – even one with the gold of Gyges – is poor if he dines alone, and if he goes out without a parasite he looks like a beggar. Just as a soldier without weapons is more contemptible, or a garment with no purple dye, or a horse without trappings, in the same way a millionaire without a parasite looks like a humble pauper.

In fact, the rich man is enhanced by the presence of the   59 parasite, but the reverse is never true. I'd especially emphasize that it's not in any way a mark against the parasite that he serves the rich man (as you assert, obviously because you're thinking of the lowlier serving the superior). Actually, keeping the parasite has two benefits for the rich man: not only does he gain enhancement through him, but he gets an increased sense of security because of his function as bodyguard. Not only would no one readily attack the rich man in a battle seeing the parasite lined up alongside him, but no one with a parasite could ever die from poisoning. After all, who'd dare to make such an attempt with the parasite pre-tasting his food and drink? Consequently, the rich man is not merely enhanced, but he's actually rescued from the greatest dangers by the parasite. His affection is so keen that he's prepared to submit to every danger: he'd never let his patron eat alone, but even prefers to share death at his table.

60   TYCHIADES: I think you've run through everything now, Simon, and with no inferiority in your technique, like the complete beginner you claimed to be, but rather like a student of one of the finest teachers. Now, finally, I want to know whether the name 'parasitic' isn't just a touch seedy.

SIMON: Well now, see if you think my answer is sufficient. Try to reply the best way you can to my questions. Tell me, what do the ancients mean by the noun *sitos*?

TYCHIADES: Food.

SIMON: And what about the verb *siteisthai*? Doesn't this mean 'to eat'?

TYCHIADES: It does.

SIMON: So haven't we agreed that the verb *parasitein* means just what it says, 'to eat (the *sit-* part) at another's side (the *para-* bit)', i.e. better?[72]

TYCHIADES: It's exactly that which seems a bit off, Simon.

61   SIMON: Well, answer me another question, then. Which of the following two things would you pick, if you'd a free choice, sailing or sailing at another's side?

TYCHIADES: Sailing at another's side for me.

SIMON: How about running or running at another's side?

TYCHIADES: The latter, of course.

SIMON: What about riding or riding at another's side?

TYCHIADES: Riding at another's side.

SIMON: How about throwing the javelin alone versus a javelin competition?

TYCHIADES: A javelin competition.

SIMON: Well, on the same basis, wouldn't you choose eating in company to just eating?

TYCHIADES: I'm forced to agree. In future I'll be arriving at your door at daybreak and after lunch, like a schoolboy, to learn your art. You've an obligation to teach me unstintingly, since I'm actually going to be your first pupil. As the proverb has it, mothers always love their first-born best.[73]

THE ART OF THE LIE

Preface

True Histories is Lucian's most famous (and probably most influential) work. We have no clear evidence by which to assign it a date, though its use of a technique from Old Comedy – see below – would place it after his fortieth year or so (see Introduction, section 2), and if, as is sometimes claimed, the *prolalia Dionysus* was designed to introduce a performance of *True Histories*, then it may belong among the works of his old age, since he speaks of himself at *Dionysus* 6 as an old man.[1] The piece is presented in its prologue as a satirical attack on fiction masquerading as truth, using fiction masquerading as truth as the mode of satire. The title itself seems formulated to reflect this design, since the word translated 'histories', *diegema*, could mean 'an unsubstantiated or false tale', and the combination *alethe diegemeta* possibly alludes to a passage of Polybius (*Histories* 1.14.6), where the historian (*c.* 200–after 118 BC) says: 'when the truth (*aletheia*) is removed from history (*historia*) the residue is a useless yarn (*diegema*)'. In that case, *True Fictions* might have been a better rendering of the title.

Lucian invites his readers to search as they read for the basis of his parodies in well-known ancient writers. He does not name his targets, because he is imitating a satirical technique believed in his time to be that of Old Comedy. Thus it has been the task of modern scholarship to track them down.[2] Lucian does tell us, however, that they include poets (such as Homer), historians (such as Herodotus and Ctesias) and philosophers (such as Plato). The comic effect is produced for the reader (as in many of Lucian's other works) by the interaction between the allusion (when located) and the absurdity of the fantastic context in which it is now encountered. As with other works, however, the substructure of literary allusion also has a more serious purpose. *True Histories* ridicules the pretence that poetry, history and philosophy can represent the truth by deviating from reality. It does this by remaking their motifs into an unmasked fiction which refuses to countenance even the first step in this charade.[3] The motif of a journey to the moon found its way into Ludovico Ariosto's poem *Orlando Furioso* (1516, 1521, 1532), cantos 34–5, while More's *Utopia* (1516) and Jonathan Swift's *Gulliver's Travels* (1726) have more than a whiff of Lucian's procedures here in their satirical use of the fantastic voyage.

NOTES

1. Georgiadou and Larmour 1995. However, the prologue of *True Histories* (1.1–2) speaks of the text as intended for reading, not performance.
2. Two major commentaries and a monograph have appeared since I began work. Commentaries: Georgiadou and Larmour 1998, von Möllendorff 2000. Monograph: Rütten 1997.
3. A companion piece, *How to Write History*, establishes literary norms (truth, absence of eulogy, etc.) for historical writing and lampoons writers who deviate from them.

TRUE HISTORIES

BOOK 1

The Prologue

Athletes and those engaged in caring for their bodies are not   1
concerned only with muscle tone and exercise. They also pay
attention to relaxation taken at the right time, and in fact
consider this to be the most important aspect of training. The
analogy operates also, in my view, for literary experts. When
they have finished a long spell of reading more serious material,
they ought to allow their intellect some recreation and put it
into more alert condition for the labour which is to follow.

Their recreation will be of the right kind if they spend their   2
leisure on the sort of reading that does not just provide them
with entertainment pure and simple because of its wit and
charm, but displays also food for contemplation of a not unliter-
ary quality. In fact, that is just the sort of judgement I suppose
they will make about the work in front of you now. It is not
only the strange subject-matter or the charm of my design that
will attract them, nor the fact that I have produced a plethora
of diverse falsehoods with convincing verisimilitude. I have also
in a manner not unconnected with comedy framed each element
of my tales as an enigmatic allusion to some of the ancient
poets, historians and philosophers who wrote much of mythical
monsters. I would give you their names, if they were not going
to be obvious to you from your reading.[1]

There have been many others who, following the same design   3
as them, have written of wanderings and foreign travels they

claim to be their own, telling tales of huge beasts, cruel men and strange lifestyles.[2] But the founding father of this sort of buffoonery and their instructor in it was Homer's Odysseus, who regaled Alcinous' court with stories of the bondage of winds, one-eyed men, cannibals, savages, and even of many-headed creatures and the drug-induced shape-shifting of his companions.[3] He talked a great deal of such marvel-ridden stuff to the Phaeacians, unsophisticated people that they were.

4   Now, when I have come across all of these writers, I have not blamed the men for telling lies. I could see that even those who profess to be philosophers are now habituated to this.[4] The thing that amazed me was that they expected no one to notice they were not telling the truth. This is the reason why I too, having the vanity to want to try to leave something to posterity, so as not to be the only writer to be left out of the fiction free-for-all, since I had nothing true to relate (I had never had any experiences worth mentioning), turned to telling fibs. Mind you, my untruth is going to be more reasonable than that of the rest, because at least I am going to tell you this one true fact: I am lying. This way, I reckon I am going to be able to escape the charge levelled by others, if I admit personally that nothing I say is true. So I am writing about what I have not seen or experienced or learned from others, things which, moreover, do not at all – and could not conceivably – exist. For this reason, those embarking on this text must avoid giving credence to them in any way.

The Voyage

5   I set off one time from the Pillars of Heracles, weighed anchor and made a voyage into the Western Ocean. I had a motive for my journey – intellectual curiosity and the urge for new experiences – and an objective, in the desire to know how far the ocean stretched and who the people were who lived on the other side. For this reason, I had put in the hold a great deal of food, I had sufficient water on board and I had enlisted fifty men of my own age with the same thoughts in their head, and, what's more, I had ensured that there was a well-equipped

armoury. I had engaged the very best helmsman by offering a
high salary and I had had the ship, which was a merchant galley
of the *akatos* class,[5] strengthened as for a long journey which
would give it a violent battering.

For a day and a night we sailed along on a following wind   6
with the land still just in sight, so the start of our voyage was
gentle enough. However, the following day as the sun was rising,
the wind freshened, the swell increased, visibility became limited
and we were not even able to furl the sail. So we entrusted
ourselves to the wind in complete surrender and weathered the
storm for seventy-nine days. On the eightieth, however, the sun
suddenly started shining and not far away we could see a high,
wooded island, ringed by the plash of waves. These were not
rough any more, since the violence of the squall was starting to
die down.

We put in to land, disembarked and lay on the ground for a
long time, as you might expect after such extended hardship.
Eventually, however, we roused ourselves and picked thirty men
to stay and guard the ship, and twenty to go forward with me
to see what was on the island.

We'd gone about three stades[6] from the sea through woods   7
when we saw a plaque made of bronze, with an inscription in
Greek letters, though faint and worn, which said, 'This was the
furthest point Heracles and Dionysus reached'. There were also
two footprints on the nearby rocks, one about a hundred feet
long,[7] and the other smaller. It is my view that the smaller
belonged to Dionysus and the other to Heracles. We paid our
ritual respects and went. We hadn't gone far when we came
across a river flowing with a wine which looked remarkably like
the Chian variety.[8] The stream was deep and wide enough even
to be navigable at some points. Now we were much more
inclined to believe the inscription on the plaque, seeing the clear
evidence of Dionysus' visit. Deciding to investigate the source
of the river, I went upstream. It was not a spring I found there,
however, but a large number of big vines, heavy with grapes.
From beside the roots of each of them there flowed drops of
translucent wine. These vines were the river's source. A lot of
fish could also be seen in the stream. They had the colour and

the taste of wine. We caught some of them and when we had eaten them became intoxicated. Of course, when we filleted them, we found that they were also full of lees. Later, though, we noticed that there were other, freshwater, fish around and by a judicious mixture of the two we managed to dilute the overpowering strength of our solid Dionysiac diet.[9]

8   After that, we crossed the river where it was fordable, and discovered a monstrous kind of vine. The part which grew from the ground was a strong, thick stem. But above that the vines were women, with a complete set of accoutrements from the thighs upwards. They looked just the way our painters portray Daphne when Apollo has just got his hands on her and she is in the process of arborification. From their fingertips, however, grew branches which were hung with grapes. The hair on their heads was formed by tendrils, leaves and grape-clusters. When we approached, they greeted us and grasped our hands. Some of them spoke Lydian, others Indian, but most of them used the Greek tongue. They also kissed us on the mouth. Anyone so kissed immediately became staggering drunk. However, they wouldn't allow us to pluck any of their fruit, but cried out in pain when we pulled at it. Some of them actually wanted to mix their fluids with our men.[10] And two of my comrades actually did have intercourse with them. But they couldn't get away afterwards. They were held fast by the genitals, which had been grafted and taken root. Their fingers had already grown branches, they were twined about with tendrils and were almost on the point where they would bear fruit themselves.

9   We left them there and fled to the ship. When we arrived, we told those who had remained behind the whole story, laying emphasis on our comrades' acts of vinosexual intercourse.[11] We then took pitchers, drew ourselves water and at the same time used the river to stock up with wine. We made camp nearby on the seashore and set sail at dawn with a wind behind us which was not too strong.

Around midday, though, when the island was already out of sight, we were suddenly struck by a typhoon, which whirled the ship round and lifted us about three hundred stades into the air. It didn't put the vessel back down on the sea. Instead, the wind fell on our sails, making them belly, and carried the ship along high in the air.

For seven days and as many nights we ran through the air.[12]   10 On the eighth day, we spotted a large tract of land in the air, like an island, bright, spherical and bathed in light. We put in there, anchored and disembarked. As we observed the country, we found that it was inhabited and cultivated. Now, during the day we could see nothing from there. But when night fell, lots of other islands came into our view nearby, some larger, some smaller, the colour of fire, and another piece of land below, with cities on it, rivers, seas, woods and mountains. So we guessed that this was our world.

We decided to go even further, but were captured when   11 we encountered the people the inhabitants call the Vulture Cavalry.[13] This Vulture Cavalry consists of men riding on large vultures and employing the birds like horses. The fact is, the vultures are huge and, for the most part, three-headed. I might best explain to you their size this way: they have wings which are each longer and thicker than the mast of a large cargo ship. The task these Vulture Cavalrymen have been given is to fly round the land and bring any foreigners they find to the king. So when they captured us, they brought us to him. He took one look at us and making the inference from our dress he said, 'Are you Greeks, then, strangers?' When we said we were, he asked, 'Well, how did you get here, then, with such a large tract of air to cross?' We told him the whole story. Then he started at the beginning and told us what had happened to him. He had been a human called Endymion. One night he had been asleep, when he was snatched off our earth, arrived here and became king of the land. He told us that his land was the one that appeared to us below as the moon. He told us to cheer up and not to have any suspicion that we might be in danger. We would have everything we needed.

'What's more,' he said, 'if I win the war I'm currently fighting   12 against the inhabitants of the sun, you'll live the most comfortable life possible with me.' We asked who his enemies were and what the reason for the conflict was. He replied, 'Phaethon, the king of the people who live on the sun, has been at war with us now for a long time. By the way, the sun is inhabited just the same as the moon is. The war began for the following reason. I once gathered together the poorest of the citizens of my realm with the intention of sending them to found a colony[14] on the Morning Star. It was empty and no one lived there. Well, Phaethon through jealousy stopped the colonization by meeting us in mid-journey with his Ant Cavalry.[15] We were beaten that time, because our forces weren't equal to theirs, and we retreated. Now I want to prosecute the war and send out the colony again. If you want, join me in the expedition and I'll give each of you one of the royal vultures and the rest of the military equipment. It's tomorrow we'll be setting off.' 'If you think it's a good idea,' I said, 'make it so.'

13   That day, we stayed with him and were treated to a feast. But next day we had to get up and into line for battle, because the scouts were indicating that the enemy were nearby. The army was one hundred thousand strong, not counting baggage handlers, engineers, infantry and foreign allies. Of these, eighty thousand were Vulture Cavalry, and twenty thousand were mounted on Vegetableplumes. This is an enormous bird which is covered all over with vegetables instead of feathers. Its quill feathers resemble most closely the leaves of a lettuce. In addition to these there were drawn up the Millet-throwers and the Garlic Warriors. There came as allies to help him from the Great Bear thirty thousand Flea Archers and fifty thousand Windrunners.[16] The Flea Archers are mounted on huge fleas, whence their name. Their fleas are each about the size of twelve elephants. The Windrunners are infantry, who fly through the air without wings. The way they do this is as follows. They wear full-length tunics, which they allow to belly out with the wind like sails and so are borne along like yachts. Most often troops like these act as peltasts[17] during battles. It was said that from the stars above Cappadocia would be coming seventy thousand Sparrow-acorns and five thousand Crane Cavalry.[18] I did not see these, because they never arrived. This is why I haven't even dared to describe their natures. I can tell you that what I was told was monstrous and incredible.

14   This is what Endymion's strength was. And everyone was

armed as follows. Their helmets were made of beans, since the beans which grow there are large and strong. Their cuirasses were all made from plates of lupin (they sew together the husks of lupins to make the cuirasses). There the husk of the lupin is as impenetrable as horn. However, their shields and swords were like the Greek ones.

When the time came, the troops were drawn up as follows. The Vulture Cavalry were on the right wing with the king, who was surrounded by the finest warriors. We were in this group too. The Vegetableplumes were on the left wing. The centre was occupied by the allies according to their own individual preference. The infantry numbered around sixty million and they were drawn up as follows. In that region are found many huge spiders, each much bigger than the Cycladic islands. They gave these instructions to web the air in the space between the moon and the Morning Star. As soon as they had done the job and made a plain, Endymion drew up his infantry on it. They were led by Nocturnal the son of the Lord of Tranquillity,[19] with two others.

The enemy's left wing was occupied by the Ant Cavalry and among them was Phaethon. They are enormous beasts, with wings, exactly like our ants except for their size (the largest of them was actually about two hundred feet long).[20] It was not just those mounted on them who fought. They joined in as well, particularly with their antennae. There were said to be around fifty thousand of these. On their right wing were drawn up the Air-gnats, also around fifty thousand in number. These were all archers mounted on giant gnats. Behind them came the Air-prancers, light-armed infantry, but also powerful fighters, since they used slings to fire oversized radishes from a distance. Anyone hit was not able to hold out long, dying as a foul smell invaded the wound. They were reported to smear their missiles with mallow poison. Next to them were drawn up the Stalk-mushrooms,[21] hoplites[22] who fought hand to hand, ten thousand in number. They were called Stalkmushrooms because they used mushroom shields and spears made of asparagus stalks. Near them stood the Dog-acorns, sent by the inhabitants of the Dog-star, five thousand men with dog's faces who fought mounted on flying acorns. Phaethon was also reported to have sent for allies who came too late, the slingers from the Milky Way and the Cloud-Centaurs.[23] The latter arrived when the battle had already been decided – I wish it had yet been otherwise. But the slingers didn't turn up at all. This was the reason they say that Phaethon got angry and later devastated their country with fire.

17   This was the army with which Phaethon was actually attacking. When the standards had been raised and both sides' asses had brayed (they use these instead of trumpeters), the armies engaged and began fighting. The left wing of the Heliot[24] forces immediately fled, not even coming to grips with the Vulture Cavalry, and we followed them, killing as we went. But their right wing defeated our left and the Air-gnats advanced in pursuit as far as the infantry. Then, when they weighed in, the enemy gave way and fled, especially when they they noticed that those on their own left wing had been defeated. The rout was comprehensive. Many were captured alive, but many too were put to the sword and a lot of blood flowed over the clouds. Consequently, they were dyed and appeared red, as they do in our world when the sun is sinking. A great quantity also dripped down onto the earth as well. I caught myself wondering whether it couldn't have been a phenomenon of the same kind that had occurred up here long ago which induced Homer to suppose that Zeus had rained blood when Sarpedon died.[25]

18   We turned back from our pursuit and set up two trophies, one to celebrate the infantry victory, on the cobwebs, the other the air-battle, on the clouds. This had only just happened when the approach was announced by our scouts of the Cloud-Centaurs, who should have come to Phaethon's aid before the battle. Indeed, we could see them as they drew near. It was a most unusual sight. They were a mixture of winged horse and human being. The human part was about the size of the Colossus of Rhodes from the waist upwards, and the horse element was as big as a large merchant ship. However, I haven't written down the number of them, for fear that its magnitude might appear incredible to people. Their leader was the archer from the zodiac.[26] When they realized that their friends had been

defeated, they sent word to Phaethon to attack again, and meanwhile drew up their forces and fell upon the disarrayed Selenites,[27] who were scattered in disorderly manner as they pursued stragglers and gathered spoils. They routed the lot of them and chased the king himself towards the city, slaughtering most of his birds. They demolished the two trophies, overran the whole plain spun by the spiders and took me and two of my companions prisoner. Phaethon had appeared by now and the enemy began setting up other trophies once more. So we were led off the same day to the sun, with our hands tied behind our backs with a piece of spider's web.

They decided not to lay siege to the city, but turned back and   19
built a wall across the middle of the air, with the result that the rays from the sun no longer reached the moon. It was a double wall, made of cloud, so that a full eclipse of the moon was effected and everything there was in the grip of continuous night. Endymion was distressed by these events and sent a messenger to beg Phaethon to tear down what they had built and not to let them live in darkness. He also promised to pay tribute, to become an ally and make war no more. In addition, he was willing to give hostages. Phaethon's people held two assembly meetings. On the first day, they did not remit one jot of their fury. However, the day after they relented[28] and peace was made on the following terms:

'On the following understandings the Heliots and their allies   20
have made a treaty with the Selenites and their allies. The Heliots are to dismantle their dividing-wall and no longer make incursions upon the moon. They shall release the prisoners, each for a fixed price. The Selenites are to leave the other stars to govern themselves, and are not to use armed force against the Heliots. Both sides are to aid the other in the event of an invasion by a third party. The king of the Selenites shall every year pay as tribute to the king of the Heliots ten thousand jars of dew. The Selenites shall give the Heliots ten thousand hostages from their own people. The colony sent out to the Morning Star shall be a joint venture, with the support of anyone else who wishes. The treaty shall be engraved on an amber plaque and set up in

mid-air on the border. The signatories are Fireball, Summerman and Fiery for the Heliots and for the Selenites Night-time, Lunarmonth and Brightspark.'[29]

21   These were the peace terms they agreed. At once the wall was demolished and they returned us prisoners. When we arrived on the moon, our comrades and Endymion himself came out to meet us and greeted us with tears. Endymion wanted us to stay there with him and participate in the new colony. He promised me his own son in marriage. I must explain that there are no women there. I had no intention of agreeing, but wanted him to send us back down to the sea below. When he realized that it was going to be impossible to persuade us to stay, he sent us on our way, after first giving us a seven-day feast.

22   Now I want to tell you the novel and unusual things I noticed during my stay on the moon. First and foremost is the fact that they aren't engendered from women, but from the men. They employ males for marital purposes and in fact don't even know the word 'woman'. Up till the age of twenty-five every individual takes the bride's part, and after that he becomes the bridegroom. Pregnancy occurs not in the womb but in the calf of the leg. The calf thickens when it receives the embryo. Later on they cut the leg open and bring out the baby dead. They bring them to life by exposing them to the wind with their mouths open. In my opinion it is from the moon that Greeks have learned the word 'calf', because there it is the calf that calves instead of the womb.[30]

    My next account, though, is more extraordinary still. There is among them a race of people known as the Treemen.[31] They are born in the following manner. They cut off a man's right testicle and plant it in the earth. From this there grows up an enormous tree, fleshy, like a phallus. But it also has branches and leaves. It bears as its crop acorns a cubit long. When they are ripe, they harvest them and hatch out the men. However, they have prosthetic genitals – the rich have them made of ivory, the poor of wood – and it is with these that they mount and have intercourse with their male consorts.

23   When the individual grows old, he does not die. He just dissolves into the air like smoke. Everyone has the same diet –

they light a fire and barbecue frogs over the coals (there are vast numbers of them there, flying around in the air). While the frogs are cooking, they sit round the fire as if it were a table and feast by gulping down the vapour of the rising smoke. Such is their solid intake. For drink, though, they squeeze air into a cup, and it yields a liquid like dew. They do not urinate and defecate. In fact, they do not have orifices in the same places we do. Boys do not offer their behinds for intercourse, but the backs of their legs, just above the calf, where they do have an opening.

Among them it is the bald and hairless who are considered beautiful. They evince a deep disgust at men with flowing locks. On the comets, it's the other way round: there they consider the long-haired beautiful.[32] I found this out because there were some visitors from that region who told me. They also grow beards just above their knees. They have no nails on their feet, but have only one toe. Above their backsides, each of them has a cabbage which protrudes like a tail. It's always fresh and doesn't get damaged when they fall on their backs.

When they blow their noses, what comes out is a very pungent 24 honey. And when they work hard or take exercise, their whole body sweats milk. In fact, they make cheese from this, by dribbling in a little of the honey. They make a smooth oil from onions which smells as good as myrrh. They have many water-bearing vines, since the berries on the bunches resemble hailstones. In my opinion, it's when the wind blows and shakes those vines that hail falls on us, because the bunches are broken apart. They use their stomachs as pouches, putting in there whatever they need, since they can be opened and closed again. They don't seem to have any innards, excepting only the thick hair with which the inside of their bellies is covered. Their young withdraw into this when they are cold.

The rich wear clothes of soft glass. Those of the poor are of 25 woven copper, since those regions are rich in copper. They work the copper by moistening it with water, as we do with wool. As regards the sort of eyes they have, I hesitate to mention it, in case anyone should think that I am lying because the story is so incredible. None the less, I'll tell you this as well. They have removable eyes and anyone who wants can take his own out and keep them safe until he needs to see again. Then he puts them in and has his vision back. Lots of people who have lost their own eyes borrow those of others to see with. There are some people, the wealthy, who keep a large store of spares. For ears they have plane-tree leaves, except for the people grown from acorns. This is the only group to have wooden ones.

26   In the king's palace, I saw yet another wonder. There is a huge mirror positioned over a shallow well. Anyone who descends into the well hears everything being said among our people on earth. If he looks into the mirror, he sees every city and every people as though he were standing next to them. On that occasion I saw my family and the whole of my native land, but whether they saw me as well I cannot further securely attest. Anyone who does not believe that this is the way things are will know that I am telling the truth if he ever gets there himself.

27   We said goodbye to the king and his entourage, embarked and sailed away. Endymion gave me gifts as well, two of the glass tunics, five of the copper ones and a suit of lupin armour. But I left them all behind in the whale. He sent us off with an escort of a thousand Vulture Cavalry which took us five hundred stades along the way.

28   In our voyage we passed many other lands by, but we put in at the Morning Star, which was just in the process of being colonized, and disembarked to get water. As we went on towards the zodiac, we passed the sun on our left, sailing very close to the land. We did not disembark there, even though my companions very much wanted to. The wind was against us. However, we did see that the land was fertile, rich, well watered and full of good things. The Cloud-Centaurs, Phaethon's mercenaries, spotted us and flew up to our ship. When they realized we were covered by the treaty, they went away again (the Vulture Cavalry had already left us by this time).

29   We sailed for the following night and day, and in the evening we arrived at the city called Lamptown,[33] already beginning our downward voyage. This city is situated midway between the Pleiades and the Hyades, but a lot lower down than the zodiac. When we disembarked, however, we found not a single human being, but lots of lamps running around, spending their time in

the market-place and the harbour. Some were tiny and like paupers. A few were the large and powerful variety, bright and visible from everywhere. They each had private houses and lamperies.[34] They all had names as well, just like human beings. We also heard them speaking. They did us no harm at all, and even offered us hospitality. Even so, we were afraid, and none of us dared to eat or sleep. In the middle of their city they have constructed an administrative centre where their chief magistrate sits all night calling each individual by name. Anyone who does not obey the call is condemned to death as a deserter. Death is by being snuffed out. We stood by and saw what went on and listened at the same time to the lamps defending themselves and giving the reasons for their delay in arriving. I actually saw and recognized our own lamp there. I spoke to it and asked how things were at home. He told me all about it.

For that night, then, we stayed there. But next day we weighed anchor and began our voyage again, already near to the clouds. That was where we saw with amazement the city of Cloud-cuckooville,[35] though we didn't set foot in it, because the wind wouldn't allow it. We heard, however, that the current king was Crow the son of Blackbird.[36] For my part, I thought of the poet Aristophanes, a wise and truthful man whose portrait of the place had been wrongly disbelieved. On the third day after this, we could actually already see the ocean clearly, though not yet land, except for the ones in the air. These appeared fiery and shone brilliantly. On the fourth day, around midday, the wind gently eased and subsided, and we were set down on the sea.

As soon as we touched the water, we were absolutely over-joyed and beside ourselves with delight. We celebrated the situation with total joy. We even jumped off the ship and swam around, since there happened to be a calm and the sea was tranquil. 30

It seems to happen often, however, that a change for the better is actually the start of greater troubles. We sailed along in good weather for only two days. At daybreak on the third, we suddenly spotted monsters and huge fish of many different kinds. One in particular, the biggest of them all, was almost one thousand five hundred stades in length. It approached with its mouth gaping, disturbing the sea a long way in front of it, creating a foamy wake all around it, and revealing teeth much taller than our Dionysiac phalluses,[37] all as sharp as stakes and as white as an elephant's tusks. We spoke to and embraced each other for the last time and waited. It wasn't long before it arrived and gulped us up ship and all. But it didn't have time to crush us with its teeth. Instead, the ship escaped through the gaps down into its belly.

31   When we were inside, at first it was dark and we could see nothing. Later, when it opened its mouth, we saw a huge cavity. It was broad and high enough to contain a city of ten thousand souls. In the middle lay small fish and many other creatures that had been smashed to bits. There were ships' sails and anchors, human bones and cargoes, and in the middle even some land with hills. I reckoned that it had formed from the mud that the creature had swallowed. Anyway, there was a forest on it and all sorts of trees had grown there, vegetables had sprung up and the whole place looked as though it was under cultivation. The land was two hundred and forty stades in circumference. Seabirds could also be seen there, gulls and halcyons,[38] nesting in the trees.

32   For the moment we wept copiously. Later, though, we got our fellows on their feet, propped up the ship, lit a fire by rubbing together sticks and made a meal from the materials to hand. In fact, lying around nearby were unlimited supplies of all kinds of fish, and we still had some water from the Morning Star. The next day we got up and got a view whenever the beast opened its mouth. Sometimes we saw mountains, sometimes just the sky, but often islands too. We realized that it was rushing quickly all over the sea. When we had finally become used to this mode of existence, I took seven of my comrades and began to walk into the forest, wishing to get a close look at everything. I hadn't gone five full stades when I discovered a temple of Poseidon (the inscription identified it as such). After a short distance there were a lot of graves, surmounted by gravestones. Nearby was a spring of clear water. What's more, we could hear a dog barking and see smoke in the distance. We guessed there must actually be a settlement there.

So we walked hastily on and came across an old man and a 33
young fellow working most enthusiastically on a garden plot
and channelling water from the spring to it. We stopped in our
tracks, delighted and afraid in equal measure. They too stood
there without a word, presumably undergoing the same emotions as ourselves. But eventually the old man said, 'Who are
you, then, strangers? Are you sea-gods or are you unlucky
human beings like us? For we're men, brought up on dry land,
who've become sea-creatures, swimming around with this beast
which embraces us. We've no clear idea of what's happening to
us. We infer that we're dead. But we believe we're still living.' I
replied to this speech as follows: 'We're also human, father, and
newly arrived. We were swallowed ship and all the day before
yesterday. Now we've come out because we wanted to find out
the situation in the forest, since it seemed so large and dense. It
was a divinity, it seems, who brought us to see you and to realize
that we're not the only prisoners shut into this monster. But tell
us about your own misfortune. Who are you, and how did you
get in here?' However, he refused to say anything or to ask us
any questions before giving us what hospitality he had available.
He took us and led us into the house, which was comfortable
and had been equipped with beds and all other conveniences.
He set before us vegetables and nuts and fish, and even poured
us some wine. When we had eaten our fill, he began to enquire
about our experiences. I told him the whole tale in the correct
order, the storm, what happened on the island, the aerial voyage,
the war and everything else right up to our descent into the
whale.

He was overwhelmed with amazement, but then began to 34
relate an account of his own experiences. 'I'm a Cypriot by
birth, strangers. I set out from my native land for the purpose
of trade, and sailed with my son, whom you see, and many other
members of my household to Italy, bringing a mixed cargo on
a large ship, which you may perhaps have seen wrecked in the
whale's mouth. We'd a fair voyage as far as Sicily. But we were
snatched away from there by a violent wind and three days later
we were swept into the ocean, where we met the whale. We
were swallowed, crew and all. The rest were killed and only the

two of us survived. We buried our companions and built a temple to Poseidon. Now we live the life you see, cultivating vegetables, and eating fish and nuts. As you can see, the forest is extensive and contains many vines, which produce the sweetest wine. Perhaps you also saw the spring, which has beautiful, ice-cold water. We make our beds from leaves and we light as many fires as we want. We hunt the birds that fly in, and catch live fish by going out into the monster's gills. We also bathe there whenever we want to. But actually, there's also a lake not far away, twenty stades in circumference, with all sorts of fish in it. We swim there and go sailing on a little boat which I constructed. This is the twenty-seventh year since our consumption.

35   'Now, the rest we can probably put up with. But our near neighbours are very difficult and troublesome, wild and unsociable people.' 'Are there really others in the whale?' I interjected. 'Lots,' he replied. 'They're inhospitable and strange in appearance. The western parts of the forest at the tail are inhabited by the Picklers. They're eel-eyed and crayfish-faced, a bold, warlike race who eat raw flesh. The areas of the other rib, on the beast's right side, are occupied by the Triton-Pans.[39] Their top half is human, but below the waist they're like swordfish. They're less unjust than the others. On the left are the Crabhands and the Tunaheads, who've made a friendly alliance with each other. In the middle area dwell the Crabbies and the Turbotfeet,[40] a warlike race which can run very fast. The eastern areas, situated near the mouth itself, are mostly uninhabited, because they're washed by the sea. None the less, I occupy this territory, paying a tribute of five hundred oysters a year to the Turbotfeet.

36   'That's what the country is like. Now you should look into how we're going to be able to fight with so many tribes and get our livelihood.' 'What number would you put on them, all told?' I asked. 'More than a thousand,' he replied. 'How are they armed?' 'With nothing but fishbones,' he said. 'In that case,' I replied, 'the best thing would be for us to go into battle against them, given that we're armed and they're not. If we defeat them, we'll live here for the rest of our lives without fear.'

That was what we decided to do. We went off to the ship to

make preparations. The pretext for war was going to be the
non-payment of the tribute, since the due date was already at
hand. Indeed, they did send to ask for their dues. But he made
a contemptuous response and chased away the messengers. As
a result, first the Turbotfeet and the Crabbies became angry at
Scintharus[41] (that was his name) and attacked with a great to-do.
We had suspected that an attack was imminent and were armed   37
and waiting. We had also set up an ambush with twenty-five
men. The ambush party had been instructed in advance to rise
and make their assault when they saw that the enemy had passed
by their position. That was what they did. They stood and cut
them down from behind, while we – also a party of twenty-five,
since Scintharus and his son were fighting alongside us – went
to meet them, joined battle and risked body and soul in our
struggle. In the end, we caused them to retreat and pursued
them right to their lairs. The enemy sustained one hundred and
seventy casualties, we only one, the helmsman, his back speared
by a mullet's rib.

For that day and night, we encamped on the battlefield and   38
set up a trophy by sticking a dry dolphin's backbone in the
ground. On the next day, the others had learned the news and
turned up. The Picklers took the right wing (led by Young
Tunny),[42] the Tunaheads the left and the Crabhands the centre.
The Triton-Pans were keeping a low profile, since they hadn't
made a prior decision to ally with either side. We began our
advance first and joined battle with them beside the temple of
Poseidon. We raised a great shout and the whale resounded as
caverns do. They were lightly armed, so we naturally routed
them. We chased them into the forest and gained possession of
the land from then on.

It wasn't long before they sent out heralds, picked up their   39
dead and began discussions about a treaty. But we decided not
to make peace. Instead, the next day we marched out against
them and cut them all down to the last one, except for the
Triton-Pans. When they saw what had happened, they ran off
through the gills and threw themselves into the sea. We occupied
the land, which was now bare of enemies, and lived in it without
fear for the rest of our time. Mostly we exercised and hunted.

We also worked the vines and gathered the harvest from the trees. All in all, we were like people luxuriating at liberty in a vast prison with no escape route. We lived this way for a year and eight months.

40   In the ninth month, on the fifth day, around the second opening of the mouth – the whale did this once every hour, so that we told the time by these openings – so, as I was saying, around second opening we suddenly heard a lot of shouting and hubbub and sounds like a boatswain's cry and rowers. This confused us, so we crept right into the monster's mouth and stood inside its teeth. From this vantage point we observed the most extraordinary sight I have ever seen. There were enormous men, each half a stade tall, sailing towards us on islands, as though they were triremes.[43] I realize that what I'm about to tell you seems incredible, but I'm going to tell you all the same. The islands were long, but not especially high, and about a hundred stades in circumference. On each of them were sailing about a hundred and twenty of those men. Some of these sat on each side of the island and rowed with huge cypress-trees, foliage and all, as though they were oars. Behind them, on what seemed to be the stern, a helmsman was positioned, with a bronze steering-paddle five stades long. At the prow about forty of them were armed and fighting. Their appearance was human in every respect, except for their hair. This was fire and was blazing, with the result that they had no need of helmets. There were no sails. Instead, the wind fell on the forest which grew abundantly on each island. It bellied out the forest and took the ship wherever the helmsman wanted. There was a boatswain in charge of them and they were quickly incited to their rowing as though they were handling warships.

41   At first we could only see two or three, but later there appeared around six hundred. They were separated into two groups and were fighting a sea-battle. Many were smashed to pieces in head-on collisions, and many too were sunk after being rammed. Others had become entangled and were fighting a valiant battle, though not finding it easy to get free, because the men drawn up on the prow were displaying great enthusiasm for boarding and slaughtering. No one was being taken alive. Instead of

grappling-irons they were casting at each other huge octopuses tied onto ropes, who would get entangled in the forest and hold the island fast. The weapons they threw and which caused wounds were oysters each big enough to fill a wagon and sponges about a hundred feet in length.[44]

The leader of one side was Aeolus-Centaur, and of the other 42 Sea-drinker.[45] Their battle had, apparently, come about over stolen property. Sea-drinker was said to have driven off many of Aeolus-Centaur's dolphin herds. We were able to hear all this because they were accusing each other and shouting out the names of their kings. In the end, victory went to the troops of Aeolus-Centaur, who sank around one hundred and fifty of the enemy islands and captured three more, men and all. The rest of the islands backed water and fled. The victors pursued them to a certain point, but when evening came they turned back towards the wrecks. They took possession of most of these and took away their own also, since no fewer than eighty of their own islands had been sunk. They also set up as a trophy of the island-battle[46] one of the enemy islands, which they impaled on the whale's head. For that night, they encamped around the monster, attaching their mooring cables to it and mooring at anchor nearby (the anchors they used were massive, strong and made of glass). Next day, they made sacrifice upon the whale, buried their kinsmen in it and sailed off, delighted with themselves and singing what sounded like paeans. This is what happened in the island-battle.[47]

BOOK 2

From then on, though, I could no longer bear my life in the 1 whale. I was fed up with hanging around and began to look for a way to escape. Our first idea was to get away by excavating a passage through the whale's right side. We began hacking, but went about five stades in without any success. So we stopped tunnelling and decided to set the forest on fire. That way, we thought, the whale would die, and if this happened it would be easy for us to get out. So we started burning, beginning with the tail area. For seven days and as many nights the whale did not feel the heat. However, on the eighth and ninth we knew that it was sick. It was opening its mouth less frequently and whenever it did do so would close it again quickly. By the tenth and eleventh day it had begun to die and had started smelling bad. On the twelfth day, we had just realized that if we didn't put some props under its teeth while its mouth was open, to stop it closing again, we would risk dying, imprisoned in the whale's corpse. So we propped open its mouth with huge beams and got the ship ready, putting on board as much water as we could and the other essential supplies. The helm was going to be taken by Scintharus.

2   Next day it was already dead. So we dragged the ship up, manoeuvred it between the gaps in its teeth, slung it from them and gently lowered it down onto the sea. Then we climbed onto the whale's back and sacrificed to Poseidon right next to the trophy. We camped there for three days, since there was a calm. On the fourth we sailed off. Right away we encountered and ran aground on many corpses of those involved in the island-battle. We were astonished when we measured the size of their bodies. For several days we sailed with a mild breeze behind us. But then a strong north wind blew up and there was a great chill which froze the whole sea, not just on the surface, but to a depth of about three hundred fathoms. Consequently, we could disembark and run about on the ice. The wind persisted, however. We couldn't stand it, and devised the following plan (actually, it was Scintharus' idea). We dug a massive cave in the water and stayed there for thirty days. We lit a fire and lived off the fish (we found them by digging in the ice). When supplies began to give out, we emerged, drew the frozen-in ship up on the ice, spread the sail and were swept along, slipping smoothly and gently over the surface as though we were sailing. On the fifth day, there was a rise in the temperature, the ice began melting and the whole sea turned back to water.

3   So we sailed about three hundred stades more and put into a small, deserted island. We stocked up with water from there (our supply had already begun to give out), shot a couple of wild bulls and sailed away. These bulls, however, did not have

their horns on their heads, but beneath their eyes, as recommended by Momus.[48] Not long afterwards, we came upon a sea of milk rather than water, with a white island visible at its centre, covered in vines. In fact, the island was an enormous round of cheese, as we later discovered by tasting it, twenty-five stades in circumference. The vines were full of grape-clusters. However, what we pressed from them and drank was not wine but milk. In the middle of the island had been constructed a temple to Galatea,[49] the daughter of Nereus, as the inscription made clear. All the time we stayed there, the land (I mean it literally) provided our bread and cheese, and we drank the milk we got from the grapes. The story was that Salmoneus' daughter Tyro was the ruler of this place. She'd received it as a reward from Poseidon after her translation from that realm.[50]

We stayed on the island for five days and on the sixth put to sea. We had a breeze escorting us and the waves were low. By the eighth day we had stopped sailing through the milk, and were now on dark and salty water, when we spotted a lot of men running on the sea. In physical appearance and in size they were completely like us. There was one difference: their feet were made of cork (and I suppose that's why they were called Corkfeet).[51] When we saw them, we were surprised by the fact that they didn't go under, but stayed on top of the waves, making their way without fear. They actually came up to us and greeted us in Greek. They said they were in a hurry to get back to Cork, their home place. For a while they accompanied us, then turned aside from our route and went on their way, wishing us a successful voyage.

Shortly after this, many islands came into view. Nearby on our left was Cork, where they had been hurrying off to. It was a city built on a massive round cork.[52] In the distance and more to the right were five very big and immensely high islands. Fire was blazing from them in great quantity. Beside the prow was another which was flat and low-lying, no more than five hundred stades away.

When we were quite near, we were engulfed by a wonderful breeze, sweet and perfumed, like the one the historian Herodotus says wafts off rich Arabia.[53] The pleasant odour which met us was like what you would get from a combination of roses, narcissi, hyacinths, lilies and violets on the one side, and myrtle, laurel and vine-blossom[54] on the other. Delighted by the scent, we had high hopes of something good after our long trials as we gradually approached the island. When we arrived, we could see all round the island lots of large, sheltered harbours, clear rivers debouching gently into the sea, and, what's more, meadows, woods and songbirds, some singing on the beaches, many on the branches of trees as well. A light atmosphere, easy on the lungs, had settled over the land. Pleasant breezes blew and gently swayed the woods, so that from the movement of the branches delicious melodies continually whistled, resembling pipe-tunes from a transverse pipe[55] played in the wilderness. We could also hear general, miscellaneous noise, not like a hubbub, but the sort you would get at a drinking-party, when some people are playing the pipes, others are shouting their approval and a few are clapping to the pipe or lyre.

6   Bewitched by all of this, we put into port, berthed the ship and disembarked, leaving Scintharus and two of our companions on board. As we went forward through a flowery meadow, we ran into the guards and their attendants. They tied us with garlands of roses (the strongest type of fetter they possess) and brought us to their ruler. On the way, we found out from them that the island was called 'the Isle of the Blest' and that its ruler was the Cretan Rhadamanthys. We were brought to him and took our place in the queue of those being tried. Our case was fourth up.

7   The first case centred on whether Ajax son of Telamon should or should not be a member of the company of heroes.[56] The prosecution's case was that he was mad and had committed suicide. In the end, when many words had been spoken, Rhadamanthys gave the following judgment: for the moment Ajax should be given a dose of hellebore[57] and handed over to Hippocrates, the doctor from Cos, but that later, when he was in his right mind, he could join the drinking-party.

8   The second trial was a matter of the heart: Theseus and Menelaus were in dispute about which of them should live with Helen.[58] Rhadamanthys decided that she should be with Menelaus, on the grounds that he had undergone so many

tribulations and dangers for the sake of his marriage. A second consideration was that Theseus had other wives as well, the Amazon and the daughters of Minos.[59]

The third suit was a contest between Alexander, son of Philip,   9 and the Carthaginian Hannibal for the seat of honour. Rhadamanthys decided that Alexander was the greater[60] and a chair was placed for him next to Cyrus the Persian, the elder.

In fourth place we were brought into court. Rhadamanthys   10 asked what had happened to us that we should set foot in a sacred place while still alive. We told him the whole story as it had happened. Then he made us leave the courtroom and for a long time pondered our situation and took counsel with his colleagues on the bench. There were many of these, including Aristides, the Athenian, known as 'the just'. When he had decided, he gave the following verdict: that we would be called to account when we died for our restless activity and our journey from home, but for now we could stay on the island for a fixed period and share the life of the heroes before we departed. The upper limit on our stay there they fixed at seven months.

At that moment the garlands fell away spontaneously and we   11 were at liberty. We were led into the city and to the drinking-den[61] of the Blessed. The city itself is made completely of gold, though the wall which surrounds it is of emerald. There are seven gates, all made of single planks of cinnamon wood. But the foundations and the ground within the city walls are ivory. The temples of all the gods are built of the precious gemstone beryl, and they contain enormous altars each made of a single block of amethyst, on which they sacrifice their hecatombs. Around the city flows a river of the finest myrrh. It is one hundred royal cubits in breadth and five deep, and so comfortable for swimming in. Their baths are large buildings made of glass, heated by cinnamon wood. However, their plunge-baths contain warm dew instead of water.[62]

For clothes they use fine spiders' webs of purple hue. They   12 themselves have no bodies, but are impalpable and fleshless, displaying only shape and form. None the less, even though they are disembodied, they look solid, they move, they think and they speak. The overall impression they give is of naked

332 CHATTERING COURTESANS AND OTHER SARDONIC SKETCHES

souls walking round dressed in a semblance of corporeality. Without touching one of them, you wouldn't have been able to say for certain that what you saw wasn't a real body. They are like upright shadows, except that they are not black. No one grows older. They all stay the same age they were when they arrived. What's more, it is never really night-time there, any more than it is ever fully day. The light which encompasses the land is like the grey twilight when the sun has not yet risen. None the less, they experience only one season of the year. For them it is always spring and the only wind that blows there is the Zephyr.

13   The land is covered with a profusion of flowers and cultivated trees, which provide shade. The vines bear fruit every month, twelve times a year. But the pomegranate, apple and other fruit-trees were said to produce thirteen times a year, because in the month they call Minoion after Minos, they bear a double crop. Instead of grain, their corn-stalks grow ready-made loaves on their ears, like mushrooms. There are three hundred and sixty-five springs of water around the city, and the same number of honey. There are five hundred of myrrh, but these are smaller. There are seven rivers of milk and eight of wine.

14   Their drinking-den they have made outside the city in the so-called 'Elysian Fields'. This is a lovely meadow surrounded by a thick wood of all sorts of different trees, which shades the participants. They have constructed the couches that support them out of flowers. The breezes are their waiters and bring them everything. But they don't serve the wine. There is no need of this, since around the drinking-den stand huge glass trees of the most limpid crystal. The crop these trees bear consists of drinking-vessels of all shapes and sizes. When a person enters the drinking-den, he picks one or two of the cups and sets them down beside him. They immediately fill up with wine. That's the way they drink. Instead of garlands, the nightingales and other songbirds pick flowers with their beaks from the nearby meadows and shower the drinkers with them as they fly singing overhead. And they get their perfume[63] in the following way. Dense clouds draw up the myrrh from the springs and the river,

then stand over the drinking-den and, with the gentle pressure
of the breezes to help, rain a fine drizzle like dew.

At their meals they devote themselves to music and songs. 15
The most popular renditions are the epic poems of Homer.[64]
The bard himself is there and shares their feast. His place is just
above Odysseus. They have choruses of boys and of girls. The
leaders[65] who sing along with them are the Locrian Eunomus,
Arion of Lesbos and Anacreon and Stesichorus. Yes, I did actually see Stesichorus there. By now Helen had patched up her
quarrel with him.[66] When these stop singing, a second chorus
comes forward, of swans,[67] swallows and nightingales. And
when these are singing, the whole wood then joins in with a
piped accompaniment orchestrated by the breezes.

The greatest aid they have for producing enjoyment, though, 16
is that there are two springs by the drinking-den, one of laughter
and the other of pleasure. Everyone drinks from both at the
start of the feast and spends the duration enjoying himself and
laughing.[68]

Now I want to tell you about the famous individuals I saw 17
there. All the demigods and those who fought at Ilium were
present, with the exception of the Locrian Ajax. He was the
only one, they said, who was undergoing punishment in the
land of the impious.[69] Of the barbarians, both the Cyruses were
there, the Scythian Anacharsis and the Thracian Zamolxis, and
Numa the Italian, and what's more Lycurgus the Spartan, the
Athenians Phocion and Tellus, and the Sages, except Periander.[70]
I also saw Socrates the son of Sophroniscus chattering with
Nestor and Palamedes.[71] Around him were Hyacinthus the Spartan, Narcissus the Thespian, Hylas and other good-looking
boys.[72] I had the impression that he had a thing for Hyacinthus.
At any rate it was him he most often refuted. There was talk
that Rhadamanthys was annoyed with him and had many times
threatened to exile him from the island if he spouted nonsense
and refused to put away his irony and get on with feasting. Plato
alone was not there. People said that he was actually living in
the city he had invented, a version of his own Republic, using
the Laws that he had composed.[73]

18   It was the groups around Aristippus and Epicurus, though, who took the first place there. They were all pleasant fellows, full of charm, and the life and soul of the drinking-den. Aesop the Phrygian was also among them. They treated him a bit like a clown.[74] Diogenes from Sinope had so thoroughly changed his ways that he had got married to Lais the courtesan[75] and would often stand up and dance when under the influence and perform other drunken tricks. None of the Stoics was present, because they were reported still to be ascending the steep hill of Virtue.[76] As far as Chrysippus was concerned, our information was that he was forbidden to set foot on the island until he had dosed himself with hellebore four times.[77] As for the Academics, people said they wanted to come, but were still suspending judgement and looking at the issue from all sides, since they hadn't even yet reached an understanding of whether or not such an island existed.[78] In my view, though, they were particularly fearful of Rhadamanthys' judgment, given that they had themselves done away with the notion of a criterion.[79] The word was, though, that lots of them had set out and had been accompanying those who had actually arrived, but had got left behind through their own indolence and lack of comprehension and then had turned back in mid-journey.

19   These were the most noteworthy of the people there. The person they respect the most is Achilles and after him Theseus. As for love-making, their ideas are as follows. They copulate openly,[80] with everyone looking on, with both women and men, without feeling in the least bit ashamed of it. Socrates is the only one to take a solemn oath that his relations with the young men are pure (but everyone thinks him guilty of perjury – at any rate, Hyacinthus and Narcissus say he has, even though he says he hasn't).[81] The women are common to all and no one is jealous of his neighbour. In this respect they are at their most Platonic.[82] Boys, by the way, never say no, but always give all those who like what they want.

20   Two or three days had not yet gone by when I approached Homer.[83] We neither of us had anything to do and so I asked him (among other questions) about his birthplace, mentioning that this was still an unresolved enigma, hotly debated in our

world. He replied that he was not unaware that some people thought he was Chian, others from Smyrna, lots a Colophonian. However, he told me he was a Babylonian, and the name he answered to among his own people was not 'Homer', but 'Tigranes'.[84] Later, he had been made a hostage by the Greeks and had changed his name.[85] My next question was about whether the athetized verses[86] were actually written by him. He claimed every last one was original. That was when I began to condemn the grammarians in the school of Zenodotus and Aristarchus for purveying nonsense. When he had given me good enough answers to these questions, I framed a third: why on earth had he started with the word 'wrath'?[87] He replied that it hadn't really been deliberate. It had just come into his head. The next thing I wanted to know was whether he had written the *Odyssey* before the *Iliad*, as most scholars reckon. He said that he hadn't. That he wasn't blind either – another of the things people say about him[88] – I knew straight away. He could see perfectly well, so I didn't even need to ask. There were lots of other occasions when I did the same thing, whenever I saw him at leisure. I would go up and ask him something, and he would reply with great enthusiasm. This was especially true after he had won the lawsuit. Thersites had brought an action against Homer for aggravated insult for the jibes he had made at him in his poem. Homer had been acquitted because Odysseus had been his advocate.[89]

About the same time, Pythagoras the Samian arrived after   21
seven transformations, having lived as the same number of living beings.[90] He had completed the circuits prescribed for his soul. His whole right side was made of gold.[91] It had been decided that he could be a citizen on the island, but there was some doubt as to whether they ought to address him as Pythagoras or Euphorbus. Empedocles turned up too, done to a turn, with his body thoroughly roasted.[92] They wouldn't let him in, though, despite the fact that he begged them for ages.

As time went on, the moment for their festival of the Death   22
Games[93] arrived. Achilles was the organizer[94] for the fifth time and Theseus the seventh. It would take me too long to tell you everything, so I'm just going to list the most important events.

Carus, Heracles' successor, won the wrestling, defeating Odysseus for the crown. The boxing was a tie. The contestants were Areius the Egyptian, who is buried in Corinth, and Epeius. There are no prizes for the *pankration*. I can't actually remember any longer who it was who won the foot-race.[95] The prize for poetry was taken by Hesiod, even though Homer was really far better.[96] Everyone's prize was a crown plaited from peacock feathers.

23   The festival had only just ended when the news broke that the prisoners in the land of the impious had snapped their chains, overpowered their guards and were heading for the island.[97] Their ringleaders were Phalaris of Acragas,[98] Busiris the Egyptian, Diomedes the Thracian and Sciron and Pityocamptes' gang.[99] When Rhadamanthys heard this, he drew up the heroes on the beach. The leaders were Achilles, Theseus and Telamonian Ajax (now back in his right mind). They joined battle and fought. The heroes were victorious, with Achilles as the most successful combatant. Socrates too, though, who was posted on the right wing, played a valiant part and fought a great deal more than he had at Delium[100] when he was alive. When four of the enemy approached him, he didn't run away and his expression remained unmoved. For this he was later awarded as a special prize for valour a large and beautiful park in front of the city, where he would have discussions with the friends he asked there. He called the place the Academy for the Dead.[101]

24   They seized and bound their defeated adversaries and sent them off to be punished even more severely. Homer wrote an account of this battle and when I left he gave me the book to bring back to people in our world. Unfortunately, we lost this along with the other stuff. The poem began:

Now sing to me Muse, of the battle of the dead heroes.[102]

Then they boiled up beans, as is their custom when they have brought a war to a successful conclusion, made a victory feast and celebrated a long festival.[103] The only one who did not participate was Pythagoras. Instead, he sat some way away, disgusted at the eating of beans.[104]

Six months had now passed. Around the middle of the seventh 25
there was an unexpected turn of events. Cinyras,[105] Scintharus'
son, a tall, handsome fellow, had been smitten for ages already
by Helen, and she did not hide her mad passion for the young
man. At any rate, they had often made signals to each other
during the drinking-sessions, proposed toasts and got up and
gone wandering around the wood on their own. By this time,
Cinyras, driven by lust and the impossibility of fulfilling it, had
decided – and it was Helen's wish as well[106] – to steal Helen and
for them to disappear off to one of the nearby islands, either
Cork or Cheeseland.[107] They had long before brought the three
most foolhardy of my companions into their plot. Cinyras did
not tell his father of it though. He knew that he would stop him.
They had made the decision and so they put the plan into
practice. They waited for nightfall (I wasn't there myself,
because I happened to be asleep in the drinking-den). They
slipped past the others, picked up Helen and quickly put to sea.

Around midnight, Menelaus woke up. When he realized his 26
bed no longer contained his wife, he let forth a yell, went to
fetch his brother and proceeded with him to King Rhadamanthys. When day began to dawn, the lookouts reported that they
could see the ship a long way off. Rhadamanthys accordingly
put fifty of the heroes onto a ship made of a single block of
asphodel[108] and instructed them to give chase. By rowing enthusiastically, they caught the runaways around midday, just as
they were entering the milky part of the ocean near Cheeseland.
That was how near they came to escaping. They tied the ship to
theirs with a chain of roses and sailed back. Helen wept, was
shamefaced and covered her head. Cinyras was interrogated
first by Rhadamanthys, to find out whether there were any others
also involved in their plan. When he said there were not, he had
him and his co-conspirators tied by the genitals and whipped
with mallow, and then sent them off to the land of the impious.

They voted to send us away from the island as well before we 27
were due to leave. We could stay the next day only.

I made indignant protests and wept with frustration to think
of all the good things I was about to leave behind in exchange
for more wanderings. But they comforted me with the promise

that in a few years I would return to them, and they showed me a chair and a couch near the greatest heroes which had already been assigned to me for the future. I went to Rhadamanthys and begged him to reveal the future and tell me about my impending voyage.[109] He told me that I would arrive back in my native land only after much wandering and many dangers. He was not willing, however, to put a time on our return. He did point out the nearby islands (there were five visible, with a sixth in the far distance). The nearby ones were, he told us, the isles of the impious, 'The ones from which you can already see vast amounts of flame belching,' he said. 'The sixth is the city of dreams. After that comes Calypso's island, though you can't see it yet. When you've sailed past them, you'll eventually arrive at the great land-mass which lies opposite to the one your people inhabit. You'll endure many trials there, pass through diverse tribes and sojourn among savage men. Eventually, you'll arrive back at the other continent.'

28 That was what he said. Then he pulled up from the ground a mallow root and handed it to me, with instructions to pray to it in times of great danger.[110] He also advised me, if I ever wanted to get back to this land, not to stir the fire with a sword, not to eat lupins and not to have intercourse with boys over eighteen.[111] He explained that if I kept these things in mind, I had hopes of returning to the island.

For the present, I prepared things for my voyage. When the right moment came, I joined their feast. The next day I went to the poet Homer and asked him to compose a two-line epigram. When he had finished, I put up a plaque made of beryl near the harbour and had the inscription engraved on it. The epigram went as follows:

> Lucian, belovèd of the blessèd gods, saw all these things
> And then returned again to his dear native land.[112]

29 I stayed that day too, but on the next put to sea with an escort of the heroes. It was then that Odysseus came up to me, taking care Penelope didn't see him, and gave me a letter to bring to Calypso on the island of Ogygia. Rhadamanthys sent the pilot

Nauplius along with me so that if we put in at the islands no one would arrest us on the suspicion that we had sailed in for some other business.

We had gone far enough to leave behind the perfumed atmosphere, when we were suddenly met by a dreadful stench, the sort you might get if you burned bitumen, brimstone and pitch together. There was also an awful and unbearable cooking smell, as though from human bodies being roasted. The air was dark and misty, and a pitchy dew dripped from it. We could also hear the sound of whips and cries of distress from many men.

We didn't put in at the rest of the islands, but I shall give you   30 a description of the one we did land on. It was round, craggy and sheer on all sides, a skeleton of rocks and stony places. There were no trees or water on it. None the less, we crept upwards over the cliffs, proceeding via a path blocked by thistles and thorns. It was a very ugly landscape. When we came to the prison and the punishment area, we were astonished first of all by the nature of the place. The ground was a garden planted everywhere with swords and stakes. It was encircled by rivers, the first of mud, the second of blood, the innermost of fire. The last was huge and uncrossable; it flowed like water and rose in waves like the sea. In it were lots of fish, some resembling torches and other, small ones lighted coals. They called them lampfish.[113]

The whole place had just one narrow entrance, and Timon of   31 Athens had been made its gatekeeper. Under Nauplius' guidance, however, we went in and witnessed the punishment of many kings, but also of many private individuals, some of whom we actually recognized. We saw Cinyras too: he was suspended by the genitals in the smoke rising from a slow fire. Our guides would add accounts of the lives of each and list the sins for which they were being punished. The biggest punishments of all were being undergone by those who had told lies of any sort during their lives or had written down things which were not true. Among them were Ctesias of Cnidus, Herodotus and many others. As I looked at them, I had good hope for the future, since I knew very well that I had never told an untruth.

I returned to the ship quickly, as I couldn't stand even looking,   32 said goodbye to Nauplius and sailed away.

The island of dreams soon came into sight nearby, though it was faint and difficult to see clearly. What kept happening to it was a bit like what goes on with dreams. As we drew near, it retreated, gradually withdrawing and getting further away. We finally caught up with it and late in the afternoon sailed into what they called Sleep harbour, near the gates of ivory, where the temple of the Cockerel stands, and disembarked. As we made our way towards the city, we saw many different sorts of dreams. But first I want to tell you about the city, since no one else has ever written an account of it, apart from Homer,[114] that is, who was not entirely accurate.

33   The whole city is surrounded by a forest, whose trees are tall poppies and mandragora plants.[115] These are crowded with bats, the only bird the island contains. Nearby a river runs past which they call the Sleepwalker and beside the gates are two springs, one called Sleep-of-the-dead and the other Allnight.[116] The city wall is high and variegated, very like a rainbow in appearance. However, there are not two gates, as Homer has maintained,[117] but four. Two of these look out over the Plain of Indolence. One is iron and the other ceramic, and it is through these that their fearsome, murderous and cruel dreams are said to go on their visitations. The other two face the harbour and the sea, one of horn and the one through which we arrived, which is ivory. As you enter the city, on your right is the temple of Night (she is the most revered of the gods among them, along with the Cockerel, whose temple stands near the harbour) and on the left the palace of Sleep. Sleep is the ruler there and has appointed as his two satraps and subordinate commanders Troubler the son of Purposeless and Fabulouslyrich the son of Imagination. In the middle of the market-place is a spring which they call Deepsleep.[118] Nearby are two temples, to Deceit and Truth. There stands also their oracular shrine. Antiphon the expounder of dreams is in charge of this and interprets, having been given the honour of this duty by Sleep.

34   The nature and form of the actual dreams is not consistent, however. Some were tall, handsome and good to look at, while others were small and ugly. Some, it appeared, were golden, others humble and shabby. Among them were some with wings,

monstrous to behold, while others were dressed up as though
for a parade, adorned as kings, gods or other such things. Many
of them we actually recognized, since we had long ago seen
them at home. They came up and greeted us, as though we were
old friends. They took charge of us, settled us on couches and
gave us the most lavish and kind hospitality. The entertainment
they provided was magnificent, but they also promised to make
us kings and satraps.[119] Some of them even took us back to our
own countries, showed us our relatives and brought us back, all
in one day.

We stayed thirty days and the same number of nights there,   35
feasting while we slept. Then a sudden clap of thunder woke us
up. We jumped up and put to sea after putting on board supplies.

Three days out from there we put in to the island of Ogygia
and disembarked. But first I opened the letter and read what
was written in it. The text went like this: 'Odysseus sends
greetings to Calypso. As soon as I sailed away from you after
building my raft, I was shipwrecked. I barely escaped, with the
help of Leucothea, to the land of the Phaeacians, who sent me
back to my own land. There I came across many suitors wooing
my wife and having a high time at my expense. I killed them all,
but later on I was done to death by Telegonus, the son I had
with Circe. Now I am on the Isle of the Blest, very much
regretting having left the life I had with you and the immortality
you were offering. So, if I get an opportunity, I am going to run
away and come to you.'[120] This was the letter's revelation. It
also mentioned that she should give us hospitality.

I went a little inland from the sea and found the cave just as   36
Homer said and Calypso at the loom.[121] When she had taken
the letter and read it over, the first thing she did was have a long
cry. But then she invited us to accept her hospitality and feasted
us lavishly. She asked about Odysseus and about Penelope.
What was she like to look at? Was she really virtuous (Odysseus
had made a lot of this aspect of her character all that time ago)?
We gave her the sort of answers we felt would please her.[122]
Then we went back to the ship and slept near it on the shore.

In the morning, we set sail, with a very strong breeze behind   37
us. After riding the storm for two days, on the third we ran into

the Pumpkin Pirates. These are savage men from the neighbouring islands who attack and rob those who sail by. As vessels
they use large pumpkins sixty cubits long. They dry out the
pumpkins, hollow them out by removing the flesh, then sail in
them, using reeds as masts and pumpkin-leaves for sails. They
attacked us and fought with two crews. They wounded many
of us by using as missiles pumpkin-seeds. The naval-battle went
on for a long time on even terms. Then around midday we
saw the Nut Sailors[123] approaching from behind the Pumpkin
Pirates. They were sworn enemies, as their reaction demonstrated, for as soon as the Pumpkin Pirates also noticed their
approach they ignored us, turned round and started a naval-
battle with them.

38   Meanwhile we raised the sail and fled, leaving them to fight.
It was obvious that the Nut Sailors were going to win, given
their superior numbers (they had five crews) and the stronger
ships they were fighting from. As vessels they used halved nut-
shells, emptied out, each half measuring fifteen fathoms in
length.

When we had lost them from sight, we tended to our wounded
and were always after that under arms, expecting some sort of
attack.

39   We were quite right to do so. The sun had not yet sunk when
from a deserted island around twenty men started heading
towards us riding on large dolphins. They were also bandits.
The dolphins carried them without mishap and, as they leapt
up, whinnied like horses. When they were near, they took up
positions on both sides of us and started pelting us with dried
cuttlefish and crabs' eyes. When we fired arrows and threw
javelins in answer, they couldn't withstand the attack, but fled
back to the island, most of them wounded.

40   Around midnight there was a calm, and without noticing it
we ran aground on the enormous nest of a halcyon. What I
mean by enormous is that it measured sixty stades in circumference. The female halcyon was floating on it. She was not much
smaller than the nest, where she was incubating her eggs. Indeed,
when she flew up she almost sank the ship with the wind
generated by her wings. However, she fled and vanished emitting

a mournful noise. When daylight began to appear, we climbed on and saw that the nest was like a huge raft constructed from a jumble of large trees. There were five hundred eggs on it, each of them larger than a Chian wine-jar. The chicks were beginning to appear from inside and were croaking. We cut through the shell of one of the eggs with axes and hatched an unfledged chick bigger than twenty vultures.

We had sailed about two hundred stades away from the nest 41 when great wonders which astonished us began to make their appearance. The goose on the ship's stern-post suddenly flapped its wings and honked,[124] and Scintharus the helmsman, who was already bald, grew hair again. But the most unusual thing of all was that the ship's mast sprouted, grew branches and bore fruit at its tip. The crop of fruit consisted of figs and black grapes, not yet ripe.[125] When we saw this, we were very alarmed, as you can imagine we would be, and started praying to the gods because of the portentous sight.

We hadn't gone five hundred stades when we saw a great, 42 dense forest of pine and cypress. We conjectured that it was a land-mass, but it turned out to be a bottomless sea planted with trees which had no roots. All the same, the trees stood motionless and upright, as though floating. When we got near and realized all this, we were at a loss about what we should do. It wasn't possible to sail through the trees, because the forest was thick and the trees were closely planted. But it didn't seem an easy course to turn around either. I climbed up the highest tree and had a look to see how things were on the other side. What I saw was that the forest stretched about fifty stades or a little more, but that there was another ocean beyond it. So we decided to set the ship on the leaves atop the trees, which were thick, and to transport it, if we could, across to the other sea. And that was what we started to do. We tied the ship with a strong cable, climbed up onto the trees and gradually winched it up. We placed it on the foliage, spread the canvas and sailed along as though we were on the sea, drawn along by the wind, which was pushing us forward. It was then that I recalled the verses of the poet Antimachus. What he says somewhere is:

To men who journey on a woodland cruise.[126]

43   Well, we overcame the forest and arrived at the water. Letting
the ship down again the same way as we had pulled it up, we
began sailing through clean and translucent water, until we
came upon a deep chasm.[127] It had been created by the separation
of the water, exactly as we often see on land canyons which are
the result of earthquakes. We took down the sails, but even so
the ship came to a halt with difficulty and barely escaped being
carried down. We peeked over the side and could see that the
chasm was about a thousand stades deep. It was absolutely
terrifying and extraordinary, because the water just stood there
as though it had been cut in two. We looked around and saw
not far off to our right a bridge which joined the two seas on
the surface, by means of a link made of water flowing from one
sea into the other. We used the oars to propel the ship, ran up
to it and with great effort crossed to the other side. We had
never expected to get there.

44   After that we came to a calm sea and a smallish island, easy
to approach and inhabited. Its occupants were savages, the
Oxheads,[128] who have horns, just the way our painters depict
the Minotaur. We disembarked and went inland to get water
and gather provisions, if we could find any from anywhere there.
We had completely run out by this time. We did find water there
close by, but there was nothing else apparent. The only thing
was that we could hear a lot of mooing in the distance. We
supposed that it was a herd of cattle, so we gradually advanced
and eventually came across the creatures. They saw us and gave
chase, capturing three of our comrades in the process, though
the rest of us escaped back to the sea. However, we didn't think
it right to stand by and leave our friends unavenged, so we
armed ourselves and fell upon the Oxheads as they were dividing
up the flesh of those they had taken away. We put them to flight,
gave chase, killed about fifty of them and captured two alive.
Then we returned with the prisoners. However, we had found
no food. So the rest of my crew advised me to slaughter the
captives. I did not agree.[129] Instead I tied them up and kept them
under guard until envoys from the Oxheads arrived asking to

ransom those we had taken. We understood that this was what they wanted, because they were nodding their heads and making mournful mooing noises as though they were supplicating. The ransom was a large quantity of cheeses, dried fish, onions and four does, each of which had three feet. They had two hind legs, but the front ones were fused together into one. On these terms, we handed back the prisoners. Then we stayed for one more day before we set sail.

We were by now seeing fish, birds were flying by and all the 45 signs that land was nearby were becoming visible. After a while we also saw men sailing along in a novel fashion. What I mean is, that they themselves were both ships and sailors. Let me enlighten you as to the way they voyaged. They lay flat on their backs in the water and hoisted their genitals (they have enormous ones), spread a sail from them and sailed along holding the ends of the canvas in their hands, while the wind propelled them. After them were others sitting on corks, driving like charioteers a pair of dolphins they had yoked together. The dolphins went ahead and pulled the corks behind them. These people did us no harm, but neither did they run away. They carried on with their ride without fear, peaceably amazed at the way we were sailing, and taking a good look at us from every direction.

By evening we had landed on a smallish island, inhabited, so 46 we thought, by women who spoke Greek. Our inference was made because they came up to us and shook our hands in welcome. They were all tricked out like courtesans, beautiful and young, trailing gowns which came right down over their feet. The name of the island was Nagland, while the actual city was called Waterlust.[130] The women allocated one of us to each of them, took us separately to their homes and entertained us. I held back a little (I had a nasty premonition) and when I looked round a bit more closely I saw piles of human bones and skulls lying around.[131] I didn't think it was a good idea to raise a shout, call my comrades together and rush into battle. Instead I took up my mallow and prayed intensely to it for an escape from the present troubles. After a while, as my hostess served me, I noticed that she did not have the legs of a woman, but the hoofs of an ass. Right then I drew my sword, took her prisoner, tied her up and asked her about everything. She told me, unwilling as she was, that they were women from the sea, called Asslegs,[132] and that they ate the guests who visited them. 'When we've got them drunk,' she said, 'we get them into bed and then attack them while they're asleep.' When I heard this, I left her tied up where she was, went up onto the roof, raised a shout and called together my friends. When they had gathered, I told them everything, showed them the bones and took them inside to the woman I had bound. But she immediately turned to water and vanished. Even so, I tested by plunging my sword into the water. It turned to blood.

47   We quickly went back to the ship and sailed away. When day began to dawn, we could already see the mainland and we guessed that it was the one which lay opposite that which we inhabit.[133] We fell down in prayer and then started to think about the future. Some thought we should just make landfall and then turn back again. Others said we should leave the ship there and go into the interior to find out about the inhabitants. While this discussion was going on, however, a violent storm engulfed us, and smashed the ship to pieces on the shore. We barely managed to swim to land, each with his weapons and whatever else he was able to grab.

Epilogue

This was what happened to me as far as the other continent, on the sea, on the islands I visited during the voyage, in the sky and after that in the whale, and when we emerged from its belly with the heroes and the dreams, and finally among the Oxheads and the Asslegs. What happened on that continent, however, I shall tell you in the books that follow.[134]

Appendix:
List of Lucian's Works

I follow here the order of Macleod OCT, which is that found in MS Vaticanus Graecus 90. Spurious works are marked with an asterisk, while those over which doubts are usually expressed are indicated by a bracketed question-mark. Greek titles can be found in Macleod OCT, vol. 1, pp. v–viii and in Anglicized form in Robinson 1979, 239–41. I give the Latin title first (sometimes in a fuller form than is found in Macleod OCT), second the Harmon–Kilburn– Macleod title, third the English title from the translation of Fowler and Fowler 1905 and fourth the title used by myself for this Penguin selection.

1. Phalaris I – Phalaris I – Phalaris I
2. Phalaris II – Phalaris II – Phalaris II
3. Hippias – Hippias, or The Bath
4. Bacchus – Dionysus – Dionysus
5. Hercules – Heracles – Heracles
6. Electrum – Amber, or The Swans – Swans and Amber
7. Muscae Encomium – The Fly – The Fly, an Appreciation – Praising a Fly
8. Nigrinus – Nigrinus – Nigrinus – The Philosopher Nigrinus
9. Demonax – Demonax – Demonax – Demonax the Philosopher
10. De Domo – The Hall – The Hall
11. Patriae Encomium – My Native Land – Patriotism – An Encomium of Fatherland
12. (?) Macrobii (or Longaevi) – Octogenarians
13. Verae Historiae I – A True Story (I) – The True History (I) – True Histories (1)

14. Verae Historiae II – A True Story (II) – The True History (II) – True Histories (2)

15. Calumniae non temere credendum (or De Calumnia) – Slander – Slander, a Warning – Slander

16. Iudicium Vocalium (or Lis Consonantium) – The Consonants at Law – Trial in the Court of Vowels

17. Symposium – The Carousal, or The Lapiths – A Feast of Lapithae

18. (?) Soloecista – The Sham Sophist – The Purist Purized

19. Cataplus – The Downward Journey, or The Tyrant – Voyage to the Lower World – The Journey down to Hades

20. Iuppiter Confutatus – Zeus Catechized – Zeus Cross-Examined

21. Iuppiter Tragoedus – Zeus Rants – Zeus Tragoedus

22. Gallus – The Dream, or The Cock – The Cock

23. Prometheus – Prometheus – Prometheus on Caucasus

24. Icaromenippus – Icaromenippus, or The Sky-Man – Icaromenippus, an Aerial Expedition

25. Timon – Timon, or The Misanthrope – Timon the Misanthrope – Timon the Misanthrope

26. Charon sive Contemplantes – Charon, or The Inspectors – Charon

27. Vitarum Auctio – Philosophies for Sale – Sale of Creeds

28. Piscator – The Dead Come to Life, or The Fisherman – The Fisher

29. Bis Accusatus – The Double Indictment – The Double Indictment – Two Charges of Literary Assault

30. De Sacrificiis – On Sacrifices – Of Sacrifice

31. Adversus Indoctum – The Ignorant Book-Collector – Remarks Addressed to an Illiterate Book-Fancier

32. Somnium sive Vita Luciani – The Dream, or Lucian's Career – The Dream

33. De Parasito – The Parasite: Parasitic an Art – The Parasite – About the Parasite: Proof that Parasitic is an Art

34. Philopseude(i)s – The Lover of Lies, or The Doubter – The Liar

35. Dearum Iudicium – The Judgement of the Goddesses – The Judgement of Paris [= Dialogues of the Gods 20]

36. De Mercede Conductis – On Salaried Posts in Great Houses –
    The Dependent Scholar

37. Anacharsis – Anacharsis, or Athletics – Anacharsis, a Discussion
    of Physical Training

38. Menippus sive Necyomantea – Menippus, or The Descent into
    Hades – Menippus

39. (?) Lucius sive Asinus – Lucius, or The Ass

40. De Luctu – On Funerals – Of Mourning – A Few Words about
    Mourning

41. Rhetorum Praeceptor – A Professor of Public Speaking – The
    Rhetorician's Vade Mecum

42. Alexander – Alexander the False Prophet – Alexander the
    Oracle-Monger

43. Imagines – Essays in Portraiture – A Portrait-Study – Images

44. De Syria Dea – The Goddesse of Surrye [= The Syrian Goddess]

45. De Saltatione – The Dance – Of Pantomime

46. Lexiphanes – Lexiphanes – Lexiphanes

47. Eunuchus – The Eunuch

48. De Astrologia – Astrology

49. (?) Amores – Affairs of the Heart

50. Pro Imaginibus – Essays in Portraiture Defended – Defence of
    the 'Portrait-Study' – In Defence of 'Images'

51. Pseudologista – The Mistaken Critic

52. Deorum Concilium – The Parliament of the Gods – The Gods in
    Council

53. Tyrannicida – The Tyrannicide – The Tyrannicide

54. Abdicatus – Disowned – The Disinherited

55. De Morte Peregrini – The Passing of Peregrinus – The Death of
    Peregrine

56. Fugitivi – The Runaways – The Runaways

57. Toxaris sive De Amicitia – Toxaris, or Friendship – Toxaris: A
    Dialogue of Friendship – Toxaris, or Friendship

58. (?) Demosthenis Encomium – In Praise of Demosthenes –
    Demosthenes, an Encomium

59. Quomodo Historia Conscribenda sit – How to Write History –
    The Way to Write History

60. Dipsades – The Dipsads – Dipsas, the Thirst-Snake
61. Saturnalia – Saturnalia – Saturnalia
62. Herodotus sive Aetion – Herodotus, or Aëtion – Herodotus and Aetion
63. Zeuxis sive Antiochus – Zeuxis, or Antiochus – Zeuxis and Antiochus
64. Pro Lapsu inter Salutandum – A Slip of the Tongue in Greeting – A Slip of the Tongue in Salutation
65. Apologia pro Mercede Conductis – Apology for the 'Salaried Posts in Great Houses' – Apology for 'The Dependent Scholar'
66. Harmonides – Harmonides – Harmonides
67. Hesiodus – A Conversation with Hesiod – A Word with Hesiod
68. Scytha – The Scythian, or The Consul – The Scythian – The Scythian, or The Honorary Consul
69. Podagra sive Tragodopodagra – Gout
70. Hermotimus – Hermotimus, or Concerning the Sects – Hermotimus, or The Rival Philosophies
71. Prometheus es in Verbis – To One who Said 'You're a Prometheus in Words' – A Literary Prometheus – 'So You Think I'm the Prometheus of the Literary World?'
72. (?) Halcyon – Halcyon
73. Navigium seu Vota – The Ship, or The Wishes – The Ship, or The Wishes – The Ship, or Prayers
74. (?) Ocypus – Swift-of-Foot
75. *Libanii De Saltatoribus (Libanius, 'On Dancers')
76. (?) Cynicus – The Cynic – The Cynic
77. Dialogi Mortuorum – Dialogues of the Dead – Dialogues of the Dead
78. Dialogi Marini – Dialogues of the Sea-Gods – Dialogues of the Sea-Gods
79. Dialogi Deorum – Dialogues of the Gods – Dialogues of the Gods
80. Dialogi Meretricii – Dialogues of the Courtesans – Dialogues of the Hetaerae – Chattering Courtesans
81. *Epistulae (Letters)
82. *Philopatris – The Patriot [c. eleventh-century Byzantine imitation]

83. *Charidemus – Charidemus
84. *Nero – Nero
85. *Epigrammata (Epigrams)
86. *Timarion [fourteenth–fifteenth-century imitation]

Notes

IN DEFENCE OF ORIGINALITY

'SO YOU THINK I'M THE PROMETHEUS OF THE LITERARY WORLD?'

1   *Prometheus*: See the Glossary entry for details relevant to picking up the Prometheus allusions in this piece. Throughout the Notes, relevant information, or further relevant information, on named individuals, places, etc. may be found in the Glossary (even when, as is often the case, the reader is not specifically directed there).

2   *Cleon's a Prometheus after the event*: Usually ascribed to Eupolis, who wrote at least one play attacking Cleon, the *Golden Race*, produced in either 426 or 424 BC. Recently, however, it has been reassigned to Aristophanes' *Farmers*, possibly produced in 424 BC (Gargiulo 1992, 161).

3   *purple robes*: See *Two Charges of Literary Assault*, n. 30.

4   *anapaestic metres*: The anapaestic metre was used for the *parabasis* ('coming forward') of a comic (Old Comedy) play, where the chorus spoke directly to the audience in the author's voice or on his behalf.

5   *walking on air . . . airy nonsense*: The examples here all come from Aristophanes' play *Clouds*, first produced at the City Dionysia at Athens of 423 BC. It lampoons Socrates as the proprietor of a school of philosophy.

6   *philosophy's solemnity*: By this Lucian means the dialogue form, the content of which was expected to be philosophical. This usage was instituted by Plato and Xenophon and followed by Aristotle. For Lucian's claim to originality in the 'comic dialogue', see further the Introduction, sections 1 and 5.

TWO CHARGES OF LITERARY ASSAULT

1   *Homer . . . on earth*: Cf. *True Histories* 1.3 for Homer's Odysseus
    as a liar and 2.20 for the 'truth' about his blindness. Homer calls
    the gods 'blessed' at *Odyssey* 6.46 among other places.

2   *his horses . . . to a crisp*: Cf. the problem Phaethon had when he
    tried to drive the Sun's (his father's) chariot.

3   *cooking up lamb-and-tortoise stew*: Croesus, king of Lydia, want-
    ing to test the perspicacity of various oracles sent a messenger
    with the question 'What is Croesus doing now?' The Delphic
    oracle answered correctly (in verse) that he was cooking lamb and
    tortoise together in a cauldron. The story comes from Herodotus,
    Histories 1.46ff.

4   *the Lydian*: Croesus (see previous note).

5   *he looks on . . . others' sorrows*: The source of the quotation is
    unknown, but it is in Ionic Greek (the accepted dialect for medical
    writing). I have marked its difference by translating the prose
    original as verse.

6   *herdsman at Nemea*: Argos.

7   *the other gods . . . its bosom*: Zeus incorporates *Iliad* 2.1–2 into
    this prose sentence, verses which begin a narrative about his
    sleeplessness while he plans to fulfil his promise to Thetis to
    honour Achilles. See also note 9 below.

8   *We'll certainly starve*: The humorous notion that the gods are
    dependent upon human sacrifice and would starve without it
    goes back to Old Comedy, notably the *Birds* and *Wealth* of
    Aristophanes.

9   *'in my heart' . . . 'in my mind'*: Zeus again invokes the language
    associated with a narrative about him in Homer (*Iliad* 2.3 and
    5). See note 7 above.

10 *lawsuit market*: This is a strange phrase (*agoran dikon*), highly
    reminiscent of the 'lawcourt bazaar' mentioned in Aristophanes,
    Knights 979, which could be an allusion to a scene in a contempor-
    ary comedy. It is possible, then, that what follows is based on, or
    alludes to, a no longer surviving Old Comedy, possibly by Crat-
    inus or Eupolis.

11 *son of Sophroniscus*: Socrates.

12 *the Eleven*: The *Hendeka* were the body of magistrates at Athens
    answerable to the archons (chief magistrates) and responsible for
    executing legal punishments and for the upkeep of the state prison
    where Socrates was put to death.

13 *hadn't even offered . . . Asclepius*: The reference is to the last

words of Socrates addressed to Crito in Plato's *Phaedo* (118a): 'Crito, we owe a cockerel to Asclepius. Make sure you don't forget to offer it.' Crito replies, 'I'll do it.' Asclepius was the god of healing and the offering suggests thanks to the deity for curing the sickness of life.

14 *old cloaks . . . your virtue*: The physical description best suits the Cynics who followed the outdoor lifestyle pioneered by Diogenes, but it was the Stoics for whom virtue was the central goal of life and philosophy.

15 *quarrels . . . hold about me*: A favourite theme of Lucian's. Cf. *The Carousal*, in which a wedding-feast attended by philosophers of different sects ends in an unseemly brawl.

16 *Pityocampteses*: As with the other denizens mentioned here, there was only one Pityocamptes ('Pinebender') – see entry for Sinis in Glossary.

17 *Pan . . . without being called*: Herodotus (*Histories* 6.105) tells the story of Pheidippides the runner's meeting with Pan on his journey to Sparta to get help from them against the Persians. He asked Pheidippides why the Athenians did not honour him for his friendliness to them, for what he had done for them in the past and would do for them in the future. After the battle, Pan's cult was established at Athens. This was because Pan was thought to have helped them at Marathon, as an inscription found in the acropolis cave-shrine shows, though Herodotus does not specifically say.

18 *pays tax . . . resident foreigner*: Resident foreigners at Athens, metics, were obliged to pay a special residence tax, known as the *metoikion*.

19 *satyrs*: These wild male creatures, represented on Athenian vases with pointed ears, horse-tails and erect phalluses, are as often associated with Dionysus as with Pan.

20 *strange words*: All these terms can be found in Plato, though later philosophers such as Aristotle and Epicurus also used them. The picture of philosophy is probably meant to be generic, as it were a layman's view.

21 *I've often seen lots of them . . .*: The sexual hypocrisy of philosophers is another favourite theme in Lucian. Cf. *Chattering Courtesans* 10.4 and *True Histories* 2.19.

22 *three obols*: In Athenian coinage, there were six obols to the drachma (see *Timon the Misanthrope*, n. 60). The ferry fare from Piraeus to Aegina was four obols, according to *The Ship* 15.

23 *Dionysius*: Dionysius the Renegade.

24   *neglect . . . wanton abuse*: Rhetoric (like Comedy in Cratinus'
     comedy *The Wine-Flask* of 423 BC) is cast as the Syrian's
     (Lucian's) wife and the charge implies, according to Athenian
     law, that she is an heiress attempting to recoup her property from
     a husband who has mistreated her. Dialogue's charge, *hybris*, is
     the most serious one that could be brought at Athens. The penalty
     was unlimited and could even be death. See further Fisher 1992
     and cf. *Timon the Misanthrope*, n. 34, *Toxaris*, n. 66 and *Images*,
     n. 53.

25   *arraigned without a name*: Old Comedy was believed to have
     gone through a period where the names of those attacked could
     not be used in the plays. Lucian is following and playing with this
     perceived convention. See also *True Histories* 1.2 with n. 1.

26   *water into the clock*: A water-clock was used at Athens to ensure
     strict time-keeping for both speeches in certain types of case
     (Harrison 1998, vol. 2, 161). See also *In Defence of 'Images'*,
     n. 17.

27   *unmixed wine*: The Greeks normally drank wine quite heavily
     diluted with water (cf. *True Histories*, n. 9). Drinking wine
     straight was considered a barbarian habit leading to severe mental
     and physical disabilities. The wine was mixed with water in a
     large bowl (*krater*), and it was from this that the cups were filled
     (Cf. *The Journey down to Hades*, n. 26).

28   *Academy . . . opposing argument well*: The Academy under
     Arcesilaus developed a form of Scepticism which involved using
     Socrates' method of inquiry to argue both sides of a case (not in
     itself a Socratic stance).

29   *lying down drinking*: Greeks (and Romans) reclined on couches
     at drinking-parties or banquets, rather than sitting down to eat
     and drink.

30   *purple cloak*: Purple dye, manufactured from certain types of
     shellfish, was expensive and regularly signifies wealth, power and
     the luxury that usually attends them.

31   *the one with the paint and elaborate highlights*: Lucian plays
     ironically here upon the decoration of the Painted Stoa (see Gloss-
     ary) and the figure of a gaudily dressed and made-up woman (a
     courtesan, in Lucian's social vocabulary: see paragraph 31 and
     Chattering Courtesans, n. 1), the fitting image, rather, of Stoa's
     opponent, Pleasure, and humorously inappropriate to the manly
     ascetic figure (*à la* the Stoic philosopher) that Stoa immediately
     presents.

32   *is taking . . . mind's elsewhere*: Euripides, *Phoenician Women* 360.

33   *'material' and 'immaterial' ... 'approved' and 'disapproved'*:
These are Stoic technical terms. The first distinction is between
things in our control (the 'material') and those not (the 'immaterial'). The second refers to the classification of things not in
our control, which depends on their contribution towards the
attainment of virtue (the 'approved' help, the 'disapproved' hinder). A more extended satire of Stoic logic can be found in
Lucian's *Philosophies for Sale* 20–25.

34   *third figure of indemonstrables*: Chrysippus produced five syllogisms which he called 'indemonstrables' because they require no
proof. The third figure runs: 'Plato is not both dead and alive; he
is dead, therefore he is not alive.'

35   *judgment*: The Greek word used here, *kriterion* (from which
English 'criterion' derives), has two senses, which are both in play
here and are the source of the humour: (1) a 'way to judge', in the
epistemological sense, i.e. whether something is true, real or not;
(2) a 'legal tribunal'. Pyrrhon's Scepticism was actually epistemological (there is no way to decide anything for sure), but he is here
being taken to make the much narrower (and more pertinent)
claim that there is no such thing as a true legal tribunal, one that can
issue valid (legal) judgments. Cf. *True Histories* 2.18 with n. 79.

36   *in future*: Rhetoric's introduction up to this point consists of
slightly adapted versions of the first sentence from Demosthenes'
speech *On the Crown* and the first sentence of his *Third Olyn-
thiac*. Lucian would certainly have expected his audience to recognize these borrowings and to judge them inept. Compare his
contemptuous treatment of the contemporary historian of the
Parthian War who began his work with the first sentence of
Thucydides' *History of the Peloponnesian War*, with only the
names changed (*How to Write History* 15).

37   *enormous dowry ... tribe ... citizen*: Claiming citizenship in
Athens involved registration with various bodies, which included
the 'tribe' (*phyle*), an association of demes from different localities
established in 508/7 BC by Cleisthenes (see *Timon the Misanthrope*, n. 43). Athenian law from 451 BC onwards denied citizenship to foreigners, except by special grant of the people. Rhetoric
implies that it was Lucian's grasp of Attic Greek which supported
his claim to being a Greek. See Introduction, section 4, Swain
1996 and Whitmarsh 2001a for the 'construction' of Greek identity in this period.

38   *He can't possibly ... only one of him*: We do not know how, if
at all, Lucian 'performed' his dialogues (see Introduction, section

5). But if he did so alone, then this is a nice irony. Lucian will be taking Hermes' part just as he denies that such a thing is possible.

39 *Do not suppose ... current needs*: More irony, if his audience already knew the *True Histories* (see previous note and *True Histories* 1.1–4).

40 *famous demesman of Paeania*: Demosthenes.

41 *'the universal periodic cycle'*: The idea referred to here may be that the universe is periodically consumed by fire and then regenerated. However, this notion is Stoic, while the dialogue form is associated with Plato (and Aristotle). However, Plato quite often uses the term 'cycle' (*periodos*) of a long period of time and it may be that Lucian is thinking of passages in *Phaedrus* (249a: reincarnation, and 246–8: circular revolutions, great circuits, of the universe), given that in the next sentence he quotes this dialogue twice (see next note).

42 *I 'trod on ... sky's back'*: The three quoted phrases are from (1) Aristophanes, *Clouds* 225, where Socrates, suspended above the stage in a basket, says: 'I tread the air and circumcontemplate the sun'; (2) Plato, *Phaedrus* 246e; (3) Plato, *Phaedrus* 247b.

43 *iambus*: A form of poetry whose central function was personal abuse. Its chief practitioners were Archilochus of Paros (seventh century BC) and Hipponax of Ephesus and later Clazomenae (sixth century BC).

44 *ancient dogs*: I.e. Cynic philosophers.

45 *not prose ... not poetry*: Traditionally, Menippean satire is defined as having mixed prose and verse together (cf. Seneca's *Apocolocyntosis*). Lucian quite often uses poetic quotation (e.g. at the start of *Zeus Rants*). But it is possible that what he means here is the deliberate use of vocabulary from poetic sources along with that of normal prose to create a hybrid style.

46 *Comedy*: Lucian means Old Comedy, the satirical drama with fantastic plots written by Aristophanes, Eupolis and Cratinus (see Preface to this section) during the fifth century BC.

47 *'Is the soul ... art of flattery?'*: Themes dealt with by Plato in *Phaedo* (*passim*), *Timaeus* (35a, 41d) and *Gorgias* (463b, d, 465c), respectively.

48 *Platonic Ideas*: The notion, outlined first in Plato's *Republic*, that everything in the real world derives its nature from a generic category (a 'Form' or 'Idea') which exists in a higher realm than ours.

49 *voting-pebble with the hole*: In the fourth century BC, ballots in Athenian courts were made in a form similar to that of a child's

top. Those for acquittal were solid, while those for condemnation were pierced through the central axis. This elaborate ending might involve reference to Philocleon, in Aristophanes' *Wasps*, who is smitten with jury-mania and is incapable of voting to acquit anyone, until cured by his son.

FAVOURITE PHILOSOPHERS

DEMONAX THE PHILOSOPHER

1 *Sostratus*: This is almost certainly the same person called 'Herodes Atticus' Heracles' and 'Agathion' by Philostratus (*Lives of the Sophists* 2.1). Philostratus' description focuses on Agathion's physical appearance, his claim to semi-divine birth, his bare-handed fights with animals, his diet of milk and barley-meal, the purity of his Attic Greek, his unusual views on Greek culture and his uncanny ability to detect a woman's hand in the milking from the mere smell of the milk offered to him. Jones (1986, 99–100) suggests that Lucian may have treated him as a self-taught philosopher and that his motive for writing the biography, now lost, may have been flattery of Herodes. However, it could rather have been his odd perspective on Greek culture that attracted Lucian's attention (compare Anacharsis' view on athletics in Lucian's *Anacharsis* with Agathion's comments on them in Philostratus and see Introduction, section 5).

2 *with unwashed feet . . . proverb has it*: The proverb appears to mean 'unprepared', though ancient sources do not explain why.

3 *not . . . skin deep*: Literally 'he had not touched them merely with the proverbial fingertip'.

4 *man from Sinope*: Diogenes. The image used by Lucian in the next sentence plays on Diogenes' family connection with banking and his exile for minting counterfeit coin.

5 *no Socratic irony about him*: Socrates was noted for his 'irony', saying one thing while meaning another. One of Lucian's best jokes has Socrates in Hades claiming that he really had meant it when he said that he knew nothing, but that everyone else thought this was irony (*Dialogues of the Dead* 6 (20).5).

6 *full of Attic charm*: In contrast to Socrates, Demonax said what he meant. His 'Attic charm' (*charis Attike*) (known in Latin as 'Attic salt') is the wit with which he took the bluntness out of his criticisms.

7 *To err is human*: Proverbial already in Xenophon (*Cyropaedia*
5.4.19) and Menander (fr. 389, *PCG*). I have borrowed 'to err
is human' from Alexander Pope's *Essay on Criticism* (1711),
l. 525.

8 *their troubles . . . overtake them*: In other words, they would soon
die. The theme of human stupidity in the face of death is explored
by Lucian in many of his Underworld dialogues, especially
Dialogues of the Dead.

9 *'Persuasion sat upon his lips'*: Eupolis was referring to the
Athenian politician Pericles. The fragment is from his play the
Demes, produced possibly in 416 BC (fr. 102.5, *PCG*). See also
The Philosopher Nigrinus 7 with n. 11 and *Images* 13 with n. 30
for other uses of this passage.

10 *garland*: It would not have been normal to wear a garland to face
a prosecution, but sacrificial victims were always so attired. As
Demonax makes clear at the end of this paragraph, his garb is a
dramatic gesture announcing potential victimhood.

11 *'I don't think . . . offerings from me'*: The same attitude towards
sacrifice is found in Lucian's *On Sacrifices*. Note especially the
final words of the piece (paragraph 15): 'Such practices and creeds
of the majority do not, it seems to me, require someone to criticize
them, but a Democritus to laugh at the ignorance of their
exponents and a Heraclitus to weep for their lunacy.'

12 *Favorinus*: Favorinus of Arles' lack of testicles and of secondary
male characteristics (the focus of the jokes in paragraphs 12–13)
may have been due to Reifenstein's syndrome, which is caused by
an endocrine disorder. On the oratory of Favorinus, see Philostratus, *Lives of the Sophists* 1.8, Aulus Gellius (*c.* 130–*c.* 180),
Attic Nights (*passim*), Bowersock 1969, Gleason 1995, Whitmarsh 2001a and Whitmarsh 2001b, 294–303.

13 *sophist from Sidon*: Jones (1986, 95) claims that this individual
cannot be identified. However, some have thought it might be
Maximus of Tyre (*c.* 125–185), author of forty-one extant
Lectures, and I have elsewhere suggested Hadrian of Tyre
(*c.* 113–193) (Philostratus, *Lives of the Sophists* 2.10; Sidwell
1986, 122–3, n. 16).

14 *we are dealing here . . . trespass on your premises*: Again English
cannot exactly capture the pun here. The ambiguity in the Greek
concerns the use of a word (the verb *peraino*, 'I conclude') to refer
to (1) a type of syllogism or (2) a sexual act. Demonax' words
could mean either (1) 'the syllogism is the type called *concluding*'
or (2) 'you are being penetrated', i.e. are submitting to anal sex.

See Jones 1986, 11, n. 25 and 96, n. 42 for the idea that this Python is from Beroea and that *The Scythian* may have been delivered there (see Preface to that piece and *Toxaris*).

15 *your own ring*: A scholiast points out that Demonax is making an obscene double entendre, since the word for ring, *daktylios*, also means 'anus'. A boy who is prepared to claim property which does not belong to him may also be susceptible to sexual corruption.

16 *He would never . . . 'Arcesilaus'*: In Greek, the joke rests on a pun between the word *arktos* ('bear') and the name *Arkesilaos*. However, it is possible that there is a further level to the humour, if Demonax insists on giving a Cynic the name of a famous Platonic philosopher.

17 *'You're not a Cynic' . . . 'You're not a human being'*: The joke in Greek relies on a double meaning of the verb *kynan*, 'to practise Cynic philosophy'. Demonax interprets it in the literal sense 'You're not a dog.'

18 *antipodeans*: Literally 'people with their feet opposite (ours)'. Philosophers speculated that the earth, being a globe, might contain another inhabited region directly opposite their own (cf. Plutarch, *Moralia* 869c). Lucian mentions the idea again explicitly at *The Ship* 44 and implicitly at *True Histories* 2.47.

19 *a great mocker . . . discourses*: Here again Demonax is in line with Lucian's own preoccupations. Compare, for example, the attacks in *Lexiphanes* and *A Professor of Public Speaking* on the arcane vocabulary of sophists.

20 *Agathocles*: Known only from this passage.

21 *Cethegus the consul*: The incident must be set before his consulship (AD 170), since he is on his way to the province of Asia to serve in a subordinate capacity.

22 *legate*: *Legati* were senators appointed to serve as governors (when of consular rank), or as legionary commanders (when of praetorian rank) under the governor.

23 *Apollonius with his Argonauts*: The joke is a pun on the name of the Alexandrian epic poet Apollonius of Rhodes, who wrote *The Voyage of the Argo*. It may also be an attack on the philosopher Apollonius' greed, since like Jason he is in search of a (different sort of) 'Golden Fleece'.

24 *Someone else . . . like everything else*: The intention of the questioner is probably to establish Demonax' philosophical creed. Demonax disallows easy categorization by appearing to accept the Platonic position (the soul is immortal) but then qualifying it

by the Epicurean idea that the soul, like everything in the universe, is made up of material (atoms) which lasts for ever, but is constantly reshaped into other things.

25   *we don't . . . one soul each*: The reference is to Plato, *Laws* 896e, where the Athenian identifies 'soul' as the cause of all things and goes on: 'One soul or more? I will answer on your behalf, "more". In any case let us assume no fewer than two, the beneficent and the maleficent.'

26   *minas*: A mina (*mna*) was the weight of 100 drachma coins (= 431 g) (and as a term for monetary value also equalled 100 drachmas – see *Timon the Misanthrope*, n. 60). Cf. *The Ship*, n. 25.

27   *man called Polybius*: Jones (1986, 96) provisionally identifies this person with the Polybius of Sardis who erected a bust of Cicero in his native city and may have written a work *On Solecism*.

28   *'I wish he'd . . . rather than a Roman'*: The point of the joke seems to be that Polybius uses *Latin* word order (*Imperator me civitate Romana honoravit*) in his Greek sentence, which order I have solecistically followed in my English translation.

29   *purple stripe . . . no more than a sheep*: Roman senators wore togas with a purple stripe. Thomas More borrowed the sheep motif in the second book of his *Utopia* (1516) to describe the Utopians' reaction to the Anemolian ambassadors' pride in their rich apparel.

30   *Hades . . . when I get there*: Lucian criticizes popular conceptions of Hades for their lack of eyewitness support in *A Few Words about Mourning* 2ff. and ironically composes such accounts in *Menippus* and *True Histories*.

31   *Admetus*: This individual is not mentioned in any other source.

32   *Spartan whipping . . . your equal*: Spartans had initiation rituals which involved their boys being whipped at an altar to test their endurance (see Lucian's *Anacharsis* 38 for a full account, and Kennell 1995, 149ff. for all the testimony). The joke involves the assumption that the whipping ritual itself represents the main qualification for being a Spartiate (one of the ruling class).

33   *Danae . . . Acrisius*: In myth, Danae was Acrisius' daughter. But here the similarity of the names is peripheral to the pun on 'Acrisius', as though it meant 'not (*a-*) judging (*krisis*)'.

34   *pestle . . . Pestleson*: The pun in Greek rests on *hyperon* ('pestle') and the name *Hyperides*. There is likely to be a further layer of humour in the inappropriateness of a Cynic's following in the footsteps of Hyperides. Possibly the fourth-century BC politician

and orator of this name is meant and the point Demonax is making is merely that his target is not a philosopher but a rhetorician.

35 *pankration*: A sport combining boxing and wrestling, it allowed kicking, wrenching and strangling, but not biting or gouging.

36 *statue . . . bronze image*: Cynegeirus' heroic loss of his hand (and life) at Marathon may have been commemorated in Polygnotus' famous painting of the battle in the Painted Stoa.

37 *Rufinus . . . lame Peripatetic*: Rufinus is known only from this passage. The joke is another pun, this time based on (1) the name of the philosophical school of Aristotle, which was taken from the *peripatoi* ('walks around'), i.e. covered porticoes, around the Lyceum, (2) the literal meaning of the word and (3) the lameness of Rufinus.

38 *Epictetus once . . . daughters, then*: The joke presumably is that Epictetus was also unmarried and childless.

39 *Aristotle's ten Categories . . . prosecutions*: Another pun, this time, as the translation suggests, on two meanings of the word *kategoria*, 'category' and 'prosecution'. (Aristotle's categories were kinds of predicates, such as substance, quantity, quality and relation.)

40 *Altar of Pity*: This well-known place of sanctuary in Athens is also mentioned at *Timon the Misanthrope* 42.

41 *The wretch . . . the same*: *Iliad* 9.320, in Alexander Pope's translation (1715–20). Literally: 'The man who achieves nothing and the man of great achievements are both equally destined to die.' Achilles is replying to Odysseus' embassy from Agamemnon and refusing the offer of reconciliation.

42 *'But I . . . Aristippus'*: Demonax' comment has a sting in the tail, since Aristippus was generally regarded as a follower of pleasure, a figure whose ideals and lifestyle were diametrically opposed to those of Socrates and Diogenes (see further *Two Charges of Literary Assault* 23).

43 *The smell will get me buried*: The futility and absurdity of funeral rituals is a theme also explored by Lucian in *A Few Words about Mourning*.

THE PHILOSOPHER NIGRINUS

1   *A LETTER TO NIGRINUS*: The letter directly, if humorously, implicates Lucian in the dialogue (as the 'Traveller'). This somewhat undermines the arguments of those who see the dialogue's

frame as satirically undercutting the seriousness of the central panel (see Preface to this section). However, it is possible that it was fabricated by a later writer anxious to commit the author to a serious stance (cf. Eunapius, *Lives of the Philosophers and Sophists* 454, where only *Demonax the Philosopher* is singled out as fully serious: see Introduction, section 6, n. 44).

2   *'Owls to Athens'*: Besides the literal absurdity (cf. 'coals to Newcastle'), there are two other resonances to 'owls to Athens': (1) the owl was the bird of Athena, patron goddess of Athens; (2) it was therefore symbolic of Athena's wisdom (and so, by extension, of philosophy).

3   *ignorance leads . . . people timid*: The point is made in the famous Funeral Oration of Pericles in Thucydides, *History of the Peloponnesian War* 2.40.3. Lucian quotes directly only the words 'ignorance [leads to] brazenness', but produces an elegant variation of the second half of the sentence, 'reasoning brings timidity'.

4   *'thrice-blessed'*: The word (*trisolbios*) is found in Sophocles, but the words 'fortunate' (*makarios*) and 'thrice-blessed' are found together in Aristophanes (*Women at the Assembly* 1129).

5   *Rome*: Lucian does not use the name of the empire's capital, but calls it merely 'the city', following the practice in Latin (*urbs*). I have used 'Rome' for clarity's sake throughout (though note the ambiguous reference in paragraph 17, where I have left 'the city').

6   *Homeric lotus*: The reference is to the episode in the *Odyssey* (9.82–104) where some of Odysseus' companions eat the lotus and become utterly forgetful of their native land.

7   *Indians*: Lucian's interest in India is manifested in the introductory piece *Dionysus*, where he uses the Indians' attitude to Dionysus' mythical conquest of India as a metaphor for his audience's reaction to his own works.

8   *'spurring a willing horse' . . . Homer*: The quotation is from Teucer's spiky reply to Agamemnon's unneeded encouragement at *Iliad* 8.293.

9   *memory-exercise*: The word used is *melete*, the term commonly employed to describe the declamations of sophists in Lucian's day, often improvised on the spot (see Lucian, *A Professor of Public Speaking* 17; Philostratus, *Lives of the Sophists* 1.21.5, 2.21, etc.). But it could also refer to a practice speech on a fictitious theme.

10 *lovers . . . affection*: The 'lovers' here are masculine and the word

translated as 'object of their affection' is *paidika*, which most often refers to a younger male.

11 *left his sting in his audience*: Said of Pericles in Eupolis' *Demes*, produced possibly in 416 BC (fr. 102.7, *PCG*). An earlier line from the same passage is deployed by the narrator in *Demonax the Philosopher* 10. See *Images* 13 with n. 30 for another use of this passage.

12 *By Hermes . . . prologue!*: The irony is reinforced by the oath, since Hermes was the patron god of orators.

13 *You've followed . . . to the letter*: Literally: 'Your prologue has been constructed according to the orators' rule.' In fact, handbooks giving clear regulations for the composition of various types of epideictic speech were available (e.g. the somewhat later manuals attributed to Menander Rhetor of Laodicea, late third century AD(?)).

14 *competition*: This picks up and extends the theatrical image, since at Athens plays were always staged at dramatic festivals in competition for prizes (cf. *In Defence of 'Images'* 29 with n. 46).

15 *look fearsome . . . gaping mouths*: Theatrical masks underwent a development from the more realistic (fifth–fourth century BC) to the grotesque (third century BC onwards). Lucian's experience is clearly of masks with an exaggerated forehead (the *onkos*, 'bulge') and wide-open mouths of the type seen in Roman art (Green 1994, figs 6.10 and 6.11). See also *Toxaris* 9 with n. 10.

16 *'every street . . . is full'*: See *Iliad* 5.642 and *Odyssey* 2.388 for use of the phrase 'all the streets are full (of)'. Aratus is the poet who developed this fuller expression (*Phainomena* 2–3). Lucian uses it elsewhere (in *Prometheus* 14 and *Icaromenippus* 24).

17 *the city*: Normally used in this piece to refer to Rome – see note 5. Here, however, the point of reference is ambiguous, since it is Athens that Nigrinus has praised, yet the previous paragraph refers to Rome. If the latter is meant, there is heavy irony.

18 *Why then . . . bright light*: This is a formulaic line, found many times in Homer, e.g. *Odyssey* 11.93–4.

19 *sykophantai*: See *Timon the Misanthrope*, n. 36. Here, in the context of imperial Rome, the term would have had the more general sense of 'informers', 'slanderers', 'backbiters', or even 'deceivers' or 'cheats'.

20 *pulled . . . and din*: Lucian paraphrases *Iliad* 11.163 and quotes line 164 in full.

21 *high up . . . watch what goes on*: The motif of 'katascopy'

('looking down from a height') on human life is common in Lucian. Cf. for example *Charon* (where the ferryman enters the upper world and watches life from a pile of mountains constructed by Hermes) and *Icaromenippus* (where Menippus observes human folly from the moon).

22 *sail past them*: As Odysseus did with the Sirens, *Odyssey* 12.158ff. The allegorical interpretation of Homer (the Sirens represent the temptations of pleasure and Odysseus' endurance the ability of the virtuous man to ignore their attraction) goes back to the sixth century BC but was especially linked later with the Stoics. See *Slander* 30 for another example of the allegorizing use of the passage, and *Images* 14 with n. 34 for a possibly ironic use of this motif and interpretation.

23 *meet through an underling*: The reference seems to be to the *nomenclator*, a slave who told his master the names of those he met while canvassing or walking in the street.

24 *ridiculous*: The motifs in this section, the clients' and hangers-on's weary round and the dinner, are highly reminiscent of Roman satire. Cf. for example Juvenal, *Satires* 1.127f. for the client's day and 5 *passim* for the dinner.

25 *claim to be philosophers ... could happen*: Once more, the hypo-critical philosopher can be found in Roman satire (e.g. Juvenal, *Satires* 2), but this theme is one beloved of Lucian (for the *soi-disant* philosopher's gluttony and bad behaviour at dinners, see his *Carousal*).

26 *circus ... individuals*: The circus (called in Greek the *hippo-dromos*) was the venue for chariot-races and is mentioned regularly in Roman satire (e.g. Juvenal, *Satires* 3.223) and Suetonius (b. *c.* AD 70) notes the enthusiasm of emperors for various chariot-racing teams (*Caligula* 55, *Domitian* 7). The Christian writer Tertullian (d. *c.* AD 225) gives an account of Roman spectacles in his *On the Games*.

27 *so that they won't ... veracity*: The satirical writer Petronius (d. *c.* AD 65) is reported by Tacitus to have written a detailed account of Nero's sexual misdemeanours in his will and sent it to the emperor (*Annals* 16.19).

28 *breaking in ... door*: The reference point cannot be traced in any of the extant plays.

29 *Momus*: This deity is mentioned often by Lucian (*Dionysus* 8, *True Histories* 2.3, *Icaromenippus* 31, *The Judgement of the Goddesses* 2, *How to Write History* 33, *Hermotimus* 20) and is found as a character in *Zeus Rants* and *The Parliament of the*

Gods. The Italian humanist Leon Battista Alberti named a Latin satirical novel (1452), inspired by Lucian, after him (see Marsh 1998, 114–29, 161).

30 *the god . . . bull*: Poseidon. Lucian uses the myth again in *Hermotimus* 20. See also *True Histories* 2.3 with n. 48.

31 *garlands . . . right place for them*: Garlands were worn on the head at drinking-parties.

32 *sponsor*: *Choregos* ('chorus-sponsor'), the wealthy man who in Athens during the fifth–fourth century BC paid for the equipping and training of choruses at the musical and dramatic festivals (see Wilson 2000).

33 *Phaeacian syndrome*: The reference is to the reaction of the Phaeacians to the narration by Odysseus of his adventures (*Odyssey* 11.333–4, 13.1–2): 'So he spoke and they remained silent, held enraptured in the shadowy halls.' It is worth pointing out that in *True Histories* 1.3, Odysseus' narrative is the archetype of the tall tale and the Phaeacians poor saps who were too naive to spot a lie. The allusion might be taken to undercut the seriousness of the central narrative. See Preface to this section.

34 *seized by . . . tongue failed*: It is almost certainly not accidental that these symptoms echo those of Sappho's famous homo-erotic ode fr. 31 (*Poetarum Lesbiorum Fragmenta*, ed. E. Lobel and D. L. Page (1955)). Note especially the inability to speak and the sweating. The reaction is that of a lover to the object of his affections. Cf. Lucian's *The Goddesse of Surrye* 17 and *Timon the Misanthrope* 17. Again, the inappropriateness of such responses could be taken to undercut the seriousness of the central narrative.

35 *'graze the surface'*: A phrase from *Iliad* 17.599.

36 *Fire thus . . . salvation's light*: The line is *Iliad* 8.282, where Agamemnon is (needlessly) encouraging the archer Teucer. A later part of this passage was used in paragraph 6.

37 *Phrygian pipes goes mad*: Some ancient mystery cults utilized the *aulos* (double-reed pipe) to induce a state of ecstasy in the worshippers. Plato mentions the way in which such music is used as therapy for mentally and emotionally disturbed individuals (*Laws* 790d–e). Here the Traveller uses the analogy to suggest that his apparent madness is in fact a sign that he is cured.

38 *go to the man . . . to heal us*: The analogy is strange, since the Traveller insisted at the start (paragraph 1) that he had become a new man because of his time with Nigrinus. What are we to make of the claim that what he has is an infection, requiring homoeopathic treatment? See also notes 33 and 34.

DAMNING DIATRIBES

SLANDER

1   *Labdacids, Pelopids . . . families*: For example, Aeschylus' *Seven
    against Thebes*, Sophocles' *Oedipus the King*, *Antigone* and *Oedi-
    pus at Colonus* and Euripides' *Phoenician Women* deal with the
    Labdacids, while Aeschylus' *Oresteia* and Euripides' *Iphigenia in
    Aulis*, *Orestes* and *Iphigenia in Tauris* treat of the Pelopids. It is
    possible that Lucian has in mind Aristotle's description of tragic
    families at *Poetics* 1453a.

2   *Ignorance . . . from a tragedy*: It is possible that Lucian is alluding
    to Aristotle, *Poetics* 1452a, where ignorance is mentioned as one
    of the central components of tragic *anagnorisis* ('recognition').

3   *He too had been slandered*: The phrasing in the Greek also
    suggests the possibility that Lucian is writing (as some of his
    fifteenth-century translators and imitators did) in response to
    personal circumstances.

4   *the whole plot*: The dates of Apelles and Ptolemy Philopator,
    fourth and third century BC, respectively, make it clear this anec-
    dote is untrue. The name and profession of Antiphilus are also
    real, but it looks as though his name ('Mutually affectionate') has
    been chosen because it is meaningful within the anecdote.

5   *talents*: See *Timon the Misanthrope*, n. 60 and *The Ship*, n. 25.

6   *Deceit . . . Remorse*: Lucian makes up his own allegorical paint-
    ing, on the Apelles model explicitly, in *On Salaried Posts in Great
    Houses* 42, and includes the figures of Deceit and Remorse in it.

7   *comedies . . . three actors*: There were three actors in tragedy too.
    Possibly, Lucian chose comedy as his theatrical model for playing
    out the drama of slander because he was trying to emphasize that
    a happy outcome (see Aristotle, *Poetics* 1453a) ought to attend
    such accusations, if his precepts are adhered to.

8   *the slanderer . . . communicated*: This set of distinctions had
    already been made by Herodotus, in the speech made to Xerxes
    by Artabanus (*Histories* 7.10): 'Slander is a most dreadful thing.
    It involves the injustice of two persons and the suffering of injus-
    tice by a third. The slanderer commits an injustice in condemning
    a person who is not present, while his hearer's crime is to be
    persuaded before he learns the true facts. The absent party suffers
    the twin injustices of being slandered by one of these men and
    being thought an evil man by the other.'

9   *the jurors swear . . . those of the other*: For example, Demosthenes
     reminds the jurors in *On the Crown* 2 of 'the laws and the oath,
     in which . . . a prime injunction is to listen to both sides with
     equal attention'.

10   *Do not . . . both speeches*: Lucian's formulation ('the supreme
     poet') implies that this is from Homer. The scholia attribute it
     to Phocylides, and Cicero to Hesiod. It is already known to
     Aristophanes in 422 BC (*Wasps* 725).

11   *gladiators*: The word Lucian uses is *monomachountes*, literally
     'men entering single combat', a classical Greek word. But he uses
     it elsewhere of a Roman gladiatorial contest (*Toxaris* 58 and 59,
     Demonax the Philosopher 57 and *Chattering Courtesans* 13.5).
     It is a good example of the way Atticists try to muffle the difference
     in culture between the world of their sources and their own times.

12   *The War God . . . killer too*: The words of Hector at *Iliad* 18.309,
     rejecting the sage advice of Polydamas to return to Troy.

13   *starting-gate is lowered*: Greek foot-races were started by the use
     of some restraining device, whose nature is still not entirely clear.
     See *The Journey down to Hades* 4 and *Timon the Misanthrope* 20.

14   *Stratonice*: Lucian tells various stories about Stratonice in *The
     Goddesse of Surrye* 17f., including one in which she slanders
     Combabos to her jealous husband (23f.), and this may be the
     basis of the allusion here.

15   *Philoxenus*: Philoxenus of Cythera (*c.* 435–380 BC) was a dithy-
     rambic poet at the court of Dionysius I of Syracuse, himself a
     dramatist. It is possible that anecdotes about his punishment by
     Dionysius are in Lucian's mind here (he sent Philoxenus to the
     stone-quarries).

16   *son of a god*: Plutarch gives an account of beliefs about Alex-
     ander's mother Olympias' pregnancy by Zeus-Ammon in the
     form of a snake (*Life of Alexander* 2–3). By 331 BC, Alexander
     was representing himself as the son of Zeus and there is anecdotal
     tradition which suggests that in 324 he wrote to the Greek cities
     suggesting that divine honours be voted to him (as well as hero
     status to Hephaestion). Lucian makes great play with Alexander's
     mortality in *Dialogues of the Dead* 12 (14) and 13 (see also 25
     (12) and *True Histories* 2.9 for Alexander's pre-eminence as a
     general, even after death).

17   *love of novelty . . . the unusual*: The 'urge for new experiences' is
     one of the reasons given by Lucian in *True Histories* 1.5 for his
     voyage, and 'the unusual' in writers of marvels like Iambulus is a
     focus for his satirical criticism of 'lying tales'.

18 *'broods in his soul's depth'*: The poet is Homer (though this
    verb, *byssodomeuein*, 'to meditate deeply', also occurs in Hesiod,
    Shield 30). Though it always occurs in Homer in the set phrase
    (formula) 'pondering evil in his heart' (see e.g. *Odyssey* 8.273,
    9.316, 17.66), Lucian uses only the verb here. This is a good
    example of the migration of poetic vocabulary into 'art prose' in
    later Greek writing.

19 *Personally . . . saying something else*: This is a paraphrase of the
    famous Homeric line from the *Iliad* (9.313) in which Achilles tells
    Odysseus, one of Agamemnon's ambassadors, that 'that man is
    my enemy as much as are the Gates of Hades who hides one thing
    in his heart and says another'. But once more Lucian uses the
    Homeric vocabulary in his allusion.

20 *Die, Proetus . . . wished it not*: *Iliad* 6.164–5. Anteia had propos-
    itioned Bellerophon and was now covering her tracks and taking
    revenge for rejection by getting her husband, Proetus, to kill the
    young man.

21 *his nickname*: 'The just'. Lucian invokes the usual picture of him
    in *True Histories* 2.10, where he is called on as an adviser in the
    tricky case of Lucian's status on the Isle of the Blest, and also at
    Timon the Misanthrope 24.

22 *advice given by Homer . . . Sirens*: *Odyssey* 12.158ff. See also *The
    Philosopher Nigrinus* 19 with n. 22 and cf. *Images* 14 with n. 34.

A FEW WORDS ABOUT MOURNING

1 *Hoi polloi . . . 'laymen'*: *Hoi polloi* (Greek for 'the many', and
   sometimes in modern English mistakenly used to mean the 'elite')
   renders 'the great multitude'. The word for 'laymen' is *idiotas*,
   literally 'private citizens' (as opposed to public men), the base
   of English 'idiot' (one who knows nothing). Here and at *True
   Histories* 1.3, the meaning is quite close to the modern English
   sense.

2 *Pluto, 'the Rich Man'*: The Greeks fancifully derived *Plouton*
   from the word for wealth, *ploutos*.

3 *a very few exceptions*: Details of these are given in paragraph 5.

4 *'Wailings', 'Fireblazings'*: *Kokytoi* and *Pyriphlegethontes*.
   Although there is only one of each, the rivers Cocytus and Pyriphlegethon, Lucian uses an ironic plural for both. The information about the rivers of Hades is found in *Odyssey* 10.513–14
   and is elaborated by Plato, *Phaedo* 113.

5 *Even the feathered . . . fly across*: This is probably a joke based

on association between Lake Avernus near Puteoli in Italy, often thought of as an entrance to Hades, and Lake Acheron. Avernus' name was derived in antiquity from *a-* ('not') and *ornis* ('bird'), because birds were said to be unable to fly across it (because of its deadly exhalations).

6   *three-headed dog*: Cerberus.

7   *meadow planted with asphodel*: Mentioned at *Odyssey* 11.539.

8   *'Forgetfulness'*: *Lethe*. Among many other places, it is mentioned at the end of Plato's *Republic* (621a).

9   *Homer's Odysseus*: Odysseus' descent into Hades in *Odyssey* 11 is part of the long account of his travels he gives to the Phaeacians. At *True Histories* 1.3, Lucian makes it clear that Odysseus' stories are the ultimate source of the genre of lying travellers' tales he is satirizing.

10   *satraps*: See *The Ship*, n. 41.

11   *Minos and Rhadamanthys*: In Plato's *Apology* 41a, Socrates numbers this pair as only two of a whole panel of jurors in Hades which parallels the live one to which he is supposedly speaking. Lucian's Underworld is despotic and authoritarian, not democratic.

12   *to a sort of colony*: From early times, Greek cities solved their space problems by sending groups of citizens to found colonies abroad. The positive representation might here be influenced by Aristophanes' bird-city utopia in the *Birds* of 414 BC.

13   *being racked ... roll rocks*: Among the more generic references to torture here are three which evoke famous sinners. Tityus, a son of Earth, lies stretched out in Homer's Underworld, being pecked at by vultures (*Odyssey* 11.574–81) as punishment for his assault on Leto. Ixion paid for his infatuation with Hera by being eternally whirled round on a wheel (Pindar, *Pythian* 2.21ff.). Sisyphus was requited (for cheating death) by having to roll a huge stone up a hill: when it reached the top, it rolled down again and he had to begin anew, and so on *ad infinitum* (*Odyssey* 11.593–600).

14   *Tantalus*: Another Homeric sinner observed by Odysseus (*Odyssey* 11.582–92). See Glossary entry on Tantalus.

15   *obol*: The smallest-denomination Athenian silver coin. A drachma consisted of six obols (see *Timon the Misanthrope*, n. 60). Cf. *The Journey down to Hades* 1 with n. 3.

16   *sent back ... once more*: Lucian plays with this idea in *Dialogues of the Dead* 2 (22), where Menippus suggests it to Charon as a solution to his inability to pay the fare.

17   *wash the corpse . . . clothing it magnificently*: Rituals involving
      washing the corpse, anointing it with oil and covering it in a linen
      shroud are described by Homer (e.g. *Iliad* 18.350–53), but Lucian
      does not seem to be referring to literary models here.

18   *'My dearest child . . . at drinking-parties'*: A literary example of
      the themes mocked by Lucian is the speech of Hecuba over
      the dead body of her grandchild Astyanax in Euripides, *Trojan
      Women* 1156–250.

19   *sacrificed . . . over the tomb*: The allusion is to Herodotus' descrip-
      tion of the way the Scythians bury their kings (*Histories* 4.71–2).

20   *Thus, then, he spoke . . . covered him o'er: Iliad* 16.502 and many
      other places (it is a formulaic line).

21   *mourning expert*: The use of professional mourners was a Roman,
      rather than a Greek, custom.

22   *cover their dead in glass*: This practice is mentioned by Herodotus
      (*Histories* 3.24) as something done by the Ethiopians.

23   *from personal observation*: Lucian in *Apology for the 'Salaried
      Posts in Great Houses'* defends a position he now holds in the
      administration of the Roman province of Egypt (see Jones 1986,
      20–21). Whether he had visited Egypt earlier is unknown.

24   *by having kept . . . for surety*: The earliest reference to this custom
      is in Herodotus, *Histories* 2.136.

25   *set up games*: The *locus classicus* is the funeral games given by
      Achilles for Patroclus in *Iliad* 23.

26   *funeral orations over the tomb*: The public funeral oration was a
      custom established by the democracy in Athens. But Lucian seems
      to be alluding rather to the Roman practice of the *laudatio
      funebris*, in which the accomplishments and virtues of the dead
      person were praised.

27   *two lines of Homer*: The first is *Iliad* 24.602, spoken by Achilles
      to Priam after he (Achilles) has seen to the washing and anointing
      of Hector's corpse. The second is *Iliad* 19.225, and is part of
      Odysseus' argument to Achilles that the Greek army cannot both
      fast (for the dead Patroclus) and fight.

28   *rhapsodes*: These were professional reciters of poetry, especially
      of Homer.

OLD COMIC DIALOGUES

THE JOURNEY DOWN TO HADES, OR
THE TYRANT

1   *TYRANT*: The word *tyrannos* was used normally for a person
    who seized power with no legitimate claim on it. The general
    portrait of the tyrant in antiquity is of a man utterly ruthless,
    often cruel and always addicted to luxury and sexual excesses.

2   *every oar oarlooped*: The oarloop was a leather strap which was
    used to tie the oar to the pin against which it was worked. In
    tandem, the oarloop and the pin acted like the modern rowlock.
    The translation mimics Lucian's use of the perfect passive
    throughout. The series of passive verbs climaxes in what for
    him was probably a reflection of Aristophanes, *Acharnians* 553
    (though there modern editors adopt a different reading) and
    underpinned the comic tone.

3   *a single obol*: An obol was traditionally Charon's charge for
    crossing over the lake into Hades. One would be placed in the
    mouth of the dead person. See *A Few Words about Mourning* 10
    with n. 15

4   *that noble corpse-guide of ours*: Hermes.

5   *wrestling with the ephebes*: An ephebe was a young man on
    the verge of citizenship. Most Greek cities had rites of passage
    marking the transition to adulthood and citizen rights. For wrest-
    ling, see *The Ship*, n. 3.

6   *asphodel, and various offerings . . . gloom, mist and darkness*:
    For these commonplaces about the Underworld, see *A Few Words
    about Mourning* 5, 9 and 18.

7   *ambrosia is plentiful . . . nectar is unstinted*: These are the food
    and drink of the Homeric gods. The particular passage which
    Lucian might have expected his audience to recall here is *Odyssey*
    5.92–5, where Calypso entertains Hermes with them.

8   *magic wand*: Hermes is usually represented with a herald's staff,
    but the word used by Lucian (*rabdos*) is that which occurs at *Iliad*
    24.343 of a wand which he uses to put men to sleep or wake them
    again (at 24.445 he puts the guards round the Greek camp to
    sleep with it so that Priam can enter unseen).

9   *beggar's pouch . . . stick in his right hand*: This is the characteristic
    costume of the Cynic philosopher.

10   *the thread spun ... run out*: Greek myth imaged fate as three
     sisters, Clotho, Lachesis and Atropos, who, respectively, span,
     drew off and cut the thread of human life. The word used here
     by Clotho and translated 'spun for him' is ironically appropriate,
     being from the verb on which her name is based (*klotho*, 'I spin').
11   *your sister*: Atropos.
12   *like runners out of their traps*: See *Slander*, n. 13.
13   *exposed infants*: Exposure of unwanted infants appears fre-
     quently in myth (e.g. that of Oedipus), and was probably practised
     occasionally as a form of family limitation.
14   *before Eucleides' archonship*: Eucleides was archon (chief magis-
     trate) at Athens in 403/2 BC, the year in which democracy was
     restored after the rule of the Thirty Tyrants. The saying derives
     from the amnesty declared for oligarchs on crimes committed
     before that date.
15   *philosopher Theagenes*: There was a second-century AD philos-
     opher called Theagenes, though it is not certain he is the one
     meant here, since there are no other contemporary references in
     the dialogue and the focus on the figure of the tyrant seems to
     locate the piece during the classical period.
16   *the frame and the cross*: The 'frame' (*tympanon*) seems to have
     been the standard form of execution in classical Athens. It was a
     board with an iron collar and ankle and wrist clamps, to which
     the criminal was strapped. The board was then lifted upright. The
     criminal who survived a period on this would be garotted (see
     A. H. Sommerstein (ed.) on Aristophanes, *Wealth* 476 (War-
     minster 2001)). Crucifixion, by contrast, was a Roman punish-
     ment. The verb Lucian employs here (*anaskolopizo*) is the same
     one he uses of the punishment inflicted on Jesus in *The Passing
     of Peregrinus* 11, a passage which had damaging repercussions
     on his reputation in Byzantium and later (see Introduction,
     section 6).
17   *Agathocles the doctor ... with them*: Once again, there was a
     first-century BC doctor called Agathocles, the writer of a treatise
     On Diet. But it is not certain that a specific real individual is the
     butt of the general joke that doctors more often than not kill their
     patients.
18   *Cyniscus*: The name identifies him as an adherent of the Cynics
     and means 'Little dog'. He is the main character in Lucian's *Zeus
     Catechized*.
19   *Hecate's dinner*: This was an offering to the goddess Hecate

consisting of bread, eggs, cheese and dog-meat, put out at
crossroads every month at new moon.

20   *raw squid*: In this, Cyniscus' death mimics that of the founder of
Cynicism, Diogenes, as reported by Diogenes Laertius (*Lives of
the Philosophers* 6.76).

21   *Megapenthes*: Like Cyniscus', his name is chosen to reflect his
character. It means 'Great grief'.

22   *with no summons from anyone*: The reading of MS Marcianus
434, *automatos*, as against Macleod OCT's *automolos* ('deserting
of my own accord').

23   *Megacles*: The name is again chosen for its meaning, 'of Great
renown'.

24   *Cydimachus*: The name means 'Fame in battle'.

25   *talents*: See *Timon the Misanthrope*, n. 60 and *The Ship*, n. 25.

26   *wine-mixers*: Greeks mixed their wine with water in vessels
specially designed for the purpose. Only the wealthiest and most
ostentatious would have gold ones. Cf. *Two Charges of Literary
Assault*, n. 27.

27   *Cleocritos*: The name means 'Chosen for glory'.

28   *Carion*: The name occurs commonly for slave characters in
fourth-century BC Greek comedy (beginning with Aristophanes'
Wealth).

29   *Glycerion*: The name means 'Sweetie' and is found as the name
of a courtesan in Lucian's *Chattering Courtesans* 1.

30   *pinned to the board*: The punishment is probably that alluded to
in paragraph 6 as 'the frame' (see note 16).

31   *Micyllus the cobbler*: This character appears also in Lucian's *The
Dream, or The Cock*, where he is persuaded by his cockerel
(who has Pythagoras' soul) that dreams of wealth are merely a
distraction and that he should accept the realities of his existence.

32   *'I'll eat Nobody last'*: The promise was made by the Cyclops
Polyphemus to Odysseus (pretending to be 'Nobody') at *Odyssey*
9.369.

33   *diametrically opposite*: The expression appears to be derived from
astronomy, and describes the relative position of planets.

34   *little molluscs from the Laconian Sea*: Purple dye was made from
these shellfish. See *Two Charges of Literary Assault*, n. 30.

35   *Gniphon*: The name means 'Niggard' (see also *Philosophies for
Sale* 23).

36   *Rhodochares*: The name means 'Rejoicing in roses', underscoring
his self-indulgent and luxury-loving nature.

37   *bring a suit ... unconstitutional measure*: In democratic Athens, this procedure was available for challenges to the constitutionality of proposals made by speakers in the assembly of the people (cf. *Toxaris* 24 with n. 41). The use of such terminology allows Lucian to create a general sense of the setting of the dialogue during the classical period.

38   *And I'll be left ... ownsome here*: I have translated this in verse because in the Greek it forms an iambic trimeter (the main metre for speeches in tragedy and comedy), though it cannot be traced in the surviving corpus of drama. It is more likely to be from comedy than tragedy, given the overall tone of the dialogue and the sentiment.

39   *give the time*: On Athenian oared ships, there was a *keleustes*, who gave time to the oarsmen. This motif was parodied in Aristophanes' *Frogs* (207f.), where Charon, who is ferrying Dionysus to the Underworld in his search for a good tragic poet, gives the time to the god, who has taken the oar. However, the Frog chorus cuts across him with an entirely different rhythm. Lucian's scene involves a sidelong look at this model.

40   *It's not proper form ... without a tear*: The Greek is slightly stronger, suggesting that crossing with dry eyes violates divinely established laws.

41   *Chinese Indopates and Heramithras*: The name 'Indopates' means 'He who walks in India', while 'Heramithras' combines the name of the Greek goddess Hera with that of the Near Eastern god Mithras. Lucian does not seem to be troubled by any real knowledge of the Far East and presumably mentions the Chinese to give a sense of how broad is the realm allotted to the Moirai ('Fates').

42   *Megillus ... Simiche ... Phryne*: Of these, only Phryne (see Glossary) appears to be historically famed for beauty. 'Megillus' is a Spartan name (e.g. Xenophon, *Hellenica* 3.4.6), but there is no reputation for pulchritude associated with any of those known. 'Simiche' seems to be merely a generic female name, used in Menander's *Bad-Tempered Man* for the old female slave of Cnemon, and in Lucian's *Chattering Courtesans* 4 for a courtesan.

43   *Eleusinian Mysteries ... dreadful threatening look*: This is another reminiscence of Aristophanes' *Frogs* (see note 39 above). Upon reaching the further shore, Dionysus and his slave Xanthias encounter a female monster (Empusa: 285ff.) and Eleusinian initiates (the chorus: 312f.)

44   *your father*: Zeus (see the Rhadamanthys entry in the Glossary).

45   *your markings ... marked man*: The Greek has a play on the words *stigmata*, 'marks' or 'tattoos', and *stigmatias*, 'a runaway slave', who has been branded or tattooed on his forehead to show that he is troublesome.

46   *Isles of the Blest ... with the heroes*: This was the place Menelaus was promised would be his final resting-place (the Elysian Fields) (*Odyssey* 4.563f.). Lucian's eyewitness account is given in *True Histories* 2.5–29.

47   *Call up his oil-lamp and bed*: Lucian uses another idea from comedy, the inanimate witness. In Aristophanes' *Wasps* (936f.), Bdelycleon calls various kitchen utensils as witnesses in the trial of the dog Labes (though in Aristophanes, the witnesses do not speak in their own voices).

TIMON THE MISANTHROPE

1   *O Zeus, god of ... thunderbolt of yours*: The epithets used by Timon do have strong poetic resonance. For example, 'lord of the lightning', 'cloud-gatherer' and 'loud-thunderer' are all regularly used in the *Iliad* (e.g. respectively 1.580, 1.511, 5.672). Some epithets are used by both Homer and Hesiod (e.g. 'lord of the lightning', *Theogony* 390; 'blazing', *Iliad* 2.415, *Theogony* 72) and 'thunderous' exclusively by Hesiod (*Theogony* 815). Many appear also in tragedy (e.g. 'lord of the lightning' in Sophocles, *Philoctetes* 1198; 'thunderous lightning' and 'blazing thunderbolt' as phrases occur in Euripides, *Phoenician Women* 182–3) or other poetry (e.g. 'loud-thunder[ing]' in Pindar, *Dithyrambs*, fr. 61.9, OCT, though not of Zeus).

2   *far-shooting*: An epithet used of Apollo in Homer (e.g. *Iliad* 1.14), but in tragedy also of Zeus (Euripides, *Ion* 213). It had been in use in Greek prose since Polybius (second century BC) to describe weapons. Given the context, it is likely that Lucian expects to evoke in his audience memories of both traditions of usage.

3   *guttering wick ... faceful of soot*: Timon's language and imagery now sink to the level of comedy. The word 'wick' (*thryallis*) is used often by Aristophanes (e.g. *Acharnians* 916), and 'a faceful of soot' recalls the shower of coal-dust which covers Dicaeopolis from the charcoal-hostage he takes (*Acharnians* 350–51).

4   *aegis*: This was a sort of goatskin pinafore, or a shield, covered in scales, with a fringe of snakes' heads and the image of the Gorgon's head in the middle. It was given to Zeus by Hephaestus

(*Iliad* 15.308–10) to terrify human beings when it was worn. After Homer, it is more usually associated with Athena.

5   *Your thunderbolt ... and violent*: An attempt has been made here to represent the comic effects of the jingling language used by Lucian. In the Greek, in the sentence 'Your thunderbolt ... skirmish' every verb has the same passive ending; in the sentence 'You produced ... style' the similes are all expressed by adverbs with the same two-syllable ending; in 'Your storms ... violent' the two adjectives have two-syllable end-rhymes. The implication of 'in low style' is that this is the language of comedy.

6   *'high-thunderer'*: Another epithet found in Homer (e.g. *Iliad* 1.354) and Hesiod (e.g. *Works and Days* 8). But Aristophanes also uses it in a parody of oracular verse in *Lysistrata* 773.

7   *thunderbolt in your right hand*: The statue of Zeus at Olympia held a representation of the goddess Victory in the right hand, not a thunderbolt, according to Pausanias (*Description of Greece* 5.11.1). Perhaps Lucian is alluding to another image, one which suffered a well-known attack, since there is no record of any assault on Phidias' masterpiece.

8   *four obols a day*: An obol was worth one sixth of a drachma (see note 60), and in fifth-century BC Athens three obols was the daily wage paid for jury service (cf. *Two Charges of Literary Assault* 12 with n. 22).

9   *whole-hecatomb*: A hecatomb literally meant a sacrifice of a hundred oxen, though it usually refers simply to a very large number of victims.

10 *liver pecked ... vultures*: Like the god Prometheus, who was punished this way for his philanthropy.

11 *forget a man ... our altars*: The Zeus of Homer makes a similar point about Odysseus (*Odyssey* 1.65–7).

12 *'virtue' and 'incorporeality'*: Although the notion of virtue is discussed often in Plato and the term 'incorporeal' (*asomatos*) is also found in his works, it seems likelier that Zeus is anachronistically objecting to the philosophical discourse of the Stoics here.

13 *temple of the Dioscuri*: The name used by Lucian here is the 'Anaceion' (temple of the Anaces, the 'Kings', i.e. the Dioscuri).

14 *ten-talent*: See note 60 and *The Ship*, n. 25.

15 *giving it all away*: The arguments of paragraphs 15 and 16 are developed from those given to Wealth and Chremylus in Aristophanes, *Wealth* 235f.

16 *your vast experience of the passion*: Zeus' amours are a favourite

topic with Lucian. See *Dialogues of the Gods* 6 (2), 7 (3), 8 (5), 10 (4).

17 *Lawbringer*: This translates *Thesmophoros*, an epithet of Demeter, who was celebrated at the festival known as the Thesmophoria. See also *Chattering Courtesans* 7.4.

18 *starting-gate . . . lowered*: See *Slander*, n. 13.

19 *Pluto . . . bestower of wealth and giver of largesse*: The Greek word for wealth is *ploutos* and a favourite etymology of the name of Pluto, god of the Underworld, connected the two. See *A Few Words about Mourning* 2 with n. 2. Wealth is saying that sudden riches are bestowed through the last will and testaments of people when they die.

20 *now bearing the name*: 'Pyrrhias', 'Dromon' and 'Tibius' are typical slave names. The new, grander, names are chosen for the implication of greatness (*mega-* means 'great', *prot-* signifies 'first') and to designate ethnic difference ('Megabyzus' is a Persian name, the other two Greek).

21 *the group who . . . substantial enough*: These people are legacy-hunters, who have been trying to worm their way with gifts ('bait') into the affections and will of the deceased. See *Dialogues of the Dead* 16–19 (6–9) for other Lucianic explorations of the theme.

22 *bowing down before the mill*: It was a characteristic punishment for a slave to be sent to work in the mill (see Euripides, *Cyclops* 240), which developed in Greece from a pair of hand-operated stones to the sort of large rotary mill operated in the Roman period by animals or slaves. The point here is probably that mill-worship is apotropaic – acknowledging the mill is a way of ensuring you aren't sent there.

23 *Zeus . . . is sending you to*: This is a development (and reversal) of Aristophanes, *Wealth* 85f., where Wealth claims that Zeus deliberately blinded him to spite humanity so that he would not be able to find the virtuous.

24 *How is it . . . so many lovers?*: See also *Dialogues of the Dead* 19 (9) for this theme.

25 *thrown themselves . . . yawning main*: This is the advice given to the poor by the Megarian elegiac poet Theognis (late seventh or mid sixth century BC), ll. 175–6.

26 *suffering from Corybantism*: I.e. 'as mad as hatters' (cf. Glossary entry on the Corybants). The Corybantic rites associated with Rhea/Cybele were commonly thought to help cure madness by

creating a sympathetic raised emotional state in the participants.

27   *Ignorance and Deceit*: For ignorance and deceit personified, see *Slander* 5. Ignorance is noted as central to the operation of slander in *Slander* 1, 5 and 32.

28   *to avoid the appearance ... unlovely things*: Lucian is very fond of the theme of surface show versus hidden reality, and often uses the image of the theatrical mask to illustrate it. Compare *The Ship* 46 and *Menippus* 16, where the contrast between the actor's role and the actor beneath the mask is used to image the unreality of life versus the reality of death.

29   *Pride, Folly ... other, similar vices*: Compare the list of dimly visible influences upon human life pointed out by Hermes to Charon at *Charon* 15 ('hope, fear, ignorance, pleasure, love of gain, anger, hatred and other such things'). For 'Wanton Injustice', see note 34 below.

30   *Poverty*: The personification of Poverty goes back to the lyric poet Alcaeus of Lesbos (seventh century BC). See further note 32 below.

31   *on earth ... in the ground*: The single Greek phrase used here means both 'on earth' and 'in the ground'.

32   *Poverty's with him as well*: Poverty appears as a character in Aristophanes, *Wealth* 415f., from where her role here is developed.

33   *Slayer of Argos*: A regular epithet of Hermes.

34   *Wanton Injustice*: The Greek term used is *hybris*, a complex idea which expressed in early Greek poetry the opposite of Justice (and not the weakened English meaning of 'hubris' as 'pride inviting a fall'). See Fisher 1992.

35   *Am I to bring ... words like this?*: Hermes quotes aptly the words of Iris to Poseidon at *Iliad* 15.202. She has brought a message from Zeus requiring Poseidon to leave the battlefield, where he has been helping the Achaeans to rally their forces against Hector. The quotation continues: 'Or will you change course?' and this is followed by a veiled threat. In the end, Hermes implies, Timon too will have to give way.

36   *sykophantes*: In Athens in the classical period, there was, for most offences, no public prosecutor, prosecution in such cases depending on the public-spirited actions of private individuals. The pejorative name of a *sykophantes* ('fig-informer') was given to a man who was believed to be abusing that role by bringing or threatening to bring (malicious) prosecutions in the courts with the (sole) intention of personal gain, either by, through pros-

ecution, gaining for himself a portion of the condemned person's property, or by blackmail, through the threat of bringing a prosecution. But it also came to mean, more generally, a common informer, false accuser, slanderer, a tale-bearer or backbiter, or, later still, a deceiver or cheat.

37   *put my case*: Once more, the idea for a formal defence comes from Aristophanes' *Wealth*, except that there it is Poverty who makes it (467f.).

38   *O Gold . . . pride and joy!*: Euripides, *Danae*, fr. 324 (*Tragicorum Graecorum Fragmenta*, ed. A. Nauck (Leipzig 1889)). An appropriate play to cite, as Danae's virginity was taken by Zeus disguised as a shower of gold.

39   *Night and day . . . you shine*: This is a slight adaptation of Pindar, *Olympians* 1.1–2: 'Water is best, but gold shines like fire blazing at night more than [other] noble wealth.'

40   *Zeus became gold . . . the ceiling*: Another allusion to the manner in which Zeus is said to have bypassed the precautions of Danae's father Acrisius.

41   *I hereby decree*: In fifth-century BC Athens, the assembly (*ekklesia*) made laws by decrees, which had to have formal proposers. The form of Timon's 'decree' (and that of Demeas at paragraph 51) does not follow any actual ancient legislative model closely, but probably takes its lead from Aristophanes (e.g. *Women at the Thesmophoria* 372f.). See Bompaire 1958, 637ff.

42   *Altar of Pity*: It is also referred to at *Demonax the Philosopher* 57.

43   *clan, phratry, deme . . . fatherland*: All Athenian citizens belonged to one of the clans, or 'tribes' (i.e. groups of demes (ten in the fifth century BC) – see *Two Charges of Literary Assault*, n. 37), and to one of the Attic demes (local administrative districts), from which they received the 'demotic' ('from X deme') as part of their name (cf. paragraph 7). Most also belonged to a phratry (religious organization). The importance of 'fatherland' is underscored in Lucian's declamation *An Encomium of Fatherland*.

44   *caught a whiff of my gold*: The idea may derive from the way Aristophanes' chorus in *Acharnians* 179 catch a whiff of the peace-treaties (actually samples of wines of different ages – cf. *Chattering Courtesans*, n. 83) being brought to Dicaeopolis by Amphitheus.

45   *Gnathonides*: The name is based on *gnathon*, meaning 'a person whose mouth is full', apt for a parasite.

46   *dithyramb productions*: The dithyramb was a choral song in

honour of Dionysus, and competitions in it were held between
choruses from the tribes at various Athenian festivals. But Lucian
makes Gnathonides speak as though it were a dramatic production from which one could pick out a lyric portion to sing at
a drinking-party (cf. Aristophanes, *Knights* 529–30). See also
True Histories, n. 65.

47   *elegies*: Elegiac verse (written in couplets containing a hexameter
and a pentameter) was used for a number of different types of
poetic composition, but the type referred to here is the *elegos*, a
sung lament.

48   *Philiades*: The name is based on the word *philos*, 'friend'.

49   *more melodious than the swans*: It was generally believed in
antiquity that swans could sing tunefully (cf. *Homeric Hymns*
21.1–3).

50   *ephebes*: See *The Journey down to Hades*, n. 5.

51   *fellow-demesmen*: See note 43.

52   *Demeas*: Another meaningful name, this time based on the word
demos, 'people'. Demeas is a public speaker in the assembly of
the people (*ekklesia*). See note 41 for decrees.

53   *Erechtheus tribe's . . . the theoric fund*: This fund (perhaps established only in the mid fourth century BC) paid for citizens to
attend the theatrical performances at festivals like the Dionysia
and Lenaea. Lucian's knowledge of Athenian tribal organization
is imperfect. Timon's deme is Kollytos, which belonged to Aegeis,
not to Erechtheus.

54   *both councils*: The Council of Five Hundred (referred to again,
as 'the council', in paragraph 51), which prepared business for
the assembly of the people (see also *Chattering Courtesans*, n. 8),
and the Areopagus.

55   *near Acharnae . . . two Spartan divisions*: The references seem
to recall the period of the Archidamian War (431–421 BC),
when the Spartans regularly invaded Attica, by way of the deme
Acharnae (see Thucydides, *History of the Peloponnesian War*
2.19.2–20.5).

56   *a thunderbolt . . . sunrays on his head*: The thunderbolt was an
attribute of Zeus, while sunrays were an attribute of the god of
the sun, Helios. Lucian may be recalling obliquely the colossal
statue of Nero, which had this latter feature.

57   *Thrasycles*: The basis of this name is the word for boldness, or
brazenness (with '-cles' signifying 'famous for').

58   *displays exactly the opposite . . . in his morning lectures*: The false
philosopher is a favourite theme in Lucian. The most developed

example is his *The Carousal*, in which various philosophers, invited to a wedding-banquet, disgrace themselves by getting drunk and behaving obnoxiously.

59   *carry him away . . . clasped around the pipe-girl*: This motif echoes the behaviour of Philocleon in Aristophanes, *Wasps* 1341f., who absconds from his drinking-party with the pipe-girl in tow.

60   *obol . . . drachmas . . . mina . . . talent*: The Athenian monetary system operated with the following relative values: 6 obols = 1 drachma; 100 drachmas = 1 mina (*mna*); 60 minas = 1 talent. Of these, only obols and drachmas were coined (cf. *Demonax the Philosopher*, n. 26 and *The Ship*, n. 25).

61   *As for me . . . Aeginetan bushels*: The point is that, while Thrasycles claims he is not asking for much, a bushel, a measure of capacity (see *The Ship*, n. 34), was, in respect of coins, very large (cf. the expression 'he measures his money by the bushel', to mean 'he is rich', in Xenophon, *Hellenica* 3.2.27).

62   *Blepsias and Laches and Gniphon*: Of these names, only 'Gniphon' is meaningful ('Niggard'; see *The Journey down to Hades* 17 and *Philosophies for Sale* 23, where it is closely associated with usury). 'Blepsias' possibly recalls comic names in Aristophanes (Blepyrus in *Women at the Assembly* and Blepsidemus in *Wealth*). 'Laches' was the name of an Athenian general of the fifth century BC and also a common character name in the comedy of Menander (see *Chattering Courtesans*, n. 38).

THE SHIP, OR PRAYERS

1   *LYCINUS*: Most scholars regard the name as a Hellenized form of the Roman *Lucianus*, and therefore a nom de plume of Lucian himself. The character appears in a large number of dialogues (those in square brackets are usually regarded as of doubtful authenticity): *The Carousal*, [*The Sham Sophist*: MSS have 'Lucian' and 'Solecist', but edns. print 'Lycinus'], *Images*, *In Defence of 'Images'*, *The Dance*, *Lexiphanes*, *The Eunuch*, [*Affairs of the Heart*], *A Conversation with Hesiod*, *Hermotimus*, [*The Cynic*]. The practice of using a pseudonym was probably derived by Lucian from what was taken to be the practice of Old Comedy (see *Two Charges of Literary Assault*, n. 25).

2   *grain-ships . . . Egypt to Italy*: Rome imported grain from Egypt as rent or tax. It was stored during the empire in public granaries from which those who had a *tessera* ('ticket') would receive a monthly ration free of charge. It is by no means clear precisely of

what tonnage the ship is envisaged to be, nor whether Lucian reports something he had himself seen. The largest shipwreck investigated by archaeologists was a vessel capable of carrying some 250 tons of cargo, and Athenaeus (*fl. c.* AD 200), *The Deipnosophists* 5.206dff. describes a gigantic ship built by Hieron II (*c.* 306–215 BC), king of Syracuse. See further Bompaire 1958, 534–6 with references and Jones 1986, 158 with n. 54.

3   *wrestling ground*: The *palaistra* ('wrestling ground' or 'wrestling school') was an enclosed courtyard, surrounded by rooms used for various purposes (e.g. undressing, washing), where young men came to train for wrestling and older men came to watch.

4   *his native language*: Elsewhere, Lucian pokes fun at himself for having up to a certain point in life retained his barbarous native language (*Two Charges of Literary Assault* 27). If Lycinus is taken to represent Lucian himself, then there may be a certain irony in the pomposity with which he criticizes the boy's Greek pronunciation.

5   *ephebes*: See *The Journey down to Hades*, n. 5.

6   *Thucydides' histories . . . first became colonists*: The reference is to Thucydides' account in his *History of the Peloponnesian War* 1.6.3.

7   *golden goose*: See *True Histories* 2.41 with n. 124.

8   *paintings*: Coloured decoration, probably applied to the parts of the ship above the water-line (see *Zeus Rants* 47).

9   *bright star at the masthead*: The phenomenon now known as 'St Elmo's fire'.

10   *the Mysteries*: I.e. the Eleusinian Mysteries.

11   *initiatory rituals . . . bright torch*: The Eleusinian Mysteries themselves contained secret revelations, but the paraphernalia of the ceremonies were well known. They took place at night, in torchlight. Here, however, Lycinus suggests a parallel erotic 'Mysteries', which also requires torchlight for its initiates.

12   *hoi polloi*: See *A Few Words about Mourning*, n. 1.

13   *'finders sharers'*: Literally 'Hermes shared'. Hermes was the god to whom lucky finds were attributed (cf. *Timon the Misanthrope* 24) and it was accepted practice for such bounty to be divided among those present when the find was made.

14   *Twelve Attic talents*: A talent was worth 6,000 drachmas (see *Timon the Misanthrope*, n. 60), making the revenue 72,000 drachmas per annum. According to paragraph 15, the current charge for a voyage from Piraeus across the Saronic Gulf to Aegina was four obols (two thirds of a drachma).

15   *Enodia*: Literally 'the goddess of the crossroads', i.e. Hecate.

16   *spitting in your lap*: A way of offering acknowledgement to, and thus warding off the attentions of, the goddess of retribution, Nemesis.

17   *ibis*: A species of bird native to Egypt. The list includes typical products associated with various parts of Egypt.

18   *stades*: The stade, the normal Greek measurement for distances (and the length of the *stadium* at Olympia), measures around 600 feet (183 metres).

19   *darics*: The daric was a Persian gold coin.

20   *dolphins . . . saved a musician*: Arion.

21   *another lad . . . on a dolphin's back*: Melicertes.

22   *bushels of gold coin*: See *Timon the Misanthrope*, n. 61 and note 34 below.

23   *immediate priority . . . a house*: Hesiod, *Works and Days* 405 says, 'First a house, a wife and a ploughing ox.' But Adeimantus is hardly interested in either women or farming.

24   *Echecrates*: The name seems to be used simply for its meaning, 'Holder of power', though it is similar to the name of Timon's father ('Echecratides': *Timon the Misanthrope* 7).

25   *weigh two talents*: The monetary talent (see *Timon the Misanthrope*, n. 60) was the sum of money equal to the talent (of silver) as a unit of weight. Cf. *Demonax the Philosopher*, n. 26.

26   *Sisyphean weight*: The allusion is to the stone Sisyphus pushes forever and again up a hill in *Odyssey* 11.594–600.

27   *People will walk . . . every morning early*: Even though the setting is Athens, and the colouring is all almost timeless, the reference here is to a Roman custom. Clients expected to receive some sort of 'dole' from their patron in return for their attendance on him at his house in the mornings (see Juvenal, *Satires* 1.95ff. and Lucian, *The Philosopher Nigrinus* 22).

28   *Cleaenetus and Democrates*: Both names belonged to real individuals of the fourth century BC, but they are probably used here only for colour. 'Cleaenetus' means 'Praised for his glory' and 'Democrates' 'Powerful over the people'.

29   *The honey will be ours*: I.e. from Attica, which was famed for this product in antiquity.

30   *bird from Phasis*: Pheasant.

31   *Homer's beggar Irus*: The reference is to *Odyssey* 18.1ff.

32   *displaying his silver . . . in the procession*: G. Husson (*Lucien: Le navire ou les souhaits*, 2 vols. (Paris 1970), vol. 2, p. 61) suggests that Dionicus lent his silverware to the city to display on it

the offerings made to the gods at religious festivals, of which processions were a central part.

33 *I'd distribute . . . metic*: Metics were foreigners who resided at Athens and paid a tax called the *metoikion* (cf. *Two Charges of Literary Assault* 9). Adeimantus' proposed distributions are absurdly generous, as comparison with the four-obol journey to Aegina (paragraph 15) and the twelve talents per annum income of the owner of the *Isis* (paragraph 13) shows. 100 drachmas = 1 mina. 60 minas = 1 talent. So 12 talents = 72,000 drachmas, which would provide 100 drachmas to only 720 citizens.

34 *I'd tell my steward . . . satirizes my prayer*: Since it was Timolaus who suggested the daydream contest (paragraph 16), it seems that Samippus is being rewarded for his suggestion (paragraph 18) that Adeimantus should wish for the pretty Egyptian boy mentioned at the beginning (paragraph 2). The Greek names for the relative measures are *medimnos* ('bushel') and *choinix* ('litre'), both measures of capacity used primarily for corn, the former the quantity of corn in which great wealth was calculated by Solon (the top class earned 500 *medimnoi* a year), the latter the standard measure for a day's ration for an individual.

35 *Phanomachus*: The name belonged to a fifth-century BC Athenian general, but does not appear to have any special significance here.

36 *hoplites*: Troops dressed in full armour, who would bear the brunt of any battle, supported by cavalry and light-armed troops.

37 *In Persian mode . . . your diadem*: For Persian greeting and manner of address, see Herodotus, *Histories* 1.134–5. The upright tiara and the diadem were attributes of the Persian king (see Xenophon, *Cyropaedia* 8.3.7) later appropriated by Alexander (see Lucian, *Dialogues of the Dead* 25 (12).3), to whose conquest of Persia there seems to be an allusion here.

38 *in charge of the centre . . . join the fray themselves*: See Xenophon, *Anabasis* 1.8.21–2 for this practice.

39 *triremes*: The trireme was an oared fighting vessel of the classical period, manned by around 180 rowers arranged in three tiers.

40 *to Artemis . . . Ionian shore*: There was a major shrine of Artemis at Ephesus, which may be the point of reference here, but Husson (*Le navire*, vol. 2, p. 76) suggests that Samippus' devotion to this goddess may arise from his Arcadian origins (see paragraph 28), since Artemis was especially worshipped in such mountainous regions.

41 *satrap of Greece*: Although 'satrap' was the name given by the Persians to their provincial governors, so that Lycinus' choice of

word may here be deliberately insulting, characterizing Samippus
as a barbarian, rather than a Greek, the word was also used in
Lucian's period for a Roman official. Cf. *A Few Words about
Mourning* 7 and *True Histories* 2.33 and 2.34.

42 *Antipater*: He was left behind to rule in Macedon when Alexander
left on his expedition to the East.

43 *phalanx*: The close-packed formation usual in hoplite battles,
anything from eight to fifty men deep.

44 *sit down under this olive-tree . . . the city*: Ironically, Lycinus
behaves as though they are in the realistic setting of a Platonic
dialogue. Socrates and Phaedrus sit under a plane-tree to shelter
from the midday heat (Plato, *Phaedrus* 229a–b).

45 *by running into the wrestling ground . . . fight it out*: Once more,
by mentioning the wrestling ground, Lycinus alludes to the real
topography of Athens and not to the fantasy being constructed
by Samippus.

46 *falling down . . . Only the barbarians, mind you*: See note 37
above.

47 *Cydias*: This name was borne by historical individuals. However,
its root is *kydos*, 'glory', and this seems to be the reason for its
selection here.

48 *Death . . . no respect at all for your diadem*: For this motif, see
also *The Journey down to Hades*, where it is centred on the tyrant
Megapenthes.

49 *the one Gyges had*: The story of the marvellous ring of Gyges is
told in Plato, *Republic* 2 (359dff.).

50 *fly high above the earth*: Lucian is fond of the flying theme, which
reappears in *Icaromenippus*, where Menippus flies to heaven to
get answers to his questions about life, the universe and
everything.

51 *antipodeans*: See *Demonax the Philosopher*, n. 18.

52 *it's nothing . . . hellebore couldn't cure*: Hellebore was a plant
used in antiquity to treat insanity. Cf. *True Histories* 2.7 and 2.18
with n. 77.

53 *those tragic actors who play . . . Agamemnon or Creon*: A favourite comparison in Lucian. Cf. *Menippus* 16, and note the use of a
generic masking motif at *Timon the Misanthrope* 27 to stress the
contrast between reality and show.

54 *dedicated followers of philosophy*: This is a surprise. Nowhere
have we been told before that Lycinus' friends have philosophical
interests. Perhaps we are supposed to infer it from the fact that
Adeimantus and Timolaus have well-known philosophical

namesakes: an Adeimantus is an interlocutor in Plato's *Republic* 362dff. and a Timolaus of Cyzicus is listed among Plato's pupils in Diogenes Laertius, *Lives of the Philosophers* 3.46. However, this does not account for Samippus. There is a possibility that the names hide contemporaries whom Lucian wishes to satirize (cf. Jones 1986, 101–16 = chapter 10, 'Concealed Victims').

NEW COMIC DIALOGUES

CHATTERING COURTESANS

1   *COURTESANS*: The Greek title is *Hetairikoi Dialogoi*. A *hetaira* (literally 'female friend', but usually translated 'court-esan') was in classical Athens (the ostensible setting for these dialogues) a free woman who could, with patience and the right approach, be persuaded into a sexual relationship. However, she was not a prostitute (*porne*), in that she controlled her own affairs and was also protected (as concubine or mistress) by the same adultery laws as wives (Xenarchus 4.18–23, *PCG* and Athenaeus, *The Deipnosophists* 13.569a). See further Davidson 1997, 109–36.

2   *Glycerion*: For the name ('Sweetie'), see *The Journey down to Hades* 12, where it belongs to the concubine of Megapenthes the tyrant.

3   *Abrotonon*: This name means 'Wormwood', but one MS writes 'Habrotonon', the name of a harp-girl in Menander's *The Arbitrators*.

4   *expose it*: See *The Journey down to Hades*, n. 13.

5   *a talent*: I.e. 6,000 drachmas (60 minas). See *Timon the Misanthrope*, n. 60.

6   *naval court*: The *nautodikai* ('naval magistrates') convened a court in which cases were heard which involved Athenian citizens who were merchants. Harrison 1998, vol. 2, 23–4.

7   *goddess of childbirth*: Artemis.

8   *prytaneum*: The building where the *prytaneis* resided while on duty. These were the members of the Council of Five Hundred, selected each year by lot from lists submitted by the ten (later twelve) tribes of Athens (see *Timon the Misanthrope*, nn. 43 and 54). The year was divided into 'prytanies' according to the number of tribes, and during their stint the councillors from each tribe in

turn would live in the prytaneum and prepare business for the
assembly (*ekklesia*).

9   *song to Hymen*: I.e. wedding song (*hymenaios*), sung by the
attendants of the bride as they led her to the house of the
bridegroom.

10 *brute*: The Greek word is *hybristes*, which denotes a person who
is thought to have no conception of, or to ignore, the basic rules
of justice and decent social behaviour.

11 *lay down . . . beside him*: See *Two Charges of Literary Assault*,
n. 29.

12 *'Sosandra' of Calamis*: A famous sculpture by Calamis, probably
of Aphrodite, evoked also in *Images* 4.

13 *Melitta and Bacchis*: 'Melitta' is Greek for 'honey bee' and
'Bacchis' for 'Bacchanal'. Plautus (*c.* 250–184 BC) wrote a play
called *The Two Bacchises*.

14 *Simiche*: The name is used by Menander in the *Bad-Tempered
Man* for a slave and by Lucian in *The Journey down to Hades* 22
for a generic beauty.

15 *fellow-ephebe*: See *The Journey down to Hades*, n. 5.

16 *a drachma . . . add seven obols*: An Athenian drachma was worth
six obols (see *Timon the Misanthrope*, n. 60). It is not quite clear
what the extra seven obols are for.

17 *She hangs them from a peg . . . I did as I was told*: Lucian's
interest in – and contempt for – magical practices is shown in a
number of places, including *The Lover of Lies*, *Menippus* and
Alexander the False Prophet.

18 *Clonarion and Leaena*: Clonarion ('Twig') is female (presumably
a fellow-courtesan, to judge by the name; cf. Musarion in dialogue
7). 'Leaena' means 'Lioness'. Possibly, given the explicit sexual
theme, there is some allusion to the sexual position called 'lioness
on the cheesegrater' (Aristophanes, *Lysistrata* 231), which was
thought of as particularly lewd.

19 *They say that . . . on Lesbos*: The association of female homo-
eroticism with Lesbos goes back to the seventh-century BC poetess
Sappho. Yet the women of Lesbos were eponymously famed for
their skill at fellatio (as the Greek verb *lesbiazo*, 'I fellate', shows).

20 *like Achilles among the maidens*: Achilles had been dressed up as
a girl by his mother, Thetis, and left with the women at the court
of King Lycomedes on Scyros because she knew he was fated to
die at Troy if he went to fight. Odysseus tricked him into revealing
his identity.

21 *something in place of the male thing*: This seems to be an oblique
    reference to the *olisbos*, a leather dildo (Aristophanes, *Lysistrata*
    109). Here Lucian seems to expect his audience to reconstruct for
    themselves the strange scenario of the *olisbos* being strapped onto
    a woman.

22 *Crobyle and Corinna*: 'Crobyle' is a feminine form of the Greek
    word for 'topknot' (and was used in later Greek to mean 'hair-
    net'), an archaic Athenian male citizen coiffure (Thucydides,
    History of the Peloponnesian War 1.6.3). 'Corinna' was the name
    of a famous Boeotian poetess (date uncertain). The names may be
    chosen to express for the mother (Crobyle) a citizen respectability
    (lost on the death of her husband; cf. Aristophanes, *Women at
    the Thesmophoria* 443f.) and for the girl (Corinna) hidden artistic
    talents.

23 *mina*: Worth 100 drachmas (a hefty amount, given that a juror's
    pay in classical Athens was half a drachma a day – cf. *Two
    Charges of Literary Assault* 12 with n. 22).

24 *two minas . . . seven months*: So Corinna has just earned three
    and a half months' living expenses in one night.

25 *two kinds of thread, for woof and warp*: The loom has a set of
    threads set lengthwise (the warp) and cloth is woven by passing
    another thread (the woof) in between those.

26 *Lyra*: The name means 'Lyre'.

27 *Adrasteia*: Literally 'She whom none can run away from'. 'Adras-
    teia' is another name for the goddess Nemesis. It is not quite clear
    why Crobyle invokes the goddess of retribution here, whether it
    is to protect her friend (Nemesis guards against excess) or herself
    (for being spiteful).

28 *in everything else she's less . . . Adrasteia*: See previous note. Here
    Crobyle definitely does step near the mark by almost claiming her
    own child's superiority over Lyra. Her address to Adrasteia shows
    her following the proverbial course recommended by the Chorus
    to Prometheus in Aeschylus' *Prometheus Bound* (936): 'Those
    who do obeisance to Adrasteia are wise.'

29 *Eucritus*: An apt name, meaning 'Well-chosen'.

30 *Musarion*: The basis of this name is *Mousa*, 'Muse'.

31 *Chaereas*: The name is common in the plays of Menander for a
    young Athenian citizen (*The Shield*, *The Bad-Tempered Man*,
    Fabula Incerta 1).

32 *goddess of earthly love . . . heavenly love, the one in the gardens*:
    The goddess in question is Aphrodite. The statue of her 'in the
    gardens' is by Alcamenes, mentioned also in *Images* 4 (see also

Pausanias, *Description of Greece* 1.19.2 and Pliny, *Natural History* 36.16). The epithets 'earthly' and 'heavenly' translate *Pandemos* and *Ourania* respectively. Although *Pandemos* means 'of the whole citizen body' and was especially used thus in Athens, what underlies the contrast drawn here by the Mother is probably Plato's use of the two epithets to describe 'common' and 'divine' love (*Symposium* 180d–181), a passage that would have readily sprung to the minds of Lucian and his audience.

33 *giver of wealth*: An epithet of Demeter.

34 *if my father . . .*: The Mother represents Chaereas as avoiding the ill-omened word 'dies' (though she is happy to use it herself in paragraph 2).

35 *the two goddesses*: Demeter and Kore (= Persephone).

36 *contribution . . . meal*: It was quite normal for classical Greeks to take their own food to a dinner (see Aristophanes, *Wasps* 1250–52). This sort of occasion was actually called an *eranos* ('contribution'), the word used by Lucian here.

37 *darics*: See *The Ship*, n. 19.

38 *Deinomache and Laches the Areopagite*: These are good Athenian citizen names, each evoking a grand pedigree (a Deinomache was the mother of the general Alcibiades, and a Laches was another fifth-century BC general). The title Areopagite (member of the Areopagus) is probably added for good measure to reinforce the idea of high status, since 'Laches' had also been a common name for characters in the comedy of Menander (*The Guardian Spirit*, *The Girl from Perinthus* and *Fabula Incerta* 1).

39 *shoes . . . two drachmas*: The shoes are quite expensive (though see also dialogue 14.2), given that Athenian jurors were only paid half a drachma a day (see note 23).

40 *Chaereas is smooth . . . the Acharnian's a little pig*: The text is difficult here. The MSS have: 'Chaereas is smooth, as they say, and the Acarnanian's a little pig.' Editors have all substituted one or other form of the word 'Acharnian' for 'Acarnanian'. However, it is not beyond the bounds of possibility that there was a proverbial expression which ran: 'X I find smooth and the Acarnanian like a little pig' (i.e. 'rough and bristly'), given the remoteness and ruggedness of Acarnania.

41 *Antiphon . . . Menecrates*: 'Antiphon' is a standard Athenian name, as is 'Menecrates'. But 'Menecrates' ('Enduring power') appears to be chosen as much for its implications.

42 *Lawbringer*: See *Timon the Misanthrope*, n. 17.

43 *of sailing off to be a soldier*: The young Moschion uses this threat

(against his father) in the final scene of Menander's *The Woman from Samos* (66off.).

44   *I hope I'm wrong*: Other MSS read: 'I hope he's not lying'.

45   *Ampelis and Chrysis*: 'Ampelis' means 'Young vine' and 'Chrysis' 'Goldie'. 'Chrysis' is the name of the Samian woman at the centre of Menander's *The Woman from Samos*.

46   *Gorgias*: The name given to a character in Menander's *Bad-Tempered Man*.

47   *never . . . more than five drachmas*: Compare the 100 drachmas (1 mina) given to Corinna for her first night in dialogue 6.1. For other payments to courtesans, ranging from 2 talents for sole use for no fixed period to 2 drachmas in kind that was still too much for two nights, see dialogues 7.3, 9.3, 11.1, 14.2–4, 15.2.

48   *Dorcas . . . Polemon*: 'Dorcas' means 'Roe', 'Pannychis' 'All-night festival', 'Philostratus' 'Army-lover' and 'Polemon' 'Warlike'. However, 'Philostratus' and 'Polemon' were real names and 'Polemon' is the name of a character (a Corinthian soldier) in Menander's *The Girl with Her Hair Cut Short*. New Comedy has certainly influenced Lucian's use of the theme of the boastful soldier and the supplanted lover.

49   *Parmenon*: The name is used for a slave character in Menander's *The Demoniac Girl*.

50   *bushels*: For the *medimnos* ('bushel'), see *Timon the Misanthrope*, n. 61 and *The Ship*, n. 34.

51   *how they'd crossed . . . against the Pisidians*: 'Tiridates' (a correction from the MSS' 'Tiridantes' or 'Tirindates') was a Persian name, then carried by rulers of Parthia and their Arsacid successors. The context seems calculated to recall the period of or after Alexander's conquests in the late fourth/early third century BC.

52   *chiliarch*: The commander of a thousand men.

53   *hoplites*: See *The Ship*, n. 36.

54   *Chelidonion and Drosis*: The names mean 'Like a swallow' and 'Dewy', respectively.

55   *Cleinias*: This was a normal Athenian name, but is also given to a character in Menander's *The Demoniac Girl* and *The Hated Man*.

56   *Diotimus*: The name means 'Honouring Zeus' or 'Honoured by Zeus'.

57   *Aristaenetus*: The name means 'With the best reputation'.

58   *Nebris*: The name means 'Fawnskin', one of the distinguishing items in the wardrobe of Dionysus and his female followers.

59   *Dromon*: An appropriate name for a messenger, since it means
     'At a run'.

60   *you know how to read, don't you?*: See also dialogue 4.3 for, in
     that case, a female slave being set to read. Chelidonion (like
     Drosis) is presumably a courtesan. In both cases it is germane to
     the plot of the piece and does not necessarily imply a high level
     of literacy among women, though it might subconsciously reflect
     Lucian's assumption about his own period.

61   *He didn't even . . . at the beginning*: Literally 'He didn't even add
     greetings (*chairein*)'. Ancient Greek letters usually began with a
     formula bidding the reader to 'rejoice' (*chaire*), the normal word
     for 'hello' and 'goodbye'.

62   *Architeles and Erasicleia*: These names have been constructed to
     sound impressive (respectively, 'Leader of the pack' and
     'Delighting in fame') rather than to reflect real usage. The first is
     attested for Athens by a story in Plutarch (*Themistocles* 7), while
     the second is found only here.

63   *because I'm virtuous . . . withstand troubles*: Aristaenetus appears
     to be teaching Cleinias Stoic philosophy, the watchwords of which
     were 'virtue' and 'endurance'. For Lucian's attitude towards
     Stoicism, see *True Histories* 2.18, *Philosophies for Sale* 21–5 and
     The Dead Come to Life 43 and 51.

64   *proverbial 'Scythian answer'*: The reference is to the answer given
     by the Scythian king Idanthyrsus to the Persian king Darius at
     Herodotus, *Histories* 4.127. When Darius asked why the Scythi-
     ans were always running away and suggested that they either
     stand and fight or pay homage to Persia, Idanthyrsus rejected
     both alternatives, the second rudely ('as for your claim to be my
     master, I tell you to go to hell').

65   *speeches about love . . . for their students*: The most obvious
     interpretation of this is that Dromon has heard Aristaenetus and
     Cleinias reading Plato's *Symposium* and *Phaedrus*, both of which
     contain speeches about love. Dromon has jumped to the con-
     clusion that the content signals Aristaenetus' homo-erotic inter-
     est. There might be something suspicious in a Stoic spending so
     much time on the works of a rival philosophical school. But
     Plato's ethics in some ways foreshadow those of the Stoics and
     Dromon's testimony as an uneducated outsider is suspect.

66   *write on the wall in the Ceramicus*: For the use of graffiti in
     manipulating attitudes, see also dialogue 4.2–3.

67   *useful accusation*: The word used here, *diabole*, is that used by
     Lucian for 'slander' in his essay *Slander* and I have translated it

'useful accusation' to give a sense of the fragility of the 'evidence' against Aristaenetus. A pun and an alliteration also underpin the sense of a devious plot here: 'support' has the same 'running' root as Dromon's name (*dram-/drom-*) and the last two words of the sentence are *Dromonos diabole*.

68   *Tryphaena and Charmides*: Tryphaena's name is based on the root *tryphe*, which means 'luxury'. 'Charmides' is a normal Athenian name, but Lucian's audience might have associated it especially with the dialogue of that title by Plato.

69   *Philemation*: The name means 'Lover of the cloak'. As it turns out, it is suitably ironic for a woman whose physical charms are not all they appear.

70   *the present commander's son*: In Athens, ten generals (*strategoi*) were elected each year. The Greek here ('the son of the man who is currently general') is not very precise. It sounds as though Lucian implies that there is only one, since he does not specify the general's name.

71   *neophyte*: The image used here is of a recent initiate into one of the Mysteries (e.g. the Eleusinian Mysteries).

72   *Moschion*: A common name for young male characters in the New Comedies of Menander. See *The Lyre Player*, *The Girl with Her Hair Cut Short*, *The Woman from Samos*, *The Sicyonian*, *Fabulae Incertae 1, 2, 5* and *7*.

73   *the coffin*: The implication is either that Philemation is very old and near death or that she will be the death of Charmides (cf. Aristophanes, *Wasps* 1365 for the latter sense).

74   *Ioessa and Pythias and Lysias*: 'Ioessa' could mean 'Violet-coloured' or 'Poisonous'. 'Pythias' was the name of Aristotle's wife and daughter. 'Lysias' is a normal Athenian name.

75   *a prytaneus*: One of the members of the Council of Five Hundred. See note 8.

76   *Phaon*: Ioessa is comparing Lysias to the mythical ferryman given good looks as a reward by Aphrodite.

77   *Lycaena ... Magadion*: 'Lycaena' is related to the word *lykos*, 'wolf'. 'Magadion' is based on the word *magadis*, a Lydian instrument with twenty strings.

78   *Thrason and Diphilus*: 'Thrason', meaning 'Bold', is a name from New Comedy, used of a bragging soldier (cf. Polemon in dialogue 9 and Leontichus in dialogue 13). 'Diphilus' (see also dialogue 3) is an ordinary Greek name.

79   *Cymbalion and Pyrallis*: 'Cymbalion' means 'Little cymbal'. 'Pyrallis' is taken from an unidentified species of bird.

80   *you took a bite . . . threw it into her lap*: The apple was regarded as a love-token, expressing sexual desire for the person to whom it was given.

81   *lifted . . . socket*: Ancient doors were not hung on hinges, but had pivots at top and bottom, which sat in sockets. If there was enough play, even a pair of doors bolted across the centre might be lifted up and removed to allow access.

82   *Lyde*: The name means 'Lydian girl', a slave name.

83   *let's have a drink . . . the peace*: There is a pun here which implies that the drink they have will actually seal the peace, because the word used for 'peace treaty' (*spondai*) is the plural form of the word for 'libation' (*sponde*) – since treaties of peace were concluded by the pouring of libations of wine.

84   *Leontichus and Chenidas and Hymnis*: 'Leontichus', a real Athenian name, also carries the connotation of 'lion-like' (i.e. brave). 'Chenidas' is not attested, but is based on the root *chen-*, which means 'goose' (known as good guards because of their noisiness, but also for their devotion to human beings: Aelian, *On the Characteristics of Animals* 12.33, 7.41). Alternatively, the root might imply 'mocking laughter'. 'Hymnis' means 'Singer of hymns'.

85   *battle against the Galatians*: The Galatians did not come into conflict with Greeks until the period of Attalus, king of Pergamum, *c.* 230 BC.

86   *phalanx*: See *The Ship*, n. 43.

87   *satrap in Paphlagonia*: The term 'satrap' was used by the Persians for the governors of their provinces (cf. *The Ship*, n. 41). The Persian hold on Paphlagonia ended after Alexander the Great's invasion and it was ruled after his death (if at a distance) by Hellenistic kings of Pontus.

88   *taxiarchs*: At Athens, a taxiarch was the commander of a contingent supplied by one of the tribes (see *Timon the Misanthrope*, n. 43).

89   *Aristaechmus . . . our best javelin thrower*: As he should be, given that his name means 'Best spearman'.

90   *But you're polluted*: In the Greek world, the shedding of blood brought a pollution (*miasma*) which required a ritual purification before the resumption of normal life. See Parker 1983.

91   *Lemnian women or Danaids*: The mythical examples Hymnis picks both relate to women who killed their husbands.

92   *Grammis*: The name is based on the root for writing, but that does not appear to have any special significance here.

93 *Dorion and Myrtale*: 'Dorion' is a real name, connected to the
    word for 'Dorian', but it may in this context also ironically recall
    the Greek word for 'gift' (*doron*). 'Myrtale' is based on the Doric
    form of the word for 'myrtle tree' (sacred to Aphrodite).

94 *bow-officer Epiuros*: The bow-officer (*prorates*) watched for
    storms (Aristophanes, *Knights* 543). Epiuros has an apt name,
    since *epiouros* means 'watcher'.

95 *five sea-bass, and four perch*: The first fish is probably the Nile-
    perch. The general point is that fish was widely regarded as a
    luxury item in antiquity (so should count high in the reckoning
    being made). But how did Dorion keep them fresh?

96 *He's the proverbial ass . . . good luck to you*: There is an untrans-
    latable pun here on 'ass' and 'good luck to you' (*onos . . . onaio*).

97 *Delphis . . . Cymbalion*: The first name means 'Dolphin'. For the
    second, see note 79.

98 *Cochlis and Parthenis*: The names mean, respectively, 'Little shell-
    fish' (of the type used for purple dye – cf. *Two Charges of Literary
    Assault*, n. 30) and 'Virgin'.

99 *with your pipes*: The girl was hired to play the double-reed pipes
    known as *auloi*, which were usually played in pairs. The *aulos*
    was used to accompany choruses in drama as well as at other,
    lighter entertainments. See also *Praising a Fly*, n. 3.

100 *Crocale . . . Gorgus*: The names mean, respectively, 'Thread' or
    'Wool' and 'Grim', 'Terrible' or 'Vigorous'.

101 *Deinomachus*: Aptly enough, his name means 'Terrible warrior'.

102 *the Megarian*: I.e. Deinomachus. Of course, he is not from
    Megara, but Aetolia. So he is called a Megarian as an insult.
    Megarian humour was reputed to be low-grade, and in general
    Megarians were believed (especially by Athenians) to be bereft of
    all the graces. Some editors change the text to make him 'the man
    from Metapa' or 'the man from Agraioi' (two places in Aetolia).

103 *Thespias'*: The name is related to the Greek word for 'prophesy'
    (*thespizo*), but also to the name of the inventor of tragedy,
    Thespis. She is presumably another courtesan.

104 *prytaneis*: See note 8.

105 *a fisherman, or a sailor . . . loads of presents*: Compare, however,
    the complaints against the poor sailor in dialogue 14.

106 *empty noise, that's all they are*: This is the general reputation of
    soldiers in New Comedy and also in these dialogues. Compare
    Polemon in Menander's *The Girl with Her Hair Cut Short* and
    Bias in his *The Fawner*. See dialogues 9 and 13, but contrast the
    Acarnanian in dialogue 1.

SCYTHIANS

THE SCYTHIAN, OR THE HONORARY CONSUL

1 *HONORARY CONSUL*: The Greek for the alternative title is *proxenos*, which was used especially in Athens of a citizen who represented the interests of a foreign state at Athens. It could also be used of a foreigner, as an honorific title granted by the city.

2 *Anacharsis*: See also Lucian's dialogue *Anacharsis*, in which the Scythian debates Greek culture with the Athenian lawgiver Solon.

3 *'pilophoric' class*: Literally, the class 'of those who wear the *pilos*'. The *pilos* was a felt cap, regarded at Athens as the mark of an ex-slave. Lucian regards it as typical of the Scythian nobility. This information is unique to Lucian in our extant sources, but there were works called *Skythika* ('Scythian doings'), now lost, which he might have used for details like this and the one about 'octapods' ('eight feet') immediately following.

4 *hoi polloi*: See *A Few Words about Mourning*, n. 1.

5 *'octapods' . . . two oxen and one wagon*: See note 3.

6 *This Toxaris*: The stress on 'this', present in the Greek, might have served to differentiate the Toxaris of this *prolalia* from the interlocutor of the long dialogue *Toxaris*, which appears to be set in a period more or less contemporary with Lucian. If so, it strengthens the argument that this piece was in conception and first performance the preamble to the larger work. See also *Toxaris*, n. 72.

7 *after his death . . . a hero*: In Greek religion, a hero was a mortal granted special power to help the people of the locality in which his sanctuary was situated. This was often established at the site – or supposed site – of his tomb. See Sophocles, *Oedipus at Colonus* 1579f. for a dramatic account of the heroization of Oedipus.

8 *not just Scythians . . . immortalize human beings and 'send them to Zamolxis'*: In *True Histories* 2.17 and *Zeus Rants* 42, Zamolxis is described as Thracian. Elsewhere in Lucian (*The Parliament of the Gods* 9) he is associated with the Getae, who are described as Scythians (though there is some disagreement among the MSS here). But Lucian was also capable of separating the Getae from the Scythians (*Icaromenippus* 16). The *locus classicus* for Lucian's audience's knowledge of Scythia was Book 4 of Herodotus' *Histories* and Herodotus' accounts of Zamolxis

(whom he calls 'Salmoxis') in chapters 93–6 make it clear that (1) he was the god of the Getae, (2) the Getae were Thracians who lived in the territory neighbouring Scythia, (3) it is the Getae who 'immortalize' human beings (believing in immortality) and send (messengers) to Zamolxis. The use of a similar word for 'immortalize' and the same for 'send . . . to Zamolxis' strongly suggests that Lucian has this passage in mind. Perhaps, then, Lucian expects his audience to spot his faux pas and interpret it as a clever adaptation of the Herodotean passage. However, it seems possible also that there is a textual error and that the true reading here was *Getae* (as it may also be in *The Parliament of the Gods* 9).

9   *great plague*: This occurred at Athens in 430–429 BC, during the Archidamian War (431–421) between Athens and Sparta and their allies.

10   *Architeles*: For this name and its meaning, see *Chattering Courtesans*, n. 62. It is impossible to know whether the story is Lucian's own invention, or derived from a lost *Skythika* (see note 3 above).

11   *The Scythian*: Toxaris.

12   *Deimainete*: The wife of Architeles. It is unusual (because against normal protocol) to hear the name of an Athenian citizen woman in classical literature. The name means 'Timid', however, and may have been invented to be suitable to the character to whom Toxaris appeared, just as Architeles' name (see note 10) and position imply high rank and authority.

13   *angel of mercy*: The Greek says 'good *daimon*'. The word *daimon* was usually used to identify divinity at work when the name of the deity responsible was not known.

14   *already a chatterbox*: The implication is both that he is now fluent in Greek and that he has abandoned the conventional Scythian reticence.

15   *Acinaces*: The word means 'sword', but is Persian rather than Scythian in origin. See also *Toxaris*, n. 61.

16   *What you've mentioned . . . completely forget them*: Lucian's erotic imagery (cf. paragraph 4) goes beyond the word 'passion' (*eros*). He has Toxaris personify Athens as a woman (the word *polis* ('city') is feminine) who uses her sexual allure to draw a man away from his wife and family. The image is probably reinforced by the mention of 'doors' (i.e. house doors, and not city gates). This may allude to the standard motif from elegiac poetry in which the lovelorn man stands outside the closed doors of the house of the woman he desires, waiting in misery to be admitted.

Lucian's portrait comically evokes the picture of Athens as court-esan (see *Chattering Courtesans*, n. 1). See further note 24 below.

17 *'No words of ill omen, please'*: Literally 'Speak well'. The com-mand was a preamble to rituals and in effect enjoined silence on the worshippers.

18 *god of strangers*: Zeus.

19 *serve as ... honorary consul*: The verb 'to serve as honorary consul' (*proxenein*) reflects the alternative title. See note 1.

20 *genuine citizen of Greece*: Of course, in the Solonian period, there was no such thing as 'a citizen of Greece'. There were only citizens of individual city-states (*poleis*) and Greeks who shared an ethnic and cultural identity. Moreover, Toxaris speaks as though contact with Solon can actually affect the legal status of Anacharsis, since the word here translated 'genuine' (*gnesios*) is the normal antithesis of *nothos* ('spurious'). Underlying this discourse, despite the classical context, are the concerns and attitudes of Lucian's own time, in which the notion of 'Greek citizenship' was not so strange in the light of the existence of 'Roman citizenship' and where 'Greekness' was acquirable through education (the way Lucian himself had obtained it). See further Introduction, section 4, Swain 1996, Whitmarsh 2001a.

21 *Theoxenus ... records this about him*: Theoxenus may be a real source, but if so he is not recorded elsewhere. It is possible, perhaps even probable, that he is an invention, given that his name means 'God's stranger', appropriate to a context in which the theme of a *xenos* ('stranger') protected by the intervention of a good *daimon* ('spirit') is central.

22 *famous young islander ... house of Menelaus*: The young islander is Telemachus, son of Odysseus, who has set out from the island of Ithaca to find his father and visits Menelaus in Sparta (*Odyssey* 4.43ff.).

23 *a flower with ... a city bloom*: The source of the quotation is unknown, but its metre is the iambic trimeter, used in tragedy and comedy.

24 *common people's ... passion*: Once more, Lucian uses the strong metaphor of sexual love, *eros*, here to express the people's attitude towards Lucian's prospective patrons and echo the passion (*eros*) of Anacharsis and Toxaris for Greek culture (paragraphs 4–5). See also note 16.

25 *so much of Aphrodite ... on his tongue*: Lucian continues to use metaphors which suggest sexual attraction. See note 24.

26 *son of Cleinias*: Alcibiades.

27 *had cause to regret the passion ... for Alcibiades*: Because he
absconded to Sparta in 415 instead of returning to Athens to
face charges in the affair of the Profanation of the Eleusinian
Mysteries.

28 *poet from Ceos*: Bacchylides, fr. 15.1–3 (*Carmina cum Frag-
mentis*, ed. B. Snell and H. Maehler (Leipzig 1998)).

TOXARIS, OR FRIENDSHIP

1 *After all, the Scythians ... the Scythian state*: The bulk of this
account follows Euripides' *Iphigenia in Tauris*, but the detail of
the murder of the king, Thoas, occurs in Hyginus, *Genealogiae*
(= *Fabulae*) 121. The priestess turns out to be Orestes' sister,
Iphigenia. See further note 7 below.

2 *Argo ... expedition to Colchis*: The reference is to the story of
Jason and the Argonauts.

3 *'Inhospitable'*: The usual Greek name for the sea was *Euxeinos*,
that is 'Hospitable', but some sources say the original name was
Axeinos, 'Inhospitable'. The fifth-century BC poet Pindar uses
both names (*Pythian* 4.203 and *Nemean* 4.49).

4 *the Bosporus*: Here it is the Cimmerian Bosporus that is meant.

5 *fishmongers*: The Greek word (*tarichopoles*) signifies that they
dealt not in fresh fish, but in salted fish. This was sold at a market
near the city gates in Athens, a location generally regarded as
much more disreputable than the Agora (see Aristophanes,
Knights 1246 with 1398–401).

6 *An account ... set up in the temple of Orestes*: There were Greek
settlements in the Crimea, in Scythian territory. Such cities (*poleis*)
tended to try to retain a link with Greece by claiming mythical
precedents. It is possible that what Lucian describes here did
actually exist in a city of this kind, though a widespread 'cult of
friendship' among the native population is difficult to believe in
and has probably been invented to underpin the moralistic point
of the friendship narratives of the dialogue. See further notes 7,
11, 13, 16, 18, 55, 61, 64, 76, 77, 78, 80.

7 *in the process of killing Thoas*: See note 1. This difference from
the account in Euripides' *Iphigenia in Tauris* has led some scholars
to suggest that these pictures were real, but that Lucian derived
his descriptions from a written source. However, the killing of
the king may simply be imported to emphasize how strange it is
that the Scythians should have come to admire Orestes. Unlike
the sculpture on Toxaris' tomb (*The Scythian* 2) or other works

of art (e.g. Apelles' *Calumny*, *Slander* 5), Lucian neither claims to have seen the paintings himself nor gives a detailed description of the temple's location. See further note 13 below.

8   *the goddess*: Artemis (i.e. a cult statue of her).

9   *they eat their fathers when they die*: This idea is mentioned also in *A Few Words about Mourning* 21. However, when the custom is mentioned by Herodotus (*Histories* 1.216 and 4.26), it is associated with the Massagetae and Issedones, not with the Scythians.

10   *empty, dumb masks ... don't emit the slightest sound*: Tragic masks in the early theatre were realistic, as vase-paintings and sculptures show, rather than exaggerated. However, the masks used on the stage from the Hellenistic period onwards show an increasing tendency towards grotesqueness, especially in the size of the mouth and the *onkos*, 'bulge', an elongation of the forehead. These are the masks which Lucian expects his audience to envisage (the image here could refer either to masks without actors behind them, or to masks on actors with no speaking part – the so-called *kopha prosopa*, the phrase used in the Greek here). See also *The Philosopher Nigrinus* 11 with n. 15.

11   *poets as witnesses ... Theseus and Pirithous and the rest*: There may be a tinge of irony here, on Lucian's part, underlying Toxaris' reference to the trustworthiness of poets, given that Lucian elsewhere (like Aristotle in the *Poetics*) tends to classify poetry and history as having entirely different goals: 'history and poetry have entirely different aims and rules. In poetry, freedom is absolute and the only rule is what the poet thinks right' (*How to Write History* 8). This will be clearer still if it is Homer to whom reference is principally made here (the *Iliad* for Achilles and Patroclus, and *Odyssey* 11.631 for Theseus and Pirithous, in this case a bare mention), since he is often satirized by Lucian for his inventions (see *True Histories* 1.3). However, no full poetic account of Theseus and Pirithous' friendship has survived and so it is not certain whether Lucian is simply recalling in general terms the story to which Homer (and Sophocles at *Oedipus at Colonus* 1593–4) alludes (as told by scholiasts and mythographers) or whether he had in mind a specific (now lost) poem.

12   *so well armed ... aimed securely at their target*: The imagery here alludes to the expertise of Scythians with the bow and arrow.

13   *described ... in ... tragic mode*: Mnesippus' use of the verb *ektragoideo* is probably in line with that found in other late Greek authors and implies exaggeration and the inappropriate use of

poetic liberty (see also note 18). Mnesippus thus casts suspicion on the reality of the temple and its paintings, but what the intended effect upon Lucian's audience was will depend on whether these were known to exist or immediately recognized to be fictional (see note 7).

14   *If yours seem . . . sharper*: Toxaris responds to Mnesippus' arrow imagery with another metaphor from the sharpness of weapons.

15   *that you'll speak the truth . . . and nothing but the truth*: Literally 'verily to tell the truth'. The words in Greek, *e men*, are a formula common in asseveration.

16   *you must swear . . . refute them*: As Lucian makes clear in *True Histories* 1.4, making up tales and representing them as the truth was not only easy, but common. However, he also says there that detecting such fictions is not difficult. The fact that Toxaris, a Scythian, demands an oath of veracity from a Greek may have been intended by Lucian to serve as a signal to his audience precisely of the fictional nature of the examples they will be hearing.

17   *Zeus in his guise as god of friends*: Zeus Philios.

18   *add no tragic frills of my own*: See note 13. The verb here has a different prefix (*epi-*) but again the implication is that 'tragedizing' would involve invention.

19   *Agathocles*: The name means 'of Good fame'. As in other pieces, Lucian signals the moral of his tale by the use of 'speaking names' (see notes on *The Journey down to Hades*, *Timon the Misanthrope* and *Chattering Courtesans*).

20   *Charicleia*: The name is once again significant; with its combination of 'charm' (*charis*) and 'fame' (*kleos*), it implies that the lady is 'famous for her charm'.

21   *apples with a bite taken out of them*: See *Chattering Courtesans* 12.1 with n. 80.

22   *courtesan-like*: See *Chattering Courtesans* generally, and n. 1 there for a definition of a courtesan (*hetaira*).

23   *ignoring him . . . interested in someone else*: The method used by Philinna in *Chattering Courtesans* 3 and the advice given by Ampelis to Chrysis in dialogue 8.

24   *played a supporting role in the comedy*: The implication may be that they acted in the comic drama as chorus.

25   *acted in countless dramas of passion*: The implication of 'acted' is that the passions were pretended, not real.

26   *talents*: See *Timon the Misanthrope*, n. 60 and *The Ship*, n. 25.

27   *drew his sword as against an adulterer*: In classical Athens, a

husband who surprised his wife in adultery technically had the right to kill her lover, though normally the aggrieved husband would accept a sum in compensation (see Lysias, *Orations* 1).

28 *generals ... harmost ... great king*: The 'great king' (*megas basileus*) in Greek of the classical period would mean 'the king of Persia'. However, it is clear from the mention of Gyarus that the story is set during the Roman imperial period. This, then, is the Roman emperor (as is the 'king' just below). The 'generals' may be the *duumviri* who administered the city where the crime was committed. The 'harmost', a word used to describe the official sent from Sparta to govern the *perioikoi* ('dwellers around Sparta'), must be the Roman provincial governor ('proconsul'). Jones (1986, 56) notes how, despite the contemporary setting, Lucian veils the Roman institutions he mentions in classical terminology.

29 *sailed to Italy*: To be tried at Rome. The implication is that Deinias was a Roman citizen.

30 *purple-fishers*: They collected the shellfish from which purple dye was made (see *Two Charges of Literary Assault*, n. 30).

31 *Euthydicus*: The name means 'Right-judging', an epithet used by the Furies of themselves in Aeschylus, *Eumenides* 312 and which can be associated with the idea of 'direct trial' (i.e. made on the merits of the case alone). But there is also a sense of immediacy implied by the root *euthy-* which will turn out to be appropriate for the man who makes his life-and-death decision both correctly and at once.

32 *when the Pleiades set*: The point is that the voyage is taking place at a time of year when the weather can no longer be trusted.

33 *Eudamidas ... Aretaeus ... Charixenus*: The three names each have special significance for the tale. 'Eudamidas', the name of the poor man, implies 'of good plebeian stock' (from the Doric *damos* = Attic *demos*, 'common people'); 'Aretaeus', the name of Eudamidas' fellow-citizen, who ultimately sees to the fulfilment of the terms of the will, implies 'virtuous' (from the word *arete*, 'virtue'); 'Charixenus', the name of the wealthy foreigner, implies 'doing favours to guest-friends' (from *charis*, 'favour', and *xenos*, 'stranger', 'guest-friend', 'host').

34 *Aretaeus, the acme of legatees*: There is a slight wordplay in the Greek. The word translated here 'acme' is *aristos* ('best') and his name *Aretaios*.

35 *nuncupative heir*: The phrase is possibly a technical one, relating to the early style of Roman wills, which were nuncupated, i.e.

sworn orally before witnesses (Plutarch, *Coriolanus* 9.2). Toxaris'
words are, however, probably meant by Lucian to be understood
ironically, implying that Eudamidas would have been just as keen
to be the heir of his rich friends, whose wills would have favoured
him in less costly ways.

36   *Zenothemis*: The name means 'Zeus' justice' and perhaps implies
that this man will surprise us by adhering to a higher law than
the usual prejudices of humans would expect.

37   *in Italy . . . for my native land*: The word translated as 'native
land' is *patris*, the same term as is used in the title of *An Encomium
of Fatherland*. He means his native city. Sophists were often sent
to Rome to present cases to the emperor for special favours (see
Bowersock 1969, chapter 4). From this anecdote, it is clear that
Mnesippus is to be thought of as an orator with high status within
his own community.

38   *hideous horror*: The word used here, *mormolykeion*, is employed
in classical literature for anything terrifying (including a type of
mask). The attitude to physical deformity and female ugliness
demonstrated by Mnesippus seems to have been usual in antiquity
(cf. Croesus' dismissive view of his deaf-mute son in Herodotus,
Histories 1.38, the laughter of the gods at Hephaestus' lameness
in *Iliad* 1.600, the Spartan king Agesilaus' own jokes at his
deformed leg in Plutarch, *Agesilaus* 2.2 and the contemptuous
reactions of Epigenes to the old women he is obliged to sleep with
in Aristophanes, *Women at the Assembly* 975f.).

39   *Menecrates*: The name means 'Remaining in power', which fore-
shadows the end of the story, where Menecrates' rights are
restored.

40   *Six Hundred*: According to Strabo (*Geography* 4.179), Massilia
had an aristocratic constitution. The Six Hundred was the ruling
council of the city, comprising the *Timouchoi* ('honour-holders'),
whose position was for life.

41   *publishing an unconstitutional measure*: This being actionable
was not unusual in Greek cities. Such a provision was also central
to the Athenian law code (see Harrison, 1998, vol. 2, 14 and
172). Cf. *The Journey down to Hades*, n. 37.

42   *Cydimache*: The name implies 'glory' (*kydos*) and 'battle'
(*mache*), perhaps suggesting that she has had to fight (against
deformity) for the status she will now receive.

43   *received the dowry . . . long ago*: This is surprising, since we have
heard nothing so far about Menecrates having given money or
property to Zenothemis.

44   *As he said this . . . taken her virginity*: The ceremony designed by
      Zenothemis has some unusual features. First of all, it takes place
      in Zenothemis' own house and not in the bride's father's house.
      Secondly, instead of a procession from the bride's father's house
      to her new husband's home, the bride is taken directly from the
      dinner in the bridegroom's house to the bedroom for the marriage
      to be consummated. Normally there would also be a number
      of other rituals associated with this procession. Perhaps this
      topsy-turvy ceremony is meant to be of a piece with the paradoxi-
      cal nature of the tale and it is possible that Lucian intends it to be
      comic.

45   *despises the criteria of . . . looks only towards his friend*: This
      would be a good philosophical position, worthy of a Cynic or a
      Stoic.

46   *Antiphilus*: The name means 'Loving in return', a theme which is
      significant for the story, though it is Demetrius whose friendship
      is put to the ultimate test.

47   *fellow-ephebes*: See *The Journey down to Hades*, n. 5.

48   *Demetrius was following . . . Antiphilus was studying medicine*:
      Demetrius of Sunium was a real Athenian name. Jones (1986, 56,
      n. 52) suggests that Lucian's audience would have thought of the
      famous Cynic philosopher of the first century AD. In the same
      place, he suggests that the audience might have thought of Alexan-
      dria as the setting for their education. It was a well-known centre
      for both Cynicism (the teacher of Peregrinus Proteus, Agatho-
      boulus, was based there) and medicine. The identity of the
      'Rhodian sophist' is unknown, though Agathoboulus has been
      suggested.

49   *whose name and nationality were 'the Syrian'*: That is, his name
      was 'Syrus', which means 'Syrian'. It was common for slaves to
      receive a generic name derived from the ethnic group from which
      they came (e.g. 'Thratta' = 'Thracian girl').

50   *Deinomenes*: An Athenian name, but it is likely that the meaning,
      'Awaiting terrible things', is meant to be uppermost in the audi-
      ence's minds here.

51   *harmost*: Here, as in paragraph 17, the word used for 'provincial
      governor' (here the prefect of Egypt) has an archaic colouring,
      being the title of a Spartan official sent to govern the *perioikoi*
      ('people living around Sparta'). See note 28.

52   *prefect of Egypt*: Interestingly, Lucian uses a direct translation of
      the Latin term *praefectus Aegypti*, instead of the classicizing
      'harmost' employed in paragraphs 17 and 32. See notes 28 and 51.

53   *a thousand drachmas*: The equivalent of ten minas, one sixth of
      a talent (see note 26), not an enormous sum.

54   *Brahmins*: A natural group for Cynics to study. In fact, Lucian
      mentions them as models for a detail in the suicide of Peregrinus
      Proteus (*The Passing of Peregrinus* 39).

55   *His defence . . . both free*: This contradicts the version implied
      at paragraph 33, where Demetrius refused to accept release on
      any grounds other than being completely cleared of any part in
      the crime. Mnesippus seems to be conflating Demetrius' self-
      incrimination (paragraph 32) with this final retrial. The slip looks
      deliberate on Lucian's part and may suggest (as did the mention of
      the ease of inventing such tales at paragraph 11) that Mnesippus'
      veracity is questionable.

56   *in so sophistic a manner*: The adverb is formed from the word
      sophistes, the term used in Lucian's day for a top-class orator (see
      Introduction, section 5).

57   *After all, you'd look . . . your native Scythia*: This remark may be
      more pointed than it appears. The Scythians were a favourite
      topic of moralistic discourse in Greek sophistic rhetoric. See
      Philostratus, *Lives of the Sophists* 2.5 (572–3) for Alexander
      Peloplaton's Scythian discourse and 2.27 (620) for that of Hippo-
      dromus the Thessalian (both *c.* first half of the second century
      AD). It was paradoxical that Scythians should use Greeks for the
      same end, and perhaps amusing to see a Scythian using the Greek
      language to praise his own people, especially given the general
      Greek view of Scythian speech (see note 58 below).

58   *not the Scythian way*: Scythians were noted in proverb for the
      brevity and rudeness of their speech (see Herodotus, *Histories*
      4.127).

59   *You live in . . . profound peace*: There is alliteration also in the
      Greek (though between 'live' (*biousin*) and 'profound' (*batheiai*),
      the last two words of the phrase). This looks very much like a
      backhanded compliment to the success of the Roman empire's
      custodianship of the Greek East.

60   *that single cut . . . to our lips and drink*: This is cleverly adapted
      to the (invented) friendship ritual from what Herodotus says
      about the way Scythians make sworn pledges (*Histories* 4.70).
      Though the detail about drinking together at the same time is not
      mentioned in Herodotus, it also appears to have been common
      practice among the Scythians (as is confirmed by a gold plaque
      from the tomb of Kul-Oba near Kertch: see Minns 1913, 203).
      Lucian may have known this from other literary sources.

61 *by the wind and by the dagger*: Herodotus (*Histories* 4.62) men-
    tions the worship of the *akinakes*, 'sword' (for which see also *The
    Scythian* 4 with n. 15), but says nothing about the wind as a
    divinity. The wind is notoriously inconstant and is used as a
    metaphor for instability (Eupolis, fr. 406, *PCG*), and in phrases
    which imply useless tasks ('to speak to the wind') or the impossi-
    bility of achieving a goal (e.g. 'to farm the winds'). It seems likely
    that this is another of Lucian's signals that claims of veracity are
    to be discounted.

62 *a lot more gods like Dagger . . . of the same kind*: These remarks
    are reminiscent of the conversation between Dionysus and
    Heracles in Aristophanes, *Frogs* 116f.

63 *'Zirin'*: The correct form of this word is difficult to reconstruct
    from the MSS, some of which give it as a masculine noun, whose
    nominative form might be *ziris*. It must mean 'friend' or
    'unarmed', but is not recorded elsewhere (though it has been
    suggested that it reflects Old Persian *zer*, 'gold').

64 *story of Belitta . . . lion*: A Scythian tale involving a lion seems
    fundamentally unlikely. The detail very likely is chosen to
    undercut Toxaris' claims to veracity.

65 *Leucanor, king of Bosporus*: Leucanor's name is not recorded
    among the known kings of (the Cimmerian) Bosporus. However,
    the name of his brother Eubiotus (paragraph 51) is found in a
    fragmentary Greek novel, *Kalligone*, set in Scythia (Stephens and
    Winkler 1995, 267–76; see also Jones 1986, 57). It seems likely
    that this tale owes its origin to that novel or one with a similar
    setting.

66 *gross insult*: The word used is *hybris*, which involved above
    all for Greeks the notion of detracting from the honour of an
    individual. See Fisher 1992.

67 *hoplites*: See *The Ship*, n. 36.

68 *I was myself*: The element of personal knowledge at second hand
    which is crucial to Mnesippus' tales and his claim to veracity
    (paragraphs 12, 19, 24) is neatly capped by Toxaris' infiltration of
    himself into the action of his third and fourth tales (see paragraphs
    57ff.).

69 *phalanx*: See *The Ship*, n. 43.

70 *bottom spike of a spear*: The MSS have a nonsensical reading
    here and the correction adopted (conjectured by Fritzsche) is
    probably the best on offer. Spears had points at both ends.

71 *tragic . . . fable*: Lucian often uses the word *tragikos* ('tragic') to
    imply that what is said is nonsense or exaggerated. The word

translated 'fable' here is *mythos*, from which the English 'myth' derives.

72   *to Athens, out of enthusiasm for Greek culture*: This produces a firm connection with the much earlier Toxaris of whom Lucian speaks in *The Scythian*, which may have been designed as an introduction to this dialogue. See Preface to this section and note 6 on that piece.

73   *sykophantai*: See *Timon the Misanthrope*, n. 36.

74   *darics*: See *The Ship*, n. 19.

75   *to fight in single combat . . . in the arena*: The practice of gladiatorial contests belongs to the Roman world of Lucian's day, though once more the word he uses, *monomachein* ('to fight in single combat'), belongs to the Attic vocabulary of the classical period.

76   *a strange Greek spectacle*: There would be no better way of insulting the Greek Mnesippus than to claim that gladiatorial shows and wild-beast hunts (*venationes*) were essentially Hellenic, rather than Roman, in origin. However, this may be another signal that Toxaris is not to be believed.

77   *anyone who wanted to fight . . . middle of the arena*: Again, this is unusual. Gladiators normally had to pass through a gladiatorial school, where they were trained by a *lanista*, and although the profession could attract volunteers (sometimes from the nobility), they would also have to submit to the same discipline. The details may once again betray Toxaris' mendacity.

78   *'It'll be easy for me . . . his affection'*: Lucian's audience are surely invited to recall a similar ending to a story in Herodotus, *Histories* 3.119 and the similar sentiments (whether interpolated or not) of Antigone in Sophocles, *Antigone* 904f. Again, the literary parallels may be designed to aim one final blow at Toxaris' veracity.

79   *hosts*: The Greek term is *xenos*, which means both 'guest' and 'host' and expresses the mutual bond between foreigners who entertain each other.

80   *I'd go even further . . . your stories*: This is double-edged, since Toxaris has shown himself to be a tall-story teller. Perhaps the joke is that Mnesippus too enjoys such fictions and regards it as possible that even better ones are to be found on Scythian soil and beyond.

THE ART OF THE EULOGY

AN ENCOMIUM OF FATHERLAND

1 *FATHERLAND*: The Greek word used throughout is *patris*, literally 'fatherland'. Though its constant repetition is slightly tedious, I have decided to retain the same term wherever it occurs.

2 *'there is nothing sweeter ... fatherland'*: This is a quotation from Odysseus' speech to the Phaeacians (*Odyssey* 9.34). He is explaining to King Alcinous that even when the goddesses Calypso and Circe each wanted him to stay with them and be their husband his heart was not persuaded, 'for there is nothing sweeter than one's fatherland'.

3 *cities*: The Greek world was still, even under the Roman empire, made up of independent city-states (*poleis*). Lucian himself often reports positively on cities which are not his fatherland (see *The Scythian* 10).

4 *islands ... birth of divinities*: For example, Apollo was closely associated in myth and poetry with Delos.

5 *laws ... against mistreatment of one's parents*: For example, at Athens parents were protected, by a specific legal procedure, from physical assault, physical neglect and the neglect of rites due to them after death, on the part of their sons (Harrison 1998, vol. 2, 77).

6 *Those who are doing well ... exile from it*: This sentiment is expressed by Odysseus in the lines which follow the quotation which opens the piece (see note 2), *Odyssey* 9.35–6: '[for there is nothing sweeter than one's fatherland or one's parents], even if a man dwells in a rich home in a land far away from his parents'.

7 *alien*: In Athens in the fifth and fourth centuries BC, most privileges were open only to citizens. If a non-Athenian claimed one, he could be accused, tried and convicted of *xenia*, i.e. 'being a foreigner' and therefore unentitled to the privilege he had claimed.

8 *autochthonous races ... thin soiled*: The autochthonous race par excellence were the Athenians, and it is their land that Thucydides describes as 'thin soiled' (*History of the Peloponnesian War* 1.2).

9 *horse-breeding ... child-rearing*: Here the writer seems to allude specifically to *Odyssey* 4.593–608, where Telemachus has the delicate task of refusing a gift of horses by Menelaus, in the process praising the open land of Sparta and contrasting the ruggedness of Ithaca. The theme of return to his home is also

hinted at there, though there is no direct eulogy of Ithaca as a land which brings forth good children (unless we are to think of Menelaus' reply, in which he praises Telemachus' speech as worthy of his 'good blood', 611). However, the adjective 'child-rearing' (*kourotrophos*) is used by Odysseus in his own praise of Ithaca at *Odyssey* 9.27.

10 *A man hastens . . . than fire elsewhere*: This paragraph, like the opening, has Odysseus especially in mind – an islander, offered marriage on Scheria to Nausicaa, immortality by Calypso and marriage by Calypso and Circe – who, Athena claims in 1.57–9, 'desires to die when he has merely seen the smoke leaping up from his fatherland'.

PRAISING A FLY

1 *her*: The Greek word for fly, *muia*, is feminine and since this fact is specifically exploited in the piece (paragraph 10), I have decided to retain the gender in translation.

2 *Indian cloth*: The reference is possibly to silk, though silk had been produced in Greece in Minoan times, as the discovery of a silkworm cocoon on Thera demonstrates.

3 *reed pipes*: The double-reed pipe (*aulos*) was used to accompany various types of Greek lyric poetry, including the choral songs of tragedy and comedy and the dithyramb. Its nearest modern relative is probably the shawm. See also *Chattering Courtesans*, n. 99 and The *Philosopher Nigrinus*, n. 37.

4 *waist*: I translate an editorial conjecture here (by E. Schwartz), which supplies a word used by Aristotle in his *History of Animals* (e.g. 487a33).

5 *fated to die early*: The adjective used here, *okymoros*, would almost certainly have recalled for Lucian's audience the figure of Achilles in the *Iliad*, of whom it is used at 1.417, 18.95, etc. The pretentiousness of the comparison enhances the irony of the encomium.

6 *When he wishes . . . style of attack*: Cf. *Iliad* 17.569–72. Menelaus has prayed to Athena for extra strength and help in avoiding missiles so that he can go to help the beleaguered Patroclus. Athena 'put strength into his shoulders and his knees and into his breast she sent the courage of a fly. Even though she is pushed away, she longs for human blood, because she relishes the blood of men.'

7 *it isn't bravado but bravery*: The distinction is between the two

words *thrasos* ('bravado') and *tharsos* ('bravery'). Actually, they are simply different forms of the same word, and both occur in Homer meaning 'courage' (e.g. *thrasos* as 'courage' at *Iliad* 14.416). The distinction made here by Lucian belongs to Attic Greek (though it is not always followed there either).

8   *And this is because ... goes for the bite*: See the previous note. Lucian is reformulating Homer's poetic language in ordinary Attic prose.

9   *gregarious flight towards the milk*: *Iliad* 2.469: 'As many as are the tribes of thronging flies that swarm about the sheep-pens in springtime, when the milk wets the milking-pails ...' Lucian's stylistic variation here moves to the fly an adjective ('gregarious', *agelaios*) more usually used with 'cattle' in Homer.

10   *when Athena diverts ... fly into his simile*: *Iliad* 4.129–31: 'she stood in front of him and warded off the sharp missile, moving it away from his flesh, as a mother shoos away a fly from her child when it is resting in sweet slumber.' Once more, the audience are meant to be aware of the skill with which Lucian substitutes a different range of vocabulary, suited to normal Attic prose, for the poetic language of Homer.

11   *'thronging' ... 'tribes'*: The reference is once more to *Iliad* 2.469, where these words (*hadinos*, *ethne*) occur (see note 9 above).

12   *Plato ... immortality of the soul*: The reference is to Plato's *Phaedo*, in which Socrates, in prison awaiting execution, discusses the immortality of the soul with his friends.

13   *nomadic, like ... the Scythians*: The Scythians were generally regarded as nomads, living in wagons (see Herodotus, *Histories* 4.11, 19, etc.). See also *The Scythian* and *Toxaris*.

14   *nor does she think ... performed in daylight*: The unspoken contrast is with human beings, who use the cover of darkness for robberies and shameful sexual acts (see *The Journey down to Hades* 27).

15   *Legend tells us ... Muia*: The Greek word for 'fly' is *muia*. See note 1. This type of myth is known as an 'aetiology', one which explains the use of a word or custom by means of a story.

16   *poetess*: Her existence is not otherwise attested, but Bompaire (1958, 144) suggests 'Muia' may be another name of the Theban poetess Corinna (fifth century BC?).

17   *courtesan*: Hetaira. See *Chattering Courtesans*, n. 1 for a definition.

18   *Muia stung him to the heart*: The fragment is unattributed (459, PCG VIII), but the phrase 'the comic poet' ought to mean that it

was from one of the major dramatists (probably of New Comedy, where the courtesan is a central figure – see Preface to *Chattering Courtesans*).

19   *'Tis strange . . . the hostile lance*: Another unidentified fragment (295, Adespota [Anon.], *TrGF*). As often in tragedy, though, there is a nod in the direction of Homeric simile (*Iliad* 17.571–2: see note 6 above for a translation of these lines). For 'hoplite', see *The Ship*, n. 36.

20   *Muia the Pythagorean*: Lucian may be using the term 'Pythagorean' in two senses, since this Muia was said to be a daughter of Pythagoras and also a Pythagorean philosopher (Clement of Alexandria, *Stromateis* ['Miscellanies'], 4.19.121, 224).

21   *child of Hermes and Aphrodite*: Hermaphroditus.

IMAGES

1   *IMAGES*: The Greek word used by Lucian for his title, *eikones* (from which the English 'iconography' and 'icon' derive), means both a pictorial image of any kind, including a statue, and a comparison or simile made in words. Since 'image' covers roughly the same ground in English, I have used this word to translate the noun *eikon* and the verb *eikazo* wherever they occur, even when the effect in English is slightly odd, in an attempt to retain Lucian's playful mingling of the verbal and visual arts.

2   *Mt. Sipylus . . . daughter of Tantalus*: Niobe lamented so much that she was turned into a rock on Mt. Sipylus. Her father Tantalus is seen in *Odyssey* 11.582–92 punished by constant thirst and hunger despite the presence of water and food. Lycinus is likened to Niobe, with the comic implication that he might turn to stone by lamenting over the lovely boys. But there is a secondary hint that he, like Tantalus, can never actually touch or enjoy what he longs for.

3   *Heracles' stone*: I.e. the magnet (which was also called the 'Magnesian stone' or the 'Lydian stone').

4   *How a young man . . . with a statue*: The story is given in a fuller version in another work (uncertainly) ascribed to Lucian, *Affairs of the Heart* 15–16.

5   *gardens at Athens*: These gardens were outside the city gates, on the banks of the river Ilissus.

6   *his Hera*: One of the Twelve Gods series. The paintings were in the stoa of Zeus Eleutherius at Athens and are described by

Pausanias (*Description of Greece* 1.3.3) and Pliny (*Natural History* 35.129).

7   *hall at Delphi*: Pausanias (*Description of Greece* 10.25.1 and 10.26.3) describes this building, known by the Delphians as the *lesche* ('place of talk'), and its paintings. It was dedicated by the Cnidians.

8   *Pacate*: Other ancient writers call her by different names ('Pancaste': Aelian, *Historical Miscellanies* 12.34; 'Pancaspe': Pliny, *Natural History* 35.86).

9   *Aëtion . . . Roxana's*: Lucian gives a description of this painting in *Herodotus, or Aëtion* 5–6. It was given new life in the Renaissance by artists in Rome (the Villa Farnesina) and Germany (Woerlitz Castle), and Botticelli copied a motif from it (Cupids playing with Alexander's armour) for his famous *Mars and Venus* (National Gallery, London).

10 *'like ivory . . . blood-red'*: *Iliad* 4.141ff.: 'As when a woman stains ivory with purple, a Maeonian or a Carian, to be a cheek-piece for horses . . . So were your thighs stained with blood Menelaus . . .'

11 *'ox-eyed'*: *Iliad* 1.551 etc. The epithet is used of the goddess Hera.

12 *Theban poet*: Pindar.

13 *'violet-eyed'*: Pindar, fr. 313, OCT, where the epithet (*ioblepharos*) was applied to Aphrodite.

14 *'laughter-loving'*, *'white-armed'* and *'rosy-fingered'*: Cf. *Iliad* 3.424 etc., 1.55 etc. and 1.477 etc. The first is used of Aphrodite, the second of Hera and the third of Dawn.

15 *'golden Aphrodite' . . . and Briseus' daughter*: Briseus' daughter is Achilles' concubine, Briseis. The reference is to *Iliad* 19.282: 'Briseis, like unto golden Aphrodite'. Aphrodite is 'golden' generally in Homer (cf. *Iliad* 3.64, *Odyssey* 8.337, etc.).

16 *book scroll . . . continuing with the rest*: In Lucian's time, books were still normally in roll form, so that reading involved rolling up the part read and unrolling to uncover the next part.

17 *'like sawn ivory'*: *Odyssey* 18.196. It is unlikely to be accidental that the passage from which this simile is taken contains a description of the beautification of Penelope by the goddess Athena while she sleeps.

18 *consort*: The Greek uses a verb, *syneinai*, meaning 'to be with', the same used later (paragraph 17) to describe Aspasia's relationship with Pericles, and again for this relationship at paragraph 22.

19 *king*: The Greek word for 'king', *basileus*, is the term used here for the Roman emperor (see paragraph 22 and *Toxaris* 17 with

n. 28). The reference is to Lucius Verus, who was co-emperor with Marcus Aurelius between 161 and 169.

20   *wife of Abradatas, king of Susa*: Panthea.

21   *heard*: Note that reading in antiquity was *viva voce* and silent reading virtually unknown (see Introduction, section 5).

22   *right-minded*: The Greek word here is related to the virtually untranslatable term of moral approbation *sophrosyne*, literally 'safeness of thinking'.

23   *Xenophon often enough praising . . . and beautiful woman*: See Xenophon, *Cyropaedia* 4.6.11, 5.1.2–18, 6.1.31–51, 6.4.2–11, 7.3.2–16. Lucian's learned audience may have been intended to understand who was meant well in advance of Polystratus (and so feel proud of their erudition), because Xenophon's Panthea is introduced with no name as 'reportedly the most beautiful woman in Asia', at the moment when she is given to the king, Cyrus, as a concubine (4.6.11), and is later portrayed with a retinue of eunuchs and serving girls (6.4.11). As it turns out, Cyrus does not actually use Panthea as his concubine, but is persuaded by her to preserve her for her real husband. Thus she keeps her chastity and Cyrus wins an important ally for his cause. All this contrasts with Lucius Verus' behaviour and may be part of an undercurrent of irony running through and undercutting the eulogy. See Preface to this section and Sidwell 2002.

24   *when she sent him into battle*: Xenophon, *Cyropaedia* 6.4.2–11.

25   *sound judgement*: Once more, Panthea is credited with the virtue *sophrosyne*. See note 22.

26   *a monkey, an ibis, a goat or a cat*: The reference is to the Egyptian style of representing their gods with animal features. For example, Anubis had the head of a jackal. Lucian makes fun of this elsewhere (e.g. *Dialogues of the Sea-Gods* 11.2). For 'ibis', see *The Ship*, n. 17.

27   *in the same measure . . . since you are able*: Cf. Hesiod, *Works and Days* 350. Hesiod is saying how one should treat a neighbour: 'Take good measure from your neighbour and give good measure in return, in the same measure, or, if you can, even better.' Lycinus reformulates the phrase 'if you can' to praise Polystratus' philosophical learning and his rhetorical abilities.

28   *'with human voice' and 'clear'*: Polystratus too is now using Homeric language. The first term is used of the goddesses Ino/Leucothea (*Odyssey* 5.334) and Circe (*Odyssey* 10.136) and the second of the Muses (*Odyssey* 24.62).

29   *old man from Pylos . . . 'sweeter than honey'*: The 'old man from

Pylos' is Nestor and the reference is to *Iliad* 1.249: '(247) And among them Nestor (248) of the sweet words jumped up, the clear [the same word as has just been applied to Panthea] speaker of the Pylians, (249) from whose tongue flowed a voice sweeter than honey.' Lucian changes the word order (and adds a definite article) in alluding to the passage, so that it effectively becomes prose.

30 *It's sweet . . . with persuasiveness*: Here Lucian's learned audience would have noticed a reformulation of the comic poet Eupolis' famous phrase about Pericles from *Demes*: 'persuasion in some form sat on his lips, so did he bewitch and alone of the orators he left his sting in his listeners' (fr. 102.5–7, *PCG*). See *The Philosopher Nigrinus* 7 with n. 11 and *Demonax the Philosopher* 10 with n. 9 for other uses of this passage.

31 *halcyons, cicadas and swans*: All these creatures were legendary in antiquity for the beauty of their song. For swans, cf. *Timon the Misanthrope* 47 with n. 49. The halcyon was a mythical bird, thought to build its nest on the surface of the sea (cf. *True Histories* 1.31 and 2.40), though Aristotle seems to have identified it with the kingfisher (*History of Animals* 616a14–19).

32 *Even Pandion's daughter . . . she sends forth*: Pandion's daughter was Procne, but the reference is to the song of the nightingale, the bird into which she was eventually turned. The word 'much-echoing' (*polyeches*) is from *Odyssey* 19.521, where Penelope tells the disguised Odysseus how she laments during the night, '(518) as when the daughter of Pandareos, the pale-green nightingale, (519) sings her beautiful song when spring has newly come . . . (521) and with swift modulations pours forth her much-echoing voice, (522) lamenting for her dear child Itylos . . .'. Lucian adapts the last half of line 521 into prose. The reference is thus not without an ominous subtext.

33 *famous Thracian . . . on top of Cithaeron*: The Thracian is Orpheus and the cattle-watcher on Cithaeron is Amphion.

34 *know what it was like to listen to the Sirens*: As Odysseus did (*Odyssey* 12.158ff.). It was his crew's ears he stuffed with wax (which the Sirens' song could not, it seems, penetrate, unlike Panthea's – cf. *In Defence of 'Images'*, n. 1). Here the focus appears to be upon the beauty of their song (*Odyssey* 12.44, 52) and not upon its deceitful or destructive nature (contrast the allegorical interpretation used in *The Philosopher Nigrinus* 19 (with n. 22) and *Slander* 30). But Lucian's audience might have sensed irony here, given the strong traditional associations of the Sirens with the destructiveness of pleasure.

35   *pure Ionic ... Attic charm*: 'Attic charm' implies that she is a
      witty speaker (cf. *Demonax the Philosopher*, n. 6), though, being
      an Ionian, she employs that dialect of Greek. This seems an
      implausible picture, since Attic Greek was the standard for edu-
      cated speakers in this period, while the *koine* ('common tongue',
      the language of the New Testament) was that of ordinary people.
      Ionic was occasionally used still for literary purposes (see Lucian's
      Astrology and *The Goddesse of Surrye*, both of which are written
      in this dialect). See Bompaire 1958, 633 for this as a contradiction
      of grammatical orthodoxy.

36   *Smyrna's original status as an Athenian colony*: Athenian myth
      held that Theseus, king of Athens, established the colony at
      Smyrna. Though such colonies often outgrew the link with their
      'mother-cities' (*metropoleis*), the *metropolis* would often cling to
      the relationship (or the claim) for political reasons, and vice versa
      (compare Corcyra and Epidamnus, and Corcyra and Corinth, in
      Thucydides, *History of the Peloponnesian War* 1.24–5).

37   *fellow-citizen of Homer*: Smyrna was only one of a number of
      places which claimed to be Homer's birthplace and it was a
      question also frequently discussed by ancient students of his
      poems. See *True Histories* 2.20 for the 'truth', as told to Lucian
      by Homer himself on the Isle of the Blest.

38   *give me back more than I doled out*: Lycinus returns to the
      citation of Hesiod, *Works and Days* 350 which was used in
      paragraph 12 (see note 27 above).

39   *Helicon's bounty*: The Muses lived on Helicon.

40   *those of Hermes and Apollo as well*: I.e. music (Apollo) and
      oratory (Hermes).

41   *in the ancient writers*: The Greek might alternatively mean
      'among those of old', implying that Panthea surpasses those
      known both in written works and in oral tradition.

42   *one actually Ionian ... a passion for their subject*: The reference
      appears to be to Aeschines the Socratic's dialogue *Aspasia*, now
      lost, in which Socrates was a central figure. In it, Aspasia – also
      an Ionian and also the mistress of a powerful man – gave advice
      on marriage to Xenophon. Lucian's learned audience might also
      have seen irony here, given that Pericles (unlike Verus) had div-
      orced his wife before cohabiting with Aspasia, and Panthea would
      be in no position to lecture on marriage. See further note 43.

43   *remarkable Olympian himself*: Lucian means Pericles, the most
      important Athenian politician of the fifth century BC. The comic
      poets, especially Cratinus (e.g. fr. 73, fr. 258, *PCG*), referred to

him and portrayed him on stage as Olympian Zeus. They were also highly critical of his relationship with Aspasia, whom they represented as a brothel-keeper. Lucian's learned audience might have read these references ironically, judging Panthea's case in light of the comic critique of Pericles and Aspasia. See also note 42 above.

44 *colossus*: In earlier Greek, this word was used for statues of any size. But since the Hellenistic period, Greek cities had built enormous statues called *kolossoi* (such as the famous 'Colossus of Rhodes', probably dedicated in 290 BC, and destroyed by an earthquake in 224 or 223 BC), and in the Roman imperial period the form was regularly used for statues of emperors (e.g. that of Nero in his 'Golden House': Suetonius, *Nero* 31.1).

45 *the present Roman empire*: The phrase used here in Greek means literally 'the present power of the Romans' and parallels that used for Athens, 'the then administration of the Athenians'. This is one of a relatively few places where Lucian mentions the Romans or Rome directly by name. Cf. *On Salaried Posts in Great Houses* 20 ('the rule of the Romans') and 24 ('the language of the Romans'), but contrast *The Philosopher Nigrinus*, where, even though the whole discourse centres on Rome, the name of the city or its inhabitants is not mentioned (see n. 5 to that piece). See further Whitmarsh 2001a, 265–79.

46 *famous Theano*: This Theano (Theano (1) in the Glossary) was associated with Pythagoras.

47 *poetess from Lesbos*: Sappho.

48 *the elegance of her calling*: I.e. poetry.

49 *Theano wife of Antenor*: See *Iliad* 6.298, where she is priestess of Athena in Troy. Her magnanimity is evidenced at *Iliad* 5.69.

50 *Arete . . . Nausicaa*: These are characters from *Odyssey* 6–8. Nausicaa shows her humanity by accepting Odysseus' supplication following his arrival on Scheria after a shipwreck, giving him clothes, leading him to the city and advising him to appeal to her mother Arete. Arete's kindness is displayed in her protection of the stranger from Phaeacian hostility to outsiders.

51 *daughter of Icarius . . . he painted*: 'Thoughtful Penelope' is the formulaic phrase used of Penelope throughout the *Odyssey* (e.g. at *Odyssey* 5.216). The adjective 'secure of mind' (*saophron*) (a derivative of *sophrosyne*: see notes 22 and 25) is used only once in the *Odyssey* (4.158), not of Penelope, but of Telemachus. This is either a rare slip by Lucian (unlikely), or is intended to recall Penelope's conversation with the nurse, Eurycleia, about

sophrosyne at *Odyssey* 23.11f., or simply to demonstrate the learned appropriation of a rare Homeric form to a character who is clearly portrayed as 'sound of mind' (and morals), even though she is not so described by Homer. Note that the words here rendered 'described' and 'painted' are both forms of the same Greek verb, *grapho*, which means 'write', 'draw' or 'paint'.

52   *wife of Abradatas . . . a little while ago*: Panthea. See paragraph 10, with notes 20, 23 and 24.

53   *Ate*: 'Ruin', described at *Iliad* 19.91–4: 'The eldest daughter of Zeus, Ate, the destructive, who injures all. She has soft feet and does not go along the ground, but walks over the heads of men, harming humans.' Lucian alludes to a well-known nexus of ideas, that such behaviour (*hybris*) regularly leads to *ate* ('loss of judgement' and 'ruin'), and is a normal concomitant of great wealth (see e.g. Pindar, *Pythian* 2.26f.: '[Ixion] received a sweet life, but could not sustain his prosperity for long . . . Instead, *hybris* drove him to overweening *ate*'). See further Fisher 1992.

54   *great king*: I.e. the Roman emperor. See paragraph 10, with note 19.

55   *a woman of whom . . . 'Athenaia' herself*: The passage alluded to (and paraphrased into prose keeping the Homeric forms for 'golden Aphrodite' and 'Athena' – 'Athenaia') is *Iliad* 9.389–90, where Achilles is rejecting an offer from Agamemnon of his daughter's hand in marriage to try to make up for the insult he inflicted in Book 1. The context is problematic here, as in the case of the Sirens earlier (paragraph 14), since it would focus attention on the fact that Panthea is not Lucius Verus' wife. But Lucian's learned audience may have taken it as yet another ironical undercutting of the apparent eulogy. See also next note.

56   *'in body . . . in action'*: The quotation here is from *Iliad* 1.115, where Agamemnon is praising the beauty of Chryseis, the girl he has been ordered to give back to her father, who as priest of Apollo has prayed for – and obtained – a plague on the Greeks. Once more, the context, in which an infatuated king takes a step towards the *ate* which will cost the life of Patroclus, is problematic, as it would reflect badly upon Lucius Verus' judgement and undercut the eulogy of Panthea. However, it may be merely the last in a series of such references which Lucian's learned audience would have understood as ironically undercutting the apparent eulogy. See Preface to this section and Sidwell 2002.

IN DEFENCE OF 'IMAGES'

1   *block my ears*: Almost certainly an allusion to the episode of the
    Sirens in the *Odyssey* (12.173ff.), where Odysseus stuffs his
    crew's ears with wax to prevent their hearing the Sirens' disaster-
    inducing song. Cf. *Images* 14 with n. 34, and paragraph 29 of
    this piece.

2   *more like a joke ... than a eulogy*: This opening paragraph
    strongly suggests that a straightforward reading of *Images* is
    mistaken (see *Images*, nn. 23, 32, 34, 42, 43, 55 and 56). Lycinus
    is ordinarily a sceptical interlocutor (see, for example, *The Ship*)
    and a natural enemy of flattery and dissimulation. The reaction
    of Panthea points to the clues: (a) the praise is overblown and
    inappropriate; (b) the purpose of overblown praise might be
    satirical. See next note.

3   *intention to flatter is obvious*: In *How to Write History* 7, Lucian
    distinguishes encomium from history as follows: 'They are two
    octaves apart, since the encomiast has only one concern, namely
    to praise and to please the object of the eulogy however he can,
    and if he is able to attain this goal by lying it won't bother him in
    the slightest.' So *Images* has failed in both of the primary goals
    of encomium, since Lycinus/Lucian has been caught out lying and
    has failed to please the work's recipient.

4   *thick-soled boots*: The Greek word is *kothornos*, which was
    originally a soft leather boot which could fit either foot and was
    used on the tragic stage (probably only for women's parts). Later
    on, when stages became higher and tragic acting more static, the
    word came to denote the high thick-soled boot (or 'buskin') seen
    in representations from the second century BC on. It is this latter
    which Lucian envisages whenever he mentions this item (see
    further Pickard-Cambridge 1968, 204–8).

5   *shaking her hand ... make the woman stand up*: As *Two Charges
    of Literary Assault* 28 shows, mild applause was registered by
    movements of the hand, while standing represented (as in our
    culture) an ovation. If the poet manages to please this subject too
    much, her applause will itself deflate his eulogy.

6   *talent*: See *Timon the Misanthrope*, n. 60 and *The Ship*, n. 25.

7   *She said that Stratonice ... non-existent locks*: The adjective
    'hyacinthine' (*hyakinthinos*) comes from Homer's description of
    Odysseus' hair as it appears to Nausicaa, once he has washed
    himself and been beautified by Athena (*Odyssey* 6.231), and
    later as he prepares finally to go to bed with Penelope (*Odyssey*

23.158). This anecdote is not elsewhere told of Stratonice (whom Lucian elsewhere mentions for being passed on to her own stepson Antiochus by his father, her husband, Seleucus I, and for falling in love with Combabos, whom Seleucus had deputed to build the great temple to Atargatis-Juno at Hierapolis-Bambyce in Syria: *The Goddesse of Surrye* 17–26; cf. also 40). If it is invented for the present work, it suggests rather the notion of the 'paradoxical encomium' (see Preface to this section), one of Lucian's favourite genres, and perhaps hints that it is to this type that *Images* (and its defence) belongs.

8   *alien . . . no resemblance to them at all*: We should not forget that the whole of Panthea's portrait, as drawn by Lycinus in *Images*, is alien to her, consisting as it does of features borrowed from the works of artists portraying other subjects. We might expect that she will go on to condemn this on the analogy she has just used.

9   *extremely superstitious . . . attitude towards the divine*: The terms used here would hardly merit the praise of the Lucian of *A Few Words about Mourning* and *On Sacrifices*, who is highly sceptical of human knowledge of and responses to the divine. In any case, 'superstition', *deisidaimonia*, was already the title of a satirical portrait of the type of behaviour Panthea is ascribing to herself in Theophrastus, *Characters* 16 (fourth century BC).

10 *I'm afraid . . . and Aphrodite*: Panthea virtually admits the inappropriateness of her own example. The Nereids were also divine and capable of punishing such a slight (see Cassiepeia entry in Glossary). Panthea also confuses the eulogist's voice with her own (it is not her responsibility what others say of her, as Lycinus points out, paragraph 28).

11 *from Cnidus and . . . in the gardens*: Sculptures of Aphrodite by Praxiteles and Alcamenes, respectively (see *Images* 4 and 6 with n. 5).

12 *An architect promised . . . extraordinary honour*: This anecdote is also reported in Plutarch (*Alexander* 72 and *Moralia* 335c), as well as in Strabo (*Geography* 14.1.23) and Vitruvius (*On Architecture* 2, preface), though with different names for the architect ('Stasicrates', 'Cheirocrates', 'Dinocrates', respectively). Note that Panthea in using this analogy explicitly claims an intelligence equal to Alexander the Great's, while missing the distinction between his rejection of a real statue and her own of the mere word-statue constructed by Lycinus. Moreover, Lucian's other mention of this anecdote (*How to Write History* 12) makes it clear that Alexander 'realized the man was a toady, and no

longer employed him as he had before on other projects'. If Panthea really thinks Lycinus is a flatterer, she ought simply to dismiss him and throw his work away (as Alexander had done to the eulogistic history of Aristobulus, also mentioned in *How to Write History* 12).

13 *you men will know ... true or not*: Panthea alludes to the prohibition on the attendance of women at the Olympic Games.

14 *Hellanodikai*: These were the chief judges at the Olympic Games.

15 *forgive this feminine response*: This suggests that *deisidaimonia*, 'fear of the gods', 'superstition' (see note 9), is to be expected from women more than from men and this would have tended to undercut the judgement Polystratus now makes of Lycinus' work.

16 *The story goes ... even if the one is Phidias*: This anecdote is not known elsewhere, but the idea of an artist listening covertly to the criticisms of the public and then responding appears to be a topos. Compare the similar story concerning Apelles in Pliny, *Natural History* 35.84–5.

17 *not having been given ... by the water-clock in which to speak*: Literally 'with no water poured out and with no (opportunity for) defence given'. In Athenian courts, strict timing of speeches in certain types of case was enforced by means of the water-clock (*klepsydra*), which consisted of two vessels, the more elevated of which emptied into the other (Harrison 1998, vol. 2, 161).

18 *poet from Himera ... palinode*: The reference is to Stesichorus and especially to his attack on Helen. The story goes that he was blinded for his attack on the goddess, but received his sight back when he wrote a palinode (a poetic retraction). The parallel is slightly mystifying, since Lycinus/Lucian has written a *eulogy* of Panthea. However, this could imply that Lucian had intended *Images* as an attack (a view which can be justified by looking at the literary allusions: see notes on *Images* and Preface to this section).

19 *people who dislike being praised*: It is worth pointing out that Panthea has not rejected all of Lycinus' eulogy, but has only asked him to modify it in certain respects.

20 *Aphrodites in Cnidus and the gardens*: See note 11.

21 *spoilt the rhythm ... too many syllables*: Literally 'was out of metre and beyond the foot'. The image here is from Greek metrics. The 'foot' is a part of the line with a particular metrical value.

22 *accountable*: The word refers to the system of *euthyna* ('accounting') undergone by all outgoing magistrates in the Athenian democracy. If their accounts or actions were suspected of illegality, they could be prosecuted.

23   *It applies even more fully . . . chariot of verse*: As Lucian says in
      How to Write History 7–8, encomium and poetry are very close,
      in that they both have complete freedom in the attempt to achieve
      their aims. Encomiasts may lie and poets may invent. Note especi-
      ally the parallel there between the method of the poet and that of
      Lucian in *Images*: 'If they want to eulogize Agamemnon, no one
      will stop him being like Zeus in head and eyes, like Zeus' brother
      Poseidon in his chest and like Ares in his waist; in a word, the son
      of Atreus and Aerope must be synthesized from all the gods,
      because Zeus, Poseidon and Ares aren't sufficient on their own
      to make a full picture of his beauty.'

24   *the poet . . . 'lion-taming'*: The poet was Pindar, but the text
      survives only in a fragment (239, OCT). Note the allusive nature
      of the reference. Panthea must be presumed to share the same
      level of learning as Lucian's normal (male) audience.

25   *renowned poet . . . steely child of Alcmene*: The son of Alcmene
      was Heracles. The poet in question is Simonides (poem 4, *PMG*).
      See previous note for the allusive nature of the reference.

26   *Croesus' son . . . than Melampus*: One of Croesus' sons was a
      deaf-mute (Herodotus, *Histories* 1.34 and 1.85), while Melampus
      could hear worms talking to one another in the roof of his prison
      cell (Apollodorus, *The Library* 1.9.12).

27   *Phineus . . . than Lynceus*: Phineus was blind, while Lynceus
      could see things beneath the earth (Apollodorus, *The Library*
      3.10.3).

28   *The encomiast would never lie . . . did not possess at all*: This is
      not what Lucian says in *How to Write History* 7. See note 3
      above.

29   *it ran across . . . them bend*: *Iliad* 20.227.

30   *'the course of storm-swift horses'*: The quotation as a whole is
      untraceable, but 'storm-swift horses' occurs in the *Homeric
      Hymn to Venus* 217 and Pindar, *Nemean* 1.6 and fr. 208, OCT.
      See also Simonides, poem 10, *PMG*.

31   *Olympian Zeus' court . . . thus within*: Said by Telemachus to his
      friend Pisistratus of the palace of Menelaus at *Odyssey* 4.74.

32   *swineherd's hut*: Another reminiscence of the *Odyssey*, where
      Odysseus spends some time in the hut of the swineherd Eumaeus
      (Book 14). However, the word for 'hut' here (*kalybe*) is not
      Homeric, while that used for 'swineherd' (*sybotes*) is, so that for
      Lucian's learned audience the phrase would have had a comic
      effect.

33   *captive Briseis . . . 'resembled golden Aphrodite'*: The reference

in the phrase 'resembled golden Aphrodite' is to *Iliad* 19.282, but the order of the words and the form of the word 'golden' have been altered, while the descriptive content of the sentence as a whole paraphrases lines 282–4.

34   *Then spoke the woman . . . to behold*: *Iliad* 19.286.

35   *critic who dared . . . considered inauthentic*: The first was Zoilus, called Homeromastix ('Whipper of Homer'), a Cynic philosopher of the fourth century BC from Amphipolis, who wrote a work called *A Censure of Homer*. The second was the famous second-century BC Alexandrian commentator on Homer, Aristarchus, who is mentioned by name at *True Histories* 2.20; following a scholarly practice that began with Zenodotus, he placed *oboli*, horizontal marginal strokes, in the left margin next to verses he thought Homer had not written.

36   *the case of Agamemnon . . . dubs 'godlike'*: *Iliad* 2.477–9 is the Agamemnon passage Lucian refers to: 'and along with them mighty Agamemnon, in eyes and head like Zeus who delights in the thunderbolt, [like] Ares in his waist and in his breast [like] Poseidon'. The text is paraphrased and the forms normalized into Attic Greek. See note 23 above for Lucian's use of this passage elsewhere. Hector is compared to manslaying Ares at *Iliad* 11.295 and 13.802 (once more, the forms are Atticized and the phrasing altered). 'The Phrygian' is Paris, called 'godshaped' at *Iliad* 3.16, and Peleus' son is Achilles, called 'godlike' at e.g. *Iliad* 1.131 and 19.155.

37   *heard Homer . . . down the mountainside*: The first quotation is from *Odyssey* 17.37 (= 19.54), said of Penelope. The second is from *Odyssey* 6.102, and refers to Nausicaa. On 'heard', see *Images*, n. 21.

38   *Euphorbus' hair . . . drenched in blood*: The reference is to *Iliad* 17.51, 'His hair, like that of the Graces, was wet with blood.'

39   *accountability*: See note 22.

40   *Hera's eyes . . . those of cows*: The allusion is to the standard epithet used of Hera in Homer, 'ox-eyed' (e.g. *Iliad* 1.551).

41   *someone else . . . Aphrodite 'violet-eyed'*: The epithet is found in Pindar, fr. 313, OCT, but Lycinus/Lucian certainly expects his audience to know the source, despite the casual lack of ascription (see *Images* 8 with n. 13).

42   *'rosy-fingered'*: This is the standard epithet used of Dawn in Homer (e.g. at *Odyssey* 2.1).

43   *accounting process for listening*: Again, see note 22.

44   *best of the philosophers*: There is debate about the identity of this

philosopher. It might be Plato (he appears as the spokesman of the revivified philosophers who attack Lucian in *The Dead Come to Life*). Cf. *Timaeus* 92c, though here it is the cosmos which is an image of the intelligible and itself a god. It could be Epicurus (cf. Cicero, *On the Nature of the Gods* 1.18). It could be the Cynic Diogenes (cf. Diogenes Laertius, *Lives of the Philosophers* 6.51), who said that *good* men were images of gods. However, the fact that Lycinus asserts that the gods have not *yet* punished this philosopher may suggest, rather, a contemporary reference. If so, it remains mysterious.

45 *I've stuffed up my ears*: Inevitably, as in paragraph 1, one recalls the episode of Odysseus and the Sirens (see note 1).

46 *audience hiss me off the stage . . . result of the contest*: All the imagery here suggests that Polystratus is to act as the producer and actor in a play, that will be entered in the theatrical competition and be judged by citizens for a prize. The reference is to practices of the fifth and fourth centuries BC, where plays were entered in competitions at festivals of Dionysus. But Lycinus' claim that he will hear the result as a member of the audience is strange and could suggest that these works were among the theatrical jokes against Verus mentioned by the *Historia Augusta* (*Verus* 7.10). If so, Lycinus/Lucian caps the ironic eulogies by referring to their true performance arena, the public stage.

ABOUT THE PARASITE: PROOF THAT
PARASITIC IS AN ART

1 *ABOUT . . . PARASITIC IS AN ART*: The title and the subtitle introduce us to the central elements of the philosophical and Platonic parody (see Preface to this section). It was common for philosophical treatises to be entitled 'About . . .' (cf. e.g. Aristotle's *About Interpretation*). The term *techne* (cf. English 'technical'), always translated here 'art', was used to refer both to professional training and to manuals which were written to facilitate it (e.g. Aristotle's *techne* of rhetoric). In Plato, adjectives ending in *-ike*, though standing alone without the noun *techne*, are used to denote the profession (e.g. *tektonike*, 'joinery'), and this is the form taken by Lucian's 'parasitic', *parasitike*. The fourth-century BC comic poet Antidotus had already presented a philosopher speaking about 'parasitic' as an 'art' (fr. 2, *PCG* preserved in Athenaeus, *The Deipnosophists* 6.240b), though it

is unclear whether the formulation 'the parasitic art' belongs to Athenaeus or Antidotus.

2   *TYCHIADES*: The name means 'Son of chance' and is given also to the sceptical reporter of the philosophers' discussion about ghosts and other paranormal phenomena in Lucian's *Lover of Lies*.

3   *SIMON*: The name means 'Snub-nosed' and is given to several characters in New Comedy (for which, see Preface to *Chattering Courtesans*), all of them old men (e.g. Plautus, *Mostellaria*; Terence, *Andria*). It is, however, entirely possible that there was a particular play (now lost) with a parasite called Simon which Lucian's character is intended to recall.

4   *spirit . . . herself*: The word used for 'spirit' is *daimon*, a general word for an unknown divinity at work – see *The Scythian*, n. 13. However, the word is feminine here and it is probable that the audience are meant to think of Lussa, the goddess of madness (*lyssa*), as personified in Euripides, *Heracles* 823ff.

5   *Phidias . . . his Zeus*: Phidias' most famous commission was the great statue of Zeus in the temple at Olympia in Elis. Cf. *Timon the Misanthrope* 4 with n. 7.

6   *Dion . . . 'to the philosopher'*: This possibly refers to the Dion who became a disciple of Plato and later expelled Dionysius II. The implication must be, however, that most people did not really regard him as a philosopher.

7   *generic term . . . individual . . . essence*: Simon begins to speak in the technical language of philosophy. Here he distinguishes between *genos* and *eidos* ('individual', i.e. species as opposed to genus) in a formulation which recalls Aristotle, *Topics* 4.1.121a12: 'The species partake of the *genus*, but the *genera* do not partake of the species.'

8   *'art is a system . . . useful for life'*: This is the standard Stoic definition of *techne* as given often in Sextus Empiricus (*fl. c.* AD 200) and (in Latin) by Quintilian (*Training an Orator* 2.17.41). It is first found in Zeno of Citium.

9   *If someone needs . . . pick him out*: *Medea* 518–19. The lines are originally a question addressed by Medea to Zeus, asking him why he has made it possible for false coins to be spotted, but not false men.

10   *'when a feast . . . skilled in cookery'*: The quotation is from *Theaetetus* 178d, a passage where (typically) Socrates is arguing on the basis that expertise is essential for true understanding in any given field.

11   *perception . . . trained perception*: See note 8 for the source of
      these terms.

12   *faculty . . . lack of art*: Once more, these are Stoic terms. 'Faculty'
      (*dynamis*) is a natural capacity, while 'lack of art' (*atechnia*)
      denotes a skill learned purely through experience, so that, in the
      examples that follow, knowing how to steer and being a chario-
      teer would indicate the possession of an art and not merely a
      skill learned through experience. Rhetoric, however, was often
      attacked as merely a 'faculty' or 'lack of art' (e.g. Quintilian,
      Training an Orator 2.15.2) – cf. paragraph 27.

13   <*TYCHIADES . . . a charioteer?*>: The angle brackets here (and in
      paragraph 26) indicate that the text has a gap in it, which has
      been filled conjecturally by the editor.

14   *philosophers . . . your objective*: Philosophical schools in
      antiquity tended to distinguish themselves from each other especi-
      ally by the definition of a 'supreme good'. For Stoicism, this
      was virtue, while for the Epicureans it was originally *ataraxia*
      ('freedom from disturbance'), though later this was popularized
      into *hedone* ('pleasure'). What follows, however, suggests that
      the Epicurean goal Simon has in mind is *eudaimonia* ('happiness').

15   *I claim that . . . in their cups*: *Odyssey* 9.5–10. The speaker is
      Odysseus, responding to the question of his Phaeacian host King
      Alcinous as to why he has been so upset by the song of the bard
      Demodocus (about the Trojan Horse).

16   *My heart . . . finest thing*: This is the very next line of Odysseus'
      speech, *Odyssey* 9.11.

17   *goal of the Stoics*: I.e. virtue.

18   *he could have mentioned it . . . 'more pleasing'*: The word trans-
      lated 'more pleasing' (*chariesteron*) is the one Odysseus used to
      the Phaeacians (*Odyssey* 9.5). Simon's argumentation is slightly
      undermined by the fact that none of these incidents is narrated
      by Odysseus in the *Odyssey*. In fact, only the spying episode
      occurs in the poem, narrated by Helen at 4.242ff. The 'bringing
      back' of Philoctetes was the subject of tragedies by Sophocles
      (extant), Aeschylus and Euripides (both lost). The prevention of
      the Greeks' desertion belongs to the *Iliad* (2.246ff.).

19   *Epicurean life . . . soft pleasures*: The phrase 'soft pleasures' (*leias
      kineseis*) (literally 'smooth moves') is used by Epicurus (fr. 411,
      Epicurea, ed. H. Usener (Rome 1963)) and earlier by the Cyrenaic
      philosopher Aristippus (fr. 193.197A–C, fr. 198.201, *Aristippi
      et Cyrenaicorum Fragmenta*, ed. E. Mannebach (Leiden 1961))

as a synonym of 'pleasure'. Lucian makes Simon deliberately obscure the difference between the goals of Epicurus and Aristippus for comic effect (see note 14 above).

20   *'Feasters . . . in a row'*: This is not an exact quotation (it doesn't scan), but a slight paraphrase of *Odyssey* 9.7–8.

21   *beside them . . . and meat*: The lines already quoted from *Odyssey* 9.8–9.

22   *pleasure subsists . . . absence of mental stress*: The vocabulary used here deliberately echoes that of Epicurus and his followers.

23   *the person who inquires . . . cosmic distress*: Again, oblique reference is being made to issues which can be traced to Epicurus' own works, which survive only in fragments. Note, for example, that Epicurus wrote works *On Gods* and *On the Objective of Life*.

24   *impunity and calm*: Once more, the vocabulary, 'impunity' (*adeia*, literally 'lack of fear') and 'calm' (*galene*), reflects terms found in Epicurean discourse. Simon's refutation of Epicurus uses Epicurus against himself.

25   *sleeps on his back . . . sailing home from Scheria*: Odysseus was ferried home to Ithaca by the Phaeacians in one of their magical ships, asleep all the while on the ship's deck (*Odyssey* 13.70ff.).

26   *Epicurus here . . . not live pleasurably*: The Stoics from Chrysippus onwards disputed at great length the Epicurean definition of pleasure as the objective of life (cf. note 14). The type of argument used here by Simon seems to owe a great deal to Stoic syllogisms, which use the technique of *diairesis* ('distinction'): A can either X or not; if he can X, then Y follows, if not then Z.

27   *a great 'and steep pathway that leads to' them*: Cf. Hesiod, *Works and Days* 289–91: 'The immortal gods placed sweat in front of Virtue. The path to her is long and steep, and rough at first.' Simon ironically adapts Hesiod's proto-Stoic lines to apply to the 'real' objective of all the arts, pleasure.

28   *thirty days each month*: The ancient Greek calendar worked on the lunar month (with adjustments), not the solar.

29   *like poetry . . . a gift from the gods*: The phrase 'a gift from the gods' is cited from Plato, *Ion* 534b. But in citing this passage, Simon risks undermining his whole argument, since the Platonic dialogue proves that poetry is not an art at all.

30   *reclining*: The convivial posture. Cf. *Two Charges of Literary Assault*, n. 29.

31   *who neither plants . . . or scattering*: The words are adapted to the sentence from *Odyssey* 9.108–9. It is unlikely to be coincidental

that the beings blessed thus by the gods are the savage and lawless Cyclopes. Once more, Simon's own examples threaten to collapse his case.

32 *for some . . . branches of science*: The 'some' were the Stoics.

33 *as far above . . . excelled her handmaidens*: The reference is to *Odyssey* 6.102–9. In fact, it is a simile in which Nausicaa's superiority in stature and beauty over her handmaidens is imaged by comparison with Artemis coming down from the mountain to hunt, joined by the nymphs of the countryside. The effect here is deliberately bizarre.

34 *substantiveness . . . subsists*: The term translated as 'substantiveness' is *hypostasis*, 'actual existence, reality', often used by ancient philosophers from Aristotle onwards as a synonym for the simpler 'being' (formed from the verb 'to be'). In the same way, the verb *hyphistamai*, rendered as 'to subsist' (i.e. to have existence as a reality), is used by Simon here for the simple verb 'to be' to give a technical philosophical flavour to the refutation of the very existence of the two *technai* considered the greatest, rhetoric and – philosophy.

35 *Now, if there were . . . not immutable*: Once more, in this sentence the technical terminology is Stoic ('mediocre', 'apprehensions', 'immutable'), as is the idea that science/knowledge is usually a firm and immutable matter.

36 *Likewise one could say . . . object of inquiry*: Once more, note the use of technical philosophical vocabulary ('substantiveness', 'proposition', 'demonstration', 'apprehension', 'singleness', 'existence'), which may derive from a Sceptic philosophical source.

37 *Nicias*: One of the generals in charge of the ill-fated Sicilian expedition, sent by Athens in 415 BC to 'help' in a local war (but really to conquer Sicily). The expedition was wiped out and Nicias killed.

38 *preliminary study . . . other arts*: The breadth of Aristotle's learning earned him criticism in antiquity for superficiality and absurdity (see Athenaeus, *The Deipnosophists* 8.352d–354a). The implication of Simon's remark is that Aristotle tried to cover too much ground ever to produce any comprehensive enough treatment of any subject for it to be called a *techne* (cf. note 1 above).

39 *hoplite*: See *The Ship*, n. 36.

40 *their ringleader . . . a used slave from him*: The reference is to Demosthenes and the passage cited is paraphrased from his *Third Philippic* (31).

41 *But before the armies clashed . . . piece of scum*: The attack on
    Demosthenes is compiled from Aeschines, *Against Ctesiphon*
    3.244 and 3.253 (cowardice at the battle of Chaeronea; see also
    Plutarch, *Demosthenes* 20) and 3.171 (Scythian origin of
    Demosthenes' mother, Cleobule).

42 *Aeschines*: Aeschines the Socratic, not the orator.

43 *wrestling school*: Cf. *The Ship*, n. 3.

44 *The only one who had the courage . . . fight a Spartan*: Plato's
    account of Socrates' valour in battle (*Apology* 28a, *Symposium*
    219a–220e, 220e–221b, *Laches* 181b) constituted the main
    ancient tradition. Simon follows a work by the late fourth-century
    BC orator Demochares (a nephew of Demosthenes), later remod-
    elled by Herodicus of Babylon in his *Against the Socrates-lover*
    (Athenaeus, *The Deipnosophists* 5.215c–216c), which sought to
    refute the Platonic claims. See also *True Histories* 2.23 with n.
    100. The reference to 'the wrestling school of Taureas' alludes to
    the beginning of Plato's *Charmides* (153a), where Socrates is
    shown on his return from the battle of Potidaea (432 BC) (not
    Delium, which is on the other side of Mount Parnes) conversing
    about philosophy and beauty in the company of good-looking
    young men. Lucian's learned audience were certainly supposed
    to notice Simon's lack of precision here (as also in the fact that
    the battle of Delium was fought against Thebans, not Spartans).

45 *from other people . . . blaming them*: This seems to be an allusion
    to Demochares or Herodicus of Babylon (see note 44).

46 *from whose tongue . . . like honey*: This is a paraphrase of *Iliad*
    1.249.

47 *He'd have taken Troy . . . old he might be*: Agamemnon says this
    in response to a long speech of advice by Nestor at *Iliad* 2.370–74.

48 *Homer likewise mentions . . . Agamemnon's parasite*: Simon
    is referring to Agamemnon's speech to Idomeneus at *Iliad*
    4.257–64.

49 *Thy cup stands . . . thine heart commands*: *Iliad* 4.262–3.

50 *'they led him to . . . Agamemnon'*: *Iliad* 7.312.

51 *Caeneus and Exadius*: These are mentioned by Nestor in his
    speech to the assembly at *Iliad* 1.264.

52 *It was Patroclus who . . . Protesilaus' vessel*: Hector smashes
    through the Achaean gate in *Iliad* 12, but the firing of the ships
    does not take place until Book 16, where Patroclus prevails upon
    Achilles to allow him to enter battle on his behalf.

53 *killed . . . Sarpedon*: The death of Sarpedon is narrated at *Iliad*
    16.477ff.

54   *a god and two human beings*: Apollo, Hector and Euphorbus:
     Iliad 16.849–50.
55   *If twenty men . . . by my spear*: *Iliad* 16.847–8.
56   *Lay not my bones . . . was I fed*: *Iliad* 23.83–4, from the speech
     made to Achilles in a dream by Patroclus after his death.
57   *Peleus then . . . as thy squire*: *Iliad* 23.89–90. The first line is
     slightly paraphrased, but the words set out as verse represent
     those kept from the original. Simon's point is that the word
     translated 'squire', *therapon*, is normally associated with those
     who give free service to a superior in various capacities, making
     them neither an equal – which a free man might aspire to, and
     which is a condition of friendship – nor a slave.
58   *although Idomeneus . . . his parasite, Meriones*: Simon bases his
     argument on *Iliad* 13.295, 328 and 528. But Lucian's learned
     audience would have known that in fact Idomeneus (along with
     Aeneas) is given the same description at 13.500 (and judged
     Simon's argumentation accordingly).
59   *The poor common citizen . . . according to Thucydides*: Thucyd-
     ides, *History of the Peloponnesian War* 6.54. However, Thucyd-
     ides makes him a 'middling citizen' and Lucian's learned audience
     have once more been provided with ammunition against Simon's
     argumentation.
60   *is now standing in a bronze version . . . in the Agora*: The bronze
     statues were by Critius and Nesiotes and date to *c.* 477–476 BC.
     Roman copies in marble are extant (in the National Museum,
     Naples). See Pedley 1998, 218–19.
61   *breakfast before . . . as Odysseus also recommends*: At *Iliad*
     19.160ff., when Achilles wants the army to fight the Trojans
     without taking food after the death of Patroclus and before his
     funeral.
62   *as Ajax did for Teucer*: The scene is described at *Iliad* 8.266–72.
63   *market-place . . . gymnasia . . . drinking-parties*: The market-
     place (*agora*) was the central business area, and political centre,
     of a city. *Gymnasia* ('exercise-grounds') were originally simply
     open areas between trees, but later developed into courtyards
     surrounded by colonnades: from the fifth century BC, however,
     they had been centres of intellectual activity. 'Drinking-parties'
     translates *symposia*, an institution that encouraged both intellec-
     tual and political networks to develop.
64   *sykophantai*: See *Timon the Misanthrope*, n. 36.
65   *learned to despise them at his feasts*: Presumably because they are
     there at his mercy on the plate.

66   *acts the sophist*: Refers to the Socratic disdain, reflected in Plato
      and Xenophon, for sophists who take payment for their services,
      rather than to the attitude to sophists in Lucian's own time.

67   *There's no need to give examples ... in exchange for his com-*
      pany: This passage is problematic and I have adopted Nesselrath's
      text (1985, 471–2). There is also the vexed question of whether
      or not some contemporary of Lucian's is meant by the old philos-
      opher taking pay from a king (which could be translated as
      'emperor'). The setting of the dialogue in general appears to be
      no later than early Hellenistic and a contemporary reference (the
      only one – though see note 71) would be intrusive. However,
      although the text translated can now be taken to refer to the
      Hellenistic period, there are no candidates readily identifiable
      (unless it is a covert reference to Aristotle's tutelage of Alexander).
      If we translate: 'demands a salary from the emperor for his
      services', the reference becomes contemporary with Lucian.
      Sextus of Chaeronea, Plutarch's nephew, who taught Marcus
      Aurelius is one candidate, Apollonius (*Demonax the Philosopher*
      31) another.

68   *the person who doesn't have ... without intelligence*: Here
      Simon's argument parodies Platonic formulations such as *Gorgias*
      497e1–3 ('Do you not call the good "good" because of the
      presence of "the good"?' Cf. 498d2–3 and 498e1–2), *Protagoras*
      332a8–c2 ('So they practise good sense through good sense?')
      and *Theaetetus* 145d11 ('I suppose it is through wisdom that the
      wise are wise?').

69   *packing a bow*: It is not clear whether this is supposed to be a
      joke (by exaggeration), whether the words contain a learned
      allusion to a now-lost comedy (for they could form the end of an
      iambic trimeter) or whether the text is simply corrupt.

70   *a 'Defence Speech' by ... rhetoricians and sages*: Simon is refer-
      ring to Plato's *Apology* (though Xenophon also wrote one),
      Aeschines 2 (*On the False Embassy*), probably Hyperides' *Against*
      Diondas and *Against Aristogiton* and Demosthenes' *On the*
      Crown.

71   *died a miserable death ... others in exile*: The obvious example
      for death by hemlock after condemnation on serious charges is
      Socrates. The likeliest referent for death by fire is Empedocles
      (who is supposed to have jumped into Mt. Etna; cf. *True Histories*
      2.21 with n. 92). Epicurus died of a kidney stone (Diogenes
      Laertius, *Lives of the Philosophers* 10.15). Aristotle died in exile.
      A second example of death by fire might be Peregrinus the Cynic,

whose self-immolation just after the Olympic Games of AD 165 was recorded by Lucian in a satirical pamphlet bearing his name (*The Passing of Peregrinus*). But since the dialogue does not seem elsewhere to allude to contemporaries (see note 67 above), and since Lucian regarded Peregrinus as a fraud, it is more likely that the references are classical.

72 *So haven't we agreed . . . better?*: The train of thought that follows is based on the similarity of the composition of the verbs: just as 'to be a parasite' is composed of the element *para-* ('alongside') plus the simple verb (in this case *siteo*, 'I eat'), so are the others (*pleo*, 'I sail', or *parapleo*, 'I sail at another's side', etc.). This style of argument is often found in Plato, but here the prefix is blatantly used in different senses in the different examples. A straight translation is virtually impossible, therefore. The difficulty is compounded by the fact that *para-* may imply either 'at another's side' or 'better'.

73 *In future I'll be arriving . . . their first-born best*: Tychiades has the last laugh on Simon, because in effect he is saying that since 'parasitic' has been shown to be an 'art', and Simon a supreme expositor of it, it is time for him to take on a pupil. That is, Simon must now take the position of Tychiades' patron and Tychiades of Simon's parasite. This proposal effectively undercuts the whole preceding argument with Socratic irony.

THE ART OF THE LIE

TRUE HISTORIES

1 *I have also in a manner . . . from your reading*: The formulation Lucian uses here alludes to the scholarship on Greek comedy. In one account of the development of Old Comedy, the Alexandrian sources focus on a change from 'open attack' to 'enigmatic attack' on the objects of satire. This was interpreted in antiquity as a suppression of the names of the targets. Lucian suggests that he is imitating the procedures of Old Comedy in giving this guessing game to his readers. He also uses in the word translated 'unconnected with comedy', *akomoidetos*, the first of many words specifically invented for the context, thus underlining, as often elsewhere, the productiveness of literary games of the sort he is playing here.

2   *There have been many others ... strange lifestyles*: The manu-
     scripts and editions contain the following passage placed before
     this sentence: 'Among these is Ctesias, son of Ctesiochus from
     Cnidus, whose account of India and the customs of its inhabitants
     contained things he had not seen himself and had not heard from
     any truthful source. Iambulus too wrote of many strange sights
     in his account of the geography of the great sea. It was obvious
     to everyone that he was telling lies, but the material he put
     together was not without its measure of entertainment.' I am
     sceptical about Lucian's authorship of this for two reasons: (1)
     there is a textual problem (which need not concern us here) and
     (2) Lucian has just said that he is going to deal *enigmatically* with
     his sources. By mentioning Homer's Odysseus, he hits at the
     earliest example of what he is satirizing and this is both sufficient
     and more pertinent, since he is going to relate, like Odysseus, a
     narrative of which he is the subject, and he is treating his readers
     (less credulous than the Phaeacians – cf. Alcinous' statement of
     trust in Odysseus' veracity at *Odyssey* 11.363–9) more honestly
     than Odysseus did his audience.

3   *stories of the bondage ... his companions*: The allusions to the
     narrative by Odysseus of his adventures to Alcinous' Phaeacians
     in *Odyssey* 9–12 are deliberately made comically generic, though
     every reader would have recognized them at once. They are
     (in order), Aeolus' gift of a bag of winds, the Cyclopes, the
     Laestrygonians, (six-headed) Scylla, and Circe's metamorphosis
     of Odysseus' companions into swine.

4   *when I have come across ... habituated to this*: This is a hit
     at Plato in particular for his use of *mythoi* ('stories') to make
     philosophical points. Lucian probably has in mind specifically
     the 'Myth of Er' at *Republic* 10 (614aff.), since there Socrates is
     made to claim that this tale will not be 'an Alcinous story' (i.e. a
     set of falsehoods).

5   *merchant galley of the akatos class*: This type of ship would carry
     a complement of 30–50 oarsmen (Casson 1971, 159–60).

6   *stades*: A stade measures around 600 feet (183 metres). See *The
     Ship*, n. 18.

7   *about a hundred feet long*: Literally 'one *plethron* long'. A
     plethron measured around 100 feet (30 metres). The passage
     parodies Herodotus, *Histories* 4.82, where the historian describes
     a footprint of Heracles 2 cubits (3 feet) in length.

8   *Chian variety*: Wines from Chios were held in high repute in

antiquity, for both their taste and their health-giving qualities (see Athenaeus, *The Deipnosophists* 1.32e–33a, 4.167e and Pliny, *Natural History* 14.73).

9   *we noticed that . . . solid Dionysiac diet*: Greeks almost always watered their wine (*oinos*) (usually with three parts water to one part wine). Here the wine and water are in solid, not liquid, form. The words 'solid Dionysiac diet' are an attempt to render a single word invented by Lucian for this context, *oinophagia*, literally 'eating wine'.

10   *mix their fluids with our men*: The Greek involves a pun based on the use of the word *mignysthai* ('to mix') to refer both to the mixing of wine (with water: see note 9) and to sexual intercourse.

11   *vinosexual intercourse*: A translation of another word invented by Lucian for the context, *ampelomixia*, literally 'sexual intercourse with vines'.

12   *ran through the air*: This phrase translates a single word, invented by Lucian for the context, *aerodromeo*, a verb meaning, literally, 'I air-run'.

13   *Vulture Cavalry*: *Hippogypoi*.

14   *colony*: See *A Few Words about Mourning*, n. 12.

15   *Ant Cavalry*: *Hippomyrmekes*.

16   *Vegetableplumes . . . Millet-throwers . . . Garlic Warriors . . . Flea Archers . . . Windrunners*: Respectively, *Lachanopteroi, Kenchroboloi, Skorodomachoi, Psyllotoxotai, Anemodromoi*.

17   *peltasts*: Light-armed troops, equipped with small shields and javelins, used in battle for skirmishing rather than hand-to-hand fighting.

18   *Sparrow-acorns . . . Crane Cavalry*: Respectively, *Strouthobalanoi* and *Hippogeranoi*.

19   *Nocturnal . . . Lord of Tranquillity*: Respectively, *Nykterion* and *Eudianax*. With the former, there is also a possible allusion to the word for 'bat', *nykteris*.

20   *about two hundred feet long*: Literally 'two *plethra* long'. See note 7.

21   *Air-gnats . . . Air-prancers . . . Stalkmushrooms*: Respectively, *Aerokonopes, Aerokordakes, Kaulomyketes*.

22   *hoplites*: See *The Ship*, n. 36.

23   *Dog-acorns . . . Dog-star . . . Cloud-Centaurs*: *Kynobalanoi* (Dog-acorns) and *Nephelokentauroi* (Cloud-Centaurs). The Dog-star is Sirius (see Glossary).

24   *Heliot*: The Heliots are the people who inhabit the sun (*helios*).

25   *rained blood when Sarpedon died*: Iliad 16.459.

26   *archer from the zodiac*: Sagittarius, represented in ancient art as
      a Centaur.

27   *Selenites*: The people who inhabit the moon (*selene*).

28   *they relented*: The learned reader would be expected to see the
      parallel here with the Athenians' reversal of their decision about
      the fate of Mytilene in 427 BC narrated in Thucydides, *History
      of the Peloponnesian War* 3.36–49.

29   *'On the following . . . Brightspark'*: The terms of the treaty con-
      tain another Thucydidean reminiscence, being similar to that
      between Athenians and Spartans in 421 BC at *History of the
      Peloponnesian War* 5.18.1–19.2. In Greek, the names of the
      signatories are, respectively, *Pyronides*, *Thereites* and *Phlogios*,
      and *Nyktor*, *Menios* and *Polylampes*.

30   *it is the calf . . . instead of the womb*: The wordplay here is based
      on the fact that the Greek for the 'calf' of the leg, *gastroknemia*,
      has as its first element (*gastro-*) the word for 'womb'.

31   *Treemen: Dendritai*.

32   *Among them it is the bald . . . long-haired beautiful*: Normally,
      Greeks considered baldness to be ugly (cf. Homer's 'long-haired
      Achaeans'). The inhabitants of the comets like long hair because
      the word for 'comet', *kometes*, means 'long-haired'.

33   *Lamptown: Lychnopolis*.

34   *lamperies*: I.e. places to keep lamps in, translates a word, *lychneon*,
      possibly invented by Lucian for the context.

35   *Cloudcuckooville: Nephelokokkygia*. Aristophanes' city was
      built between heaven and earth by the birds in his *Birds* of 414
      BC.

36   *Crow . . . Blackbird*: Respectively, *Koronos* and *Kottyphion*.

37   *our Dionysiac phalluses*: Large phalluses were carried in the
      procession which preceded the City Dionysia festival at Athens.
      But the word 'our' has suggested to some commentators that it
      refers to the 300 fathom (1,800 feet) high phallic pillars dedicated
      by Dionysus himself in the temple of Atargatis-Juno at Hieropolis-
      Bambyce in Lucian's native Syria, described in his *The Goddesse
      of Surrye* 16, and 28–9. This suits the massive size of the whale
      much better, since it is a space which must contain not only
      Lucian's ship and comrades, but a whole host of other beings and
      a large piece of land.

38   *halcyons*: Cf. 2.40 and *Images*, n. 31.

39   *Picklers . . . Triton-Pans*: Respectively, *Tarichanes* and *Triton-
      omendetes*. Triton was a sea-god and Mendes the Egyptian Pan

(Herodotus, *Histories* 2.46). However, there was also a city called Mendes, on the Nile delta, where much salted fish (*tarichos*) was produced, and the name *Tritonomendetes* may be intended to play on that of the Picklers, *Tarichanes*, just before, which derives from *tarichos*.

40   *Crabhands . . . Tunaheads . . . Crabbies . . . Turbotfeet*: Respectively, *Karkinocheires, Thynnokephaloi, Pagouridai, Psettopodes*.

41   *Scintharus*: Possibly based on the word *skinthos*, 'a diver'.

42   *Young Tunny*: *Pelamos*. The name derives from *pelamys*, 'young tunny'. Tunny was among the most regularly salted fish (*tarichos*), and it is therefore in keeping that the leader of the Picklers (*Tarichanes*) should be so named.

43   *triremes*: See *The Ship*, n. 39.

44   *about a hundred feet in length*: See note 7.

45   *Aeolus-Centaur . . . Sea-drinker*: Respectively, *Aiolokentauros* and *Thalassopotes*.

46   *island-battle*: The Greek word is *nesomachia*, a word invented by Lucian for the present purpose, on the basis of the word *naumachia*, 'naval-battle'.

47   *This is what happened in the island-battle*: The phrasing here is directly borrowed from Thucydides, *History of the Peloponnesian War* 7.87.6 ('this is what happened around Sicily'). By using it, Lucian ensures we understand that his parody in this last section has been aimed at the Greek historian (though a writer less inclined to the marvellous – he dismisses it with contempt in his first book (1.22) – it would be hard to imagine). Adam Bartley (2003) suggests that the allusions to Thucydides in *True Histories* are positive and show approbation for his historical method (cf. *How to Write History*).

48   *These bulls . . . by Momus*: Momus, son of Night (Hesiod, *Theogony* 214), personifies mockery and criticism and is a favourite figure in Lucian (*Zeus Rants* 19–31, *Icaromenippus* 31, *How to Write History* 33). He was said to have attacked Poseidon's design of the bull on the ground that with the horns above its eyes it could not see when it butted its opponent. Another criticism of his alluded to by Lucian (*Hermotimus* 20) is that the gods did not make men with a window in the chest so that their intentions could be easily read. See also *The Philosopher Nigrinus* 32 with nn. 29–30.

49   *Galatea*: Her name recalls the Greek word for milk, *gala*, but also brings to mind that she is the nymph whom the Cyclops Polyphemus tries to woo in Theocritus, *Idyll* 11.34–7. Poly-

phemus in *Odyssey* 9 also lived on an island and Homer's narrative is being satirized generally in this passage.

50 *Tyro . . . translation from that realm*: There is a pun here in Tyro's name on the Greek word for cheese, *tyros*. The story of her love for the river Enipeus, and Poseidon's deceitful rape of her in Enipeus' shape, is told in *Odyssey* 11.235–59, and Lucian has the two gods discuss her in *Dialogues of the Sea-Gods* 13. In the Greek, 'from that realm' reads simply 'from there' (*enteuthen*), which could mean either from where she had come from, i.e. her home or homeland (Thessaly), or from the earth, i.e. after her death. The word rendered 'translation' here (*apallage*) may also suggest that Tyro is dead (as she is when Odysseus meets her). The passage may be a parody of Plato's theory of the soul's existence after death (*Phaedo* 64c4–8). Thus, here Tyro's soul may be presiding over a punning version of her cheesily beautiful body.

51 *Corkfeet*: Phellopodes. See also note 52.

52 *Cork . . . built on a massive round cork*: The Greek name for the island-city here is *Phello*, which puns on *phellos*, 'cork'.

53 *wafts off rich Arabia*: Herodotus, *Histories* 3.113.

54 *vine-blossom*: Ampelanthe, a word invented by Lucian for the context, the usual one being *oinanthe*. He is perhaps punning on the idea of metamorphosis which every ancient reader would see in the mention of laurel (*daphne*) – Daphne loved by Apollo and changed into the laurel – since Ampelus was a young man loved by Dionysus and changed into a vine (*ampelos*) after being gored to death by a bull (Nonnus, *Dionysiaca* 10.178–11.350 and 12.102).

55 *transverse pipe*: The *aulos* was a reed pipe (see *Praising a Fly*, n. 3). The *plagiaulos*, 'transverse pipe', by contrast appears to have been more like the modern flute.

56 *heroes*: A class of beings in between gods and men, the powerful dead, who were worshipped at shrines and thought to have particular power in the region containing their tombs. Cf. *The Scythian* 1 with n. 7.

57 *dose of hellebore*: An ancient cure for madness. Cf. *The Ship* 45.

58 *which of them should live with Helen*: The issue arises because of a tradition that Theseus abducted Helen before she was of marriageable age (Plutarch, *Theseus* 31) and so had her before Menelaus (who had to fight in Troy for her return).

59 *the Amazon and the daughters of Minos*: Hippolyta, and (in turn) Minos' daughters Ariadne and Phaedra.

60 *contest between . . . Alexander was the greater*: Lucian dramatizes

this event, with a third contestant, the Roman general Scipio Africanus, and Minos as judge, in his *Dialogues of the Dead* 25 (12), where the result is 1. Alexander, 2. Scipio, 3. Hannibal. The Renaissance manuscript collector Giovanni Aurispa, who brought a Lucian MS back from Byzantium in 1423, wrote a 'translation' of this piece which changes the decision to favour Scipio (and ascribes the alteration to the later Greek writer Libanius). See Marsh 1998, 30–1.

61   *drinking-den*: I have chosen to translate thus the word *symposion* (translated 'drinking-party' otherwise) since it is here a place rather than an institution.

62   *The city itself is made . . . instead of water*: The description of the city is generally held to be a parody of the New Jerusalem in Revelation 21:10ff. Lucian clearly knew about Christianity, as can be seen from his brief sketch of the new religion in *The Passing of Peregrinus* 11–13. However, there are also classical parallels and it seems unlikely that Lucian would have expected his learned readers to have read and remembered a text which in no way belonged within the classical tradition, even if he had.

63   *garlands . . . perfume*: Sensory pleasure at *symposia* was often enhanced by expensive scents (see Xenophon, *Symposium* 2.3, where Callias offers to have some perfume brought in, though Socrates refuses on the ground that it is unmanly). For garlands, see *The Philosopher Nigrinus*, n. 31.

64   *music and songs . . . epic poems of Homer*: Performances of epic poetry were accompanied by the lyre and sung (cf. the bard Demodocus in *Odyssey* 8.492 and 8.537).

65   *leaders*: The lyric genre especially associated with such 'leaders' (*exarchoi*) was the dithyramb, a choral song in honour of Dionysus, supposedly invented by Arion, and certainly appropriate at this *symposion*. Cf. *Timon the Misanthrope*, n. 46.

66   *her quarrel with him*: Stesichorus was said to have been blinded for writing a poem criticizing Helen for her behaviour and to have had his sight restored when he wrote a palinode. See also *In Defence of 'Images'*, n. 18.

67   *swans*: See *Timon the Misanthrope*, n. 49.

68   *The greatest aid . . . and laughing*: The two springs may be parodying the fourth-century BC rhetorical historian Theopompus of Chios, who described two rivers running round a place called Anostos ('No return'), one of sorrow and one of pleasure, with corresponding trees beside them bearing fruit which bring sorrow or joy (Aelian, *Historical Miscellanies* 3.18).

69 *punishment in the land of the impious*: For boasting of his seizure
    of Cassandra from Athena's temple at Troy (see *Odyssey* 4.499–
    511). Traditionally, sinners were incarcerated in Tartarus, a part
    of the Underworld, but for the purpose of his narrative Lucian
    envisages them on a group of five islands within sight of the Isle
    of the Blest (paragraphs 4, 27, 29–31).

70 *Of the barbarians ... the Sages, except Periander*: The list of
    barbarians probably ends with Zamolxis, since Lucian avoids
    classifying the Romans in this way. Thus Numa, second king and
    lawgiver of Rome, is paired (as in Plutarch's *Parallel Lives*) with
    Lycurgus the Spartan lawgiver here, rather than the last of the list
    of barbarians. The missing Sage of the seven, Periander, as a
    tyrant is probably consigned by Lucian to the isles of the impious,
    where many kings are being punished (paragraph 31).

71 *Socrates ... Nestor and Palamedes*: Here Lucian asserts the
    reality of Socrates' picture of the afterlife at Plato, *Apology* 41a–
    b, where he imagines talking with Homer and meeting Palamedes
    and Ajax son of Telamon, among other heroes who met their
    death through an unfair verdict. Socrates is talking nonsense
    with Nestor and Palamedes in Hades in *Dialogues of the Dead*
    6 (20).4, and at *Menippus* 18 Odysseus is an additional member
    of the group of chatterers.

72 *Around him were ... good-looking boys*: Socrates' interest in
    youthful male beauty can be seen clearly at Plato, *Charmides*
    153d and is satirized by Lucian in *Dialogues of the Dead* 6 (20).6.
    For the punchline, see paragraph 19.

73 *a version of ... he had composed*: Literally 'using his own *Consti-
    tution* and the *Laws*'. The title of Plato's *Republic* in Greek is
    Politeia, which means 'Constitution'. For the *Laws*, see his entry
    in the Glossary.

74 *clown*: The *gelotopoios* was a sort of stand-up comic, brought on
    to entertain the drinkers after the meal was over (see Xenophon,
    Symposium 1.11ff. and Athenaeus, *The Deipnosophists*
    14.613dff.).

75 *got married to Lais the courtesan*: In life, Diogenes forswore
    marriage and children in his search for self-sufficiency (Diogenes
    Laertius, *Lives of the Philosophers* 6.54).

76 *steep hill of Virtue*: An allusion to Hesiod, *Works and Days* 290:
    'The path to [Virtue] is long and steep' (cf. *About the Parasite* 14
    with n. 27). Compare Lycinus' criticism of the Stoic pursuit of
    virtue in Lucian's *Hermotimus* 78 – it takes so long, they are dead
    before they obtain their goal.

77 *As far as Chrysippus ... hellebore four times*: Hellebore was a cure for madness (see note 57). Chrysippus was supposed to have taken the cure (cf. *Hermotimus* 86, and note the assertion of the Stoic in *Philosophies for Sale* 23 that 'a man may not become a sage until he has drunk hellebore three times').

78 *As for the Academics ... island existed*: The Sceptics (who are meant here by the term 'Academics'), like the Stoics, are denied ultimate felicity by their own philosophical position. *Epechein*, 'to suspend judgement', was a technical term used by Pyrrhon and his followers.

79 *judgment ... criterion*: In the Greek the pun is more forceful, since the word for (a legal) 'judgment', *krisis*, has the same basic root as the word *kriterion* ('criterion'). Cf. *Two Charges of Literary Assault* 25 with n. 35.

80 *copulate openly*: This is a reversal of the norms usually associated with Greeks and barbarians. At Herodotus, *Histories* 3.101 it is the Indians who make love in public, in Xenophon, *Anabasis* 5.4.33–4 it is the Mossynoeci, a people living in a region bordering on the Black Sea.

81 *Socrates is the only one ... he says he hasn't*: A parody of the Platonic claim that Socrates, though attracted to beautiful young men, never actually touched them. At Plato, *Symposium* 216c2–219d2, it is one of these young men, Alcibiades, who relates his vain attempt to get to grips with Socrates.

82 *women are common to all ... most Platonic*: In his *Republic* (457c–d), Plato famously floats this idea for the 'Guardians' in his ideal city.

83 *I approached Homer*: Lucian here experiences what Socrates imagined as an advantage of the afterlife at Plato, *Apology* 41a, a meeting with Homer. A similar idea lies behind the conversation between Lycinus and Hesiod in *A Conversation with Hesiod*. The questions Lucian asks Homer were all of great concern in antiquity.

84 *he was a Babylonian ... 'Tigranes'*: Zenodotus said that Homer was Chaldaean, i.e. Assyrian (a scholium on *Iliad* 23.79), and this is perhaps a parody of his view.

85 *made a hostage by the Greeks ... changed his name*: 'Homer' (*Homeros*) meant 'hostage' in Greek.

86 *athetized verses*: I.e. those marked out by Alexandrian textual critics as spurious (from *athetein*, 'to set aside'). Cf. *In Defence of 'Images'* 24 with n. 35.

87 *started with the word 'wrath'*: In Greek, the first line of the *Iliad*

starts *menin aeide, thea*, literally '(About) wrath sing, goddess'. The wrath was that of Achilles, kindled by Agamemnon's treatment of him. In fact, without the wrath there could be no *Iliad*.

88   *blind . . . people say about him*: The ancient tradition that he was blind derives from a section of the *Homeric Hymn to Apollo* (169–73) in which the bard proclaims his identity: 'he is a blind man, and he lives in rocky Chios'. In antiquity, the *Hymns* (eighth–sixth century BC) were all ascribed to Homer.

89   *Thersites had brought . . . Odysseus had been his advocate*: This vignette is created from the scene at *Iliad* 2.212–77 where Thersites ('the ugliest man who came to Troy', 216) criticizes Agamemnon and is then silenced and beaten with the golden sceptre by Odysseus.

90   *having lived as . . . living beings*: He turns up as a cockerel belonging to the cobbler Micyllus in *The Dream, or The Cock* (see especially paragraphs 4, 13, 17 and 19–20).

91   *His whole right side was . . . gold*: The usual tale was that he had a golden thigh (Diogenes Laertius, *Lives of the Philosophers* 8.11).

92   *Empedocles . . . thoroughly roasted*: Another of Lucian's favourite philosophical targets, Empedocles appears in *Dialogues of the Dead* 6 (20).4 and on the moon in *Icaromenippus* 13, both times in the company of the Cynic philosopher Menippus. For his leap into the crater of Mt. Etna, see Diogenes Laertius, *Lives of the Philosophers* 8.69.

93   *Death Games*: Thanatousia. The name of the festival (based on *thanatos*, 'death') is modelled on those of Olympia, Nemea, Pythia, etc. There are two Homeric models behind this parody, the athletic contests among the Phaeacians (*Odyssey* 8.104–235) and the funeral games for Patroclus (*Iliad* 23.257–897).

94   *organizer*: The Greek is the technical term, *agonothetes*, used for all ancient festivals (for Olympia, see Pausanias, *Description of Greece* 5.9.4–6).

95   *pankration . . . foot-race*: For the *pankration*, see *Demonax the Philosopher*, n. 35. The foot-race was the oldest and most important of the events at the Olympic Games, the first contest among the Phaeacians (see note 93) and the event won by Odysseus in the *Iliad* (23.740–97).

96   *prize for poetry . . . far better*: Many games included poetry contests (see Plutarch, *Table-Talk* 674d–675d on their introduction to the Pythian Games). The myth of a contest between Homer and Hesiod won by the latter goes back possibly to the sixth

century BC, but is preserved in *The Contest of Homer and Hesiod*, of uncertain date.

97   *prisoners . . . heading for the island*: Possibly a parodic reminiscence of Plato, *Republic* 615dff. in the Myth of Er, where tyrants and other sinners attempt to cross through the opening into the happy life and are repulsed by savage, fiery men.

98   *Phalaris of Acragas*: He is the subject of two of Lucian's paradoxical rhetorical pieces, *Phalaris I* and *Phalaris II*, which rebut the charges usually made against him.

99   *Busiris . . . Pityocamptes' gang*: Busiris and Diomedes were killed by Heracles, while Sciron and Pityocamptes were dealt with by Theseus (who will be up against them once again).

100   *Socrates . . . than he had at Delium*: The primary reference is to Alcibiades' account of Socrates' bravery at Delium (Plato, *Symposium* 221a–b). But later writers denied Plato's veracity. See *About the Parasite* 43 with n. 44 for this tradition, to which Lucian also alludes here.

101   *Academy for the Dead*: Nekrakademia. The name puns on Plato's Academy.

102   *Now sing to me Muse . . . heroes*: Homer's new epic's opening line takes elements from *Odyssey* 1 ('sing to me Muse') and *Iliad* 4 ('of heroes') and is in the same metre (hexameter).

103   *Then they boiled up beans . . . a long festival*: A parodic version of the festival of the Pyanepsia as instituted by Theseus (again among the victors here) after his unexpected arrival home from Crete, the island of Minos (the judge of Hades in Lucian's Underworld pieces). At the Pyanepsia (named after the *pyanos*, 'bean'), dishes of beans were offered to Apollo. The festival was held in the month of Pyanepsion.

104   *Pythagoras . . . eating of beans*: The ban on eating beans was a well-known motif of Pythagoreanism. Lucian plays with it also in *Dialogues of the Dead* 6 (20).3 and *The Dream, or The Cock* 4, where there are allusions to a pseudo-Pythagorean verse which states that bean-eating is like eating the heads of one's parents. The phrase 'eating of beans' translates the single word *kyamophagia*, a word invented by Lucian for the context (*kyamos*, 'bean') (cf. *oinophagia* in 1.7: for which see note 9 above). There is a punning allusion to the word *omophagia*, the eating of raw flesh, an uncivilized practice also associated with Dionysiac myth.

105   *Cinyras*: Commentators note that he shares the name of a king of Cyprus (this is where he and Scintharus come from: see 1.34), grandson of Pygmalion, who was famous for having unwittingly

begotten an incestuous child (Adonis) from his daughter. However, the reader would have been more likely to have been alerted
what to expect from him (sexual frustration and lust) by the fact
that his name (like that of a close parallel, Cinesias in Aristophanes, *Lysistrata* 852) begins with *kin-*; *kino* is one of the Greek
words for 'copulate'.

106 *Helen's wish as well*: Lucian playfully suggests thus that the
ancient versions of the abduction of Helen by Paris in which she
was a willing partner were the correct ones (Herodotus, *Histories*
1.4, Euripides, *Trojan Women* 987–8).

107 *Cork or Cheeseland*: These islands were described at 2.3–4,
though Cheeseland (*Tyroessa*) is named for the first time here.

108 *single block of asphodel*: The asphodel was a plant associated
with the Underworld (e.g. *Odyssey* 11.539), though it did not
grow large enough to produce ship-hulls.

109 *reveal the future . . . impending voyage*: The learned reader would
be forcefully reminded of the role of Tiresias in *Odyssey*
11.100–149.

110 *mallow root . . . in times of great danger*: See also 1.16 and 2.26.
The mallow is a plant associated with the dead, and its leaves were
considered sacred by Pythagoras (Aelian, *Historical Miscellanies*
4.17: see also next note). But here it also echoes the magical moly
root given by Hermes to Odysseus in *Odyssey* 10.287–306 to
protect him against Circe's magic.

111 *He also advised me . . . over eighteen*: The first of these injunctions
is a precept of Pythagoras (Diogenes Laertius, *Lives of the Philosophers* 8.17), and the other two are parodies of Pythagorean
rules.

112 *Lucian . . . dear native land*: The lines are in the usual epic metre
(hexameter) and the phrase 'To his dear native land' echoes a
Homeric formula (see e.g. *Odyssey* 1.290).

113 *lampfish*: Lucian here invents a diminutive of a word, *lychnos*,
which means both 'lamp' and a type of fish.

114 *gates of ivory . . . temple of the Cockerel . . . Homer*: *Odyssey*
19.560ff. for the gates of horn (true dreams) and ivory (false
dreams) and 24.12 (the people of dreams). The temple of the
Cockerel is Lucian's invention. On one level its significance is
obvious – dreams end at cock-crow. But there may also be an
allusion to the story of Alectryon ('Cockerel'). Placed on guard
by Ares while he slept with Aphrodite, the youth fell asleep,
thus allowing Hephaestus, Aphrodite's husband, to discover the
adultery. Ares changed Alectryon into a cockerel.

115 *poppies and mandragora plants*: Both associated in antiquity with sleep-inducing narcotics.

116 *Sleepwalker ... Sleep-of-the-dead ... Allnight*: Respectively, *Nyktiporos, Negretos, Pannychia. Negretos* is an epithet used of sleep in *Odyssey* 13.80.

117 *not two gates, as Homer has maintained*: See note 114. See also *The Dream, or The Cock* 6 for more criticism of Homer's description of these gates.

118 *Indolence ... Troubler ... Purposeless ... Fabulouslyrich ... Imagination ... Deepsleep*: Respectively, *Blakeia, Taraxion, Mataiogenes, Ploutokles, Phantasion, Kareotis.*

119 *promised to make us kings and satraps*: In Lucian, dreams often make lavish and unrealistic promises. See *The Dream, or Lucian's Career* and *The Dream, or The Cock*, especially 12ff. And the desire to dream, even while awake, of unrealizable things is also continually criticized (see *The Ship passim*). For 'satrap', see *The Ship*, n. 41.

120 *'Odysseus sends ... and come to you'*: Odysseus' letter gives an abbreviated account of the events in *Odyssey* 5–24, together with the story of the *Telegony* by the sixth-century BC poet Eugammon of Cyrene. There is a hint of criticism of Homer's account, however, in two details. First, Homer said Odysseus travelled for seventeen days before being shipwrecked (*Odyssey* 5.278). Secondly, Tiresias tells Odysseus that his death will be gentle and that he will be old, surrounded by a prosperous people (*Odyssey* 11.134–7).

121 *just as Homer said and Calypso at the loom*: Homer apparently *is* accurate in some details (*Odyssey* 5.57–62).

122 *the sort of answers we felt would please her*: Lucian probably means to imply that he denigrated her beauty and chastity. For the learned reader, the first idea would have sprung to mind when he recalled Odysseus' words to Calypso on parting from her (*Odyssey* 5.215–17): 'I know perfectly well that wise Penelope is less well-endowed than you in looks and stature.' The second would have followed on reflection on the ancient tradition which denied Penelope's chastity and claimed that she had been seduced by the suitor Antinous and driven out of the palace by Odysseus (Apollodorus, *The Library*, Epitome 7.38).

123 *Pumpkin Pirates ... Nut Sailors*: Respectively, *Kolokyntho-peiratai* and *Karyonautai.*

124 *goose on the ship's stern-post ... honked*: The goose was regularly used as an ornamental figure at the prow or stern of Greek

ships (cf. *The Ship* 5). Only the *Argo*, however, had a speaking stern-post (Apollonius of Rhodes, *Argonautica* 4.580–83), which supplies the background for the parody here.

125 *great wonders . . . grapes, not yet ripe*: These marvels attest the miraculous vivifying force of the god Dionysus, as exemplified by his treatment of the Tyrrhenian pirate-ship by which he is captured in the *Homeric Hymn to Dionysus* (see especially 38–42 for the vine-covered mast). Lucian and his crew are right to be worried by the omen, recalling what had happened to their comrades the last time Dionysus made his presence felt (1.7–9).

126 *To men . . . on a woodland cruise*: Lucian takes literally what was intended as a metaphor in Antimachus, referring to the Argonauts' need to convey their ship across the deserts of Libya to get from one sea to another (the adjective 'woody' (*hyleeis*) was used in Antimachus' verse to mean 'muddy').

127 *deep chasm*: This strange phenomenon may well invite the learned reader to recall a passage of Herodotus (*Histories* 4.85) where the phrase 'sea chasm' (meaning a 'strait') is used.

128 *Oxheads*: Boukephaloi.

129 *I did not agree*: In this, Lucian learns a good lesson from his Homeric model for this episode, the incident on the Island of the Sun, where Odysseus' men kill and eat the forbidden cattle (*Odyssey* 12.260–402). Lucian holds out against his men, whereas Odysseus was unable to prevent the killing of the sacred cattle, because of the men's hunger and the gods' desire for him to sleep.

130 *Nagland . . . Waterlust*: There is a problem with both these names, because the MSS vary in the first case between a word based on 'trickery' (*kobala*) and one based on 'horse' (*kaballes*) and in the second make no sense at all. The text I translate reads Kaballousa ('Nagland') and Hydamargia ('Waterlust'), both appropriate to the context.

131 *I held back a little . . . skulls lying around*: Like his model in the *Odyssey*, Odysseus, Lucian can read the signs of entrapment. The parody is based on the episodes with Circe (*Odyssey* 10.312ff., where Odysseus draws his sword on Circe) and the Sirens (12.45–6, where Circe mentions the piles of human bones on the Sirens' island).

132 *Asslegs*: Onoskeleis. Lucian may be alluding to the story, reported in the early fifth-century AD compiler Johannes Stobaeus' *Anthology* (4.20.74), of a young man who had sexual intercourse with a female ass, which gave birth to a daughter named Onoscelia

('Asslegs'). But a similar name, 'Onoscelis' is given to an Empusa (a monster familiar from Aristophanes, *Frogs* 285ff.) in a scholium to Aristophanes, *Women at the Assembly* 1048.

133   *mainland ... opposite that which we inhabit*: The 'other continent' (see paragraph 27) may parody the Atlantis myth (Plato, *Timaeus* 24e) or the 'only continent' mentioned by Silenus to Midas in Theopompus of Chios (as reported by Aelian, *Historical Miscellanies* 3.18). But see *Demonax the Philosopher* 22 with n. 18 and *The Ship* 44 for the idea that there was another inhabited area on the opposite side of the globe.

134   *What happened ... I shall tell you in the books that follow*: Though we know from the narrative itself and the many hints within it that Lucian survives his adventures on the other continent and returns home, the promise of 'more books' is, as a scholiast noted, 'the greatest lie of all'. It is also parodic of contemporary book-closure (e.g. Athenaeus, *The Deipnosophists* 3.127: 'So let this book be at an end ... We will begin the banquet in the ones that follow').

Glossary of Names

Abradatas King of Susa, husband of Panthea, whose beauty and loyalty to her husband are recorded in Xenophon's *Cyropaedia*.

Academics Followers of the philosophical school established by Plato, but usually associated with the Scepticism of Pyrrhon.

Academy A grove outside the Dipylon Gate to the north-west of the city of Athens, used by Plato as a meeting-place for his philosophical school, also known by this name.

Acarnania A region on the coast in western Greece, north of the Corinthian Gulf.

Achaeans The name given to the Greeks in Homer.

Acharnae An Attic deme (local administrative district) to the north of the city of Athens.

Acheron The lake which the dead must cross on Charon's ferry to get into Hades.

Achilles Son of Peleus, from Phthia in Thessaly. The central character in the *Iliad*. He withdraws from the battle against the Trojans in response to an insult by King Agamemnon, and returns only after his best friend Patroclus, having taken his place, has been killed by Hector.

Acragas A city in Sicily.

Acrisius Legendary king of Argos, father of Danae.

Admetus A poet known only from *Demonax the Philosopher* 44.

Adonis A young male deity beloved of Aphrodite. His name became a metaphor for a handsome lover.

Aeacus Son of Zeus and the nymph Aegina, father of Peleus and Telamon. One of the judges in the Underworld.

Aegean Sea The sea between Greece and Asia Minor.

Aegeus Legendary king of Athens, father of Theseus. His name was given to one of the demes (local administrative districts) of Athens.

Aegina An island in the Saronic Gulf, where Mysteries were performed in honour of Hecate.

Aeschines (*c.* 397–*c.* 322 BC) Athenian orator, opponent of Demosthenes and a central figure in the political debate about how to handle the growing power of Macedon in the 340s.

Aeschines the Socratic (fourth century BC) A follower of Socrates, writer of Socratic dialogues, now known only in fragments. Spent some time at the court of Syracuse, returning to Athens in 356 after Dionysius II's expulsion.

Aeschylus (*c.* 525–*c.* 456 BC) Athenian tragic dramatist, the earliest of those whose works survive. Seven plays are extant, though one (*Prometheus Bound*) is possibly spurious.

Aesop the Phrygian A legendary figure, said to have been a slave, regarded in antiquity as the writer of fables, moralistic stories often involving speaking animals.

Aëtion (fourth century BC) Painter. According to Lucian (*Herodotus, or Aëtion*), he painted the *Wedding of Alexander and Roxana*.

Aetolia A region in west-central Greece on the Corinthian Gulf.

Agamemnon Son of Atreus, king of Argos, brother of Menelaus and leader of the Greek forces against Troy. He is a central character in the *Iliad* and featured also in Greek tragedy.

Agathoboulus (*fl.* first–second century AD) From Rhodes, a Cynic philosopher who taught Peregrinus Proteus and who was known to Demonax, he may appear also in one of the stories in *Toxaris* (27).

Agathocles (1) A Peripatetic known only from *Demonax the Philosopher* 29. (2) A doctor (first century BC?), writer of a treatise *On Diet*, who may be the person mentioned in *The Journey down to Hades* 6, though the identification is uncertain.

Agathocles of Samos An infantry commander of Alexander the Great. Nothing is known of this individual beyond the information in *Slander* 18.

Agora The business and political centre of Athens, located at the foot of the acropolis to the north-west. The word *agora* was used for the place with these functions everywhere in the Greek world.

Aidoneus Another name for Hades (Pluto).

Ajax (1) Son of Telamon, king of Salamis, in the *Iliad* the mightiest of the Greek warriors at Troy after Achilles. After Achilles' death, when the verdict went against him and Achilles' arms were awarded to Odysseus instead of to himself, Ajax went mad and killed a herd of cattle, thinking them to be the Greek commanders. When he recovered his senses, he was so ashamed that he killed himself.

Ajax (2) Son of Oileus, from Locris, leader of a contingent of ships to

Troy in the *Iliad*, often paired with Telamonian Ajax (Ajax (1)) and hence called the 'Lesser Ajax'. In the *Odyssey*, he is reported drowned by Poseidon for blasphemy against the gods. Another story, often illustrated on vases, has him dragging Cassandra away from the statue of Athena at Troy.

Akamas A promontory on the north-west tip of Cyprus.

Alania A region beyond the Caucasus mountains and bordering the Caspian Sea, inhabited by Alans.

Alans Nomadic pastoralists who inhabited the region of Alania during the early centuries AD.

Alcamenes (*fl.* second half of the fifth century BC) Athenian or Lemnian sculptor, pupil of Phidias. He produced many cult statues, including a Hermes and a Hecate for the acropolis at Athens (copies survive). His 'Aphrodite in the gardens' is sometimes connected with figures of Venus genetrix.

Alcestis Daughter of Pelias and wife of Admetus, king of Pherae in Thessaly. The Fates allowed Admetus to escape death if he could find a substitute. The only willing person was Alcestis, but she was returned to life by Heracles (in Euripides' *Alcestis* he wrestles Death for her).

Alcibiades (451/50–404/3 BC) Son of Cleinias, Athenian politician and general, famed for his flamboyant style of dress and speech. Originally one of the commanders of the Sicilian expedition (415), he was exiled after refusing to return to Athens to face charges in the affair of the Profanation of the Eleusinian Mysteries (a group of young aristocrats was accused of mocking these rituals of Demeter and her daughter). He gave aid to Sparta (415–412), then to the Athenian fleet at Samos, until he secured his return to Athens in 407. He soon lost his position again and was eventually murdered in Phrygia.

Alcinous King of the Phaeacians, inhabitants of the island of Scheria, where Odysseus lands at the end of Book 5 of the *Odyssey* and to whom he relates the story of his adventures (Books 9–12).

Alcmene Mother of Heracles.

Alexander (356–323 BC) III, 'the Great', king of Macedon, son of Philip II and Olympias. Tutored by Aristotle. He conquered Persia, Egypt and a vast tract of territory as far east as India.

Alopeke An Attic deme (local administrative district), to the south of the city of Athens.

Altar of Pity A well-known place of sanctuary in Athens, sometimes identified with the Altar of the Twelve Gods or with that of Zeus Agoraios.

450   GLOSSARY OF NAMES

Amastris City on the south coast of the Black (Euxine) Sea.

Amazons A mythical race of warrior women.

Ammon Amun, the chief divinity of the Egyptians, identified with Zeus. He had an oracular shrine at Siwa in the Libyan desert, visited by Alexander the Great in 331 BC.

Amphion One of the twin sons of Zeus and Antiope, born in a cave on Mt. Cithaeron. A gifted lyre-player, Amphion is said to have moved stones with his music to form the walls of Thebes.

Anacharsis A Scythian, said to have lived in the sixth century BC, to have admired Greek customs and to have been exceptionally wise. Later his name was sometimes included among those of the Seven Sages. Letters and sayings (dating from the Hellenistic period) are attributed to him.

Anacreon (*fl. c.* 536 BC) Lyric and iambic poet from the Ionian coastal city of Teos, who spent time at the court of Polycrates in Samos and the court of the Pisistratids at Athens.

Anaxagoras (*c.* 500–*c.* 428 BC) From Clazomenae, settled at Athens, but left, with his pupil, friend and patron Pericles' aid, after a trial for impiety in 437/6. His claim that the sun was a fiery stone upset contemporaries and was part of what led to the image of him as atheistic.

Anaxarchus (mid–late fourth century BC) From Abdera, philosopher and teacher of Pyrrhon. He went with Alexander the Great to Asia.

Anteia Wife of Proetus, king of Tiryns. She tried to seduce Bellerophon, but when rebuffed told her husband that Bellerophon had tried to seduce *her*. Proetus sent Bellerophon to Anteia's father Iobates, king of Lycia, carrying a sealed letter with instructions to kill the bearer. Iobates set Bellerophon several deadly tasks (including fighting the Chimaera), which he survived.

Antenor A Trojan elder, husband of Theano.

Antimachus (*fl.* 400 BC) From Colophon, poet, author of an epic (the *Thebaid*) and a narrative elegy (the *Lyde*), rife with Homeric allusion and with a tendency to scholarly obscurity.

Antipater (*c.* 397–319 BC) Representative of the Macedonian kings Philip II and Alexander the Great. Left in charge of Europe from 334 during Alexander's eastern campaigns.

Antiphilus (*fl.* late fourth century BC) From Egypt, a painter noted for the facility of his technique.

Antiphon Possibly the contemporary of Socrates mentioned by Xenophon in the *Memorabilia* (1.6), who wrote a treatise on interpreting dreams.

Antisthenes (mid fifth–mid fourth century BC) Friend of Socrates, a philosophical writer, who stressed especially the ascetic life and was regarded by later ages as the founder of Cynicism (see CYNICS, CYNICISM).

Anubis An Egyptian god of the dead, usually represented as a human being with a jackal's head.

Anytus (*fl.* 399 BC) Athenian general in 409, best known as one of the prosecutors of Socrates.

Apelles (*fl.* 332 BC) From Colophon, and later Ephesus, one of the most frequently mentioned painters of antiquity. Besides the *Calumny*, his works included *Aphrodite Rising* and portraits of Alexander the Great and a girl called variously Pacate, Pancaste or Pancaspe.

Aphrodisia Festival of Aphrodite.

Aphrodite Goddess of love, sometimes said to be daughter of Zeus and Dione, associated in legend and cult especially with Cyprus (hence the epithet 'Cyprian'). The famous statue, the Aphrodite of Cnidus, was sculpted by Praxiteles.

Apollo Son of Zeus and Leto, god of healing and purification, prophecy, care of ephebes, poetry and music. Especially associated with Delphi and Delos, he is always depicted as a handsome, beardless youth, with bow and laurel.

Apollonius (1) (*fl. c.* 270–245 BC) Known as Apollonius Rhodius, 'of Rhodes', but possibly from Naucratis, he was Royal Librarian at Alexandria. A scholar and poet, his only extant work is an epic in four books of hexameters about the voyage of the *Argo*, called *Argonautica*.

Apollonius (2) (*fl.* AD 150) A Stoic philosopher criticized for his greed by the emperor Antoninus Pius (AD 138–161).

Arabia Region between Egypt and India.

Aratus (*c.* 315–before 240 BC) From Soli in Cilicia, he studied in Athens, spent time at the courts of Antigonus in Macedonia and of Antiochus in Syria. A scholar and poet, his main extant work is a didactic poem called *Phainomena*, which deals with constellations and weather signs.

Arcadia The central region of the Peloponnese.

Arcesilaus (316/15–242/1 BC) From Pitane in Aeolia, a Platonic philosopher, head of the Academy from *c.* 268. He was later known as the founder of the Middle Academy, and credited with the introduction of Scepticism.

Archelaus King of Macedon (413–399 BC), a friend of Athens who established a theatre festival at Dium and gave patronage to artists and writers, including Zeuxis and Euripides.

Architeles Supposedly a member of the Areopagus, this individual appears to have been invented by Lucian to suit the needs of his argument at *The Scythian* 2.

Areius the Egyptian He may have been an athlete of the Hellenistic era, though his name is only found in one other source, asserting that he was never defeated in a boxing contest.

Areopagus The 'Hill of Ares' at Athens, and the council associated with it. In early times an aristocratic body, its wider powers were removed in the early fifth century BC, leaving it as a court primarily judging homicide cases. Its prestige grew again in the fourth century BC and it regained some power. Associated with both location and council was a shrine of the 'Dread Goddesses', the Eumenides. In *Two Charges of Literary Assault*, Lucian uses the Areopagus as though it were a normal lawcourt.

Ares Son of Zeus and Hera, god of war.

Arete Wife of Alcinous, king of the Phaeacians, and mother of Nausicaa, her goodwill is essential to Odysseus' reception in Scheria in the *Odyssey* (Book 6).

Argo The ship in which Jason led the expedition to bring back the Golden Fleece from Colchis.

Argonauts The name given to the crew of the *Argo*.

Argos (1) A city in the Peloponnese, associated in Greek tragedy with the family of Agamemnon, including his son Orestes.

Argos (2) A monster with many eyes and never asleep. Set by Hera to guard Io, one of Zeus' lovers, who had been turned into a heifer, he was tricked and killed by Hermes, who was hence known as 'Slayer of Argos'.

Arion (late seventh–early sixth century BC) From Methymna in Lesbos, a poet and musician at the court of Periander. Herodotus relates that he was thrown overboard on his way back to Corinth from a trip to Italy and Sicily, but arrived back safely at Taenarum on the back of a dolphin (*Histories* 1.23–4).

Aristarchus (c. 216–144 BC) From Samothrace, at one time head of the Royal Library at Alexandria. He wrote commentaries on various authors, and treatises on the *Iliad* and *Odyssey*, but is best known for pioneering work of textual criticism.

Aristides (d. c. 467 BC) Athenian politician, known as 'the just', ostracized in 483/2, often contrasted favourably with Themistocles.

Aristippus (late fifth–early fourth century BC) From Cyrene, a member of Socrates' circle. Regarded as the founder of the Cyrenaic school of philosophy. Lucian always represents him as a hedonist (taking his cue from Xenophon's vignette in his *Memorabilia*).

Aristogiton (late sixth century BC) Executed for his part with Harmodius in a plot to kill the Athenian tyrant Hippias in 514. The plot misfired and only Hippias' brother Hipparchus was murdered. Later, the two were regarded as heroes by the emerging democracy and bronze statues of them erected.

Aristophanes (*c.* 450–*c.* 386 BC) Writer of comedy in the 'iambic form' (usually known as 'Old Comedy'). Eleven of his plays survive. They generally engage critically with the political figures of the day in plots marked by their use of fantasy, e.g. the *Birds* (414 BC), where two humans found a bird city in mid-air, 'Cloudcuckooville', and one eventually usurps Zeus' tyranny. In *Clouds* (423 BC), Socrates is represented as the proprietor of a school which teaches students how to make the weaker argument the stronger. An old man, Strepsiades, has his wastrel son Pheidippides educated there in order to weasel out of the debts his son's chariot-racing has led him to incur.

Aristotle (384–322 BC) From Stagira in Chalcidice, he studied with Plato in the Academy at Athens, later became tutor to Alexander the Great, and in 336/5 established his own philosophical school in the Lyceum, outside the city of Athens. Its covered walks (*peripatoi*) gave him and his followers the name 'Peripatetics'. Aristotle's work covered logic (including the *Categories*), metaphysics, nature, life, mind, ethics, politics, rhetoric and poetry.

Aristoxenus (b. *c.* 370 BC) From Tarentum, a writer on music, philosophy and history. He composed several biographies of philosophers, including Plato. Lucian associates him with Neleus, a pupil of Aristotle.

Arles Ancient Arelate, a city in Gaul on the Rhône.

Armenians Inhabitants of a region of eastern Anatolia.

Artemis Daughter of Zeus and Leto. A virgin goddess depicted as a huntress, with bow, arrows and deer. She was associated with mountains and with female transitions, especially childbirth. One of her rituals (the cult of Artemis Tauropolos at Halae) was explained by the myth of Orestes' theft of the statue of Artemis from the Taurians, from whom she demanded human sacrifice. She had an important cult centre at Ephesus.

Asclepius God of healing.

Asia In general, the area known now as Asia Minor. In Roman times (from 133 BC), the province of Asia.

Aspasia (*fl.* 445 BC) From Miletus, consort of Pericles. She was reputed to teach rhetoric and to have debated with Socrates.

Ate ('Ruin') Personification of mental infatuation which leads to disaster. In Homer, the daughter of Zeus.

Athena Daughter of Zeus, from whose head she was born. A virgin goddess, concerned as much with the womanly crafts as with the manly art of war (source of the epithet *Stratios*, 'of the Army'). She was patron goddess of Athens under the title *Polias* ('Protectress of the City').

Athos (Mt.) A mountainous headland on the easternmost promontory of Chalcidice.

Atlas A Titan, son of Iapetus and brother of Prometheus. Father of Calypso.

Atropos One of the three Moirai ('Fates'), Clotho and Lachesis being the others. Atropos cuts the thread spun by Clotho and apportioned by Lachesis and thus ends a person's life.

Attic Orators By Lucian's time, the recognized canon of Athenian oratory was: Lysias, Isaeus, Hyperides, Isocrates, Dinarchus, Aeschines, Antiphon, Lycurgus, Andocides and Demosthenes.

Attica The territory of Athens, divided into demes (local administrative districts).

Babylon A city situated to the south of modern Baghdad (Iraq), capital of the Babylonian empire, and later an important centre for Persian and Seleucid kings. In Lucian's day it was under the control of the Parthians.

Bacchus See DIONYSUS.

Bacchylides (*c.* 520 – *c.* 450 BC) From Ceos, a lyric poet, most of whose victory odes along with some dithyrambs survive in a papyrus found in 1986.

Bactra Capital of Bactria, a country located in parts of what are now Afghanistan, Uzbekistan and Tajikistan.

Bellerophon In Homer, son of Glaucus. As a part of his punishment for the (false) accusation made against him by Anteia, he was sent by King Iobates to slay the Chimaera (see ANTEIA).

Bithynia A region in north-west Asia Minor.

Black Sea Also known as the Euxine Sea, it was colonized from at least the sixth century BC by Greeks and always had important trade links with the Mediterranean.

Boeotia A region in central Greece, Athens' immediate northern neighbour.

Boreas The North Wind.

Borysthenes A river in Scythia (river Dnieper).

Borysthenites A people living along the north bank of the river Borysthenes. Their city at *Toxaris* 61 may be Olbia.

Bosporus (1) The narrow strait which separates the Propontis (Sea of Marmara) from the Black (Euxine) Sea.

Bosporus (2) The Cimmerian Bosporus, a narrow strait separating the

Black (Euxine) Sea from the Maeotis (Sea of Azov), and the name of a kingdom encompassing the straits.

Bousiris A mythical Egyptian king, who killed foreign visitors at the altar of Zeus. He was killed by Heracles.

Brahmins Collective name for the Indian priestly cast.

Branchidae Another name for Didyma, an oracular shrine of Apollo, situated just south of Miletus. Strictly speaking, the name of the priestly clan which administered the shrine.

Briseis In the *Iliad*, daughter of Briseus, from Lyrnessus, given as a prize to Achilles, but later taken away by Agamemnon.

Briseus Father of Briseis.

Busiris See BOUSIRIS.

Caeneus A Lapith, mentioned by Nestor in the *Iliad* (1.264) as one of the great men of the past known to him.

Calamis (*fl.* 475 BC) A sculptor in marble, bronze, gold and ivory. His works (including the Sosandra) have not been identified among extant sculpture.

Callias (*c.* 450–370 BC) Son of Hipponicus. A wealthy Athenian nobleman, often satirized by comic poets.

Calliope The Muse of epic poetry.

Calypso ('Concealer') A nymph, daughter of Atlas. In the *Odyssey* (Book 5), she detains Odysseus on the island of Ogygia for seven years, offering him immortality, before letting him leave on the orders of Zeus, conveyed by Hermes.

Cambyses The name of two kings of Persia, the father and the son of Cyrus the Great.

Canopus A city in Egypt, near Alexandria.

Cappadocia A region in Asia Minor.

Carambis A city on the southern shore of the Black (Euxine) Sea.

Caria A region in the south-west of Asia Minor.

Carus (or **Caprus**) Caprus (MSS read 'Carus') of Elis was the first man after Heracles to win both wrestling and *pankration* at the Olympic Games – in 212 BC.

Carystus A city on the southern end of Euboea.

Caspian Sea A large lake east of the Black (Euxine) Sea.

Cassandra The most beautiful daughter of Priam (by Hecabe), raped by Ajax of Locris during the capture of Troy. In later tradition, she had prophetic powers but was always disbelieved.

Cassiepeia (or **Cassiopeia**) When she boasted that she was prettier than the Nereids, her daughter, Andromeda, was exposed as a sacrifice to a sea-monster (later killed by Perseus) set upon the land as a punishment for her presumption.

Castor One of the two Dioscuri. The other was Polydeuces (or Pollux).

Caucasus A mountain range extending from the Black (Euxine) Sea to the Caspian Sea.

Cecrops A mythical king of Athens.

Cenchreae A port on the Saronic Gulf.

Centaurs Mythical creatures, with the body of a horse and the torso and head of a human being. They were often portrayed in sculpture and painting, a favourite scene being their drunken and murderous behaviour at the wedding-feast of Pirithous and Hippodamia, where they fought the Lapiths.

Ceos An island in the Cyclades, home of Bacchylides.

Ceramicus (*Kerameikos*) A large area in the city of Athens, between the Dipylon Gate and the Agora, named from the potters who worked there. Also the cemetery beyond the Dipylon Gate.

Cerberus The monstrous dog who guards the entrance to Hades, most often described as three-headed. His theft was the last of the twelve labours of Heracles, according to Apollodorus (*The Library* 2.5.12).

Cethegus M. (Gavius) Cornelius Cethegus, *consul ordinarius* in AD 170.

Chaeronea Site of a crucial battle in 338 BC. See further PHILIP II.

Chalcis The main city of Euboea.

Charon Ferryman of the dead, who demands an obol as fare for the crossing of Acheron.

Chelidones The Chelidonian Islands lie off a promontory which divides the Lycian Sea from the Pamphylian Sea on the south coast of Asia Minor.

Chimaera A monster made up of a lion in front, a she-goat in the middle and a snake at the back. Killed by Bellerophon.

Chios Large island off the coast of Asia Minor. Famous for its wine (Chian) and for its claim to be Homer's birthplace.

Chrysippus (*c.* 280–207 BC) From Soli in Cilicia, head of the Stoa from 232. Through his many writings he established what was later regarded as Stoic orthodoxy (see STOA, STOICISM, STOICS).

Cilicia A region in southern Asia Minor.

Circe In the *Odyssey*, a sorceress who lives on the island of Aeaea. She turns all but one of Odysseus' men into pigs. Odysseus forces her to return them to human form and stays with her for a year. In later legend, their son Telegonus unwittingly kills his father when raiding Ithaca.

Cithaeron A mountain on the borders between Attica and Boeotia.

Clazomenae A Greek city on a small island just off the coast of Ionia.

Cleinias Father of Alcibiades, died at the battle of Coronea in 446 BC.

Cleon (d. 422 BC) Athenian politician and general attacked by Thucydides in his history and in the plays of Aristophanes, especially *Knights*, as a low-born rabble-rouser.

Clio The Muse of history.

Clotho One of the Moirai ('Fates'). She spins the thread which represents the span of a person's life and which Atropos cuts (see also ATROPOS).

Cloudcuckooville (*Nephelokokkygia*) The city of birds built in mid-air to attack the Olympian gods in Aristophanes' *Birds* (414 BC).

Cnidus A Greek city located in the Gulf of Cos, in the south-west of Asia Minor.

Cocytus ('Wailing') The name of one of the rivers of Hades.

Codrus A legendary king of Athens.

Colchis A region at the eastern end of the Black (Euxine) Sea associated in myth with the voyage of Jason and the *Argo*.

Colophon A Greek city in Ionia. It claimed to be the birthplace of Homer. Nearby was the famous oracle of Apollo at Claros.

Colossus of Rhodes A bronze statue of Helios ('the Sun') *c.* 105 ft (32 m) tall, sculpted by Chares (*fl.* 300 BC), erected on a hill overlooking the harbour at Rhodes. It was one of the Seven Wonders of the ancient world.

Corinth A city in the Peloponnese on the Corinthian Gulf. It commands the Isthmus and a fertile coastal plain.

Corybants Male supernatural beings, associated with Rhea because of their madness (Lucian, *Dialogues of the Gods* 20 (12).1, *The Dance* 8; cf. *Icaromenippus* 27 and *The Parliament of the* Gods 9).

Crates (*c.* 368/365–288/285 BC) From Thebes, Cynic philosopher and follower of Diogenes.

Cratinus A major poet of the Old Comedy, active between *c.* 450 and 423 BC, when he won a victory at the Dionysia festival with *The Wine-Flask* against Aristophanes' *Clouds*.

Creon In tragedy, brother of Jocasta, the mother and wife of Oedipus, king of Thebes. He ruled after Oedipus' fall and is a central character in Sophocles' *Antigone*.

Crete A large island in the Aegean Sea, legendary birthplace of Zeus, Minos and Rhadamanthys.

Croesus The last king of Lydia (*c.* 560–546 BC), fabulously rich. His name became a byword for wealth. Herodotus tells us that he made offerings to Delphi after testing the oracle's veracity with a question asking what he was cooking at the time (lamb-and-tortoise stew). He had a deaf-mute son. Croesus lost his position and wealth to Cyrus the Great after famously misinterpreting a Delphic oracle ('If you invade Persia you will destroy a great kingdom').

458   GLOSSARY OF NAMES

Cronus Father of Zeus and husband of Rhea. He was the youngest of the Titans, overthrew his father Uranus and was in turn overthrown by Zeus.

Croton A Greek city on the toe of Italy.

Ctesias (*fl.* late fifth century BC) From Cnidus, son of Ctesiochus. A writer of histories of Persia and India and of a geographical work. Regarded in antiquity as notoriously unreliable.

Ctesiphon Originally a village on the river Tigris, north of Babylon, it became the chief city of Babylonia in the later second century AD.

Cupids In Greek, *Erotes*, indicating a plurality of 'Loves'. The god Eros/Cupid is associated with Aphrodite and personifies the (mental and physical) desire which draws lovers together.

Curetes An Aetolian people, living in Pleuron, mentioned by Homer at *Iliad* 9.529ff.

Cyclades A group of around thirty islands in the southern Aegean Sea.

Cyclops One-eyed giant. In the *Odyssey* (Book 9), a whole tribe of them live as pastoralists on a remote island. Odysseus and his companions are trapped in the cave of one named Polyphemus, who begins to eat them one by one. Odysseus, pretending that his name is 'Nobody', gets the Cyclops drunk, and then blinds him and escapes with his remaining companions from the cave under Polyphemus' sheep. In Hesiod, the three Cyclopes are the craftsmen who make Zeus' thunderbolts.

Cynaethus This individual is known only from *In Defence of 'Images'* 20 and 22 and may be an invention (though the name itself is real).

Cynegeirus (d. 490 BC) Brother of the tragic poet Aeschylus. He died at Marathon, after having had chopped off with an axe the hand with which he was grasping the stern of a Persian ship.

Cynics, Cynicism Followers of/the principle of living according to nature, as do dogs, from the Greek word for which (*kyon*, *kynos*) the term is derived. This lifestyle, first followed by Diogenes and later by Crates and others, later developed literary forms which are associated with satire (see MENIPPUS) and influenced the formulation of the philosophical doctrines of the Stoics. Cynic practice declined in the second and first centuries BC, but underwent a revival under the Roman empire.

Cyprus A large Greek island in the eastern Mediterranean.

Cyrene A Greek colony in Africa, founded *c.* 630 BC from Thera.

Cyrus (1) Cyrus the Great ('the Elder'), *fl.* 550 BC, who conquered Media, Sardis, Lydia and Babylonia to form the Persian empire; (2) Cyrus the Younger, second son of Darius II, commander of Asia Minor from 408 BC, served by the Athenian historian Xenophon as a mercenary in his failed attempt to take the throne from his brother Artaxerxes II in 401.

Daedalus Legendary inventor and craftsman, who escaped from Crete by flying with wings held together with wax (see also MINOS, MINOTAUR). His son Icarus was less successful.

Danae Daughter of Acrisius, king of Argos. Imprisoned by her father when an oracle predicted that her (future) son would murder him, she was visited by Zeus in the form of a shower of gold falling into her lap through a vent in the ceiling and thus gave birth to Perseus, with whom Acrisius set her adrift at sea in a chest, though they arrived safely at the island of Seriphos.

Danaids The fifty daughters of Danaus, who (except for one) killed their husbands on their wedding night. In the Roman period, they are represented as punished in Hades by continually attempting to fill a leaking water-jar.

Daphne Daughter of a river-god. Apollo fell in love with her, but her prayer for help was answered and she was turned into a laurel-tree, which became Apollo's plant.

Darius (d. 486 BC) I, king of Persia, responsible for crushing the Ionian Revolt (c. 500–493) and for sending a fleet against Athens in 490 under the command of Datis.

Datis (fl. 490 BC) A Mede, commander of the Persian fleet which Darius sent against Athens and which was defeated at Marathon in 490.

Delium A temple of Apollo on the coast of Boeotia, where the Athenians were defeated in battle in 424 BC. Socrates was a participant.

Delos A small island in the Cyclades, birthplace of Apollo and Artemis, location of an important shrine of Apollo.

Delphi A pan-Hellenic sanctuary, located on the southern slopes of Mt. Parnassus, north of the Corinthian Gulf, sacred to Apollo, site of an oracular shrine and the Pythian Games. The wealth of the offerings stored there was renowned. See also CROESUS, POLYGNOTUS.

Demades (c. 380–319 BC) Athenian politician, taken prisoner in the battle of Chaeronea (338). Philip II used him to negotiate peace with Athens.

Demeter The goddess of corn, celebrated especially at the Thesmophoria and the Eleusinian Mysteries. Her priestesses, unlike those of other deities, remained unmarried.

Demetrius (1) A Platonic philosopher, a contemporary of Ptolemy Dionysus. Nothing is known about him except what is reported at *Slander* 16.

Demetrius (2) At *Demonax the Philosopher* 3, possibly the Cynic philosopher who lived in Rome under Gaius ('Caligula'), Nero and Vespasian. He may also be the same as or the basis for the Demetrius of Sunium of *Toxaris* 27ff.

Demetrius Poliorcetes (336–283 BC) Demetrius I of Macedonia, son of Antigonus I, he gained his epithet 'The Besieger' (*Poliorketes*) after a year-long siege of Rhodes in 305–304, for the relief from which the Rhodians commissioned the Colossus, which they paid for by the sale of Demetrius' abandoned siege-equipment.

Democritus (b. 460–57 BC) The originator of the 'atomic' theory of matter, mentioned in ancient satire as a philosopher whose re-action to human folly was to laugh uproariously (Juvenal, *Satires* 10.28–35).

Demosthenes (384–322 BC) From the deme of Paeania, Athenian politician vigorously opposed to making peace with Philip II of Macedon. His most famous speeches against Philip are the *Olynthiacs* and *Philippics*. He was in the canon of Attic Orators.

Deucalion In mythology, the son of Prometheus and husband of Pyrrha. He and his wife were the only survivors of the flood sent by Zeus as a punishment on the human race. They escaped drowning by build-ing a chest in which they lived until the waters receded.

Diasia An Athenian festival of Zeus held outside the city at Agrae in late February.

Diogenes (*c*. 412 or 403–*c*. 324 or 321 BC) From Sinope, son of the banker Hicesias. Known as the founder of Cynicism. Exiled from his own city, for making counterfeit coin with his father, he lived then in Athens and Corinth a 'dog-like' existence, relying on the minimum of possessions, begging for food or living off the land, training in physical endurance, performing natural functions in public and attacking all forms of convention with witty rhetoric.

Diomedes Son of Tydeus. A major hero in the *Iliad*.

Diomedes the Thracian Son of Ares and Cyrene, king of the Thracians, famous in myth for his team of man-eating mares, the capture of which was Heracles' eighth labour. In some versions, Diomedes is fed to his own horses.

Dion (*c*. 408–353 BC) Son of Hipparinus and son-in-law of Dionysius I of Syracuse. A follower of Plato, he was banished by Dionysius II, returned at the head of an army in 357 and eventually captured Syracuse in 355, but was assassinated after losing support for a plan to instigate a political system inspired by Plato's doctrines.

Dionysia A festival of Dionysus at Athens, in March, the occasion for competitions in dithyramb, tragedy, comedy and satyr-play.

Dionysius I (*c.* 430–367 BC) Tyrant of Syracuse. Also a tragic dramatist, whose play the *Ransom of Hector* won the prize at the Athenian Lenaea in 367.

Dionysius II Eldest son of Dionysius I. Tyrant of Syracuse (367–357 BC) before retiring into private life at Corinth. An enthusiastic convert to philosophy, he entertained a number of leading practitioners at his court, including Plato and Aeschines the Socratic.

Dionysius the Renegade (*c.* 330–250 BC) A philosopher. Originally a pupil of Zeno, he switched from Stoicism to the Cyrenaic school of Aristippus, allegedly after a bout of ophthalmia.

Dionysus Son of Zeus and Semele, god of wine, but also associated with ritual madness, masked impersonation and the theatre (see DIONYSIA). Sometimes known under the cult name 'Bacchus'. Dionysiac Mysteries also connect the god with the promise of happiness in the afterlife.

Dioscuri (Literally 'Sons of Zeus') Castor and Polydeuces (Pollux), brothers of Helen. Worshipped as divinities in various centres, especially Sparta and Athens, they were believed in particular to bring help to those in peril on the sea, manifesting themselves as 'St Elmo's fire'.

Diotima Fictional or actual priestess of Mantinea (*c.* 440 BC), from whom Socrates in Plato's *Symposium* asserts that he learnt his understanding of love.

Dipylon Gate A double gateway in the city wall of Athens at the north-west corner, leading from the Ceramicus to the cemetery of the same name outside.

Dracon (*fl. c.* 621 BC) The first Athenian lawgiver, noted for the harshness of his penalties.

Dread Goddesses The Eumenides ('Kindly ones'), who had a shrine beneath the Areopagus rock and were associated with the Areopagus court which sat there.

Echo A nymph, vainly loved by Pan, who in revenge maddened shepherds to tear her to pieces.

Egypt Large region of north Africa, governed by Macedonians from its conquest by Alexander in 332 BC, it was annexed by Rome as a province in 30 BC and was an important source of grain. It remained a province under the Byzantine empire until taken over by the Arabs in AD 642.

Elaphebolion A month of the Athenian calendar, covering roughly the second half of March and the first half of April.

Eleusinian Mysteries A pair of annual festivals (the 'Lesser' in spring and the 'Greater' in early autumn) to Demeter and her daughter Kore (or Persephone), connected with the myth of Demeter's recovery of her daughter from Hades. After purification rituals, initiates (no one was debarred) processed from Athens and at Eleusis were eventually admitted to the Telesterion ('Mystery Building'), where things were 'done, said and shown'. In contrast with other Greek ritual practices, the Mysteries promised personal salvation through initiation.

Eleusis An Attic deme (local administrative district), west of the city of Athens, most famous for the Eleusinian Mysteries held there.

Eliaea A meeting of Athenian citizens in their capacity as jurors, later the name given to all the courts or to any individual one, as well as to a particular court building.

Elis A region in the north-western Peloponnese, where the Olympic Games were held (see OLYMPIA).

Elysian Fields A paradise where the famous or the good live on after death (see also ISLE(S) OF THE BLEST).

Empedocles (c. 492–c. 432 BC) From Acragas in Sicily, a philosopher, who was reputed to have died after throwing himself into the crater of Mt. Etna to confirm the belief that he was a god (one of his bronze slippers was thrown back up, disclosing how he had perished) (Diogenes Laertius, *Lives of the Philosophers* 8.69).

Endymion A good-looking boy with whom the moon-goddess Selene fell in love.

Epeius In the *Iliad* (23.664–99) he wins the boxing contest at the funeral games for Patroclus, but is less successful in the weight-throwing (23.839–40).

Ephesus A city on the west coast of Asia Minor.

Epictetus (mid first–mid second century AD) From Hierapolis in Phrygia, a Stoic philosopher, whose oral teachings were published as *Discourses* by Arrian, who had attended his lectures and noted down what he said.

Epicurus (341–270 BC) Born of Athenian parents in Samos, he moved to Athens in around 306 and established his school there in 'the Garden'. His philosophical goal was to achieve a happy life (often over-simplified as the pursuit of pleasure), his physical theories adopted the atomism of Democritus and he believed that though the gods exist they have no interest in the world and live a life of untrammelled happiness.

Epimenides A Cretan holy-man (seventh or sixth century BC), reputed to have lived to a great age and once to have fallen asleep only to awake fifty-seven years later.

Epimetheus ('Afterthought') Son of Iapetus and brother of Prometheus. Implicated in the woes brought to men by Pandora, the first woman, sent as a gift to him by Zeus to punish both Prometheus (whom Zeus knew to be too canny to accept such a 'gift' himself) and the human race (see PANDORA, PROMETHEUS).

Erechtheus A mythical king of Athens, regarded along with Cecrops as ancestor of all Athenians, he was also the eponymous hero of the Erechtheus tribe. He was worshipped on the acropolis (at the Erechtheum), where he was identified with Poseidon.

Etesian winds Seasonal winds blowing from the north to north-east during a forty-day period beginning in mid-July.

Ethiopia A name applied to the region of Africa south of Egypt. In Homer, it is a land favoured by the gods because of its inhabitants' generosity of sacrifice.

Etna (Mt.) An active volcano, situated on the east coast of Sicily.

Eucleides Athenian archon in 403/2 BC, the year the democracy was re-established after the rule of the Thirty Tyrants with a general amnesty for oligarchs.

Eumolpus the Thracian Mythical ancestor of the Eumolpidae clan of Eleusis and founder of the Eleusinian Mysteries. In some versions he inherited a Thracian kingdom, and died when recalled to fight a war for Eleusis against Erechtheus of Athens.

Eunomus of Locri A harp-player from Locri in southern Italy.

Euphorbus A Trojan. In the *Iliad*, he wounds Patroclus and is then killed by Menelaus. Pythagoras claimed to have been him in a previous life.

Euphranor (*fl. c.* 370–330 BC) Greek sculptor and painter, he also wrote on proportion and colours. Among his painted subjects were the Twelve Gods.

Euphrates The longest river in western Asia. Originating in Armenia, it flows south-west to the Taurus mountains, then south-east into Babylonia.

Eupolis (d. 411 BC?) A poet of the Old Comedy, a contemporary and rival of Aristophanes.

Euripides (*c.* 480–407/6 BC) Tragic playwright, writer of about ninety plays, of which eighteen survive (one of them a satyr-play).

Evagoras (*c.* 435–374 BC) King of Salamis in Cyprus.

Exadius A Lapith, mentioned by Nestor in the *Iliad* (1.264) as one of the great men of the past known to him.

Favorinus (*c.* AD 85–155) A sophist and philosopher from Arles, the teacher of Herodes Atticus, and thought in antiquity to have been a eunuch. He wrote miscellanies, declamations and works on philosophy (he claimed to be a Sceptic in the tradition of the old Academy).

Furies The Erinyes, originally chthonian deities who exact retribution for crimes committed within the family and implement a mother's or father's curse. Later, generalized into avenging spirits, who punish crime in the afterlife (see also TISIPHONE).

Galatea ('Milky') A sea-nymph, daughter of Nereus. Polyphemus the Cyclops attempts to woo her in Theocritus, *Idyll* 11 by telling her how much cheese and milk he has.

Galatia A region in central Asia Minor. After 25 BC, the name of a Roman province.

Gaul A region stretching from the Alps and the Pyrenees to the English Channel and the Rhine, conquered for Rome by Julius Caesar in the first century BC and divided into four provinces by Augustus at the end of the century.

Geryon A three-headed, three-bodied giant. Heracles' tenth labour was to steal his cattle, according to Apollodorus (*The Library* 2.5.10).

Getae A Thracian tribe, living on the lower Danube.

Giants The sons of Earth, monsters who did battle with the Olympian gods under Zeus and were defeated.

Glaucus of Carystus A famous boxer, winner of the contest at Olympia (*c.* 520 BC), Delphi (twice) and at the Nemean and the Isthmian Games (eight times each).

Gobares Son of Oxyartas. A Persian name, probably a figure invented by Lucian for *The Journey down to Hades* 6, rather than a reference to a real person killed in a contemporary war.

Gorgon One of three monstrous sisters (see MEDUSA) whose appearance turned men to stone.

Graces The Charites, daughters of Zeus, sometimes three in number and named Aglaea ('Radiance'), Euphrosyne ('Happiness') and Thalia ('Flourishing'). They personify grace, beauty and charm and are associated with Aphrodite, enjoying song, dance and poetry.

Gyarus A small island in the Cyclades, used during the Roman imperial period as a place of exile.

Gyges King of Lydia (*c.* 680–645 BC), he initiated the recovery of gold from the river Pactolus. His wealth enabled him to send extravagant offerings to Delphi and became proverbial (see CROESUS). Legend attached to an ancestor of the same name possession of a gold ring which made the bearer invisible (Plato, *Republic* 359dff.).

Gythium A coastal city in Laconia.

Hades The Underworld, the gloomy realm of Hades (Pluto), the god of the same name, son of Cronus and Rhea, brother of Zeus and Poseidon, where the dead are conveyed (see CHARON). The 'cap of Hades' made its wearer invisible. See also PLUTO.

Haloa An Attic festival dedicated to Demeter and Dionysus, mainly celebrated by women, in the month of Poseideon (December/ January).

Halys (river) The longest river in Asia Minor.

Hannibal (247–183 or 182 BC) General from Carthage, famous for his invasion of Italy with elephants, his defeat of the Romans at the Trebbia in 218, Lake Trasimene in 217 and Cannae in 216 and his defeat by Scipio Africanus at Zama in north Africa in 202.

Harmodius Athenian tyrannicide (see ARISTOGITON).

Harpies ('Grabbers') Mythical winged women (two or three in number) who are blamed for mysterious deaths or disappearances. In the story of the Argonauts, they continually snatch away or defile the food of the Thracian king Phineus, before being put to flight by the sons of Boreas.

Hecabe (or **Hecuba**) Wife of Priam, king of Troy, featured briefly in the *Iliad*, but a central figure in Euripides' *Hecabe* and *Trojan Women*.

Hecate A divinity associated by the fifth century BC with magic, often worshipped at crossroads. 'Hecate's dinner' was an offering of bread, eggs, cheese and dog-meat put out at crossroads every month at new moon. Mystery cults to Hecate existed in various places (e.g. Aegina).

Hector Eldest son of Priam and Hecabe. In the *Iliad*, the mainstay of Troy's defence. After single combat with Ajax, an assault on the Greek camp and the killing of Patroclus, he is killed in revenge by Achilles, and his body, after being abused by Achilles, is ransomed to Priam.

Helen Daughter of Zeus and Leda, wife of Menelaus, her abduction by Paris was the cause of the Trojan War. Theseus is said to have abducted her with the help of his friend Pirithous before she was of marriageable age. The two cast lots for her and Theseus won (Plutarch, *Theseus* 31). The poet Stesichorus wrote a poem blaming Helen for her behaviour, was punished with blindness (for insulting a goddess) and received his sight back after writing a palinode (a poetic retraction).

Helicon A mountain in Boeotia sacred to the Muses, often used as a metaphor for the gifts endowed by them.

Heliots The people who inhabit the sun (*helios*) in *True Histories* 1.

Hephaestion (d. 324 BC) A Macedonian noble, close friend of Alexander the Great, whose death was mourned deeply by him. The oracle of Ammon decreed that honours should be paid to him as a hero, and temples were begun in Alexandria and on Pharos.

Hephaestus God of fire, of blacksmiths and artisans, the son of Hera and husband of Aphrodite. He was lame from birth.

Hera Daughter of Cronus and wife of Zeus, a goddess closely associated with marriage.

Heraclea A city on the south coast of the Black (Euxine) Sea.

Heracles Son of Zeus and Alcmene, the greatest of the heroes, who became a god after his death. Harassed by Hera, he was bound in vassalage to Eurystheus, king of Argos, at whose command he performed his (usually twelve) labours (see CERBERUS, DIOMEDES THE THRACIAN, GERYON). His might in combat, both armed and unarmed, was unbeatable, and he is sometimes said to have founded the Olympic Games (see OLYMPIA). He was a favourite figure of cult for men and consequently appears often in male oaths ('By Heracles!'). His madness (inflicted by Hera) and his death (by a 'love-potion' administered by his wife Deianira) are the subjects of tragedies by Euripides and Sophocles.

Heraclitus (*fl. c.* 500 BC) A philosopher whose fundamental doctrine was that everything is in flux, in ancient satire he is portrayed as the sage who finds the vagaries of human behaviour so hard to bear that he weeps to see them (Juvenal, *Satires* 10.28–32).

Herm A four-cornered pillar of marble or bronze, fronted by an erect phallus and topped by a bust, located at various key points (at crossroads, at doorways, in sanctuaries, etc.) and considered as a protector, representing Hermes.

Hermaphroditus Half-male and half-female child of Hermes and Aphrodite, depicted with breasts but male genitals.

Hermes Son of Zeus and the nymph Maia, father of Pan and Hermaphroditus, in myth primarily a messenger of Zeus. He is a guide, most particularly of the dead to Hades. He presides over prosperity, is the god of trade and is often appealed to as the god of luck or of gain. Skilled from birth in trickery, he is patron of thieves. As a persuasive mediator, he is also the protector of orators. He is a great inventor (e.g. of the lyre) and at times a musician. He is the god of athletes. He is the slayer of Argos.

Herminus (*fl.* second century AD) A Peripatetic philosopher and the teacher of Alexander of Aphrodisias, who wrote a commentary on Aristotle's *Categories*.

Hermotimus Legendary early philosopher, whose soul was said to have passed to him from Euphorbus, then after his death to Pyrrhus (a fisherman) and then to Pythagoras.

Herodes Atticus (*c.* AD 101–177) Lucius Vibullius Hipparchus Tiberius Claudius Atticus Herodes, consul at Rome in 143, from Athens, sophist and public benefactor, he endowed many buildings at Athens and elsewhere. His writings (lectures and diaries) do not survive, but Philostratus gave an account of him in his *Lives of the Sophists*.

Herodotus (*c.* 480–*c.* 420 BC) From Halicarnassus, his *Histories*, beginning with the fall of Lydia in 546 BC and centred on the conflict between Persia and the Greeks in the early fifth century (see MARATHON), are the first extended historical narrative in Greek. His account often stops to give ethnographic information or anecdotes. Thucydides began the assessment of him as a mere storyteller, and in later antiquity he was sometimes regarded as a liar (see especially Plutarch's *On the Malice of Herodotus*).

Hesiod (*fl. c.* 700 BC) From Ascra in Boeotia, a poet whose surviving works are the *Theogony* (an account of the genealogy of the gods) and *Works and Days*, which gives moral advice and practical instruction, and ends with a list of auspicious and inauspicious days. Among other works attributed to him in antiquity are *The Shield* and *The Catalogue of Women*. There was a legend that he and Homer had been involved in a poetry contest won by Hesiod.

Himera A city on the north coast of Sicily.

Hippocrates (*fl.* fifth century BC) From Cos, the most famous doctor of antiquity, under whose name a large body of medical writing was preserved.

Hippolyta An Amazon, in some versions wife of Theseus and mother of Hippolytus.

Hippolytus Son of Theseus and an Amazon (in some versions Hippolyta), he rejects the worship of Aphrodite and cultivates only Artemis. His stepmother Phaedra falls in love with him and when rejected kills herself, leaving a letter denouncing Hippolytus, which leads to his death. He was worshipped at Troezen as a hero alongside Aphrodite. Dramatic treatments survive by Euripides and Seneca.

Hipponicus (d. 424 BC) An Athenian general, from one of the richest families in Athens, father of Callias.

Homer (eighth century BC?) Regarded in antiquity as the composer of the two great epics, the *Iliad* (set during the Trojan War and telling the story of Achilles' wrath and its consequences) and the *Odyssey* (set ten years after the end of the Trojan War, relating the tale of Telemachus and the homecoming of Odysseus), as well as other poems. Various cities claimed him as their own, including Chios, Smyrna and Colophon. He was reputed to be blind.

Honoratus A Cynic philosopher known only from Lucian's *Demonax the Philosopher* 19.

Hyacinthus A beautiful young favourite of Apollo, killed accidentally by the god's discus. Worshipped as a hero at Amyclae near Sparta.

Hyades ('Rainers') A group of stars named from the fact that their rising (17 October) and setting (12 April) fall within the rainy season.

Hylas Son of Theiodamas the Dryopian, whom Heracles killed. He went along with Heracles on the voyage of the Argonauts, but disappeared when nymphs dragged him into the water where he had gone to fill a jar. Often regarded as Heracles' lover.

Hymen God of marriages.

Hymettus (Mt.) A mountain south-east of Athens.

Hyperbolus (d. 411 BC) Son of Antiphanes. Athenian politician often attacked in Old Comedy (see ARISTOPHANES, EUPOLIS), ostracized in 417, 416 or 415 and killed in Samos by oligarchs.

Hyperboreans Legendary race living in the far north, in a paradise visited in winter by Apollo.

Hyperides (389–322 BC) Athenian politician, who vocally opposed the growing power of Macedon and was murdered for it by the Macedonians after the collapse of Greek resistance. In antiquity, one of the canon of Attic Orators.

Iambulus (third century BC?) Writer of a lost travel story (preserved in outline in Diodorus Siculus, *Library of History* 2.55–60). The author relates his journey to an island of the Sun, the life of the remarkable people who live there, his expulsion and his return home via India.

Iberia The ancient name for (1) Spain and (2) the eastern part of Georgia.

Icarius Father of Penelope.

Icarus Son of Daedalus. During their escape from Crete on wings crafted by his father, he ignored injunctions not to fly too close to the sun. The wax holding the feathers together melted, and he plunged to his death into what became the Icarian Sea.

Idomeneus Son of Deucalion and grandson of Minos, in the *Iliad* the leader of the Cretans at Troy, and one of nine heroes who volunteer to engage in single combat with Hector.

Iliad See HOMER.

Ilissus A river running past the walls of Athens to the south-east.

Ilium Another name for Troy.

India In the early period, often confused with Ethiopia and like that region a land of fable, its geography and ethnography became better known when parts of the north-west came under Greek control after the conquests of Alexander the Great. Under the early Roman empire, trade was vigorous, some settlements were established on the west coast, and Sri Lanka was circumnavigated.

Ino See LEUCOTHEA, MELICERTES.

Ionia Coastal area of central-western Asia Minor colonized by Greeks some time after the collapse of Mycenaean civilization. Later, Athens claimed to be the mother-city (*metropolis*) of Ionia. The local dialect, Ionic, is related to Attic, and was the dialect first used for literary prose (see HERODOTUS, HIPPOCRATES). Several cities in Ionia (Chios, Colophon, Smyrna) claimed to be the birthplace of Homer. Certainly, later on Ionia was a centre for science and philosophy (e.g. Thales and Xenophanes).

Ionian Sea An alternative name for the Adriatic, the waters between the Balkan peninsula and Italy.

Iphigenia Daughter of Agamemnon and Clytemnestra, sacrificed to Artemis at Aulis to gain favourable winds for the expedition against Troy. In some versions, Iphigenia is substituted at the last moment by a hind. In Euripides' *Iphigenia in Tauris*, she becomes a priestess of Artemis among the Taurians (in the Tauric Chersonese, the Crimea), where she is forced to perform human sacrifice. When her brother Orestes arrives and is designated as a victim, she flees with him and the statue of Artemis to Brauron in Attica (where in historical times she received a hero-cult and was connected with the ritual of the *arkteia*, a rite of passage for young girls, held every four years).

Irus In the *Odyssey*, a beggar in Odysseus' house with whom the disguised Odysseus has a fight.

Isis Egyptian goddess of women, maternity and agricultural fertility.

Isle(s) of the Blest Mythical place where the privileged dead live a life of unending pleasure. Later identified with Madeira or the Canary Islands (see also ELYSIAN FIELDS).

Isocrates (436–338 BC) Athenian orator, pupil of Prodicus and Gorgias, he devised a training in rhetoric which greatly influenced his many pupils (among them the orators Hyperides and Isaeus). He did not participate in public debate, hampered as he was by physical frailness and a weak voice, but wrote speeches for others to use in court and political tracts which reflect a distaste for the radical democracy of Athens.

Isthmia The Isthmian Games, held at Corinth in honour of Poseidon, a pan-Hellenic festival celebrated biennially.

Isthmus The narrow neck of land joining northern Greece to the Peloponnese.

Italy Originally the Greek name given just to the 'toe', it came to be used of the whole peninsula by Greek writers from the second century BC.

Ithaca Island home of Odysseus, off the west coast of the Peloponnese.

Jason From Iolcus in Thessaly, son of Aeson and Alcimede, he was the leader of the Argonauts (see also MEDEA, PELIAS).

Kollytos A city deme (local administrative area) of Athens.

Labdacids The family of Labdacus, son of Polydorus, son of Cadmus, kings of Thebes. His son Laius was the husband of Jocasta and the father of Oedipus, who in ignorance married his own mother and killed his own father. Oedipus' sons, Eteocles and Polynices, fought and killed each other for the kingship, while his daughter Antigone lost her life after defying a decree by her uncle, Creon, not to bury Polynices' corpse.

Laconian Sea The gulf between Cape Taenarum and Cape Malea on the coast of Laconia in the south-east of the Peloponnese.

Lais A famous courtesan from Corinth, who numbered among her lovers Diogenes the Cynic and Aristippus.

Lazi A Scythian people living in Colchis on the Black (Euxine) Sea.

Lemnian women Women from Lemnos, reputed in myth to have killed their husbands (see also DANAIDS).

Lemnos An island in the north Aegean.

Lenaea A festival of Dionysus at Athens, in January/February, at which competitions for tragedy and comedy were held.

Lesbos Large island off the north-west coast of Asia Minor.

Lethe ('Forgetfulness') The dead drink the water of Lethe when they enter Hades and thus forget all that they were in their lives on earth.

Leto A female Titan, mother of Apollo and Artemis. She was responsible for the death of Niobe's children. Also the name of the wife of Evagoras, king of Salamis in Cyprus.

Leucothea A goddess, also known as Ino, who saves Odysseus from drowning when he is shipwrecked in the *Odyssey* (Book 5).

Locri A Greek colony in southern Italy.

Locris A region in central Greece.

Lyceum A sanctuary of Apollo Lyceius, outside the city walls of Athens to the east, the location of the school of Aristotle and the Peripatetics (see ARISTOTLE).

Lycia A region in south-west Asia Minor.

Lycian Sea The sea which skirts Lycia.

Lycoreus A village above Delphi on the slopes of Mt. Parnassus, where Deucalion's chest finally landed after the flood.

Lycurgus (*c.* 390–*c.* 325/4 BC) Athenian politician, opponent of Macedon, one of the canon of Attic Orators. He played an important role in controlling the finances of Athens after the battle of Chaeronea (338 BC).

Lycurgus the Spartan The lawgiver to whom were attributed Sparta's laws and institutions.

Lydia A wealthy region in western Asia Minor, the kingdom of Croesus before its incorporation into the Persian empire. Later conquered by Alexander, it came under first Seleucid, then Attalid control, until taken over by Rome in 133 BC.

Lynceus Son of Aphareus and Arene, a member of the expeditions against the Calydonian boar and with the *Argo*, he had proverbially sharp eyesight, which amounted to X-ray vision.

Macedon(ia) A region to the north-east of mainland Greece, which became the centre of an empire under first Philip II, then Alexander the Great and his successors.

Machlyans The name of the tribe inhabiting Machlyene.

Machlyene A territory which seems entirely fictional, located somewhere to the north-east of Scythia.

Maeotis The Greek name for the Sea of Azov.

Malea The most southerly promontory on the eastern side of the Peloponnese.

Mantinea A city in eastern Arcadia in the Peloponnese.

Marathon A deme (local administrative district) on the north-east coast of Attica, site of the battle of 490 BC, in which the Athenians fought off a Persian naval attack led by Datis.

Massilia A Greek colony founded in southern France (modern Marseilles) around 600 BC.

Medea Daughter of Aeetes, king of Colchis, she used magic and fratricide to assist Jason in capturing the Golden Fleece. She fled with Jason to Corinth. There, according to Euripides in *Medea*, when Jason decides to marry the king's daughter, she not only conspires to kill her, but also murders her own children to avenge Jason's treachery.

Medes Inhabitants of Media.

Media The country of the Medes, a mountainous region south-west of the Caspian Sea, conquered by Cyrus, king of Persia, in 549 BC.

Medusa The name of the Gorgon whose head Perseus cut off with the help of Athena and Hermes while she slept. Even after death, the head still turned to stone anyone who looked at it.

Megara A city located between Athens and Corinth.

Melampus A mythical seer, ancestor of Greece's most famous family of seers, the Melampodids. When he was a child, snakes cleaned out his ears, with the result that he could understand the language of birds (and hence tell the future).

Meletus Son of Meletus, of the deme Pitthos, he was the titular accuser of Socrates at his trial in 399 BC.

Melicertes Son of Ino (see LEUCOTHEA), who threw him, as well as herself, into the sea while being pursued by her husband Athamas.

His body was brought to shore at the Isthmus by a dolphin. The Isthmia (Isthmian Games) were instituted in his honour.

Melpomene The Muse of tragedy.

Memnon A mythical king of Ethiopia, who fought at Troy and was killed by Achilles. The statue of Memnon was one of two gigantic statues of Amenophis (Amenhotep) III at Thebes in Egypt, known as 'the Colossi of Memnon'. It gave out a sound at dawn, until the earthquake damage which caused the phenomenon was repaired by the emperor Septimius Severus in the early third century AD.

Memphis An important city in Egypt.

Menelaus King of Sparta, younger brother of Agamemnon and husband of Helen, whose abduction by Paris caused the Trojan War. In *Iliad* 4.141ff., he is wounded by an arrow fired by the Trojan Pandarus. His house is visited by Telemachus in the *Odyssey*.

Menippus (first half of the third century BC?) A Cynic, he was widely regarded in later antiquity as the originator of a form of satire which mixes prose and verse (Menippean satire) and of the idea of the serio-comic (i.e. the mixture of moralism and humour). His appearance as a character in Lucian does not guarantee that his works are being in any way closely imitated.

Meriones In the *Iliad*, son of Molus, 'squire' of Idomeneus and a subordinate leader of the Cretan contingent at Troy.

Mesopotamia The area now covered by northern Iraq.

Midas Mythical king of Phrygia, who judged a musical contest between Apollo and Pan, gave the prize to Pan and was rewarded by Apollo with the ears of an ass. In his quest for an understanding of the secrets of life, he captured Silenus, leader of the satyrs, and was told that it was best not to be born, or, if born, to die as soon as possible. When he returned Silenus safely, Dionysus granted him a wish. He chose the famous 'golden touch', but thought better of it when his food and drink turned to gold and left him starving.

Miletus A city of Ionia.

Milon (late sixth century BC) From Croton, an athlete victorious six times each at the Olympic and Pythian Games.

Miltiades (*fl.* 524 BC) Athenian noble, archon in 524/3 and a general in 490/89 (the year of Marathon). Sent to take back control of the Thracian Chersonese (Gallipoli peninsula) in 524, he later submitted to Persia. Involved in the Ionian Revolt in the early 490s, he eventually had to flee to Athens, where he was arraigned for having been a tyrant in the Chersonese (he was acquitted). After Marathon, he was again tried, this time after his failure to take Paros, and fined fifty talents (he died before he could pay, but his son settled the debt).

Minos Son of Zeus and Europa, legendary king of Crete. With his brother Rhadamanthys, he gave mankind its first laws and acted as a judge both on earth and in Hades. Among his daughters were Ariadne and Phaedra, with both of whom, in turn, Theseus consorted, after killing their half-brother, the monstrous Minotaur hidden in the labyrinth Daedalus had constructed for Minos.

Minotaur The half-bull, half-human son of Minos' wife, Pasiphae, and the bull Poseidon sent to Minos for sacrifice in answer to a prayer. In punishment for Minos' retention of the bull for himself, Poseidon made Pasiphae fall in love with the bull, a passion consummated with the help of Daedalus' inventiveness.

Mithridates The name of six kings of Pontus, one of the Hellenistic kingdoms carved out by the successors of Alexander the Great.

Mitraean mountains A range located to the north-east of Scythia, from which Machlyene is reached. It does not appear on maps of the ancient world and, like Machlyene, is probably a fiction of Lucian's or someone else.

Momus ('Blame') Son of Night. A god who personifies mockery and criticism, he is a favourite figure in Lucian (e.g. *Zeus Rants*).

Muia ('Fly') Said to have been the name of a daughter of Pythagoras and of the wife of Milon of Croton.

Muses Goddesses connected with the inspiration towards creativity, especially in poets, but also in other artists. Nine in number, they are most usually named as Calliope, Clio, Erato, Euterpe, Melpomene, Poly(hy)mnia, Terpsichore, Thalia and Urania, and each presides over a different area (see individual entries for those Lucian mentions).

Mycenae A citadel in the Peloponnese which was in legend the home of the family of Atreus, including Agamemnon and his son Orestes, and fabulously wealthy.

Myrrhinous A deme (local administrative district) in the south-east of Attica.

Mysteries See DIONYSUS, ELEUSINIAN MYSTERIES, HECATE.

Narcissus A beautiful young man from Thespiae in Boeotia, son of the river Cephissus and a nymph named Liriope. He did not fall in love until he saw his own reflection in water. He pined away and was turned into the eponymous flower.

Nauplius A navigator for the Argonauts, he caused the Greek fleet to be wrecked on the way back from Troy by lighting false beacons on Euboea in revenge for the death of his son Palamedes.

Nausicaa The daughter of Alcinous and Arete, in the *Odyssey* she is the first to encounter Odysseus after his arrival on the island of Scheria (Book 6).

Neleus (fourth century BC) A pupil of Aristotle and Theophrastus (Aristotle's successor as head of the Lyceum), and inheritor of his library. See ARISTOXENUS.

Nemea A region in the Peloponnese, the site of a pan-Hellenic sanctuary to Zeus and the Nemean Games held in his honour.

Nemesis ('Retribution') A daughter of Night. A goddess who punishes wrongdoing or excess (of riches, pride, etc.). Cults of Nemesis were widespread.

Nereids The daughters of Nereus, nymphs of the calm sea.

Nereus A sea-god of the 'old man of the sea' type (like Proteus), father of the Nereids by Doris, a daughter of Oceanus.

Nestor Son of Neleus and Chloris, king of Pylos, the oldest of the Greek leaders at Troy, a major character in the *Iliad* with a cameo role in the *Odyssey*. He is depicted as a wise counsellor, a fine (if prolix) speaker, fond of stories about the distant past, a great warrior and a close confidant and table-companion of Agamemnon.

Nicias (*c*. 470–413 BC) Athenian politician, a general on the ill-fated Sicilian expedition of 415. He was captured and executed after his troops were defeated at the river Assinarus.

Nile The river of Egypt. Speculation about its source was rife in antiquity.

Niobe Daughter of Tantalus, wife of Amphion, she boasted that she was better than Leto, because she had more children. Leto asked her own children, Artemis and Apollo, to avenge the insult and they killed all Niobe's offspring. Niobe was inconsolable and would not eat. Finally, however, she relented and took food, and later was turned into a rock on Mt. Sipylus.

Nireus The handsomest of the warriors at Troy after Achilles. This unwarlike individual came to stand for masculine beauty.

Numa Numa Pompilius, legendary second king of Rome (dated traditionally 715–673 BC), regarded in antiquity as a lawgiver and credited with the creation of the framework for Roman public religion.

Numidia A region in north Africa south and west of Carthage, later a Roman province.

Odrysians A Thracian tribe, who in the fifth and fourth centuries BC held sway over a large territory in the north-eastern Aegean.

Odysseus King of Ithaca, son of Laertes, husband of Penelope, father of Telemachus by Penelope and of Telegonus by Circe. He is a major figure in the *Iliad*, where he is a brilliant adviser (for example, persuading the leaders to give their troops breakfast before battle in Book 19), a fine speaker (he makes short shrift of the complaints of Thersites in Book 2), a brave warrior and a cunning wrestler (he ties the contest with Ajax in Book 23). In the *Odyssey*, he is the central figure, famed for his intelligence, but none the less held captive for seven years by Calypso. He tells amazing stories to the Phaeacians (Books 9–12), including that of his encounter with the Sirens and his visit to Hades, before being transported asleep back to Ithaca on one of their magic ships. Outside Homer, he is presented less well, for example as having conspired with Diomedes to bring about the death of Palamedes in revenge for his having exposed as a pretence the madness Odysseus feigned to try to dodge the Trojan War draft.

Odyssey See HOMER, ODYSSEUS.

Oenoe A deme (local administrative district) in the far north-west of Attica.

Ogygia Island home of Calypso.

Olympia Pan-Hellenic sanctuary of Zeus, located beside the river Alpheus in Elis, the site of the four-yearly Olympic Games. Contests included wrestling, boxing, *pankration*, foot-races and chariot-races. The list of victors begins in 776 BC.

Orestes Son of Agamemnon, exiled from Argos for the killing of his mother Clytemnestra in revenge for her murder of his father. Several versions of his story are told in tragedy, including that of his adventures in Tauris (see IPHIGENIA). He is often paired with a close friend named Pylades.

Orion A mighty hunter, eventually transformed into a constellation.

Orpheus Son of Apollo and a Muse, a lyre-player and singer so powerful that he could move inanimate objects (see also AMPHION).

Pacate A girl from Larissa in Thessaly, first love of Alexander the Great, painted by Apelles.

Paeania A deme (local administrative district) in the middle of Attica.

Painted Stoa Situated in the north-east part of the Agora at Athens, the *Stoa Poikile* was a roofed colonnade, its back wall decorated with panel paintings with various mythological and historical scenes by famous painters (see POLYGNOTUS). It was much used by Zeno, and from it his philosophical school (the Stoics) was named.

Palamedes Son of Nauplius and Clymene. Odysseus conspired to bring about his death by forging a letter from Priam promising him a certain sum of gold to betray the Greeks and then hiding the same sum in Palamedes' tent. Agamemnon read the letter and condemned Palamedes to be stoned. Traditionally clever, he is said to have invented some letters of the Greek alphabet, and the games of draughts and dice.

Palestine The coastal region south of Phoenicia, in Roman times in the province of Judaea.

Pamphylia A region on the south coast of Asia Minor.

Pamphylian Sea The sea off the coast of Pamphylia.

Pan Son of Hermes, a shepherd god from Arcadia, half-man and half-goat, who received a cult in Athens after the help he was thought to have given at the battle of Marathon.

Panathenaea A festival of Athena held every year in Hekatombaion (July/August). At the Great Panathenaea, held every four years, a new embroidered robe was presented to Athena and athletic and musical contests open to all Greeks were held.

Pandion A mythical king of Athens, one of the eponymous heroes who gave their names to Athenian tribes. His daughters were Procne and Philomela.

Pandora In Hesiod (*Works and Days* 53–105), the first human female, created on Zeus' command by Hephaestus to punish Prometheus (for the theft of fire) and the whole human race he had aided (see also EPIMETHEUS).

Paphlagonia A region in the north of Asia Minor, on the coast of the Black (Euxine) Sea.

Paris Son of Priam and Hecabe, his abduction of Helen precipitated the Trojan War. An archer, he was responsible for the death of Achilles.

Parnassus (Mt.) A mountain in the Pindus range around Delphi.

Parnes (Mt.) The mountain range which separates Attica from Boeotia.

Parrhasius (*fl.* fifth century BC) A famous painter, son and pupil of the Ephesian Euenor, he became an Athenian.

Parthenium (Mt.) A mountain in the Peloponnese connected with Pan.

Parthians The name of a people inhabiting a region to the east of the Caspian Sea.

Patara An important city in Lycia.

Patroclus Son of Menoetius, in the *Iliad* he is Achilles' closest companion. He persuades Achilles to allow him to enter the battle in his place. When he is killed by Hector, Achilles kills Hector and then holds funeral games in Patroclus' honour.

Pelasgicum Either the ancient wall of the acropolis at Athens or an area below that wall.

Peleus Father of Achilles and husband of Thetis.

Pelias Son of Poseidon and Tyro, king of Iolcus. He sent Jason to get the Golden Fleece to dispose of him. When Jason returned successful, he and Medea persuaded Pelias' daughters to try the same magical rejuvenation process she had used with Jason's father Aeson (viz. cutting him up and boiling him in a cauldron). Pelias did not survive.

Pelopids The descendants of Pelops, son of Tantalus, father of Atreus and Thyestes, and grandfather of Agamemnon. The family was cursed because of Pelops' behaviour in winning his wife Hippodamia from her father Oenomaus. Atreus killed Thyestes' sons and fed them to his brother. Agamemnon was killed by his wife, Clytemnestra, and she in turn by their son Orestes.

Pelusium A city on the easternmost mouth of the Nile in Egypt.

Penelope Daughter of Icarius and wife of Odysseus, her patience and self-control in waiting for her husband's return from Troy for twenty years and her cunning in putting off the suitors' requests for a decision on remarriage are central features of her characterization in the *Odyssey*.

Perdiccas (d. 321 BC) Macedonian noble who rose to the rank of chiliarch under Alexander the Great.

Peregrinus Proteus From Parium, a Cynic philosopher and one-time Christian convert, Peregrinus publicly burned himself to death just after the Olympic Games of AD 165. Lucian's satirical biography, *The Passing of Peregrinus*, is one of the chief sources of 'information' about him.

Periander Tyrant of Corinth (*c.* 627–587 BC). For some the archetype of the oppressive ruler, but for others he was among the Seven Sages.

Pericles (*c.* 495–429 BC) Athenian politician, early on a leader in radical democratic reform of the Areopagus, he was later elected general every year from 443 until his death of the plague, and is credited with the policies which led to the outbreak of the Peloponnesian War in 431. Thucydides regarded him as a quasi-monarch, and comic poets dubbed him 'the Olympian'. He was associated with the sophistic movement through Anaxagoras, was the guardian of Alcibiades and had a long relationship with the Milesian Aspasia.

Peripatetics The philosophical school started by Aristotle in the Lyceum, and continued by Theophrastus.

Persephone Daughter of Demeter and Zeus, wife of Hades and queen of the Underworld. Often known as Kore ('Maiden daughter'), her abduction by Hades, her mother's search for her and the subsequent agreement that she live half the year above and half below the earth was the central myth underpinning the Eleusinian Mysteries.

Persia A region to the south of Media, it became the centre of a massive empire under Cyrus the Great, and unsuccessfully attempted to encompass Greece between 490 and 479 BC.

Phaeacians In the *Odyssey*, the inhabitants of Scheria, ruled by Alcinous, the audience bedazzled by Odysseus' wonder-packed tales of his wanderings (Books 9–12).

Phaedra Daughter of Minos, wife of Theseus, stepmother of Hippolytus, whose death she caused.

Phaethon Son of Helios (the Sun) and Clymene (hence an appropriate ruler of the sun and the Heliots in *True Histories* 1). When he learned his father's identity, he visited him and asked for a favour as proof. Granted leave to ask for anything, he requested the job of driving the chariot of the Sun for a day. The horses bolted and the world was close to conflagration when Zeus killed him with a thunderbolt. In some versions, the conflagration caused by Phaethon is, like Deucalion's flood, used to punish mortals for their sins.

Phalaris Tyrant of Acragas in Sicily (*c.* 570–*c.* 549 BC), he was for ancients the epitome of cruelty, said to have roasted his enemies alive in a bronze bull. Lucian's *Phalaris* orations spring (ironically) to his defence.

Phaon A mythical ferryman, sometimes said to be from Lesbos, given youth and beauty by Aphrodite and a byword for male comeliness.

Pharos An island off Alexandria in Egypt, linked by a causeway to the mainland by Alexander the Great, and site of a famous lighthouse built under Ptolemy II.

Phasis A Greek colony at the mouth of the river Phasis at the eastern end of the Black (Euxine) Sea.

Phidias (*fl. c.* 465–425 BC) Athenian sculptor, famous for his massive chryselephantine statues of Athena Parthenos at Athens and of Zeus at Olympia (Elis). What are thought to be copies of his Lemnian Athena and Amazon are extant.

Philip II (382–336 BC) King of Macedon, father of Alexander the Great. Author of an expansionist policy which led to Macedon's victory over the southern Greek alliance at Chaeronea (338 BC) and effective control over the Greek world by the time of his assassination. Athenian politicians had been bitterly divided about how to deal with him (see further AESCHINES, DEMADES, DEMOSTHENES, HYPERIDES, LYCURGUS, PHILOCRATES).

Philocrates (*fl.* 350 BC) Athenian politician, deeply involved in the Peace of Philocrates concluded between Athens and Philip II of Macedon in 346. He fled into exile in 343 after prosecution by Hyperides.

Philoctetes Son of Poeas, he was leader of a small contingent of ships to Troy, but was left behind on Lemnos suffering from a festering wound caused by a snake-bite. Eventually, the Greek leaders were forced to bring him to Troy, when it was learned from the Trojan seer Helenus that the city could not be captured without him.

Phineus A blind seer-king from Thrace, punished by the gods for revealing their plans by having his food stolen or defiled by the Harpies, until rescued by the Argonauts.

Phocion (402/1–318 BC) Athenian politician and general, nicknamed 'the good'. An opponent of Demosthenes, he was influential with the Macedonians and was executed in the democratic revolution of 318.

Phoenicia A region along the coast of the eastern Mediterranean, including the cities of Sidon and Tyre, populated by the Phoenicians, a sea-going people, deeply involved in trade.

Phrygia A large region in west-central Anatolia.

Phryne (fourth century BC) A courtesan famous for her exceptional beauty, sculpted by Praxiteles (possibly the model for his Aphrodite) and painted (as model for his *Aphrodite Rising*) by Apelles.

Pillars of Heracles The name of the promontories on the coasts of Spain and north Africa at the entrance to the Atlantic Ocean. The straits (of Gibraltar) were known to the Greeks as the straits of Heracles (*Herakleios porthmos*).

Pindar (518–after 446 BC) Lyric poet from the village of Cynoscephalae near Thebes in Boeotia, composer of hymns, paeans, dithyrambs and victory odes for winners at pan-Hellenic festivals, among many other types of poetic composition.

Pinebender See SINIS.

Piraeus The harbour of Athens, some 4–5 miles (7 km) south-west of the city, connected with it in the classical period by the Long Walls.

Pirithous King of the Lapiths (see CENTAURS). In Athenian myth an inseparable friend of Theseus, whom he helped to abduct Helen and who then accompanied him to Hades. In some versions, Pirithous did not return.

Pisidia A mountainous region in southern Asia Minor.

Pityocamptes See SINIS.

Plato (*c.* 429–347 BC) Athenian, follower of Socrates, he established the philosophical school called the Academy, is supposed to have visited the court of Dionysius II in Sicily, and wrote a large number of philosophical works, in dialogue form, often with Socrates as the main interlocutor. These include the *Apology* (an account of the trial of Socrates), the *Phaedo* (a discussion about the immortality of the soul set in Socrates' prison cell as he prepares to drink hemlock), the *Theaetetus* (on the nature of knowledge), the *Republic* (an exploration of the question of justice and the attempt to sketch an alternative society, in which, famously, women and children are held in common) and the *Laws* (another sketch of an ideal state). Plato's central doctrine involved the notion that there is a reality beyond what we see and that everything gains its character from these universals (the 'Theory of Forms' or 'Ideas').

Pleiades A constellation of seven stars in Taurus, called by Hesiod the daughters of Atlas and Pleione. They were used as a weather sign and navigational aid by the ancients. The sailing season was defined by their rising and setting (in the fifth century BC, 19 May and 8 November, respectively).

Pluto Brother of Zeus, husband of Persephone, the god who rules the Underworld, also known as Hades. His name was often etymologized in antiquity from *ploutos* ('wealth'), because of his wealth in corpses.

Pnyx A hill in Athens, south-west of the Agora, where the assembly (*ekklesia*) of democratic Athens held its meetings.

Polemon Athenian philosopher, head of the Academy 314/13–270/69 BC. Dissolute in his youth, he had been converted to philosophy by Xenocrates (d. 314/13), his predecessor as head. He dismissed theoretical philosophy and promoted the ideal of 'living according to nature' (a goal taken up by his pupil Zeno, founder of Stoicism). He taught that virtue brings happiness and that bodily and external goods do exist.

Pollux (or **Polydeuces**) One of the Dioscuri.

Polycrates Tyrant of Samos from *c.* 535 BC, his good fortune and wealth were legendary, but his life ended badly when, *c.* 522, he was lured to the Persian mainland by the satrap Oroetes and crucified.

Polydamas A famous athlete from Scotussa in Thessaly, winner of the Olympic *pankration* in 408 BC.

Polydeuces (1) (or **Pollux**) One of the Dioscuri, whose boxing skill was displayed at its best during the expedition of the Argonauts, when he beat Amycus, king of the Bebryces, who forced all comers to fight him on condition that the loser become the winner's chattel.

Polydeuces (2) Name of a young favourite of Herodes Atticus.

Polygnotus (*fl.* mid fifth century BC) From Thasos, a painter, he later became an Athenian citizen. He painted *The Sack of Troy*, presumably including a scene with Cassandra, in the hall of the Cnidians at Delphi, had a *Battle of Marathon* in the Painted Stoa and was famed for expressive faces and transparent drapery.

Polymnia (or **Polyhymnia**) The Muse of hymns and pantomime.

Polyxena A daughter of Priam and Hecabe, sacrificed on Achilles' tomb by his son Neoptolemus.

Pontus The part of northern Asia Minor which includes the south coast of the Black (Euxine) Sea between Paphlagonia and Colchis and reaches as far south as Cappadocia. The name of a Hellenistic kingdom.

Poseidon The god of the sea, earthquakes and horses, brother of Zeus and Hades (Pluto), father of the Cyclops Polyphemus.

Potidaea A Corinthian colony situated on the Pallene peninsula in Chalcidice. A member of the Delian League, an Athens-led league of Greek cities against the Persians, created in 478 BC, it revolted from Athens in 432 and was defeated in 430 BC.

Praxiteles (*fl. c.* 375–330 BC) Athenian sculptor, who worked in bronze and marble. His Cnidian Aphrodite, supposedly modelled on Phryne, was the first completely nude representation of the goddess, and it survives in many copies.

Priam King of Troy, father of Hector and Paris, husband of Hecabe.

Procne Daughter of Pandion and sister of Philomela. Philomela was raped by Tereus, Procne's husband. He cut out her tongue to silence her, but she communicated the story to Procne in a tapestry. Procne then killed their son Itys and served him to Tereus as a meal. Tereus pursued the women, but was changed into the hoopoe, while Philomela was metamorphosed into the swallow and Procne into the nightingale.

Prodicus (fifth century BC) A renowned sophist from Ceos who taught rhetoric and had an interest in the correct use of words. His writings are lost except for Xenophon's account of his 'Choice of Heracles' from *The Seasons* (*Memorabilia* 2.1.21f.).

Proetus King of Tiryns, husband of Anteia.

Prometheus ('Forethought') A Titan, son of Iapetus, brother of Epimetheus, he formed human beings out of clay, subsequently gave them fire, tricked the gods into accepting bones and fat as their share of sacrifice and was punished by Zeus by being chained to a rock in the Caucasus with a vulture pecking out his liver afresh each day. He was eventually freed in return for a piece of knowledge Zeus required to keep his position. He was worshipped at Athens along with Hephaestus by potters.

Protesilaus Leader of the Thessalians at Troy, the first of the Greeks to disembark and to die (his ship is at the centre of the fighting when the Trojans attack the Greek camp in the *Iliad*). His wife Laodamia grieved so much that the gods allowed her a three-hour visit from him, after which she killed herself.

Proteus A sea-god of the 'old man of the sea' type (see NEREUS), who can change shape at will and has knowledge of the future to impart to anyone who can trap him (as Menelaus does in the *Odyssey*).

Ptolemy Name given to monarchs of the (Macedonian) Ptolemaic dynasty in Egypt (see PTOLEMY DIONYSUS, PTOLEMY PHILOPATOR, PTOLEMY, SON OF LAGUS).

Ptolemy Dionysus (d. 51 BC) Ptolemy XII, *Neos Dionysus* ('The new Dionysus'), also known as *Auletes* ('Pipe-player'), king of Egypt from 80 BC.

Ptolemy Philopator (*c.* 244–205 BC) Ptolemy IV, king of Egypt from 221.

Ptolemy, son of Lagus (367/6–282 BC) Ptolemy I Soter ('Saviour'), king of Egypt from 305, a general of Alexander the Great, who got hold of Alexander's corpse, took Egypt and moved the capital from Memphis to Alexandria.

Pylades In myth, son of Strophius, from Phocis, he grew up with Orestes and is always represented as his trusty companion.

Pylos A city in the western Peloponnese, capital of Nestor in Homer.

Pyriphlegethon ('Burning with fire') The name of one of the rivers of Hades.

Pyrrhon (*c.* 365–*c.* 275 BC) The founder of Scepticism, he had been a painter before he turned to philosophy. He claimed that there are no grounds for making a judgement about the truth or falsehood of anything and that this lack of assertion leads to tranquillity.

Pythagoras (*fl.* sixth century BC) From Samos, he founded a philosophico-religious sect in Croton. He is associated with the doctrine of transmigration of souls (he was reported to have been able to recall his own past lives: see EUPHORBUS), with mathematics (cf. Pythagoras' theorem) and its relation to music (the ratios between length of string and basic harmonies), and with a lifestyle which involved a sort of vegetarianism (though beans were disallowed as much as meat) and periods of complete silence.

Python A Macedonian noble, contemporary with Demonax. Nothing is known about him outside *Demonax the Philosopher* 15.

Regilla Wife of Herodes Atticus.

Rhadamanthys Son of Zeus and Europa, from Crete, ruler and judge in the Elysian Fields. Also a judge of the dead in Hades with his brother Minos and Aeacus.

Rhea Wife of Cronus and mother of Zeus, associated with ecstatic rituals at *The Philosopher Nigrinus* 37 in a way that suggests identification with Cybele, the Phrygian Mother Goddess.

Rhodes A large island in the Aegean, off the coast of Asia Minor.

Roxana (d. *c.* 311 BC) Daughter of a Bactrian noble, she was captured by Alexander the Great and subsequently became his first wife. The wedding was the subject of a famous painting by Aëtion, described by Lucian in *Herodotus, or Aëtion*.

Rufinus the Cypriot A Peripatetic philosopher, known only from *Demonax the Philosopher* 54.

Sages See SEVEN SAGES.

Salmoneus Son of Aeolus and king of Salmone in Elis, pretended to be Zeus (with torches for lightning, and his chariot-wheels for thunder), until Zeus killed him with a thunderbolt. The father of Tyro.

Samos A city on the Aegean island of that name, off the coast of Asia Minor.

Sappho (*fl.* late seventh century BC) Lyric poetess from Lesbos, her poetry was collected in nine books in antiquity. Many of her surviving poems deal with love between women or girls.

Sarpedon In the *Iliad*, the son of Zeus and Laodamia, leader of the Lycian allies of Troy. Zeus wishes to save his son, but in the end he is killed by Patroclus, and Zeus makes a bloody rain fall in honour of his death.

Sauromatai (or **Sarmatae**) A nomadic tribe, related to the Scythians and living east of the river Tanais until *c.* 250 BC, when they began to move westwards and displace the Scythians.

Sceptics Philosophers holding no doctrine and suspending judgement on all issues. See ACADEMICS, PYRRHON.

Scheria In the *Odyssey*, the island of the Phaeacians, ruled by Alcinous, where Odysseus lands (in Book 6) after being shipwrecked on his way from Calypso's island, Ogygia, and from where he is magically conveyed home to Ithaca, asleep.

Sciron A brigand from Megara killed by Theseus on his journey to claim Athens as his inheritance.

Scythia The region from the Danube to the Don, Caucasus and Volga. The Scythians were a nomadic people and have ascribed to them by Greek writers many uncivilized practices, such as eating their dead and using arrows tipped with poison, though Anacharsis was sometimes listed among the Seven Sages.

Sea of Azov See MAEOTIS.

Selene The goddess of the moon (see ENDYMION).

Selenites The people who inhabit the moon (*selene*) in *True Histories* 1.

Seleucia A city north of Babylon, near Ctesiphon, founded by Seleucus I as his capital.

Seleucus (*c.* 358–281 BC) Seleucus I Nicator ('Victor'), a general of Alexander the Great and later founder of the Seleucid empire (stretching from Anatolia to Central Asia via Babylon).

Seven Sages The canonical list of the Seven Sages of Greece comprised Thales of Miletus, Bias of Priene, Cleobulus from Lindus on Rhodes, Pittacus of Mytilene, Solon from Athens, Chilon of Sparta, and Periander, tyrant of Corinth.

Sicily A large island off the toe of Italy, widely colonized by Greeks.

Sicyon A city north-west of Corinth with a rich coastal plain.

Sidon A major city in Phoenicia.

Simonides (b. *c.* 556 or 532 BC) A poet from Ceos, writer of choral lyric, elegies and epigrams.

Sindiani The inhabitants of Sindice, an area adjacent to the Cimmerian Bosporus on the southern shore of Maeotis and ruled by Bosporus (though the usual Greek for them is *Sindi* not *Sindiani*).

Sinis A son of Poseidon who attacked and killed travellers by tying them to two bent pine-trees and tearing them apart (hence he was known as 'Pityocamptes', 'Pinebender'). He was eventually killed by Theseus.

Sipylus (Mt.) A mountain near Smyrna in Asia Minor.

Sirens In the *Odyssey*, they live on an island near Scylla and Charybdis and charm sailors to their deaths with the beauty of their song. Odysseus, on the instructions of Circe, has himself tied to the mast and blocks his sailors' ears with wax so as to hear their song and survive. Classical writers regarded this story as an allegory of how to avoid temptation.

Sirius The Dog-star, the brightest star in the sky, situated in the constellation Canis Major (the Great Dog).

Sisyphus Son of Aeolus, founder of Corinth and a man of legendary cunning. He cheated death and was consequently punished in Hades. In the *Odyssey* (Book 11), Odysseus sees him there endlessly having to push a massive boulder up a hill, watch it roll back and begin again.

Smyrna A city in Ionia on the west coast of Asia Minor, one of the places which claimed Homer as a native.

Socrates (469–399 BC) Athenian, son of Sophroniscus and Phaenarete from the deme of Alopeke. He avoided involvement in politics, except to do his duty as a soldier (as at the battle of Delium in 424), and when the lot fell on him as a member of the Council of Five Hundred. Though his admirers claimed that he was never a teacher and did not take fees, he was surrounded by a group of young intellectuals, some of whom (Critias, Charmides and Alcibiades) later did damage to the democracy. His trial in 399 (see ANYTUS, MELETUS), in which he faced charges of impiety and corrupting the young, led to his execution by hemlock (both Plato and Xenophon wrote accounts of his defence speech). He wrote nothing, but was made immortal by his followers (notably Plato) as the protagonist of philosophical dialogues in which he challenges established views of knowledge and the virtues. He was noted especially for his trenchant interrogation of all and sundry, for his view that he knew that he knew nothing, for his irony and for his trust in an internal divine sign (his *daimonion*) which prevented him, he claimed, from doing certain things.

Solon (*fl.* 600 BC) Athenian politician, poet and lawgiver (see also DRACON), whose reforms radically altered the socio-political landscape of Athens by abolishing debt slavery and the feudal obligations which had caused it. Regarded as one of the Seven Sages, he was said to have met Croesus and Anacharsis.

Sophocles (*c.* 496–406 BC) Athenian tragic dramatist. Of his vast output, only seven plays are extant.

Sosandra A statue by Calamis, probably of Aphrodite.

Sostratus A strong man from Boeotia, subject of a lost biography by Lucian. See *Demonax the Philosopher* 1 with n. 1.

Sparta A city in the Peloponnese, the leader of the league that defeated Athens in the Peloponnesian War (431–404 BC). The Spartans were noted for their toughness in battle and for the discipline and training they received as children.

Steiria A deme (local administrative district) on the east coast of Attica, belonging to the Pandionis tribe.

Stentor In Homer, a man with a brazen voice, as loud as that of fifty men together.

Stesichorus (*fl. c.* 600–550 BC) A lyric poet, possibly from Himera in Sicily. He wrote extended works on mythical topics, including *Oresteia*, *Sack of Troy* and *Helen* (see HELEN for his blinding and his 'palinode').

Stoa, Stoicism, Stoics A philosophical school, based in the Painted Stoa, founded by Zeno and developed by Chrysippus. Its teaching covers the fields of logic (where they developed a philosophy of language and epistemology), physics (where they held that everything in the world is composed of objects and their interactions, but that all is in the hands of providence, though humans are still free to act and are morally responsible) and ethics (where they saw the goal of human life as virtue, which is sufficient for happiness).

Stratonice From 299/8 BC, second wife of Seleucus I.

Sunium The southernmost part of Attica, including the promontory (Cape Sunium), where there were temples to Poseidon and Athena.

Susa The winter capital of the Persian empire under Darius I, it later became a Greek city named Seleucia-on-the-Eulaeus under the Seleucids.

Syracuse A Greek city on the east coast of Sicily, the focus of the Athenian expedition of 415 BC (see NICIAS).

Syria A region on the eastern coast of the Mediterranean, in Lucian's day a Roman province, which included Lucian's native city, Samosata in Commagene.

Taenarum The central peninsula of the Peloponnese and its cape, traditionally the site of one of the entrances to Hades.

Tanais A river which flows into Maeotis, known today as the Don.

Tantalus Son of Zeus and father of Pelops and Niobe, he abused his privilege of dining with the gods (in one version by cooking Pelops as dinner for them) and was punished in Hades by perpetual hunger and thirst, though he is forever 'tantalized' by the water in which he stands and fruit hanging in front of him, which he cannot drink from or eat.

Taureas A professional trainer, owner of the *palaistra* where Plato's dialogue *Charmides* is set.

Telamon An Argonaut, son of Aeacus and father of Ajax (1) and Teucer.

Telamonian Ajax See AJAX (1).

Telegonus Son of Odysseus by Circe. In search of his father, he came to Ithaca and killed him unwittingly.

Telemachus Son of Odysseus and Penelope, in the *Odyssey* he leaves Ithaca in search of his father, visiting Nestor at Pylos and Menelaus in Sparta.

Telephus Son of Heracles and Auge, born a Greek, he became king of the Mysians (in north-west Asia Minor). In resisting the Greek expedition on its way to Troy, he was wounded by Achilles' spear. His wound was healed by rust from the same spear eight years later after an oracle stating that Telephus must go back to the man who wounded him to be healed. He then guided the Greeks to Troy. The story was the subject of a famous play by Euripides produced in 438 BC, but no longer extant.

Tellus An Athenian awarded the first prize for human happiness by Solon in Herodotus (*Histories* 1.30), because he had fine sons and many grandchildren, died fighting bravely for his city and was given a public funeral on the spot where he fell.

Ten Attic Orators See ATTIC ORATORS.

Terpsichore The Muse of lyric poetry and dancing (especially choral dancing).

Teucer Son of Telamon, half-brother and faithful companion of Ajax, in the *Iliad* a great archer. Exiled by Telamon, he later founded Salamis in Cyprus.

Theagenes A Cynic philosopher from Patrae, a disciple of Peregrinus Proteus, he died at Rome in the reign of Marcus Aurelius (AD 161–180), killed by his doctor according to Galen, though Lucian says he committed suicide for love of a Megarian courtesan, if he is the person mentioned in *The Journey down to Hades* 6 (see note on that passage).

Theano (1) The wife (or perhaps a pupil or daughter) of Pythagoras; (2) in the *Iliad*, wife of the Trojan counsellor Antenor, priestess of Athena, who was magnanimous enough to rear Pedaeus, a bastard son of her husband's, as her own child.

Thebes Chief city of Boeotia, the birthplace of Heracles, Tiresias and Pindar.

Themistocles (c. 524–c. 459 BC) Athenian politician, archon in 493/2, the architect of Athens' naval strength and general during the Persian invasion of 480, where he played a major role in the victory at Salamis. Ostracized in the 470s, he was suspected of collusion with the Persians and condemned to death by the Athenians *in absentia* in 465. He ended his life as governor of Magnesia under the Persian king Artaxerxes I.

Theodotas A mistake for Theodotus, a general of Ptolemy Philopator, who in 219 BC betrayed his king, occupied Ptolemais and Tyre and handed them over to the Seleucid king Antiochus III, who made him governor of the conquered domain.

Theoxenus A historian who wrote about the Scythian Anacharsis. Nothing is known about him beyond the reference in Lucian's *The Scythian* 8 (see note on that passage).

Thermopylae ('Hot Gates') The name of a narrow pass connecting northern to central and southern Greece.

Thersites In the *Iliad* (2.212ff.), the ugliest man who came to Troy, who attacks Agamemnon in the assembly and is silenced by a beating from Odysseus.

Theseus Son of Aegeus, or, in other versions, of the god Poseidon (whose gift of effective curses allows him to be responsible for the death of his son Hippolytus), a legendary king of Athens and a great hero. His exploits include the defeat of Sciron and the Minotaur, the kidnapping of Helen with the help of his close friend Pirithous and helping Pirithous in the attempt to bring back Persephone from the Underworld. His wives included Ariadne, her sister Phaedra and the Amazon Hippolyta or Antiope, the mother of Hippolytus. In legend, also the founder of Smyrna.

Thesmophoria A festival in honour of Demeter, celebrated by women
alone.

Thespis A pipe-player at the court of Ptolemy, son of Lagus. Nothing
is known about him apart from the reference in '*So You Think I'm
the Prometheus of the Literary World?*' 4.

Thessaly A region of northern Greece, in mythology home of the
Centaurs and Lapiths and famed in antiquity for its witches.

Thetis A sea-nymph, daughter of Nereus, wife of Peleus and mother
of Achilles.

Thirty Tyrants The name given to the thirty men chosen to run Athens
according to the terms of the peace imposed by Sparta upon victory
in the Peloponnesian War in 404 BC. Their misrule led to some 1,500
executions and an uprising, which succeeded in restoring democracy
in September 403 BC.

Thoas Mythical king of the Taurians, who hands over strangers to the
priestess of Artemis, Iphigenia, for sacrifice. In some versions, after
pursuing Orestes, Pylades, Iphigenia and the cult statue of Artemis
to the island of Sminthe, he is killed there by Orestes and Chryses
(Lucian's version in *Toxaris* 6 is slightly different).

Thrace A region between Greece and the Black (Euxine) Sea, traditionally peopled by warlike tribes, the home of Orpheus.

Thucydides (*c.* 460–*c.* 400 BC) The author of the *History of the
Peloponnesian War*, which covers the period to mid-winter 411 and
then breaks off in mid-narrative. He was general in 424, but was
exiled after failure in the campaign at Amphipolis against Brasidas.

Timocrates From Heraclea, a Stoic philosopher, one of the teachers of
Demonax.

Timon of Athens A misanthrope, probably legendary, first mentioned
by Aristophanes.

Tiresias A Theban seer, consulted in Hades by Odysseus in *Odyssey*
11. One story told that he had disturbed snakes copulating and had
been turned into a woman, then later had seen them again and been
turned back into a man.

Tisiphone The name of one of the Furies.

Titans Immortals of the generation before the Olympians, including
Cronus, Rhea, Leto and Prometheus, battled and defeated by the
Olympian gods under the command of Zeus.

Toxaris (1) A contemporary of Solon; (2) the interlocutor in the
dialogue *Toxaris*, set roughly in the contemporary world of Lucian.

Triton A merman, sometimes in human form, but more usually
portrayed as a human with a fish-tail.

Troy The city in north-western Asia Minor, also known as Ilium, captured and sacked after ten years of war by a Greek contingent under the leadership of Agamemnon, in pursuit of revenge against Paris for the abduction of his brother Menelaus' wife Helen.

Tyre A city in southern Phoenicia.

Tyro Daughter of Salmoneus and grandmother of Jason, she loved the river Enipeus, but was deceived in his shape by Poseidon, to whom she bore the twins Pelias and Neleus. Her name is often connected with the word for cheese (*tyros*), presumably because of her white complexion.

Western Ocean Atlantic Ocean.

Xanthus A city in Lycia, where there was an important sanctuary of Leto, mother of Apollo.

Xenophon (*c.* 430–*c.* 354 BC) An Athenian writer, who enlisted as a mercenary with the Persian Cyrus the Younger after the defeat of the Thirty Tyrants in Athens (404/3) and later composed an account of Cyrus' rebellion (the *Anabasis*). He also wrote an account of the life of Cyrus the Great, the *Cyropaedia*, a continuation of Thucydides' *History of the Peloponnesian War*, called *Hellenica*, several pieces in praise and defence of Socrates, including the *Memorabilia*, *Symposium* and *Apology*, and other works including themes as diverse as hunting, the Spartan constitution and the organization of the household.

Zacynthus An island off the west coast of Greece.

Zamolxis (or **Zalmoxis**) A god of the Thracian Getae, who promised his devotees immortality. Or a human being, a former slave of Pythagoras, who faked death and resurrection by hiding in an underground chamber for several years and than reappearing.

Zeno (335–263 BC) From Citium in Cyprus, the founder of Stoicism, who taught in the Painted Stoa at Athens. The name is derived from that of Zeus.

Zenodotus (b. *c.* 325 BC) From Ephesus, the first head of the Royal Library at Alexandria. He was the first editor of the *Iliad* and *Odyssey* and famous for his use of a marginal horizontal stroke (*obelos*) to indicate verses he considered spurious.

Zephyr The West Wind, which characterizes spring for ancient writers.

Zeus Son of Cronus and Rhea, the king of the Olympian gods, often known simply as 'the Olympian'. He is invoked under a large number of different guises (as god of friendship, protector of strangers, god of the hearth, god of oaths) and has a number of epithets, especially in Homer, suggestive of his power over the weather ('lord of the lightning', 'cloud-gatherer', 'loud-thunderer'). Oaths 'by Zeus' are among the commonest in Greek literature. He was worshipped at

many festivals, including the Diasia at Athens and at the pan-Hellenic
sanctuary in Olympia in Elis, where there was a famous cult statue
by Phidias and he was honoured with games every four years (see
OLYMPIA). In Homer and Hesiod, he is the head of a large household,
which includes his two brothers Poseidon and Hades (Pluto), his
wife Hera and the children they have in common (e.g. Ares), as well
as those they have with others or alone (e.g. Athena, Dionysus,
Hermes, Apollo and Artemis are Zeus' and Hephaestus is Hera's).
His philandering tendencies were well established in myth and he
had many mortal children by extramarital liaisons (see HERACLES,
MINOS, RHADAMANTHYS, SARPEDON), some of which led him to
transform himself into non-human form (a swan for Leda, a bull for
Europa, a shower of gold for Danae).

Zeuxis (*fl.* 430 BC) From Heraclea in Lucania, a painter famous for his
subtle use of colour and highlights, as well as for unusual subject-
matter (Lucian describes his *Centaur Family* in detail in *Zeuxis, or
Antiochus*) and the effective portrayal of emotion in his figures.

References

Harmon–Kilburn–Macleod	*Lucian*, 8 vols., ed. and trans. A. M. Harmon, K. Kilburn and M. D. Macleod (Loeb Classical Library; Cambridge, Mass. and London 1913–67)
Jacobitz	*Lucianus*, 4 vols., ed. C. Jacobitz (Leipzig 1836–41)
Macleod OCT	*Luciani Opera*, 4 vols., ed. M. D. Macleod (Oxford Classical Text; Oxford 1972–87)
*OCD*³	S. Hornblower and A. Spawforth (eds.), *Oxford Classical Dictionary*, 3rd edn. (Oxford 1996)
OCT	Oxford Classical Text
PCG	*Poetae Comici Graeci*, ed. R. Kassel and C. Austin (Berlin and New York 1983–)
PMG	*Poetae Melici Graeci*, ed. D. L. Page (Oxford 1962)
SIG	*Sylloge Inscriptionum Graecarum*, ed. W. Dittenberger (Leipzig 1883)
TrGF	*Tragicorum Graecorum Fragmenta*, ed. B. Snell, R. Kannicht and S. Radt (Göttingen 1971–)

Anderson, G. (1976) *Lucian: Theme and Variation in the Second Sophistic* (Leiden)

—— (1978) 'Lucian's *Nigrinus*: The Problem of Form', *Greek, Roman and Byzantine Studies* 19, 367–74

Bartley, A. (2003) 'The Implications of the Influence of Thucydides on Lucian's "Vera Historia" ', *Hermes* 131, 222–34

Baumbach, M. (2002) *Lukian in Deutschland: Eine forschungs- und rezeptionsgeschichtliche Analyse vom Humanismus bis zur Gegenwart* (Munich)

Berti, E. (1985) 'Uno scriba greco-latino: Il codice Vaticano Urbinate

Gr. 121 e la prima versione del *Caronte* di Luciano', *Rivista di Filologia e di Istruzione Classica* 113, 416–43

—— (1987a) 'Alla scuola di Manuele Crisolora: Lettura e commento di Luciano', *Rinascimento* 27, 3–73

—— (1987b) 'Alle origini della fortuna di Luciano nell'Europa occidentale', *Studi Classici e Orientali* 37, 303–51

Bompaire, J. (1958) *Lucien écrivain: Imitation et création* (Paris)

Bowersock, G. W. (1969) *Greek Sophists in the Roman Empire* (Oxford)

Bowie, E. L. (1970) 'Greeks and Their Past in the Second Sophistic', *Past and Present* 46, 3–41 (repr. in rev. form in *Studies in Ancient Society*, ed. M. I. Finley (London 1974), 166–209)

Branham, R. B. (1985) 'Introducing the Sophist: Lucian's Prologues', *Transactions and Proceedings of the American Philological Association* 115, 237–43

—— (1989) *Unruly Eloquence: Lucian and the Comedy of Traditions* (Cambridge, Mass.)

Caccia, N. (1907) *Luciano nel Quattrocento in Italia: Le rappresentazioni e le figurazioni* (Florence)

Casson, L. (1971) *Ships and Seamanship in the Ancient World* (Princeton)

Cast, D. (1981) *The Calumny of Apelles: A Study in the Humanist Tradition* (New Haven and London)

Craig, H. (1921) 'Dryden's Lucian', *Classical Philology* 16, 141–63

Davidson, J. (1997) *Courtesans and Fishcakes: The Consuming Passions of Classical Athens* (London)

Elsner, J. (2001) 'Describing Self in the Language of the Other: Pseudo (?) Lucian at the Temple of Hierapolis', in Goldhill 2001a, 123–53

Fisher, N. R. E. (1992) *Hybris: A Study in the Values of Honour and Shame in Ancient Greece* (Warminster)

Fowler, H. W. and F. G. Fowler (1905) *The Works of Lucian of Samosata*, 4 vols. (Oxford)

Gargiulo, T. (1992) 'Cleone, Prometeo e gli Oracoli', *Eikasmos* 3, 153–64

Georgiadou, A. and D. H. J. Larmour (1995) 'The *Prolaliae* to Lucian's *Verae Historiae*', *Eranos* 93, 100–12

—— (1998) *Lucian's Science Fiction Novel True Histories: Interpretation and Commentary* (Leiden)

Gleason, M. W. (1995) *Making Men: Sophists and Self-Presentation in Ancient Rome* (Princeton)

Goldhill, S. (ed.) (2001a) *Being Greek under Rome: Cultural Identity, the Second Sophistic and the Development of Empire* (Cambridge)

—— (2001b) 'The Erotic Eye: Visual Stimulation and Cultural Conflict', in Goldhill 2001a, 154–94.

Green, J. R. (1994) *Theatre in Ancient Greek Society* (London)

Hall, J. (1981) *Lucian's Satire* (New York)

Harrison, A. R. W. (1998) *The Law of Athens*, 2 vols. (London and Indianapolis; repr. of Oxford 1968 and 1971 edn.)

Holzberg, N. (1988) 'Lucian and the Germans', in *The Uses of Greek and Latin: Historical Essays*, ed. A. C. Dionisotti et al. (London), 199–209

Jones, C. P. (1986) *Culture and Society in Lucian* (Cambridge, Mass.)

Kennell, N. G. (1995) *The Gymnasium of Virtue: Education and Culture in Ancient Sparta* (Chapel Hill)

Korus, K. (1981) 'The Motif of Panthea in Lucian's Encomium', *Eos* 69, 47–56

Mace, N. (1996) *Henry Fielding's Novels and the Classical Tradition* (Newark and London)

Macleod, M. D. (1979) 'Lucian's Activities as a μισαλάζων', *Philologus* 123, 326–8

—— (1991) *Lucian: A Selection* (Warminster)

Marsh, D. (1998) *Lucian and the Latins: Humor and Humanism in the Early Renaissance* (Ann Arbor)

Massing, J.-M. (1990) *Du texte à l'image: La Calomnie d'Apelle et son iconographie* (Strasbourg)

Miller, H. K. (1961) *Essays on Fielding's 'Miscellanies': A Commentary on Volume One* (Princeton)

Minns, E. H. (1913) *Scythians and Greeks* (Cambridge)

Nesselrath, H.-G. (1985) *Lukians Parasitendialog* (Berlin)

—— (1990) 'Lucian's Introductions', in *Antonine Literature*, ed. D. A. Russell (Oxford), 111–40

Parker, R. (1983) *Miasma* (Oxford)

Pedley, J. G. (1998) *Greek Art and Archaeology*, 2nd edn. (London)

Peretti, A. (1946) *Luciano: Un intellettuale greco contro Roma* (Florence)

Pickard-Cambridge, A. (1968) *The Dramatic Festivals of Athens*, 2nd edn., rev. by J. Gould and D. M. Lewis with supplement and corrections (1st edn. 1953) (Oxford)

Reardon, B. P. (1965) *Lucian: Selected Works* (Indianapolis and New York)

Robinson, C. (1979) *Lucian and His Influence in Europe* (London)

Rütten, U. (1997) *Phantasie und Lachkultur: Lukians 'Wahre Geschichten'* (Tübingen)

Schwartz, J. (1965) *Biographie de Lucien de Samosate* (Brussels)

Seminar Classics 609 (1975) *Mazaris' Journey to Hades* (*Arethusa* Monographs V)

Sidwell, K. (1975) *Lucian of Samosata in the Italian Quattrocento* (unpublished Cambridge Ph.D. dissertation)

—— (1986) *Lucian: Selections* (Bristol)

—— (1990) 'Greek Inspiration for Mickey Mouse and Roger Rabbit', *Omnibus* 20, 8–9

—— (2002) 'Damning with Great Praise: Paradox in Lucian's *Imagines* and *Pro Imaginibus*', in *Pleiades Setting: Essays for Pat Cronin on his 65th Birthday*, ed. K. Sidwell (Cork), 107–26

Stephens, S. A. and J. J. Winkler (1995) *Ancient Greek Novels: The Fragments* (Princeton)

Strohmaier, G. (1976) 'Übersehenes zur Biographie Lukians', *Philologus* 120, 117–22

Swain, S. (1996) *Hellenism and Empire: Language, Classicism and Power in the Greek World, AD 50–250* (Oxford)

Tarrant, H. A. S. (1985) 'Alcinous, Albinus, Nigrinus', *Antichthon* 19, 87–95

Thompson, C. R. (1940) *The Translations of Lucian by Erasmus and St Thomas More* (Ithaca)

Turner, P. (1961) *Lucian: Satirical Sketches* (Harmondsworth)

von Möllendorff, P. (2000) *Auf der Suche nach der verlogenen Wahrheit* (Tübingen)

Whitmarsh, T. (2001a) *Greek Literature and the Roman Empire* (Oxford)

—— (2001b) ' "Greece is the World": Exile and Identity in the Second Sophistic', in Goldhill 2001a, 269–305

Wilson, P. (2000) *The Athenian Institution of the Khoregia: The Chorus, the City and the Stage* (Cambridge)

Index of Names and Subjects

Index of Authors and Works

General references (if any) to a work are given first, then any specific references, these following the citations, in bold type, of the passages in question using the paragraph or line numbering system common to the work.